JAMES ROSS SWEENEY is Associate Professor of History at The Pennsylvania State University. STANLEY CHODOROW is Associate Vice Chancellor–Academic Planning and Dean of Arts and Humanities at the University of California, San Diego.

D1104485

Popes, Teachers, and Canon Law
in the Middle Ages

BRIAN TIERNEY

# Popes, Teachers, and Canon Law in the Middle Ages

EDITED BY

James Ross Sweeney and
Stanley Chodorow

WITH A FOREWORD BY

Stephan Kuttner

*Cornell University Press*

ITHACA AND LONDON

First published 1989 by Cornell University Press.

International Standard Book Number 0-8014-2264-7
Library of Congress Catalog Card Number 88-47930
Printed in the United States of America
*Librarians: Library of Congress cataloging information appears on the last page of the book.*

*The paper in this book is acid-free and meets the guidelines for permanence and durability of the Committee on Production Guidelines for Book Longevity of the Council on Library Resources.*

# Contents

# Contents

# Foreword

I first met Brian Tierney early in 1951 when I visited Cambridge during my residence as a visiting fellow at All Souls, Oxford. Walter Ullmann had invited me to come to a seminar session with his research students. I still see the bright young scholars before me as they were then, although most of them are by now distinguished, white-haired members of academe, or even emeriti. Brian at the time was about to complete his Ph.D. thesis on the fundamental significance the books of canon law and the canonists' doctrines had for the growth of medieval conciliarism: a rich lode of sources—many of them only extant in manuscript—which historians of the Great Schism and its aftermath had deplorably neglected.

I returned to Cambridge toward the end of Trinity Term as an external examiner for Tierney's doctoral defense. Years later he told me how terrified he was when he learned of this appointment: he had always thought that the man who was rumored "to know everything" about the decretists' and early decretalists' writings, whether printed or unpublished, was at a safe distance across the ocean. But as it turned out, his defense of the dissertation in the relaxed setting of David Knowles's rooms at Peterhouse showed him at his best, a good partner in a good scholarly debate. And the book that eventually grew out of this dissertation, *Foundations of the Conciliar Theory* (Cambridge, 1955), was to become a classic for every serious student of medieval ecclesiology and constitutional thought.

Brian Tierney came to Washington in the fall of 1951 as an instructor in the Catholic University of America, where he advanced to assistant and associate professorships. Those were the years of congenial daily contact and a growing friendship of our families. (It should perhaps be recorded that, contrary to academic gossip, his appointment at Catholic University was not my doing but that of the late Aloysius K. Ziegler, then chairman of the History Department, who had intuitively recognized the potential of the young medievalist when he accepted a paper of his on Hostiensis for publication in the *Catholic Historical Review* while the author was still a research student in Cambridge.) These Washington years also saw the birth pangs and the foundation in 1955 of the Institute of Medieval Canon Law. Brian became the first employee of the fledgling corporation as secretary to the president, an invaluable help to the latter and a very modest help to the family finances of an underpaid young faculty member. We had to part company in 1959, when he accepted the offer of a full professorship from Cornell.

Ithaca has remained his home ever since. His remarkable success as a teacher, from 1977 on in the prestigious Bowmar Chair of Humanistic Studies, is reflected in the decision of many students to do graduate work in areas of research related to his own primary concerns: ecclesiology and constitutionalism in the Middle Ages. There were students who had originally come to Ithaca with entirely different interests—like one of the editors of this festschrift, who had planned to be a veterinarian until he became fascinated by Tierney's undergraduate lectures.

What I have just called "his own primary concerns" of course include much more than one could describe by these abstract labels: they should rather be understood as a kind of conceptual shorthand for the complex reality in which ideas and doctrines as well as the personalities of their authors, social conditions, and political events are inseparable. Brian has time and again examined these historical configurations and often returned to the *droit savant*, especially the canonists, as a sure guide for an intellectual history that remains in touch with the world of facts: their unmistakable influence in the judiciary and the governance of church, kingdoms, principalities, and city-states belies the cliché that for the "real" history of law it matters only what the courts do, not what the professors teach.

Brian Tierney has never shunned controversy, or even the painful task of tactfully criticizing his own mentor. But his manner in controversy is quite different from Walter Ullmann's temperamental outbursts. The criticism of his own *Origins of Papal Infallibility* (1972) by an esteemed fellow historian of canonical thought, Fr. Alfons M. Stickler—now Cardinal Librarian and Archivist of the Roman Church—prompted a reply by him and a rejoinder by the reviewer. It was quite in style that this exchange of strong disagreements in 1974–75 remained a gentlemen's performance: not a duel but a fencing match.[1]

The essays of former students assembled in this volume are a testimonial to Tierney's basic perception of intellectual history as an indis-

1. For his criticism of Ullmann see "Some Recent Works on the Political Theories of the Medieval Canonists," *Traditio* 10 (1954): 596–625, at pp. 597–99. The stages of the debate with Stickler—also in its Italian version—are recorded in the "Select Bibliography" of the *Bulletin of Medieval Canon Law*, n.s. 5 (1975), at p. 158.

pensable part of the recurring crises and conflicts in the body politic, ecclesiastical and secular, of Western Christendom. The growth of medieval canon law and canonistic doctrine by decree and decretal, by learned interpretation and advice, remains in a haze unless we recognize that political life and jurisprudential reason are interlocked. It remains for the historian to read this often enigmatic relationship "from within," not with the bias of one kind or another that has bedeviled so much historiography ever since the Reformation. This is not to say that there is always only one way to evaluate the interplay between ideas and events, and the essays that follow here on popes, teachers, and canon law in the Middle Ages will often differ in their understanding of texts, or personalities, or situations. But the teacher to whom these essays are dedicated was never one to make his pupils "iurare in verba magistri."

What is more, merely browsing through this volume before he reads it, Brian must see what the essays have in common in all their diversity: they show how greatly his own work has expanded the frontiers of medieval history in America.

STEPHAN KUTTNER

*Berkeley, California*

# Preface

This book of essays honors Brian Tierney, Bryce and Edith Bowmar Professor in Humanistic Studies at Cornell University, on his sixty-fifth birthday. Both as a teacher and as a scholar, Professor Tierney has made major contributions to medieval studies. An engaging and popular lecturer, he has brought the medieval world to life for generations of Cornell undergraduates, some of whom have gone on to become professional medieval historians themselves. Through his excellent textbook, *Western Europe in the Middle Ages,* and other works for undergraduates, he has reached countless students in American universities and colleges, and his *Crisis of Church and State* is fairly described as a classic sourcebook, used in history, political science, and other courses here and abroad.

Since his arrival at Cornell in 1959, the instruction and supervision of graduate students has been an equally important dimension of Professor Tierney's role as a teacher. To his graduate students, he has given that balance of encouragement and constructive criticism that marks the work of a superb teacher. Long after they have received the doctorate, his students still turn to him for advice and assistance and are rewarded with the same patience and interest they remember from their student days.

As a scholar, Professor Tierney has written works of profound importance for the history of medieval ecclesiology. Brilliantly conceived and a joy to read, his books and articles are notable for their remarkable clarity, judiciousness, and meticulous scholarship. They have changed our understanding of medieval political thought as it applied to the church. Beyond the world of scholarship, his *Foundations of the Conciliar Theory* and *Origins of Papal Infallibility* have helped to frame the twentieth-century Catholic debate about ecclesiology. In this way, he is in our time like the medieval canonists in whom he has had such a profound interest; he is a scholar who has never been merely a specialist distant from the world of affairs but is a man engaged in the study of history for its relevance to our world.

The genesis of this volume of essays dates from the meeting of the Sixth International Congress of Medieval Canon Law on the campus of the University of California, Berkeley, in July 1980. Seven of the congress participants, former students of Professor Tierney, met to initiate and organize a volume in his honor. The editors and contributors have made a conscious effort in the organization of the book to show the effect of Professor Tierney's ideas and historical interests. Through the topics examined here, we hope to highlight and develop those subjects and methods that he taught us and that continue to influence our work. With these essays we give back to him a small fragment of what he imparted to us. We are pleased that Professor Kuttner, whose close association with Professor Tierney dates from their years together on the faculty of the Catholic University of America, has provided reflections on Professor Tierney to serve as the Foreword to the volume.

The editors acknowledge with thanks the wise counsel and helpful assistance of all those who labored to bring this collection into existence. In particular, we are indebted to Richard M. Fraher, Stephan Kuttner, Karl F. Morrison, Kenneth Pennington, Edward M. Peters, and the Rev. Edward A. Synan for their many kindnesses and suggestions. The secretarial staff of the History Department of the Pennsylvania State University, especially Monica Perchonok, Sherri Miller, and Judy Gentzel, have over a period of years worked cheerfully on a variety of tasks associated with the editing of this collection. In addition, the staff of the Dean of Arts and Humanities of the University of California, San Diego, especially Peggy Thompson and Christina Snofsky, helped in many ways despite the burdens of the dean's normal business. We thank them all for their help.

7 May 1987

JAMES ROSS SWEENEY
STANLEY CHODOROW

*University Park, Pennsylvania*
*La Jolla, California*

# Abbreviations

The following works are cited throughout in abbreviated form.

| | |
|---|---|
| *DA* | *Deutsche Archiv für Erforschung des Mittelalters* |
| Friedberg, *CIC* | Emil Friedberg, *Corpus iuris canonici*, 2 vols. (Leipzig, 1879–81) |
| Mansi | J. D. Mansi, *Sacrorum conciliorum nova et amplissima collectio*, 31 vols. (Florence and Venice, 1759–98) |
| Migne, *PL* | J. P. Migne. *Patrologia latina*, 222 vols. (Paris, 1844–64) |
| *MIOG* | *Mitteilungen des Instituts für österreichische Geschichtsforschung* |
| *MGH* | *Monumenta Germaniae historica* |
| *Auct. ant.* | *Auctores antiqui* |
| *Dip* | *Diplomatum regum* |
| *Epp* | *Epistolae* |
| *LdL* | *Libelli de Lite* |
| *LL* | *Leges* |
| *Poetae* | *Poetae latinae* |
| *Schr* | *Schriften* |
| *SS* | *Scriptores* |
| *Mon. iur. can.* | *Monumenta iuris canonici* |
| *QF* | *Quellen und Forschungen aus italienischen Archiven und Bibliotheken* |
| *ZRG*, Kan. Abt. | *Zeitschrift der Savigny-Stiftung für Rechtsgeschichte, kanonistische Abteilung* |

# PART I

# [1]

## Paschal II, Henry V, and the
## Origins of the Crisis of 1111

### STANLEY CHODOROW

In early February 1111, Pope Paschal II and King Henry V of Germany reached an agreement about lay investiture—a significant achievement after nearly forty years of dispute between the two powers. Given the positions on investitures that had been staked out by the two sides during the dispute, the terms of the agreement of 1111 were startling, and historians have speculated a good deal on why the pope and king suddenly left the beaten paths of their political ideologies. In this essay I argue that the agreement was the result of the politics of expediency, particularly on the side of the German king.

The treaty was negotiated as Henry led a substantial army toward Rome, where he intended to be crowned emperor. Of course, the coronation would not take place unless the king and pope reached an agreement on investitures. During the early stages of negotiation, Henry was represented by a team dominated by Archbishop Bruno of Trier and other bishops. Paschal's negotiators were apparently led by Pierleoni, a powerful Roman noble whose son Peter was later elected pope.[1] The first negotiations got nowhere because both sides held to the positions they had developed during previous attempts at reconciliation. Then Henry changed his embassy, making his chancellor Adalbert its leader and giving prominence to other laymen, and an agreement was worked out at Santa Maria

---

1. Pierleoni swore on behalf of the pope and promised to support the king if Paschal failed to live up to the agreement. Peter became a cardinal shortly after 1111 and was elected pope as Anaclet II in the double election of 1130. See F. J. Schmale, *Studien zum Schisma des Jahres 1130* (Cologne, 1961), pp. 15–28; P. Fedele, "Le famiglie di Anacleto II e di Gelasio II," *Archivio della R. Società Romana di storia patria* 26 (1904): 399–433; and idem, "Pierleoni e Frangipani," *Roma* 15 (1937): 1–12.

in Turri in the Leonine city on 4 February. Henry accepted the terms at Sutri, just north of Rome, on 9 February and then marched his army to the city, which he reached on the eleventh.[2]

In the agreement, Paschal promised to force the German bishops to give back to the king all the regalian rights they had held since the time of Charles the Great. Henry gave up his claim to the right to invest bishops.[3] In a stroke the German church, which was then fully integrated into the structure of secular power, would cease to exist as contemporaries knew it, and a new vision of the church was promulgated. The image of a church supported solely by tithes and pious donations and wholly separate from secular authority and affairs reverberated in the consciousness of the generation of church leaders who were coming of age about 1111. Bernard of Clairvaux, Gerhoch of Reichersberg, and Gratian held the church of Paschal's promise to be the ideal.[4]

2. The story of the negotiations was told in the *Annales Romani*, ed. L. Duchesne, *Le liber pontificalis*, vol. 2 (Paris, 1892), pp. 338–40, which also transmitted the treaty documents, and by the German chronicler Ekkehard of Aura, *Chronicon*, ed. G. Waitz, *MGH SS*, 3:243–45. Ekkehard says that he relied on the lost account of the Scot David, who had accompanied the king to Rome. On David, see notes 14 and 51 below. In general, see G. Buchholz, *Ekkehard von Aura* (Leipzig, 1888). King Henry himself transmitted some of the documents, with his own interpretation of the events, in a letter he wrote after the agreement collapsed. The copy addressed to Parma is preserved in the *Codex Udalrici*, no. 149, ed. P. Jaffé, *Bibliotheca rerum Germanicarum*, vol. 5, Monumenta Bambergensia (Berlin, 1869), pp. 269–74. Both sources provide evidence of who the representatives of the two sides were. The king's new embassy consisted of Chancellor Adalbert, the three counts Hermann, Frederick, and Gottfried, and the *ministerialis* Folkmar. These are the signators of the royal document; see *Ann. Romani*, p. 338. For a narrative history of the events based on the sources, see G. Peiser, "Der deutschen Investiturstreit unter König Heinrich V. bis zu dem päpstlichen Privileg vom 13. April 1111" (diss., Leipzig, 1883), and G. Schneider, "Der Vertrag von S. Maria in Turri und dessen Folgen" (diss., Rostock, 1881), pp. 17–19.

3. See *Ann. Romani*, pp. 338–39. The king promised to give up "omnem investituram ecclesiarium in manu domni pape" (p. 338). The pope, acting through Pierleoni and other unnamed representatives, promised to order "episcopis presentibus in die coronationis eius [the king's—set for Sunday, 12 February] ut dimittant regalia regi et regno, que ad regnum pertinebant tempore Karoli, Lodoici, Heinrici et aliorum predecessorum eius, et scripto firmabit . . . ne quis eorum vel presentium vel absentium vel successorum eorum intromittant se vel invadant eadem regalia" (p. 339). In his exculpatory letter (*Cod. Udal.*, no. 149, pp. 270–71), the king quoted the text of the pope's side of the treaty but was vague about his own promises. Henry said he promised "omnibus episcopis abbatibus et omnibus ecclesiis omnia, quae antecessores mei reges vel imperatores eis concesserunt vel tradiderunt. Et quae illi pro spe eternae retributionis obtulerunt Deo, ego peccator pro timore terribilis iudicii ullo modo subtrahere recuso." This promise does not appear in the texts of the treaty transmitted by the *Annales Romani*, and it looks like an attempt by the king to present himself as having held to the traditional imperialist view of the regalia as rights that the kings had granted. In this view, churches ought to be integrated into the structure of the secular kingdoms, and regalia were the vehicle through which this integration was effected. See note 10.

4. All of these men were about twenty years old in 1111. The clearest expression of this ideal is in the *Dictum Gratiani*, post C. 23 q. 8 c. 20, Friedberg, *CIC*, 1:959. "Quosdam episcopos Leuitica tantum portione esse contentos. . . . His nichil commune

The treaty connected the settlement of the investiture controversy with the coronation of Henry V as emperor. The terms of the agreement were to be announced to the members of the Roman church and of Henry's entourage, assembled in St. Peter's on 12 February 1111, and afterward the pope was to crown the king. But it seems that only Paschal actually read his side of the agreement, because the churchmen present objected strenuously enough to block the completion of the ratification process. In his encyclical to the people and churches of the empire, Henry said that bishops, abbots, and other churchmen on both sides objected to Paschal's offer to give up the regalia. The *Annales Romani* say that, after hearing the pope's oath, the Germans withdrew to consult with the king and that they refused to permit the king to carry out the agreement.[5] In the aftermath of these events Henry seized the pope, several cardinals, and some laymen and retreated from the city. He held Paschal and the others for two months until Paschal gave in, granting Henry the right to invest bishops and crowning him emperor on 13 April.[6]

Paschal's submission to the king raised calls for his abdication, and in March 1112 the Lenten synod in Rome coerced the pope into condemning his grant to Henry as a *pravilegium*.[7] Henry had returned to Germany

---

est cum principibus seculi, quia temporalia penitus abiciunt, ne eorum occasione legibus inperatorum obnoxii teneantur. Talibus nulla occasio relinquitur occupationis secularis miliciae, quia, cum de decimis et primiciis vivunt tamquam summi regis filii in omni regno a terrenis exactionis liberi sunt." Cf. the famous complaint of St. Bernard that the papal palace resounded with litigation of this world, *De consideratione*, 1.4.5, ed. J. Leclercq and H. M. Rochais, *Opera omnia*, vol. 3 (Rome, 1963), p. 399. See R. Benson, "The Obligations of Bishops with 'Regalia': Canonistic Views from Gratian to the Early Thirteenth Century," in *Proceedings of the Second International Congress of Medieval Canon Law* (Vatican City, 1965), pp. 123–37; S. Chodorow, *Christian Political Theory and Church Politics in the Mid-Twelfth Century* (Berkeley and Los Angeles, 1972), pp. 260–65.

5. *Ann. Romani*, pp. 340–41, "Ille [Henry] cum episcopis suis et principibus secessit in partem iusta secretarium; ibi diutius quod eis placuit tractauerunt. . . . Cum autem longior se hora protraeret, missis nuntiis pontifex conventionis supradicte tenorem repetiit adinpleri. . . . Set post paululum familiares regi dolos suos paulatim aperire ceperunt, dicentes scriptum illut quod conditum fuerat non posse firmari auctoritate et iustitia. Quibus cum evangelica et apostolica obiceretur auctoritas . . . illi tamen in dolositate sua et pertinacia permanebant." This account implies that the two sides tried to renegotiate the treaty on the spot. In his encyclical, Henry said only (*Cod. Udal.*, no. 149, p. 272), "Cum ergo supradictae postulationi insisterem, scilicet ut cum iusticia et auctoritate promissam mihi conventionem firmaret—universis ei in faciem resistentibus et decreto suo planam heresim inclamantibus, scilicet episcopis abbatibus, tam suis quam nostris, et omnibus ecclesiae filiis."

6. *Annales sancti Disibodi*, ed. G. Waitz, MGH SS, 17:20–22. Henry V's account of the events of 12 February is understandably vague (*Cod. Udal.*, no. 149, pp. 269, 270, 272). Cf. *Ann. Romani*, pp. 340–41. See Peiser, "Investiturstreit unter König Heinrich V." (note 2 above), and Schneider, "Vertrag von S. Maria in Turri" (note 2).

7. See, in general, C. Servatius, *Paschalis II. 1099–1118*, Päpste und Papstuum 14 (Stuttgart, 1979), pp. 296–325. See *Relatio registri Paschalis II*, MGH Const, 1:147; Johannes, cardinal bishop of Tusculum, *Epistola*, PL, 160:col. 1047. Henry's supporters

immediately after his coronation and was soon faced by episcopal opposition led by the very man who had negotiated the Sutri agreement and
whom Henry had installed as archbishop of Mainz. The opposition led by
the bishops disturbed Henry's reign for a decade.[8]

These events realized the risks inherent in the original agreement, and
what is surprising is that Paschal and Henry—particularly the latter—
were willing to take them. The agreement constituted a direct attack on
the German episcopate and would have radically altered the distribution
of power in the kingdom. Although events rendered the matter moot and
the sources are silent, one can wonder how the church outside Germany
would have reacted to the agreement. In one sense, Paschal had stuck to
the reformers' old ideal of an independent church responsible for the
spiritual leadership of the world, but it had never been suggested that the
church could or should carry out this role by giving up its traditional
sources of worldly power. Because of the captivity and the capitulation of
Paschal, pro-papal churchmen virtually forgot about the agreement of
Sutri, but the pope certainly had taken a risk in making it. The descriptions of the commotion in St. Peter's on 12 February do not show conclusively that members of the papal entourage objected to the agreement,
since only Henry suggests that they did, but the sources do indicate that
the German bishops and abbots reacted strongly. At the end of the day, the
coronation had not been performed, and Henry found himself in the
awkward position of holding the pope prisoner.

Historians have interpreted the February agreement against its ideologi-
cal background, from which it stands out in sharp relief, and they have
concluded that Paschal was its principal author.[9] He is credited with a

---

in Italy sent him descriptions of what happened at the Lenten synod of 1112. See *Cod.
Udal.*, nos. 161–62. On the Lenten synod, see P. R. McKeon, "The Lateran Council of
1112, the Heresy of Lay Investiture, and the Excommunication of Henry V," *Mediaevalia et Humanistica* 17 (1966): 3–12, and U.-R. Blumenthal, *The Early Councils of
Pope Paschal II: 1100–1110* (Toronto, 1978). On the background and contemporary
interpretation of the *pravilegium*, see H. Hoffmann, "Ivo von Chartres und die Lösung
des Investiturproblems," *DA* 19 (1963): 423–24.

8. On Adalbert's break with Henry, see F. Haussmann, *Reichskanzlei und Hofka-
pelle unter Heinrich V. und Konrad III., MGH Schr* 14:27–34. The origin of the break is
unknown, although in December 1112, when Henry imprisoned his former chancellor,
he wrote a manifesto against Adalbert (Stumpf 3093). Henry was anxious to put out his
version of the events, as he had done the previous year. It is striking that Paschal soon
wrote to Henry urging him to free Adalbert (JL 6339; *Cod. Udal.*, no. 163, pp. 290–91,
dated from Benevento, 25 January 1113). On the civil strife in Germany after 1111, see
G. Meyer von Knonau, *Jahrbücher des deutschen Reiches unter Heinrich IV. und
Heinrich V.*, vol. 6 (Leipzig, 1907), pp. 25off.

9. For the traditional view, see W. Giesebrecht, *Geschichte der deutschen Kai-
serzeit*, 4th ed., vol. 3, 2 (Leipzig, 1877), pp. 807–11, and A. Hauck, *Kirchengeschichte
Deutschlands*, vol. 3, 2 (Leipzig, 1896), p. 892. Cf. Meyer von Knonau, *Jahrbücher*,
6:142–43. K. Jordan, "Investiturstreit und fruhe Stauferzeit," in B. Gebhardt, *Handbuch
der deutschen Geschichte*, 9th ed., vol. 1, ed. H. Grundmann (Stuttgart, 1970), pp. 322–

bold, though naive, stroke to resolve a dispute that increasingly had appeared to be unresolvable. In the proposed agreement, historians see the pope as trying to realize a vision of a spiritual church that was the simple extension of the ideas of the papal reform movement. The terms of the agreement could also be traced to the old imperialist idea that the king should govern worldly affairs and the church should pray for his success.[10]

The traditional papal position rested on the idea that the *episcopatus* is indivisible and simply ecclesial and that therefore a bishop must receive his office from the church. The regalian rights that nearly all bishops possessed were considered part of the *episcopatus*, to be handed over with the pastoral office through investiture with ring and staff.[11]

The German king and his supporters only slowly came to recognize the

---

67. M. J. Wilks holds that the agreement was consistent with the papal ideas about *regalia*; see "*Ecclesiastica* and *Regalia*: Papal Investiture Policy from the Council of Guastalla to the First Lateran Council, 1106–1123," *Studies in Church History* 7 (1971): 69–85. See now Servatius, *Paschalis II.*, pp. 217–19, 221–27. On the history of papal and imperial ideology, see notes 11 and 12.

10. See the letter of Charlemagne, attributed to the pen of Alcuin, to the newly elevated Pope Leo III, Boehmer 330, printed in *MGH Epp*, 4:136. A poem dated 799 expressed a similar idea: "Rex pater Europae et summus Leo pastor in orbe" (*MGH Poetae*, 1:366).

11. For the most part, reformers did not distinguish between the *spiritualia* and *temporalia* of an *episcopatus*. Humbert of Silva-Candida specifically rejected such a distinction when he wrote against simony and lay investiture; see *Adversus simoniacos libri III*, lib. 3, cap. 1, ed. F. Thaner, *MGH LdL*, 1:198, "Contra eos, qui dicunt se non consecrationem [i.e., *spiritualia*], sed res ecclesiae comparasse." The prohibition of lay investiture grew out of the condemnation of simony and rested on the same notion of the ecclesiastical office as a unity. For example, Humbert moved from his discussion of the former directly to the latter, ibid., cap. 6, p. 205, "De baculis et anulis per manus saecularium potestatum datis." Thirty years later, Deusdedit made the same argument, quoting an apocryphal letter of Paschal I, *Libellus contra invasores et symoniacos*, ed. E. Sackur, *MGH LdL*, 2:318, "Nam cum corporalis ecclesiae episcopus vel abbas sine rebus corporalibus exterioribus in nullo proficiat, sicut nec anima sine corpore temporaliter vivit, quisquis eorum alterum vendit, sine quo alterum habere non provenit, neutrum non venditum derelinquit." In the early 1080s, the pro-Gregory writer Manegold of Lautenbach implied the distinction between *temporalia* and *spiritualia* of the bishopric and even between the regalia and other *temporalia* when he said that benefices were held under secular law, while tithes were received under divine authority. See Manegold, *Ad Gebehardum liber*, ed. K. Francke, *MGH LdL*, 1:399, "Unde et illud, de ecclesiasticis beneficiis quod dicunt [Wenrich of Trier, see ibid., p. 297] ab omni secularium iure perpetua immunitate auferendis, penitus falsum repperit, quemcumque eius [Gregory VII] decreta perlegere non piguerit. Nam nusquam beneficiorum mentionem fecit, sed decimas tantum, quas tam sub lege quam sub gratia ad usus tantam pietatis concessas divina testatur auctoritas." See A. Scharnagl, *Der Begriff der Investitur in den Quellen und Literatur des Investiturstreites*, Kirchenrechtliche Abhandlungen 56, ed. U. Stutz (Stuttgart, 1908); R. Schieffer, *Die Entstehung des päpstlichen Investiturverbots für den deutschen Königs*, *MGH Schr*, vol. 28 (Stuttgart, 1981); G. Schmid, *Der Begriff der kanonischen Wahl in den Anfangen des Investiturstreites* (Stuttgart, 1926), pp. 126–30; I. Ott, "Die Regalienbegriff im 12. Jahrhundert," *ZRG Kan. Abt.* 45 (1948): 234–304; and J. Fried, "Der Regalienbegriff im 11. und 12. Jahrhundert," *DA* 29 (1973): 450–528.

central importance of investiture, but once this was recognized, imperialist writers developed a rationale for lay investiture that presumed the
*episcopatus* had a dual nature. The bishops were subject to the king—and
to his investiture—because they held property, which was the creature of
secular law, and because they exercised royal rights. This novel analysis of
the *episcopatus* seems to have arisen in the Anglo-Norman realm as a
means of explaining the role of the king in the selection of bishops, but it
was most clearly and influentially stated by the great French canonist Ivo
of Chartres in a letter to the committed Gregorian Archbishop Hugh of
Lyons (1097).[12] A few years later, imperialist writers used this idea to
justify lay investiture. They held that though the church had authority
over the *spiritualia*, no one who was unacceptable to the king and who
had not given him homage and fealty could exercise the regalian rights.[13]

The agreement completed at Sutri was based on the royal conception of
the *episcopatus*, and under its terms the bishopric would, at least in

12. See Ivo, ep. 60, ed. E. Sackur, *MGH LdL*, 2:645, "Reges nichil spirituale se dare
intendant, sed tantum aut votis petentium annuere, aut villas ecclesiasticas et alia bona
exteriora, que de munificentia regum optinent aecclesiae." On the background of this
idea, see Hoffmann, "Ivo," pp. 393–405. Until the turn of the century, imperialists did
not concern themselves with the nature of the *episcopatus*, but only with the relationship between the two powers—*regnum* and *sacerdotium*. The anonymous author of the
imperialist tract *De unitate ecclesiae conservanda* never considers the nature of the
bishopric. The closest he comes is to say that the properties given to the church must be
used for divine rather than human purposes, but his aim here is to attack the Gregorians
(or as he calls them, Hildebrandists) who use ecclesiastical property—i.e., the regalia—
to support usurpers; see *De unitate eccl. cons.*, ed. W. Schwenkenbecher, *MGH LdL*,
2:240. In general, see G. Tellenbach, *Libertas: Kirche und Weltordnung im Zeitalter des
Investiturstreites* (Stuttgart, 1936) pp. 77–108, 176–78.

13. The locus classicus of this idea is the royalist treatise *De episcoporum investitura*
(1109), ed. E. Bernheim, *MGH LdL*, 1:498, "Non consecretur episcopus, qui per regem
vel imperatorem non introierit pure et integre, exceptis papa Romanus investire et
consecrare debet ex antiquo dono regum et imperatorum cum aliis que vocantur regalia,
id est a regibus et imperatoribus pontificibus Romanis data in fundis et reditibus," and
p. 502, "iura civitatum in theloneis, monetis, villicis et scabinis, comitatibus, advocatiis, synodalibus bannis per reges delegata." For a discussion of the authorship and
purposes of this tract, see notes 14 and 40. The distinction had been suggested by
Sigebert of Gembloux, who may have been the author of the *De episc. invest.* (see note
42), in a letter he wrote against Paschal in 1103, *Epistola adversus Paschalem papam*,
ed. E. Sackur, *MGH LdL*, 2:458–59, "Dominus noster episcopus communicat regi et
imperatori suo, cui ex regalibus eius acceptis fidelitatem iuravit. Nimium effluxit
tempus, quo haec consuetudo incepit; et sub hac consuetudine migraverunt a seculo
sancti et reverentes episcopi, reddentes caesari que erant cesaris et Deo que erant Dei."
Although Manegold of Lautenbach had approached this idea in the early 1080s (see note
11), it was only after 1111 that papalist writers really accepted it, and their treatment of
it seems to stem from the negotiations of February 1111. See Placidus of Nonantula,
*Liber de honore ecclesiae* (late 1111), ed. L. Heinemann and E. Sackur, *MGH LdL*, 2:615,
"Pastor aecclesiae . . . de rebus aecclesiae sibi commissis imperiale praeceptum ex-
petat." Cf. Gottfried of Vendôme, *Libelli*, book 3 (1119), ed. E. Sackur, *MGH LdL*, 2:691,
"Non enim possessiones haberet aecclesia, nisi sibi a regibus donarentur et ab ipsis non
quidem divinis sacramentis, sed possessionibus terrenis investiretur."

Germany, be purged of its regalian attributes. Then the king would cease to have any justification for investing men with it.[14]

Although the pope gave up an important principle in the agreement by consenting to the idea that the *episcopatus* had a dual nature, events prevented papalists from giving a considered response to this radical departure from papal ideology. From February to April, the pope and several cardinals were Henry's prisoners, and the outrage of April preoccupied papalists thereafter. From late 1111 on, however, papalist writers accepted the dualist view.[15]

Henry's situation was different. His commitment to the failed agreement of February revealed his political intentions and undermined his political support. That this was the case is shown by the encyclical letter written soon after 12 February to which reference has already been made. In the letter, the king presented himself as a reluctant participant in the agreement, which, he said, had been formulated by Paschal. He had not wanted, he went on, to accept Paschal's proposal because it meant depriving the churches of the *regalia* they had received since the days of Charles the Great, but he agreed to the pope's plan because Paschal himself promised to force the German bishops to relinquish their regalian rights. He asserted that he knew all along that the pope could not do it. Finally, he explained the events of 12 February as in large part the result of the pope's failure to carry out the treaty.[16]

14. Bernheim noted that a key phrase in the pope's document of February 1111 could be traced to the *De episcoporum investitura*. Compare *De episc. invest.*, p. 502, "Iura civitatum in theloneis, monetis, villicis et scabinis, comitatibus, advocatiis, synodalibus bannis per reges delegata," with Paschal's undertaking in February 1111 to force the bishops to give up "regalia, id est civitates, ducatus, marchias, comitatus, monetas, teloneum, mercatum, advocatias regni, iura centurionum et curtes que manifeste regni erant" (*Ann. Romani*, p. 339; *Cod. Udal.*, no. 149, p. 271 [with slight variation]). Moreover, the parties to the agreement emphasize the importance of Charlemagne, as does the author of the *De episc. invest.*, who relies on the false privilege of Pope Hadrian I for Charles. In his encyclical, Henry quoted a purported statement of Paschal reaffirming the terms of the agreement, in which the list of regalian rights accords almost exactly with *De episc. invest.*; see *Cod. Udal.*, no. 149, p. 273. Sigebert of Gembloux, a moderate imperialist, appears to have based his account on Henry's letter. See Sigebert, *Chronicon*, ed. L. Bethmann, *MGH SS*, 6:372–73. Karl Pivec argued that the agreement was actually drafted by the imperial servant David, a Scot who had been *scholasticus* of Würzburg and who, Pivec thought, replaced Adalbert as Henry's principal adviser during the journey to Rome. David accompanied the king on the visit and wrote an account, which became the basis of Ekkehard of Aura's chronicle of the events (see Ekkehard, p. 243, and note 2 above), but Pivec's opinion of his central role has never been accepted. See K. Pivec, "Studien und Forschungen zur Ausgabe des Codex Udalrici," *MIOG* 46 (1932): 272–73. For a judgment on Pivec's opinion, see Fried, "Regalienbegriff," p. 476 n. 81. In general, see E. Bernheim, *Das Wormser Konkordat und seine Vorurkunden* (Breslau, 1906).

15. See note 13.

16. *Cod. Udal.*, no. 149, p. 269, "Notum esse volumus . . . ea quae inter nos et domnum P. papam erant, . . . scilicet de conventione inter me et ipsum," ibid., p. 270.

In sum, Henry proposed to excuse his violent treatment of the pope by citing the pontiff's failure to carry out an agreement that the king admittedly recognized to be unworkable. It is difficult to understand why the king made such a disingenuous argument, much less why historians have accepted it.

The ostensible purpose of the encyclical was to justify the seizure of the pope, but it reveals Henry's bigger problem. Most of the letter is devoted to the agreement and Henry's protestation of innocence in bringing it about. The young king had colluded with the pope to deprive the bishops of their traditional role in the German kingdom, and he had to assuage them and calm the fears of the magnates (who must have been unsettled by the king's attempt to change their political world).[17] He needed strong support to bring the crisis to a successful conclusion and to rebuild the political status quo ante. The ploy was partially successful. The king was able to force Paschal to give in, but the political situation in Germany was seriously disturbed.

Sutri was a watershed in Henry's reign, and he played a large role in creating it. The question is: Why did he join with Paschal to make an agreement that was so likely to put him in a difficult position? The same question can be asked of Paschal. The answers to these questions will provide the basis for reinterpreting the origins and aims of the agreement and the nature of the crises that followed.

## The Road to Sutri

Henry V rebelled against his father Henry IV shortly after Christmas 1104. Young Henry's decision to rebel must have rested on his assessment of the politics of the kingdom, which would in turn have rested on the experience of his older brother Conrad's unsuccessful rebellion of 1093 to 1098. Conrad's movement had united the papal curia, Countess Mathilda of Tuscany, the Lombard communes, and the bishops and magnates of Germany.[18] It showed two principal things: how difficult it was to hold

---

Paschal said, "Ecclesiae decimis et oblationibus suis contentae sint; rex vero omnia praedia et regalia . . . recipiat et detineat. Ad hec cum nostri responderent, nos quidem nolle ecclesiis violentiam inferre nec ista subtrahendo tot sacrilegia incurrere, fiducialiter promisit . . . si hec, uti praemissum est, complesset—quod tamen nullo modo posse fieri sciebant [Henry's representatives]—me quoque investituras ecclesiarum, uti querebat, refutaturum." Henry then tells of the attacks of the Romans against him and his men when they entered Rome on 12 February.

17. The *Ann. Romani* say that Henry withdrew to reconsider the pact "cum episcopis suis et principibus" (p. 340) and describe those who came back to the altar to treat with Paschal only as "familiares regi" (p. 341). See note 5.

18. The principal source for the history of Conrad's rebellion is Bernold, *Chronicon*, ed. G. Pertz, *MGH SS*, 5:385–467. See Giesebrecht, *Geschichte*, 3, 1:661–67; Jordan, "Investiturstreit," pp. 347–49.

such a coalition together and that the success of a rebellion would depend on German, not Italian or international, politics.

By the time young Henry committed himself to rebellion, he did not have to be very acute to see that a rebellion against his father could succeed only if it suited the self-interest of the three centers of power in Germany—the magnates, the bishops, and the *ministeriales*. None of these elements could be counted on.

Conrad's rebellion had shown that the magnates suffered from chronic political myopia, which was proved again during young Henry's rebellion. Even after the old king had been forced to abdicate at the Christmas court of 1105, he was soon gaining support among the magnates of Lotharingia. Only the old king's death in August 1106 saved Henry V from losing substantial magnate support elsewhere in the kingdom.[19]

The German bishops could be counted on to support a rebellion against Henry IV, and their political vision was more sweeping than that of the nobility, but the young king could not count on their undivided attention or unquestioning adherence. While the bishops were most concerned about German affairs—about their own competition with the burghers and about their role in royal government—for decades they had also been involved in papal politics, which had been among the factors that had weakened Henry IV.

Young Henry had justified his rebellion on the grounds of his father's excommunication, but there was no indication that the young king supported the papal views of investiture. Pro-papal bishops, led by Gebhard of Constance, introduced into the politics of his rebellion a fastidiousness about investiture and the proper role of the monarchy in ecclesiastical affairs. Moreover, Bishop Gebhard was probably the vehicle for the appeal to Pope Paschal that young Henry made immediately after breaking with his father.[20]

The support of the pope was essential, but young Henry based his attempt to depose his father on German political elements, including bishops who had little or no connection with the papacy. From very early in the rebellion, Archbishop Ruthard of Mainz, who had been elevated by Henry IV, joined with Gebhard in bringing the church into Henry V's camp. Yet Ruthard played a role different from that of the Gregorian

19. Ekkehard, *Chronicon*, pp. 236–37. Cf. Meyer von Knonau, *Jahrbücher*, 5:290. Henry IV wrote letters to the magnates seeking to win back their support. One such letter is transmitted in the later recensions of Ekkehard, pp. 236–37; another example is in *MGH LL*, sect. 4, 1:131.

20. See Ekkehard, pp. 225–26; *Libellus de rebellione Heinrici V.*, in *Annales Hildesheimenses*, ed. G. Pertz, *MGH SS*, 3:107. On the independence of this pro-Henry IV tract, see G. Buchholz, *Die Würzburger Chronik* (Leipzig, 1879), pp. 70–71. On the controversy over authorship, see Meyer von Knonau, 5:196 n. 3. See also K. Henking, *Gebhard III., Bischof von Constanz 1084–1110* (Stuttgart, 1880), and E. Heyck, *Geschichte der Herzöge von Zähringen* (Freiburg im Breisgau, 1891). The author of the *Libellus* called Gebhard "domni papae cooperator fidelissimus" (p. 108).

bishop. While Gebhard, as papal legate, carried out a reform of the church, Ruthard, the royal bishop, received the submission of bishops formerly loyal to the old king.[21] Young Henry's ecclesiastical support appears to have been built by Ruthard and connected, somewhat loosely, to the papacy by Gebhard.[22]

The import of the papal role became evident after Henry captured his father in December 1105. The young king held his Christmas court at Mainz. It was a grand success. All the great men of the kingdom came, and those churchmen who had remained loyal to Henry IV were reconciled to the church and to the young king through the agency of the papal legates, Gebhard of Constance and Richard of Albano. The old king abdicated in favor of his son.[23]

Through his legates at Mainz, Paschal had complained about the state of the German church, and the assembled magnates and bishops had joined the young king in promising to end abuses and to support reform. The pope's remonstrance must have reminded the king and his supporters that they needed to resolve the controversy over investitures, and they decided to send a distinguished embassy to the pope. The embassy would be well suited, "de obiectis rite rationem reddere et de incertis sagaciter investigare ac per omni utilitatibus ecclesiasticis sapienter consulere."[24]

This description of the ambassadors' aims comes from the chronicle of Ekkehard of Aura and sounds like authentic diplomatic rhetoric. After thirty years of controversy, the king and churchmen recognize only that some things may have to be explained to the pope and that there are problems of misunderstanding.

This was the first of several unsuccessful attempts to resolve the investiture contest, and it is difficult to judge Henry's seriousness. On the one

21. *Libellus de rebellione*, p. 108. The passage relates what happened at the synod of Nordhausen in the week before Pentecost (28 May 1105) and indicates that Gebhard presided over the synod's legislative actions. Henry's commitment to Ruthard is measured by the effort he made in June 1105 to reestablish him in Mainz, from which Ruthard had been driven in 1098. See ibid., p. 108. Cf. Ekkehard, p. 227. Henry went directly from Nordhausen to Mainz.

22. On the gathering of episcopal support for Henry V, see Ekkehard, pp. 227–29; *Annales Patherbrunnenses*, ed. P. Scheffer-Boichorst, *Eine verlorene Quellenschrift des XII. Jahrh.* (Innsbruck, 1870), p. 109; Meyer von Knonau, 5:229–30 n. 2 and 5:230–52 (for a detailed history of the rebellion in the second half of 1105). Cf. Hauck, *Kirchengeschichte*, 880–82.

23. On the Christmas court and synod, see Ekkehard, pp. 230–31; *Vita Heinrici IV imperatoris*, ed. W. Wattenbach, *MGH SS*, 12:279–80; cf. Henry IV's letter to Hugh of Cluny, ed. L. d'Achery, *Spicilegium sive Collectio veterum aliquot Scriptorum*, vol. 3 (Paris, 1723), pp. 441–42.

24. Ekkehard, p. 231. On the legation, compare recensions C, D, and E of the *Chronicon* (p. 233); cf. *Ann. Patherbrunnenses*, p. 112. Buchholz argued that Ekkehard consciously portrayed the embassy as representative of the kingdom (*Ekkehard von Aura*, p. 260) and interpreted the phrase "de obiectis . . ." as referring specifically to investiture and the pope's complaint as an attack on Henry V's actions (p. 259). But the pope was unlikely to try to undermine Henry's rebellion; the young king had proclaimed a desire to settle the conflict between the monarchy and the papacy.

hand, he needed papal support to consolidate his position in Germany, and he had the example of his father to show what the consequences of prolonged conflict might be. On the other hand, the composition of the embassy indicates that he was taking a traditional imperialist stance in dealing with the pope. The embassy was made up of six powerful bishops and an unspecified number of lay nobles. In the sources, the bishops are identified by duchy as well as see; Lotharingia, Saxony, Franconia, Bavaria, Swabia, and Burgundy each had an episcopal representative. Therefore, contemporaries seem to have seen the embassy as representative of the kingdom and its interests rather than as a party sent to Rome to compromise old customs. Ekkehard's description of the embassy's purpose supports this interpretation.

Henry IV's resurgence after the Mainz court spoiled the embassy, and the three bishops—Gebhard of Constance, Wido of Chur, and Otto of Bamberg—who actually reached Rome only invited Paschal to come to Germany for the next Christmas court. There a reconciliation would take place.[25]

In preparation for going to Germany, Paschal held a great council at Guastalla in October where he hoped to conclude peace between himself and Henry.[26] The king sent a delegation, but the pope did not treat the king's ambassadors well and the talks collapsed. The delegation was led by Archbishop Bruno of Trier, who had been elevated by Henry IV in 1102. At the council, Paschal suspended Bruno for three days because he had received his see from a layman.[27] At the same time, the pope also attacked the actions by which Ruthard and Henry had won the German church over to the rebellion. He condemned the reconciliations Ruthard and Henry of Magdeburg had effected the previous year, and shortly after the council he ordered the rehabilitated Bruno of Trier to perform Archbishop Henry's reconciliations again.[28]

25. Ekkehard, pp. 234–35.
26. JL 6076, 31 March 1106, to Archbishop Ruthard and his suffragans, is the only extant summons to Guastalla. The council was to be held (*Cod. Udal.*, no. 130, p. 247) "pro ecclesie ac regni pace, pro ecclesiarum ordinibus." It was held 22 October. See Blumenthal, *Early Councils of Pope Paschal II*, pp. 32–73.
27. See *Gesta Treverorum*, ed. G. Waitz, *MGH SS*, 8:192; cf. *Translatio sancti Modoaldi*, ed. P. Jaffé, *MGH SS*, 12:295. On Bruno's career, see N. Gladel, "Die trierischen Erzbishöfe in der Zeit des Investiturstreits" (diss., Cologne, 1932), pp. 61–65, and H. Schlechte, "Erzbischof Bruno von Trier" (diss., Leipzig, 1934). The suspension of Bruno may have been part of an attempt by the pope to enact a formal reconciliation of the German bishops to the papacy, creating thereby a direct relationship between pope and bishops. At the end of the council, Paschal issued a canon of reconciliation: Blumenthal, *Early Councils of Pope Paschal II*, p. 53, "Tot igitur filiis in hac strage [i.e., in schism] iacentibus, christiane pacis necessitas exigit ut super hos materna Ecclesie viscera aperiantur . . . prefati regni episcopos in scismate ordinatos, nisi aut invasores aut symoniaci aut criminosi comprobentur in officio episcopali suscipimus."
28. See *Ann. Patherbrunnenses*, p. 115; *Libellus de rebellione*, p. 108; *De Eginone et Hermanno*, ed. P. Jaffé, *MGH SS*, 12:438 (on Hermann of Augsburg's case); Ekkehard, p. 240. For Paschal's order to Bruno of Trier, see JL 6099, *Epistolae Bambergenses*, no. 14

Having done these things, the pope did not go to Germany after the council, though the German court still expected him.[29] Instead, he went to France, where he could wait to see the results of his actions at Guastalla. While there, he settled the investiture controversies in France and England by making compromises that permitted the kings of those countries to participate in choosing bishops but not to invest them.[30] The agreements with France and England rested on the analysis of the *episcopatus* and *regalia* offered by Ivo of Chartres ten years earlier. The agreements permitted the kings to invest bishops with the regalia *after* they had been consecrated. This was a true compromise of the disputed points because it recognized the secular character of the regalia and the rights of kings in them and implied that the *episcopatus* was a unity by making investiture with the regalia merely the completion of an act begun when the new bishop was consecrated. One could say that consecration entailed the right to the regalia and that the king, although he had authority over the regalia, had an obligation to confer them.

It is apparent that Paschal viewed these agreements as temporary arrangements born of political necessity. Had he been committed to the idea of shared authority over bishops, he might have used it in his subsequent negotiations with Henry V, but he had accepted the terms of the French and English agreements only because he needed the support of the two kings more than ever. At Guastalla, he had challenged Henry V by asserting both his authority over the German church and the traditional papal view of investiture.[31]

---

(10 November 1106), ed. P. Jaffé, *Monumenta rerum Germanicarum*, 5:508–9. The pope may have intended this action to drive a wedge between Bruno and his fellow bishops. Shortly after Henry V appointed Adalbert chancellor—at the latest in early February 1106—Bruno and he became embroiled in a power struggle; see Gladel, *Trierische Erzbischöfe*, p. 68. Paschal may have wanted to exploit the possibilities in that competition.

29. See Ekkehard, p. 241; *De Eginone et Hermanno*, p. 438; *Ann. Patherbrunnenses*, p. 115.

30. See Suger, *Vita Ludovici Grossi*, ed. A. Molinier, *MGH SS*, 26:49–50. B. Monod, *Essai sur les rapports de Pascal II avec Philippe Ier*, Bibliothèque de l'Ecole des Hautes Etudes 164 (Paris, 1907), p. 47. A. Becker, *Studien zum Investiturproblem in Frankreich* (Saarbrücken, 1955), pp. 121–22. Z. N. Brooke, *The English Church and the Papacy from the Conquest to the Reign of John* (Cambridge, 1931). N. F. Cantor, *Church, Kingship, and Lay Investiture in England, 1089–1135* (Princeton, 1958).

31. There is no prohibition of investiture among the canons of Guastalla transmitted by Cardinal Boso, which are the basis of all modern editions up to Blumenthal; see Blumenthal, *Early Councils of Pope Paschal II*, pp. 48–57. However, Blumenthal, pp. 57–64, argues that a series of canons transmitted as interpolations in early twelfth-century copies of Anselm of Lucca's collection and in the *Collection in Thirteen Books* (Vat. Lat. 1361) were from the Council of Guastalla. These canons repeat the prohibition of investiture: ibid., p. 60, "Constitutiones sanctorum canonum sequentes statuimus ut quicumque clericorum ab hac hora in antea investituram ecclesiae uel ecclesiasticae dignitatis de manu laica acceperit, et qui ei manum imposuerit, gradus sui periculo subiaceat, et communione privetur."

That the pope did not want to make a similar agreement with the German king is shown by what followed. After inconclusive negotiations held in the spring of 1107, Paschal reasserted the traditional papal view of investiture at the Council of Troyes (held in May) and then repeated it at the Lenten Council of 1110. When the two sides finally did come to an agreement in February 1111, it rested on an idea of *regnum* and *sacerdotium* radically different from the one that supported the agreements with France and England. Even in April 1111, when Paschal was a defeated man, he does not appear to have tried to get out of his predicament by offering Henry the compromise solution of 1107. But the "agreement" of April 1111 may have been dictated by a king who thought he needed complete constitutional control over a church whose leaders knew he had betrayed them. The question is, why, even after years of trying to settle the German investiture controversy, did Paschal view the compromise agreements with France and England as unacceptable for Germany?

The answer may be that he really was committed to the traditional papal definition of the *episcopatus*—and, consequently, of investiture— and really did view the agreements of 1107 merely as political expedients. The record of Paschal's later actions supports this interpretation. But it is also possible that he thought the compromise would not work in Germany, where the bishops were fully integrated into the constitution of the monarchy. Considering the importance of every episcopal appointment, the German king could not be expected to observe the niceties of the compromise that seemed to obligate him to hand over the regalia to a man canonically elected and consecrated. Paschal may have been convinced that there was a strong possibility the German king would withhold the regalia from properly elevated bishops.

The attempts to resolve the investiture controversy in Germany therefore continued to fail. In 1107, while Paschal was in France, he agreed to meet Henry's envoys yet again. He had summoned a new council to meet at Troyes in May 1107, and in preparation he met Henry's embassy in Châlons, on the border of the German kingdom. The king sent a large and distinguished embassy, again led by Bruno of Trier.[32] By now both sides knew that negotiations would be difficult, and they made careful preparations for them.

The royal embassy appears to have represented the range of political opinion in the coalition that had formed to support the new king. Among the bishops were Reinhardt of Halberstadt, who was a representative of Archbishop Ruthard, Erlung of Würzburg and Burchard of Münster, who had once supported Henry IV but had been reconciled with the young king, and Otto of Bamberg, a scrupulous follower of papal doctrine, if not

32. Suger, p. 50; *Ann. Patherbrunnenses*, p. 117; cf. *Chronica regia Coloniensis*, ed. G. Waitz (Hannover, 1880), p. 46.

an open supporter of the pope.[33] The laymen also represented the politics of the coalition. There was Duke Berthold of Zähringen, a supporter of the pope, Count Herman of Winzenburg, who had been an early partisan of Henry V and was probably a strong supporter of royal prerogative in investiture, and Wiprecht of Groitsch and Welf of Bavaria, men who could only be considered typical of the class of self-interested magnates.[34]

At the outset, each side stated its traditional position on investiture, but the magnates in Henry's legation, led by Welf of Bavaria, reacted violently to the speech by the papal representative.[35] Welf and his associates were not patient with the technicalities of canon law. They had a good young king and expected the pope to embrace him.

The magnates' violent outburst broke up the meeting, and afterward Paschal sent a small delegation to Adalbert, Henry's chancellor, who had remained on the German side of the Marne. The two sides decided that

33. Bishop Reinhardt had been consecrated by Ruthard on 30 March 1107. The Annalista Saxo says that he was elected by order of King Henry and by the counsel and violence of the magnates. *Annalista Saxo*, ed. G. Waitz, *MGH SS*, 6:745; *Epistolae Moguntinae*, ed. P. Jaffé, *Monumenta rerum Germanicarum*, vol. 3, nos. 34–36; *Epp. Bambergenses*, vol. 5, nos. 15, 17, 19 (= JL 6500); JL 6144 (= *Cod. Udal.*, no. 139). Erlung and Burchard were appointees of Henry IV who switched their allegiance late in the rebellion. On Erlung, see Ekkehard, p. 241. Burchard was with Henry IV as late as November 1105; see Stumpf, no. 2975, and *MGH Dip*, 6.2:667–69. Meyer von Knonau says that Burchard made peace with Henry V at Mainz (Christmas 1105) but does not cite any sources for the information (5:281). Henry IV held Burchard in captivity during the summer of 1106; see *Libellus de rebellione*, p. 111, and *Ann. Patherbrunnenses*, p. 114. On Otto, see *Cod. Udal.*, nos. 122, 125, 128, which show him wavering between the two Henrys in 1105 and seeking consecration directly from the pope. See C. H. Friedrich, *Die politische Thätigkeit des Bischofs Otto I von Bamberg, eine Studie zur Geschichte des Investiturstreits* (Königsberg, 1881), and M. H. Kotner, *Otto I., Bischof von Bamberg in seinem Verhältnisse zu Heinrich V. und Lothar III.* (Giessen, 1868).

34. Berthold was Bishop Gephard of Constance's brother and a strong supporter of the papacy; see Heyck, *Geschichte der Herzöge von Zähringen* (note 20 above), and Meyer von Knonau, 5:23–24. Hermann had joined young Henry early; see E. von Uslar-Gleichen, *Geschichte der Grafen von Winzenburg* (Hannover, 1895), and Meyer von Knonau, 6:44 n. 20. On the reinstatement of Hermann's relative, Bishop Uto of Hildesheim, see *Ann. Patherbrunnenses*, p. 113, and JL 6145. Wiprecht was an important easterner and strong royalist who came over to Henry V at the end of 1105 after actively supporting the old king; see Meyer von Knonau, 5:266–67. Welf had a history of being closely self-interested. On his behavior during the rebellion of Conrad, see Bernold, *Chronicon*, pp. 449, 452, 461, 463; cf. Ekkehard, p. 208.

35. Suger, p. 50, "Teutonici impetu frendentes tumultabant, et, si tuto auderent, convicia eructuarent, inivias inferrent. 'Non hic,' inquiunt, 'sed Romae gladiis hec terminabitur querela.'" Suger was an eyewitness to the negotiations, but he wrote his account about thirty years after the events. The speeches were reconstructed to give narrative structure to his memory and interpretation of the events. He appears to have been influenced by later events. He calls Henry "imperator" four years before such a title would have been justified. In addition, Bruno of Trier's speech uses a definition of *regalia* that seems to have originated in the tract *De episcoporum investitura*, which was composed in 1109; see below and note 37. In his account, Ekkehard emphasized the king's disappointment when Paschal did not come to Germany and mentions the meeting at Châlons only briefly (p. 242). Cf. *Ann. Patherbrunnenses*, p. 117.

nothing would be accomplished here, and they agreed to put off further negotiations, apparently until Henry could come to Rome the next year.

Probably the pope appealed to Chancellor Adalbert in the hope that he could control the magnates, but also, perhaps, it was because the chancellor was the counterweight to Archbishop Bruno in the royal court. For his part, Adalbert certainly saw that exerting authority over the dukes and counts would be very risky to his own position, and he may also have wanted to avoid helping Bruno. Paschal apparently recognized the nature of Henry's position, because, as Suger reports, he took a positive and patient attitude toward Adalbert.[36]

Beyond this, Bruno's carefully traditional speech at Châlons revealed that the bishops were anxious about a resolution of the investiture controversy. As Suger reported, Bruno said, "Temporibus antecessorum vestrorum sanctorum et apostolicorum virorum . . . hoc ad ius imperii pertinere dinoscitur, ut in omni electione hic ordo servetur: antequam electio in palam proferatur, ad aures domini imperatoris perferre, et si personam deceat, assensum ab eo ante factam electionem assumere, deinde in conventu secundum canones peticione populi, electione cleri, assensu honoratoris proferre, consecratum libere nec simoniace ad imperatorem pro regalibus, ut anulo et virga investiatur, redire, fidelitatem et hominium facere."[37] With these words, Bruno affirmed that he and his fellow bishops represented a German episcopate that valued its close relationship with the monarchy and, therefore, revealed that the bishops were as much of an obstacle to an agreement on the investiture issue as were the king himself and the magnates, who, as was said, seem to have had little patience with the legal argument.

Now, either Henry and Adalbert did not yet see the futility of negotiations based on the positions Bruno enunciated or they could not yet shift their ground. In either case, the need for a reconciliation with Paschal remained great, for, as the makeup of the royal embassy showed, Henry's power rested on a disparate coalition, and the conflict with the papacy was a ready-made excuse for elements of it to go into opposition.

Suger's tone in reporting the consultations between the pope and Adalbert indicates that they agreed to cooperate in bringing about the reconciliation. They agreed to put off further negotiations, and one can only suppose that the purpose of the delay was to permit Adalbert, and the king, to build a political basis for successful negotiations. To do this, the

36. Suger, generally critical and distrustful of the German king and his advisers, reports that the pope and chancellor held a cordial meeting (pp. 50–51). Giesebrecht (3.2:784) says that the pope turned to Adalbert because the chancellor, being close to the king, appeared to be the best person to bring about a compromise. This implies that the pope wanted a compromise, presumably like the ones he had recently made with the kings of France and England. But there is no evidence that Paschal was willing to compromise with Henry.

37. Suger, p. 50.

king and his chancellor had to strengthen magnate support for the monarchy, for the problem was that the king had to be able to defy the episcopate. The bishops were royalists, but they were powerful enough to force the king not only to recognize but to protect their constitutional position by continuing to insist on investiture. To effect a reconciliation with the papacy, Henry and Adalbert had to create an independent base of support in the nobility.

They seem to have thought that they could reduce the fickleness of the nobility by helping them to further their ambitions for land and wealth. So long as the king's wealth and power also grew, he might build a lasting alliance with the great families. By hindsight the idea seems unrealistic, but it may have looked good from the young king's unstable throne.

A difficult time followed these failures of 1105–7. The king could not yet rely on magnate support, and consequently he continued to invest bishops.[38] When Henry sent a new embassy to the pope in 1109, it was again dominated by bishops whose conservative stance hindered any progress.[39]

The treatise *De episcoporum investitura*, which was apparently written to serve as instructions for the embassy, expresses the limits of the bishops' willingness to compromise. Its author, who may have been Sigebert of Gembloux, asserts the traditional imperialist position. He argues that the bishopric has a dual nature. It is subject to the church in *spiritualia* and to the king in *temporalia*. Therefore, elevation of a bishop is a joint action of the two powers, and the king has the right to invest bishops with the regalian rights.[40]

During the next two and a half years, the king devoted most of his

38. After Châlons, Henry prohibited the German bishops from going to Paschal's council at Troyes, for which the pope punished them; see *Ann. Patherbrunnenses*, p. 117, and Ekkehard, p. 242. For Henry's installation of bishops, about which Paschal complained at Troyes and afterward, see *Ann. Patherbrunnenses*, pp. 117–18; cf. Meyer von Knonau, 6:54–55 n. 30.

39. The delegation of 1109 was made up of Bruno of Trier, Frederick of Cologne, chancellor Adalbert, and Hermann of Winzenburg, among others. See *Gesta Treverorum*, p. 193.

40. The view that the treatise was written specifically for the embassy rests on its literary character. It lacks many of the formal characteristics of polemical tracts meant for publication. It was written in the diocese of Liège, perhaps by Sigebert of Gembloux, who had already established a reputation as a royal publicist, but certainly under his influence. The tract was revised in a shorter version, which may have been intended to serve as instructions for the new negotiations of 1111. This version is toned down somewhat. The original treatise was first edited by E. Bernheim, *MGH LdL*, 1:495–504. It has been reedited, with a clear indication of the differences between the two versions, by J. Krimm-Beumann, "Der Traktat 'De investitura episcoporum' von 1109," *DA* 33 (1977): 37–83. See E. Bernheim, "Über den Traktat De investitura episcoporum," *Forschungen zur deutschen Geschichte* 16 (1876): 279–98, and J. Beumann, *Sigebert von Gembloux und der der Traktat de investitura episcoporum* (Sigmaringen, 1976). H. Fuhrmann, *Germany in the High Middle Ages: C. 1050–1200*, trans. T. Reuter (Cambridge, 1986), p. 87, accepts the attribution to Sigebert.

attention to a series of military campaigns that served the interests of his lay supporters and promised to solidify their adherence to him. First, he led an army against Count Robert of Flanders, who had been disturbing the western regions. The campaign was not particularly successful, but it resulted in a settlement that ensured peace.[41] Then Henry turned his attention to the complicated affairs of Poland and Bohemia, where some of his most powerful supporters had interests.[42]

Eastern affairs occupied Henry from the summer of 1108 to the end of 1109, but he seems to have achieved little. By the end of 1109, his political outlook was bleak. He had not succeeded in binding the magnates to his crown by giving them the wealth and security that victory would have brought. He was therefore more than ever dependent on the church, whose support remained precarious because of the conflict with Paschal. To understand the events of 1111, we must appreciate that by early 1110 Henry was in a very difficult, if not desperate, position.

At the beginning of 1110, he was working on two projects to shore up his monarchy—reconciliation with the pope and the establishment of a family alliance with the king of England, Henry I.[43] Around Christmas 1109, he began working toward reconciliation with Paschal, and he received Mathilda, Henry I's young daughter, in March 1110.

Reconciliation was now more important than ever. The continuing controversy over investitures made the threat of excommunication a matter of grave concern, for already at Guastalla the pope had added to the law on investitures the stipulation that not only those who receive ecclesiastical office from laymen, but also the giver of investiture would be subject to excommunication.[44] It is even possible that the alliance with Henry I depended on the promise of the imperial crown.

41. Meyer von Knonau, 6:65–71.

42. See *Annales Pegavienses,* ed. G. Pertz, *MGH SS,* 16:235; G. A. von Mulverstedt, *Regesta archiepiscopatus Magdeburgensis,* vol. 1 (Magdeburg, 1876), p. 340. See Meyer von Knonau, 6:61–65, for a summary of the politics of Bohemia and Poland, based primarily on Cosmas, *Chronicon Boemorum,* vol. 3, chaps. 19–28, ed. R. Kopke, *MGH SS,* 9:110–16.

43. K. Leyser, "England and the Empire in the Early Twelfth Century," *Transactions of the Royal Historical Society,* ser. 5, 10 (1960): 61–83. See Henry's letter to Queen Mathilda of England, wife of Henry I, seeking her support and friendship and concerning an embassy the German king had sent to her and her husband; *Cod. Udal.,* no. 142, p. 259, dated by Jaffé only 1106–9.

44. For Guastalla, see note 31. Blumenthal (*Early Councils of Pope Paschal II,* p. 106) points out that at Guastalla Paschal had already added the threat of excommunication against the giver as well as the receiver of lay investiture. Older authorities had argued that the pope first added the threat to the lay invester at the synod of Benevento in 1108. See Peiser, pp. 47–49, and Meyer von Knonau, 6:90. Blumenthal agrees with Peiser and Meyer von Knonau in seeing the decree issued at Benevento as directed against Henry. From Benevento, Paschal wrote Archbishop Anselm of Canterbury stating the threat; JL 6206 (Benevento, 12 October 1108), PL 163, col. 246, "Rex [Henry V] vero si in paternae nequitiae tramite perseveraverit, Beati Petri gladium quem iam educere coepimus procul dubio experietur."

While strengthening the law against lay investiture, the pope had also meddled in German politics. He repeatedly tried to bring the German bishops into obedience to him and under the papal rules about investiture. Already at the Council of Guastalla in 1106, when he was supposed to be preparing to go to Germany, he had asserted his authority over the German episcopate.[45]

He renewed his efforts at the synod of Troyes in May 1107. About the time of the council, Paschal suspended Ruthard for reinstating Uto of Hildesheim and for consecrating Reinhard of Halberstadt, remonstrated with Gebhard of Constance for consenting to the consecration of Gottschalk of Minden and for participating in the consecration of Henry of Magdeburg, and suspended Frederick of Cologne and his suffragans for failing to answer the summons to the council.[46]

On their face, Paschal's actions at Troyes appear to have been a continuation of what he had done at Guastalla, where both in his treatment of Bruno of Trier and in his legislation he seems to have taken a hard line with the Germans, but the actions of 1107 may also have been related to what had happened at Châlons. The position represented at Châlons by Bruno of Trier indicated that the bishops opposed the papal view of investitures, and their prominence in the delegation showed that they held enough power to obstruct progress toward reconciliation on any but their own terms. If, as suggested earlier, Paschal and Adalbert agreed at Châlons to delay negotiations while Henry worked to balance the power of the bishops in Germany, then the actions of Troyes may have been designed to help him by applying papal discipline to the situation.[47]

The combined efforts of the king and pope to reduce the influence of the bishops failed. Throughout the period when he was occupied with the eastern frontier, Henry was surrounded by bishops, and of necessity he continued to build an episcopate loyal to him. The centerpiece of this policy was the appointment of his chancellor Adalbert as archbishop-elect of Mainz in May 1109.[48] But the king did not invest Adalbert, perhaps because the investment of a new primate would have made opening new negotiations nearly impossible. The status of Adalbert was a challenge to Paschal: either the pope and king would be reconciled, or Henry would consolidate his control over the episcopate by the investiture of his close friend.

At the end of 1109, Henry tested the willingness of the pope to deal with him by sending Walcher, who had been deposed from the bishopric of

45. See note 27.
46. *Ann. Patherbrunnenses*, pp. 117–18, and JL 6143 (= *Epp. Mogunt.* no. 37).
47. Shortly after Troyes, Paschal wrote strong denunciations to the German bishops; see JL 6143, 6144, 6145, and 6146. All these letters date from late May 1107.
48. Ruthard died on 2 May 1109, and Henry appointed Adalbert immediately. See Ekkehard, p. 243; *Annales Corbeienses*, ed. G. Pertz, *MGH SS*, 3:7; *Ann. Patherbrunnenses*, p. 132.

Cambrai for receiving it from the king, as a representative in advance of a new embassy. If the pope received Walcher, it would be a clear signal that Paschal was ready to deal with Henry himself. The king got his signal. The pope received Walcher and granted him the dignities that he had held before his illicit elevation to Cambrai.[49]

At the beginning of 1110, Henry sent a new embassy, led by Archbishops Frederick of Cologne and Bruno of Trier and Archbishop-Elect Adalbert (who remained chancellor). Paschal's answer to the new approach was encouraging and vague. He said he would receive Henry if he showed himself to be a good Catholic king and if he admitted the canonical rights of the church. Paschal, on his side, would not demand anything that would damage the king's rights.[50] This was encouraging, but it made Henry responsible for taking the initiative.

In 1106, it had been Paschal who was supposed to travel to Germany for a reconciliation. In 1107, the two men had approached one another along the border of the French and German kingdoms. Now Henry had to go to Rome. As in 1106, it was risky for one party to go to the other's territory for a meeting. If something went wrong, the danger of military action was high and the conflict would become even more intractable than it was. To prepare for every eventuality, Henry had to go to Rome strongly supported. If the reconciliation succeeded, all those there would reflect his glory. If it failed, he would need strong forces to extricate himself.

From mid-1110, Henry worked on making a grand march to Rome. He collected a large army in the western part of the kingdom, while Welf V of Bavaria and other eastern magnates gathered a similar force in the east. The two armies crossed the Alps separately in mid-August and met at Roncaglia. From there, Henry made a procession through Lombardy and over the Apennines. In January, he sent a new embassy—composed of churchmen like the earlier ones—from Arezzo. This delegation received another vague response, which did not move the parties any closer to reconciliation.

It did not seem that Henry could make Paschal leave the realm of diplomatic niceties and enter into real bargaining on the issues, and unless this happened the trip was unlikely to turn out well. Either Henry would have to use force, or he would have to go home uncrowned and very much weakened. It was at this point that he took the radical step of changing his

---

49. On Walcher, see the *Vita vel actus Galcheri episcopi Cameracensis* ed. G. Waitz, *MGH SS*, 14:183–210; *Gesta Odonis episcopi Cameracensis, MGH SS*, 14:210–11; cf. JL 6250 and 6251. Walcher had held offices in the churches of Reims and Brabant before his adventure in Cambrai. The *Ann. Patherbrunnenses* (p. 120) do not mention Walcher as a member of the embassy sent by the king.

50. *Ann. Patherbrunnenses*, pp. 120–22; Donizo captured the tone of the exchange in *Vita Mathildis*, vv. 1131–34, ed. L. Bethmann, *MGH SS*, 12:401, "Pontifices magnos comiters direxit [Henry] et altos / Magnificam Romam, pro regni quippe corona. / Filius esse Petri si vult rex atque fidelis, / Papa *dabo Romam* respondit *eique coronam.*"

negotiators. He sent a new delegation, led by Chancellor Adalbert and composed of magnates, to meet the pope's envoys at Santa Maria in Turri in the Leonine city.[51]

Paschal had maneuvered Henry into this position, but as the royal army moved closer to Rome it put pressure on the papal court. That the pope felt the pressure is shown by his appeal in January to the Lombards and Normans for support. When he received only promises, which his supporters recognized as empty (as the Chronicle of Montecassino put it, "qui verba ferebat, verba recepit"),[52] he too was ready to negotiate at Santa Maria.

Notwithstanding the testimony Henry gave in his encyclical to his bishops and magnates, there is no direct and incontrovertible evidence that identifies the originator of the bold new ideas embodied in the agreement. Long ago, Bernheim showed that certain crucial phrases in the agreement echo the royalist tract *De episcoporum investitura*.[53] Nonetheless, the treaty departed definitively from the position taken in the tract. It could be that the negotiators, putting together a radically new solution to the problem of investitures, used whatever came to hand in existing documents, but the failure to use papal and conciliar decrees as well as the royalist treatise weakens this interpretation. Rather, it seems that Adalbert and his counterparts sought to make the agreement sound as if it grew directly out of the positions expressed by the German bishops.

The concern of the negotiators was probably focused on the reaction of the German bishops, who were indeed among the principal objectors when the agreement was announced in St. Peter's on 12 February. Further, although the bishops did not go into rebellion immediately—because the treaty failed and they were left in their powerful position—the attempted agreement undermined the relationship between them and the king and was probably a principal cause of the episcopal opposition that began after the return to Germany and lasted until the Concordat of Worms.

Why was Henry willing to risk so much in the agreement of Santa Maria? By 1111, it was clear that the king could not rule without controlling the bishops and their regalia. Therefore, he could neither accept the papal law of investiture nor remain in dispute with the pope. At the synod

---

51. Ekkehard, pp. 243–45. Ekkehard acknowledges that his account is based on a work by the Scottish scholar David, whom Henry took on the campaign as historian. David's book is lost. He was then the regent of the cathedral school in Würzburg. The king wanted to record the expected resolution of the Investiture Controversy and his coronation; see Ekkehard, p. 243. For an analysis of the sources see Meyer von Knonau, vol. 6, excursus 1, pp. 369–90. Pivec thought that during the journey south David became the dominant figure in the king's entourage and that he was responsible for drafting the documents of the agreement reached in S. Maria, but there is no evidence that Adalbert lost any influence until 1112. For the literature, see note 14.

52. Petrus, *Chronicon monasteriae Casinensis*, ed. W. Wattenbach, *MGH SS*, 7:779.

53. See note 14.

of Benevento in 1108 Paschal directly threatened the king with excommunication, which had been his father's downfall.[54] By depriving the German bishops of their regalia, the agreement cleared away these problems. Henry could not hope to hold onto the regalia, but the windfall would give him the wherewithal to gain the firm support of the magnates, which had been a particular goal since 1107, and some of the regalia would surely stay in his hands.

These considerations may explain Henry's motivation in agreeing to, perhaps even proposing, the agreement's radical terms, but why would the pope join him? He and his predecessors had wanted to make the church *as it was* free of secular control. Now, he was agreeing to take it as the imperialists said it would have to be—deprived of the regalia—if it were ever to be completely free of the emperor's (and kings') control. This is not what he had meant to accomplish when he made the temporary compromises with the French and English kings.

One interpretation of his willingness to give up so much is the one that has become traditional—that he was an idealist who hoped to create a purely spiritual church. A person with such ideals would have been the proposer of the agreement, as Henry said in his encyclical.

But remember that what broke the barrier to an agreement was a change in the king's team of negotiators, not anything the pope did. There is no good reason for supposing that the pope ended the stalemate by proposing the agreement. Furthermore, one can interpret the pope's motivation in accepting the agreement as essentially pragmatic. Paschal probably saw the risk to be primarily Henry's. Whether the treaty succeeded or failed, Henry would have to deal with the consequences. He would have to assure the magnates that they would share in the regalia, a matter in which good timing would be critical. He would also have to deal with the opposition of the bishops, a group of powerful men who would either be fighting to retain their status or irate that the king had tried to deprive them of it. If, as Henry later wrote, Paschal promised to help recover the regalia, he must have made the promise with a measure of cynicism. For years he had been trying unsuccessfully to gain the obedience of the German bishops; he was merely promising to keep trying.

In fact, Paschal was a practical politician. He had inherited a papacy that had high international prestige but could not maintain itself in Rome.[55]

54. See note 44.
55. When Urban II died in 1099, the procession bearing him to burial had to skirt the city. *Liber pontificalis*, 2:294, "Qui Christi confessor [Urban] et bonus Christi atleta apud sanctum Nicolaum in Carcere, in domo Petri Leonis, IIII kl. aug. animam Deo reddidit; atque per Transtiberim propter insidias inimicorum in ecclesia beati Petri, ut moris est, corpus eius delatum est et ibi honorifice humatum." The Pierleoni lived in the Teatro di Marcello, near San Nicola in Carcere, and controlled the Transtevere. The center of medieval Rome was around Santa Maria in Rotunda and was controlled by antipapal families. See D. Zema, "The House of Tuscany and of Pierleoni in the Crisis of Rome in the Eleventh Century," *Traditio* 2 (1944): 155–75.

During the first decade of his reign, he had reestablished control over the city. Part of that activity was a building program that restored some important churches, including at least one that had been ruined during the Norman invasion of 1085.[56] Paschal had also restored the administration of the papal estates outside Rome.[57] In early 1111, all this work was threatened. The Normans had effectively refused assistance against the advancing German king, and the Romans were untrustworthy.[58] Henry and his army could undo Paschal's patient work of restoring papal authority and income in and around Rome. The pope was impelled to make an agreement.

In the event, Paschal was the first one to face the risks inherent in the treaty concluded at Sutri. While the pope was a prisoner, the king endangered a decade's work, and Paschal's sudden capitulation in April may have been motivated by a desire to send Henry and his troops home rather than by a weakness of character. Certainly, Paschal's strength against the pressures put on him to abdicate and to excommunicate Henry, leading up to the Lenten synod of 1112, do not make him appear weak willed. Although he repudiated the capitulation of April 1111, he refused to excommunicate the king, and he never repudiated the agreement of Sutri.[59] He may have thought that the consequences of the crisis for Henry would induce him to renew efforts to be reconciled to the Roman church as soon as he could. The terms of the agreement of Sutri remained ground on which the two practical politicians could meet.

It is only a slight exaggeration to say that the ideal of a purely spiritual church expressed in the agreement was generated by men whose concerns

56. The *Liber pontificalis* (2:297–99) says that Paschal brought peace to the city, drove out Wibert (the antipope Clement), gained control of Cività Castellana, which had been the last refuge of the antipopes, and of Benevento, and defeated the noble family of the Corsi, which had seized part of the city. See Servatius, *Paschalis II.*, pp. 73–85, 87. The *Liber* (p. 305) names three churches consecrated by Paschal. One of them was the church of Sancti Quattro Martiri, which had been destroyed by the Normans in 1085. He also reconstructed San Clemente, which had been his titular church.

57. Paschal played an important role in the history of papal financial and curial administration. See Servatius, *Paschalis II.*, pp. 58–69. K. Jordan, "Zur päpstlichen Finanzgeschichte im 11. und 12. Jahrhundert," *QF* 25 (1933–34): 61–104, and "Die Entstehung der Romischen Kurie," *ZRG*, Kan. Abt., 29 (1938): 97–152.

58. During his march south, Henry wooed the Romans, writing directly to them; see *Cod. Udal.*, no. 148, p. 269, dated by Jaffé December 1110–January 1111, "Volumus, quatinus idoneos nuncios, vestrae utilitatis providos et nostri honoris devotos, nobis obviam mittatis." The Romans sent a delegation that met him at Aquapadente; see Ekkehard, p. 244.

59. On the Lenten Council, see note 7, and S. Chodorow, "Ecclesiastical Politics and the Ending of the Investiture Contest," *Speculum* 46 (1971): 623 with nn. 27–28. Paschal continued dealing with Henry throughout 1111; see JL 6293, 6295, 6296, 6299, 6300, 6305 (= *Cod. Udal.*, nos. 152, 154, 155, 156, 157, 158). He wrote Henry again to demand that he release Archbishop Adalbert of Mainz—whom Henry had invested!—from captivity; JL 6339 (*Cod. Udal.*, no. 163).

were purely temporal. And even adding the qualifications that might have to be admitted to this view, it is paradoxical that idealists like Bernard of Clairvaux and Gerhoch of Reichersberg found their dream of a spiritual church so powerfully revealed in the extraordinary agreement of Sutri. The crises in church and state that followed the announcement of the treaty enhanced its ideational power as they obscured its origins.

# [2]

## Innocent III, Canon Law, and
## Papal Judges Delegate in Hungary

### JAMES ROSS SWEENEY

The earliest documented instance of delegated papal jurisdiction in lands subject to the Hungarian king dates from the reign of Pope Alexander III (1159–81), although it is likely that here as elsewhere in Europe the practice had become common in the first half of the twelfth century.[1] In 1161, Alexander III directed Peter of Narni, the archbishop of Spalato (Split) in Dalmatia, to see that one of his suffragans, the bishop of Knin, accept the sentence of deposition promulgated in a prior mandate of Eugenius III or else suffer the sentence of excommunication upon himself

I thank Professors Erik Fügedi (Budapest), Othmar Hageneder (Vienna), Richard Helmholz (Chicago), and Kenneth Pennington (Syracuse) for reading an earlier draft of this chapter and for generously offering helpful criticisms. I have benefited from their advice even if I did not always follow their suggestions. Research for this essay was supported in part by a grant from the Alexander von Humboldt Stiftung, Bonn, Germany.

1. Dietrich Lohrmann has drawn attention to the use of papal delegated jurisdiction as early as the era of the eleventh-century Reform Papacy; "Papstprivileg und päpstliche Delegationsgerichtsbarkeit im nördlichen Frankreich zur Zeit der Kirchenreform," in *Proceedings of the Sixth International Congress of Medieval Canon Law, Berkeley California, 28 July–2 August 1980* (Mon. iur. can., ser. C, Subsidia, vol. 7 (Vatican City, 1985), pp. 535–50. Evidence for judicial delegation is more abundant and widespread from the pontificate of Paschal II (1099–1118) and thereafter. For an excellent introduction to twelfth-century developments see Jane E. Sayers, *Papal Judges Delegate in the Province of Canterbury, 1198–1254* (Oxford, 1971), pp. 9–11, who notes that England possesses "more material to illustrate the development of papal delegated jurisdiction before 1198 than probably any other country" (p. 3). For the province of Rheims in the same period see Ludwig Falkenstein, "Appellationen an den Papst und Delegationsgerichtsbarkeit am Beispiel Alexanders III. und Heinrichs von Frankreich," *Zeitschrift für Kirchengeschichte* 97 (1986): 36–65; for the Austrian areas of the province of Salzburg see Othmar Hageneder, *Die geistliche Gerichtsbarkeit in Ober- und Niederösterreich* (Linz, 1967), pp. 24–36.

and interdict upon his see. Archbishop Peter was further commanded to inquire into the truth of reports of uncanonical irregularities in the election of another suffragan, the bishop of Traù (Trogir), which were brought to papal notice by Peter, cardinal deacon of Sant'Eustachio, and certain others. If after ascertaining the truth of the matter the archbishop were to find that the situation was as reported to Rome, he was to compel the bishop's removal and the cessation of episcopal functions through ecclesiastical penalties without the right to appeal.[2] The Dalmatian church, comprising the provinces of Zara (Zadar) and Spalato, was in 1161 subject to the Hungarian king Géza II as ruler of Croatia and Dalmatia, although the Dalmatian provinces were never regarded as integral parts of the Hungarian church.[3] Somewhat later, in 1177, Alexander III gave a mandate to another archbishop of Spalato, Rainerius, and his suffragan, Michael of Traù, to secure the restitution of stolen papal letters and other diplomatic correspondence as well as sixty marks of silver, all taken by naval pirates based in the town of Sebenico (Šibenik) from two papal legates en route from the royal court of Sicily. Failing that, the archbishop was to place the town of Sebenico under interdict.[4] The archbishop and his colleague were further instructed to excommunicate the piratical

2. T. Smičiklas, *Codex diplomaticus regni Croatiae, Dalmatiae et Slavoniae*, vol. 2 (Zagreb, 1904), p. 92, no. 90; Philip Jaffé, *Regesta pontificum Romanorum*, 2d ed. (Leipzig, 1885–88), no. 10676 (1 September 1161). Peter of Narni came to Spalato from Umbria in Italy and possessed a reputation for great learning, especially in medicine. He died in 1166 while at the Hungarian royal court in Székesfehérvár; see Thomas of Spalato, *Historia Salonitanorum pontificum atque Spalatensium*, ed. F. Rački (Zagreb, 1894), p. 65. For Peter de Mizo, cardinal deacon of Sant'Eustachio and later cardinal priest of S. Lorenzo in Damaso, see Werner Maleczek, *Papst und Kardinalskolleg von 1191 bis 1216* (Vienna, 1984), pp. 242, 249. Cardinal Peter had been sent to Spalato in the summer of 1161 to bestow the pallium on Archbishop Peter; see Smičiklas, *Codex diplomaticus*, 2:91, no. 89; Jaffé, *Regesta pontificum*, no. 10669 (2 July 1161).

3. In the twelfth century Hungarian monarchs since the time of King Coloman (Kálmán, 1095–1116) styled themselves kings of Croatia and Dalmatia. They repeatedly arranged for the election of clerics from the royal court to the archiepiscopal see of Spalato. Spalatan archbishops were frequent visitors at the Hungarian royal court; see Thomas of Spalato, *Historia*, pp. 61, 64–65. It is also worth noting that the German imperial notary, Burchard of Cologne, reported that in 1161 Alexander III had granted King Géza of Hungary the right to bestow the pallium on Hungarian archbishops following their election, and had agreed that bishops and clerics should not proceed to Rome except with royal consent; see H. Sudendorf, *Registrum oder merkwürdige Urkunden für die deutsche Geschichte*, 3 vols. (Jena and Berlin, 1849–54), 2:134, no. 55; Jaffé, *Regesta pontificum*, no. *10682. Whether or not Burchard's report is credible in all details, it appears that the Dalmatian church was excluded. Walther Holtzmann has argued that Gerhoch of Reichersberg independently confirmed that portion of Burchard's report dealing with the prohibition of appeals to Rome; "Papst Alexander III. und Ungarn," in *Beiträge zur Reichs- und Papstgeschichte des hohen Mittelalters* (Bonn, 1957), pp. 151–52. The existence of such an agreement between the papacy and Hungary, moreover, may help to explain why evidence for appeals to Rome from Hungary in the middle of the twelfth century is lacking.

4. Smičiklas, *Codex diplomaticus*, 2:144, no. 142; Jaffé, *Regesta Pontificum*, no. 12889 (23 July 1177).

leaders and their associates for having laid hands on one of the legates. Since Archbishop Rainerius was serving as *legatus* in his own province, this case may properly be considered an example of a papal legatine commission rather than an instance of delegated jurisdiction. Dalmatia by this time was no longer subject to the Hungarian king but was administered and garrisoned as a Byzantine province.[5] No other piece of evidence, however, remotely touches upon the question of the exercise of delegated papal authority in Hungary or its dependencies after 1161 until the pontificate of Innocent III.

In the first years of Innocent's pontificate we find clear evidence for delegated jurisdiction in Hungary that also sheds light on the closing years of the twelfth century. Writing on 15 June 1198 to Bishop Adrian of Transylvania, Innocent confirmed the terms of a settlement worked out by Gregory of Sancto Apostolo, cardinal deacon of Santa Maria in Portico, in 1192, when he was serving as legate in Hungary.[6] From Innocent's text we can reconstruct the central issues in the dispute and note the role the papacy played in resolving the case. In 1189 King Béla III had founded the collegiate church of Nagyszeben (Hermannstadt, Sibiu) in eastern Transylvania to serve as the spiritual center for the large community of German settlers known as Transylvanian Saxons, who had earlier immigrated to this region.[7] Shortly after Béla's grant an appeal was lodged in Rome, probably by the bishop of Transylvania, protesting the extent of the spiritual jurisdiction claimed by the newly established provost of Nagyszeben. The pope, Celestine III, remitted the case to Cardinal Gregory, his legate in Hungary. In settling the case the cardinal restricted the extent of the provost's jurisdiction to those Transylvanian Saxons subject to the provost at the time of the church's foundation and to those living in the wilderness of Transylvania (*in deserto*), but all other German settlers in Transylvania were to be subject to the authority of the bishop. The effect of the legate's judgment and of Innocent III's subsequent confirmation was to preserve the integrity of episcopal jurisdiction.

For the entire pontificate of Innocent III we possess a total of forty-three references to delegated jurisdiction in the correspondence addressed to Hungarian recipients. The papal register, so valuable to historians in other contexts, preserves thirteen papal letters explicitly concerned with cases

---

5. See John Kinnamos, *Deeds of John and Manuel Comnenus*, trans. C. M. Brand (New York, 1976), pp. 186–87; Gyula Moravcsik, *Byzantium and the Magyars* (Amsterdam, 1970), p. 83; Jadran Ferluga, *Byzantium on the Balkans* (Amsterdam, 1976), pp. 193–213; and Jadran Ferluga, *L'amministrazione bizantina in Dalmazia* (Venice, 1978), pp. 256–69.

6. *Innocentii III Regesta*, 1:272, in Migne, *PL*, 214:228 (hereafter *Inn. III Reg.* or *Reg.*), and in O. Hageneder and A. Haidacher, *Die Register Innocenz' III.*, vol. 1 (Graz, 1964), p. 375, no. 272; A. Potthast, *Regesta pontificum Romanorum* (Berlin, 1874–75), no. 284. For Cardinal Gregory of S. Maria in Portico see Maleczek, *Papst und Kardinalskolleg*, pp. 93–94.

7. See I. Szentpétery and I. Borsa, *Regesta regum stirpis Arpadianae*, 2 vols. (Budapest, 1923–61), no. 150 (hereafter *Reg. Arp.*).

appealed to Rome and subsequently remanded to local judges.[8] There exist also ten papal letters omitted from the register but preserved by the recipients, which deal with the same sort of circumstances.[9] Valuable additional information on one case appealed to Rome and delegated to an auditor in the *audientia*, the famous Cardinal Guala Bicchieri, is found only in a decretal letter included in the *Decretales* of Gregory IX.[10] The text of a sentence rendered by a panel of three Hungarian papal judges delegate has also come down to us. Drafted in 1215, it is the oldest document of its kind known in Hungary.[11] From these documents and several others it is possible to identify an additional eighteen lost letters, or *deperdita*, most in the form of mandates to Hungarian prelates serving as judges delegate.[12]

From these documents and allusive references collectively constituting the earliest body of evidence for the work of judges delegate in Hungary we are able to ascertain patterns in the character and processes of litigation and in the selection of judges. The following analysis sets out to illuminate one of the several forms of contact and communication between representatives of the Hungarian church and the papal court at a crucial time in the development of Western ecclesiology. The interaction between Hungary and Rome in the resolution of legal disputes, moreover, furnishes comparative evidence for a Europeanwide assessment of the efficacy of the system of delegated jurisdiction. When the Hungarian cases are scrutinized with reference to those cases contemporaneously arising from England and France which have been examined by modern scholars such as Jane Sayers and John C. Moore, we find confirmation of the broad outlines of established practice as well as some regional peculiarities. In

8. *Inn. III Reg.* 1:272; Potthast 284, Hageneder, *Register*, 1:272. *Reg.*, 1:510; Potthast 508; Hageneder, *Register*, 1:510. *Reg.*, 1:544; Potthast 583; Hageneder, *Register*, 1:541. *Reg.*, 1:546; Potthast 582; Hageneder, *Register*, 1:543. *Reg.*, 1:540; Potthast 584; Hageneder, *Register*, 1:537. *Reg.*, 2:89; Potthast 749; O. Hageneder, W. Maleczek, and A. E. Strnad, *Die Register Innocenz' III.* (Rome and Vienna, 1972), 2:89. *Reg.*, 8:49; Potthast 2184. *Reg.*, 8:98; Potthast 2547. *Reg.*, 9:75; Potthast 2791. *Reg.*, 9:113; Potthast 2837. *Reg.*, 13:12; Potthast 3930. *Reg.*, 15:7; Potthast 4401. *Reg.*, 16:62; Potthast 4737.

9. *Monumenta romana episcopatus Vesprimiensis*, 4 vols. (Budapest, 1896–1907), 1:11, no. 13; 16, no. 19; 16, no. 20; 17, no. 21 (Potthast 3369); 18, no. 23; 19, no. 26; 29, no. 31 (Potthast 4918); 30, no. 32 (Potthast 4987); 36, no. 39 (Potthast 5102); 38, no. 40 (Potthast 5109); 4:305, no. 239 (hereafter *Mon. rom. ep. Vesprim.*).

10. X 3.30.31. Friedberg, *CIC*, 2:567–68.

11. *Mon. rom. ep. Vesprim.*, 1:33, no. 35.

12. Reference to now-lost mandates is made in texts printed in A. Theiner, *Vetera monumenta Slavorum Meridionalium historiam illustrantia*, vol. 1 (Rome, 1863), p. 58, no. 82 (hereafter *Mon. Slav.*) (Potthast 1398) and p. 59, no. 135 (Potthast 1457); and in *Mon. rom. ep. Vesprim.*, 1:10, no. 12; 33, no. 35; 41, no. 45; 43, no. 48 (three *deperdita*); 65, no. 78; 74, no. 88; and in *Inn. III Reg.*, 6:196 (Potthast 2086), *Reg.*, 7:128 (Potthast 2280), *Reg.*, 9:74 (Potthast 2793) and *Reg.*, 15:7 (Potthast 4401); and in A. Theiner, *Vetera monumenta historica Hungariam sacram illustrantia*, vol. 1 (Rome, 1859), p. 61, no. 129 (hereafter *Mon. Hung.*) (Potthast 7477). Although a mandate ordering the archbishop of Esztergom to respond to charges brought against him in the *audientia* has been lost, the sentence rendered by the auditors is preserved in *Mon. rom. ep. Vesprim.* 1:35, no. 38.

James Ross Sweeney

view of the notorious scarcity of medieval Hungarian historical documentation, the present discussion may also demonstrate the value of exploiting ecclesiastical and legal sources as a way of deepening our understanding of the operation of key institutions within the kingdom in general. The identification of the specific prelates frequently chosen as papal judges, for example, suggests that these were the clerics most respected by their contemporaries for their fairness or judicial impartiality. This insight is a valuable complement to analyses of dynastic connections and social standing in the ongoing historical investigations of Hungarian higher clergy in the Middle Ages.

The surviving evidence, although fragmentary, permits us to identify those prelates whom Innocent III called upon with some frequency to serve as papal judges delegate. Between the years 1198 and 1216, the pope sent a mandate to the bishop of every diocese in both provinces at least once. The bishops of Veszprém (Esztergom province) and Csanád (Kalocsa province) received commissions more often than most of their colleagues, while the bishops of Győr, Ugrinus and Peter together, served more frequently than any other prelate. The primate, the archbishop of Esztergom, appears to have functioned as a judge delegate relatively more often than the archbishop of Kalocsa, but neither metropolitan appears to have been asked to act in this capacity with any regularity. Although this seems somewhat unusual, special circumstances may account for such infrequent service. During Innocent's pontificate both archiepiscopal sees experienced vacancies: Esztergom suffered through a prolonged election dispute, and the archbishop-elect of Kalocsa waited years before receiving papal approval for his consecration.[13] The Dalmatian archbishops, with one exception, do not appear as judges delegate.[14]

During Innocent's pontificate the abbot of the Benedictine foundation at Tihány was called upon to serve as a judge more often than the abbots of Székszard, Pécsvárad, and Bakonybél. But no other Benedictine abbot, except the abbot of Traù in Dalmatia, is mentioned as a judge delegate despite the fact that there may have been in the first half of the thirteenth century as many as one hundred Benedictine abbeys of widely differing size and prominence in Hungary.[15] The abbot of St. Martin of Pannon-

13. For circumstances concerning the vacancy at Esztergom see J. R. Sweeney, "Innocent III and the Esztergom Election Dispute: The Historical Background of the Decretal Bone Memorie II (X.I.5.4)," Archivum historiae pontificiae 15 (1977): 113–37.

14. Inn. III Reg., 5:110 (Potthast 1768). The activities of judges delegate in Dalmatia during Innocent's pontificate are sparsely documented. See, for example, Reg., 2:299 (Potthast 789), and 11:105 (Potthast 3440). In any case the Dalmatian church has been excluded from consideration in this chapter.

15. J. L. Csóka, Geschichte des benediktinischen Mönchtums in Ungarn (St. Ottilien, 1980), p. 80. "Somit kann mit Gewissheit angenommen werden, dass es in Ungarn in der ersten Hälfte des 13. Jahrhunderts mehr als 100 Benediktiner-Klöster gegeben hat." A somewhat more conservative estimate of the number of Benedictine communities in Hungary before the Mongol invasion is given by E. Fügedi, "Koldu-

halma, the oldest, richest, and most prestigious Benedictine abbey in the kingdom, is notable for his absence. This is explicable. Abbot Urias (Oros) of Pannonhalma was the most litigious prelate in early thirteenth-century Hungary.[16] Many of the cases of delegated jurisdiction between 1213 and 1216 arose from disputes in which Abbot Urias was one of the litigants. Among the Cistercian houses Innocent III commissioned the abbots of Zirc and Cikádor more often than their colleagues. The abbot of Zirc, John of Limoges, moreover, was a man of wide learning familiar with the law.[17] Together with the abbots of Pilis, Egres, and Szentgotthárd, the abbots of Cikádor and Zirc were the only Cistercians to serve as papal judges, no doubt because these five abbeys were the oldest communities of the order in Hungary.[18] No Cistercian abbot from the monasteries of more recent foundation is recorded as having functioned as a judge delegate. As the Cistercian abbots were given mandates as judges delegate more than twice as often as Benedictines, even though the Cistercians had only nine houses in Hungary before 1216, there existed in Hungary an apparent preference for the white monks.[19]

Among the lesser prelates Innocent called upon a number of archdeacons and provosts of collegiate churches or cathedral chapters. While none of the lesser prelates served with the frequency of a bishop or an abbot, the archdeacon[20] and the provost of Székesfehérvár are especially prominent. The inclusion on one occasion of the *scholasticus* of Székesfehérvár is also significant. The town of Székesfehérvár was not an episcopal see, but it was the site of the basilica of St. Stephen and a favored residence of the

---

lórendek és városfejlődés Magyarországon" [Mendicants and urban development in Hungary], *Századok*, 1972, p. 73. Exclusive of mendicant houses Fügedi confirms the existence of 121 foundations, of which 68 were Benedictine, 17 Cistercian, 33 Premonstratensian, and 3 Augustinian canons.

16. Csóka, *Geschichte des benediktinischen Mönchtums*, pp. 193–94.

17. John of Limoges, the former prior of Clairvaux, served as abbot of Zirc from 1208 to 1218. From his activity as a papal judge delegate we may assume he possessed at least a working knowledge of canon law while in Hungary, despite the Cistercian order's general antipathy toward legal study. Later, after he returned to France, he played an active role in the legal defense of the Cistercians' claim to exemption from episcopal jurisdiction; see Dom Jean Leclercq, "Un opuscule inédit de Jean de Limoges sur l'exemption," *Analecta sacri ordinis Cisterciensis* 3 (1947): 147–54.

18. For the history of the medieval Cistercian houses in Hungary see F. L. Hervay, *Repertorium historicum ordinis Cisterciensis in Hungaria* (Rome, 1984) (hereafter *Rep. hist. ord. Cist.*).

19. Cf. J. Sayers, "English Cistercian Cases and Their Delegation in the First Half of the Thirteenth Century," *Analecta sacri ordinis Cisterciensis* 20 (1964): 85–102; and idem, *Papal Judges Delegate*, pp. 123–24, where the Cistericans rank third after the Augustinians and Benedictines in the number of English cases heard.

20. As the archdeacon of Székesfehérvár was a member of the chapter of Veszprém and resided in the episcopal see, his presence in the royal town cannot be assumed, although his administrative obligations would necessitate close association with the town's affairs. I am indebted to Professor Erik Fügedi for drawing my attention to this archdeacon's membership in the chapter of Veszprém.

Árpád kings. The clergy of the town, therefore, seem to have received a higher proportion of mandates than those of any other urban center.[21]

From time to time Innocent delegated jurisdiction over cases involving Hungary to non-Hungarian clerics, but this was exceptional. One well-known instance is recorded in the first book of the papal register. Eager to apprehend the clerical miscreants, Italian and Hungarian, who stole a quaternion from the register of Pope Alexander III, Innocent commissioned the bishop of Győr and the abbot of Zirc in Hungary and the patriarch of Grado in Italy to summon and interrogate the suspects and to suspend and excommunicate them if the charges against them proved true.[22] In another case, which arose in 1206, the pope commissioned Eberhard, archbishop of Salzburg, and Albert, provost of Salzburg, to examine the qualifications of Berthold of Andechs-Merania, provost of Bamberg and brother-in-law to the Hungarian king, to be archbishop of Kalocsa.[23] In accordance with the papal mandate they proceeded in the spring of 1207 to the frontier of Hungary, and there in the presence of two suffragans of Kalocsa they examined the archbishop-elect. They determined that he was approximately twenty-five years of age rather than the canonical age of thirty and was well versed neither in canon law nor in Scripture ("nec in jure canonico nec in divino eloquio").[24] When the report of the judges delegate was received in Rome, Innocent discussed the case with the cardinals and decided not to confirm the election but to postpone confirmation for several years. The choice of the archbishop of Salzburg and his associate appears to have been motivated by both political and legal considerations. Eberhard of Salzburg was a trusted papal envoy who had already been commissioned to resolve the politically sensitive question of the second marriage of King Ottokar of Bohemia to Constance, the sister of the Hungarian king.[25] No Hungarian prelate would have been suitable to examine the qualifications of the archbishop-elect of Kalocsa. The suffragans of Kalocsa as copetitioners for the confir-

21. For the historical importance of Székesfehérvár (Stuhlweissenburg, *Alba Regalis*) in the Middle Ages see J. Deér, "Aachen und die Herrschersitze der Arpaden," *MIOG* 79 (1971): 5–31; and E. Fügedi, "Der Stadtplan von Stuhlweissenburg und die Anfänge des Burgertums in Ungarn," *Acta historica Academiae Scientiarum Hungaricae* 15 (1969): 103–34.

22. *Inn. III Reg.*, 1:540; Hageneder, *Register*, 1:537 (Potthast 584: 30 January 1199). Although the apparatus of the Hageneder edition (p. 776) identifies the abbot *de Boccan* as the abbot of the Benedictine house at Bakonybél, the monastery in question is the Cisterican foundation at Zirc; see Hervay, *Rep. hist. ord. Cist.*, p. 208.

23. The mandate has not survived but is mentioned in *Inn. III Reg.*, 9:74 (Potthast 2793: 7 June 1206).

24. *Inn. III Reg.*, 10:39 (Potthast 3073: 5 April 1207).

25. *Inn. III Reg.*, 9:60 (Potthast 2762: 26 April 1206). The archbishop of Salzburg had also been directed to discipline the bishop of Passau for refusing to restore to the Hungarian king 2,000 marks needed to finance Hungarian crusade efforts; *Regestum Innocentii III papae super negotio Romani imperii*, ed. F. Kempf (Rome, 1947), no. 70 (Potthast 1736: 2 October 1202).

mation would have been excluded. The archbishop of Esztergom, himself only recently translated from Kalocsa, thereby creating the vacancy, may likewise have seemed an inappropriate choice. The suffragans of the province of Esztergom, in light of the well-established rivalry between the two provinces and the obvious opportunity for the king to use his influence upon them on his brother-in-law's behalf, were also unsuitable. Non-Hungarian judges, therefore, were better able to carry out the papal mandate by preserving independence of judgment and of action.

On the basis of the extensive surviving English materials for the first half of the thirteenth century, Jane Sayers has demonstrated that the plaintiff who initiated the case regularly proposed the names of the judges delegate.[26] The Hungarian cases offer no specific confirmation of this practice between 1198 and 1216, but it can be inferred. In several instances the initiators of suits in Rome can be identified. For example, in 1211 Robert, bishop of Veszprém, was sent to Rome by King Andrew II to present a compromise plan to resolve the conflicting claims to royal coronation rights and to create a new diocese with its center at Nagyszeben. Although Innocent III refused to approve either proposal, Bishop Robert availed himself of the opportunity presented by his visit to Rome to initiate a case against the brothers of St. Abraham who, he claimed, retained certain tithes which were rightfully his. The judges appointed by a mandate of 26 January 1212 which names Robert of Veszprém as the plaintiff were Bishop Peter of the neighboring diocese of Győr and the abbot of Tihány and the provost of Vasvár.[27] If these judges were not proposed by the plaintiff, he was certainly fortunate that none of his known ecclesiastical adversaries were given a commission in this case. Somewhat more suggestive are the circumstances associated with the suit brought by Abbot Urias of Pannonhalma in 1214 against Archbishop John of Esztergom concerning the rights to the tithes of St. Mary in Sala near Pozsony (Bratislava). Innocent III delegated the case to Bishop Robert of Veszprém, Thomas, provost of Veszprém, and the archdeacon of Székesfehérvár with a mandate to hear and decide the case without appeal.[28] But a year later no progress had been made on the suit. In the spring of 1215 Abbot Urias was in Rome, where he personally complained that to his knowledge Bishop Robert and his fellow judges had taken no action in the case, largely because the bishop had been, for reasons not associated with this case, placed under sentence of excommunication by Archbishop John, who in turn refused to respond to the suit before an excommunicated bishop. The pope committed the case to new judges, Peter, bishop of Győr, the abbot of Tihány, and the archdeacon of Raba, who were instructed to hear and settle the case if both parties were willing to accept a settlement;

26. Sayers, *Papal Judges Delegate*, p. 112.
27. *Mon. rom. ep. Vesprim.*, 1:19, no. 26.
28. Ibid., 1:29, no. 31 (Potthast 4918: 5 May 1214).

otherwise the judges were to direct both parties to send fully instructed envoys to Rome, where Innocent proposed to resolve the dispute personally during the forthcoming sessions of the Fourth Lateran Council.[29] Although Robert of Veszprém did not always have cordial relations with Urias of Pannonhalma, the selection of Robert—a prelate embroiled in a bitter feud with the archbishop over the bishop's traditional right to crown the queen, which led to his excommunication—points to Urias as the canny nominator of this papal judge. The later selection of Bishop Peter may also suggest the choice of a judge likely to be independent of the archbishop, if only because this bishop was so often called upon by Rome to perform judicial service.

For the entire pontificate of Innocent III thirty-five Hungarian prelates can be identified as having served as papal judges. Doubtless there were many more for whom the evidence is now lost. Where did these judges acquire legal skills? Although judges delegate were not required to have formal training in canon law, it was expected that they would be familiar with it.[30] Hungary could boast of no university or *studium generale*. Some Hungarian prelates were educated in Paris—for example, Bishop Adrian of Transylvania, a former royal chancellor.[31] Probably, in view of the frequent journeys of papal envoys in one direction and Hungarian litigants in the other, some were educated in Italy as well. We know that when the underage archbishop-elect of Kalocsa, Berthold of Andechs-Merania, needed to acquire the rudiments of an education, he and his whole entourage, to the shock and embarrassment of Innocent III, moved to the newly founded university at Vicenza in 1208.[32] Thomas, the future archdeacon of Spalato, is known to have studied *ars dictaminis* in Bologna in 1222, but he is unlikely to have been the first Bolognese-trained archdeacon in the lands of the Árpád kings.[33] Some foreigners, moreover, notably Master Robert of Lille, who after serving as provost of Székesfehérvár and royal chancellor was elected to the bishopric of Veszprém, were trained in western European schools.[34] It is possible that there may have been one or more local Hungarian schools where the learned law could have been

29. Ibid., 1:30, no. 32 (Potthast 4978: 6 May 1215). Excommunicates were prohibited from serving as judges delegate; see R. Helmholz, "Canonists and Standards of Impartiality for Papal Judges Delegate," *Traditio* 25 (1969): 391.

30. See Helmholz, "Canonists and Standards," citing the opinion of Hostiensis, p. 393 n. 29.

31. See I. Hajnal, *L'enseignement de l'écriture aux universités médiévales*, 2d ed., ed. L. Mezey (Budapest, 1959), p. 192.

32. *Inn. III Reg.*, 11:220 (Potthast 3613: 16 January 1209).

33. Thomas of Spalato, *Historia*, p. 98. On the general question of the familiarity of Hungarian clerics with canon law in the twelfth and thirteenth centuries see G. Bónis, "Die Entwicklung der geistlichen Gerichtsbarkeit in Ungarn vor 1525," *ZRG*, Kan. Abt. 49 (1963): 188–97; and idem, "Men Learned in the Law in Medieval Hungary," *East Central Europe* 4 (1977): 182–83.

34. F. Knauz and L. C. Dedek, *Monumenta ecclesiae Strigoniensis*, 3 vols. (Esztergom, 1874–1924), 1:257.

studied at least in a rudimentary way. Our evidence neither confirms nor denies the existence at the beginning of the thirteenth century of a school at Veszprém, although a much later diploma of King László IV from 1276 grandly compares the study of the liberal arts at Veszprém to that at Paris and pointedly refers to the preservation of a devotion to justice ("cultus iustitie ad regni iura conservanda").[35] Circumstantial evidence from Innocent III's reign, however, points to Székesfehérvár as another possible center of instruction. The inclusion of the *scholasticus* of Székesfehérvár among the papal judges delegate commissioned to hear a case between the abbey of Pannonhalma and the Hospitalers in 1216 lends support to this hypothesis as the presence of a *scholasticus* presumes the existence of a school, in all likelihood in association with the royal palace.[36] A knowledge of canon law could also be acquired through practical necessity. Many Hungarian prelates at the end of the twelfth century and in the opening decades of the thirteenth, moreover, served as judges in Hungarian secular courts. Practical experience in the administration of justice in a general sense may thus have been acquired by Hungarian prelates through service in both secular and ecclesiastical courts.[37]

The cases heard by Hungarian judges delegate fall into three broad categories. Judges delegate were sometimes commissioned to enforce prior mandates and the discipline of the canon law. For example, in 1198 the archbishop of Kalocsa and the bishops of Győr and Zagreb were instructed to investigate reported irregularities in the elections of the archbishops of Spalato and Zara, both of whom were believed to have violated a mandate of Celestine III prohibiting aid to the rebellious duke of Croatia and Dalmatia.[38] If the reports proved true, the elections were to be quashed and the intruders into these archiepiscopal sees excommunicated. In 1204 the bishop of Nagyvárad, the abbot of Zirc, and the provost of Székesfehérvár were chosen to inquire into the disputed election of the abbot of St. Egidius in Somogy in which four monks alleged that at the king's insistence Bernard (O.S.B.), the archbishop of Spalato, was imposed upon the monastery as abbot. The judges were instructed to inflict canonical sanctions upon the archbishop if the allegations proved true and he refused to correct his excesses.[39] In the same year the bishop of Győr and

35. The charter, issued after a fire caused widespread destruction of the church of Veszprém, makes plain that the school was already well established by that time. It is preserved in the private archives of the cathedral chapter at Veszprém (Veszprémi káptalan magán levéltára, 1276, fok 2) and published in Jenő Gutheil, *Az Árpád-kori Veszprém* [Veszprém in the Árpád period] (Veszprém, 1977), p. 278. Cf. Szentpétery and Borsa, *Reg. Arp.*, no. 2747. I am indebted to Erik Fügedi for drawing my attention to this important document.

36. See *Mon. rom. ep. Vesprim.*, 1:36, no. 39 (Potthast 5102: 20 April 1216).

37. See Bónis, "Entwicklung der geistlichen Gerichtsbarkeit," p. 193.

38. *Inn. III Reg.*, 1:510 (Potthast 508: 30 December 1198).

39. Although the mandate to the judges no longer exists, the case is described in full in a letter to King Imre with an *a-pari* letter to Bernard of Spalato, *Inn. III Reg.*, 7:128 (Potthast 2280: 14 September 1204).

five other bishops were mandated to make a secret *inquisitio* into the rumored accusations of incest on the part of the aged bishop of Pécs and to permit the bishop to clear himself canonically through the administration of the *purgatio canonica* to be conducted by the bishop of Győr and his associates.[40] This commission could not be carried out because the bishop of Pécs became embroiled in the disputed Esztergom election, which rendered all his fellow bishops unsuitable. Although he did not believe it to be legally necessary, Innocent, urged by the bishop's proctor in Rome, delegated the bishop of Csanád and the Cistercian abbot of Cikádor together with two bishops and three abbots to conduct the purgation. This, however, did not take place either. The bishops refused to participate. One claimed he was ill, and the other would not act in the absence of his colleague. In 1206 Innocent once more directed the bishop of Csanád and the abbot of Cikádor to carry out the prior mandate and ordered that those bishops who willfully refused to participate should be sent to Rome, where they would be suspected of lying and hatred and would be liable at law to feel the full force of apostolic indignation.[41] As Innocent was obligated to reissue this mandate three years later, the required purgation presumably had not been carried out.[42]

Most cases, however, arose as the result of an appeal to Rome by one ecclesiastical litigant against another. A large number of these concern the right to tithes, as when the bishop of Győr contended with the Hospitalers;[43] the bishop of Veszprém with the abbot of Pannonhalma, the chapter of Esztergom, or the Hospitalers;[44] the abbot of Pannonhalma with the abbot of St. Egidius (O.S.B.), the archbishop of Esztergom, the bishop and chapter of Veszprém, the bishop of Zagreb, the *custos* of Székesfehérvár, the Hospitalers, or the abbot of Pilis (O. Cist).[45] As quar-

40. The mandate has not survived but is mentioned in *Inn. III Reg.*, 6:196 (Potthast 2086: 7 January 1204) and *Reg.* 9:113 (Potthast 2837: 7 July 1206). The latter text entered the law books as X 2.23.15.

41. *Inn. III Reg.*, 9:113. On the bishop of Pécs's candidacy for the see of Esztergom, see Sweeney, "Innocent III and the Esztergom Election Dispute," pp. 126–28.

42. *Inn. III Reg.*, 13:112 (Potthast 3930: 9 March 1210).

43. *Mon. rom. ep. Vesprim.*, 1:18, no. 23. The frequency of appeals to Rome from ecclesiastical litigants contesting rights to tithes or patronage or property is reflected in contemporary cases arising in Upper and Lower Austria; see Hageneder, *Geistliche Gerichtsbarkeit*, p. 27. No cases concerning clerical patronage, however, have been found in the Hungarian evidence for the early thirteenth century.

44. *Inn. III Reg.*, 15:7 (Potthast 4401: 3 March 1212). *Inn. III Reg.*, 16:62 (Potthast 4737: 26 May 1213). Reference to a lost mandate concerning the dispute with the Hospitalers is found in Honorius III, *Reg.* 10:50 (Potthast 7477: 16 September 1225), printed in Theiner, *Mon. Hung.*, 1:61, no. 129.

45. The papal mandate for the St. Egidius (St. Gilles) case is mentioned in the judicial *actum* found in *Mon. rom. ep. Vesprim.*, 1:33, no. 35. Other mandates are cited in *Mon. rom. ep. Vesprim.*, 1:29, no. 31, and 30, no. 32. The mandate in the suit against the chapter of Veszprém is mentioned in *Inn. III Reg.*, 5:7. Another letter of Honorius III (Potthast 6466: 2 January 1221) printed in L. Erdélyi, *A pannonhalmi főapátság tör-*

rels over tithes often hinged on conflicting claims to land, they constitute a form of property dispute. In other cases rights to land were at the heart of the suit, for example, when the chapters of Kalocsa and Székesfehérvár disputed rights to three villages or when the bishop of Veszprém claimed that the abbot of St. Egidius wrongfully occupied three churches.[46] In other suits jurisdictional rights were at issue, as in the case between the bishop of Transylvania and the provost of Nagyszeben mentioned earlier, or the complaints arising out of the Esztergom-Kalocsa rivalry, or the bishop of Veszprém's defense of his rights to grant holy orders, provide chrism, and offer other ecclesiastical *sacramenta* to religious houses in his diocese.[47]

The third category of lawsuit involved members of the laity, some who had committed injuries against clerics and others who were petitioners for ecclesiastical justice. Evidence from 1207 records that the newly founded Cistercian abbey of Borsmonostor (Marienberg) was subject to violent attacks by laymen associated with the village of Ukas (Kroatisch-Minihof), which was an integral part of the abbey's original endowment. Following the complaints of the abbot and convent, Innocent III delegated the archbishop of Esztergom, the bishop of Győr, and the provost of Székesfehérvár to serve as judges of a case against a certain P. of Ukas and unnamed others from Koronczó who shed blood in laying violent hands on some of the monks and taking their goods.[48] The judges were directed, if the charges were true, to excommunicate these laymen publicly, compel them to make satisfaction, and send them to Rome with letters from the judges in order to be absolved. At the same time, in a separate letter to the same judges, Innocent commissioned them to give judgment in a case against a certain Aianus and his sons Mic and Pau and others who reportedly took certain possessions and goods that had been granted to Borsmonostor at the time of its foundation.[49] The judges were to see that proper restitution was made to the abbey and that the settlement was guaranteed by the threat of ecclesiastical sanctions. In both cases the

---

*ténete*, 6 vols. (Budapest, 1902–16), 1:648, no. 64. See also ibid., 1:673, no. 84. Honorius III, *Reg.*, 2:935 (Potthast 5725: 20 March 1218), printed in *Mon. rom. ep. Vesprim.*, 1:43, no. 48; *Mon. rom. ep. Vesprim.*, 1:36, no. 39 (Potthast 5102: 20 April 1216). The mandate for the Pilis case is mentioned in a letter of Honorius III (22 January 1218) printed in *Mon. rom. ep. Vesprim.*, 1:41, no. 45.

46. The mandate to hear the case between the churches of Kalocsa and Székesfehérvár is mentioned in Theiner, *Mon. Slav.*, 1:58, no. 82 (Potthast 1398: May–June 1201). For the mandate in the case between the bishop of Veszprém and St. Egidius see *Mon. rom. ep. Vesprim.*, 1:11, no. 13.

47. See above, note 6; and Theiner, *Mon. Slav.*, 1:59, no. 135 (Potthast 1457: August 1201); and *Mon. rom. ep. Vesprim.*, 4:305, no. 239.

48. *Mon. rom. ep. Vesprim.*, 1:16, no. 19 (13 February 1207). See also I. Szentpétery, *A Borsmonostori apátság Árpádkori oklevelei* (Budapest, 1916), p. 111.

49. *Mon. rom. ep. Vesprim.*, 1:16, no. 20 (13 February 1207), and Szentpétery, *Borsmonostori oklev.*, p. 111.

James Ross Sweeney

defendants were denied the right to appeal. When the Count Palatine
wrote to Innocent requesting a dispensation for his marriage to his wife of
many years to whom he was related in the second degree, the pontiff
commissioned the archbishop of Esztergom and the bishop of Eger to act
as judges.[50] The count maintained that he did not know of the relationship at the time of the marriage. The judges were to examine the circumstances and, if they were as the count claimed, the judges were to grant a
papal dispensation. When a layman attempted to prevent the terms of a
will from being enforced, Innocent sent the bishop of Veszprém and the
abbot of Zirc a mandate to hear the case.[51] According to the complaint of
the Hospitalers, the deceased Princess Margaret, aunt of King Andrew II
and widow of Andreas count of Somogy, had willed her dowry to the
Hospitalers, but Andronicus, the son of Count Andreas, retained it contrary to law. Innocent directed the judges to see that Andronicus hand over
the bequest to the Hospitalers without difficulty, but should he retain it
after having been duly warned they were to compel him through the
application of ecclesiastical sanctions without the right to appeal. In each
of these instances—attacks on clerics, despoliation of ecclesiastical property, the validity of marriages, and the enforcement of testimentary
grants—the ecclesiastical courts were exercising well-established jurisdiction.

Several cases appealed to Rome from Hungary were heard in sessions of
the *audientia* before being remanded to local judges. The earliest of these
arose out of a dispute between the Benedictine abbot of Földvár and the
bishop of Pécs.[52] The abbot claimed that his house was exempt from
episcopal jurisdiction, visitation, and collation on the basis of the foundation charter bestowed by King Béla II in the first half of the twelfth
century, but the bishop contested this. The abbot maintained that he had
resolved to go to Rome and had collected a sum of money for the journey,
but the bishop had seized the charter and the money and with violence
imprisoned him in a Cistercian monastery, permitting him to appeal
neither to the king nor to Rome. Later, however, the bishop permitted him
to return to his abbey. But when the bishop, having himself taken the
charter and the money, lied in the presence of the king, the abbot appealed
to Rome. According to the abbot, the bishop permitted the appeal and
agreed to appear in Rome by the feast of St. Luke (18 October 1198), yet
only a few days later he excommunicated the abbot. The bishop of Pécs
offered a very different narrative of events. He maintained that the abbot
of Földvár had forged two charters and had been tried and convicted of this
crime, to which the abbot later confessed. Consequently, the bishop sent
him to do penance in the Cistercian house at Cikádor, but the abbot,

50. *Inn. III Reg.*, 9:75 (Potthast 2791: 7 June 1206).
51. *Mon. rom. ep. Vesprim.*, 1:17, no. 21 (Potthast 3369: 13 April 1208).
52. *Inn. III Reg.*, 1:544; Hageneder, *Register*, 1:541 (Potthast 583: 30 January 1199).

without having completed the penance, returned to his abbey with the physical assistance of laymen. Then, according to the bishop, the abbot seized parish property belonging to churches pertaining to the bishop and drove their clergy from their homes. For his contumacy the abbot was excommunicated, but he nevertheless celebrated mass after the sentence was imposed and violently seized and abused the goods of the monastery. These arguments were presented by the abbot in person and by master Obertus the envoy of the bishop, both of whom appeared before the auditor Gerard, cardinal deacon of San Nicola in Carcere Tulliano.[53] For Cardinal Gerard, a Cistercian and former abbot of Pontigny, this was one of the first cases he heard as auditor since his elevation to the cardinalate, and it presented him with irreconcilable accounts. After hearing the case he persuaded both sides to accept the bishops of Vác and Csanád and the Cistercian abbot of Zirc as judges delegate. The sentence of excommunication against the abbot was lifted. The papal mandate committing the case to these judges carefully instructed them to determine two key points: whether the monastery licitly enjoyed exemption from episcopal jurisdiction, in which case silence was to be imposed on the bishop and the abbot was to be reinstated, and whether the bishop had excommunicated the abbot before or after he lodged his appeal to Rome. If before, then the abbot's deposition from office was to be confirmed; if after, the bishop was to be suspended for contempt of the Apostolic see. We have no more evidence about this suit, but as no mention of the suspension of the bishop of Pécs from office is found in the later extensive discussion of scandals rumored (falsely) about the bishop, it is possible that he had the better case.

Sometime in 1211, or possibly early in 1212, a dispute over ecclesiastical prerogatives and the collection of tithes from certain parishes in Somogy county between the abbot of Pannonhalma and the bishop of Veszprém was heard in the *audientia* by Hugolino, cardinal bishop of Ostia, the future Pope Gregory IX.[54] The abbot's claim to the tithes rested on royal grants to the abbey, especially that of King Stephen I, and on subsequent papal letters of confirmation from Paschal II, Alexander III, and Clement III.[55] The bishop attempted to cast doubt on the earliest of the diplomas—those of King Stephen and Pope Paschal. Cardinal Hugolino brushed aside the bishop's arguments, however, and confirmed the validity of the charters. In so doing he also recognized the monastery's right to the disputed tithes. But the dispute over ecclesiastical prerogatives— namely, the receiving of chrism and holy oil, the consecration of altars

53. For the career of Cardinal Gerard see Maleczek, *Papst und Kardinalskolleg*, pp. 125–26.

54. See *Inn. III Reg.*, 15:7 (Potthast 4401: 3 March 1212).

55. The texts of these four charters are printed in Erdély, *Pannon. főapátság tört.*, 1:589, no. 1; 592, no. 3; 606, no. 18; 613, no. 25.

and churches, the ordination of clerics, and the status of clergy attached to churches and chapels pertaining to the monastery within the boundaries of the diocese of Veszprém—was settled in favor of the bishop, to whom the monastery was directed to apply in these matters. The key to the settlement of this aspect of the case was the auditor's close scrutiny of the twelfth-century papal letters of confirmation, wherein he determined that the earlier bulls of Paschal II and Alexander III explicitly acknowledged the rights of the diocesan bishop, but that the bull of Clement III, lacking any reference to the existence of the diplomas of Paschal II and Alexander III, equally explicitly granted the monastery the right to obtain these episcopal benefits from whatever bishop they might wish, provided he be a Catholic in communion with the Apostolic see.[56] This discrepancy prompted Innocent III to question whether the monastery's putative privilege had been renounced by the abbot when seeking confirmation from Alexander III but later asserted when seeking confirmation from Clement III, or whether the privilege had been asserted knowingly and in bad faith after obtaining Alexander's letter and hence was uncanonical. The judges delegate chosen to help resolve the case—Berthold archbishop-elect of Kalocsa and the abbots of Székszard and Cikádor—were informed that the sentences of excommunication and interdict imposed by the bishop of Veszprém during the dispute were to be lifted. The judges were commanded to hear witnesses from both sides concerning those issues in the case on which the pope had been unable to secure full information and to send back their report in writing authenticated by their seals. What they reported to Rome is unknown. In 1215, Abbot Urias sought and obtained from Innocent III explicit confirmation of the tithes and properties in dispute in this case.[57] When somewhat later, however, the abbot was in the Holy Land accompanying the Hungarian king as a participant in the Fifth Crusade, the bishop took advantage of his absence to compel parishioners of the disputed churches in Somogy county to pay tithes to him. Honorius III in a mandate of 1218 recommitted the case to judges delegate, the abbots of Pécsvárad, Székszard, and Cikádor, with instructions to convene the parties and resolve the dispute.[58]

From a letter of Honorius III we learn that sometime during Innocent

56. The original bulls of Paschal II and Alexander survive in the archives of the archabbey (Pannonhalma. Pannonhalmi főapátság rendi levéltár, no. 6, Capsa 39.I. and no. 27, Capsa 68.A.). Unfortunately, the controversial bull of Clement III is preserved only in later transcriptions, the earliest of which is a figured copy prepared at the direction of King Andrew II and intended for transmission to Pope Honorius III for authentication (Pannonhalma. Pannonhalmi főapátság rendi levéltár, no. 67, Capsa 31.G.).

57. Innocent issued two letters. The first is dated 28 July 1215 ("Cum inter vos") and printed in Erdély, *Pannon. főapátság tört.*, 1:633, no. 47 (Potthast 4986). The second, from 9 September 1215 ("Constitutis in presentia") is in ibid., 634, no. 48 (Potthast 4993).

58. Erdély, *Pannon. főapátság tört.*, 1:644, no. 56 (Potthast 5684: 1 February 1218).

III's reign a suit between the Hospitalers and the abbot and monks of the abbey of the Holy Spirit in the diocese of Pécs was initiated in Rome and given to Cinthius, cardinal priest of San Lorenzo in Lucina, as auditor.[59] The suit centered on conflicting claims to the church of the Holy Spirit and its appurtenances. The Hospitalers were represented before Cardinal Cinthius by their proctor, but the monks sent no proctor. The bishop of Pécs, however, was represented by three proctors, a Master Boniface and a certain I. and O. who spoke against the monks, asserting that they had despoiled the Hospitalers. For this reason and to cover the expenses of the suit, the monks were fined one hundred marks. Innocent delegated the archbishop of Esztergom, the bishop of Transylvania, and the provost of Arad to impose the fine, and the archbishop and provost were further directed to settle the case on its merits. Since these judges, according to a later complaint, failed to resolve the issue, Honorius recommitted the suit to the Cistercian abbot of Zirc and to the provost and the cantor of Székesfehérvár.

Another letter of Honorius III provides valuable information about one of a series of legal disputes initiated by the abbey of Pannonhalma concerning the right to tithes in Somogy county.[60] Sometime in 1214 or 1215, before the convening of the Fourth Lateran Council, Abbot Urias brought suit against the bishop and chapter of Zagreb in Rome, where both parties seemingly agreed to the selection of the bishop of Győr and unnamed cojudges to hear the case. The bishop of Zagreb, however, later frustrated the work of the bishop of Győr and his colleagues by refusing to permit them to examine relevant materials. The abbot, in Rome for the council, succeeded in placing the case before an auditor, Gregory of Crescentio, a subdeacon and papal chaplain who later in 1216 would be created cardinal deacon of San Teodoro.[61] Subdeacon Gregory appears to have been unable to resolve the case because of conflicting claims to lands in Somogy county "beyond the Drave." Thus a new panel of judges delegate was commissioned late in 1215 or early 1216 with a mandate to determine the facts of the case and settle the dispute finally. The bishop of Vác and unnamed colleagues were appointed to hear the case, but their work was never completed because of issues arising out of the hearing of the case itself and because Innocent III's death ended their commission. Honorius III subsequently delegated the case first to the provost of Veszprém and the archdeacons of Veszprém and Székesfehérvár, but when they failed to bring about a settlement, then to the abbot of Zirc and the provosts of Esztergom and Győr.

59. A letter of Honorius III (Potthast 7404: 9 May 1225) is printed in Theiner, *Mon. Hung.*, 1:55, no. 117. For Cardinal Cinthius see Maleczek, *Papst und Kardinalskolleg*, pp. 104–6.

60. Two lost mandates of Innocent III are mentioned in a letter of Honorius III (20 January 1221) printed in Erdélyi, *Pannon. főapátság tört.*, 1:648, no. 64.

61. For Cardinal Gregory see Maleczek, *Papst und Kardinalskolleg*, pp. 183–84.

James Ross Sweeney

At about the same time, Gregory of Crescentio also served as auditor in another suit brought by Abbot Urias and the monks of Pannonhalma against the cathedral chapter of Veszprém, which arose from a long-standing dispute over the church of the Holy Savior in the village of Tard in Somogy county and over certain other tithes in the same county, especially those from the church of St. Appollinaris, which the abbot claimed the chapter had usurped. The abbot complained that in addition to violating Pannonhalma's right to these churches and their tithes the chapter had despoiled the abbot's men, their cattle, and other property and had committed unnamed offenses associated with the disputed tithes against the archdeacon, rectors of churches, priests, and people of Somogy county. For more than sixteen years the abbot and convent had sought justice by obtaining several papal letters of commission for diverse judges to hear the case ("ad diversos iudices diversas a sede apostolica commissivas litteras impetrarint"). But they labored without useful result. No trace of this earlier litigation, which presumably occurred throughout the pontificate of Innocent III, now exists. Nor do we know how the papal subdeacon and chaplain Gregory attempted to resolve this case. The sole source of our knowledge—a mandate of 1226 of Honorius III committing the case again to three Hungarian judges delegate[62]—is silent on Gregory's disposition of the case, if any. Yet it reveals that a new pope, new auditors, and new judges delegate were prepared to search for a just resolution of the protracted suit.

An interesting and historically important case arising from a dispute between the bishop of Veszprém and the archbishop of Esztergom was heard by auditors in Rome who, without recourse to local judges delegate, brought the case to a successful conclusion. In 1215 while in the city to attend the Lateran Council, Bishop Robert of Veszprém obtained a papal mandate citing the archbishop of Esztergom to respond to a complaint that the archbishop had violated the bishop's right to crown Hungarian queens and had usurped episcopal rights associated with the royal abbeys and collegiate churches and elsewhere within the diocese of Veszprém. Archbishop John of Esztergom, who was also in attendance at the council,

---

59. A letter of Honorius III (Potthast 7404: 9 May 1225) is printed in Theiner, *Mon. Hung.*, 1:55, no. 117. For Cardinal Cinthius see Maleczek, *Papst und Kardinalskolleg*, pp. 104–6.

62. Erdély, *Pannon. főapátság tört.*, 1:673, no. 84 (11 July 1226); omitted by Potthast. László Erdély, the modern editor of the text ("Cum olim . . abbas"), silently emended the name of one of the churches to read: "ecclesia Sancti Salvatoris de Tord," whereas the original mandate, preserved in the archabbey's archives (Pannonhalma. Pannonhalmi főapátság rendi levéltár, no. 84, Capsa 45.N.), has "de Zord." It was common, however, for the papal chancery to make such errors in Hungarian placenames. The addressees of the letter were the bishop of Vác, the abbot of Pilis, and the archdeacon of Pest, to whom the case was recommitted after another hearing in the *audientia* before Pelagius, the cardinal bishop of Albano, and Otto, the papal subdeacon and chaplain, who later replaced Cardinal Pelagius on the case.

appeared in person at the *audientia*. The case was assigned to Pelagius, cardinal bishop of Albano and papal legate to Hungary, and to Stephen of Fossanova, cardinal priest of the Basilica of the Twelve Apostles, the papal chamberlain, serving as joint auditors. Both litigants in person set out their arguments which, for each, rested on local custom. What is striking in this case is how the auditors understood their papally mandated function to be not so much that of judges as negotiators of a lasting resolution of the issues in a form agreeable to both parties ("post altercationes multiplices, unanimi voluntate consensum est ab utroque, quod nos, iuxta domini pape mandatum, questiones propositas amicabili, si possemus, concordia vel iudicio sopiremus"). Since both litigants were present and the issues did not turn on testimony of absent witnesses as in so many other cases, the auditors were able to fashion a satisfactory agreement on the spot. The text of this agreement expressed in the form of the auditors' sentence issued on 11 April 1216 has been preserved in the archives of the chapter of Veszprém. In the matter of the queen's coronation the sentence specified that the bishop of Veszprém should anoint and crown her if her coronation should occur at the same time as that of the king, who was to be anointed and crowned by the archbishop. In the event of the coronation of the queen alone, the archbishop was to perform the anointing and the bishop the imposition of the diadem. In the absence of the archbishop, however, the bishop might perform both rituals.

A similar spirit of compromise is reflected in the settlement of the other issues in the case. The rights of the archbishop over the confirmation, institution, and deprivation of the provosts and canons of the royal collegiate churches at Buda and Dömös and over the jurisdiction of cases arising from these churches were to continue as before but now with the permission of the bishop. But both foundations were to receive chrism and holy oil for baptisms, confirmations, and ordination only from the bishop of Veszprém, whose exclusive right to confirm the children of these locations was also asserted. Within the diocese of Veszprém the customs of the royal abbeys were to remain unchanged while the *sacramenta* were to be administered to Cistercian monasteries in accordance with the sense of their charters without opposition from the archbishop. As the archbishop enjoyed considerable authority over all royal abbeys observing the Benedictine rule, this too was a compromise respecting the rights of each prelate within distinct monastic communities. Finally, the archbishop was to leave the parish church in Segesd peacefully in the hand of the bishop.[63] The auditors' sentence under normal circumstances would have

---

63. The auditors' sentence is the earliest document of its kind preserved in Hungary. It is printed in *Mon. rom. ep. Vesprim.* 1:35. no. 38 (with facsimile). For the careers of cardinals Pelagius and Stephen, see Maleczek, *Papst und Kardinalskolleg*, pp. 166–69 and 179–83. Honorius III issued confirmation of the auditors' settlement on 18 December 1220; see Theiner, *Mon. Hung.*, 1:26, no. 45 (Potthast 6450).

been confirmed by papal letter, but the death of Innocent III on 16 July 1216 intervened. In December 1220, however, Honorius III at the request of Robert of Veszprém promulgated the definitive sentence of the case confirming the text of the agreement drafted by cardinals Pelagius and Stephen.

Two other cases involving auditors date from the closing months of Innocent's pontificate. Abbot Urias of Pannonhalma brought suit in Rome against the Hospitalers of the province of Hungary in the spring of 1216 over the payment of tithes from Hospitaler villages and properties in Somogy county. The case was referred to Cardinal Leo Brancaleone of Santa Croce in Gerusalemme as auditor.[64] The choice of Cardinal Leo as auditor suggests that in this instance it was helpful to entrust the case to an auditor personally familiar with the country. Cardinal Leo had been a papal legate to Hungary and Bulgaria in 1204, although the experience could not have been a happy one, since he had been imprisoned by the Hungarian king.[65] Abbot Urias appeared in person to represent his monastery, and the Hospitalers were represented by a certain proctor B. The abbot's case was straightforward. He claimed that the tithes in question were well known to pertain to the abbey, that this was confirmed by papal privileges and confirmations, and that the Hospitalers had wrongfully injured the monastery's rights.[66] He asked for the restitution of the tithes. The Hospitalers' proctor argued that the abbey's privileges were outmoded because the abbey had failed to collect the tithes for more than forty years, during which time the Hospitalers had peacefully possessed them. This could be proved by the fact that the abbey could produce no witnesses. Such witnesses would be able to prove that for twenty years before the death of King Béla III (d. 1196) and for three years thereafter the

64. *Mon. rom. ep. Vesprim.*, 1:36, no. 39 (Potthast 5102: 20 April 1216). For Cardinal Leo see J. M. Bak, "Leone Brancaleone," *Dizionario biografico delgi Italiani* 13 (Rome, 1971): 814–17; and Maleczek, *Papst und Kardinalskolleg*, pp. 137–39.

65. See J. R. Sweeney, "Innocent III, Hungary and the Bulgarian Coronation: A Study in Medieval Papal Diplomacy," *Church History* 42 (1973): 323–30.

66. The earliest papal confirmation of privilege for Pannonhalma, issued by Paschal II on 8 December 1102 (Jaffé 5962), somewhat obliquely confirms to the abbey the tithes from the church of St. Michael and other grants made for the protection of the nation, the welfare of the kingdom, and the increase of the faith by King Stephen of pious memory. The passage is more explicit in a privilege of Alexander III given on 16 December 1175 (Jaffé 12526), where the tithes in the region of Somogy which the abbey had held for the past forty years and other grants made for the protection of the nation, the welfare of the kingdom, and the increase of the faith by a charter of King Stephen are confirmed. The same language is repeated in another bull of Alexander III (12 January 1181, Erdélyi, *Pannon. főapátság tört.*, 1:610, no. 21 (not in Jaffé), and a bull of Urban III (8 May 1187, Jaffé 15968). In the solemn privilege of Clement III (11 March 1189, Jaffé 16387), the text has been compressed to say that tithes the monastery is recognized to have possessed for the past forty years are confirmed to the abbot and monks by apostolic authority.

abbey made no use of its privileges and that only in the reign of King Imre (1196–1204) did the abbot, resorting to violence, coerce the Hospitalers for about seven years into paying the tithes from these lands. The order's proctor argued that in view of the forty years when the Hospitalers retained the tithes, the failure of the abbey to use its privileges, and the abbot's behavior toward them, Pannonhalma neither had rightful title to the tithes nor possessed them in good faith. Because Cardinal Leo in Rome could not easily hear the testimony of witnesses in Hungary, the case was committed to judges delegate: the bishop of Győr, the archdeacon of Nyitra, and the *scholasticus* of Székesfehérvár. The judges were instructed to show preference for the abbot's case, since the tithes had been granted long ago to the monastery and had been confirmed by numerous Roman popes. Thus, with the consent of proctors for both sides (it appears that the abbot, although present, employed a proctor also), the judges were ordered to provide the Hospitalers a period of four months to produce witnesses and prove their good faith; otherwise the tithes were to be restored to the abbey, and the Hospitalers were to be ordered to silence on this matter. Further impetrations from Rome were prohibited. Implementation of this mandate, however, proved impossible. The death of Innocent III and the departure of the bishop of Győr for the Fifth Crusade terminated the commission. But on 27 August 1217 Pope Honorius III renewed it for the archdeacon of Nyitra and the *scholasticus* of Székesfehérvár.[67] We do not know what action they took, if any. A lengthy mandate of Honorius III from 28 May 1225 provides details for the subsequent fate of the suit.[68] Honorius, with the concurrence of the parties, recommitted the still unresolved suit to the archbishop of Kalocsa and other judges with a mandate to settle it, but the parties for differing reasons refused to appear. The Hospitalers then obtained new letters from Rome designating the bishop of Zagreb and other judges to hear the case. The abbot challenged the impetration of the Hospital and was heard in person by Pelagius, cardinal bishop of Albano, who, because of the absence of the proctor of the Hospitalers, committed the suit to yet another set of judges delegate—the provosts of Győr and Székesfehérvár and the Cistercian abbot of Pilis. It is clear that the Hospitalers were attempting to evade a settlement, but Abbot Urias was a persistent opponent, who had meanwhile secured first from Innocent III and then from Honorius III solemn privileges confirming Pannonhalma's rights and possessions, including the disputed tithes from Somogy.[69]

A somewhat similar case is known to us chiefly through a decretal of

67. Theiner, *Mon. Hung.*, 1:8, no. 15 (Potthast 5597).
68. *Mon. rom. ep. Vesprim.*, 1:65, no. 79 (Potthast 7414).
69. Erdélyi, *Pannon. főapátság tört.*, 1:640, no. 53, and 654, no. 67 (Potthast 5123), and the letter of Honorius III (Potthast 7413: 26 May 1225).

Innocent III included in the *Decretales* of Gregory IX (3.30.31: *Dudum adversus fratres*).[70] The suit, initiated by the bishop of Veszprém also against the knights Hospitalers of the priory of St. Stephen at Székesfehérvár, alleged that tithes from two villages, Csurgó and Ujudvár, belonged by right to the bishop. The case was heard in the *audientia* by the well-known Guala Bicchieri, cardinal priest of San Martino.[71] Whereas the bishop claimed the tithes on the grounds of the *ius commune*, the Hospitalers rested their claims on a royal charter and papal confirmations of privilege. The prior of the Hospitalers produced a copy of the charter of King Béla III of 1193 wherein the rights to the tithes of these two villages were confirmed. Several later copies of this charter exist, and we learn from them that Archbishop Martirius of Esztergom (ca. 1150–58) had intended to endow the Hospitaler priory of St. Stephen the King at Székesfehérvár but was prevented from doing so by death.[72] Subsequently, Queen Euphrosyne of Kiev (d. 1175), for herself and her husband, King Géza II (1141–62), and her son, the future Béla III, generously endowed the foundation. Béla's charter of 1193 confirmed this gift in perpetual alms. The prior could also show the auditor a papal privilege confirming the order's possessions in Hungary. The decretal text identifies the pope who granted the privilege as Clement (III), but if the papal privilege confirmed the terms of the charter of 1193—as later papal confirmations did—then the correct pope would be Celestine III. The prior also claimed the existence of an even earlier privilege of Lucius III, but this was not produced in evidence. By contrast with the preceding example, sentence was given in Rome. In a letter to the bishop of Veszprém, which became the basis of the decretal text, the case was decided in favor of the bishop despite the fact that the *ius commune* was not here applicable to tithes. The royal and papal privileges with which the Hospitalers were armed were of no avail. Innocent explained that donors had no authority to confer the things they did not possess de jure and that in bestowing churches and ecclesiastical things the crime of sacrilege had been committed.[73] In conferring these

70. Friedberg, *CIC*, 2:567–68; Theiner, *Mon. Slav.*, 1:69, no. 195 (Potthast 5298: 22 February 1215–16 July 1216).

71. Although the abridged decretal text merely identifies the auditor as "G. presbyterum cardinalem," he is cited as "tit. S. Martini" in *Comp. IV*. 3.9.3, see Friedberg, *CIC*, 2:567. Guala Bicchieri was cardinal priest of S. Martino from 1211 to 1227; see Maleczek, *Papst und Kardinalskolleg*, pp. 141–46.

72. The circumstances surrounding the endowment of the Hospitaler priory at Székesfehérvár are set forth in Béla III's charter (Szentpétery and Borsa, *Reg. Arp.*, no. 155) and subsequent confirmation charters such as that of Pope Innocent IV of 13 February 1252 (Budapest, Hungarian National Archives, MODL 28).

73. Royal grants of ecclesiastical privileges were viewed in Rome with deep suspicion. See, for example, Alexander III's rejection of an English royal grant of ecclesiastical exemption given to Battle Abbey in Kenneth Pennington, *Pope and Bishops: The Papal Monarchy in the Twelfth and Thirteenth Centuries* (Philadelphia, 1984), pp. 158–59.

two churches with their tithes and appurtenances upon the Hospitalers, the king in his original grant was legally incapable of disposing of that portion of the tithes which by right belonged to the bishop in accordance with local custom. The subsequent papal privileges, furthermore, even if authentic, would in no way diminish episcopal rights. Thus the Hospitalers were forbidden to impede the bishop's collection of the tithes, which he was to possess in peace in the future. The abbots of Tihány and Zirc were given a mandate to enforce the sentence.

Although Innocent's decision in this case would be firmly established in canon law through inclusion first in the *Compilatio quarta* and later in the *Decretales*, within a few years it was reopened. In 1225 the Hospitalers appealed to Honorius III to reexamine the merits of the case.[74] The well-known Cardinal Pelagius was designated as auditor. The Hospitalers through their proctor R. claimed that the process under Innocent III had been flawed because their case had been conducted by a false proctor (whether by a sham proctor or by a proctor who betrayed them is not clear). Moreover, vital testimony and proofs had been omitted from the first hearing which, it was argued, had they been heard would have led to the restitution of the tithes to the Hospital. The bishop of Veszprém replied that he was not answerable for the proctor, that he had been given possession of the tithes through the execution of the earlier sentence by the abbots of Tihány and Zirc, and that although the Hospitalers had at the time of the sentence accepted it, they later despoiled him of the tithes. The bishop, therefore, asked Cardinal Pelagius that he not be obliged to stand in court thus despoiled. Honorius's response was to recommit the case to the Cistercian abbot of Szentgotthárd, the provost of Székesfehérvár, and Master Enoch, the archdeacon of Nyitra, with instructions first to restore the tithes to the bishop in their entirety, then to hear the Hospitalers on the questions of the false proctor and the omitted proofs, and finally to send a detailed report to Rome, where the case would be resolved.

The foregoing cases provide graphic evidence for one of the apparent problems of the system of delegated jurisdiction, the difficulty of securing a lasting settlement. The refusal of the litigants to plead before certain judges or the inability of a judge to carry out his mandate resulted in the committing of the case to new judges and inevitably in new delay. A suit initiated by the abbot of Pannonhalma in 1214 against the *custos* of Székesfehérvár (the clerical guardian of the royal diadem) concerning rights to tithes in Somogy county is another case in point. Innocent first commissioned the bishop of Veszprém, the provost of Veszprém, and the

74. Honorius III, *Reg.* 10:50 (Potthast 7477: 16 September 1225), printed in Theiner, *Mon. Hung.,* 1:61, no. 129.

James Ross Sweeney

archdeacon of Székesfehérvár to hear the suit.[75] Yet in less than a year the case was given to new judges led by the bishop of Győr, who were instructed to gather information and send a report to Rome by the time the Fourth Lateran Council assembled. When the *custos* refused to accept the judgment of the bishop of Győr or to make satisfactory responses before the convening of the Lateran Council, a third mandate was given to the abbot of Tihány and colleagues to compel the *custos* to pay court costs and to decide the case, if the parties were willing; otherwise they were to remit the case to Rome with sufficient information for a settlement and to fix a time when the parties should present themselves in Rome.

Obviously the willingness of the parties to end the litigation was also a crucial factor. Jane Sayers has drawn attention in the English evidence to frequent instances of the termination of suits by composition rather than by judicial sentence. The Hungarian documentation is too sparse to permit generalization.[76] The sole surviving *actum* of Hungarian judges delegate for the pontificate of Innocent III, however, points in the direction of composition. Probably in 1214 or possibly in early 1215, Innocent issued a mandate, now lost, to the bishop of Győr and the Benedictine abbots of Pécsvárad and Bakonybél to hear and settle a case between the two Benedictine abbeys of Pannonhalma and St. Egidius concerning tithes in Somogy county. These tithes of fields, gardens, cellars, and people of the parish of the chapel of St. Peter were said to belong to the monastery of St. Egidius, a daughter house of the abbey of St. Gilles in Toulouse.[77] Urias of Pannonhalma claimed that they had been sold for debt and by right and possession properly belonged to his house. The monks of St. Egidius acknowledged and swore in the presence of the three judges delegate that the tithes were indeed owed to Pannonhalma. The abbot of St. Egidius, Herveus, promised in the presence of the judges to recognize the concession to Pannonhalma both by oath and by letter, the text of which was included in the judges' *actum* dated 1215.[78] It is instructive that in this case the parties were prepared to agree, or more properly, that one side recognized the legitimacy of the opponent's argument, without the need for a sentence to be imposed by the judges. Without other judicial *acta* we cannot know how often Hungarian cases were ended through composition.

75. Only the third of three Innocentian mandates survives, but it refers to the preceding two; see *Mon. rom. ep. Vesprim.*, 1:43, no. 48.
76. Sayers, *Papal Judges Delegate*, pp. 239–40.
77. For a review of the historical ties between the French Benedictine community of St. Egidius in Hungary and its mother house of St. Gilles in Toulouse, see F. Baumgarten, "A Saint-Gillesi apátság összeköttetései Magyarországgal," *Századok* 40 (1906): 389–411.
78. The *actum* was subsequently preserved in a *vidimus* of the Count Palatine Denis from 1238; see *Mon. rom. ep. Vesprim.*, 1:33, no. 35.

We should remember, however, that the most passionately contested cases, for example, the dispute between Pannonhalma and the Hospitalers discussed above, were precisely those likely to leave a body of evidence appearing to show that cases of delegated jurisdiction failed to effect lasting legal resolution of disputes appealed to Rome. Although the survival of the settlement of the case between St. Egidius and Pannonhalma is purely fortuitous, it serves as a reminder that much evidence of a similar character has likely been lost.

In the interest of an orderly judicial system, decisions rendered in Rome or by local judges delegate needed to be lasting and beyond challenge. But it is well known that even when the right of appeal was explicitly denied by papal mandate one of the sides could resourcefully find grounds to evade that prohibition.[79] A system so intimately bound up with the right of appeal was constantly vulnerable to the abuse of appellate procedure. Innocent III in a case arising in Hungary showed himself aware of this weakness, desirous of providing a remedy, but not wholly successful in fashioning a procedural solution to the problem. The case involved the conflicting claims of the bishop of Transylvania and the provost of Nagyszeben touched upon earlier in this essay. Innocent's letter of 1198, as we have seen, confirmed a settlement propounded by an earlier papal legate which preserved many of the bishop's jurisdictional rights and limited those of the provost.[80] A year later, however, the provost and his allies were moving to challenge the decision. In this effort the provost was joined by the archbishop of Esztergom, who was his ecclesiastical superior—for all royal abbeys and collegiate churches were subject to the metropolitan—and by certain unnamed Transylvanian Saxon priests. Their objective was to overturn that part of the judgment which obliged the Transylvanian Saxons to pay certain tithes from the lands of the cathedral church of St. Michael in Gyulafehérvár (Alba Julia, Karlsburg). To this end they sought and obtained, apparently by deception, a papal rescript reversing the earlier sentence.[81] In a letter to the bishop from late 1199, the pope not only declared the improperly obtained rescript invalid, he explicitly granted the bishop the right to appeal to Rome even if appeal

79. There is no shortage of examples; see the discussion of the York-Durham dispute in R. Brentano, *York Metropolitan Jurisdiction and Papal Judges Delegate (1279–1296)* (Berkeley and Los Angeles, 1959), p. 151.

80. See above, note 6.

81. This papal letter does not survive but is cited in Innocent III's letter to the bishop of Transylvania; see next note. Such falsely obtained rescripts were a long-standing problem; see S. Chodorow, "Dishonest Litigation in the Church Courts, 1140–98," in *Law, Church and Society: Essays in Honor of Stephan Kuttner*, ed. K. Pennington and R. Somerville (Philadelphia, 1977), pp. 187–206.

were to be forbidden by papal letters of commission if, in the future, his enemies should obtain inimical or suspect judges to hear the case.[82] Innocent's purpose in granting this privilege to appeal when appeals were prohibited was, somewhat paradoxically, to preserve the stability of previous judicial decisions. As he told the bishop of Transylvania, "Those things which have been reasonably decided through the process of judicial examination ought not lightly to be rescinded, but rather ought to be confirmed through constant steadfastness."[83]

The system of papal delegated jurisdiction at the beginning of the thirteenth century was far from perfect, but it gave the appearance of functioning in order to resolve cases fairly and in accordance with recognized legal norms. The bureaucratic court machinery at Rome, in the process of further development in the opening decades of the century, gave promise for the creation of a more efficient and effective central judicial administration.[84] That this promise was not realized in its entirety does not compel us to hold Innocent III or his successors accountable for all shortcomings of the system. John C. Moore, after analyzing the evidence for delegated jurisdiction in France during Innocent's pontificate, concluded that as mediators local judicial authorities were as fair as papal judges delegate and more efficient.[85] He maintains that the system of delegated jurisdiction weakened the authority of episcopal courts by removing cases from local ecclesiastical courts and that this in turn led to an expansion of secular courts. Furthermore, Moore says, the way appeals were accepted in Rome was "mindless" and "indefensible."[86] A review of the Hungarian evidence does not support this negative assessment. Moore does not take into account that local justice, whether ecclesiastical or secular, was more prone to prejudice and to ignorance of the law and was more susceptible to external political pressure. The system of papal delegated jurisdiction, on the other hand, had the advantage of fostering the interplay between the

82. *Inn. III Reg.*, 2:244. Hageneder, *Register*, 2:235 (Potthast 901: 14 December 1199). The standard phrase beginning "appellatione postposita" was intended to prohibit interlocutory judgments lodged purely to prolong the proceedings and was never designed to prevent all appeals regardless of legitimate merit; see P. Herde, *Audientia litterarum contradictarum*, 2 vols., Bibliothek des Deutschen Historischen Instituts in Rom, 31–32 (Rome, 1970), 1:235 n. 10.

83. Ibid. "Quoniam ea, que per ordinem judicialis examinis rationabiliter sunt decisa, nulla debent temeritate rescindi, sed perpetue stabilitatis robore confirmari."

84. See, for example, J. Sayers, *Papal Government and England during the Pontificate of Honorius III (1216–1227)* (Cambridge, 1984); Herde, *Audientia litterarum contradictarum*, and idem, *Beiträge zum päpstlichen Kanzlei- und Urkundenwesen im 13. Jahrhundert*, 2d ed. (Kallmünz, 1967).

85. J. C. Moore, "Papal Justice in France around the Time of Pope Innocent III," *Church History* 41 (1972): 295–306, esp. p. 301.

86. Ibid., p. 306.

impartial statement of the law at the papal court and the fact-finding and enforcement of decisions at the local level. Mediation and arbitration, as Moore has correctly shown, were also effective ways to resolve legal disputes locally, but mediation was not incompatible with papal delegated jurisdiction.[87] In Hungary, too, mediation was employed, but the bulk of our evidence is drawn from secular justice. The statistics adduced by R. C. van Caenegem in his analysis of the Hungarian secular ordeal register from Nagyvárad for 1208 to 1235 reveal that out of 308 cases where the outcome is known, 75 cases were settled by agreement, with an additional 25 resolved through the withdrawal of the complaint.[88] This is nearly one-third of the cases. Thus in secular courts, which had greater means of physical coercion to enforce judicial decisions, mediation was a significant factor. The increasing influence of secular courts in the thirteenth century, futhermore, can be explained by a wide variety of factors, one of which was that these courts achieved new standards of fairness and efficiency in the thirteenth century precisely because they adopted Romano-canonical procedures.[89] Canon law courts and especially the highest Christian tribunal in Rome were unique institutions grounded in a religious conception of justice. The freedom of any Christian to appeal to Rome sprang from a compassionate religious idealism that was far from "mindless," although it was open to abuse and exploitation. Criticisms of judicial confusion at Rome and long delays experienced in receiving final settlement in a case are documented in many instances. These complaints are such a standard feature of antibureaucratic rhetoric, however, that they come close to constituting a topos. What is sometimes overlooked is that the system of delegated jurisdiction permitted local prelates on the periphery to share both function and authority with the center of power precisely at the time that the centralization process was accelerating. The result was a firmer, tighter relationship between the judicial center and its outlying parts than had ever existed previously. No similar integration of central authority with local expertise can be found in contemporary secular bureaucracies. The system of papal judges delegate was not just a way to employ litigious prelates in harmless tasks or a means of financial support for legists; rather, it was an agent in the homogenization of ecclesiastical legal practices, a way of standardizing ecclesiastical justice

87. Ibid., pp. 301–3. For the composition and local enforcement of decisions in England, see Sayers, *Papal Judges Delegate*, pp. 274–75.

88. R. C. van Caenegem, "Methods of Proof in Medieval Law," trans. J. R. Sweeney and D. A. Flanary, *Academiae Analecta: Mededelingen van de Koninklijke Academie voor Wetenschappen, Letteren en Schone Kunsten van België* 45 (1983): 90.

89. See the arguments advanced in H. J. Berman, *Law and Revolution: The Formation of the Western Legal Tradition* (Cambridge, Mass., 1983), pp. 115–18, 199–224, and passim.

James Ross Sweeney

across international boundaries from England to Scandinavia, from Spain to Hungary.[90]

90. Moore, "Papal Justice in France," p. 304, has taken out of context the perceptive observations of R. Brentano in his *Two Churches: England and Italy in the Thirteenth Century* (Princeton, 1968). Brentano's full text (p. 171) is balanced and persuasive: "Cases before delegates' courts implemented a government of self-help and good compromise. This government defined the reality of local power and, in defining it, avoided disorder. The disputed endings of cases before delegates were not really inane; they were part of a workable, although elaborate, expensive, and intermittent system. They, in fact, used effectively the necessary deflection between stated purpose and act that inefficient official government made universal in thirteenth-century Europe." The Hungarian cases analyzed above support and augment these conclusions.

# [3]

## Gregory IX, Emperor Frederick II, and the Constitutions of Melfi

### KENNETH PENNINGTON

In September 1231 Frederick II issued a new code of laws for the Kingdom of Sicily while his court resided at Melfi. This code, called the Constitutions of Melfi or, since the nineteenth century, the *Liber Augustalis*, was the first major codification of royal law during the High Middle Ages. It remained in force until 1809 in Naples and 1819 in the Kingdom of Sicily. Frederick introduced his new code into the curriculum of the university he had established at Naples in 1224, and between 1270 and 1280 Marinus de Caramanico wrote his apparatus that became the Ordinary Gloss for it. His gloss, along with that of Andrea d'Isernia, was printed several times from the fifteenth to the eighteenth century.[1]

Frederick appointed a commission to work on a new law code in 1230. Only one member is known with certainty, Jacobus archbishop of Capua. There has been a lively discussion of whether Jacobus directed the committee. A tradition dating from the middle of the thirteenth century credited Petrus de Vinea with compiling the Constitutions. Historians have debated whether Jacobus or Petrus was primarily responsible for the compilation, but unless new evidence surfaces, the problem will remain unsolved.[2]

My thanks to Professors Stephan Kuttner, Hans Martin Schaller, and Armin Wolf for reading this essay and offering useful criticism.

1. *Constitutiones Regni Siciliae* (Naples, 1475; reprint Glashütten, 1973); *Constitutiones, capitula, ritus, et pragmaticae utriusque Siciliae . . . commentariis illustrata* (Venice, 1590); A. Cervonius, *Constitutionum Regni Siciliarum libri III* (Naples, 1773).

2. The evidence for Jacobus's role is the letter of Gregory IX discussed below. A summary of the problem may be found in Norbert Kamp, *Kirche und Monarchie im staufischen Königreich Sizilien*, vol. 1, *Prosopographische Grundlegung: Bistümer und Bischöfe des Königreichs 1194–1266* (Munich, 1973–82), pp. 126–27 n. 140, and Her-

The commission worked swiftly. Each province sent four representatives who declared local law. The finished product, however, incorporated few examples of differing provincial customs. The commission drew material from the royal statutes of the Norman kings of Sicily and those of Frederick II. Lombard, Roman, canon, feudal, and Byzantine law also left their marks on the compilation to varying degrees.[3]

Since the nineteenth century, historians have noted that Pope Gregory IX wished to suppress publication of the new code, and they have connected Frederick's determination to codify the laws of Sicily with his strained relationship with the papacy. Hermann Dilcher most recently summarized this position: "It is not certain whether Frederick had already decided to promulgate his own code of laws during 1230. In any case, at the beginning of 1230 he ordered the judges of Sicily to observe the Norman Assizes as valid law. For that reason it is not unlikely that Frederick's plans for new legislation took shape during his peace negotiations with Pope Gregory IX. Consequently Gregory also considered Frederick's legislation a challenge. He warned Frederick on 5 July 1231 not to issue it and forbade Archbishop Jacobus of Capua to participate in the work of the commission."[4] Thus historians have considered the *Liber Augustalis* a challenge to papal authority and another gauntlet thrown down in the great struggle between the empire and the papacy.

The evidence for these assumptions is contained in two papal letters. The first, addressed to Frederick II, was edited from the registers of Gregory IX by Odorico Rinaldi in his continuation of Baronius's *Annales ecclesiastici.*[5] Unfortunately, although from his own interpretation of the letter we can see that he read the entire text, Rinaldi edited it only in part. In the nineteenth century, Rodenberg, Huillard-Bréholles, and Casertano reprinted the letter from Rinaldi's truncated edition.[6] The second letter,

---

mann Dilcher, *Die sizilische Gesetzgebung Kaiser Friedrichs II.: Quellen der Constitutionen von Melfi und ihrer Novellen* (Cologne and Vienna, 1975), pp. 20–22.

3. Dilcher, *Gesetzgebung*, pp. 29–57.

4. Ibid., p. 20. See also Eduard Winkelmann, *Kaiser Friedrich II.* (Leipzig, 1897), 2:266–75; Ernst Kantorowicz, *Kaiser Friedrich der Zweite*, 4th ed. (Düsseldorf and Munich, 1964), pp. 238–39; Sten Gagnér, *Studien zur Ideengeschichte der Gesetzgebung*, Acta Universitatis Upsaliensis, Studia Iuridica Upsaliensia 1 (Stockholm, Uppsala, and Göteborg, 1960), p. 309; Armin Wolf, "Die Gesetzgebung der entstehenden Territorialstaaten," in *Handbuch der Quellen und Literatur der neueren europäischen Privatrechtsgeschichte*, ed. Helmut Coing (Munich, 1973), pp. 698–99; Kamp, *Kirche und Monarchie*, pp. 126–27, and again Hermann Dilcher, "Die sizilische Gesetzgebung Friedrichs II., eine Synthese von Tradition und Erneuerung," in *Probleme um Friedrich II.*, ed. J. Fleckenstein (Sigmaringen, 1974), pp. 24–25.

5. Odorico Rinaldi, *Annales ecclesiastici ab anno quo desinit Card. Caesar Baronius* (Coloniae Agrippinae, 1693), 13:376–77.

6. C. Rodenberg, *Epistolae saeculi XIII e registis pontificum romanorum* (Berlin, 1883), 1:357–58. J. L. A. Huillard-Bréholles, *Historia diplomatica Friderici secundi* (Paris, 1857), 3:289. Antonio Casertano, "Sull'autore delle Costituzioni Melfiesi: Nota critica," *Archivio storico campano* 1, 1 (1889): 161–72 at pp. 165–66.

to Jacobus, archbishop of Capua, was printed by Huillard-Bréholles with numerous errors.[7] Both letters are here edited anew from the Vatican registers and printed below in the Appendix.

The complete letter of Gregory to Frederick does not solve all the problems connected with the promulgation of the *Liber Augustalis*, but it does shed considerable light on Gregory's concerns. The letter begins with a striking proverb: "Where there is love, there rests the eye, where there is pain, the finger often moves to [ease it]." The proverb's more common form was "Ubi amor, ibi oculus; ubi dolor, ibi manus" (Where love resides, there rests one's eye; where pain, there presses one's hand). Gregory's slight change of hand to finger in his version of the proverb may have reminded Frederick and his counselors of the biblical "writing finger" and might just possibly have been a subtle reference to the pope's role in directing the spiritual welfare of Christian society.[8]

After his short arenga, Gregory came to the point of his letter: "We understand that either through your own will or as a result of the unwise counsels of perverse men you intend to issue new constitutions from which it necessarily follows that you shall be called a persecutor of the church and a destroyer of public liberty" (text 1, lines 6–10). On the basis of this passage Winkelmann and other historians have concluded that Gregory did not want Frederick to publish a new code of laws. The term "nove constitutiones" could indeed refer to a new code of laws, and several contemporaries refer to the *Liber Augustalis* with this or similar language.[9] But since only a handful of laws in the completed code refer to the church or its clergy, one may wonder whether historians have correctly understood Gregory's apprehensions. Further, since the papacy never objected to other royal codifications or laws—unless they contained laws harming the interests of the church—Gregory's objection would be a singular moment in the development of legislation and legislative theory in the West. Certainly, none of the provisions in the promulgated version of the *Liber Augustalis* was obviously damaging to the church; most of those touching the church and the clergy either are tangential to ecclesiastical affairs or incorporate commonly accepted doctrines.[10] Gregory did not object to the *Liber Augustalis* after its publication, and none of the later commentators remark that particular laws were controversial in ecclesiastical circles, either in Rome or in the Schools.

7. Huillard-Bréholles, *Historia*, 3:290.

8. Hans Walther, *Proverbia sententiaeque latinitatis medii aevi* (Göttingen, 1963–67), no. 32036. Walther lists a proverb "ubi dolor, ibi digitus," no. 32040. The "writing finger" is found in Exod. 31:18, Deut. 9:10, with the most familiar being John 8:6: "Iesus autem inclinans se deorsum digito scribebat in terra."

9. Winkelmann, *Kaiser Friedrich II.*, p. 267 n.3.

10. The chapters of the *Liber Augustalis* touching either the clergy or the church are: 1.7, 1.31, 1.33, 1.45, 1.49, 1.64, 1.68, 1.69, 1.71, 1.82, 1.84, 3.2, 3.20, 3.28, 3.60, and 3.83. Most are quite trivial mentions.

Kenneth Pennington

Odorico Rinaldi did not understand Gregory's words to be directed
against the Constitutions as a whole. He noted that Gregory wished to
admonish Frederick not to issue laws inimical to the church.[11] The section of the text from the registers that he omitted gives a clear indication
of Gregory's concerns: "Lest therefore what never should have been begun
should be completed, we ask, warn, and implore your imperial highness in
the name of Jesus Christ, who is the Prince of princes, to take prudent
heed that these sorts of novelties usually cause serious scandal and never
to permit yourself to be seduced in proceeding to anything for which
blame could be attached to you or us" (text 1, lines 29–35). Even if the first
part of the letter might be interpreted as warning Frederick not to issue his
new codification, this section does not forbid "nove constititiones" but
prohibits "novitates" contrary to ecclesiastical rights or liberties. If Gregory had objected to the entire codification, he hardly would have used this
phraseology in his concluding admonition.

We do not know what these "novelties" may have been, and speculation about them must be conjectural. It is most likely that Frederick
ordered legislation drafted that reasserted royal rights in ecclesiastical
affairs. During the 1220s Frederick had attempted to exercise rights in
Sicilian churches that the papacy found improper; Gregory had been especially offended by Frederick's practice of leaving bishoprics and monasteries bereft of their prelates for uncanonical durations in order to collect
the revenues attached to those offices. As feudal lord of the Regno, Gregory may also have wished to protect the liberties of the Regno's city-
states. The new constitutions severely restricted these rights, and when,
for example, the imperial justiciar wished to apply the Constitutions in
Messina, the city revolted.[12] We may deduce from a letter of 1236 that
Gregory may have objected to Frederick's arbitrary abolishment of the
cities' liberties and privileges to elect their own magistrates and to render
their own justice. He noted that Frederick's harsh rule permitted no one in
the Regno to move a hand or foot unless the emperor commanded it.[13] He
may, however, have understood Frederick's "urban policy" and sym-

11. Rinaldi, *Annales*, 13:376–77: "Cum enim Fridericus iniquiores leges ecclesiasticis intulisset, mox excitatus zelo Gregorius Capuanum qui improbarum ferendarum
legum auctor extiterat, perstrinxit; imperatoremque ut eas rescinderet, oratione gravis-
sima est adhortatus."
12. G. Tabacco, "La lotta per il potere nelle città dominanti e l'instabilità delle
istituzioni," in *Storia d'Italia* (Turin, 1974), 2:202–3.
13. Rodenberg, *Epistolae*, 1:602: "Indigne ergo super oppressionibus predictarum
ecclesiarum et hominum regni, in quo nullus manum vel pedem absque tuo movet
imperio, affirmativam nostre propositionis negativa ignorantie imperialis interimis,
quibus consensum vel originem prestitisse, cum nuntiis et litteris apostolicis ac clamo-
ribus passorum iniurias, eas tuis auribus pluries inculcatas non solum scire set etiam
plene potueris emendare, minime dubitaris." My thanks to H. M. Schaller for bringing
this passage to my attention. Frederick's legislation restricting or abrogating communal
rights is found in book 1 of the Constitutions, title 50 to the end of the book.

[56]

pathized with it. He too demanded that the cities of the papal states submit to papal overlordship in similar matters.[14] Unfortunately, all of this conjecture is meager evidence from which to deduce Frederick's intentions and Gregory's objections.[15]

The tone of Gregory's letter to Jacobus, the archbishop of Capua (letter 2 in Appendix), leaves no doubt that the pope viewed Frederick's planned legislation as a serious infringement of ecclesiastical liberties. Beginning with a reference to Isa. 10:1, Gregory heaped both sarcasm and rebuke on Jacobus for his insensitivity to ecclesiastical rights and for his vainglory. The letter reveals that there had already been an exchange of letters between the two. Gregory rejected Jacobus's excuse in the earlier letter that he was merely a scribe and not a legislator. "You sew a girdle from fig-leaves [to cover your nakedness]," he thundered. Rather, Jacobus should have opposed the legislation (text 2, lines 8–13). The archbishop of Capua was a well-known figure at the curia, a "court bishop," and a frequent representative for Frederick in imperial affairs. Gregory's tone has all the flavor of that used when two men know each other well enough to speak sharply.[16]

Jacobus was almost certainly a member of the commission that Frederick appointed to draft the *Liber Augustalis*. This letter is the only piece of evidence for this conclusion and falls just short of being conclusive. Most modern historians have interpreted it as establishing Jacobus's position on the commission and as commanding that he stop working on the Constitutions. I think the letter can bear only the first assumption without too much difficulty.[17] Gregory had learned that new legislation touching the church had been drafted in Frederick's curia, and he wrote to Jacobus, who admitted that he helped draft new legislation. We may assume that Jacobus must have been a member of the commission whose work was in full swing and that these laws were destined for the *Liber Augustalis*. Gregory's parting admonition did not, however, preclude Jacobus's participation in the work of the commission, but directed him to be more sensitive to ecclesiastical rights. Gregory warned him that, as imperial counselor, he must remind the emperor of his duties to the church: "So, therefore,

14. D. Waley, *The Papal State in the Thirteenth Century* (London, 1961), pp. 104–41.
15. For an analysis of Frederick's relationship with the church in Sicily see H. J. Pybus, "The Emperor Frederick II and the Sicilian Church," *Cambridge Historical Journal* 3 (1929–31): 134–63; James M. Powell, "Frederick II and the Church in the Kingdom of Sicily, 1220–1224," *Church History* 30 (1961): 28–34, and idem, "Frederick II and the Church: A Revisionist View," *Catholic Historical Review* 48 (1963): 487–97.
16. Kamp, *Kirche und Monarchie*, pp. 121–28, has written a fine biography of Jacobus, outlining his importance to Frederick. See also the dated but still useful study of J. L. A. Huillard-Bréholles, *Vie et correspondance de Pierre de la Vigne, ministre de l'empereur Frédéric II* (Paris, 1865; reprint Aalen, 1966), pp. 15–18, 123–32.
17. Winkelmann, *Kaiser Friedrich II.*, p. 269, Conrad, "Gesetzgebung," p. xlv, Dilcher, quoted above note 4, and Wolf, "Gesetzgebung," p. 699, believe that in the letter Gregory forbade Jacobus to participate further in the work of the commission.

that this warning may keep you safe from punishment, we carefully admonish you by firmly commanding through [these] apostolic letters that, keeping in mind [your] episcopal office, you must not only not obey an unlawful command, but rather should strive to make amends for the previous offense" (text 2, lines 17–22). Huillard-Bréholles's editing of this passage has helped to mislead subsequent readers. He left out the "non solum" of line 20, an omission that lessens the emphasis that Jacobus should not obey unjust commands *and* should make amends. Jacobus would have been hard pressed to make good his earlier sin of omission if he were no longer part of the commission.[18]

In their analysis of this episode historians have generally not emphasized that Gregory's protest was successful. In a letter dated a month later (27 July 1231), Gregory assured Frederick of his goodwill.[19] Although it is not certain that this letter is connected with those of 5 July, it is probable. And if so, we may conclude that Frederick had abandoned whatever objectionable legislation he intended to include in the *Liber Augustalis*. This should not be surprising. After the long and now successfully negotiated peace treaty in which Jacobus had played a key role (1230–31), Frederick had good reason to avoid conflict with the papacy. But even more telling evidence can be adduced. Gregory did not protest the promulgation of the *Liber Augustalis* a few months later. It is inconceivable that Gregory would have remained silent if his primary concern had been the new codification.

Jacobus may even have undertaken the risky task of persuading Frederick to remove the offending legislation from the Constitutions. He seems to have successfully continued to balance his allegiance to Frederick against his loyalty to the church. This was not an easy task, for Frederick was a hard master. A striking example of his difficult situation is found in a letter of Jacobus to a cardinal at the curia in response to the cardinal's request that the son of an imperial notary be punished. Jacobus wrote that he would do anything he could, "especially in those things in which imperial goodwill was not injured and in which nothing was contrary to the emperor's honor."[20] This is not the stuff from which martyrs are made, but is probably not different from the sentiments of many bishops who cared for their flocks on the lands of powerful lords.

18. In the course of arguing that Petrus de Vinea was the author of the *Liber Augustalis*, Casertano, "Sull'autore delle Costituzioni," p. 166, also noted that "Or è chiaro che, in questa secunda lettera, il pontefice non afferma con precisione che l'Amalfitani lavorasse intorno a quelle leggi, e vi lavorasse da solo, ma dice essergli pervenuto all'orecchio questo fatto, e disuade il suo subordinato dal prendere parte ad opera contraria alla Chiesa e alla libertà dei popoli."

19. *Epistolae*, 360; Vat. Reg. 15, fol. 110r–v, no. 100. Potthast 8775. Rodenberg's edition is accurate.

20. Karl Hampe, "Zu der von Friedrich II. 1235 eingesetzten sizilischen Regentschaft," *Historische Vierteljahrschrift* 21 (1922–23): 76–79: "presertim in hiis, in quibus et ex quibus favor imperialis non leditur et honori suo contrarium non occurit." It is not absolutely certain, but it is likely, that Jacobus was the author of this letter.

The last piece of evidence that Gregory achieved his aims is Jacobus's success at the papal court in the years after 1231. In the summer of 1234, Gregory rendered a judgment for Jacobus against the Abbey of Santa Maria di Capua, and in July 1235 he delegated an important case to him.[21]

To sum up, I think that the evidence does not support the generally accepted contention that Gregory considered the Constitutions of Melfi a threat to the church. Historians have been deceived by faulty evidence, but also by anachronistic assumptions. We must be cautious not to attribute motives to historical characters that are persuasive for us but completely alien to them. The debate surrounding the purpose of Pope Honorius III's *Super speculam* is another, nearly contemporary, example of analyzing legal problems with modern rather than medieval notions. In 1218 Honorius forbade the teaching of Roman law at the University of Paris. A number of historians have attributed political motives to Honorius or a fear of Roman law. Recent research has, however, emphasized the pope's pastoral concerns, which led him to restrict the study of Roman law to a small number of clergy.[22] More work remains to be done on *Super speculam*, but we shall not return, I think, to the old interpretation that the decretal was prompted by hatred of Roman law in the Roman curia.[23] By 1218 Roman legal concepts and definitions had been so integrated into canon law that its study was unthinkable without a thorough knowledge of Roman jurisprudence. Every curial lawyer would have understood this basic fact.

In the end, it is not surprising that Gregory did not oppose the publication of the *Liber Augustalis*. If he had, his opposition to a codification of secular law would have been an anomaly in the history of church-state relations. That Frederick intended to secure what he considered royal rights over ecclesiastical institutions in the Regno and that these royal prerogatives may have been at odds with Gregory's conceptions of ecclesiastical liberty cannot be denied. The drafting of such legislation would conform to what we know of Frederick's policies. Nevertheless, Frederick would not have planned his codification as an instrument of antipapal policy. Such ideas simply do not conform to medieval presuppositions about the purpose and function of legislation in society.

21. Lucien Auvray, *Les registres de Grégoire IX* (Paris, 1896–1955), nos. 2392, 2393, and 2685. See Kamp, *Kirche und Monarchie*, p. 128.

22. Especially Stephan Kuttner, "Papst Honorius III. und das Studium des Zivilrechts," in *Festschrift für Martin Wolf*, ed. E. von Caemmerer et al. (Tübingen, 1952), pp. 79–101; reprinted with valuable additional notes in *Gratian and the Schools of Law, 1140–1234* (London, 1983). Also emphasizing the nonpolitical origins of the decretal but minimizing the role of Honorius in its genesis is Ernst Pitz, *Papstreskript und Kaiserreskript* (Tübingen, 1971), pp. 171–91. His thesis has not been generally accepted. Pitz answered his critics in "Die römische Kurie als Thema der vergleichenden Sozialgeschichte," *Quellen und Forschungen aus italienischen Archiven und Bibliotheken* 58 (1978): 286–89 (pages treating *Super speculam*).

23. For details of the earlier literature, see Kuttner, "Papst Honorius," pp. 82–83. I am currently editing the glosses to *Super speculam* in the Lisbon and Florence manuscripts.

Kenneth Pennington

Appendix

Text 1

Vat. Reg. 15, fol. 105r–v, lib. 5, no. 91, 5 July 1231. Potthast 8760. Auvray 676.

F. illustri Romanorum imperatori semper augusto et regi Sicilie.

Quia iuxta uulgare prouerbium, "ubi amor, ibi oculus; ubi dolor, ibi sepe digitus admouetur,"[24] ex amore fit quod in benefactis tuis intimis affectibus exultamus, de contrario contrarium sentientes. Intelleximus siquidem quod uel proprio motu uel seductus inconsultis consiliis peruersorum nouas edere constitutiones intendis ex quibus necessario sequitur ut dicaris ecclesie persecutor et obrutor publice libertatis, sicque tibi contrarius contra te tuis uiribus moliaris, nam cum speretur per manum tuam iura tam ecclesie quam imperii resarciri, et alias que solidanda fuerint solidari, clerus grauatus fauorem hiis exhibuerit inuitus, et alii cum de seruitute in libertate soleant prouocare, nequaquam rem ex animo prosequentur. Sane si ad id ex te forte moueris, timemus multum de gratia te[25] esse subtractum dum sic patenter famam propriam negligis et salutem. Si uero impulsus ab aliis, miramur quod talibus consiliariis acquiescis qui spiritu uexati nequitie te intendunt Deo et hominibus constituere inimicum, ut taceamus alia potius silentio intelligenda quam uerbo. Que utinam a te tacite intellecta fortius in auribus cordis sonent quatinus quieti tue ac fame nostre prouide consulens utrumque ab imprecationibus populi serues immunem. Cum enim montes pacem susceperint,[26] cur pauperes populi debent esse pacis expertes ut in pace amaritudo amarissima sit eorum? Aut quis posset indurato corde ululatus quos quodammodo preuidemus tot flentium obaudire? Ne igitur ueniat ad progressum quod non est ullatenus inchoandum, imperialem celsitudinem rogamus, monemus et obsecramus in Christo Jesu qui principibus principatur, quatinus prudenter aduertens quod huiusmodi nouitates grauia solent scandala suscitare nequaquam te seduci permittas ut procedas ad aliquid quo tibi uel nobis nota posset impingi, cum sicut nec te id agere ita nec nos deceret equanimiter tolerare. Dat. Reat. iii. Non. Iulii Pont. nostri anno quinto.

24. Hans Walther, *Lateinische Sprichwörter und Sentenzen des Mittelalters,* cf. nos. 32036 and 32040.
25. Tibi–*Reg.* Rinaldi gave the text of the Register at this point but suggested "Dei gratiam tibi esse subtractum." Huillard-Bréholles and Rodenberg adopted Rinaldi's emendation without indicating that it departed from the Register's text. Rinaldi's phrase is commonly used in the papal chancellery; I have chosen "te" for "tibi" because it required only a single change in the text and may be, for that reason, the more likely reading.
26. Ps. 72:3.

[60]

Text 2

Vat. Reg. 15, fols. 105v–6r, lib. 5, no. 92, 5 July 1231. Potthast 8761. Auvray 677.

Archiepiscopo Capuano.

Ve[27] qui condunt leges iniquas siue qui scribunt iniustitiam,[28] uideto quid te sperare ualeas uel timere dum sicut nobis est procerto relatum, carissimo in Christo filio nostro F. illustri Romanorum imperatori semper augusto et regi Sicilie constitutiones destitutiuas salutis et institutiuas enormium scandalorum edenti uoluntarius obsequens eas dictas, consuens tibi forsan ex foliis ficuum perizoma,[29] in excusationem friuolam pretendendo quod non legum dictator sed calamus es scribentis,[30] quibus deberes esse patentissimus contradictor quantumcumque tibi econtra discriminis immineret. Sed in hoc non innoxie forsitan gloriaris quod datum est tibi tuam ex hoc scientiam ostentare, non timens Deo scientiarum domino[31] displicere nec nos ueritus prouocasse qui tandem illas nequaquam equanimiter pateremur. Vt igitur premissa monitio te premuniens a pena preseruet immunem, fraternitatem tuam monemus attente per apostolica scripta firmiter precipiendo mandantes quatinus memor officii presulatus non solum non obsequaris illicite iussioni, sed potius offensam studeas redimere precedentem. Dat. ut supra.

27. MS Siue—Stephan Kuttner suggested this emendation and thought that a rubricator might have been responsible for the error. If we read "Siue" for "Ve," the grammar of the sentence is quite awkward, although not impossible. Most important, the passage in Isa. 10:1 begins "Ve." However, the letters "iue" are clearly in the hand of the scribe who wrote the text of the letter; thus the error, if it is one, precedes the copyist who entered the letter in the Register.
28. Isa. 10:1.
29. Gen. 3:7.
30. Cf. Ps. 45:2.
31. 1 Sam: 2:3.

# [4]

# Boniface VIII as Defender of Royal Power: *Unam Sanctam* as a Basis for the Spanish Conquest of the Americas

## JAMES MULDOON

In the early seventeenth century, Juan de Solórzano y Pereira, an official of the Spanish imperial government, compiled a two-volume work designed to present all of the arguments that lawyers, philosophers, and theologians had advanced over the previous two hundred years in defense of the Spanish conquest of the New World. His *Disputatio de Indiarum iure: Sive, de iusta Indiarum Occidentalium inquisitione, acquisitione et retentione* was a veritable summa of the academic debate about the legitimacy of the conquest that Lewis Hanke termed "The Spanish struggle for justice in the conquest of the Americas."[1]

In the second book of the first volume, Solórzano traced the arguments that dealt with *dominium*, that is, with the nature of legitimate possession of land and government. Did the inhabitants of the New World legitimately possess the lands that they occupied? The answer to this question was crucial to the entire debate about the conquest, because if the Indians did possess their lands legitimately then the conquest could not be justified on the grounds that the Spanish were only taking from the inhabitants land to which they had not been entitled in the first place. On the other hand, if the Aztecs, Incas, and other peoples of the Americas did not hold their lands legitimately, if they did not possess *dominium*, then the Spanish could claim that they were not depriving the inhabitants of what was rightfully theirs. Furthermore, even if the Indians did originally acquire their lands legitimately, it might be possible to demonstrate that their subsequent actions would justify conquest by Christian armies.

---

1. Ioannes de Solórzano Pereira, *Disputationem de Indiarum iure: Sive, de iusta Indiarum Occidentalium inquisitione, acquistione et retentione*, 2 vols. (Madrid, 1629–39); Lewis Hanke, *The Spanish Struggle for Justice in the Conquest of America* (Philadelphia, 1949; reprint, Boston, 1965).

In discussing the nature of *dominium*, Solórzano presented a wide range of materials that stretched back to the mid-thirteenth century when canon lawyers first began to treat the question of the existence of *dominium* in infidel societies. For the most part the materials he presented were the ones that had been traditionally included in the debate, although he did add some new materials, among them *Unam sanctam*, Boniface VIII's most famous letter. The use of this letter by a royal official in the seventeenth century is, at first glance, surprising in the light of the common opinion that Boniface's forceful assertion of papal power signified the high-water mark of papal pretensions to universal authority. According to the conventional opinion, the tides of history flowed away from the strong popes of the thirteenth century, of whom Boniface VIII was the last, through the period of the Avignon papacy and the Great Schism, bringing the papacy to its lowest point during the Reformation of the sixteenth century.[2] In this view, *Unam sanctam* remained a piece of flotsam tossed up at the tidemark to indicate the heights of papal pretensions and the extent of the subsequent papal fall.

If the conventional view of *Unam sanctam* is correct, why would a seventeenth-century lawyer cite it in support of Spanish claims to the New World? One might, of course, take the old-fashioned view that Spain was so deeply rooted in medieval obscurantism that a Spanish intellectual would know no other way of dealing with a contemporary problem than applying outdated medieval formulas. This would make Solórzano a scholarly Quixote, seeing the contemporary world through medieval glasses that distorted reality. In recent years historians have done much to lay to rest the ghost of a decadent Spain sinking into decline because of some innate weakness.[3] Solórzano's Spain was still strong and perceived as such by contemporaries. Spanish universities were still successfully developing the medieval Scholastic tradition in significant ways. Indeed, the attempt of Spanish officials and intellectuals to wrestle with the problem of justice in the conquest of the Americas suggests an awareness of the moral problems associated with overseas expansion not found elsewhere, and the solutions proposed, while rooted in the medieval legal and moral tradition, were creative responses showing more concern for the well-being of the inhabitants of the Americas than other European nations were to demonstrate until the nineteenth century.

To understand why Solórzano used *Unam sanctam*, we will have to

2. The most convenient introduction to the basic literature concerning Boniface's views and to *Unam sanctam* in particular is Charles T. Wood, ed., *Philip the Fair and Boniface VIII*, 2d ed., European Problem Studies (New York, 1971). See also James Muldoon, "Boniface VIII's Forty Years of Experience in the Law," *Jurist* 31 (1971): 449–77; Walter Ullmann, "Die Bulle Unam sanctam: Rückblick und Ausblick," *Römische historische Mitteilungen* 16 (1974): 45–77, and idem, "Boniface VIII and His Contemporary Scholarship," *Journal of Theological Studies* 27 (1976): 58–87.

3. For an extensive discussion of this issue, see J. H. Elliot, "The Decline of Spain," *Past and Present* 20 (1961): 52–75.

make one assumption and revise one historical opinion. The assumption one must make is that Solórzano did not collect and organize these documents relating to the legitimacy of the conquest of the Americas simply out of antiquarian interest; he judged this medieval material relevant to the contemporary imperial situation.

The historical opinion that needs revision concerns subsequent papal reaction to the *Unam sanctam*. In spite of what is sometimes believed, none of Boniface VIII's successors ever formally rejected the claims made in *Unam sanctam*. When Clement V (1305–14) issued the letter *Meruit* in response to French pressure to denounce Boniface and all his works, Clement did not modify or qualify what his predecessor had written. What he said was: "We do not wish or intend that any injustice be done to the king and the kingdom [of France] because of the definition and declaration of our predecessor of good memory Pope Boniface VIII which began *Unam sanctam*. The king, the kingdom, and the aforementioned people of that kingdom are no more subject to the Roman church as a consequence of that letter than they had previously been. They are to be understood as being in the same state as they were before the aforementioned statement."[4] Clement's letter suggests that Philip the Fair and his advisers had overreacted to Boniface's letter, perhaps responding to the very forceful way Boniface had expressed himself rather than to the substance of the letter, which was essentially traditional in nature. Thus, while *Unam sanctam* did contain a number of forceful images and dramatic phrases about papal power unrelieved by any qualifying remarks, the language itself consisted of images and phrases that popes and canonists had been using for a century. They formed a pool of ideas and rhetoric that Boniface and his successors were to draw on simply because it was the common vocabulary of papal letters.

Another sign of the continued significance of *Unam sanctam* was that it attracted attention from canon lawyers, who treated it as earlier important papal letters had been treated. It was glossed and made the subject of commentaries. Joannes Monachus (ca. 1250–1313) wrote a gloss on it, and Petrus Bertrandus (1280–1349) wrote a lengthy commentary.[5] These writers took different but related approaches to Boniface's letter.

For Joannes Monachus, the most important aspect of *Unam sanctam* was its discussion of the image of the two swords. After rehearsing the traditional arguments about the meaning of the image, the glossator concluded that the swords representing the spiritual and the temporal powers

---

4. *Extravagantes communes*, 5.7.2, in *Corpus iuris canonici*, 4 vols. (Venice, 1595), 4:243.

5. When *Unam sanctam* was published as *Extravagantes communes*, 1.8.1, pp. 142–49, in 1503, the gloss of Joannes Monachus and the commentary of Petrus Bertrandus were published with it. Concerning these writers, see *Dictionnaire de droit canonique*, ed. R. Naz, 7 vols. (Paris, 1935–65), 2:cols. 789–92, and 6:cols. 112–14.

belonged by right to the church, but that it could directly use only the spiritual sword, an argument that the glossator noted came from a letter of Bernard of Clairvaux to Pope Eugenius III (1145–53).[6] The temporal sword was in the hands of the secular rulers, who employed it under papal direction.[7]

Having demonstrated the relationship between the pope and the two swords, the glossator concluded his remarks with a brief discussion of the hierarchical relationship between the two swords. This line of argument reinforced what the glossator saw as the major theme of the letter, the necessity of subordination to the pope if one wished to be saved. He argued that subordination of the temporal sword to the pope was essential, because only in such circumstances would there exist the subordination to the pope that was essential to salvation.[8]

In these comments, the glossator did little more than restate Boniface's own words. He drew on the mainstream of the canonistic tradition, just as Boniface had done, in order to discuss the nature of relations between the two swords and the spheres of jurisdiction they represented. He avoided drawing any new conclusions about the meaning of Boniface's letter, giving his remarks the air of an academic exercise designed to provide a gloss to fill a margin rather than to develop further the substance of the letter or to explicate its original meaning to an audience that would not be aware of the context within which Boniface had functioned.

Petrus Bertrandus took another, and in the long run more important, approach to the meaning of *Unam sanctam*. Picking up where Joannes Monachus left off, Petrus asked whether the doctrine of the two swords meant that the spiritual power "ought to dominate the temporal." His answer was that it should not. The direction of secular matters should be left in the hands of secular rulers, because the two spheres of jurisdiction represented by the two swords were distinct, not unified. For the pope to play a direct role in secular affairs would be an unwarranted invasion of

6. "Consequens est igitur, quod uterque gladius sit Ecclesiae, et in potestate Ecclesiae. Notandum etiam, quod istam sententiam tenet Bernardus ad Eugenium iiii. [sic] dicens: Aggredere eos, idest malos Christianos, non ferro, sed verbo: innuens esse duos gladios, unum spiritualem, qui ferit verbo, et alium materialem, qui ferit ferro" (Joannes Monachus, *Extravagantes communes*, 1.8.1, at *Certe, qui in potestate*, p. 146.

7. "Hic vult ostendere non eodem modo utrunque gladium ad Ecclesiam pertinere: ideo ait, quod uterque est in potestate Ecclesiae spiritualis scilicet gladius, et materialis: non tamen eodem modo is quidem, i. materialis pro Ecclesia: ille vero, i. spiritualis ab Ecclesia exercendus. Ille, idest, spiritualis, sacerdotis manu. Is, idest, materialis, manu regum, et militum: sed ad nutum, et patientiam sacerdotis" (ibid., at *uterque ergo est*, p. 146).

8. "Quia, ut patet, principalis intentio, huiusmodi decre. est ostendere, quod subesse summo Pontifici est de necessitate salutis, prout ultima conclusio manifeste declarat: et quia ex ordine gladiorum hoc aperte patet: . . . oportet autem gladium esse sub gladio: et temporalem auctoritatem subiici spirituali potestati, quasi dicat, quod hi gladii habent hunc ordinem, quia gladius est sub gladio, cum temporalis, et materialis sit sub spirituali" (ibid. at *Oportet autem gladium etc*, pp. 146–47).

the secular ruler's jurisdiction.[9] Taking this argument one step further, Petrus Bertrandus argued that if the pope could intervene directly in secular matters it would mean that he possessed all temporal *dominium*, that is, he would be the sole possessor of land and governmental authority.[10] This would mean that the only legitimate governments would be those that recognized the pope as the source of their right to govern. All other rulers, and all possessors of land anywhere, would be usurpers.

With the introduction of the issue of *dominium*, Petrus Bertrandus moved *Unam sanctam* away from the conflict that embroiled Philip the Fair and Boniface VIII and into another area that was less volatile. Since the mid-thirteenth century canonists had discussed the issue of *dominium*, but not in connection with conflicts between the papacy and European secular rulers. Rather, they considered it in connection with wars against infidel societies. Could Christians attack infidels and occupy their lands simply because they were infidels? In other words, did *dominium* depend upon being a member of the church and subject to the pope?

The issue was initially raised by the canonist-pope Innocent IV (1243–54) when he commented upon a decretal of Innocent III (1198–1216) that dealt with the vows crusaders took and the indulgences granted them. According to Innocent IV, *dominium* was to be found among all kinds of societies, not only among Christians. Therefore, the crusaders could not attack the Holy Land simply because Moslems occupied and ruled it. He then justified the Crusades on the grounds that the Moslems had taken the Holy Land from its rightful possessors in an unjust war. The crusaders were simply acting to restore the land to its rightful, that is, Christian, rulers. As for other infidel lands, the Christians had no right to invade and occupy them unless the inhabitants were violating natural law, which, Innocent IV assumed, was known to all men.[11]

Not surprisingly, there were canonists who argued the other side of the question. The most important of these writers was the canonist known as Hostiensis (d. 1270), a student of Innocent IV. Hostiensis argued that with the coming of Christ, *dominium* could be claimed only by those who were subject to the pope, because he, as vicar of Christ on earth, was heir to

9. "Quero utrum potestas spiritualis debeat dominari temporali? Et videtur, quod non, quia iurisdictiones sunt distinctae. . . . Non ergo Papa debet se intromittere de potestate temporali: sed debet temporalia dimittere Imperatori, Regibus, et aliis dominis temporalibus" (Petrus Bertrandus, *Additio ad Extravagantes communes,* 1.8.1, p. 149).

10. "Praeterea si potestas spiritualis dominaretur temporali, haberet dominium temporalium. Sed dominium earundem rerum non potest esse simul, et semel insolidum eodem tempore apud plures . . . ergo nullus alter haberet dominium, quod est falsum" (ibid.).

11. The most extensive discussion of *dominium* is James Muldoon, *Popes, Lawyers, and Infidels: The Church and the Non-Christian World, 1250–1550* (Philadelphia, 1979), pp. 5–15. See also Benjamin Z. Kedar, *Crusade and Mission: European Approaches toward the Muslims* (Princeton, 1984), pp. 159–61.

Christ's power over everyone and everything that exists. This being so, the pope was the possessor of Christ's *dominium*, and only those who accepted papal headship could claim that they legitimately possessed their lands and power. Therefore, any Christian campaign against the infidels could be justified simply on the grounds that the infidels were usurpers because they did not acknowledge the pope as the source of their *dominium*.[12]

Petrus Bertrandus presented both sides of the debate about *dominium*. Initially he discussed Hostiensis's argument, the most extreme position on the nature of papal power. He then moved to consider the opposing view. In the first place, he argued, both spiritual and temporal powers came from God, but they were distinct. The superiority of the spiritual power came from the fact that its purpose was more important than that for which temporal power existed. The relationship between the two powers was symbolized in the consecration ceremonies for bishops and kings. Bishops were anointed on the head, whereas kings were anointed on the arm, indicating that as the arm acts at the direction of the head, so kings exercise their power at the direction of the church. At the same time, however, this functional subordination did not mean that the pope possessed "*dominium* over all temporal goods."[13]

Having denied that the spiritual power's superiority of purpose meant that the pope possessed *dominium* over all temporal goods and power, essentially the position of Innocent IV, Petrus Bertrandus went on to analyze the nature of *dominium*. He argued that there were two kinds of *dominium*, one created by divine law, the other by human law. The first kind is that which God possesses over his creation. Everything that exists is God's and so is in his power, his *dominium*. As for the other kind of *dominium*, what he terms human or legal *dominium*, Petrus Bertrandus argued that it came from natural law. It was not created by civil or imperial law. When the laws of secular governments deal with *dominium*, they deal only with the means of acquiring it, not with its creation. In the final analysis, men have acquired *dominium* from God, who delegated its exercise to his creatures. As a result, anyone who has acquired land or power by legitimate means possesses true *dominium* and cannot be deprived of it by the pope or anyone else "except for just cause," the opinion that Innocent IV also held.[14]

---

12. Muldoon, *Popes, Lawyers, and Infidels*, pp. 15–18, and Kedar, pp. 169–71.

13. "Ad tercium argumentum dico, quod licet, ut sup. dictum est, omnis humana creatura subsit Papae, et sic potestati spirituali; non tamen sequiter, quod habeat dominium omnium rerum temporalium." Petrus Bertrandus, *Additio ad Extravagantes communes*, 1.8.1, p. 150.

14. "Ad cuius declarationem sciendum est, quod est duplex dominium. Est enim quoddam dominium iure divino: quoddam aliud iure humano. . . . Divinum dominium est illud, quod est apud Deum super omnem creaturam. . . . Istud dominium est verum dominium, simplex, et absolutum, et unus est Dominus omnium creaturatum Deus. Et

James Muldoon

It was not only the theoreticians of papal power who continued to discuss *Unam sanctam* and to employ its main ideas. Boniface VIII's successors at Avignon continued to use phrases reminiscent of those found in Boniface's bull, though not in letters to European Christian kings. Instead, these popes went in the direction that contemporary canonists were moving, directing statements of papal claims to universal power to schismatic and infidel rulers who lived along the frontiers of Europe. While none of these popes directly quoted *Unam sanctam* in letters to such rulers, they did inform them that membership in the church was essential for salvation and that the pope was responsible for the salvation of all men.[15] These statements were just as uncompromising as anything Boniface VIII had said. These phrases assumed that salvation required subordination to the pope, just as the famous concluding lines of *Unam sanctam* had done. In addition to using language similar to Boniface's, one of the popes at Avignon even had a copy of Boniface's letter made for his own use. The registers of Gregory XI (1370–78) included a copy of *Unam sanctam* because, as a brief note indicates, Gregory XI wished to have authentic copies of the bulls that his predecessors had issued.[16] Inasmuch as it was also Gregory XI who moved the papacy from Avignon back to Rome and whose death there precipitated the Great Schism, it is tempting to see a special meaning in his having ordered a copy of *Unam sanctam*, the most forceful statement of papal power ever made. Was ordering a copy of *Unam sanctam* linked to returning the

ideo proprie loquendo omnes creaturae proprietates, res, et possessiones, et bona alia in nullius bonis sunt vere, absolute, et proprie, nisi Dei. . . .

"Aliud est dominium, quod secundum legistas vocatur legale dominium . . . secundum vero canonistas vocat humanum. . . . Innuens expresse, quod rerum dominia, et obligationes sunt de iure naturali, idest, de iure gentium. Non autem a iure civili, vel Imperatore . . . quod a iure gentium descendunt dominia: sed per leges principum distinguuntur modi, per quos rerum dominia acquiruntur. . . . Videtur mihi, quod dominium rerum legale, vel humanum fuit a Deo collatum humanae creaturae, et non fuit ab initio introductum iure gentium, vel civili. Nam Deus omnia quae creavit, fecit propter rationalem creaturem, et omnia subiecit rationali creaturae. . . . Prout vero cuilibet appropriatur, vel acquiritur hoc dominium, sic consideratum est iuris gentium. Et tale dominium non est apud Papam tamen, sed apud omnes, qui iuste acquirunt: et ex quo semel acquisitum est, non licet Papae, vel aliciui alteri auferre, vel occupare sine iusta causa" (ibid.).

15. For examples, see James Muldoon, "The Avignon Papacy and the Frontiers of Christendom: The Evidence of Vatican Register 62," *Archivum historiae pontificiae* 17 (1979): 125–95, at pp. 136–40 and 175–76.

16. "Aequitas suadit et necesitas exposcit interdum, ut tenores litterarum Summorum Pontificum, qui in Domino quieverunt, cum sint necessarii et bullis eorumdem haberi nequeunt, de ipsorum Registris sumantur fideliter atque plene et sub bulla supervenientium successorum in forman authenticam redigantur. Hinc est, quod Nos tenorem quarumdam litterarum apostolicarum felicis recordationis Bonifacii papae VIII praedecessoris nostri"; Gregory XI, *Acta Gregorii P.P.XI (1370–1378)*, ed. Aloysius L. Tautu, Pontificia commissio ad redigendum codicem iuris canonici orientalis, *Fontes*, ser. 3, 12 (Vatican City, 1966): 331–32.

papacy to its traditional home? Was he hoping to restore the papacy to the position Boniface had claimed for it?

The fourteenth-century papal and canonistic use of *Unam sanctam* and of phrases describing papal power and responsibility when dealing with infidel societies marked an interesting redirection of Boniface's letter. Instead of using these phrases in conflicts with European Christian rulers who could be expected to express outrage at such strong statements about the nature of papal power, Boniface's successors directed such statements at an audience—infidel rulers—that was in no position to attack the papacy directly. The scene at Anagni would not be repeated with infidels playing the roles that Philip the Fair and William de Nogaret had played in the original version.

The task of redirecting Boniface's assertions about papal power away from Europe and toward the infidel world continued through the fifteenth century in the work of canon lawyers. At the Council of Constance, for example, the Polish canonist Paulus Vladimiri cited *Unam sanctam* in a discussion of the claim of the Teutonic Knights to hold Lithuania on the basis of a grant from the Holy Roman emperor. According to Vladimiri, since the conquest of Lithuania was predicated on the fact that the Lithuanians were infidels, the salvation of their souls was involved. Therefore, he argued, the pope, who is ultimately responsible for the salvation of all men's souls, is the only person who can authorize the conquest of infidel lands. In support of this conclusion, the Polish canonist quoted the concluding lines of *Unam sanctam*, "that it is necessary for salvation to believe that every human creature is subject to the Roman Pontiff."[17] Vladimiri's willingness to cite these words in this connection indicates that Boniface's language was still very much a part of the canonistic vocabulary.

The scattered references to *Unam sanctam* and to phrases similar to those found in the bull would not by themselves explain why Juan de Solórzano y Pereira chose to include Boniface's letter in his defense of the Spanish conquest of the Americas. What these references do indicate, however, is that neither the rhetoric nor the substance of *Unam sanctam* had been forgotten by subsequent generations of popes and canonists. Furthermore, the application of Boniface's words to relations with non-Christian societies suggests why the letter could be of interest to a Spanish scholar writing to justify two centuries of Spanish imperial expansion.

---

17. Paulus Vladimiri, "Opinio Hostiensis," in *Paulus Vladimiri and His Doctrine concerning International Law and Politics*, ed. Stanislaus F. Belch, 2 vols. (London, 1965), 2:864–84, at p. 874; see also Muldoon, *Popes, Lawyers, and Infidels*, pp. 112–19; and Frederick H. Russell, "Paulus Vladimiri's Attack on the Just War: A Case Study in Legal Polemics," in *Authority and Power: Studies on Medieval Law and Government Presented to Walter Ullmann on His Seventieth Birthday*, ed. Brian Tierney and P. Linehan (Cambridge, 1980), pp. 237–54.

The text of *Unam sanctam*, along with the texts of a number of other papal letters from the fourteenth and fifteenth centuries, circulated as appendixes to manuscript and incunabula editions of canon law until the early sixteenth century. In 1500 and again in 1503, Jean Chappuis, a French lawyer, published these letters in two small collections. The first of these, the *Extravagantes Johannis XXII*, contained twenty of Pope John XXII's (1316–34) decretals. The latter contained seventy-four letters, of which fourteen, including *Unam sanctam*, were from Boniface VIII's pontificate. There were six letters, including *Meruit*, from the reign of Clement V. These collections had no official standing until they were included in the revised edition of canon law, the *Corpus iuris canonici*, that was published at the direction of Pope Gregory XIII (1572–85) in 1582. In a brief introduction to Boniface's letter, Chappuis summed up the letter's significance as he saw it: "It is necessary for salvation that all Christians be subject to the Roman pontiff, who holds both swords, and who judges all men and is judged however by no one. This letter, however, did not subject the king and the inhabitants of France to the Roman church more than they had been previously: as is clear, below, de privil. meruit."[18] The introductory note to *Meruit* was similar. For Chappuis, *Unam sanctam* was not a radical departure from the canonistic tradition, nor were the ideas that Boniface expressed in it to be avoided in the future. Two of the statements that compose the compiler's introduction, papal possession of the two swords and the exemption of the pope from human judgment, were standard positions among canonists. One slight change that Chappuis made concerned who had to be subject to the pope in order to be saved. While Boniface asserted that all men had to be subject to the pope to be saved, Chappuis says only that all Christians must be. If this were to be taken literally, it would suggest that the salvation of infidels was not dependent upon membership in the church, only that schismatics and heretics had to return to the papally headed church if they wished to be saved.

In addition to the text of *Unam sanctam*, Chappuis included a gloss on the text and a lengthy canonistic commentary on the letter. The gloss was that of Joannes Monachus, while the commentary was that of Petrus Bertrandus. Thus, by the early sixteenth century there was available in a printed edition not only the text of Boniface's letter but a convenient selection of canonistic commentary on it. Furthermore, the tradition of canonistic commentary on the text had shifted the focus of interest away from its implications for papal relations with European Christian rulers and toward infidel societies outside Europe, a refocusing that made *Unam sanctam* potentially useful to those who sought to justify the conquest of the New World.

---

18. *Extravagantes communes*, 1.8.1, p. 143.

When Juan de Solórzano y Pereira came to write his massive defense of the Spanish conquest of the New World, he had at his disposal not only the mass of contemporary materials that missionaries, imperial officials, and others had provided about the conquest of America, but also over four centuries of canonistic debate about the legitimacy of such conquests. In the second book of the first volume, Solórzano displayed a wide-ranging knowledge of all this material. The preliminary chapters of this book concerned the general problem of *dominium:* Who could possess, and in what circumstances could a society be legitimately deprived of, *dominium?* His treatment of the issue rested upon an analysis of the opinions of Innocent IV and Hostiensis. *Unam sanctam* appeared toward the end of the book when Solórzano moved from discussing the broad question of *dominium* to applying the principles derived from that analysis to the conquest of the Americas. The question concerned the Spanish assertion that their occupation of the Americas rested on papal authorization, specifically Alexander VI's (1492–1503) bull *Inter caetera,* issued in 1493. On what basis could a pope authorize such a conquest? Solórzano dealt with *Unam sanctam* just before dealing with *Inter caetera* and just after a brief mention of the Donation of Constantine.

In keeping with contemporary historical practice, Solórzano provided his readers with lengthy extracts from the documents relevant to his argument. In the case of *Unam sanctam* he included approximately two-thirds of the text.[19] He omitted the opening section of the bull with its numerous traditional images that emphasized the church's unity. He began his excerpt at the point at which Boniface began his discussion of the two swords and continued on to the end, thus including the famous concluding lines. In Solórzano's argument *Unam sanctam* provided an important part of the foundation upon which Alexander VI could justify his grant of the New World to the Spanish, because the basis for Alexander's action was the spiritual nature of the primary Spanish goal in the Americas, the conversion of the inhabitants. The pope was employing the secular sword toward the achievement of a spiritual goal, precisely as the theory of the two swords dictated. So, under the direction of the papacy, the Spanish were engaged in the task of bringing the Indians to the true faith and membership in the church which was headed by the pope. In this way, and only in this way, could their salvation be achieved. Thus, Boniface VIII's grandiose assertion of papal power could be employed by a secular ruler to justify the creation of a worldwide empire.

Solórzano's use of *Unam sanctam* in this fashion could be seen as nothing more than a cynical ploy on the part of a decadent imperial power to legitimize bloodthirsty imperialism in the name of religion. It could also be seen as an example of Spanish antiquarianism, another charac-

19. Solórzano, vol. 1, bk. 2, chap. 23, pars. 119ff.

teristic of a decadent society nostalgically recalling medieval glories instead of facing contemporary realities. Both of these interpretations miss
the point. In the first place, Spain was still a world power when Solórzano's first volume appeared in 1629, and it continued to be so for some
decades afterward. By 1640 the empire was verging on collapse, but even
then the collapse was not inevitable. Until the early nineteenth century
the Spanish continued to control a great deal of the non-European world.
The problems with which Solórzano was concerned continued to be real
issues of colonial government as well. In the second place, while Solórzano's style and method were traditional, this was not due to nostalgia
for the Middle Ages. He was operating within an intellectual framework
that stretched back to the initial phases of the conquest and before that to
medieval tradition, because that was the way his contemporaries functioned. The Spanish had long cited papal grants as a basis for a variety of
activities beginning with the *reconquista* itself. Working within a tradition that required justifying important actions in legal terms, Solórzano
simply presented the reader with the precedents and the arguments that
justified the conquest of the Americas. Opponents of the conquest such as
Bartolomé de Las Casas employed precisely the same kind of argumentation when opposing Spanish rule in the Americas. For Solórzano, *Unam
sanctam*, as it was understood in the sixteenth century, provided another
argument for the Spanish conquest of the Americas.

Given all the medieval and early modern precedents and arguments in
support of the conquest's legitimacy, it was not necessary for Solórzano to
develop a new body of arguments to justify it. Indeed, new arguments to
replace the traditional ones might even have had some serious drawbacks.
In the first place, the Spanish claims rested on the right, even the responsibility, of the pope to employ the material sword to achieve spiritual
ends. If, in fact, the pope did not have the right to authorize the conquest of
the Americas in order to secure the salvation of the inhabitants' souls, not
only could Alexander VI not have authorized the conquest of the Americas, but his predecessor Innocent VIII (1484–92) could not have granted
the Spanish Crown the right of patronage to all ecclesiastical benefices in
the Kingdom of Granada, which was conquered in 1492. Spanish rights
over the infidels of the New World were in the tradition of this form of
patronage. If one was invalid, so must the other be also. In the long run, as
a result of the bull issued by Pope Julius II (1503–13), the Spanish Crown
was to acquire "a unique power over the Church in its American possessions."[20] All of these powers, the entire legal basis for the Spanish empire,
rested on the assumption that the pope had universal jurisdiction in
spiritual matters and that the means for achieving the ultimate goal of the
spiritual sword, the salvation of all men, could be delegated to secular
officials. In a paradoxical way, the Spanish monarchy justified ascendency

20. Elliot, p. 100.

over its empire as a charge delegated by popes claiming authority over secular rulers. Thus, from an assertion of papal control over European Christian rulers, *Unam sanctam*, in the hands of lawyers, was transformed into a basis for asserting a European Christian ruler's right to conquer the New World.

In putting *Unam sanctam* to a use not envisaged by its author, Juan de Solórzano y Pereira was engaging in a common practice of lawyers, taking an argument developed for one situation and extending its application to a new situation that seemed related. Sixteenth- and seventeenth-century lawyers in countries far removed from Spain continued to rely on traditional materials when faced with new situations just as Solórzano did. His contemporaries, the Puritan lawyers in England, did the same thing with Magna Carta, reinterpreting it to serve as a basis for Parliament's right to limit the power of the Stuarts. In both cases, the language of a medieval document was reinterpreted to deal with a contemporary political situation. Old and familiar words and phrases were given new meanings or emphases without regard to the context which generated them in the first place.[21] One reason for this was that in spite of various new currents, the European intellectual world changed slowly at the level at which the lawyers functioned. Even if the individual lawyers who were doing the reinterpreting were involved in the new intellectual currents, the audiences they were addressing were not as likely to be. The audiences required traditional language, even if that language disguised new meanings. What Fernand Braudel has said about the continuity of material life in Europe between 1400 and 1800 can be said of much of intellectual life as well.[22] Medieval intellectuals provided a full arsenal that with some modification, or outright twisting, continued to be useful long after the Middle Ages are conventionally said to have ended. In using *Unam sanctam*, Solórzano demonstrated that while twentieth-century scholars have found it a pretentious piece of papal rhetoric and have judged it outmoded even in its own day, a seventeenth-century intellectual could find it useful and relevant to his own work, the defense of a king's right of conquest.

21. See Faith Thompson, *Magna Carta: Its Role in the Making of the English Constitution, 1300–1629* (Minneapolis, 1948), and J. G. A. Pocock, *The Ancient Constitution and the Feudal Law* (Cambridge, 1957).

22. "It is a fact that every great centre of population has worked out a set of elementary answers—and has an unfortunate tendency to stick to them out of that force of inertia which is one of the great artisans of history"; Fernand Braudel, *Civilization and Capitalism, 15th–18th Century*, vol. 1, *The Structure of Everyday Life*, rev. trans. Sian Reynolds (New York, 1981), p. 561.

# [5]

# John XXII and the Franciscans:
# A Reappraisal

### Thomas Turley

Pope John XXII's attack in 1322 on the Franciscan doctrine of the absolute poverty of Christ was perhaps the worst moment in the history of the order. It certainly has proved a most puzzling moment for historians who have struggled to discover a satisfactory motive for the pope's action. The attack seems quite inconsistent with John's previous policy toward the Franciscans. Between 1316 and 1320, he worked closely with the order's leaders to stamp out its radical Spiritual faction, which for decades had been a source of dissension. As a result, by the early 1320s the order was experiencing a tranquillity it had not felt for many years. Then in March 1322, with no apparent provocation, John seized upon a dispute between a Franciscan and a Dominican inquisitor in Narbonne to open discussion of the orthodoxy of the Franciscan poverty doctrine. In November 1323 he condemned the doctrine. The resulting controversy threw the order back into turmoil, led to schism between the pope and the Franciscan minister-general, and triggered a twenty-year polemical war.[1] These serious consequences have drawn historians to examine John's motives

1. This controversy has been reviewed many times. See especially Decima Douie, *The Nature and Effect of the Heresy of the Fraticelli* (Manchester, 1932), pp. 1–202; Malcolm Lambert, "The Franciscan Crisis under John XXII," *Franciscan Studies* 32 (1972): 123–43, and idem, *Franciscan Poverty* (London, 1961), pp. 149–246; Gordon Leff, *Heresy in the Later Middle Ages*, 2 vols. (Manchester, 1967), 1:51–258; John Moorman, *A History of the Franciscan Order* (Oxford, 1968), pp. 180–204, 307–31; and Brian Tierney, *Origins of Papal Infallibility, 1150–1350* (Leiden, 1972), pp. 171–204. Also Charles T. Davis, "Ubertino da Casale and His Conception of *altissima paupertas*," *Studi Medievali* 22 (1981): 1–56; and Conal Condren, "Rhetoric, Historiography, and Political Theory: Some Aspects of the Poverty Controversy Reconsidered," *Journal of Religious History* 13 (1984): 15–34. I thank David Burr, Charles Davis, James John, and Delno West for reading a draft of this chapter and offering many useful comments.

closely, but the results have been inconclusive. This, in turn, has thwarted a full understanding of John's policy regarding the Franciscans.

In the absence of a clear statement of John's motives, scholars have turned to indirect evidence to resolve the problem. Since the 1930s, Josef Koch's hypothesis that John attacked the Franciscan doctrine because he believed it stood in the way of a total condemnation of the Spiritual Peter Olivi has received wide acceptance.[2] According to Koch, Franciscan poverty was not the pope's real target. John intended his campaign to condemn the Franciscan doctrine as merely a subordinate episode in the condemnation of Olivi. But recently a number of critics, including Brian Tierney, have questioned Koch's theory. This essay reviews some of Koch's key evidence and offers an alternative explanation of Pope John's actions.

The background of Pope John's decision is a long and complicated controversy among Franciscans, Dominicans, and secular clergy over the validity of the Franciscan teaching on Christ's poverty. It began in the mid-1250s, when the seculars' attacks on mendicancy prompted certain Franciscan apologists to respond that absolute poverty was an essential teaching of Christ. These apologists asserted that Christ and the apostles had embraced a poverty so complete that they renounced all possessions, both individual and communal. This in itself was a novelty, for it was believed conventionally that Christ and the apostles had been poor in the sense that most monastic orders were poor: propertyless as individuals, but retaining rights to communal possessions. The Franciscan apologists went further, however. They claimed that this absolute poverty was the way of life most conducive to Christian perfection, the essence of the evangelical rule. This meant that owning nothing "individually or in common" was a more perfect state of life than any which permitted possession of things, because it was more conducive to perfection. And as the Franciscan Rule was the only one in the church which forbade both individual and communal possessions, it also implied that the Franciscan state of life was more perfect than any other and that the Franciscan Rule was closer than any other to the gospel's essential teachings on perfection.[3]

2. Josef Koch, "Der Prozess gegen die Postille Olivis zur Apokalypse," *Recherches de théologie ancienne et médiévale* 5 (1933): 302–15.

3. For a bibliography and general outline of the dispute see Decima Douie, *The Conflict between the Seculars and the Mendicants at the University of Paris in the Thirteenth Century* (London, 1954); Yves Congar, "Aspects ecclésiologiques de la querelle entre mendiants et séculiers dans la seconde moitié du XIIIe siècle et le début du XIVe," *Archives d'histoire doctrinale et littéraire du Moyen Age* 36 (1961): 44–52; and M.-M. Dufeil, *Guillaume de Saint-Amour et la polémique universitaire parisienne, 1250–1259*, 2 vols. (Paris, 1972). Thomas of York and Bonaventure were the major Franciscan apologists in the controversy. Thomas stated the Franciscan position quite bluntly in his *Manus quae contra omnipotentem tenditur* (pub. 1256), ed. Max Bierbaum, in *Bettelorden und Weltgeistlichkeit an der Universität Paris* (Münster-in-

Thomas Turley

These claims not only enraged the seculars but also alienated the Dominicans, who until that time had been allies of the Franciscans against the seculars. Both groups attacked the Franciscan teaching as a challenge to the church's right to possess property and to the authenticity of its traditional teachings on Christian perfection. In 1279 their protests were cut short by Pope Nicholas III, who intervened in favor of the Franciscans. His decree *Exiit qui seminat* declared that Christ and the apostles indeed had lived without individual or communal possessions and that they had been "showing the path of perfection" in doing so.[4] Nicholas also confirmed three other important aspects of the Franciscan position: the Franciscan belief that St. Francis had received a special inspiration from the Holy Spirit in conceiving his rule; the Franciscan equation of the rule's teachings on poverty with the gospel's essential teachings on perfection; and the legal arrangements made earlier in the thirteenth century which permitted the Franciscans to deny common ownership of their goods by transferring ownership to the papacy. Having decided in favor of the Franciscan teaching, Nicholas forbade any further discussion of the question of Christ's poverty.[5]

*Exiit*'s threat of excommunication seems to have ended most open criticism of the Franciscan position on poverty, but the seculars and Dominicans did not give up their opposition.[6] Nor were all Franciscans modest about the implications of their doctrine. Cardinal Vital du Four, for example, explained to John XXII in 1322 that the perfection of those

---

Westfalen, 1920), esp. pp. 43–59. Though much more sophisticated and conciliatory, Bonaventure too emphasized that absolute poverty was most conducive to Christian perfection. *Apologia pauperum* (pub. 1269), 2. 19, 7.1–4; *Opera omnia*, 11 vols. (Quaracchi, 1882–1902), 8:249b, 272a–73a.

4. Sext. 5.12.3, Friedberg, *CIC*, 2:1112. The text of this and other important sections of *Exiit* are reproduced by Lambert, *Franciscan Poverty*, pp. 142–43, and Tierney, *Origins*, pp. 98–99. Both discuss Franciscan influence on Pope Nicholas.

5. Friedberg, *CIC*, 2:1110, 1113–20, 1121. The legal arrangements referred to here were *Quo elongati* (1230) and *Ordinem vestrum* (1245). By assuming ownership of Franciscan goods in these decrees, the papacy allowed the Franciscans to claim that they owned nothing whatever, not even the food they ate, but simply used the property of the papacy. The decrees' distinction between ownership and use is discussed by Fidelis Elizondo, "Bullae 'Quo elongati' Gregorii IX et 'Ordinem vestrum' Innocentii IV: De duabus primis regulae Franciscanae authenticis declarationibus," *Laurentianum* 3 (1962): 349–94.

6. Four months after the promulgation of *Exiit*, the Dominican master-general felt it necessary to warn his friars not to dispute with the Franciscans about their rule; *Litterae encyclicae magistrorum generalium Ord. Pr. saec. XIII et XIV*, ed. B. Reichert (Rome, 1900), p. 114. The directive was not always obeyed. See, e.g., the controversy at Oxford described by Franz Pelster in "Eine Kontroverse zwischen Englischen Dominikanern und Minoriten über einige Punkte der Ordensregel," *Archivum Fratrum Praedicatorum* 3 (1933): 57–80. The rivalry between Franciscans and Dominicans extended far beyond the matter of Christ's poverty. See Yves Dossat, "Les origines de la querelle entre Prêcheurs et Mineurs provençeaux: Bernard Délicieux," in *Franciscains d'Oc: Les Spirituels ca. 1280–1324*, Cahiers de Fanjeaux 10 (Toulouse, 1975), pp. 315–54.

who lived with possessions in common could compare "in no way" to the perfection of those who lived with neither individual nor communal possessions.[7] These occasional bald assertions of the perfection of Franciscan practice only encouraged their opponents—among whom, by the late 1310s, were several important advisers of Pope John.

Dominican hostility to the Franciscan teaching was the cause proposed by Franz Ehrle in the first modern attempt to solve the problem of Pope John's attack. Ehrle observed that during their twenty-year struggle against the rigorous interpretation of the observance of poverty espoused by the order's radical Spiritual faction, the Franciscan community or "Conventuals" allowed a laxity and legalism to develop in their own observance which contrasted sharply with their lofty theoretical claims.[8] Earlier, according to Ehrle, the poor lives of Franciscans had added cogency to their arguments regarding poverty. By the early 1300s, however, the community had as many houses and goods as other orders in the church. Franciscans still claimed apostolic poverty because their houses and goods were not legally in the order's possession, having been assumed as the property of the papacy. But their claims seemed to many to be no more than a legal fiction—a pretense that rendered secular and Dominican criticisms of Franciscan teachings on Christ's poverty all the more persuasive. Ehrle argued that the Dominicans, who had special influence with Pope John, used the contradictions between Franciscan theory and practice to convince the pope to lift *Exiit*'s restrictions on the discussion of Christ's poverty and to investigate the orthodoxy of its doctrine.[9] That the immediate occasion of Pope John's questioning of *Exiit*'s teachings in 1322 was a dispute between a Dominican and a Franciscan over the nature of Christ's poverty seemed to reinforce Ehrle's hypothesis.[10] So did the

7. "Ad hoc respondeo quod habere res temporales in communi per modum proprietatis vel dominii nullo modo est tante perfectionis sicut nichil habere in communi et in speciali." Vat. MS lat. 3740, fol. 15ra. This characterizes the whole of Vital's response, fols. 3ra–16ra. It seems to have infuriated the pope, who called it heretical. See the account of Michael of Cesena in S. Baluze and J. Mansi, *Miscellanea*, 4 vols. (Lucca, 1761–64), 3:270b.

8. Franz Ehrle, "Die Spiritualen, ihr Verhältnis zum Franziskanerorden und zu den Fraticellen," *Archiv für Literatur- und Kirchengeschichte des Mittelalters* 4 (1888): 45–50. The Spirituals taught that the Franciscan Rule demanded an actual frugality in day-to-day use of goods—a "poor use"—as well as abandonment of all legal rights to them. The Conventuals contended that the rule demanded only the latter.

9. John had been raised by the Dominicans, and during his reign he favored both the order and the doctrines of its most prominent theologian, Thomas Aquinas. Lambert, "Franciscan Crisis," pp. 125–27, 135, cites particular instances of John's partiality toward the Dominicans during the poverty controversy. Also Pierre Mandonnet, "La canonisation de Thomas d'Aquin," in *Bibliothèque Thomiste*, vol. 3 (Paris, 1934), pp. 1–48. The Franciscan chronicler John of Winterthur, writing in the 1340s, attributed Pope John's attitude toward Franciscan poverty to Dominican influence. *Chronica*, ed. F. Baethgen, *MGH SS*, n.s. 3:93, 95, 98.

10. This dispute began during the examination of a Beguin—a lay follower of the Spirituals—at Narbonne in late 1321. John of Belna, a Dominican inquisitor, listed the

Thomas Turley

enthusiastic support given John by the Dominicans and their sympathizers in the relatively brief period during which the orthodoxy of the Franciscan doctrine was debated.[11] Published in 1888, Ehrle's work remained the common explanation of Pope John's actions for over forty years.[12]

In 1933 a hypothesis was offered which generally has supplanted Ehrle's. In that year Josef Koch attempted to place Pope John's attack on the Franciscan poverty doctrine within a broader context by linking it with the concurrent papal investigation of Peter Olivi's *Lectura super Apocalipsim*.[13] Olivi, who died in 1298, had formulated some of the essential teachings of the Spiritual Franciscans. Though he himself had been loyal to the papacy, his writings—and especially his *Lectura super Apocalipsim*—had proved an important source for the radical antipapal speculation of later Spirituals.[14] Naturally, both the Franciscan community and Pope John saw the condemnation of the *Lectura* as a necessary part of their suppression of the rebellious Spirituals. In June 1318 the pope set a commission of eight masters of theology from his curia to investigate the work. The report the commissioners delivered sometime during 1319 listed sixty passages from the *Lectura* in which they found heresy.[15] The report also suggested a barrier to total condemnation of Olivi's doctrines, however. In article 22 the commissioners observed that the decree *Exiit*

---

Franciscan doctrine of Christ's poverty among the heresies he found in the Beguin. Berengar Talon, a Franciscan member of Belna's inquisitorial panel, objected that the teaching was sound doctrine defined in *Exiit*. When Belna demanded that Talon recant, Talon appealed to the Holy See. Instead of handling the matter by invoking the authority of *Exiit*, Pope John ordered the issue debated in consistory. In the course of the debate on 6 March 1322 he showed a strong prejudice against the Franciscan doctrine. Greatly alarmed, the Franciscan leadership protested that *Exiit*'s ban on discussion of their poverty doctrine made John's proceedings illegal. John responded before the month's end with the decree *Quia nonnunquam* (25 March 1322), which lifted *Exiit*'s ban on discussion and solicited opinions on the matter from all interested theologians.

11. E.g., Felice Tocco, *La questione della povertà nel secolo XIV* (Naples, 1910), p. 32; Douie, *Fraticelli*, pp. 154–55; Patrick Gauchat, *Cardinal Bertrand de Turre O.F.M.: His Participation in the Theoretical Controversy concerning the Poverty of Christ and the Apostles under John XXII* (Rome, 1930), pp. 12–24.

12. Marie-Thérèse d'Alverny lists many of the works surviving from the Dominican-Franciscan controversy that broke out after Pope John opened discussion of the Franciscan poverty doctrine in "Les écrits théoretiques concernant la pauvreté évangélique depuis Pierre Jean Olieu jusqu'à la bulle *Cum inter nonnullos*," in *Positions des thèses des élèves de l'Ecole des Chartres* (1928), pp. 7–8. Once the pope had initiated discussion he moved very quickly, considering the importance of the issue and the vehemence of Franciscan opposition. Within nine months he had abrogated papal ownership of Franciscan goods in *Ad conditorem* (6 December 1322); within another eleven months he had condemned the Franciscan teaching in *Cum inter nonnullos* (23 November 1323). See especially Lambert, *Franciscan Poverty*, pp. 226–42; and Tierney, *Origins*, pp. 171–81.

13. Koch, "Prozess," pp. 302–15.

14. On Olivi see David Burr, *The Persecution of Peter Olivi* (Philadelphia, 1976).

15. See note 25 below for the attitude of the commission toward Olivi. On the date of the commission's report, see Koch, "Prozess," p. 306.

permitted one extremely important, suspect teaching of Olivi's to be interpreted as orthodox: his claim that the Rule of St. Francis was "truly and properly the evangelical rule which Christ himself observed, imposed upon the apostles, and caused to be written down in the gospels." The commissioners declared that Olivi was heretical if he meant that the Rule of St. Francis was identical to the gospel of Christ, that Christ had observed everything in the rule, or that the pope had no power over the rule. But they added: "If he comprehends these words according to the understanding and explanation of the decree *Exiit qui seminat*, he speaks the truth."[16] According to Koch, the commissioners' connection of *Exiit*'s formulation of the Franciscan poverty doctrine with Olivi's teaching convinced Pope John that a total condemnation of Olivi's *Lectura* could come only after the teaching in *Exiit* had been abrogated. So John sought an opportunity to attack *Exiit*'s teaching.[17]

Though Koch's theory has received wide acceptance since its publication, it has not gone unchallenged. In the late 1930s, J. G. Sikes ignored Koch's theory in proposing that Pope John attacked the Franciscan doctrine because he realized that acceptance of it would have led necessarily to an attack on the papacy's possessions. Léon Baudry made a similar suggestion in the late 1940s, again ignoring Koch.[18] Recently, several direct criticisms of Koch's position have appeared. Both Gordon Leff and Brian Tierney have emphasized the hypothetical nature of Koch's argument. Like Sikes and Baudry, Tierney has suggested that Pope John's attack was aimed not at Olivi but at the Franciscan doctrine of Christ's poverty itself, because the teaching implied a "wounding criticism" of the hierarchical church and its wealth. H. S. Offler, reviewing Tierney, has proposed that the attack came because John perceived that the divergence

16. "Dicit sic: 'Ex quo igitur per Romanae Ecclesiae authenticam testificationem et confirmationem constat regulam Minorum per beatum Franciscum editam esse vere et proprie illam evangelicam quam Christus in seipso servavit, et Apostolis imposuit, et in evangeliis suis conscribi fecit. . . .' Ubi videtur de regula beati Francisci, 'quam vere et proprie illam evangelicam' et caetera quae de ipsa adiungit, quod si haec verba capit secundum intellectum et declarationem decretalis *Exiit qui seminat*, verum dicit. Si autem intelligit, sicut ipse alibi declarat, et sui sequaces asserunt, quod regula beati Francisci sit vere et proprie idem et idipsum quod Christi evangelium et e converso, et quod Dominus Papa non habet potestatem super eam sicut nec super evangelium, vel quicquid est in regula beati Francisci, totum Christus ad litteram servaverit et Apostolis imposuerit observandum, hoc totum simpliciter reputamus haereticum et ridiculum et insanum; nec istud probatur per aliquod testimonium quod inducat." Baluze and Mansi, *Miscellanea*, 2:261b.

17. Koch, "Prozess," pp. 308–9.

18. J. G. Sikes, "Hervaeus Natalis: De paupertate Christi de apostolorum," *Archives d'histoire doctrinale et littéraire du Moyen Age* 12–13 (1937–38): 216. According to Sikes, John came to this realization only after the poverty question had been disputed in the curia in March 1322. Léon Baudry, *Guillaume d'Occam*, 2 vols. (Paris, 1949), 1:106. Michael Bihl also expressed doubts about Koch's thesis in a recension of "Prozess," *Archivum Franciscanum Historicum* 29 (1936), pp. 254–57.

between the Franciscans' theory and practice of poverty was producing intolerable administrative disorder, while the theory itself was based on suspect theological grounds. Edith Pásztor, in articles that carefully review the curial investigations of Olivi between 1318 and 1326, has concluded that these focused primarily on his Joachimism and his attacks on the Roman church, not his views on poverty, even after the condemnation of the Franciscan poverty doctrine in 1323. The poverty dispute, she contends, was a separate matter. And David Burr has argued that Koch was half right: Pope John did become interested in the poverty question as a result of his investigation of Olivi, but soon saw the issue as important in its own right.[19]

A reexamination of Koch's evidence, especially of the preliminary reports on Olivi and his followers produced in the curia while the commission of eight masters deliberated in 1318–19, verifies much of this recent criticism. Although Pope John was made aware of the poverty question through his investigation of Olivi, as Koch contends, he seems almost immediately to have understood the poverty issue as more important than Olivi's condemnation, because the reports emphasized that the traditional Franciscan doctrine of Christ's poverty was the source of Olivi's error. Moreover, these early reports offer substantial support for Ehrle's contention that the Dominicans were instrumental in prejudicing the pope against the Franciscan position.

Two of these early reports survive. One is a list of errors extracted from Olivi's *Lectura* under the direction of Nicholas Alberti de Prato, the Dominican cardinal of Ostia. The actual author is unknown.[20] Used eventually by the eight masters as a basis for their report, Alberti's list of errors is predictably hostile toward Franciscan claims about Christ's poverty. The other report is an analysis of a pamphlet by an anonymous Catalan Beguin—a lay follower of the Spirituals—allegedly reflecting Olivi's doctrines. It was requested by Pope John from two Thomist theologians serving on the commission of eight masters: Pierre de la Palu, a prominent Dominican, and Guido Terreni, the general of the Carmelite

---

19. Leff, *Heresy*, p. 161 n.2; Tierney, *Origins*, pp. 174–75; H. S. Offler, review of *Origins*, *American Historical Review* 78 (1973): 666; Burr, *Peter Olivi*, p. 87; Edith Pásztor, "Le polemiche sulla 'Lectura super Apocalipsim' di Pietro di Giovanni Olivi fino alla sua condanna," *Bullettino dell'Istituto Storico Italiano per il medio evo e Archivio Muratoriano* 70 (1958): 365–424, and idem, "Giovanni XXII e il Gioachimismo di Pietro di Giovanni Olivi," ibid., 82 (1970): 81–111. Also significant has been Malcolm Lambert's "Franciscan Crisis," pp. 123–43, which explores John's deep prejudices against the Spiritual interpretation of poverty, notes the pope's conviction of the "hollowness" of the Franciscan theory, and revives Ehrle's emphasis on Dominican influence in Pope John's decisions.

20. This is preserved in Paris MS BN lat. 3381 A, fols. 1r–277v; and Vat. MS lat. 11906, fols. 63r–188v. Both manuscripts are described by Koch, "Prozess," pp. 303–4. Koch thinks the author was William of Laudun, a Dominican member of the committee of eight masters.

order.[21] It too has a heavily Dominican bias.[22] Why Pope John chose these three men to render the reports is uncertain, although his admiration for the advice of Thomist theologians, especially Dominicans, is well established. It is also unclear whether the report of Palu and Terreni was known to their fellow commissioners. Both reports were produced in the summer of 1318, as the commission of eight masters began its work; both were submitted long before the commission reached its conclusions.[23]

The work of Palu and Terreni is the shorter of the two reports and in many ways the more direct. It has not been considered much in discussions of Pope John's views, although Palu and Terreni were close advisers of the pope. Perhaps because they dealt with a contemporary Beguin's brief polemical interpretation of aspects of Olivi's thought rather than the subtleties of Olivi's own writings, Palu and Terreni stated the issues they felt confronted Pope John more clearly than the author of Nicholas Alberti's report.[24] Like the rest of the commission of eight masters, Palu and Terreni were deeply prejudiced against the doctrines of Olivi and so focused on two errors the full commission would later treat in examining the *Lectura:* the Beguin pamphleteer's heretical understanding of the authority of the Roman church and his identification of the Franciscan Rule with the teaching of the gospel on perfection.[25] But to these they

21. Edited by José Pou y Martí in his *Visionarios, Beguinos y Fraticellos catalanes (siglos XIII–XV)* (Vich, 1930), pp. 483–512. Koch discusses this report in "Prozess," p. 305. Also Bartomeu Xiberta, *Guiu Terrena, Carmelita de Perpinyà* (Barcelona, 1932), pp. 67–68; Paul Fournier, "Gui Terré, théologien," *Histoire littéraire de la France* 36 (1927): 435, and idem, "Pierre de la Palu, théologien et canoniste," ibid., 37 (1938): 45–46.

22. Terreni considered himself a Thomist and so had strong ties with the Dominicans. Xiberta, "De doctrinis theologicis magistri Guidonis Terreni," *Analecta ordinis Carmelitarum* 5 (1923–26): 248–49.

23. Koch seems to assume that John did not read these reports because they were preliminary to the fuller report of the eight masters. This is possibly true of Alberti's list of errors, but Palu and Terreni's brief report was requested independently by the pope. Moreover, even if John did not read these works immediately, he certainly would have reviewed them after the report of the eight masters revealed difficulties with the condemnation of Olivi in 1319.

24. When the Spirituals were suppressed by Pope John in late 1317 and early 1318, the Beguins rallied to their support, hiding Spirituals who would not submit and continuing the circulation of Spiritual doctrines. Like the most radical Spirituals, the Beguins began to see the Roman church's persecution of the Spirituals as a fulfillment of Olivi's apocalyptic predictions, denouncing it as the whore of Babylon and the seat of the Antichrist. The Catalan pamphlet Palu and Terreni examined is one of the earliest of these denunciations. It undoubtedly helped spur the series of inquisitions which wiped out the Beguins by 1330. See Raoul Manselli, *Spirituali e Beghini in Provenza* (Rome, 1959), esp. pp. 151–208.

25. See especially Pou y Martí, *Visionarios,* pp. 496, 511, 493. Palu and Terreni approached the Catalan pamphlet much as they and their fellow commissioners did Olivi's *Lectura* later. It is widely recognized that the commission was prejudiced against Olivi because of what he symbolized to the Spirituals. Because the commissioners saw the Roman church as an unchanging institution, they refused to come to terms with Olivi's dynamic and evolutionary approach to its history. They ignored his subtleties as

Thomas Turley

added a third error: the belief that Christ had renounced both individual and communal possessions. This last error, they argued, was closely connected to the first two. According to Palu and Terreni, the anonymous Beguin's erroneous conviction that Christ had lived without communal possessions led him to reject the Roman church and its authority, declaring it a carnal church and a "Babylon of confusion" because it held communal possessions.[26] It was also the essence of the Beguin's equation of the Franciscan Rule with the gospel in its teaching on perfection, and it caused him to condemn the rest of the church for failing to revive the life of evangelical perfection taught in the rule.[27] Finally, the Beguin's beliefs about Christ's poverty induced him to assert not only that the Franciscans alone practiced evangelical perfection, but that the Roman church had lost the teachings of evangelical perfection from the time of the apostles to the time of St. Francis.[28] Throughout their report, Palu and Terreni reiter-

---

well as his attempts to avoid precisely the implications they drew from many of his teachings. Moreover, they identified Olivi with the rebellious Spirituals and Beguins of their own day and so read into his doctrines the interpretations of these contemporary Spirituals and Beguins. David Burr has shown, however, that while the commission distorted and oversimplified some of Olivi's teachings in the Lectura, they read him correctly in certain essential ways. The commissioners were correct when they declared that Olivi envisioned radical changes for the church, especially in its hierarchy, and when they asserted that he believed the forces of evil would someday capture the highest offices in the church and lead an attack on evangelical perfection from Rome. As these last were the two views most commonly condemned in the commissioners' report, it can be said that the impression among modern scholars that Olivi's censure was the result of misunderstanding of his views is false. The teachings the commissioners found most objectionable were authentic. Burr, Peter Olivi, pp. 83–85.

26. "Si enim vocet ecclesiam carnalem Ecclesiam Catholicam habentem possessiones in communi, in qua aliqui carnaliter vivunt, clare patet quod dicit heresim male sentiens de sancta matre Ecclesia, que non Babilon confusionis sed est Jerusalem et velut castrorum acies ordinata. . . . Nec habere eas in communi adversatur evangelice perfectioni." Pou y Martí, Visionarios, p. 486. There follows a denial of the imperfection of communal possessions, pp. 486–90. Pope John had already condemned the radical Spirituals' distinction between their own "spiritual" church and the "carnal" church of Rome in Gloriosam ecclesiam (23 January 1318), ed. Konrad Eubel, Bullarium Franciscanum (Rome, 1898), 5:137b–42b.

27. "Sed vocat iste renovationem vite evangelice in sexto statu vivere secundum perfectionem evangelicam, imo secundum istum vita et perfectio evangelica est in abdicatione habendi in proprio et communi. . . . Igitur renovatio ad vitam evangelicam non est nisi in vita secundum observantiam regule beati Francisci. Regula autem beati Francisci precipit nichil habere in communi; ergo ecclesia habens in communi divitias non est reparata nec renovata ad vitam evangelice perfectionis, et sic dapnat totam ecclesiam aliam ab ordine Minorum, lapsam a vita apostolorum et perfectione evangelica." Ibid., p. 491. A discussion of the primitive church's communal possession follows.

28. "In quarta pagina dicit, 'quod sextus status, de quo supra dixit quod in eo fiet renovatio vite evangelice, incepit tempore beati Francisci.' Istum articulum ex eadem causa dapnandum reputamus, nam tota universalis ecclesia tempore Francisci non abjecit divitias in communi, sicut nec nunc abjicit nec aliqui de ecclesia abjiciunt omnia in communi, nisi soli fratres de ordine Minorum: igitur ecclesia in nulla sui parte renovabitur ad statum evangelice perfectionis nisi in solis fratribus Minoribus, quod est

ated that the poverty doctrines of the anonymous Beguin pamphleteer were the source of his other errors. By implication, Olivi's errors were attributable to the same cause.

Palu and Terreni's report made no reference to *Exiit* by name, but their explicit condemnation of the anonymous Beguin's position on Christ's poverty implicitly condemned the traditional Franciscan interpretation expounded in *Exiit*. This is not to say that the traditional interpretation asserted Franciscan perfection as radically as did the Spirituals and their Beguin followers, or that its proponents ever advocated refusal of submission to the Roman church. On the contrary, Franciscans were among the most extreme supporters of papal authority from the earliest days of their order, and they vociferously condemned Spiritual attacks on the papacy.[29] Even as Palu and Terreni's report was submitted to the pope, the Conventuals were depending upon the Roman see to stamp out the Spirituals. But as stated in *Exiit*, the traditional Franciscan position did equate the renunciation of individual and communal possessions with the highest perfection taught in the gospel. Moreover, it identified the poverty teachings of the rule with the gospel's essential teachings on Christian perfection. According to Palu and Terreni, these doctrines had led their Beguin, and presumably his Spiritual masters, first to condemn the church's right to possess property, then to condemn the Roman church and rebel against its authority. Their arguments implied that these doctrines could produce open heresy and rebellion in the rest of the Franciscans as easily as they had in the Spirituals and Beguins. It is unlikely that Pope John missed their point.

About the same time Palu and Terreni delivered their report to Pope John—probably shortly before—Nicholas Alberti's report was submitted.[30] Long and somewhat redundant, it extracted eighty-four errors from Olivi's *Lectura*. The conclusions were similar to those of Palu and Terreni, if less emphatically stated. The author asserted that Olivi's essential error was his identification of the Franciscan Rule with the teachings of the gospel on perfection, and that to claim as Olivi did that the rule's teaching on communal poverty was taught by Christ in the gospel was to claim that the whole church had lost evangelical perfection from the time of the primitive church to the time of St. Francis.[31] Like Palu and Terreni,

---

absurdum." Ibid., pp. 491–92. An extended version of this argument on pp. 502–3 claims that the Beguin denies the church perfection from the time of the apostles to Francis.

29. See the examples quoted by Pásztor, "Polemiche," pp. 371–72.

30. The report is dated 1318 in manuscript; a reference establishes that it could not have been composed before 7 May (Koch, "Prozess," p. 304 n. 11). As the commission of eight masters worked from this report, and as it is likely that Palu and Terreni were asked to review the Catalan pamphlet after appointment to the commission, Alberti's report was probably written shortly before Palu and Terreni's.

31. On the identification of the rule and the gospel, Paris MS BN lat. 3381 A, fols. 66v–70r; on the church's loss of perfection, fols. 3v, 19r, 100r.

he made no explicit reference to *Exiit* in his condemnation of Olivi's poverty doctrines, but he did refer to it by name in discussing related questions.[32]

While neither of these reports explicitly connected *Exiit* with the Spirituals' poverty teachings, both identified as an essential error of the Spirituals and their followers a poverty doctrine similar to that taught in *Exiit*, and Alberti's report introduced *Exiit* into the discussion of that error. It seems unlikely that Pope John would have taken very long to see the similarity.[33] However, even if Koch is correct in assuming that John failed to see the connection until the report of the commission of eight masters was delivered in 1319, these earlier reports ensured that the pope's reaction to the commission's report would be somewhat different from the one Koch suggests. Koch argues that when John understood *Exiit*'s content, he considered abrogation because the decree barred condemnation of Olivi's views on poverty and thereby limited censure of Olivi's apocalyptic beliefs regarding the Roman church. It is more probable that the pope considered abrogation because he had been brought to believe that the poverty doctrine in *Exiit* was a dangerous error. Certainly John saw abrogation of *Exiit* as related to the condemnation of Olivi; Alberti, Palu, and Terreni had emphasized that the doctrine of Christ's absolute poverty was at the center of Olivi's errors. But the poverty doctrine went beyond Olivi, the Spirituals, and their followers. It touched the whole Franciscan order. It implicitly challenged both the church's possession of property and the integrity of its teaching on Christian perfection. And it might produce open heresy and rebellion if it were not exposed and condemned as error. These seem the reasons John turned his attention from Olivi to *Exiit*.[34]

This interpretation of Pope John's motives is supported by other evidence we have about his investigations of Olivi and of *Exiit*'s teaching. The report of the commission of eight masters, for example, is very revealing. It contains surprisingly little reference to the Franciscan Rule and poverty, despite the commission's use of Nicholas Alberti's report as a basis for its investigations and the presence of Palu and Terreni among the

32. E.g., he cited *Exiit* in an argument showing that the rule did not contain all of Christ's counsels and precepts and therefore was not equal to the gospel. Later he used it to demonstrate that the rule had been altered by papal authority—a thing which could not be done to the gospel. Paris MS BN lat. 3381 A, fols. 68r, 103v–4r.

33. As Koch notes, John seems to have had only a vague conception of *Exiit*'s poverty doctrine before these reports were delivered. In *Quorundam exigit* (7 October 1317), he described *Exiit* as "salubriter editas, soliditas quidem et claras, et lucidas multaque maturitate digestas." *Extrav. Ioan. XXII* 14.1, Friedberg, *CIC*, 2:1220. He was referring to measures in *Exiit* which granted the friars the use of things the Spirituals claimed the rule prohibited. *Quorundam* did not address poverty but concerned the disobedience of the Spirituals. Later in *Quorundam* he said: "Magna quidem paupertas, sed maior integritas bonum est, obedientia maximum, si custodiatur illaesa." Ibid., 2:1223.

34. Koch's argument also rests on a presumption that the condemnation of Olivi proceeded rapidly after the teachings of *Exiit* had been abrogated late in 1323. But in fact there is no evidence of haste, as the Appendix below explains.

eight commissioners. Only six articles of sixty refer to the rule. Two of these deserve special attention: one on the Spiritual doctrine that St. Francis was the most perfect observer of the evangelical rule since Christ and the Virgin Mary, and one on *Exiit* and Olivi's teaching on the relationship between rule and gospel. Both are treated in this report with formulas suggesting some kind of conflict between the Franciscans and their critics.[35]

Nicholas Alberti's report had responded to the claim that St. Francis was the most perfect observer of the evangelical rule since Christ and Mary by listing the many saints who had achieved perfection in the twelve hundred years between Christ and Francis. This challenged traditional Franciscan interpretations of Christ's poverty by implying that those saints had achieved the highest perfection without observing the absolute poverty the Franciscans attributed to Christ. The report of the eight masters avoided repeating Alberti's challenge. It merely asserted that the saints "of the New Testament" were as perfect in following the evangelical rule as Christ and Mary had been.[36] The change apparently was made to fit Conventual Franciscan teaching, which contended that the practice of absolute poverty had been lost sometime after the New Testament period.[37]

Similarly, the reports of Alberti, Palu, and Terreni had condemned flatly the equation of the Franciscan Rule with the evangelical rule. The report of the eight masters carefully distinguished a sense in which this equation could be sustained and a sense in which it could not; a general sense in which it agreed with *Exiit* and so was orthodox, and a literal sense in which it was heretical. Here again, the report of the eight masters seems to have been tailored to avoid conflict with Conventual Franciscan doctrine.[38]

The report's handling of both these questions indicates a strong reaction on the part of the Franciscan members of the commission—Bertrand de la Tour and Arnold Royard—to the report of Nicholas Alberti, and very probably to the attitudes of fellow commissioners Pierre de la Palu and Guido Terreni as well. The leaders of the order seem to have gotten their way here, but to do so they must have stated vigorously their views on the absolute poverty of Christ—and made very clear to the pope the similarity of their views to those condemned by Alberti, Palu, and Terreni.

35. Articles 28 and 22. The six articles which refer to the rule are 22, 23, 25, 28, 29, 30. Baluze and Mansi, *Miscellanea*, 2:261b, 262a, 263b, 264b.

36. Article 28; ibid., 2:263b: "Quia hoc est ipsum [Francis] praeferre omnibus sanctis novi testamenti, quod specialiter propter apostolos temerarium est, et credimus esse falsum." Nicholas Alberti's comments are in Paris MS BN lat. 3381 A, fol. 107r.

37. Tierney, *Origins*, pp. 67–74.

38. Article 22. The text is in note 16, above. Burr, *Peter Olivi*, p. 87, notes other evidence of tension in the report. This, he suggests, led Pope John "beyond Olivi to the order itself."

Thomas Turley

Significantly, at about the same time the report of the eight masters was being completed in 1319, Pope John seems to have begun pressuring Michael of Cesena, the minister-general of the Franciscans, to change the order's teaching on Christ's poverty. Michael himself provides evidence of this in the letter to the Franciscan order he issued in July 1328, shortly after he had broken with the pope over the poverty issue.[39] He complains that Pope John had been trying to induce the order to alter the state of life handed down to it by St. Francis "incessantly and harshly" for nine years—that is, since 1319.[40] If Pope John had become convinced of the error of the Franciscan poverty doctrine in 1319, the most sensible course open to him would have been to seek the cooperation of the Franciscan leadership in changing it. Michael seems to be complaining that John followed just such a course.[41]

Although Josef Koch provided a more complete and sophisticated description of the events surrounding John XXII's attack on Franciscan poverty than any historian before him, his explanation of the pope's motivation for the attack is not supported by the evidence. John's desire to condemn Peter Olivi certainly played a part in his decision, and the investigation of Olivi drew his attention to the Franciscan doctrine, but the key factors were apparently the hostility of the Dominicans and their supporters toward the Franciscan doctrine and the influence of this group

39. *Universis ministris*, ed. Konrad Eubel, *Bullarium Franciscanum*, 5:347a–48b.
40. Ibid., p. 348b: "Siquidem a IX annis ordinem nostrum et meam personam indesiniter et atrociter persecutus multifarie nos videbatur omnes inducere ad mutandum statum, quem novimus nobisque tradidit almus Christi confessor Franciscus." Michael's comment is noted by Gauchat, *Bertrand de Turre*, p. 24, and Johann Hofer, "Die Geschichte der Armutsstreites in der Chronik des Johann von Winterthur," *Zeitschrift für Schweizerische Kirchengeschichte* 21 (1927): 242. Another indication that John was privately investigating the Franciscan doctrine of Christ's poverty long before he opened the matter to public discussion in March 1322 is a Franciscan response on the subject written before 21 August 1321. Tocco, *Quistione*, pp. 50, 58–59.
41. Better known than Michael's fairly brief July letter is a long appeal to the Christian faithful he issued two months later, in September 1328. This seems to be the source of much of the confusion regarding Pope John's motives in questioning the Franciscan poverty doctrine. Unlike the July letter, this September appeal offers a history of John's actions. Unfortunately, the account begins abruptly with the hostile decrees of 1322, ignoring the pope's apparent attempts to deal privately with Michael and thereby leaving a strong impression that John acted precipitously and inexplicably. Michael's appeal was eventually incorporated into the so-called chronicle of Nicholas the Minorite—actually a collection of documents—and its history paraphrased in the chronicle's preface. The chronicle, in turn, has become the main account for modern historians of the struggle between Pope John and the Franciscan leadership.
The chronicle is edited in Baluze and Mansi, *Miscellanea*, 3:206a–358b. Michael's version of Pope John's attack is on pp. 270a–71a, the preface which repeats Michael's description of the attack on 207a–b. See Konrad Eubel, "Zu Nicolaus Minorita," *Historisches Jahrbuch* 18 (1897): 375–86. Michael's July letter is also included in the chronicle (244b–46a), but its cryptic reference to Pope John's attempts to coerce Michael in 1319 is perhaps the only hint at the pope's motives in the entire work.

with the pope. The reports Pope John received from Dominican theological advisers in 1318 argued emphatically that a poverty doctrine very similar to that held by the Conventual Franciscans lay at the root of Olivi's errors. It is likely that John then came to see this doctrine as an error distinct from, and potentially more important than, the problem of Olivi. When he opened debate on the orthodoxy of *Exiit*'s teaching, it was the Franciscan poverty doctrine itself, not Olivi, which was the pope's main concern.

## Appendix

Koch's claim that Pope John was concerned principally with the condemnation of Peter Olivi when he attacked *Exiit*'s poverty doctrine requires that Olivi's condemnation should have followed closely on *Cum inter nonnullos*, the decree in which John declared the Franciscan doctrine to be error. In fact, John waited over two years to condemn Olivi (12 November 1323–8 February 1326). To account for this, Koch asserts that the investigation of Olivi—suspended soon after the attack on Franciscan poverty had begun—did indeed proceed at a faster pace once *Cum inter* was promulgated. He implies that the two-year interval was filled with two intensive probes of Olivi's doctrines. The first, according to Koch, reconvened the commission of eight masters to render a new report in light of *Cum inter;* the second conducted a careful examination of four errors extracted from this report, on the basis of which Olivi was finally condemned.[42] A close look at Koch's evidence does not support his contention, however: it appears that the commission of eight masters was never reconvened. Its report certainly was used in determining the four errors for which Olivi was ultimately examined. But the commission did not meet again to repeat its work. This leaves the comparatively simple examination of Olivi's four errors as the only investigation carried out in the twenty-seven months between the promulgation of *Cum inter* and Olivi's condemnation.

Koch's only evidence for the reconvening of the commission of eight masters consists of two jumbled texts in which the authors have either confused the date of the commission's investigation or deliberately changed its date for polemical purposes. The first is a list of events leading up to the condemnation of Olivi composed sometime between 1328 and 1340, the *Series condemnationum et processuum contra doctrinam et sequaces Petri Joannis Olivi*. It records the report of the eight masters twice, suggesting that a second report was submitted. But its second

42. Koch, "Prozess," pp. 309–10. Bihl, in his recension of "Prozess," p. 257, expresses unspecified doubts about Koch's conclusions here. Pásztor does not directly address this part of Koch's argument.

reference clearly confuses the report with the actual instrument of Olivi's final condemnation in 1326, a papal document which the *Series* never mentions. This throws the accuracy of the *Series* into grave doubt, especially on this matter. Koch's second text is preserved in book 2, article 59, of Alvarus Pelagius's *De planctu ecclesiae*. It is part of a pamphlet composed sometime between 1324 and 1326 by a Franciscan loyal to John XXII.[43] The author is attempting to reconcile *Exiit*'s teaching on poverty with Pope John's condemnation in *Cum inter* by denying that *Cum inter* really condemned the doctrines contained in *Exiit*. He finds his evidence in the report of the eight masters. Asserting that the report of the eight masters was submitted after *Cum inter* had been promulgated, the Franciscan quotes article 22 of the report, which cites *Exiit* as a doctrinal authority in its treatment of Olivi's poverty teachings. Then he argues that Pope John could not possibly have condemned *Exiit*'s poverty teaching in *Cum inter* if he permitted *Exiit* to be cited as a doctrinal authority on apostolic poverty in a report made after *Cum inter*'s promulgation. Unfortunately, the importance of the date of the commission's report to this Franciscan's argument makes his testimony very questionable. Neither of these texts is very strong evidence for Koch's contention. Pope John does not seem to have been in a great hurry to deal with Olivi after his condemnation of the Franciscan poverty doctrine.

Edith Pásztor's research on Olivi's condemnation offers an explanation for John's slowness. She has emphasized that there were two phases to the investigation of Olivi's doctrines. The first phase focused on the Spirituals in 1318–19 and culminated in a papal commission's condemnation of the *Postilla super Apocalypsim*. Pope John did not directly participate. After this, John was content to let consideration of Olivi move very slowly, apparently because the Spirituals were suppressed and the Beguins were on the run. But in May 1324 the German emperor Lewis of Bavaria issued an appeal at Sachsenhausen which employed new Olivian arguments against the pope and the Roman church. Investigation of Olivi again became a priority, and he was condemned by papal decree in February 1326. Pásztor's analysis is compelling, though she seems to react too strongly to Koch's claims regarding the part the Franciscan poverty doctrine played in the first investigation. She apparently sees no link at all between the 1318–19 proceedings and the later poverty dispute.[44]

43. Koch actually finds the text in the chronicle of the Franciscan Nicholas Glassberger, who took it from Alvarus's work. "Prozess," p. 309 n. 30. Pásztor, "Polemiche," p. 379 n. 2 discusses the origin and authorship of this text.

44. Pásztor, "Polemiche," pp. 366ff., 386ff.; "Giovanni XXII," pp. 82ff., 109–111. Burr, *Peter Olivi*, pp. 86–87, follows Pásztor on the phases of the investigation of Olivi, but integrates Koch's hypothesis. His conclusion is similar to mine: the investigation brought the Franciscan poverty doctrine to Pope John's attention, but he soon saw the issue as important in its own right.

# PART II

# [6]

## Ennodius in the Middle Ages:
## Adonics, Pseudo-Isidore,
## Cistercians, and the Schools

### Richard H. Rouse and Mary A. Rouse

Ennodius (ca. 474–521), cleric of Milan and (from ca. 513) bishop of Pavia, was a rhetorician trained in the ancient manner. The body of his work comprises 470 separate items, including letters, verses, *dictiones*, epitaphs, and epigrams, as well as an account of his own life, a panegyric on the Arian king Theodoric, and a life of the bishop-saint Epiphanius of Pavia. Correspondent of Boethius and mentor of the much younger Arator, Ennodius embodied "perhaps the last . . . futile attempt to reconcile a radically pagan culture with the profession of the Christian religion."[1] By no means an elegant stylist—his seventeenth-century editor Andreas Schott called him "auctor horridus atque obscurus"—Ennodius today is primarily of historical rather than of literary interest.

The transmission of Ennodius's works was studied in depth at the end of the nineteenth century by Hartel and by Vogel, the one following close upon the other.[2] A century later, Vogel's edition of 1885 remains the accepted text. Hartel and Vogel, however, address none of the questions

We thank Robert L. Benson, David Ganz, and Carol D. Lanham, who read this essay in manuscript and generously shared their knowledge with us, and Sister James M. Dyer, who assisted in the early stages of the research.

1. Frederick J. E. Raby, *A History of Christian-Latin Poetry*, 2d ed. (Oxford, 1953), p. 117. Concerning Ennodius's life and works see J. Fontaine, "Ennodius," in *Reallexikon für Antike und Christentum* 5 (1962): 398–421, and the bibliography cited there.

2. The edition cited here is that of Friedrich Vogel, *Magni Felicis Ennodi Opera*, MGH Auct. ant. 7 (Berlin, 1885). The edition of Wilhelm von Hartel, *Magni Felicis Ennodi Opera omnia*, Corpus scriptorum ecclesiasticorum latinorum 6 (Vienna, 1882), is likewise dependable; Hartel, however, followed Jacques Sirmond (edition of 1611) in arranging the works of Ennodius according to literary type, producing a sequence which is found in no surviving manuscripts and which ignores the almost unvarying order of the works (Vogel's) found in all manuscripts before the fourteenth century.

that interest historians: Where, when, by whom, and how was this text disseminated? Or further, why was this unappealing text copied at all? Since Vogel's edition, a substantial amount of information has been unearthed concerning the manuscripts of Ennodius, as the study of medieval scriptoria and libraries has advanced. To Vogel's stemma can now be added information about the date, origin, and home of each of the surviving manuscripts and about the nature of those parts of the picture now missing. The stemma examined in this fashion becomes a revealing piece of historical evidence for avenues of intellectual contact. Moreover, as the paucity of manuscripts implies—only seven survive from before the fourteenth century—Ennodius was seldom copied and even more seldom read in the Middle Ages because of his overblown and obscure Latin style. The transmission seen in its historical setting reveals, as no bare stemma could, the variety of purposes at different times and in differing circumstances that ensured the survival and motivated dissemination of this corpus. Ennodius is one of those rare texts whose fortunes can be traced almost from the moment the ink dried in the early sixth century until its appearance in print in the sixteenth and seventeenth centuries.

At an early date, presumably after the Pavian bishop's death, an edition of his works, made perhaps by one of his protégés, brought them together in roughly chronological order.[3] That edition or a descendant of it forms the archetype of all surviving manuscripts. Vogel demonstrates that there are only two independent witnesses to the archetype, both dating from the ninth century: B, without issue, and V, source of all the remaining manuscripts. Schematically, Vogel's stemma for the pre-fourteenth-century manuscripts is as shown in the accompanying diagram. Vogel's two oldest

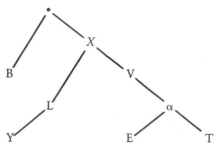

surviving manuscripts appear as if from nowhere, in two seemingly widely separated monasteries, Lorsch (B) and Corbie (V). The older of these is Brussels, Bibliothèque Royale 9845–48, B,[4] written in the first third of

3. Whether the works are entirely, or just largely, chronological is a subject of dispute. See Fontaine, "Ennodius," p. 400.

4. Joseph Van den Gheyn, *Catalogue des manuscrits de la Bibliothèque Royale*, vol. 2 (Brussels, 1902), no. 1218; Vogel, pp. xxxii–xxxvii.

the ninth century; much the better of the two textually, it is assumed to be a direct copy of the archetype. Although B belonged to the abbey of Lorsch (it is recorded in the Lorsch catalog of ca. 830),[5] Bernhard Bischoff has shown by paleographic evidence that it was written for Lorsch at some West Frankish center, almost certainly St-Vaast in Arras. At the time B was written, Adalung abbot of Lorsch was simultaneously abbot of St-Vaast (A.D. 808–38); the Western dissemination of the *Chronicon Laureshamense breve* from St-Vaast and the appearance of St-Vaast hands of the first half of the ninth century in Lorsch manuscripts point to the close connection between the scriptoria and the libraries of the two houses.[6] The *stemma codicum* of Ennodius begins to make geographical sense, then, if the two oldest manuscripts were written at Arras and Corbie, some thirty miles apart; Corbie is just off the Roman road linking Arras with Amiens to the south.

How, when, and why did the source of these, and of all surviving manuscripts, come to be in the North? The answer was supplied by Michael Lapidge in his study of Carolingian adonic verse.[7] An adonic verse (dactyl + trochee, or dactyl + spondee) was originally employed at the end of a stanza of poetry, to vary the meter. From the second century A.D., poets sometimes composed in consecutive adonics, a light, racing verse form. Ennodius, however, was an innovator in the use of consecutive adonic verses, in that he was the first to employ this metric form as the graceful conclusion of a letter to a friend, Faustus: "Lux mea, Fauste, / spesque salusque, / litterularum / munera parva / suscipe laetus," and so on. As Lapidge has shown, the use of adonics for epistolary purposes was introduced to the Carolingian court from the Ennodian model, and the appearance of adonics in letters is a clear indication of the presence of Ennodius. Paul the Deacon (d. 797), who came to the Carolingian court in 782, initiated there the use of epistolary adonics, which soon became fashionable among writers associated with the court. Paul the Deacon was the earliest writer to quote Ennodius (the *Vita Epifani*), in his *Historia romana*, and he had been educated by the grammarian Flavianus at Pavia, Ennodius's home. Paul must have found there a manuscript of Ennodius's works, perhaps in the chapter library itself, and brought this manuscript or a copy of it north to Charlemagne's court.

Unquestionably the text of Ennodius was still available in the late eighth century in the neighborhood of Pavia, since there are even later local traces: Ennodius's *Vita Epifani* is quoted in the eleventh century at

5. Gustav Becker, *Catalogi bibliothecarum antiqui* (Bonn, 1885), p. 109, no. 37:379, "Liber Ennodii epistolarum multarum in uno codice." For the date of this (Bischoff's catalog 1) see Bernhard Bischoff, *Lorsch im Spiegel seiner Handschriften* (Munich, 1974), pp. 10, 16.

6. Bischoff, pp. 32–35, 39.

7. Michael Lapidge, "The Authorship of the Adonic Verses 'ad Fidolium' Attributed to Columbanus," *Studi medievali*, ser. 3a, 18, 2 (1977): 249–314, esp. pp. 256–58.

Milan (some twenty miles north of Pavia), and a manuscript of his works
is recorded in the eleventh-century catalog of the library at Bobbio (some
thirty miles south of Pavia).[8] The secondary literature tells one also that,
in the ninth century, popes Nicholas I and John VIII quote briefly from
Ennodius's *Liber apologeticus,* mentioning the author by name; but, as
we shall see, these snippets come from an intermediate source and do not
represent a manuscript of Ennodius in ninth-century Rome.[9] There are no
further southern traces, and no independent southern manuscript tradition. Instead, the manuscript known in, and presumably brought to, the
North by Paul the Deacon was the sole source of the text of Ennodius as
we have it today.

The Carolingian enthusiasm for epistolary adonics doubtless derived
primarily from Paul's own use of them rather than directly from Paul's
model, Ennodius. Nevertheless, a few of Paul's contemporaries, among
them Alcuin, clearly knew Ennodius's verses at first hand, suggesting that
Paul's manuscript of Ennodius circulated at court.[10] It is reasonable to
suppose that circulation continued after Paul's death (as the vogue for
adonics demonstrably did). Circulation of the archetype among court
figures must explain the only ninth-century witness to Ennodius that is
not associated with the surviving manuscripts: A sequence of three dis-
tichs of Ennodius (carm. 2.26, 27, 28; Vogel 134, 134a, 134b) appears in
Paris, BN lat. 8071, fol. 57. This famous collection of pagan and Christian
verse was compiled in the second half of the ninth century, perhaps at
Fleury or perhaps farther south, and belonged in the seventeenth century
to Jacques de Thou.[11] It is unlikely that these six lines represent a lost
manuscript of Ennodius; rather, someone at the end of the eighth century
or the beginning of the ninth—a figure such as Theodulf, for example—

8. Ennodius's *Vita Epifani* was used in the *De situ civitatis Mediolani* and the
*Historia Mediolanensis* of Landulfus at the end of the eleventh century; see Fedele
Savio, *Gli antichi vescovi d'Italia . . . : La Lombardia,* vol. 1, *Milano* (Florence, 1913),
pp. 701–10, and Vogel, p. 333. For the Bobbio catalog, which dates from the eleventh
century, see Becker, *Catalogi,* p. 69, no. 32:377, "Librum Ennodii episcopi unum, in quo
& alia continentur opuscula." The manuscript may have come to Bobbio much earlier,
of course.

9. See below, at note 26. Concerning the manuscript reported from Pavia in the
fifteenth century, see note 77 below.

10. Lapidge (p. 272) demonstrates the verbal dependence on Ennodius of the controversial Columbanus, whom he tentatively identifies with an unknown abbot of St-
Trond near Liège, ca. 780–ca. 820. Although the grounds for this specific identification
seem slight, the circumstantial evidence for a Carolingian dating of Columbanus's *Ad
Fidolium* is convincing. Lapidge also states (p. 273) that Alcuin used Ennodius; he gives
no examples, but there seems to us to be a close structural parallel between successive
lines of Alcuin's epistolary verse to "Eulalia" (*MGH Poetae* 1:303; quoted by Lapidge,
p. 258), "Ut tua mitis / tempora Christus / tota gubernet" and the "sic tua summus /
germina Christus / lucida servet" of Ennodius's letter to Faustus (Vogel, p. 29).

11. There is a very substantial bibliography on aspects of this collection. For an
introduction, see E. K. Rand, "Vade Mecum of Liberal Culture in a Manuscript of
Fleury," *Philological Quarterly* 1 (1922): 276–77 and n. 48.

may have copied the verses from the archetype when it was at court and brought them to the library where MS 8071 was compiled.

Certainly the archetype survived Paul's death for a number of years, whether at court, in private hands, or in a monastic library. Evidently it came to be lodged at a place or with a person known to Adalung; logically, it must have been located somewhere appreciably closer to Arras than to Lorsch, such as Corbie. Therefore, we assume, Adalung borrowed the archetype and had the St-Vaast scriptorium produce a copy for Lorsch.

B, sent off to Lorsch, apparently remained uncopied, for no manuscript descendants survive. The subsequent fortunes of B are unknown,[12] until it appears in the hands of the German scholar Francis Modius in 1585.[13] B probably left Lorsch at least for a time, since the entry was stricken, perhaps in the tenth century, from a catalog of the abbey's books (Bischoff's catalog III*).[14] The manuscript itself bears a note on folio 206v concerning the cult of the eleven thousand virgins, which flourished at Cologne; and, while Modius acquired a number of his manuscripts from the cathedral library in Cologne, he is not known to have acquired any from Lorsch.[15] Bischoff, however, lists B among those books that "sicher oder wahrscheinlich" left Lorsch but were subsequently returned.[16]

The next oldest surviving manuscript of Ennodius, V, dates from the mid-ninth century. But earlier than V, both chronologically and stemmatically, was X, the text of Ennodius (no longer extant) that was used in compiling the Pseudo-Isidorian forgeries.[17] Consideration of Pseudo-Isi-

12. The text of B was employed, in the *editio princeps* by J. Grynaeus (Basel, 1569), to fill lacunae in his base text; see below, at note 90, and Vogel, pp. xlix–l. One does not know where Grynaeus found and used B, however.

13. See Paul Lehmann, *Franciscus Modius als Handschriftenforscher*, Quellen und Untersuchungen zur lateinischen Philologie des Mittelalters 3, 1 (Munich, 1908). Modius must have acquired the volume by 1585, for in that year he wrote to Joachim Camerarius proposing to edit a series of patristic authors, Ennodius among them (Lehmann, p. 33). Modius used Ennodius in his *Pandectae triumphales*, published in 1586, and Ennodius appears in the catalog of Modius's library, 1588. A collation of the *Panegyricus in Theodericum* in B was sent to Jacques Bongars (d. 1613) via the German scholar Fr. Sylburg (d. 1596) and used in Bongars's Lyons edition of that work. In 1593 B and others of his books were sent for safekeeping to Aire (near Nantes), where Modius had been a canon since 1590; and on his death in 1597 they became the property of Richard de Pan, a longtime friend and fellow canon. In 1598 de Pan moved the books to St-Omer, where he was archdeacon; B appears in the catalog of his books made there in 1605. After his death in 1614 the collection dispersed, and B came into the possession of the Jesuits of St-Omer. From St-Omer B went to the Jesuits of Antwerp, and thence to the Burgundian Library, basis of the Royal Library in Brussels (Lehmann, pp. 127–28, 132–33).

14. Bischoff, *Lorsch*, pp. 59 and 85 n. 53.

15. See Lehmann, pp. 92–98 and passim.

16. Bischoff, p. 85 n. 53.

17. See Vogel's stemma, p. xlvi. Elsewhere (pp. xi–xii) Vogel lists the readings that demonstrate X's affiliation with the Ennodius family now preserved in V and its descendants, as well as the indications (p. xlv) that X was one step closer to the archetype than V.

dore's use of X will illuminate the transmission of Ennodius. More unexpected is the fact that the reverse is true: The textual transmission of Ennodius brings one very close indeed to the compilation of the forgeries.

Recent scholarship has imposed some much-needed order on the unruly topic of Pseudo-Isidore.[18] Therefore, two of the questions most pertinent to the transmission of Ennodius now have at least approximate answers: Where and when were the forgeries produced? The considered judgment of Horst Fuhrmann on the location of Pseudo-Isidore has had no serious challenge: somewhere among the opponents of Archbishop Hincmar of Reims (845–82) and the supporters of Ebbo of Reims (d. 851).[19] Moreover, Fuhrmann has narrowed the date of the forgeries to the years between A.D. 847 and 852/57.[20]

The evidence for Pseudo-Isidore's Ennodius and the evidence for the surviving early manuscripts dovetail neatly. B, the oldest surviving Ennodius, was copied from the archetype at Arras, in the archdiocese of Reims, by about 830. Pseudo-Isidore's X, source of the texts that he/they carved out of Ennodius, was also very probably a copy of the archetype, and thus a gemellus of B. When and where X was written is unknown, save that it antedates Pseudo-Isidore's use (847–57); but it was likely written in the ninth century (whether before or after B) and surely in the archdiocese. Finally, virtually at the same time as its use by Pseudo-Isidore, X served as exemplar for Vatican Vat. lat. 3803 (V, discussed below), written also in the archdiocese of Reims, at Corbie.

The amount of material that Pseudo-Isidore borrowed from Ennodius may seem negligible, compared with the whole bulk of the forgeries. The reverse of the coin is a different matter: Compared with contemporary knowledge and use of Ennodius, the amount of material borrowed by Pseudo-Isidore is astonishing. At the time Pseudo-Isidore was making extracts from X, no one else was reading, citing, or copying Ennodius. B was already sequestered at Lorsch. Paul the Deacon and his associates were long dead. Moreover, Paul, although he was presumably instrumental in bringing Ennodius north, actually quoted from the text nothing but some bits of the *Vita Epifani* and the verses at the end of a letter. A half-century later the forger(s), doubtless relying upon the contemporary ignorance of this text, borrowed three works wholesale from Ennodius, the lengthy *Liber apologeticus* (or *Libellus pro synodo,* Vogel's no. 49) and two short epistles (nos. 214, 174), all three of which Pseudo-Isidore at-

18. See especially Horst Fuhrmann, *Einfluss und Verbreitung der pseudoisidorischen Fälschungen,* 3 vols., *MGH Schr.* 24 (Stuttgart, 1972–74); also Schafer Williams, *Codices Pseudo-Isidoriani: A Palaeographico-Historical Study, Mon. iur. can.,* ser. C, Subsidia 3 (New York, 1971).

19. Fuhrmann, 2:595.

20. The double terminus ante quem refers to the first possible (A.D. 852) and the first unmistakable (A.D. 857) citation of the forgeries; Fuhrmann, 1:191. Also, the dates refer to the time of completion, not to the time when the forger(s) began to compile the collection of forgeries.

tributed to Symmachus.[21] In addition, there are some forty brief snippets from Ennodius that Pseudo-Isidore has scattered among the forged decretals attributed to some nineteen other popes.[22] Such ready familiarity with the contents of the Ennodian corpus, quite unmatched earlier, was not even to be approached thereafter until the late twelfth century.

Moreover, with the exception of the previously mentioned couplets in BN lat. 8071, Pseudo-Isidore's manuscript, X, was responsible for all near-contemporary knowledge of, and copies of, Ennodius. And since B had no discernible influence until the late sixteenth century, this implies as well that Pseudo-Isidore bears indirect responsibility for all the subsequent medieval transmission. The immediate influence of Pseudo-Isidore upon the circulation of Ennodius is traceable through Corbie; and for the supposed knowledge of Ennodius, we shall make a detour to Rome.

Corbie, at and just after the middle of the ninth century, saw a sudden if short-lived surge of interest in Ennodius. V, copy of X and progenitor of all surviving Ennodius manuscripts save B, was written at Corbie at or just after midcentury, according to Bischoff;[23] it is recorded in the eleventh- and twelfth-century catalogs of the abbey.[24] (We do not know when or how it eventually left Corbie, to appear in the Vatican collection by the sixteenth century.) For V to have been written at Corbie necessarily implies, of course, that Pseudo-Isidore's X, V's exemplar, must also have been physically present at Corbie, at least during the time when the copy was being made. Though we cannot know the particulars of how and why X was at Corbie, a connection is easily imagined. The fact that the forger(s) sought out a manuscript of Ennodius (for purposes unspecified, one assumes) may have alerted Corbie to the existence and supposed desirability of this text, which the abbey therefore copied, to produce V. V, in turn, served as exemplar for another manuscript of Ennodius, Lambeth Palace 325 (L, discussed below), which Bischoff dates slightly later than V itself; and we assume that L may also have been written at (though presumably not written for) the abbey of Corbie. Finally, Radbert of Corbie, in a letter which has been dated about 856, included an unattributed but unmistakable quotation from Ennodius.[25] Radbert's isolated borrowing, a turn of

21. Paul Hinschius, *Decretales Pseudo-Isidorianae* (Leipzig, 1863), pp. 664–75, 684–86, prints these texts not from manuscripts of Pseudo-Isidore but from Sirmond's edition (1611) of Ennodius. For the variants between Pseudo-Isidore's version of these texts and the original, see Vogel, pp. 48–67 (no. 49), 171–72 (no. 214), and 153–54 (no. 174).

22. See the list in Vogel, p. 333.

23. We thank Bernhard Bischoff for the date and localization of this and the other ninth-century manuscripts of Ennodius (B, L).

24. Leopold Delisle, *Le cabinet des manuscrits*, vol. 2 (Paris, 1874), p. 430 (catalog 2, no. 128), "Ennodii liber"; ibid., p. 438 (catalog 3, no. 243), "Ennodius. Exameron Basilii." The latter entry is a mistaken conflation of two entries, nos. 89 and 128, from catalog 2.

25. For Radbert see *MGH Epp*, 6, Karolini aevi 4 (1925), p. 147, lines 33–34, "Exhausti maties ingenii iam arescit," quoting Ennodius (Vogel 1, lines 13–14), "Exhausti macies ariscat ingenii."

phrase taken from the first paragraph of the first work, suggests only a superficial acquaintance with Ennodius. It is striking to realize, however, that, just after midcentury at Corbie, any one of three manuscripts of Ennodius could conceivably have been Radbert's source: Pseudo-Isidore's X, V, or even L.

The Pseudo-Isidorian connection with this author at Rome explains away a supposedly "lost manuscript" of Ennodius. Aside from Pseudo-Isidore and the Corbie manuscripts (and the six lines in BN lat. 8071), the only traces of Ennodius in the second half of the ninth century—indeed, the only other traces between about 850 and about 1100—are two previously mentioned quotations, in a letter of Pope Nicholas I in 865 and a letter of Pope John VIII in 872/73;[26] almost certainly, both of these were written for the popes by Anastasius Bibliothecarius.[27] The excerpts, both from Ennodius's *Liber apologeticus*, are each attributed by name to "Ennodius, bishop of Pavia."

Circumstantial evidence clearly indicates that Pseudo-Isidore prompted these quotations. As Fuhrmann has shown, Anastasius knew the False Decretals; arguably, he was the first person in Rome who did so.[28] As we have said, the entire *Liber apologeticus* comprised much the largest borrowing from Ennodius by the forger(s). Moreover, the forger(s) prefaced this work with a rubric some ninety words in length, detailing the (fictitious) circumstances of its composition: It reports (says the rubric) a synod held by the authority and in the presence of Pope Symmachus, and the record was written "*at the direction of the deacon Ennodius*, on the authority of the pope and of all the assembled bishops."[29] In the whole of the forgeries, the only mention of Ennodius's name is in connection with this one text, and this one text provides Anastasius's only quotations from Ennodius. Clearly, Anastasius took the rubric to mean that the actual author of the report was Ennodius, an interpretation that suited his needs, as we shall see.

Did Anastasius thereupon seek out a manuscript of Ennodius's works

26. See above at note 9. For Nicholas I see *MGH Epp*, 6, Karol. aev. 4, ep. 88, p. 469, lines 4–5 (Migne, *PL*, 119:942, ep. 86); for John VIII see *MGH Epp*, 7, Karol. aev. 5 (1928), ep. 1 among the fragments, p. 274, lines 16–17 (Migne, *PL*, 126:944, ep. 344).

27. Concerning Anastasius see Girolamo Arnaldi, "Anastasio Bibliotecario," in *Dizionario biografico degli Italiani* 3 (1961): 25–37 and the bibliography cited there. It is generally accepted that Nicholas's letter was drafted by Anastasius—see, e.g., Fuhrmann, 2:325 n. 77; nor is there any doubt that he could have drafted John VIII's letter. We suggest that the inclusion of a reference to Ennodius in the latter changes a possibility into a near certainty.

28. See Fuhrmann, 2:271–72 and the bibliography cited there.

29. See Vogel, p. 48n, "Ab Ennodio diacono precepto et ab auctoritate memorati papae atque omnium episcoporum qui in eandem synodum convenerunt scripta." The first sentence of the immediately following *Actio* (Hinschius, *Decretales*, p. 675)—a report of the so-called Fifth Synod of Symmachus (concerning its source, see Fuhrmann, 1:189 and n. 114)—reiterates that the preceding work, the *Liber apologeticus*, had been drafted by Ennodius, "Libellus . . . ab Ennodio conscriptus."

(a manuscript for whose existence there is no other evidence), in order to quote the original? Surely not, in light of the context and the phrasing of the earlier two quotations by Anastasius. In A.D. 865 Anastasius wrote on the earlier of the two quotations on Nicholas I's authority to the Eastern emperor Michael a lengthy letter condemning the arrogance of the Eastern empire and the Eastern church in refusing to acknowledge the primacy of the bishop of Rome; the letter details the protracted history of this dispute, citing all the supposed precedents. It is in this context that Anastasius writes, "That great confessor of Christ Ennodius, bishop of Pavia—he who was sent to Constantinople by Pope Hormisdas of blessed memory, and who, for the faith of Christ and the good of the Church, more than once suffered innumerable miseries from the savage behavior of the Greeks—recalls from the prophet words pertinent to this matter: 'Shall the axe vaunt itself over him who hews with it, or the saw magnify itself against him who wields it?' (Isa. 10:15)."[30] Anastasius's words obviously display biographical information about Ennodius that he could not have gleaned from Pseudo-Isidore. More to the point, however, is the fact that this information is likewise unavailable in the edition of Ennodius's works. Only one known source reported that an Ennodius, bishop of Pavia, had twice been sent on official errands to Constantinople by Hormisdas, namely, the *Vita Hormisdae* in the *Liber pontificalis*.[31] Happily for Anastasius's purposes, the *Liber pontificalis* enabled him to make the necessary connection: The bishop Ennodius who had gone on legations to the East was one and the same with Pseudo-Isidore's "Ennodius diaconus" who had drafted such an uncompromising justification of papal authority against obstreperous subordinates (nothing to do with Greeks at all). Anastasius, therefore, did not know a manuscript of Ennodius's works but merely cobbled together the quotations from Pseudo-Isidore and the identification from the Life of Hormisdas.

An examination of Pseudo-Isidore has helped to clarify the transmission of Ennodius; conversely, evidence from the transmission of Ennodius contributes two small pieces of information about Pseudo-Isidore. The first involves the much-disputed questions of whether, or when, or to what extent, the forgeries were known in the Rome of Nicholas I. As we have seen, Anastasius's first quotation from "Ennodius" is really a quota-

---

30. *MGH Epp*, 6:469: "Magnus Christi confessor Ennodius, Ticinensis episcopus, qui ab Hormisda apostolicae memoriae Constantinopolim missus innumeras miserias a Graecorum vesania pro Christi fide et statu ecclesiae non semel pertulit, ex propheta de his meminit: 'Numquid gloriabitur securis contra eum, qui secat in ea? Aut exaltabitur serra contra eum, qui trahit eam?'"

31. Louis Duchesne, *Le Liber pontificalis*, 2d ed., 3 vols. (Paris, 1955–57), 1:269, lines 4–16. Paul the Deacon's *Historia Romana* also mentions that Ennodius was sent to Constantinople by Hormisdas: Hans Droysen, ed., *Eutropi Breviarium ab urbe condita cum . . . Pauli Landolfique additamentis*, MGH Auct. ant. 2 (Berlin, 1879), p. 217, lines 16–22 (bk. 16.5). Only the *Liber pontificalis*, however, mentions two trips for Ennodius, the source of Anastasius's "non semel."

tion from Pseudo-Isidore, solid evidence that the forgeries were available in Rome by September 865. The second matter lies closer to the creation of the forgeries themselves. That Radbert of Corbie in about 856 could quote from a manuscript of Ennodius—whether Pseudo-Isidore's X, or the copy of X, or the copy of that copy—establishes a terminus ante quem for the presence of X at Corbie. This tallies with the fact, previously established by Fuhrmann and others, that the library and scriptorium of Corbie were very much up to date in the literature of the forgeries, on the one hand possibly serving as source of some of the texts used by Pseudo-Isidore (e.g., the Corbie Ecclesiasticus) and, on the other, producing probably the oldest surviving manuscripts of the forgeries themselves (Vatican Vat. lat. 630 and Leipzig Universitätsbibliothek II.7).[32] Ironically enough, Radbert's casual quotation from Ennodius provides the earliest fixed point in the interchanges between Corbie and Pseudo-Isidore's circle, wherever the latter may have been.

It is illuminating, to studies both of the transmission of Ennodius and of Pseudo-Isidore's milieu, to establish that X was at Corbie by 856. It would be still more helpful if one could say not only where X went, but where it came from. The crucial evidence, X itself, is unfortunately lacking. Let us examine instead some possibilities that might fit with the evidence that does survive. We have assumed, following Vogel, that X was a gemellus of B, both having been copied from the archetype. It is surely not impossible that, in the early decades of the ninth century, the archetype of Ennodius belonged to St-Vaast of Arras where B was written; and perhaps X was also written there, and borrowed from there by Pseudo-Isidore. A much more plausible suggestion, however, is that the archetype belonged to Arras's more cosmopolitan neighbor, Corbie. Corbie was the most important abbey and library in the archdiocese of Reims in the late eighth and early ninth centuries. It is known to have been the source of texts represented in the library of St-Vaast;[33] it may, as well, have provided the exemplar for Adalung's Ennodius, B.

With this as a working hypothesis, further suggestions fall into line: (1) X would have been written at Corbie itself, perhaps in the early decades of the ninth century; the purpose would have been to replace the archetype, written presumably in a pre-Caroline script dating from A.D. 782 at the latest, with a readable text in the newly evolved Caroline script, whose development owed much to the Corbie scriptorium. (2) Again, we have suggested above that Pseudo-Isidore's seeking out a text of Ennodius must somehow have spurred the Corbie monks to make a copy of that text. With X hypothetically located at Corbie, the explanation is simplified.

32. See especially Fuhrmann, 1:178–79 and 1:195–96 n. 1; see also his index s.v. "Corbie."

33. See Philip Grierson, "La bibliothèque de St-Vaast d'Arras au XIIe siècle," *Revue bénédictine* 52 (1940): 117 n. 1.

Corbie in the time of Hadoard was intensely active in the collection and circulation of all sorts of literature, classical, patristic, and Carolingian;[34] and virtually any notable ecclesiastic in the archdiocese (and many well outside those boundaries) could have had contact with this busy cross-roads, borrowing books from Corbie to copy and visiting the abbey in person. If *X*, perhaps a book of the previous generation, was borrowed by Pseudo-Isidore from Corbie itself, the scriptorium would have made the abbey a new copy, V. Given V's early date, it is conceivable that V was in fact copied before *X* was used by the forger(s).

This suggestion concerning the home of the archetype and of *X*, while possible and even plausible, is of course only speculation. We must leave it to others to consider the implications of this hypothesis regarding the methods by which, and the place(s) at which, the forgeries were created, and to determine on that basis whether the suggestion is useful and usable for Pseudo-Isidore scholarship. In terms of the transmission of Ennodius, however, the hypothesis makes very good sense ideed.

We can now turn to the descendants of V, and ask how the text of Ennodius reached the twelfth century. Through what routes did the books of the ninth century pass to the libraries of the twelfth?

The mid-ninth-century V engendered at least two copies, only one of which survives. This is Lambeth Palace 325 (L), shown by Vogel to be a direct copy of V.[35] Though not in an identified Corbie script, L is written in a good small northwest Frankish minuscule; according to Bischoff, it cannot be dated more precisely than the third or possibly fourth quarter of the ninth century. Sometime before the mid-twelfth century L was taken to England, where it came to rest at Durham Cathedral. It can be identified, from the opening words of its second folio, with number 17 in the catalog of cathedral books made in 1391.[36] There is no record of how or when L came to Durham, though we assume that it came after the Conquest; the list of French personal names on L's flyleaf (fol. lv), which M. R. James assigns to the eleventh century, would support that assumption.[37] L embodies a shift in this study; itself a product of the Carolingian interest in Ennodius, L's descendant belongs to the twelfth century, when interest in Ennodius revives.

34. See Bernhard Bischoff, "Hadoardus and the Manuscripts of Classical Authors from Corbie," in *Didascaliae: Studies in Honor of Anselm M. Albareda*, ed. S. Prete (New York, 1961), pp. 39–57 and the bibliography cited there.

35. Montague R. James and Claude Jenkins, *A Descriptive Catalogue of the Manuscripts in the Library of Lambeth Palace* (Cambridge, 1930–32), pp. 426–27. See Vogel, pp. xxxviii–xxxix.

36. Roger A. B. Mynors, *Durham Cathedral Manuscripts to the End of the Twelfth Century* (Oxford, 1939), p. 26, no. 17; James Raines, *Catalogi veteres librorum ecclesiae cathedralis Dunelm.*, Surtees Society Publications 7 (London, 1838), pp. 32A (ter), 109A (quater).

37. James and Jenkins, pp. 426–27.

Presumably after L had reached Durham, it was copied to produce Berlin, Staatsbibliothek Phillipps 1715 (Rose 172), Y, written in an English hand of the mid-twelfth century.[38] Y was given to the Cistercians of Fountains Abbey in Yorkshire by the physician Atenulf: "Liber sancte marie de fontan. quem dedit ei pro redemptione anime sue magister Atenulfus medicus. Anima eius requiescat in pace, amen."[39] Atenulf is otherwise unknown.[40] Y left Fountains at the Dissolution in 1536 and reemerged at the Jesuit Collège de Clermont in Paris later in the sixteenth century. In the early seventeenth century Y belonged to Nicholas Fabri, who lent it to Sirmond for use in his edition of 1611.[41]

Aside from Y, there are no surviving English manuscripts of Ennodius. There are reports of manuscripts in the catalogs of two English monastic libraries, namely, in the early fourteenth-century catalog of Christ Church Canterbury and in the fifteenth-century catalog of Leicester.[42] Given the links of Christ Church with Bec and the lateness of the Leicester record, these manuscripts may represent the Continental tradition; it is certainly possible, however, that one or both were descendants of L.

The other surviving manuscripts of Ennodius are Continental, descended from a lost copy of V called α. Like its gemellus L, α produced no surviving descendants until the twelfth century; whether α was also, like L, another ninth-century manuscript disseminated from Corbie we of course cannot say. By the twelfth century, at any rate, α seems to have been located at a place more central to the scholarly activity of that period than was Corbie. At least four twelfth- and thirteenth-century manuscripts descend from α, and it is probably also both the ancestor of the Ennodius (now lost) that belonged to Philip of Bayeux and the ultimate source of the various collections of extracts from Ennodius. An examination of these suggests where α may have been.

38. Valentin Rose, *Verzeichniss der lateinischen Handschriften der Königlichen Bibliothek zu Berlin* i (Berlin, 1893), pp. 387–89, no. 172; Vogel, p. xl ("Cheltenhamensis 1715").

39. Printed by Rose, p. 387. The ex libris dates from the twelfth (Vogel) or thirteenth (Rose) century.

40. See Ernest Wickersheimer, *Dictionnaire biographique des médecins en France au Moyen Age*, 2 vols. (1936; reprint Paris, 1979), 2:9, and ibid., vol. 3, ed. Danielle Jacquart (Paris, 1979), p. 12; Charles H. Talbot and E. A. Hammond, *Medical Practitioners in Medieval England: A Biographical Register* (London, 1965), p. 19. Both Jacquart and Talbot and Hammond explicitly discount the possibility that the Santa Maria de Fontanis of the ex libris was Fountains in Yorkshire, rather than a Continental house (Wickersheimer's suggestion), ignoring the fact that the text (Y) is a direct copy of the Durham Cathedral manuscript (L). Atenulf is not mentioned by Edward J. Kealey, *Medieval Medicus: A Social History of Anglo-Norman Medicine* (Baltimore, 1981).

41. Rose, pp. 387–88. Concerning Fabri and Sirmond's edition, see note 93 below.

42. Montague R. James, *The Ancient Libraries of Canterbury and Dover* (Cambridge, 1903), p. 31, no. 125; and see also note 61 below. Idem, *Catalogue of the Library of Leicester Abbey* (Leicester, [1941?]), p. 129, no. 567 (reprinted from *Transactions of the Leicestershire Archaeological Society* 19 [1936–37]: 111–61, 377–440, and 21 [1939–41]: 1–88).

The oldest surviving descendant of α is T, a curious three-part text now in Troyes MSS 658, 461, and 469, written by the Cistercians of Clairvaux in the second half of the twelfth century.[43] The three manuscripts contain, respectively, Ennodius's works 1–119, 120–406, and 407–68; and although each of the three parts was written by a different scribe, the quire numbering reveals an intent to bind them together as one volume.[44] Inexplicably, they were instead each bound in a different volume comprised primarily of other texts. A further oddity is the fact that the Clairvaux text has omitted—deliberately, one assumes—virtually all of Ennodius's verse. The three volumes were still at Clairvaux in 1472, to be recorded in Pierre Virey's catalog (Clairvaux E.45, I.22, I.23).[45] T was doubtless the source of the extracts from Ennodius found in two later Clairvaux manuscripts, the passage quoted in the thirteenth century by a Frater Dionysius, in Troyes MS 1761, fol. 144 (Clairvaux L.72), and the excerpts made in 1471 by Jean de Voivre, prior of Clairvaux, in Troyes MS 1452.[46] An earlier set of extracts from Ennodius appears on folio 20r–v of a short patristic florilegium written in the late twelfth century at the Cistercian abbey of Vauclair (Laon MS 176); since Vauclair was a daughter house of Clairvaux, it is probable that these excerpts also come from T.

A second Cistercian descendant of α is E, Escorial D.3.22, a thirteenth-century manuscript that belonged to St. Stephen of Fossa Nuova in Rome, a Cistercian house of the Clairvaux family.[47] According to its ex libris, E was given to the Roman Cistercians by a "d. Pertussus," about whom nothing else is known. E is not descended from T; but their textual filiation is so close that Hartel's apparatus has taken E to stand for T in editing the verses that T omits.[48]

---

43. *Catalogue général des manuscrits des bibliothèques publiques des départements*, 4° ser., vol. 2 (Paris, 1855), pp. 275, 207, and 209, respectively.

44. See Hartel's edition, p. v. The text of Ennodius is not the only indication of a mistake in Clairvaux's binding of these three manuscripts. The works of Rupert of Deutz, bound at the head of MSS 461 and 469, were also meant to follow in sequence; fol. 1 of MS 461 begins with the fifteen lines (now crossed out) that were missing from the end of Rupert's *De divinis officiis* in MS 469. (The lines were added to MS 469 in another hand, evidently by the expedient of scraping away the first fifteen lines of the portion of Ennodius bound in that manuscript.) We thank J. F. Genest for this information. Hartel and Vogel concur that the three parts of T derive from a single, presumably whole, exemplar.

45. André Vernet, *La bibliothèque de l'abbaye de Clairvaux du XIIe au XVIIIe siècle*, vol. 1, *Catalogues et répertoires* (Paris, 1979), pp. 115, no. 412 (E.45), and 162, nos. 752 (I.21) and 753 (I.22).

46. "Frater Dionysius" is otherwise unknown; see Vernet, p. 191, no. 987. MS 1452 is described, with the shelf number O b XIII, in the Clairvaux catalog of Mathurin de Cangey, ca. 1551; edited by Vernet, p. 545, no. 1432. Concerning Jean de Voivre, "sans doute aussi bibliothécaire de l'abbaye," see Vernet, pp. 33–34 and the bibliography cited there.

47. G. Antolín, *Catálogo de los códices latinos de la Real biblioteca del Escorial*, vol. 1 (Madrid, 1910), pp. 499–502.

48. See Hartel, p. vii, and notes to the edition passim.

Richard H. Rouse and Mary A. Rouse

The making of the two manuscripts E and T is explicable in terms of Cistercian emphasis on the Fathers.[49] We are reminded that Y, the only surviving Ennodius of English origin, belonged to the Cistercian house of Fountains. Despite the stemmatic and geographic distance between Y and TE, the motive for their circulation and survival was the same.

The twelfth-century Loire schools—Vendôme, Chartres, Orléans—are the other major element in the twelfth- and thirteenth-century circulation of Ennodius. Focusing on a training in the *ars dictaminis*, the schools drew on model letters, such as those of the younger Pliny, Symmachus, Sidonius, and also Ennodius. Because of his difficult style, however, Ennodius in particular was much better known at the schools in florilegia than in whole texts. In contrast with monastic florilegia, the school's florilegia were designed strictly for use as examples of epistolary style and as collections of sententious remarks for use in composition. The school florilegia not only account for the main way Ennodius was read in the Middle Ages but they also witness the existence of a copy of α or α itself in the Orléanais.

For Ennodius, the earliest and most significant collection is the *Florilegium Angelicum*, which survives in at least twenty copies.[50] The list of its other contents indicates both the company Ennodius kept and the purposes for which he was excerpted in the dictaminal schools: excerpts from Macrobius's *Saturnalia*, the *Proverbia philosophorum*, the epistles of Jerome and Gregory I, the works of Apuleius, Pliny the Younger's epistles, Cicero's shorter orations, Sidonius's epistles, the *De beneficiis* and epistles of Seneca, the *Sententiae philosophorum*, and *Praeceptae Pithagorae*, and *Aenigmata Aristotilis*, Cicero's Tusculan disputations, Aulus Gellius, Cicero's Verrine orations, Martin of Braga's *Formula honestae vitae*, the Pseudo-Plautine *Querolus*, and Censorinus's *De die natali*. The *Florilegium Angelicum* was compiled at Orléans just after the middle of the twelfth century, evidently dedicated to Pope Alexander III, and it provided Gerald of Wales, its best-known user, with the knowledge of several classical authors.[51] Included in this collection, between the excerpts from the Verrines and those from Martin of Braga, is a lengthy set of extracts from virtually all of Ennodius's prose works, filling from four to six folios in the manuscripts. Among his other borrowings from the *Florilegium Angelicum*, Gerald of Wales took one passage from Ennodius

---

49. See Jean Leclercq, *The Love of Learning and the Desire for God*, trans. C. Misrahi (New York, 1961), pp. 111–38, esp. 118–22.

50. Concerning this work see Richard H. Rouse and Mary A. Rouse, "The *Florilegium Angelicum*: Its Origin, Content, and Influence," in *Medieval Learning and Literature: Essays Presented to Richard William Hunt*, ed. J. J. G. Alexander and M. T. Gibson (Oxford, 1976), pp. 66–114.

51. See André A. Goddu and Richard H. Rouse, "Gerald of Wales and the *Florilegium Angelicum*," *Speculum* 52 (1977): 488–521.

which he cited in five different works: "Ut ait Enodius, 'Ruina preceden-
tium posteros docet et cautio est semper in reliquum lapsus anterior.'"[52]
Some of the collections of extracts from Ennodius were doubtless independent efforts. That is the case for Paris, BN lat. 2638, fols. 24–31v, a
single quire (bound now into a collection) written in France in the late
twelfth or early thirteenth century. Folios 24–31 contain a selection of the
letters of Sidonius; on folio 31 is a brief "Excerptum ex quadam historia"
(beg. "Eodem tempore quo Galli Senones duce Brenno . . ."). The rest of
folio 31r and all of 31v contain five letters of Ennodius, to Decoratus (ep.
4.17, Vogel 149), Agapitus (4.16, Vogel 146), Apollinaris (4.19, Vogel 151),
Boethius (6.6, Vogel 271), and Avienus (8.2, Vogel 376). A sample collation
reveals only that these five letters were copied from a manuscript of the α
family.[53] Probably the scholar who put together this little quire of epistolary models made his selection from Ennodius on the basis of the supposed
recipients, with his chronology slightly askew, mistaking Agapitus for
Pope Agapetus I (A.D. 535–36), Apollinaris for Sidonius himself (d. 487),
and Avienus for the fabulist Avianus/Avienus (fl. A.D. 400), while correctly taking Boethius for the author of the Consolatio. (The writer's
interest in "Decoratus" is a mystery.)
Most of the late twelfth- and early thirteenth-century florilegia of Ennodius, however, seem to be interrelated, in a way not yet discovered. We
know of five, and there are doubtless others: Bourges, Bibl. mun. 400, fols.
126v–133, s. xii[2], belonged to the cathedral of Bourges;[54] Vatican, Ottob.
lat. 687, fols. 13–28, s. xii[2], was also written in France;[55] Oxford, Bodleian

52. And in one of the five, Gerald's *Speculum duorum*, he uses the passage twice, at
1.295 and at 2.1207; Goddu and Rouse, p. 513 (cf. Vogel, p. 100, line 26). See also Goddu
and Rouse, p. 512.
53. For example, at 143.22 (= page and line of Vogel's edition) it has the correct
"vestri silentia" with V against B's erroneous "vestris laetitia"; thus, it is not from B. At
143.2 it reads "esse lingua" against "lingua esse" of CP in error, and at 143.7 "quid"
against "quod" CP in error; hence, it is not from β (descendant of α and common
ancestor of CP, discussed below). MS 2638 agrees with T in error (against BVL) at 143.25
"rancessit" and at 144.4 "si estis mei." The editions do not report readings of T's gemelli
E and León MS 33 (discussed below), so that we do not know whether these errors are
common to all descendants of α.
54. *Catalogue général des manuscrits des bibliothèques publiques de France: Départements*, vol. 4 (Paris, 1886), p. 91.
55. *Les manuscrits de la reine de Suède au Vatican: Réédition du catalogue de
Montfaucon et cotes actuelles*, Studi e testi 238 (Vatican City, 1964), p. 96, no. 1699.
Curiously, Vogel (pp. xlii–xliii) treats this manuscript as a fragmentary full text and
gives it a siglum (O); and he suggests that the extracts in     come directly from L, the
Durham manuscript, stating that O and L are joined "ex lectionibus quibusdam." Since
he does not specify these readings, one cannot assess the strength of the connection.
Vogel's other arguments for O's direct dependence on L are unconvincing: that O omits
Ennodius's *carmina* because they are marked in L with the Greek letters α–ω; and that
O also omits those *epistulae* which in L bear the same α–ω marks. This overlooks the
facts that none of the florilegia, of whatever source, include the *carmina*, and that, in

Library Bodl. 678, fols. 56v–60, s. xiii in., was written in England and belonged to Dover Priory;[56] London, British Library Royal 8 E.iv, fols. 1–49, s. xiii[1], probably belonged to the Cistercian abbey of Rievaulx in Yorkshire;[57] and Brussels, BR 10098–10105, fols. 29–37, s. xiii[1], was written in France and belonged to the Liège Carthusians in the fifteenth century.[58] In addition, there are eleven excerpts from Ennodius in Vincent of Beauvais's *Speculum historiale,* about 1244.[59]

The five manuscripts begin with extracts from Ennodius's *Dictio I,* the first work in the corpus.[60] In four of the manuscripts (all save Bodl. 678) the first extract begins "Usu rerum . . ." (1.6 = page and line of Vogel's edition); their second extract, beginning "Superflua scribere . . ." (1.11), is the first excerpt in Bodl. 678 (as well as the first of Vincent's handful). Thereafter, the five continue for a while almost in step: "Verborum abundantiam . . ." (1.20), "Formido facessat . . ." (1.23), "Sine culpa . . ." (1.25), "Marcida est . . ." (1.29), "Libet dicendi . . ." (2.2). At an undetermined point shortly thereafter the contents of the florilegia of Ennodius diverge. The early *Florilegium Angelicum,* mentioned above, also includes excerpts that begin like the seven listed here, though the wording varies from that of the five later manuscripts. Of the five manuscripts, most will omit one or two of these seven, and most will insert one or two additional *sententiae;* and the length of the individual extracts may vary widely from one manuscript to another. The overall length of the Ennodian florilegia also varies considerably, from a fairly brief collection (four folios) in Bodl. 678 to the forty-nine folios in Royal 8 E.iv. Moreover, an initial survey shows that most, if not all, of the five manuscripts each contains material not found in any of the other four.

We must leave the sorting out of this complex tradition to others. On present evidence, we suggest the possibility that all the individual florilegia used, as one source, a collection of extracts which circulated at the

---

addition to the few marked portions, O also omits the vast majority of the unmarked prose available in L.

56. Falconer Madan and Herbert H. E. Craster, *A Summary Catalogue of Western Manuscripts in the Bodleian Library,* vol. 2, 1 (Oxford, 1922), p. 443, no. 2595.

57. George F. Warner and Julius P. Gilson, *Catalogue of Western Manuscripts in the Old Royal and King's Collections,* vol. 1 (London, 1921), p. 252. This is evidently the volume that John Leland saw at Rievaulx in the sixteenth century; see Neil R. Ker, *Medieval Libraries of Great Britain,* 2d ed. (London, 1964), p. 159.

58. Van den Gheyn, *Catalogue des manuscrits,* no. 1334. See also Hubert Silvestre, "Notices et extraits des manuscrits . . . 10098–105 . . . de la Bibliothèque Royale de Bruxelles," *Sacris erudiri* 5 (1953): 187–89. This small florilegium (forty-two folios), with extracts from Solinus, Fulgentius, Cicero, Claudian, and Horace, also includes two segments from the *Florilegium Angelicum,* but the latter was not its source for the extracts from Ennodius. See Rouse and Rouse, "*Florilegium Angelicum,*" p. 102.

59. Vincent of Beauvais, *Speculum historiale* (Douai, 1624), bk. 21.28.

60. Exceptionally, in Brussels 10098–10105 the Ennodian section begins (fol. 29) with excerpts from Ennodius's second work (carm. 1.6, Vogel's no. 2); the excerpts from *Dictio I* appear at the very end, fols. 36v–37, beginning "Usu rerum. . . ."

schools of dictamen on the Loire, and that many of the compilers supplemented this with material taken from a full text of Ennodius. For example, Royal 8 E.iv, probably from Rievaulx, might have derived its additional material from Y, the Ennodius at nearby Fountains; and Bodl. 678 from Dover, a priory of Christ Church Canterbury, may include some additions from the text of Ennodius (now lost) recorded in the early fourteenth-century Christ Church catalog.[61] Certainly, there must have been a manuscript of Ennodius, perhaps α itself, at Orléans, where the *Florilegium Angelicum* was compiled. Moreover, a manuscript remained available to the mid-thirteenth-century scholar who filled the margins of his copy of Papias, Bern MS 276, with lexicographical references from texts that he found in and around Orléans; among them are twenty-four examples of usage taken from Ennodius.[62]

Ennodius was known to medieval writers through florilegia far more than through whole manuscripts. From this text, too difficult to be read as a whole yet interesting for style, energetic compilers snipped out the useful portions and assembled them with cuttings from other texts in florilegia.

From the schools Ennodius occasionally made his way back into the old abbey and cathedral libraries, via chancery clerks sent off to schools such as Orléans to be trained in *dictamen*. The Ennodius listed in the mid-twelfth-century catalog of Bec is a good example.[63] It was given to Bec in 1164 by Philip, bishop of Bayeux. Philip, an able Norman clerk, rose rapidly in the service of the Angevin monarchy. He amassed a private library of approximately 130 manuscripts, probably the largest recorded from the twelfth century. Among these books are a number which must have come from either Chartres or Orléans, such as the younger Pliny's letters, Cicero's *Partitiones oratoriae* and *De finibus bonorum et malorum*, and Pomponius Mela's *Cosmographia*.[64] Ennodius, available at

61. James, *Ancient Libraries*, p. 31, no. 125 (catalog of Christ Church, Canterbury); Bodl. 678 appears in the Dover catalog (ibid., p. 418, no. 199, and p. 452, no. 119) under the name of the first work in the codex, the *Elucidarius*.

62. Concerning this annotator's activities see Michael D. Reeve and Richard H. Rouse, "New Light on the Transmission of Donatus's *Commentum Terentii*," *Viator* 9 (1978): 235–49, and Richard H. Rouse, "Florilegia and Latin Classical Authors in Twelfth- and Thirteenth-Century Orléans," *Viator* 10 (1979): 131–60, esp. pp. 142–50.

63. Becker, *Catalogi*, p. 201, no. 86:55, "In alio [volumine] Ennodius."

64. Concerning the books of Philip of Bayeux see Rouse and Rouse, "*Florilegium Angelicum*," 85 and n. 3; Richard H. Rouse and Mary A. Rouse, "The Medieval Circulation of Cicero's 'Posterior Academics' and the *De finibus bonorum et malorum*," in *Medieval Scribes, Manuscripts and Libraries: Essays Presented to N. R. Ker*, ed. M. B. Parkes and A. G. Watson (London, 1978), pp. 333–67, esp. pp.346–55; Catherine Gormley, Mary A. Rouse, and Richard H. Rouse, "The Medieval Circulation of the *De Chorographia* of Pomponius Mela," *Mediaeval Studies* 46 (1984): 266–320; and Richard H. Rouse and Mary A. Rouse, "*Potens in opere et sermone*: Philip, Bishop of Bayeux, and His Books," in *The Classics in the Middle Ages*, ed. A. Bernardo and S. Levin, forthcoming.

Orléans, should be added to the list. While nothing is known of Philip's early life, it is a reasonable assumption that, as a future chancery clerk, he would have passed through the schools at Orléans.

Philip's manuscript is probably the copy referred to in the only known medieval literary assessment of Ennodius. In 1160 Arnulf, bishop of Lisieux, wrote to Henry of Pisa, "I am sending you the book of Ennodius. It belongs to someone else, but if you decide that you like it, I shall have a transcript of it sent to you as soon as possible."[65] Henry of Pisa, a Cistercian, was cardinal-priest of Sts. Nereus and Achilleus and a papal legate. Peter Classen has suggested that, as legate to France for Alexander III early in 1160, Henry may have spent some time at the Cistercian house of Fontenay in Burgundy; for Fontenay somehow came into possession of the manuscript of a treatise on the Psalms, now Paris, BN lat. 4236, that its author Gerhoch of Reichersberg had presented to Henry two years earlier.[66] Perhaps Henry had heard of Ennodius through his Cistercian connections at Fontenay; or perhaps, instead, he had come across the name, and copious extracts from the text, of Ennodius in the *Florilegium Angelicum* at the court of Alexander III, its presumed dedicatee. Whatever the cause, the curiosity about Ennodius originated with Henry, for Arnulf remarks that he himself had never seen the work until Henry mentioned it. The letter continues with the famous diatribe on Ennodius's turgid style ("Once having seen it, I was amazed that an author should have had the gall to publish it, or that others should have been disposed to make copies of it," etc.), concluding that the perpetrator should more aptly be called "Innodius" (complicated, convoluted) than "Ennodius" (open, plain). Philip of Bayeux was a fellow Norman bishop, whom Arnulf knew well, as witness his strongly supportive letter on Philip's behalf to Eugenius III (ca. 1153).[67] Very likely, then, Philip was the "someone else" from whom Arnulf borrowed a copy of Ennodius to fill Henry of Pisa's request, and Henry must thereafter have returned it, for it was included in Philip's bequest to Bec four years later. One cannot say whether Henry, in the teeth of Arnulf's scathing critique, had a copy of Ennodius made for himself, but at least there is no trace of such a copy.

The third surviving descendant of α is probably a product of the same Arts Faculty milieu. León Cathedral MS 33 (S) was not known to Hartel and Vogel and is hitherto unreported.[68] The León Ennodius is a small

65. "De cetero, librum Ennodii uobis mitto, alienum quidem, sed si experientia uestra probauerit, transcriptum cum quanta fieri poterit festinatione remittam." The letter is edited by Frank Barlow, *The Letters of Arnulf of Lisieux*, Camden Ser. 3, vol. 61 (London, 1939), pp. 36–38, ep. 27; also printed by Vogel, pp. lx–lxi.

66. In 1679 this manuscript was purchased from Fontenay by the agents of Colbert (no. 4841). See Peter Classen, "Aus der Werkstatt Gerhochs von Reichersberg," pt. 3, "Das im Original erhaltene Widmungs-Exemplar einer Streitschrift: cod. Paris BN lat. 4236," *DA* 23 (1967): 47–56, esp. p. 53.

67. Barlow, pp. 11–12, ep. 8.

68. Zacarias García Villada, *Catálogo de los códices y documentos de la catedral de León* (Madrid, 1919), pp. 62–63.

book, 8½" × 6", about the size of an open hand. It contains thirty long lines per page, ruled with a lead point. S is written in a well-formed small text hand, with attention to serifs and finishing strokes. Space has been left for initials, which were never entered; the texts for the rubrics, also left uncompleted, are entered vertically in the outer margins. The text is carefully punctuated, double *ii* is stroked, and words are properly divided and hyphenated at line ends. S looks to have been written in France. The only distinctive letters are the majuscule *A*, which is reminiscent of the Anglo-Norman initial leaning *A*; the terminal tall *A* occasionally rising above the line; and the *r*, with its nose invariably touching the following letter. The manuscript was written toward the end of the twelfth century—at the beginning of the last quarter, to judge from the absence of ampersands and the rare use of the cedilla. The occasional paragraph marks in gibbet form also suggest a date in the 1170s or 1180s.

A collation of folios 1–10 of the León manuscript provides preliminary information regarding its place on Vogel's stemma: (1) S, as one would expect, descends ultimately from Corbie's V; (2) its agreement in error with other of V's progeny shows that S must derive from α; (3) S is not descended, however, from any of the known surviving manuscripts.[69] It seems likely that S was brought to León by a member of the cathedral or diocesan clergy who, like Philip of Bayeux of Arnulf of Lisieux, had been to Orléans to receive his training in *dictamen*. The number of late twelfth- and thirteenth-century books of northern French origin found in the chapter libraries of northern Spanish cathedral libraries is significant, and documents a close involvement in the intellectual currents of northern Europe.

In addition to the surviving T, E, and S, there was at least one other independent descendant of α, called β, which is known from its two fourteenth-century descendants. The first of these, Vatican Reg. lat. 129, fols. 11–12, 26–36, 55–57, 79–80 (C), contains a selection of works from the corpus: the lives of Epiphanius and Antonius, and Ennodius's "Eucharisticum." C was written by two scribes, probably in Italy or southern France.[70] Its early provenance is unknown. The second manuscript, Vienna, Nationalbibliothek 745 (P), belonged to Adalbertus Ranconis de Ericinio, rector of the University of Prague, in the middle of the fourteenth century. Adalbertus, a master of arts at Paris and a fellow of the Sorbonne, is known to have traveled in the West, purchasing books in Paris and Avignon and sending them to Prague.[71] While β may, like its gemelli,

69. The following examples must suffice (page and line numbers from Vogel's edition): 5.7 adnitente (anni- VL) BVL, annuente αS; 6 v. 11 sic BVL, si αS; 6 v. 33 quatiam V (*recte*), quantiam B, que iam αS. S does not repeat the individual errors of T, the only surviving descendant of α old enough to have been the source of S; e.g., 5.7 me *om*. T, *hab*. S; 5.15 nescire T, nesciere S (*recte*); 5.21 radicem T, indicem S (*recte*).

70. André Wilmart, *Codices Reginenses latini*, vol. 1 (Vatican City, 1937), pp. 304–5.

71. Concerning Adalbert's book collecting in the West, see Richard H. Rouse, "The Early Library of the Sorbonne," *Scriptorium* 21 (1967): 42 n. 3. Ivan Hlaváček, "Studie k

have been written in the Orléanais, we can surmise from its progeny that by the early fourteenth century it had been carried south, perhaps to or by way of Avignon. Catalog entries indicate that there was a text of Ennodius in the papal library at Avignon by 1369 at latest.[72] While place and date are suggestive, there is of course no way to know whether the papal manuscript was related to β, or to say anything at all about its textual filiation. The *secundo folio* reference confirms that this was something other than the ninth-century V, which eventually reached the papal library. The Avignon manuscript is last mentioned in the catalog of 1411.

One final manuscript of Ennodius, undated but possibly medieval, survived the centuries to perish by fire in 1870. This was Strasbourg, Bibl. univ. C.V.26, known only from its entry in the catalog: "Ennodii et Symmachi epistolae, mbr. 4."[73]

Many texts, Christian as well as pagan, that had survived from late antiquity in a single manuscript and had enjoyed only a minimal circulation through the long medieval centuries, were then rediscovered and enthusiastically proliferated by the Italian humanists. The transmission of Ennodius, which thus far has followed the pattern, unexpectedly pulls up short. Only four surviving manuscripts of Ennodius were written in fourteenth- and fifteenth-century Italy, all descendants of a single manuscript (δ)[74] of the α tradition.[75] Paris, BN lat. 2177 was written in Italy in the fourteenth century.[76] In 1426 it is recorded in the *Consignatio librorum* of the dukes of Milan.[77] Textually akin to it is Milan, Ambros. D

Dějinám Knihoven v Čeakém Státě v Době Předhusitské," *Acta Universitatis Carolinae: Historia Universitatis Carolinae Pragensis* 6, 2 (1965): 60–61 edits a list of books Adalbert purchased in Avignon and sent to Prague.

72. Franz Ehrle, S.J., *Historia bibliothecae romanorum pontificum*, vol. 1 (Rome, 1890), p. 354, catalog of 1369, no. 879: "Item epistole Ennodii, cooperte corio viridi, que incipiunt in secundo folio: *tentarum*, et finiunt in penultimo folio: *subripere*"; and Anneliese Maier, in *Archivum historiae pontificiae*, vol. 1 (1963), p. 119, catalog of 1411, no. 64, with virtually identical wording.

73. Vogel, p. xliv.

74. Perhaps δ is descended by way of β; understandably, with the source of this half of the tradition in hand (V), editors do not bother to record *variae lectiones* from the *recentiores*, except for a selection (see the next note).

75. For the readings that demonstrate the filiation of these texts with α, see Vogel, p. xliii.

76. Philippe Lauer, *Bibliothèque Nationale: Catalogue général des manuscrits latins*, vol. 2 (Paris, 1940), p. 354.

77. Elisabeth Pellegrin, *La bibliothèque des Visconti et des Sforza, ducs de Milan, au XVe siècle*, Publications de l'Institut de Recherche et d'Histoire des Textes 5 (Paris, 1955), p. 214, no. 639. Vogel, p. xliii, mistakenly names N. Fabri as possessor of this manuscript; see note 38 above. It is this manuscript, in the ducal library at Pavia, and not a potentially early text from the cathedral chapter's library, which is recorded in the catalog designated by Manitius as "Pavia 1431" (a misreading of the date "MCCCCX-XVI"); see Max Manitius, *Handschriften antiker Autoren in mittelalterlichen Bibliothekskatalogen*, ed. Karl Manitius, Zentralblatt für Bibliothekswesen Beiheft 67 (1935; reprint Wiesbaden, 1968), p. 300.

117 sup. (F), written for Francesco Pizzolpasso, archbishop of Milan 1435–43;[78] F was copied from an exemplar whose quires were out of order.[79] The other descendants of δ come from an intermediate in which the sequence of the works had been rearranged in order to group them according to literary type—first the prose works, followed by the letters and concluding with "Epitaphia et distica."[80] The earliest of these rearranged manuscripts, and perhaps the earliest of all the surviving Italian manuscripts, is Florence, BN Conv. soppr. I.vi.29 (M), written in the third quarter of the fourteenth century.[81] M belonged to Pietro da Moglio (d. 1383) in Bologna. It was acquired from his estate by Coluccio Salutati sometime between 1385, when he wrote a letter requesting it, and 1394, when he mentions the manuscript as his. From Salutati M passed to Cosimo de' Medici and thence to the library of San Marco.[82] A second rearranged corpus is Vatican, Urb. lat. 61 (U), written in Italy in the second half of the fifteenth century; it belonged to Duke Federigo of Urbino (d. 1482).[83] Finally, one might note a belated representative of this rearranged tradition, Munich Clm 110 (D), written in the middle of the sixteenth century.[84]

Three Renaissance manuscripts contain extracts from Ennodius: Escorial Q.3.18, a fourteenth-century manuscript of Cassiodorus, has extracts from Ennodius, Juvenal, and other poets on the final two flyleaves, added in a fourteenth-century hand.[85] Ennodius is included in a small florilegium, more patristic than classical (Augustinus, Alanus, Ambro-

78. It is doubtless not a coincidence that Pizzolpasso, who commissioned this manuscript, was like Ennodius a former bishop of Pavia (1427–35). Concerning Pizzolpasso see Remigio Sabbadini, *Le scoperte dei codici latini e greci ne' secoli XIV e XV* (1905; reprint with additions, Florence, 1967), pp. 120–22.

79. Vogel, p. xliii, describes the textual relationship of F and BN lat. 2177.

80. This rearrangement, though perhaps similarly motivated, is not at all the same as the rearrangement found in the editions of Sirmond and Hartel; see note 2 above.

81. The manuscript is described by Berthold L. Ullman, *The Humanism of Coluccio Salutati*, Medioevo e umanesimo 4 (Padua, 1963), p. 173. Concerning this and the other Renaissance manuscripts, we are grateful to Dr. A. C. de la Mare for sharing with us her knowledge of fourteenth- and fifteenth-century Italian hands.

82. Concerning da Moglio see Giuseppe Billanovich, "Giovanni del Virgilio, Pietro da Moglio, Francesco da Fiano," *Italia medioevale e umanistica* 6 (1963): 203–34. Regarding Salutati's acquisition of the volume see Ullman, *Humanism*, pp. 227, 266. Along with Salutati's annotations, the manuscript bears a list of contents in the hand of Poggio; see Albinia C. de la Mare, *Handwriting of Italian Humanists*, vol. 1, 1 (Oxford, 1973), pp. 34, 73 n. 4. Concerning its acquisition by Cosimo, see Ullman, *Humanism*, p. 278. For its passing to San Marco see Berthold L. Ullman and Philip A. Stadter, *The Public Library of Renaissance Florence*, Medioevo e umanesimo 10 (Padua, 1972), pp. 21, 223, no. 849, and 283, no. M210.

83. See Paolo d'Ancona, *La miniatura fiorentina*, vol. 2 (Florence, 1914), p. 585, no. 1164. U is no. 98 in the catalog of Federigo's books, compiled just after his death; the catalog is published in the *Giornale storico degli archivi toscani* 6 (1862), esp. p. 144.

84. Vogel, p. xliii, notes that the text of Ennodius in this codex follows a work dated 1553.

85. Antolín, *Catálogo*, p. 437.

sius, Anselmus ... Ennodius, etc.), which appears on folios 57–73v in Berlin, Staatsbibl. Ham. 540, an Italian manuscript of the first half of the fifteenth century; it probably belonged to the Franciscans of Ferrara.[86] And Venice, Bibl. marc. lat. class. II 40, also from the fifteenth century, contains excerpts from Ennodius on folios 9–10. Finally, extracts from Ennodius are listed among the contents of a florilegium compiled by "Fr. Bonifacio de Thomar, Cistercian monk of Estremadura," in the catalog description of Alcobaca MS 73,[87] dating from the fifteenth or sixteenth century; the manuscript presumably perished when the library burned in 1811. Despite the late date, this florilegium does not reflect the spirit of southern humanism but rather represents the conservative Cistercian piety of Alcobaca. In sum, the text of Ennodius is extraordinary, in the fact that a work so rare in the Middle Ages—a work, moreover, that passed through the hands of that prodigious disseminator Salutati—should be even rarer in the Renaissance, to the point that surviving manuscripts from the fourteenth and fifteenth centuries should be handily outnumbered by those from the ninth, twelfth, and thirteenth centuries.[88]

Interest in Ennodius revived briefly in the second half of the sixteenth century with the great editions of patristic authors produced by Counter-Reformation scholarship.[89] Johannes Grynaeus produced the first printed edition of Ennodius in 1569 at Basel, essentially a transcription of the Vienna manuscript (P). P, however, had a number of lacunae, many of which Grynaeus filled from the Lorsch manuscript (B).[90] A second edition was produced in 1611 at Tournai by the Jesuit scholar Andreas Schott and dedicated to Frederic Borromeo, cardinal archbishop of Milan. Schott emended the text of the Basel edition against B.[91] In the same year a third edition was published at Nivelles by another Jesuit, Jacob Sirmond, who dedicated it to Nicholas Fabri.[92] Besides the two earlier editions, Sirmond

86. Helmut Boese, *Die lateinischen Handschriften der Sammlung Hamilton zu Berlin* (Wiesbaden, 1966), pp. 258–59.

87. *Index codicum bibliothecae Alcobatiae* ... (Lisbon, 1775), p. 50.

88. Likely the humanists' assessment of Ennodius paralleled that expressed earlier by Arnulf of Lisieux (see above), and the later opinion of Andreas Schott, editor of Ennodius, who called him an "auctor horridus atque obscurus" (Vogel, p. l).

89. This is also the context from which emerged the four latest manuscripts of Ennodius, two of the sixteenth century (Escorial F.2.9 and Vatican Ottob. lat. 2366) and two of the seventeenth (Vatican Ottob. lat. 485 and Vat. lat. 6057), all copied from V after it had reached the Vatican Library; see Vogel, p. xxxix.

90. See Lehmann, *Franciscus Modius*, pp. 132–34; see also notes 12 and 13 above.

91. Schott requested, in vain, the loan of the Ambrosiana manuscript (F) as well; see Vogel, p. l.

92. Note that one has here two separate editions of an obscure author, Ennodius, both appearing in 1611, both edited by Jesuits, both published in the Netherlands in cities only some forty miles apart. Moreover, as Vogel shows (p. li), Sirmond knew and used Schott's slightly earlier edition but makes no mention of his predecessor, despite acknowledging another and lesser source. An interesting story must lie behind this; but since it is likely to be concerned exclusively with seventeenth-century personalities and politics rather than with Ennodius, we leave it for others to uncover.

used Fabri's manuscript of Ennodius (Y) and two others that have not been identified.[93] While these editions were reprinted a number of times, the majority of the manuscripts did not come to light until the editions of Hartel and Vogel.

Although clearly never popular, the text of Ennodius was more widely known in the Middle Ages than one might have expected. A number of unrelated factors determined the survival of, and the episodic flurries of interest in, this corpus. That Ennodius was made available in the North, wellspring of the whole tradition, resulted from the fortuitous fact that Paul the Deacon brought the text with him from Italy and shared with his friends at court Ennodius's model for epistolary adonic verses. The subsequent close connection among Carolingian Corbie, Arras, and Lorsch ensured the survival of Ennodius. The surge of interest in Ennodius centered on Corbie in the third quarter of the ninth century was fueled, if not initiated, by the work of the Pseudo-Isidorian forger(s). Two further impulses, each originating in the twelfth century and carrying over into the thirteenth, virtually complete the picture. First was the expansion of the Cistercian order in the twelfth century and its singular focus on the Fathers as the core of authority, which clearly account for a significant proportion of the interest in Ennodius manifested in that century. Second, quite distinct from Cistercian spirituality, was the role played by the twelfth-century schools in training men skilled in the *ars dictaminis* for service in the episcopal chanceries. This interest accounts for several separate collections of extracts from Ennodius known in some two dozen manuscripts; and it doubtless accounts as well for the copying of whole texts, such as the León manuscript and the lost codex of Philip of Bayeux. Interest in Ennodius waned with the Middle Ages, and revived only slightly with the focus on patrology that accompanied the Counter-Reformation.

93. See Vogel, pp. l–li. Vogel (pp. xliii, li) assumed, on misinformation provided by Pertz, that Fabri's manuscript was the fourteenth-century BN lat. 2177; see note 41 above, for Valentin Rose's correction. Sirmond's two other manuscripts are identified, in his preface, merely as "a Vatican exemplar" (not V) and "a more recent exemplar."

# [7]

# The Church as Play: Gerhoch of Reichersberg's Call for Reform

## KARL F. MORRISON

With the eye of a teacher, Johan Huizinga saw long ago that "civilization grows in and as play." With the eye of a historian, he saw that
"holiness and play always tend to overlap," following rules "other than
those of logic and causality."[1] Huizinga argued that play was not simply
an instrument for the development and transmission of cultural values
but that it was precisely culture in the act of self-transformation. For in
play culture claimed and explored an area where one could venture beyond normal logic and the dominant plausibilities of everyday existence.
In play, culture created a little world whose inner coherence was defined
by its own rules, one that had no purpose outside itself. In the game,
players assumed characters other than ones they had in the world outside
the game. For the time being, they changed into other persons. Their
identities depended on conflict and victory in the play.

Huizinga's theory is illustrated by Gerhoch of Reicherberg's commentary on Psalm 64 (*"Te decet hymnus"*), which is the subject of the present
essay. Gerhoch's call for church reform in that commentary is in part a
tissue of logical contradictions. I maintain that principles of play reconcile those contradictions on a nonlogical level of discourse: namely, on
the level of feeling. Gerhoch's theology and—even more—his training in
rhetoric and an early enthusiasm for the theater convinced him of the
primacy of feeling. Because of its disjunction between logical and affective
discourse, Gerhoch's commentary stands in marked contrast with Ber-

---

1. Johan Huizinga, *Homo Ludens: A Study of the Play Element in Culture* (Boston,
1962), pp. 48, 119, 140. See also the very extensive analysis of Gerhoch's hermeneutic
principles in my book, *"I Am You": The Hermeneutics of Empathy in Western Literature, Theology, and Art* (Princeton, 1988), pp. 191–237.

nard of Clairvaux's *De consideratione,* another call for church reform exactly contemporary with Gerhoch's treatise and, like it, addressed to Pope Eugenius III.[2] I suggest that Gerhoch's violations of logic provide a particularly clear instance in which Huizinga's theories about play can be applied to doctrines of church reform, for they expose an area in which the church itself was seen to grow as play.

Gerhoch delivered his plea for reform to Eugenius in person. Paradoxically, he presented it at the time when he was also defending Cardinal Octavian (later the antipope Victor IV) against charges that he had acted with extreme avarice on his visitation of the sees of Augsburg and Eichstätt (1151), when Gerhoch had attended the cardinal. He included his critique of papal government in a wider discussion of ecclesiastical abuses, masquerading as a commentary on Psalm 64. Gerhoch attached such importance to this treatise that he presented it twice as a program for reform: first, to Pope Eugenius in 1152, at Octavian's defense, and second, to another legate, Cardinal Henry of Sts. Nereus and Achilleus, as that prelate was undertaking a visitation in Augsburg (1158). The commentary, with its complaint that the extension of papal jurisdiction into secular matters, notably those involving bloodshed, had defiled the Roman church and changed it into the Roman court, was an important step toward the moment when Gerhoch turned away from pope and cardinals and toward a general council as an agent of reform.[3]

In this essay I describe some strategies of proof (or apparent proof) that Gerhoch employed in his treatise. To be sure, Gerhoch incorporated a number of diverse arguments into his commentary, each of which had its own proof. But all were subordinate to his overarching argument that the church was one, bound together by affective union in heart and soul.

Gerhoch referred to his commentary as *"psalmi expositio et oratio."*[4] The predominance of the *oratio* (on abuses) over *psalmi expositio* is indicated by the fact that 102 chapters out of the entire 176 contain no

2. Gerhoch was one of the earliest writers to refer to the *De consideratione.* See Peter Classen, *Gerhoch von Reichersberg: Eine Biographie* (Wiesbaden, 1960), pp. 363–64. John D. Anderson and Elizabeth T. Kennan, trans., *Five Books on Consideration: Advice to a Pope* (Kalamazoo, Mich., 1976), p. 187.

3. Prefaces *A* and *B. MGH LdL* 3:439–40. Because Sackur omitted mainly theological sections from the *Monumenta* edition (thus presenting a version that lacks many of the sections which Gerhoch himself regarded as crucial), references will be made to two editions: to the *Monumenta* version for sections that Sackur included and to Migne's *Patrologia* for those that he omitted. Unlike any other commentaries by Gerhoch, that on Psalm 64 is divided into chapters that do not correspond with the chapters of the Psalm. Citations of the commentary on Psalm 64 follow this literary division, while citations of other commentaries follow the division by verses. For general discussions of the commentary on Psalm 64, see Classen, *Gerhoch von Reichersberg*, pp. 141–49, 419. Damian Van den Eynde, *L'oeuvre littéraire de Géroch de Reichersberg*, Spicilegium Pontificii Athenaei Antoniani 11 (Rome, 1957), pp. 92–107.

4. Chap. 75. *MGH LdL*, 3:471.

Karl F. Morrison

references to Psalm 64.[5] Gerhoch composed the work chiefly in the epideictic (or ceremonial) mode of oratory.

I propose that Gerhoch's doctrine of "unity in heart and soul" in God
(Acts 4:32) was the keystone of all his arguments and the source of the
logical contradictions with which we are concerned. Gerhoch visualized
that doctrine in metaphors of eating. Believers, he wrote, consume the
Eucharist, but they are consumed by Christ as doves are eaten by hawks.
In this way they become bone of his bone and flesh of his flesh. They are in
him and he in them. The Apostle Peter, too, is in Christ, and Emmanuel
lives in him.[6] But it is also true, according to Gerhoch, that believers live
in Peter. Gerhoch recalled that, while entranced in prayer, Peter had seen a
vessel let down from heaven containing animals and birds. Commanded
to kill and eat them, he refused because they were common and unclean,
obeying when admonished, "What God hath cleansed, call not thou common" (Acts 11:5–11). So, Gerhoch observed, believers passed into Peter's
body by instant obedience, as had that banquet divinely set before him.[7]

To be Peter was to share in the apostolic principate that broke stubborn
emperors and received the kingly crowns of Antioch and Rome in tribute.
It was to share the authority of confirming the brethren that Christ gave
not to a king or an emperor, but to a fisherman. It was also to be assimi-
lated to the apostle who submitted to admonition and correction by other
believers without prejudice to his authority, to be at one with the apostle
who in weakness denied the Lord while loving him, who was healed of
that infirmity by bitter contrition, and who, as pastor of his Lord's flocks,
yearned to be dissolved and to be with Christ.[8] And yet, a fundamental
tension existed in Gerhoch's doctrine of the church because his reasoning
was moral as well as institutional. He held that all believers partook of
Peter's power and, equally, that Peter's obedience was binding on them
all, including bishops. But was that obedience necessarily institutional?
Gerhoch knew that obedience to Christ's commands and institutional
conformity did not always coincide; for despite the principate of Peter,
Satan (or Antichrist), the king of Babylon, could usurp the principate over
the church and over any faithful soul, even the souls of those who held the
highest offices in the church.[9] Perhaps, in the end, a general council
provided the most secure defense of ecclesiastical purity.[10]

5. See Appendix, part 2.
6. Chap. 70. MGH LdL, 3:469.
7. Chap. 110. Migne, PL, 194:73.
8. On the powers of Peter, chaps. 25, 68, 150. MGH LdL, 3:450, 468, 485. On Peter's
contrition, chaps. 8, 69, 101, 103, 157. Migne, PL, 194:68. MGH LdL, 3:444, 469. Migne,
PL, 194:69, applying words of the letter to the Philippians (1:23) to Peter, MGH LdL,
3:488. Chap. 12. MGH LdL, 3:446. Cf. chap. 124. MGH LdL, 3:472.
9. Chaps. 29, 159. MGH LdL, 3:452 (praecipuas dignitates), p. 489 (summos hon-
ores).
10. It is not clear whether Gerhoch drew on any practical experience other than that
of the "general council" that had met in Rheims (1148), whose decrees, he knew, were
ignored. Karl Joseph von Hefele-Henri Leclerq, Histoire des conciles, vol. 5, 1 (Paris,

This tension indicates a profound cleavage between Gerhoch's role as apologist for sacerdotal privilege and his role as prophetic destroyer of priestly abuse. Often in conflict with the Schoolmen of Paris and their disciples, many of whom were laymen, Gerhoch extolled the sacerdotal dignity. The priest, he wrote, was truly a shepherd, a biped standing erect among and over his quadruped, grazing flock.[11] Gerhoch argued that the purity achieved in the apostolic church by unity in heart and soul in God (Acts 4:32) had, after the dispersal of apostles and their followers from Palestine, been safeguarded by the hierarchic order of bishops, priests, and deacons.[12] Yet, he also contended, even in the heyday of unity, apostolic purity had not extended to such as Simon Magus, Nicholas, Judas, Ananias and Sapphira, and that spiritual counterparts of those primitive heretics infested the hierarchic order in his own time.[13] He portrayed the church, the Body of Christ, as the temple of equity,[14] and yet he charged that, among all who ruled the church, there were no teachers or leaders of justice, and that Christians were denied in the church the justice for which they hungered and thirsted.[15] An apologist for sacerdotal privilege, he argued that the historical success of the church—the conversion of pagan temples and palaces into churches and the accumulation of wealth—manifested the truth of Christianity.[16] And yet, as prophetic iconoclast, he denounced the emptiness and filth enclosed within the glittering opulence of the church, and he invoked the destruction of the temple in Jerusalem, once so overweening in its stately grandeur and so much the object of the vainglory of the Jews, as an admonition from the Spirit to the church.[17]

Contradiction marked Gerhoch's discussions of two matters vital to his apology: the defense of the *vita apostolica*, as codified in the Augustinian

---

1912), pp. 823–38. Of course, he knew and drew on texts of councils in the patristic era. Nikolaus M. Häring, "Gerhoch von Reichersberg and the Latin Acts of the Council of Ephesus (431)," *Revue de théologie ancienne et moderne* 35 (1968): 26–34.

11. Chap. 127. *MGH LdL*, 3:474.

12. Chaps. 40, 113. Migne, *PL*, 194:33, 74.

13. Chap. 12. *MGH LdL*, 3:446. Cf. chap. 124. *MGH LdL*, 3:472. In an illuminating fashion, Classen compared Gerhoch's free and easy use of the word "heresy" with Anselm of Havelberg's much more sparing use, notably in Anselm's (putative) debate with Nicetas of Nicomedia over doctrinal, disciplinary, and liturgical differences between the Greek and Latin churches. See Peter Classen, "Der Häresie-Begriff bei Gerhoch von Reichersberg und in seinem Umkreis," in *The Concept of Heresy in the Middle Ages (11th–13th C.)*, ed. William Lourdaux and D. Herhelst (Louvain, 1976), pp. 40–41. See also my essay "Anselm of Havelberg: Play and the Dilemma of Historical Progress," in *Religion, Culture, and Society in the Early Middle Ages: Studies in Honor of Richard E. Sullivan*, ed. Thomas F. X. Noble and John J. Contreni (Kalamazoo, Mich., 1987), pp. 225–26. 231.

14. Chaps. 82–84. Migne, *PL*, 194:59.

15. Chap. 34. *MGH LdL*, 3:454.

16. Chap. 70. *MGH LdL*, 3:469.

17. Chaps. 169, 171. Migne, *PL*, 194:113–14. The king of Babylon has usurped principate over the church: chap. 67. *MGH LdL*, 3:468.

Rule, and the assertion of papal authority. Gerhoch regarded the apostolic church as the perfect model of Christian faith and order, and he particularly judged that the external discipline set forth by the Augustinian Rule preserved the outward order and inward unity of heart and soul described in Acts 4:32. Early in his career, he emphatically taught that it should be imposed even upon secular clergy. He insisted on the continuity of "holy rules and patristic traditions" as a test of authenticity.[18] He pointed with satisfaction to forms of discipline in postapostolic days, the falsity of which had been proved when they dried up as rivulets cut off from the mainstream of life.[19] And yet, aware that the *vita apostolica* had been revived in comparatively recent times, he found it necessary to acknowledge that the *vita apostolica* itself had fallen into disuse after the apostolic church was dispersed from Jerusalem, and that it had experienced centuries of "long sterility."[20] Moreover, his argument that material prosperity could certify spiritual authenticity clashed with his portrayal of those who lived the *vita apostolica*, Christ's poor. He portrayed them as paupers and simple folk, chosen by God to confound the powerful and worldly wise, as Christians living piously in Christ and being bone of his bones and flesh of his flesh. Yet, despite their exalted mission and intimate union with Christ, Christ permitted those who held the highest offices in the church and professedly Christian kings to persecute them while he slept.[21]

Gerhoch's arguments concerning the pope were equally inconsistent. On the one hand, he declared that Christ's commission to St. Peter had established papal headship of the church. Indeed, he wrote, the rulers of Antioch and Rome had ceded their thrones to Peter, and, crowned with many golden crowns, Emmanuel was in the pope.[22] Defending the legitimacy of the Donation of Constantine, Gerhoch exulted in the power of popes to name and to depose secular rulers, a power symbolized in the glorious "spectacle" of kings and emperors performing groom's service for popes.[23] However, he emphasized the defectibility of Peter, notably in denying Christ and in readily submitting to rebuke and correction by other believers.[24] When he observed that popes were almost universally

18. Chap. 123. *MGH LdL,* 3:472.

19. Chap. 114. Migne, *PL,* 194:75.

20. Chaps. 43, 161. *MGH LdL,* 3:456 (the *vita apostolica* lasted into the days of Pseudo-Urban I), p. 489. See also chap. 128, a decree of Pope Urban II. *MGH LdL,* 3:474.

21. Chap. 97. Migne, *PL,* 194:66.

22. Chaps. 67–70, 80, 95. *MGH LdL,* 3:468–69. Migne, *PL,* 194:58, 65.

23. Chap. 67. *MGH LdL,* 3:468. See A. J. Carlyle, *A History of Medieval Political Theory in the West,* vol. 4 (London, 1950), pp. 361–63. Gerhard Laehr, *Die konstantinische Schenkung in der abendländischen Literatur des Mittelalters bis zur Mitte des 14. Jahrhunderts,* Historische Studien 166 (Berlin, 1926), pp. 51–54, 67–68. Erich Meuthen, *Kirche und Heilsgeschichte bei Gerhoh von Reichersberg,* Studien und Texte zur Geistesgeschichte des Mittelalters 6 (Leiden, 1959), p. 108. See also chap. 110. Migne, *PL,* 194:73, and below, note 111.

24. Chaps. 69, 101, 110. *MGH LdL,* 3:469. Migne, *PL,* 194:69, 73.

disobeyed,[25] Gerhoch weakened his argument that pompous displays of worldly power vindicated papal headship. His complaint that the Roman church had been debased into a Roman court by its exercise of secular jurisdiction and his defense of the "two sword" doctrine hardly support his portrayal of popes disposing of kingdoms and empires. Indeed, in other treatises, he vehemently denounced a painting in Rome—one that he himself may have seen—depicting an emperor in the act of performing groom's service to a pope. He asserted that the picture unmasked Rome as the new Babylon, confounding the papal with the imperial office.[26]

A number of implied criticisms also modified Gerhoch's assertions of papal headship. In his commentary on Psalm 64, Gerhoch denounced bishops who took up the sword and polluted with human blood hands consecrated to make the Body of Christ.[27] While in the commentary he deplored the abomination of desolation that stood in St. Peter's church and the instruments of warfare that had been erected above the apostle's tomb,[28] he neglected to mention events still fresh in memory: Pope Innocent II's capture on the field of battle and Pope Lucius III's death from wounds received in battle against the Romans. He also failed to recall Pope Eugenius III's responsibility for the slaughters of the Second Crusade or his own rebuke to Eugenius, the recipient of the commentary, for fighting against the Romans with the sword of iron.[29] As an apologist for the Augustinian Rule for canons regular and as an enemy of the Aachen Rule, Gerhoch invoked papal decrees supporting his case, as well as relevant canons of the Council of Rheims (1148). But Pope Eugenius III's name was conspicuously absent from the catalogue of popes who had legislated in favor of the Augustinian Rule, and the canons that Eugenius had proclaimed with his own mouth at Rheims had not been enforced.[30] Gerhoch lamented that dangerous abuses could have been averted if only Pope

25. Chap. 52. MGH LdL, 3:460–61.
26. De investigatione Antichristi, 1.72 (book 1 was written before 1155 or 1158; book 2, 1160–62). De quarta vigilia noctis, chap. 12 (written 1167). MGH LdL, 3:393, 511–12. Classen, Gerhoch von Reichersberg, pp. 421–24, 426–27. Cf. Otto of Freising, Gesta Friderici Imperatoris, 3.10, ed. Georg Waitz and Bernhard von Simson (Hannover, 1912), MGH SS, rer. Germ., p. 177. On the two-power theory and the Donation of Constantine in Rupert of Deutz, who greatly influenced Gerhoch, see John H. Van Engen, Rupert of Deutz (Berkeley, 1983), pp. 268, 290, 296.
27. Chap. 62. MGH LdL, 3:465.
28. Chap. 52. MGH LdL, 3:461.
29. De investigatione Antichristi, 1.64, 68. MGH LdL, 3:380, 384. Ep. 17 (to Pope Alexander III). Migne, PL, 193:568–69.
30. Chaps. 35, 44. MGH LdL, 3:455, 457 (Eugenius proclaimed the decrees at Rheims "sermone apostolico"). Bernard of Clairvaux, De consideratione, 3.5.19–20, emphasizes that Eugenius uttered the decrees with his own mouth. J. Leclercq and H. M. Rochais, eds., Tractatus et Opuscula, S. Bernardi Opera, vol. 3 (Rome, 1963), p. 446. On Gerhoch's place in the history of the Augustinian Rule, see Luc Verheijen, La règle de Saint Augustin, vol. 1 (Paris, 1967), p. 126, and vol. 2 (Paris, 1967), p. 47. Ironically, though he went to Rome to obtain an authentic copy of the rule, Gerhoch was misled by Norbert of Xanten and defended a later conflation.

Paschal II's decree against the Aachen Rule had been universally applied; he asserted that the popes (meaning Eugenius) could purge the Aachen Rule of its "depraved" elements if they wished.[31] Clerical discipline could be restored if only a decree went out "from the throne of God, who wishes to make all things new, from those who hold the place of Christ on earth," constraining bishops to replace irregular clerics with those professed to follow the Augustinian Rule.[32] Indeed, a major cause of disorder in the church, he said, was the lapse of swift apostolic vigilance, such as Pope Gregory I had exercised over the whole church, without waiting for formal processes against patent malefactors.[33]

Errors intruded by unwilling workers in the Lord's harvest could be corrected by willing and worthy ones. Evidently Gerhoch included "pontiffs of the apostolic see, cardinals, and legates" in both categories.[34] Even without directly referring to other abuses in the see of Peter—such as constricting legalism and venality—that he explicitly denounced elsewhere, Gerhoch set forth in his commentary on Psalm 64 an imposing array of grievances against the see of Peter and the reigning pope.

Gerhoch's methods permitted him to tolerate, and required him to employ, contradiction. The use of metaphor in particular and figurative language in general requires the fundamental contradiction of seeing two things in one, of misapplying the name that is proper to one thing to another quite different thing. The object is to reveal a hidden similarity in dissimilars, and the method of figurative association entails a deliberate violation of the "logic of reasoning" in order to exercise a "logic of discovery."[35] The detection of metaphor, Aristotle wrote, could not be learned from others. The figurative method of association by likeness depended on feeling and, indeed, not on the unaided feeling of the average person. Evading logical processes, it came by intuition, through the inspiration or touch of madness that made a poet.[36]

There is a parallel with Gerhoch's concept of exegesis and, in fact, with that of the whole Christian life. Intoxicated by the Holy Spirit, exegetes spoke not their own words, but Christ's. Logical contradictions betraying hidden truths expressed their inebriated self-alienation. More generally, Gerhoch wrote that Christ, the eternal wisdom of God, exulted before the creation, then played on earth, delighting to be with the sons of men.[37] For Gerhoch the phrase "sons of men" had a specific meaning: the re-

31. Chaps. 133, 137, 150, 151. *MGH LdL*, 3:478–79, 484–85.
32. Chap. 48. *MGH LdL*, 3:459.
33. Chaps. 72, 74. *MGH LdL*, 3:470–71.
34. Chap. 168. *MGH LdL*, 3:492.
35. Paul Ricoeur, *The Rule of Metaphor*, trans. Robert Czerny et al. (Toronto, 1977), pp. 21, 22, 24. Aristotle, *Poetics*, 1457b, 1459a.
36. Aristotle, *Rhetoric*, 1408b; idem, *Poetics*, 1455a, 1459a.
37. Chap. 29. *MGH LdL*, 3:453, an allusion, as Professor Bernard McGinn kindly indicated, to Prov. 8:31. On inebriated exegetes, see below, notes 101–3.

deemed.[38] Gerhoch believed that the creative play of God's wisdom over the primordial waters was replicated over the waters of baptism.[39] "Just as, in the creation of the world, He commanded and they were created, so now, abiding with the elect until the end of the world, He speaks and they become. He commands and sends His Spirit, and they are created."[40] Gerhoch's reference to baptism contains an implied reference, common in his day, to the religious life of continual penance as a second baptism.[41] Through the contemplative knowledge that the formative play in first and second baptisms opened, the human reason in the elect became partaker of the eternal wisdom "which is nothing else than the Son of God himself,"[42] expressing itself through the tongues of teachers and the swiftly writing pens of exegetes. Of the perfect God said, "This is now bone of my bones," and of the imperfect, yet still men of goodwill, "and flesh of my flesh."[43]

Clearly, for Gerhoch's argument logical contradictions were not elementary errors. They were incorporated in his method of figurative association. They issued from the charismatic inebriation of the exegete and, indeed, expressed the play of God's wisdom in and through him. For Gerhoch, there was more in his commentary than the text, the level of logical discourse. The greater part of discourse, the text's content, was invisible, hidden within the "positive values" on the surface. It was made up of "negative values": the Word of God contained in the feeling that was contained in the words of the author that, in turn, were contained in the text that, finally, was contained in the musical setting of psalmody. Such negative values had to be disclosed by indirect methods of exegesis. There was one further "negative value": namely, the text in the reader. For Gerhoch's entire object was to absorb the negative values in the Psalm, to make his own the spirit playing in it. Thus, explaining contradictions in the text has led to the task of explaining the "union of heart and soul" in God that produced discourse. Just as in psalmody Gerhoch listened to the words within the sweetness of music, so when he contemplated Psalm 64, he saw the text and, within the words, a person (the psalmist), and within the person, the feeling that informed the words, and, within the feeling, the Word, or wisdom, of God, all of which, he thought, he could, and did, assimilate to himself.

Thus far, I have suggested that the contradictions in Gerhoch's commentary were introduced by his charismatic mentality. That mentality

38. E.g., *Tractatus in Ps.*, 35:8b. Gerhoch of Reichersberg, *Opera inedita*, ed. Damian Van den Eynde and Odulph Van den Eynde, vol. 2, 2 Spicilegium Pontificii Athenaei Antoniani 10 (Rome, 1956), pp. 434–35.
39. Chap. 30. *MGH LdL*, 3:453.
40. Chap. 64. *MGH LdL*, 3:466.
41. Van Engen, *Rupert of Deutz*, p. 264.
42. *Tract. in Ps.*, 7:2. Migne, *PL*, 193:725.
43. Chap. 65. *MGH LdL*, 3:466. For the references to exegetes, see below, note 105.

taught him how, in some circumstances, one person could be transfused into another. Encountering negative values of discourse leads further: namely, to practical methods of persuasion (including the use of irony) conveyed by the rhetorical tradition. Indeed, Gerhoch's task was to bridge three kinds of ironic distance: (1) between the words and the feeling in the text; (2) between the feeling and the author in the text; and (3) between the author and the text in the audience. Consequently, I have organized the following comments according to three categories of persuasion identified by Aristotle and canonized in that tradition, categories that allude to three kinds of ironic distance and to negative values that were thought to bridge them: (1) the feeling in the words, (2) the author in the text (or, in Aristotle's terms, the author's commendation of himself to the audience), and (3) the text in the reader (i.e., the author's transformation of his own feelings into his audience by exciting their emotions and refreshing their memories).[44]

I suggest that these categories of persuasion were thought to correspond with three kinds of experience that bridged ironic distances: (1) the feeling in the words, with play (specifically, the play of God's wisdom in the human soul); (2) the author in the text, with performance (that is, with the enactment of his role as a vessel of the word of God); and (3) the text in the reader (or audience), with imitation (namely, with the mental assent of the audience to recapitulate the role enacted before it).

## The Feeling in the Word: Play

Text, words, and person were vessels of discourse. Indeed, any word uttered by the body (in speech or in writing) was informed by two negative values: intent (the word of the heart) and thought (the word of the mind). Each of the three words was linked to the others by likeness, except of course in cases of conscious deception. The interpreter's task was to establish a bonding between the content of the physical words and the content of the human soul—his own and, if possible, the souls of others. Gerhoch stated that the object of his commentary on Psalm 64 was "insofar as, with God's favor, we can, to arouse ourselves and those who are to read what we write to the same affect of praising and praying that the words both of the Psalms and of patristic expositions on them contain." He described his own work as a rustic basket, or a chamberpot, filled with the attitudes (sensus, denoting both feeling and meaning) of the Fathers, chosen for those purposes.[45] Notably, Gerhoch did not here use the word

---

44. Aristotle, Rhetoric, 1356a, 1403b, 1419b.
45. Tract. in Ps., 44:2. Migne, PL, 193:1565. Chap. 75. Migne, PL, 194:55. Cf. Quintilian's statement that a father pleading for justice for some wrong should "transfuse a portion of his own sorrowful feeling into the breasts of his audience." Institutes, 11.1.53.

*sententiae,* denoting verbal quotations, though they too were present in abundance.

Thus understood, the content of the words was a living thing. It was a vivid feeling, a spiritual movement, or even more. Like other exegetes of his day, Gerhoch addressed his text with four analytical categories in mind: *materia, intentio, modus tractandi,* and *titulus libri.* Unlike others, however, he did not refer these categories to the positive values—the text—of the Psalms. The *materia* of the Psalms, he wrote, was "the whole Christ, that is, the head with all [its] members." The *intentio* was "to provoke those members to conformity with the head." The *modus tractandi*—whether narrative, dramatic, or mixed—conformed the affects of those singing the Psalms with the affects of those who wrote them. The *titulus libri,* giving the name of the author and the *materia* of the work— was rendered in the opening words of the first Psalm: Christ was the *beatus vir.* Arranging the Psalms in order and assigning them individual titles, Esdras did not presume to set a title above the first Psalm, knowing that Christ had already done so, saying, "In the head of the book, it is written concerning me" (Heb. 10:7). For such reasons, the Psalms could be called not only "the book of hymns," because it contained many lauds and songs of divine mysteries, but also "the book of soliloquies," since the prophecy that it conveyed was bestowed on man by the Holy Spirit alone, without any human teaching (*magisterio*).[46]

The organization of Gerhoch's commentary on Psalm 64 plainly reflects one aspect of his theory: namely, that the *materia,* or content, of the Psalms was "the whole Christ." Gerhoch had resolved to avoid the discursive questions and detours that characterized his earlier commentaries and to follow a straight path of discourse.[47]

Still, the diversity of subjects considered in his commentary on Psalm 64 and his irrepressible penchant for digression rather obscure the structure that he did follow. As the Appendix below indicates, however, Gerhoch's citations of the Psalm divide his commentary into five sections. Regarding one of them further precision is possible, for Gerhoch himself affirmed that the second section, which he called a "digression," began in chapter 14 and ended after chapter 75.[48] A "digression," of course, was a standard device in oratory for affording pleasure to the audience, and according to Quintilian digression was one of the arts that gave life and energy to oratory.[49] One may therefore take Gerhoch's conscious and extended "digression" as evidence of design.

46. On the general use of this *accessus ad auctores,* Nikolaus M. Häring, "Commentary and Hermeneutics," in *Renaissance and Renewal in the Twelfth Century,* ed. Robert L. Benson and Giles Constable (Cambridge, Mass., 1982), p. 186. Gerhoch's discussion is in the general prologue to his entire commentary on the Psalms, Migne, *PL,* 193:630–36. See also *Tract. in Ps.,* 64, chap. 80. Migne, *PL,* 194:58, on Ps. 1:1.

47. *Tract. in Ps.,* 51, prologue to part 6. Migne, *PL,* 193:1609.

48. Chaps. 14, 75. *MGH LdL,* 3:446. Migne, *PL,* 194:55.

49. Quintilian, *Institutes,* 9.1.29, 9.2.4.

Karl F. Morrison

It is at least possible that Gerhoch enlarged an original commentary on Psalm 64 by interpolating in segments a longer treatise on ecclesiastical abuses,[50] but the existing text is by no means a random agglomeration of excursus, digressions, and interpolations. As noted earlier, Gerhoch referred to the work as "psalmi expositio et oratio."[51] His mastery of rhetoric taught him that a complete oration consisted of five or, alternatively, six parts.[52] Dividing orations (and letters) in this way was part of an oratorical tradition that Cicero canonized for the West,[53] and it was natural for Gerhoch to use the structure in a ceremonial masterpiece destined for the eyes of popes and cardinals.

Indeed, his structure is part of his message. In another commentary, Gerhoch elucidated the sixfold division as he thought he found it in one scriptural episode: Christ's rebuke to Simon for thinking ill of him when he permitted a "woman of the city" to anoint his feet with balm and wash them with her tears (Luke 7:36–50).

The first section (*exordium*), he wrote, consisted of two parts: the *principium*, the shorter one, to capture the attention and goodwill of the hearer (perhaps as short as the statement, "The Lord said these things"), and the *insinuatio*, the longer of the two, an elaborate circumlocution drawing the listeners into its coils and putting them in a frame of mind receptive to the following argument (Luke 7:36–43). The second main section, the *narratio*, could be brief ("Do you see this woman?" Luke 7:44), simply establishing the matter of the oration. The *partitio* followed, distinguishing correct from incorrect and what was to be affirmed from what was to be refuted (Luke 7:44–45). The fourth and fifth parts, the *confirmatio* ("Many sins are forgiven, for she loved much," Luke 7:47) and the *confutatio* ("To whom little is given, the same loveth little," Luke

50. The original commentary would have been organized approximately as follows:

| chapter of commentary | verse(s) of Psalm 64 |
| --- | --- |
| 1–14 | 1, 2 |
| 65 | 3 |
| 75–122 | 4–12 |
| 169–76 | 13–14 |

The distribution of references to the conflict between Babylon and Sion indicates that this leitmotiv was imposed in a random fashion on an already existing text. The rarity of references to the conflict and their concentration at three points suggest an afterthought. The distribution of these references by chapter is as follows (with concentrations italicized): *Exordium:* 5, 6, 7, 9, 13; *Narratio:* 14; *Partitio:* 15, 28, 29, 34, 39, 44, 49, 50, 51, 52, 67; *Confirmatio:* 79, 81, 97; *Confutatio:* 133, 134, 135, 136, 137, 150; *Conclusio:* 169, 174, 175. For a fuller diagram, see Appendix, part 2.

51. Chap. 75. Migne, *PL*, 194:55.

52. The division into six parts is given in *Tract. in Ps.*, 6:1 (*exordium, narratio, partitio, confirmatio, confutatio, conclusio*). The division into five parts is given in *Tract. in Ps.*, 7:1 (on prayer) and *Tract. in Ps.*, 17:21 (*propositio, ratio, confirmatio, exornatio, conclusio*). Migne, *PL*, 193:712–14, 724, 870–71.

53. James J. Murphy, *Rhetoric in the Middle Ages: A History of Rhetorical Theory from Saint Augustine to the Renaissance* (Berkeley, 1974), pp. 12–13, 205–7, 221, 225.

7:47) continued this discussion. The final part, the *conclusio*, artfully made the point of the *oratio* ("Thy faith hath saved thee; go in peace," Luke 7:50).

Gerhoch enlarged the *conclusio* of the Gospel episode with his own artful allegory. The woman, he wrote, had fulfilled the penitential psalm not with words, but with the affect of her heart and the effect of outward service. Christ was the psaltery that the woman touched as, by feeling and action, she sang the penitential psalm that her service was. Because of her inmost faith, he could save her, despite her lack of good conscience and reputation, even as he could save the church, a sinner, polluted in conscience and repute, if she turned to him in ardent faith.[54]

This discussion illustrates Gerhoch's confidence that formal expository structure enabled an orator to capture the feelings of his audience. It also indicates the functions that he assigned to the different parts of his commentary on Psalm 64 in the task of exposing the discourse in the text. These are summarized below in tabular form.[55]

Content and organization make it clear that Gerhoch employed the rhetorical device of self-deprecation when he wrote that he had inclined to omit, from the written version of his commentary, his "doctrines [*sententiae*] concerning the glorification of human substance in the Son of God" but retained them because of Pope Eugenius III's approval.[56] The effect of this statement was to draw the reader's attention to the precise center of Gerhoch's argument and, moreover, to enhance it with papal commendation.

Thus far, it might appear that few contradictions would arise from the negative value of the Word (or feeling) in the text. But such was not the case. The living content of the text was hidden from the many. It was disclosed to the few, but only partially revealed even to them. Satan (or Antichrist), the king of Babylon, gloried that his sons and daughters were multiplied beyond the number of Jerusalem's children,[57] and indeed the testimonies of the Lord were incredible to the world, demented and entranced as it was by lies and inebriated by the turgid waters of Babylon.[58]

A wide area of conflict existed between those to whom access to the living content of Scripture had been opened and those to whom it was closed. Gerhoch's call for reform hinged precisely on the insight that the wicked majority prevailed within the church. They had acceded to the highest offices; they wielded great power. Although some were bishops, those too were bestial, carnal men, evil laborers in the Lord's vineyard who conspired to kill his Son. Defending their titles with armed violence

---

54. *Tract. in Ps.*, 6:1. Migne, *PL*, 193:712–14.
55. See the Appendix.
56. Preface A. *MGH LdL*, 3:440.
57. Chap. 34. *MGH LdL*, 3:454–55.
58. Chap. 139. *MGH LdL*, 3:480.

and legal coercion, they persecuted and all but suppressed the righteous few.[59]

Gerhoch's ideas about how readers gained access to the feeling in the words of Scripture and were set apart from the wicked are summed up in the sentence "Wherever a true Christian is, there is Christ."[60] The interpreter did not confront the text as a dead object. He entered the living spirit that it contained, and it entered into him. Projecting himself into the text, he absorbed that spirit into himself. There was no longer any gap between the interpreter as subject and the Psalm as object, or between the interpreter and Christ, the *materia* of the Psalm. Gerhoch described this cyclical movement: "Showing my heart to you as an instrument of psalmody, I shall sing to be filled, and I shall be filled to sing, to you, O Lord. I shall sing, I say, and, singing to my capacity, I shall be filled. Filled, I shall be made a vessel among 'the vessels of the Psalms,'" filled with the spirit of wisdom and understanding, with the spirit of counsel and fortitude, with the spirit of knowledge and piety; and the spirit of the fear of the Lord "will fill me from 'the vessels of the Psalms,'" which vessels, Gerhoch added, had been turned and rounded by the fingers of God.[61]

As this statement about filling and being filled indicates, Gerhoch held that the interpreter became the feeling in the text and that this transformation occurred by two actions: the ecstatic assumption of the believer into God, and the infusion of God into him. Gerhoch found the basis for this idea of discourse in a doctrine of personal unity that, in turn, had its prototype in Christology. The Council of Chalcedon (451) declared that two natures (divine and human) coexisted in the one person (*prosopon*) and one substantial individual (*hypostasis*) of Christ. They coexisted in him, indivisible and inseparable, but unchanged by confusion, mingling, or blending. By a communication of idioms, the attributes of the divine could be predictated on the human nature, but the reverse was not so. Emptying himself, Christ became obedient unto death, yet he retained the eternal impassibility of his divine nature. When he spoke of union between Christ and the faithful, Gerhoch likewise argued that believers retained the substance of their humanity and their personal identities, even as they "passed over" into Christ's body. Again, the communication of idioms ran from the divine to the human, but not in reverse; for, annihilating their former lives by obedience, human beings were changed into Christ, not he into them, even though Scripture did employ the

59. Chaps. 30, 64, 69, 147, 161, 163, 166, 167. *MGH LdL*, 3:453, 466, 469, 483, 489, 490, 492.

60. Ep. 7. Migne, *PL*, 193:497.

61. *Tract. in Ps.*, 70:23. Migne, *PL*, 194:308–9. For a conventional reference to St. Paul as *vas electionis*, see chap. 8. *MGH LdL*, 3:445. The disciples were dispersed from Jerusalem, "sancte conversabantur in medio nationis pravae ac perversae verbum vitae continentes." Chap. 40. Migne, *PL*, 194:33.

rhetorical device of *transumptio* (or *metalepsis*) to refer to Christ while stating what literally applied only to his members.[62]

The faithful "passed over" into the Body of Christ through the Eucharist, but that transforming passage was not possible even for those who performed the Eucharist if they consumed its elements without purity of heart or orthodoxy of belief. Turning to the first of the two unitive acts, Gerhoch described the mental process by which the believer was ecstatically assumed into God.

Like Quintilian, Gerhoch reasoned that "all knowledge depends on memory."[63] He described the intellect, spurred on by a sensual *figura* (a sound or sight), diligently dredging the vat of memory and then integrating its discoveries according to mental habit and moral discipline.[64] Forgetfulness in the form of ingratitude to God was man's greatest iniquity, according to Gerhoch, and the hallmark of Christ's mediation was that he taught men, for the first time, how to give thanks to God. In the Eucharist, he enabled them to give thanks to the Father in and through him, just as he did in and through them.[65] The mental process leading to the soul's union with God in this commemorative action began in terror of God's fearful wrath.

Terror recalled memory of God's past benefits, thus feeding faith, exciting hope, and delighting love. Ingratitude, as forgetfulness, closed the way to future benefits, but gratitude revealed what might yet be gained. By recollection, the soul dwelled on God's works, reading, meditating, learning, teaching, keeping vigil, and praying. Especially through the Eucharist, performed in memory of Christ, the soul realized that the living memory of holiness was, in fact, the body of Christ. Raised above itself thereby, it exulted in foretastes of divine affections; united to Christ as a branch to the vine, it was vivified by his life and sanctified by his holiness. For the soul in this ardent union, absorbing what it dredged from the vat of memory, the experience was as described in the Song of Solomon, when "the king brought me into a cellar of wine; he ordained the love in me."[66]

Mental habit and moral discipline, operating on memory, shaped a person's affects into conformity with the affects contained in the Psalms.[67]

62. Preface to all commentaries on the Psalms, Migne, *PL*, 193:638. On Christ's self-emptying, chap. 88. Migne, *PL*, 194:61. The trace of a dialogic relation is indicated by Gerhoch's statement that Christ's majesty is enhanced by a believer's penitential return to him and diminished by the defection of a soul to the king of Babylon. Chap. 67. *MGH LdL*, 3:468.

63. Quintilian, *Institutes*, 11.2.1.

64. *Tract. in Ps.*, 8:1. Migne, *PL*, 193:740.

65. Chap. 85, 86. Migne, *PL*, 194:59–60.

66. *Tract. in Ps.*, 29:5–6, 76:12–14. Migne, *PL*, 193:1257–59. Migne, *PL*, 194:427–29. *Tract. in Ps.*, 8:1. Migne, *PL*, 193:740, quoting Cant. 2:4. On the gender ambiguity of Gerhoch's spiritual eroticism, see the chapter on Gerhoch in my book, *"I Am You": The Hermeneutics of Empathy in Western Literature, Theology, and Art*, esp. pp. 219–224.

67. Above, notes 45, 64.

Karl F. Morrison

Gerhoch's apology for the Augustinian Rule expressed his conviction that habits of mind imparted by its discipline, above all others, enhanced affective union. But in his commentary on Psalm 64 and in other writings, there are many references, not directly related to exegesis or forms of discipline, that establish the kinship between Gerhoch's thought and wider currents of affective spirituality. Like other affective writers, he oriented his whole thought toward the God in man, as is clear from his Christology and meditations on scenes from the life of Christ.[68] Like other writers, he gave great prominence to psalmody, reading, and prayer as meditative exercises and to the mortification of the flesh and the cultivation of penitential sorrow. Like them, he repeatedly portrayed the exultation of those who were one with God, the inebriation in which their human substance was divinized, the ecstasy of being dissolved to be with Christ as metal takes on the form of the fire that melts it,[69] and the sleep in which, with unspeakable joy, the soul felt the gentle touch of its divine spouse.[70]

This union was free of time and space. Participating in the life of God, the soul also participated in the "eternal today" in which God lived.[71] It entered into the continual creation by which God's eternal wisdom played among the sons of men,[72] the "continual resurrection" of Christ in penitent sinners.[73] The soul's transformation from difference into identity was also undefined by space, since it was measured not by nearness of distance, but by strength of affect, and by the degree of change in human nature.[74]

Gerhoch's concern was with man's moral life and particularly, with the emotions. Understanding that human nature was uniform, and not the creation of variable social forces, he could only imagine that the experience of virtue and vice was also uniform, while it varied proportionately according to the goodness or evil of individuals. The moral dimension lacked space and time.

Further, Christ was the common object of desire in all holy affective unions. All who were one in heart and mind in God participated *in idipsum*, and thus in the eternity and the ubiquity of the glorified Christ.[75]

68. E.g., on Christ in the crib, chaps. 22, 24. *MGH LdL*, 3:449–50. In chap. 22, Gerhoch identified Christ's crib as the dwelling of those who served Christ in monasteries.
69. *Tract. in Ps.*, 72:19–20. Migne, *PL*, 194:349–50.
70. *Tract. in Ps.*, 4:7, 25:8. Migne, *PL*, 193:684, 1170.
71. *Tract. in Ps.*, 2:7. Migne, *PL*, 193:664. Cf. David belonged to the "fertile year" that was Christ, although he was born before it began. Chap. 121. Migne, *PL*, 194:80.
72. Above, note 38.
73. *Tract. in Ps.*, 7:8. Migne, *PL*, 193:730.
74. *Tract. in Ps.*, 75:12; 64, chaps. 23, 24, 91, 115, 116. Migne, *PL*, 194:409, 63, 75–77. *MGH LdL*, 3:449–50. The church itself had been despatialized when, with the diaspora of the apostles, it spread from Judaea, "a wretched little corner of the earth," to every land. Chaps. 94, 118. Migne, *PL*, 194:64, 78.
75. Cf. *De investigatione Antichristi*, 2.51–54. Friedrich Scheibelberger, ed., *Ger-*

The timelessness and spacelessness of affective union reduced all affective unions to the same plane. Under the aspect of the "eternal today," they were simultaneous, like the dots of a circle, equidistant from the center that informed and defined them. Like prophecy, they encompassed past, present, and future.[76] Chronology was suspended. Though Gerhoch quoted from Rupert of Deutz a reference to the four world monarchies— Babylon, Persia, Macedon, and Rome—that exegetes read into the prophecies of Daniel, he employed the reference not to establish a sequence of events, but rather to illustrate the ever-recurrent actions by impure spirits of magic, poetry, and philosophy.[77]

When he turned to the infusion of God—the second act by which the believer became at one with feeling in the text—Gerhoch could describe effects, but not process. In and with the sons of men, the play of God's eternal wisdom was creative at the beginning of the world and in the calling of the elect, the vessels of the Psalms, turned and rounded by the fingers of God. Gerhoch characteristically described this creative play as analogous to sexual generation. Within the text of Psalm 64, Gerhoch detected numerous parallels between flesh and earth, inebriation and fecundation, and sexual engendering and the fertilization of crops. The verse, "Thou hast visited the earth and inebriated it" (Ps. 64:10), he found, illuminated the conception of Christ. After the Fall "that cursed female earth," the flesh, was sterile of good but fertile of evil, until at the Incarnation the Lord visited the "blessed earth" of the Virgin's flesh and the torrent of his delight inebriated it, setting it apart from the earth that germinated briars and nettles and fecundating it to bear the Savior.[78] What occurred in the Blessed Virgin, "not tilled with the plow of male operation," was recapitulated in each redeemed soul, the spouse of Christ, inebriated and filled with his richness at the nuptial banquet, exulting in abundance, and, germinating Christ, bringing him—the power and wisdom of God—forth in the fruit of good works.[79] Gerhoch expressed this complex of ideas when he spoke of his own role as spiritual mother.[80] The same creative play was continually recapitulated across the ages and in

---

hohi Reichersbergensis praepositi opera hactenus inedita (Leipzig, 1875), pp. 299–305. Sackur omitted books 2 and 3 of De investigatione Antichristi from the MGH edition, just as he omitted the theological sections of the commentary on Psalm 64.

76. Van Engen, Rupert of Deutz, p. 278. For the metaphor of the circle, and related figures, see Tract. in Ps., 18:11; Tract. in Ps., 45:6; De aedificio Dei, chap. 3. Migne, PL, 193:930, 1575–76. Migne, PL, 194:1203. Cf. Tract. in Ps., 75:12. Migne, PL, 194:410, on Jesus in the midst of the apostles, "vel Spiritum sanctum, quem posuit Jesus in medio discipulorum, id est in cordibus eorum, quia locus cordis medietas est animalis."

77. Chap. 141. MGH LdL, 3:480, quoting Rupert, Comm. in Apoc. Migne, PL, 169.1123–24.

78. Chap. 104. Migne, PL, 194:70.

79. Chaps. 117, 171. Migne, PL, 194:77, 114.

80. E.g., Tract. in Ps., 16:8; 70:24. Expositio super canonem, "Collatio missae." Migne, PL, 193:851. Migne, PL, 194:312. Damian Van den Eynde and Odulph Van den

the experience of individual souls, which would know the fullness of its rapture in the heavenly Jerusalem.

Gerhoch's comments illustrate that affective union—the feeling in the text—was real in the moment when it was felt. Testimonies to it could be rightly assessed only by those who retained comparable experiences in memory. Gerhoch himself knew occasions when his passionate concentration was broken, when he was distracted from his devotions by the beauty of music, by practical concerns, or by fearful onslaughts of carnal lust.[81] Even those who had prophetic gifts of understanding, interpreting, and proclaiming the Scriptures knew that the affective union in which they filled, and were filled by, the content of Scripture existed only during the actual play of Christ in their hearts and souls. Words in a text were only memorials of the event.

Gerhoch's comments on the feeling in the word took for granted that the ironic distances between God and the authors and interpreters of Scripture were bridged by lines of participation running from the word of the mouth to that of the heart and, finally, to that of the mind. Each differed from the others in kind; each exhibited likeness to the others; but by participation all were identical in truth, present in and through them in different ways. Gerhoch's comments on the relationship between Christ and the mouths, hearts, and minds that uttered those words also posited difference in kind, similarity in form, and identity in content. He visualized that relationship as a cyclical filling and being filled as believers passed over into Christ and Christ was infused into believers.

From what has been said, it is evident how this assumption of affective union entered into the contradictions mentioned at the outset. As a priest, confident in his experience of affective union with Christ, Gerhoch both defended sacerdotal privilege and rebuked the abuses of those who, despite their priestly or episcopal orders, were manifestly excluded from participation in God's eternal Word. He was able to exult in the power and opulence of the church as outward signs of its triumph over the world and yet to deplore the inward pollution introduced into the church by those who, in their spiritual blindness, usurped the church's wealth in the self-worshiping passions of avarice and lust.

A number of the contradictions mentioned at the beginning were historical. To elucidate them, we shall turn to another negative value in Gerhoch's commentary: the author in the text.

---

Eynde, eds., *Opera inedita*, vol. 1, Spicilegium Pontificii Athenaei Antoniani 8 (Rome, 1955), p. 24.

81. *Tract. in Ps.*, 1:Gloria, 41:6; 54:20; 136:8; 37:7. Migne, *PL*, 193:656–57, 1505–6, 194:908. Damian Van den Eynde and Odulph Van den Eynde, eds., *Opera inedita*, vol. 2, 2, Spicilegium Pontificii Athenaei Antoniani 10 (Rome, 1956), pp. 628–29.

## The Author in the Text: Performance

Aristotle stressed that the speaker's own character was virtually "the most effective means of persuasion he possesses." The demonstration of his goodness, indeed, could be yet more persuasive than the proof given by his words.[82] Quintilian, too, taught that, to win the goodwill of his audience and to excite their feelings, the speaker must commend himself to his hearers, and this was notably true of epideictic oratory, in which the speaker's "success concerns his reputation and not his cause."[83]

Gerhoch wrote that an artist unified his work and gained the attention of others by infusing it with his own nature (*ingenium*). People, he said, praised and loved the artist in his work, rather than the work itself.[84] One characteristic of his commentary on Psalm 64 is exactly the self-revelation of the author, partly intended and partly inadvert, and this characteristic of self-revelation is all the more striking by contrast with the anonymity under which other exegetes in Gerhoch's day released their works, assuming, even when they modulated it, "the neutral voice of tradition."[85]

His commentary on Psalm 64 was a performance of the feeling in the word, the feeling that consisted in the believer's ecstatic passing over into Christ, and Christ's infusion into the believer. The commentary is polemical. It enacts charismata and the living ardor of affective union, and the enactment is agonistic. Like Rupert of Deutz, whom he adopted as a source and model of exegesis, Gerhoch continually engaged in dispute. Again like Rupert's, his doctrines more than once stirred up accusations of heresy. His extreme advocacy of the *vita apostolica* had led him to deny the validity of sacraments performed by secular priests. His doctrine that Christ had assumed humanity into divinity smacked of Monophysitism.[86] Without mentioning the charges of heresy that had resulted, Gerhoch yet made his doctrines on those two matters the chief substance of his commentary on Psalm 64, and in his preface he brazenly flaunted them before the noses of his critics.

Gerhoch's deliberate and assertive self-revelations in the course of his

82. Aristotle, *Rhetoric*, 1356a, 1378a.

83. Quintilian, *Institutes*, 8.3.12, 9.2.3.

84. *Tract. in Ps.*, 27:2; 144:4. Migne, *PL*, 193:1224, 194:964. Gerhoch's assertion of his own qualifications would appear to be at least a partial exception to Brian Stock's conclusion that, from the twelfth century on, "literacy created a set of lexical and syntactical structures which made the *persona* of the speaker largely irrelevant." Brian Stock, *The Implications of Literacy: Written Language and Models of Interpretation in the Eleventh and Twelfth Centuries* (Princeton, 1983), p. 86; see also p. 529.

85. Häring, "Commentary and Hermeneutics," pp. 176, 179, 181, 184–85.

86. Classen, *Gerhoch von Reichersberg*, pp. 47–57, 89–98, 167–73, 248–72. Heinz Hürten, "Neue Arbeiten über Gerhoch von Reichersberg," *Historisches Jahrbuch* 80 (1961): 268. Hefele-Leclerq, *Histoire des conciles*, 5:841.

defense belong to the positive values of his work. He endeavored to establish his credit by asserting that he had delivered his commentary to Eugenius III (an assertion reinforced by a direct address to Eugenius in the second recension, casually retained after the pope's death) and, in particular, that the pope had been well pleased by the Christological section.[87] At various moments in the discourse, he took occasion to note that he had moved in the highest circles in the see of Peter. He had defended the legality of the Donation of Constantine against a jurisconsult there.[88] He was familiar with strategies by which popes divided and conquered insurgent Romans.[89] When he was present at the Roman curia (1132) during the aftermath of the divided papal election of 1130, Archbishop Walter of Ravenna (1119–44) invited him to compile authoritative texts on whether sacraments performed by heretics were valid. With satisfaction, Gerhoch stated that Cardinal Aimeric, Innocent II's chancellor, approved the collection and its negative conclusion, a judgement that, as Gerhoch must have known, Innocent II mercilessly enforced against the acts and supporters of Anacletus II at the Second Lateran Council (1139). Gerhoch's elaborate affirmations of papal decrees in favor of the *vita apostolica* are further aspects of the effort to enhance his own credit by identifying himself with Rome and with Jesus, living in Peter.[90]

His advocacy of the ascetic morality of the *vita apostolica* was also occasion for polemical self-commendation. Gerhoch portrayed himself as a rigorist, discharging the prophetic duties of vigilance and fraternal rebuke. Defending a mode of life that (as he thought) the evangelist Luke himself certified as apostolic, and that safeguarded the purity of the priesthood,[91] Gerhoch denounced the specious holiness of its enemies. He displayed his knowledge of canonistic texts and the confirmity of his own teaching with testimonies of prophets, evangelists, and apostles.[92] Frequently speaking through the personae of prophets, and always speaking as one of those who have the firstfruits of the Holy Spirit,[93] Gerhoch portrayed himself as one of the rare exegetes—one in thousands—who possessed both wisdom and faithfulness, one of those not alien to the same gift of prophecy that had inspired David the psalmist, men who had the power of rightly understanding the Scriptures, interpreting them, and wisely proclaiming them in the church.[94] He evidently included himself when he asserted that all catholic pastors and teachers were angels of the

87. Preface A; chap. 44. *MGH LdL*, 3:439–40, 457.
88. Chaps. 15, 19. *MGH LdL*, 3:447, 448.
89. Chap. 56. *MGH LdL*, 3:462.
90. Chaps. 68, 70. *MGH LdL*, 3:468, 469.
91. Chaps. 41, 160. Migne, *PL*, 194:33. *MGH LdL*, 3:489.
92. Chaps. 15, 22. *MGH LdL*, 3:447, 449.
93. Chaps. 75, 78–79. Migne, *PL*, 194:55, 57.
94. Ep. 3, and general prologue to the commentaries on the Psalms, Migne, *PL*, 193:490, 638.

Lord of hosts in his apocalyptic harvest, separating the sons of hell from the sons of the kingdom as, by their words and writings, they taught clergy how to live in the eternal tabernacles and laymen how to be received into them.[95]

Neither Gerhoch's devotion to Roman primacy nor his ascetic morality produced logical aberrations in the agonistic performance he gave as exegete. They clearly gave him the ambiguous "is/is not" character of union by participation in which believers both were, and were not Christ—Christ by participation, themselves by birth. Beyond these positive values, Gerhoch informed his commentary with negative values that bridged the ironic distance between the inspired feeling in the text and the author in the text. Those values were elements of his thinking that he sometimes deliberately veiled in paradox. The illuminations of contemplative spirituality, he wrote, were like women who were not allowed to speak in the church, because what they received in secret ought to be kept as a secret for themselves. Those illuminations were waters that one ought to keep for oneself and to which others should not be admitted, although they were also the fountainheads from which exegetes drew streams that could be conveyed to others for their use.[96] Toward the end of his life, Rupert of Deutz was forced to reveal the visions that had formed the secret core of his spiritual life. Gerhoch escaped being coerced into comparable self-disclosure; but it is clear that one such illumination came during the terrifying and painful illness, associated with the loss of his virginity, that brought Gerhoch to seek clerical orders at the age of sixteen or seventeen.[97]

Gerhoch imagined his own life as a constant interplay between the *vita activa* and the *vita contemplativa* (or *theorica*).[98] With its emphasis on hierarchic obedience and cenobitic discipline, the commentary on Psalm 64 moves largely in the area of the *vita activa*. However, it was in the *vita theorica* that human reason learned to despise and use earthly things (in the *vita activa*), but to burn in holy desire for heavenly, and that it partook of the eternal wisdom.[99] The contemplative fonts of Gerhoch's spirituality appear in several ways in the commentary, and they indicate—as positive values do not—how Gerhoch's portrayal of the author in the text had a part in giving rise to the contradictions in his argument; for they plainly identify ways in which, by participation, the author both was and was not Christ.

95. Chap. 154. *MGH LdL*, 3:486.
96. *De investigatione Antichristi*, 2.75. Scheibelberger, pp. 333–36. On Rupert of Deutz's disclosure (under duress) of visions that he regarded as the basis of his authority, see Van Engen, *Rupert of Deutz*, pp. 346, 349–51.
97. *Dialogus inter clericum saecularem et regularem (epistola ad Innocentium papam)*, *MGH LdL*, 3:203.
98. Meuthen, *Kirche und Heilsgeschichte*, pp. 29–37.
99. *Tract. in Ps.*, 7:2; 64, chap. 170. Migne, *PL*, 193:725, 194:114.

Again, as in regard to the words of mouth, heart, and mind, Gerhoch was guided by three coordinates: difference in kind between the author in the text and Christ as individual persons; likeness in form between effects of the author and those contained in the words of Scripture; and identity in content, achieved in affective union of the author's soul with Christ. Gerhoch was confident that he himself—the author in his text—wrote under divine inspiration, "God ruling our spirit and pen."[100] He recalled how the disciples at Pentecost had been intoxicated by the infusion of the Holy Spirit and so alienated from themselves that their inebriated earthly substance became entirely heavenly.[101] Having drunk the waters of saving wisdom, they understood what they must seek and desire; being one in heart and soul in God, they neither possessed nor said what was their own.[102] Likewise exegetes, filled with the Holy Spirit and inebriated by the streams of God, obeyed a will other than their own.[103] They uttered God's words, not theirs. To seek not what was Christ's but what was one's own in the divine service was to commit idolatry; for "our sufficiency is of God, who hath also made us worthy ministers of the New Testament, not by letter but by spirit. For the letter killeth, but the Spirit giveth life."[104] Thus, Gerhoch frequently turned to the verse (Ps. 45:2): "My tongue is the pen of a scrivener that writeth swiftly," for the tongue of teachers confirmed the word (*verbum*) of God that had been spoken to them, and that informed the word (*sermo*) that raced through the mouths of teachers and the pens of scriveners writing swiftly.[105]

Speaking words not their own, exegetes played roles in the ever-recurrent conflict of good and evil desire. Like Augustine, Gerhoch as a young man had been infatuated with the theater, but after conversion to a life of austerity, he turned against theatrical performances. Like Augustine, Gerhoch retained, even after conversion, patterns of thought and expression borrowed from the theater. He tenaciously viewed the world in terms of disguise, a habit well suited to his doctrine that different persons could, through likeness, partake of the same identity. Evil was masked in many

100. *Princeps Mundi, MGH LdL,* 3:241. See also *Tract. in Ps.,* 31:prologue, and 34:24–28. Damian Van den Eynde and Odulph Van den Eynde, eds., *Opera inedita,* vol. 2, 1, Spicilegium Pontificii Athenaei Antoniani 9 (Rome, 1956), pp. 8, 402. *Tract. in Ps.,* 51: prologue. Migne, *PL,* 193:1609.

101. Chap. 105. Migne, *PL,* 194:71.

102. Chaps. 107, 115. Migne, *PL,* 194:71, 76.

103. Chaps. 105, 109, 110, 114. Migne, *PL,* 194:71–75.

104. Chap. 5. *MGH LdL,* 3:444. Among the apostles, Judas alone stubbornly held to his own understanding. Chap. 101. Migne, *PL,* 194:68. On the fatal allure of human curiosity, chap. 141. *MGH LdL,* 3:480. The quotation of 2 Cor. 3:5–6 occurs in chap. 95. Migne, *PL,* 194:65.

105. Chaps. 23, 24, 107. *MGH LdL,* 3:450. Migne, *PL,* 194:72. Gerhoch frequently turned to this verse in other works. Cf. Gerhoch's analogies between the tongue and God the Father, the pen and Jesus, and the scribe and the Holy Spirit. *Tract. in Ps.,* 45:2. Migne, *PL,* 193:1566.

ways, most perniciously when it appeared as a counterfeit good.[106] But wherever it appeared, it was always Satan in the wicked withstanding Christ.[107] Christ was in his faithful people; he was in his priests, visibly and corporally crowned with glory and honor, and in popes.[108] He was in exegetes and in texts that embodied their inspired thoughts.

As Huizinga wrote, an actor on stage both is and is not another being.[109] In the timelessness and spacelessness of affective union, the believer "was" Christ by participation. In the time and place of his own existence he "was not" Christ. In the same way, the prophets were great and unshakable in God's power, though in themselves they were lowly and weak.[110] The sins of Judas, Nicholas, and Simon Magus were not only events marring the unity of the apostolic church, but also sinful affects of envy, avarice, and lust that persisted and, indeed, aroused the abuses in his own day that Gerhoch deplored. The prophet Daniel was not merely God's witness in a distant age and hostile environment, but he was also at one with the affects of praise and prayer active in the midst of the Babylon that tyrannized the twelfth-century church. Gerhoch cast his own enemies in the roles of Judas, Nicholas, and Simon Magus. He cast himself as Jeremiah, the prophet of the exile, as Daniel, and as the three boys subjected to persecution in the Babylonian furnace, whose hymn, appended to the book of Daniel, he made the leitmotiv of his commentary.

Like liturgical drama, the agonistic play of virtue and vice "extended backward and forward from its center."[111] Whenever and wherever it was performed, the agonistic play of good affects against evil ones was simultaneous in Christ and equidistant from him. Thus, the historical contradictions in Gerhoch's argument are resolved on the level of affective spirituality. The argument that its temporal splendor and wealth vindicated

---

106. Chaps. 142–43. *MGH LdL*, 3:481–82. Gerhoch recalled that, during his service as *magister scholarum et doctor juvenum* at the cathedral in Augsburg (ca. 1117 to ca. 1120), he was in charge of theatrical productions. He later grieved that he had not only supervised, but also given them an enthusiastic stimulus "pro affectu stultitiae quo tunc infectus eram, et in quo supra multos coaetaneos meos profeceram." Others plainly shared his enthusiasm. The canons, he said, neither slept in the dormitory nor ate together in the refectory except on rare festivals, most of all those on which they represented "Herod, the persecutor of Christ and slayer of children," or "ludis aliis aut spectaculis quasi theatricalibus exhibendis," the canons came to the otherwise empty refectory. *Tract. in Ps.*, 133:3. Migne, *PL*, 194:890–91. Classen, *Gerhoch von Reichersberg*, p. 18. See notes 18 and 129.

107. Chap. 96. Migne, *PL*, 194:65.

108. Chaps. 99, 114. Migne, *PL*, 194:67, 75. Familiarity with the use of costumes may be indicated by Gerhoch's statement that the impious, seeing Antichrist face to face, put on his face, just as the poor are clothed in the face of Christ. *Tract. in Ps.*, 16:8. Migne, *PL*, 193:852.

109. Huizinga, *Homo Ludens*, p. 13.

110. Chaps. 65, 96. *MGH LdL*, 3:466–67. Migne, *PL*, 194:66.

111. O. B. Hardison, Jr., *Christian Rite and Christian Drama in the Middle Ages* (Baltimore, 1965), p. 285, on the *Quem queritis* trope.

the church in Constantine's day or in Gerhoch's did not contradict Gerhoch's lament over the inward corruption in the church. For Gerhoch cast his argument on a concentric scale, not a rectilinear one. Likewise, it was by no means contradictory to deride modes of life in the apostolic church whose falsity was proved by their early extinction, to embrace continuous tradition as a mark of authenticity, and yet to accept the *vita apostolica* as authentic although it withered after the era of the apostles and passed through centuries of sterility before being revived in comparatively recent times. For these events too occurred in a dimension that, like drama, negated time.

The fecundating, creative play of God's eternal wisdom was timeless and spaceless in its continual recapitulations. But it was agonistic in its dramatic performance.

Huizinga's comment on classical Greek drama is appropriate to Gerhoch's concept of role playing in, but not, of time and place. "The player, withdrawn from the ordinary world by the mask he wore, felt himself transformed into another ego which he did not so much represent as incarnate and actualize. The audience was swept along with him into that state of mind."[112]

How did Gerhoch seek to sweep his audience up into his vision of the church? I have indicated some ways in which he believed that the barriers between character and actor could be removed. Turning to our third negative value, I may now suggest ways in which he hoped to remove barriers between the character internalized by the actor, and the audience.

## The Text in the Audience: Imitation

Aristotle's third mode of persuasion was the orator's arousing the emotions of his audience, partly by appealing to memories.[113] The speaker's task was to persuade his hearers that happiness would be gained by doing what he advised and lost by doing what he opposed. Thus, he stimulated perceptions of pleasure and pain and corresponding emotional responses that determined whether the audience would cleave to the good (i.e., the case defended by the orator) and reject the bad (i.e., that opposed by him). Employing rhetoric—which he considered a "secular science" for capturing the affects[114]—Gerhoch set out to excite not only himself, but also his readers to the affects contained in the Psalms. He strove to go beyond what rhetoricians and dramatists achieved; for, he wrote, unlike those in comedies and tragedies—mere theatrical follies—who simulate grief or

---

112. Huizinga, *Homo Ludens*, p. 145.
113. Aristotle, *Rhetoric*, 1419b.
114. *Tract. in Ps.*, 6:1. Migne, *PL*, 193:1712–13. Above, note 59.

joy, he wished that he and his readers might actually be conformed, by true devotion, with the affects of those whose words they repeated.[115]

As noted above, memory was central to affective bonding as Gerhoch understood it. The attempt to engage the affects of his audience by stimulating perceptions of pleasure and pain—especially with reference to eternal rewards and punishments—exerted demands on his argumentation. The principles of play with which he responded entailed some of the logical contradictions that I mentioned at the outset.

Although he wished that something could be written to disclose to his adversaries the wrath of God hanging over them, it is clear that Gerhoch did not include in his intended audience those clerics whom he condemned for their Babylonian debaucheries with shameless women or, indeed, any who found the good intolerable; for they themselves, he wrote, were to be shunned.[116]

Gerhoch's intended audience consisted of two categories. The one, to which Gerhoch specifically addressed the commentary on Psalm 64, was Pope Eugenius III and his cardinals. The other, to which he generally addressed all his commentaries on the Psalms, was the "weak and poor" whom God chose to confound the powers of this world, "Christ's true paupers" living according to monastic rule.[117]

Gerhoch's address to pope and cardinals exemplified Quintilian's advice that one should use forbearance and decorum when speaking against a person of great dignity. All Gerhoch's implicit criticisms of papal actions conform with Quintilian's advice that the orator use circumlocution, profess grief at circumstances that brought him to complain, and censure the behavior of exalted persons tacitly, by describing applicable categories of reprehensible conduct and permitting the audience to draw its own conclusions, as Hamlet designed his play within a play to "catch the conscience of the King."[118] Likewise, Gerhoch's emphatic characterization of the power of the papal office and of the Apostle Peter as penitent conform with Quintilian's counsel that, when pleading with a judge of doubtful impartiality, an advocate should put the judge in mind of the dignity of his office, profess respect for the opinions of earlier judges (in an appellate process), and suggest that the presiding judge should fear incurring disgrace by rejecting the plea.[119]

115. General prologue to the commentaries on the Psalms, Migne, PL, 193:633–34. Gerhoch was therefore consciously appealing to, or seeking to form, what Brian Stock has defined as a "textual community." Stock, Implications of Literacy, pp. 88, 90–91. See also Stock's distinction between real and fictive audiences, p. 333.

116. Chaps. 49, 163. MGH LdL, 3:459, 490.

117. Chaps. 65, 133. MGH LdL, 3:466–67, 479. See also Van Engen, Rupert of Deutz, pp. 302–3.

118. See the acknowledged evasion in chap. 52. MGH LdL, 3:461. Quintilian, Institutes, 11.1.68–73, 85–90; 11.3.177.

119. Quintilian, Institutes, 11.1.75–78.

Karl F. Morrison

The occasion of Gerhoch's commentary justified the suppression of some grievances that Gerhoch expressed in other treatises. In the second preface to the commentary, he complained bitterly to Cardinal Henry against the perversion of justice in the church. Fear of retribution might keep a righteous man from openly blaming wicked judges, Gerhoch wrote, but he could at least keep truth in his heart, as Joseph of Arimathea had done when he silently refused to assent to the unjust judgment against Christ and yet dared openly to bury him. With Joseph, the righteous man could dare to bury Christ, silently venerating truth buried in his heart, and he could be certain that when it rose from the hiddenness of its tomb, truth would claim all power in heaven and on earth. Even so, Christ had stood silent before Pilate but proclaimed his word to all after the Resurrection; and the apostolic church in Rome, encircled by its Babylonian enemies, had taken refuge in "crypts and other hiding places,"[120] to be exalted in latter days with imperial pomp.

The cautious play of decorum evidently explains some of the contradictions between Gerhoch's assertion of papal dominance and his implied rebuke to the pope and cardinals for rebuilding Babylon within the walls of Jerusalem.

Play was at the heart of Gerhoch's address to his wider audience, just as it was in that specifically to pope and cardinals. The addresses and correspondingly the forms of play differed, however. When he spoke to the Roman clergy, Gerhoch employed the play of decorum. He revealed less than he saw, and he applied tactics of suppression and indirect inference. Speaking for and to the large, anonymous audience of Christ's poor, his object was to reveal more than the visible evidence of their captivity to the children of the curse, and he applied tactics of amplification, disclosing what was imperceptible.

True to exegetical convention, Gerhoch cast the paradoxical circumstances of Christ's poor in a dramatic setting inherited from the pre-Christian theater: the sequence of pathos, peripety, and theophany. The effect of drama composed on this scheme depended upon the reversal from suffering into apotheosis. As Gerhoch read Psalm 64, it figuratively described the passage of the righteous from bitter and degrading exile in Babylon to joyful and glorious return into Jerusalem, where their spirit was forever one with God.[121] The counterpart of pathos was exile; that of peripety, conversion through penance; that of theophany, the final affective union with God.

In the ancient theater, dramatic irony was used to stimulate an imitative emotional response in the audience, the irony by which events turned probability and fitness into mockery of themselves, an outcome expected by the audience but slowly revealed to the characters by experience.

120. Preface B; chap. 16, 51. MGH LdL, 3:441, 447, 460.
121. Chap. 172. Migne, PL, 194:115.

[138]

Dramatic irony elucidates the apparent contradiction in Gerhoch's portrayal of Christ's poor. Christ sleeps, permitting his disciples to suffer so that in their anguish and terror they may call upon him the more fervently, and so that in their wretchedness they may recognize that the redemption that he promised them is at hand.[122]

Christ played with terror; his poor, as viewers of the drama, recognized the irony that they, as characters, were enacting. Dramatic irony, turning on fear, also attended the mortifications that Christ's poor willingly embraced. Those very few who in purity kept celibate had heard God roaring with the voice of terror, threatening destruction of the earthly temple and its priesthood.[123] They followed the example of the three boys tried in the Babylonian furnace and of Daniel the prophet who, castrating themselves for the sake of the kingdom of God, were worthy to sing a hymn to God, to see visions of the heavenly kingdom, and to judge lewd old men. In the agonistic play of which their celibacy was part, they became the fields fecundated by the Lord and abounding with corn.[124]

A different irony operated with regard to clergy not numbered among Christ's poor. Denied the knowledge imparted to the audience, they were but actors in the drama and not knowledgeable spectators. The emotional catharsis of the performance, the change from wrong opinion to true knowledge, was not for them. They played with careless self-indulgence, like fish in Babylon's river, unaware how soon God's wrath would sear away the foul waters that sustained their lives.[125]

Retaining, as he did, vestiges of his earlier enthusiasm for the theater, and considering the life of the just a playing out of a dramatic progression, Gerhoch quite naturally employed theatrical tactics to evoke associations reaching beyond the pathos of Christ's poor to their theophany. Gerhoch knew that, as Aristotle observed, his tactics must give great vividness and immediacy to his presentation, removing barriers between audience and characters so that the audience feared for itself what it saw in others. Gerhoch's tactics included the lyric stimulus of the Psalm itself. Acutely sensitive to the emotional effects of music, Gerhoch may also have employed in delivery—and expected all familiar with psalmody to associate with his text—a "chanting tone," such as Quintilian advised to excite pity, "a kind of musical cadence and plaintive sweetness of the voice by which the mind is strongly affected and which is extremely natural."[126]

122. Chaps. 97–98. Migne, *PL*, 194:66–67.
123. Chap. 169. Migne, *PL*, 194:113.
124. Chaps. 39, 120–22, 173. Migne, *PL*, 194:32–33, 79–81, 115.
125. Chap. 138. *MGH LdL*, 3:479.
126. Aristotle, *Rhetoric*, 1386a. Quintilian, *Institutes*, 11.3.167, 170, 172. Cf. *Institutes*, 11.1.56, against using a "chanting tone." Cf. the occasional appearance of neumes over scriptural and liturgical texts in Gerhoch's commentary on the Psalms. Classen, *Gerhoch von Reichersberg*, pp. 115–16. On psalmody opening the heart to grace, Van Engen, *Rupert of Deutz*, pp. 303, 306.

He employed a "mixed style" of narrative and dramatic portrayal, rarely in dialogue and normally in soliloquy, freely impersonating prophets and other characters in the drama.[127] He lavishly extracted figures from the Psalm to evoke vivid tableaux in the minds of his hearers, his *benevoli spectatores*.[128] Convinced of the agonistic character of the play that he had to describe, he again and again referred to those tableaux as *spectacula*, a word for him kept the twofold sense of gladiatorial conflict and theatrical amusement. The "amazing spectacle" of Pharaoh drowning in pursuit of those who fled to refuge with God, the "wretched spectacle" of Babylonians infesting the citadel of Jerusalem (the church), the "joyful spectacle" of Armageddon, were displayed as *spectacula*,[129] so that the audience could experience them as actual events, vicariously seeing with the mind's eye the wonderful works of God that resounded inside the words of Scripture.[130] For *spectacula* delighted the eyes, as stories did the ears and banquets the taste; by sensory experiences, the mind was put in memory of God's power, wisdom, and goodness; and by remembering, it passed, through gratitude, to affective union.[131]

Gerhoch could assume that his readers would place Psalm 64 and his commentary on it in another dramatic context: that of the Eucharist. He himself located his discourse on the Eucharist at the focal point of his treatise and at the heart of divine wisdom's play with the sons of men. Like the terrible anguish of their lives, the Eucharist offered Christ's poor life after death, triumph after persecution, exultation after sorrow, and riches after poverty. "I see in this, your table," Gerhoch wrote, "a sublime miracle, a sublime spectacle." The people who are to enter into union with God approach the altar. They are to be slain, "just as, when a dove is incorporated into a falcon [*herodius*] or hawk, it is entirely destroyed, for one bird can not be incorporated into another bird so long as it keeps its earlier life."[132] Such were the poor, deserting the world and deserted by it. But before they could pass eucharistically into the Body of Christ, believers, slain and consumed in obedience, passed into the body of Peter who submitted to correction by his brethren, even as he confirmed them. They alone knew the course of events, because, annihilating their former lives by being digested into the body that they consumed, they entered into the richness of that body, the Holy Spirit.[133]

Play as imitation could address those who were not, but were yet to

127. An example of dialogue occurs in chap. 35. *MGH LdL*, 3:455. On personification, see chap. 75. Migne, *PL*, 194:55–56.
128. Chap. 73. *MGH LdL*, 3:471.
129. Chaps. 49, 52, 67, 87, 118, 149. *MGH LdL*, 3:459–60, 460–61, 468. Migne, *PL*, 194:61, 77. *MGH LdL*, 3:484. See above, notes 23, 106.
130. Cf. chap. 68. *MGH LdL*, 3:468.
131. *Tract. in Ps.*, 76:14. Migne, *PL*, 194:428–29.
132. *Tract. in Ps.*, 22:5. Migne, *PL*, 193:1051.
133. Chaps. 64, 172. *MGH LdL*, 3:466. Migne, *PL*, 194:114.

be, one in heart and soul.[134] As such, it encompassed another audience touched by God's creative and fecundating play. It widened the focus from the ineffable play of God in the hearts and minds of those already redeemed, and its expression by them in performance, to encompass also the impact of their performance upon the outside world, including those who were still to be born as "sons by faith and imitation."[135]

Gerhoch's commentary on Psalm 64 was one such performance, "this small gift from the hand of [his] poverty," which he wished to serve the increase of blessedness.[136] It was, he clearly hoped, part of the ministry hastening the return of God's people from Babylonian captivity into Jerusalemite freedom, part of the preaching of the word of God that became for hearers the efficient cause of salvation.[137] The same river of God ran in all spiritual men, Gerhoch wrote, so that, as they multiplied, inebriated by those waters, they might also irrigate the earth, germinating Christ and bringing him forth in the abundant and joyful tillage of justice, spiritual power, and penance.[138] Thus, in itself, the play of God's wisdom was creative; in performance, it was agonistic; in imitation, it was procreative.

*To summarize:* Huizinga's perception that "civilization grows in and as play" elucidates Gerhoch's call for church reform. The church, Gerhoch believed, was the sacramental union of heart and soul in God. That union was a dynamic movement by which Christ played in and through "the sons of men," and they played in and through the eternal wisdom and power that was Christ. Gerhoch's commentary presupposed three ways in which this play was experienced: directly, in the play of feeling itself; mediately, through the performance of roles (in this case, the role of author); and imitatively, as an audience, spiritually reenacting the role performed before them, conformed their affects with those inspired through the play of feeling and enacted in performance. In itself, the play had the effect of creation; as performance, that of conflict; as imitation, that of propagation.

Gerhoch consciously worked in the area of "is" and "is not," where character, actor, and audience were both themselves and one another; where, like the material elements of sacraments, they all were changed by sanctification into something different from what they had been and yet retained their original identities.[139]

134. Chap. 122. Migne, *PL*, 194:81, referring to the Jews.
135. Chaps. 42, 169. *MGH LdL*, 3:456. Migne, *PL*, 194:113. On imitation as a means of spiritual procreation, see my study *The Mimetic Tradition of Reform in the West* (Princeton, 1982), pp. 90, 126, 157, and passim. Gerhoch denounced performances of Antichrist plays in churches for many reasons, but notably because the performances incited emulation of the bad. *De investigatione Antichristi,* 1.5. *MGH LdL*, 3:315.
136. Preface B. *MGH LdL*, 3:442.
137. Chap. 174. Migne, *PL*, 194:115.
138. Chaps. 120, 173, 176. Migne, *PL*, 194:79, 115, 116.
139. Cf. *Princeps mundi,* chap. 25. Migne, *PL*, 194:1360.

Weaving together acknowledged and unacknowledged citations of other exegetes, Gerhoch built many positive components into his discourse: historical, dogmatic, and apologetic; moral, ascetic, and mystical; and, above all, sacramental. But it would be difficult to limit his doctrines to any of these modes of theology. In its manifold character and emphases, Gerhoch's thinking resembles the theology of feeling, developed by Schleiermacher from varied materials, including some from the twelfth century. Certainly, Schleiermacher's theology of feeling resembles Gerhoch's doctrines about the church in stressing the theologian's sense of affective union with God and in its critical object of penetrating positive values of a text—the logical screen of expression—to partake of the negative values, the emotional truth, that it contained. Gerhoch lacked the historical components that were essential to Schleiermacher's theology of feeling. Even so, for each writer discourse about the center of his reflections—the progression from difference through likeness to affective identity—was possible only by indirect methods; that is, by exposing the negative values in discourse itself. It was appropriate, therefore, that Gerhoch drew so many of his metaphors from the performing arts.

Behind Gerhoch's call for church reform lay the assumption that, like a song, oration, or drama, the church as play existed in the actual experience. In the case of the church, the play was affective union, experienced both immediately and at second hand through the reflective function of memory. Such experiences were possible, he argued, only in the hierarchic church. The affective union of persons in one common identity was limited to few, however, and it obliged them to struggle against those who had no access to the mysteries of Christ, even against those who held the supreme offices of the church. The communion that the sanctified few inwardly beheld and impersonated actually reproached the community in which they lived. They moved between contrary demands of spiritual obedience and institutional conformity. And it was through the church as agonistic play, as dramatic irony in action, continually in the process of resolution, that they advanced from captivity in the Babylon within the church into exultant freedom as living stones in the temple that was Christ their king, that eternal temple wondrous in equity where priests and prelates neither fell away into injustice nor played God or the Christian people false.[140]

140. Chaps. 175, 176. Migne, *PL*, 194:116.

## Appendix
## Table of Organization

1. Schematic Outline of Gerhoch's Commentary on Psalm 64

    I. *Exordium* (chaps. 1–13).
        A. *Principium* (chaps. 1, 2): A brief section to capture attention and goodwill

Summary: The Psalm looks to the end of the world. Gerhoch allegorizes its two alleged authors, Jeremiah and Haggai, as representing (respectively) the elect in exile and the elect in their return to Jerusalem. Jeremiah's sufferings are "planted together" in Christ's passion. There are further allegorical interpretations of Peter, representing the active life, and John the Evangelist, representing the contemplative life.

B. *Insinuatio* (chaps. 3–13): A longer section to entangle the audience in the subject and prepare its mind to receive the *narratio*.
Summary: Gerhoch explains the allegory of Babylon and Sion as a figurative way of talking about corruption in church history.

II. *Narratio* (chap. 14): A brief section stating the matter of the oration.
Summary: Gerhoch begins his "digression" against those who want to destroy the walls of Jerusalem and rebuild the walls of Babylon: in other words, to paganize Christendom. He recounts earlier persecutions of the faithful and discusses the conversion and the Donation of Constantine as a model for Christian rulers. He insists that Constantine was baptized by Pope Sylvester I, not by the heretical bishop Eusebius of Nicomedia.

III. *Partitio* (chaps. 15–74): Distinguishes what is to be confirmed from what is to be confounded.
Summary: Gerhoch continues the discussion of Constantine's benefactions to the church. He considers the need of clerical purity and complains of its contamination in modern times by avarice, chiefly through the confusion of spiritual and secular jurisdictions by kings and clergy. He praises the apostolic life (as defined by the Augustinian Rule) and papal authority as safeguards of clerical purity.

IV. *Confirmatio* (chaps. 75–122): Sets forth what is to be confirmed.
Summary: Gerhoch devotes this section to the Christological basis of his doctrines. Beginning with the expectation of Christ's eschatological return, he turns to Christ's glorification of human nature and to the salvation of the elect through his mediation, portraying Christ as the temple of equity and the faithful as living stones incorporated into that temple. He discusses the Eucharist as a particular means of Christ's mediation and asserts the invalidity of sacraments administered by heretics. He contrasts the sterility of heretics with the fecundity of those obedient to Christ.

V. *Confutatio* (chaps. 123–69): Sets forth what is to be rejected.
Summary: Gerhoch largely devotes this section to a discussion of how to deal with the corruption of the apostolic life by the Aachen Rule. He considers the apocalyptic plagues of unclean spirits and false prophets that visit suffering upon the good. He insists that, according to Christ's command, the tares are to be left to grow among the wheat until the harvest, but he offers the good the comfort of knowing that eventually the wicked will be confounded and brought to nothing.

VI. *Conclusio* (chaps. 170/71 to 176): Artfully states the point of the oration.
Summary: Gerhoch describes the consummation of the apocalyptic harvest. He contrasts the blighted sterility of the reprobate with the endless

abundance and jubilation that will reward those who have been faithful under persecution and who have returned to Jerusalem from their Babylonian exile. Those whose spirit adheres to God are made one with him. As king of justice, humbling no one whom faith and humility commend, Christ rebukes the Jews, his own brethren, for their wrongdoing and does not repel the Gentiles from the glory prepared for saints. The whole Christian people, returned to Jerusalem, brings him glory and honor in the fruits of justice and penitence.

## 2. Sections of Gerhoch's Commentary on Psalm 64

Chapters in which there is *no* reference to Psalm 64 are italicized. Chapters in which initial references occur to verses in Psalm 64 are marked with lowercase roman numerals, indicating the verse.

| | |
|---|---|
| *Exordium*[141] | 1 (i, ii), 2, 3, 4, 5, 6 (vi), 7, 8, 9, 10, 11, 12, 13, |
| *Narratio* | 14 |
| *Partitio* | 15, 16, *17*, *18*, 19, 20, 21, 22, 23, 24, 25, 26, 27, 28, 29, 30, 31, *32*, *33*, *34*, *35*, *36*, *37*, *38*, *39*, 40, 41, 42, 43, 44, 45, 46, 47, 48, 49, 50, *51*, *52*, *53*, *54*, *55*, *56*, *57*, *58*, *59*, 60, 61, 62, 63, 64, 65 (iii), 66, 67, 68, 69, 70, 71, 72, 73, 74, |
| *Confirmatio* | 75, 76, 77, 78 (iv), 79 (v), 80, 81, *82–84*, *85*, 86, 87, 88, 89, 90, 91, 92, 93, 94 (vii), 95, 96 (viii), 97, 98, 100 (ix), *101*, *102*, *103*, 104 (x), *105*, 106, 107, 108, 109, *110*, 111, 112, 113, 114, 115, 116, 117, *118*, *119*, 120 (xii), *121*, 123, |
| *Confutatio* | *123*, *124*, *125*, *126*, *127*, *128*, *129*, *130*, *131*, *132*, *133*, *134*, *135*, *136*, *137*, *138*, *139*, *140*, *141*, *142*, *143*, *144*, *145*, *146*, *147*, *148*, *149*, *150*, *151*, *152*, 153, *154*, *155*, *156*, *157*, *158*, *159*, *160*, *161*, *162*, *163*, *164*, *165*, *166*, *167*, *168*, |
| *Conclusio* | 169, *170*, 171 (xiii), *172*, 173 (xiv), *174*, *175*, 176 |

Without relating the sections to rhetorical theory, Classen also proposed a thematic division of the commentary into five parts. *Gerhoch von Reichersberg*, pp. 142–43. The issue is whether Gerhoch imposed a deliberate outline (as proposed here), or allowed an outline to emerge as he worked his way through a series of excursus and digressions.

---

141. The *exordium* can be divided into the *principium* (chaps. 1, 2) and the *insinuatio* (chaps. 3–13).

# [8]

## Praeter Politicos Principatus Ponendum: Priests as Magistrates and Citizens in Medieval Texts Using Aristotle's *Politics*

### Susan M. Babbitt

In a well-known monograph Martin Grabmann described the influence of Aristotelian philosophy on medieval theories of spiritual-temporal relations.[1] The examples of this influence or, better, this use of Aristotle, which are classified in this essay, show an ingenuity of application that medievalists have come to know and even to admire. Grabmann's Schoolmen, whatever their stripe, were determined to take full advantage of the work of the Philosopher. One may wonder, however, why they did not make more of the *Politics*. I do not speak now of the indirect effects of Aristotle's depiction of the natural origins and independent moral value of secular associations. I am thinking of a more direct connection. In the *Politics*, the role of priests in real and ideal states is considered. Why is there so little mention of these texts?

The simple part of the answer is the practical part. The scholars of the West did not have a Latin *Politics* until about 1260. Even then the perplexing translation of William of Moerbeke could not really be used, only puzzled out sentence by sentence.[2] This was a temporary problem, of course. But one might also argue, to get to the complex part of the answer,

---

1. Martin Grabmann, "Studien über den Einfluss der aristotelischen Philosophie auf die mittelalterlichen Theorien über das Verhältnis von Kirche und Staat," *Sitzungsberichte der Bayerischen Akademie der Wissenschaften zu München: Philosophisch-historische Abteilung*, 1934, no. 2.

2. The complete translation of Moerbeke was edited by Franz Susemihl, *Aristotelis Politicorum libri octo, cum vetusta translatione Guilelmi de Moerbeka* (Leipzig, 1872). For the earlier incomplete translation see Pierre Michaud-Quantin, *Politica: Translatio prior imperfecta interprete Guillelmo de Moerbeka (?)*, vol. 29¹ of *Aristoteles Latinus* (Bruges and Paris, 1961). See also Martin Grabmann, *Guglielmo di Moerbeke, O.P., il traduttore delle opere di Aristotele* (Rome, 1946).

that the better a medieval writer knew the priesthood of Aristotle, the less likely he was to mention it. After all, what was it but a "dignified sinecure"?[3] In Aristotle's ideal polity one might serve when young as a soldier, when in vigorous middle age as a counselor or judge, and when elderly as a temple guardian. This priesthood was not a separate class, but a function or office occupied by male members of the upper class or *honorabilitas* at a particular time of life. There was no vocation, no division of loyalties; no place for a Hildebrand, a Becket, a Boniface VIII.

Aristotle treats these elderly caretakers almost as an afterthought. They appear in his most famous enumeration of the (six) parts of the state, in *Politics*, 7.8.1328b, but not in a longer list in 4.4.1291a–b. Perhaps they deserved no attention at all from Christians. I suggest, however, that the principles implied in the description of this priesthood were pertinent to the integration of a strongly political clerical organization into increasingly aggressive secular states.

In this matter, as in others, Aristotle provided balance, along with an ambiguity that allowed considerable room for maneuvering. On the one hand, his clergymen have no pedestal. They are no more than a part of the state and can even be overlooked. Aristotle, unlike Marsilius of Padua, would not have made a strong a priori argument from unity to prove this; it hardly needed proving, for the priesthood of Greece was not a faction. On the other hand, as a mere part or office of the polis, it was no less than these things. Its position was stabilized, because it could neither rise above nor fall below a certain point. As officers and as members of the ruling class, the priests had a secure standing within the state.

The ambiguity in the position of these undoubted officers enters with the question whether they are also magistrates, that is, endowed with the power of "deliberating, deciding, and giving instructions." Aristotle excluded them from this class in 4.15.1299a, saying that "we can hardly include [as magistrates], for example, the priests of the public cults, whose office must be reckoned as something different from the political magistracies." His meaning seems quite clear: priests cannot give instructions, "which is the special mark of the magistrate."[4] For Marsilius of Padua such a statement was most helpful. He used it in *Dictio* 2 as well as in *Dictio* 1: indeed, it is one of only two citations of the *Politics* in the second part of his treatise, where it serves to reinforce his denial of power to the clergy.[5]

In fact the matter is not as unequivocal as might have pleased him. For

---

3. W. L. Newman, *The Politics of Aristotle*, 4 vols. (Oxford, 1887–1902), 1:329.

4. *Politics*, 4.15.1299a. This translation is from Ernest Barker, *The Politics of Aristotle* (Oxford, 1946), pp. 194–95.

5. *Defensor pacis*, 1.19.12 (p. 136 in the edition of Richard Scholz [Hannover, 1932]); 2.9.8 (p. 239 in Scholz). Marsilius refers to this latter citation in 2.30.5 (p. 597 in Scholz) without quoting it. The other *Politics* citation in *Dictio* 2 is in 2.2 (p. 143 in Scholz), where he refers to 2.10.1272a.

one thing, Aristotle himself, as noted by Newman, seems in *Politics*, 6.8.1322b to imply that priests are public, if not political, officers of some kind.[6] For another, Moerbeke's Latin for the crucial phrase in 4.15.1299a, "reckoned as something different from the political magistracies," is a flexible one.[7] This translation provided medieval writers with a nose of wax, which they did not fail to turn in more than one direction.

Even here, then, clerical prerogative can be defended. These priests might be considered magistrates in some sense, as well as officials and members of the *honorabilitas*. This would ensure their rights to property and jurisdiction, a solution very different from that of Marsilius.

Marsilius must be considered the first and foremost of those who made use of Aristotle's discussion of the priesthood, although earlier literal commentaries on the *Politics* dealt, however routinely, with the whole of the text.[8] Peter of Auvergne (who completed the commentary of Thomas Aquinas) and Albertus Magnus treated the temple guardians as part of ancient error. When explicating 4.4.1291a–b, where Aristotle fails to mention priests among the parts of the state, neither Peter nor Albertus made an objection.[9] As for the consideration of priests as magistrates in 4.15.1299a, Peter's explication does not get us very far, but Albertus's version does contain at least the germ of an interpretation favorable to the clergy: those concerned with sacred things are not subject to the political order.[10] But this is as far as he will go. Nor do their commentaries on 6.8.1322b discover the suggestion Newman found there, that priests might be public officers of some sort. Peter is clearly speaking of a vanished institution. He makes nothing of the statement in this chapter that these ancient religious officials were sometimes called kings. Albertus has little more to say.[11]

Their treatment of the clergy as part of Aristotle's ideal city in book 7 is no more extensive. Peter paraphrases, and Albertus, like Peter, speaks of a pagan priesthood.[12] Peter did become unusually expansive when agreeing

6. Newman, *Politics of Aristotle*, 1:514–15; 4:564.

7. Susemihl, p. 440, line 12: "praeter politicos principatus ponendum."

8. Alan Gewirth, *Marsilius of Padua: The Defender of Peace*, 2 vols. (New York and London, 1951–56), 1:93. I have been unable to consult Marino Damiata, *"Plenitudo potestatis" e "Universitas civium" in Marsilio da Padova*, Biblioteca di Studi Francescani 16 (Florence, 1983), and the papers of the *Atti del convegno internazionale di Padova del 18–20 settembre 1980* (of which Marsilius was the subject), which appeared in 1982 in *Medioevo: Rivista di storia della filosofia medievale*.

9. Peter: Raimundo M. Spiazzi, ed., *In libros politicorum Aristotelis expositio* (Turin and Rome, 1951), pp. 198–99, nos. 560–68. (Aquinas's part in this commentary goes to 3.6, inclusive.) Albertus: *Opera omnia*, 38 vols. (Paris, 1890–99), 8 (1891): 335c–338k.

10. Peter: Spiazzi, p. 235, no. 683: "Principatus autem iste est alter a civilibus principatus." Albertus: *Opera omnia*, 8:405b.

11. Peter: Spiazzi, p. 336, no. 1042. Albertus: *Opera omnia* 8:614y.

12. Peter: Spiazzi, p. 367, nos. 1132, 1134. Albertus: *Opera omnia*, 8:671e, g.

with Aristotle that temples should be guarded by elderly citizens, not by farmers and mechanics. Aristotle specified that priests should be "weary with years" to keep them from exercising political influence, but Peter saw weariness less as a hindrance to one activity than as an aid to another, that is, contemplation. Albertus for once had less to say and hardly developed this theme.[13] Aristotle's assignment of a portion of public property to "the service of the gods" evoked only the briefest of comments from the two men.[14]

One last passage should be mentioned, although the mention will not advance this study. In 7.12.1331b, there is a final contribution to the subject of priests as magistrates: "The directors of the state include priests as well as magistrates." Moerbeke's version makes the distinction clear.[15] Unfortunately, it seems that none of the writers mentioned here, including Marsilius, made anything of this statement.

Marsilius has other predecessors who spoke of the priesthood as was done in the *Politics* without mentioning that text. These writers witnessed the attempts of aggressive secular rulers to broaden the state's jurisdiction and its access to the property of its citizens. The rulers saw the clergy in its local aspect, as a group of subjects responsible to the commonwealth. John of Salisbury treated the clergy as officials of the republic long before the reappearance of the *Politics*.[16] While not surprising or momentous in itself, this suggests that Aristotle's account of the priesthood would not seem alien to the first readers of the Latin *Politics*.

The intricacies of question 9.31 of the *Quodlibeta* of Henry of Ghent, where he considers whether priests, as part of the city, are liable to the same exactions as others, may reflect the problems of hard-pressed administrators as well as the scholastic love of distinction mongering.[17] Indeed, such circumstances were to lead to a celebrated papal-royal controversy, which produced a literature displaying a leveling attitude toward clerics. This is seen in a letter of Philip IV himself, who held that all members of the body politic must contribute to its defense.[18] The author of *Antequam essent clerici* said that any part of the kingdom which does not support the

13. *Politics*, 7.9.1329a; Barker, p. 303. Newman, *Politics of Aristotle*, 1:329, says that "the history of the Papacy may be quoted against [Aristotle and Plato, who agreed about separating age and influence], perhaps not altogether conclusively." (Peter: Spiazzi, p. 371, no. 1141. Albertus: *Opera omnia*, 8:679–80g).

14. Aristotle: *Politics* 7.10.1330a; Barker, p. 305. Peter: Spiazzi, p. 374, no. 1151. Albertus: *Opera omnia*, 8:686c–d.

15. Barker, p. 310. Susemihl, p. 293, lines 9–10.

16. John of Salisbury, *Policraticus*, 5.2, ed. Clemens C. I. Webb, *Ioannis Saresberiensis Episcopi Carnotensis Policratici sive de Nugis Curialium . . . ,* 2 vols. (Oxford, 1909), 1:284, which is part of the famous exposition of the analogy of the body politic, taken from "Plutarch."

17. Henry of Ghent, *Quodlibeta*, 2 vols. (Venice, 1613), fols. 127v–128v.

18. Joseph R. Strayer, "Defense of the Realm and Royal Power in France," in *Medieval Statecraft and the Perspectives of History* (Princeton, 1971), p. 291.

whole is to be considered inharmonious, useless, almost paralytic.[19] The soldier in the *Disputatio inter clericum et militem* spoke of a moral rather than a biological imperative. He contrasted the hardships of temporal governors with the security and luxury of the clergy, declaring that anyone who is protected by the government should help to preserve it.[20] Here priests are required to promote the general welfare rather than restrained from harming it, to share their wealth rather than surrender it, but the anonymous author, like Marsilius, saw them as a part of the state.[21]

Marsilius, whose defense looks from some perspectives like an offense, may be taken, both for his decisiveness and for his extensive use of both Aristotle and Scripture, to be the culminator of this aggressive attitude. His work has been described as an infernal machine.[22] Such a description might not have seemed excessively vivid to the clerical victims of a scheme designed to expose them to every possible disadvantage, to catch them between the strictures of Aristotle on the one side and those of the New Testament on the other, in a trap contrived to close with all the force of logic. The *Politics* could be used to bring them down to the level of other public officials and, at the same time, to make them less than these officials by denying the title of magistrate. In losing this title priests lost the coercive power that was all-important to Marsilius, and they lost as well all authority beyond that of an expert witness.[23]

The New Testament was used by Marsilius further to handicap the church. Although the first part of his treatise was dominated by Aristotle

19. Pierre Dupuy, *Histoire du différend d'entre le pape Boniface VIII et Philippes le Bel roy de France* (Paris, 1655), p. 22.

20. Norma N. Erickson, "A Dispute between a Priest and a Knight," *Proceedings of the American Philosophical Society* 111, 5 (October 1967): 298–99. A nearly identical text is found in Melchior Goldast, *Monarchia seu Romani imperii*, 3 vols. (Hannover, 1611–14), 1:16, 17.

21. There is a similar statement in *Defensor pacis*, 2.8.9 (ed. Scholz, p. 230). See also Gewirth, *Defender*, 1:26–27.

22. G. Piovano, "Il Defensor pacis di Marsilio Patavino," *Scuola Cattolica*, 5th ser., 22 (1922): 64, cited in Conal Condren, "Marsilius of Padua's Argument from Authority: A Survey of Its Significance in the *Defensor Pacis*," *Political Theory* 5 (1977): 215.

23. *Defensor pacis*, 1.5.1 (hereafter *DP*), from *Politics*, 7.8.1328b. See also *DP*, 1.5.13, from his discussion of those who may properly become priests, taken from *Politics*, 7.9.1329a. For Marsilius's discussion of the need for unity under a single sovereign authority, see 1.15.10, which takes support from *Politics*, 5.3.1302b and 3.12–13.1282b, and 1.17.3.

This argument reappeared in the *Somnium viridarii* and in its French analogue the *Songe du Vergier*, whose author or authors almost surely borrowed it from Marsilius, while using also his statement that those who enjoy the benefits of civil government should share in its expenses (an echo as well of the *Disputatio inter clericum et militem*): *Somnium viridarii*, 1.65 (Goldast, *Monarchia*, 1:80); *Songe du Vergier*, 1.64, edited by Jean Louis Brunet as vol. 2 of Pierre Dupuy, *Traitez des droits et libertez de l'église gallicane*, 4 vols. (Paris, 1731–51), p. 69. For the statement echoing the *Disputatio*, see *Somnium* 1.102 (Goldast 1:91) and *Songe* 1.60 (Brunet, p. 66).

On the importance of coercive power, see *DP*, 1.10.4 and 1.12.6. On the denial to and the second by Scripture, the two sections and sources are presented as consistent and complementary.[24] A clergy that followed the self-denying precepts of Christ, looked only to a kingdom not of this world, and gave Caesar his due should subordinate itself to the unity of the city. Furthermore, since property is essentially, according to Marsilius, a right that can be defended at law,[25] the poverty observed by Christ and the apostles would agree with the denial of jurisdiction to the clergy, which had been built upon an Aristotelian basis in *Dictio* 1.[26] The Legislator, or his deputies, or donors within the state, should preserve the evangelical purity of the priesthood by managing its modest goods.[27]

It would seem that Marsilius managed to reconcile Athens and Jerusalem, and perhaps Padua as well.[28] Unfortunately, however, his Aristotle wars against his New Testament. It is true that both sources can be used to deny temporal authority to the clergy, but they cannot be applied to this purpose at the same time without contradiction. Broad inconsistencies within the *Defensor pacis* have been noted by writers including Labanca, who wrote a century ago, Passerin d'Entrèves, Gewirth, and Quillet.[29] Gewirth and others have asked how the priests, who are members of the upper class and of the human legislator, according to *Dictio* 1, can be so thoroughly stripped of temporal jurisdiction in *Dictio* 2.[30] Gewirth cites

priests of all authority beyond that of the expert witness or "judge in the first sense," see *DP*, 1.19.12; 2.7.4; 2.7.5; 2.9.2; 2.9.8; and 2.10.2. In 2.7.3 Marsilius gives an example of his notion of the noncoercive role of priests, quoting Ambrose by way of Peter Lombard (Scholz, p. 217, from *Sent.*, lib. 4, dist. 18, cap. 4 [Migne, *PL*, 192:886]).

John of Jandun, sometimes alleged to be the collaborator of Marsilius, mentioned Aristotle's sixfold classification in his questions on the *Metaphysics*, 1.18, but he was principally concerned with the role of the philosophers, whom he considered to be apart from but not inferior to the city. See Jeannine Quillet, "Brèves remarques sur les *Questiones super metaphysice libros I–VI* (Codex Fesulano 161 f° 11a–41va) et leurs relations avec l'aristotélisme hétérodoxe," *Miscellanea Mediaevalia* 10 (1976): 380. See also Gregorio Piaia, "L'averroismo politico e Marsilio da Padova," in *Saggi e ricerche*, ed. Carlo Giacon (Padua, 1971), p. 42.

24. *DP*, 1.1.8.

25. Ibid., 2.12.13.

26. What Marsilius wanted to do was quite different from what the Spiritual Franciscans wanted to do: he wished to laicize clerical property (Jeannine Quillet, *La philosophie politique de Marsile de Padoue* [Paris, 1970], p. 214).

27. *DP*, 2.14.8.

28. See Gewirth, *Defender*, 1:26–27, for a description of the strict regulation of the clergy in Padua.

29. Baldassare Labanca, *Marsilio da Padova: Riformatore politico e religioso del secolo XIV* (Padua, 1882), pp. 209–10; Alexander Passerin d'Entrèves, *The Medieval Contribution to Political Thought* (London, 1939), p. 50; Gewirth, *Defender*, 1:299–300; Quillet, "L'Aristotélisme de Marsile de Padoue," *Miscellanea Mediaevalia* 2 (1963): 705. Gewirth speaks of a "double dialectic, alternately dualistic and monistic," rather than of a contradiction between Aristotle and the New Testament, but one could argue that the former contradiction arose from the latter or that it is associated with Marsilius's attempt to serve both spiritual and political ends.

30. *DP*, 1.5.1; Gewirth, *Defender*, 1:298–99 and n. 42. See also J. W. Allen, "Marsilio of Padua and Medieval Secularism," in *The Social and Political Ideas of Some Great Mediaeval Thinkers*, ed. F. J. C. Hearnshaw (New York, 1923), p. 185; Quillet, "L'orga-

texts from the *Defensor minor* that express what he calls "Marsilius' hesitation between the two poles of popular sovereignty (which would admit the priests to a share in coercive authority) and a completely non-coercive, non-political priesthood."[31] In these two similar texts, Marsilius says that "spiritual ministers" of whatever rank are by no means constituents of the human legislator, unless perhaps they may be considered as such because they are part of the city.[32] (The *Politics* is not mentioned in these chapters.)

Quillet shows how this contradiction extends to the matter of property. It is as paradoxical to deny property to an honorable estate as it is to deny political power to it. Furthermore, to put the matter the other way around, if the clergy has no property, it cannot be an element in the "weightier part" of the state, which is determined by quality (that is, by wealth) as well as by quantity.[33] It looks as though priests, despite their gentle origins and exalted rank, have none of the attributes of citizens.

It seems that the synthesis of Marsilius was at cross-purposes with itself. One could argue all the same that the *Politics* taken alone provided a more promising model for those who wished to weaken the clergy than for those who wished to exalt it. Nevertheless a few clerical supporters used this text, as well as others discussed by Grabmann, to provide churchmen with independence, and more than independence. In a series of related works the association of priests and judges, which was merely nominal or sequential in Aristotle, became subject to a sort of sympathetic magic whereby priests acquired the powers of judges and kings.[34]

Some opposed to Marsilius their own interpretations of the *Politics*. In an anonymous treatise *De potestate ecclesiae*, dated by Scholz to about 1324–32, the career of the Greek gentleman suffers a strange transformation.[35] Some, said the author, deny active political power to the clergy

---

nisation de la société humaine selon le Defensor pacis de Marsile de Padoue," *Miscellanea mediaevalia* 3 (1964): 194, 197; Jean-Pierre Royer, *L'église et le royaume de France au XIVe siècle d'après le "Songe du Vergier" et la jurisprudence du Parlement* (Paris, 1969), pp. 42–43 and n. 42, who speaks of a conflict between Aristotelianism and Augustinianism in the work of Marsilius.

31. Gewirth, *Defender*, 1:299 n. 42, citing *Defensor minor*, 13.9 and 16.4.

32. *Defensor minor*, 13.9, 16.4.

33. Quillet, "Organisation de la société," p. 197.

34. Of course one could call them judges and kings, as one could call them part of the city, without help from Aristotle. James of Viterbo cited the *Politics* in *De regimine christiano*, but he did not mention it in 2.3 when he made this connection (H. X. Arquillière, ed., *Le plus ancien traité de l'église, Jacques de Viterbe, De regimine christiano [1301–1302]* [Paris, 1926], p. 180).

As Gewirth says (*Defender*, 1:99 and n. 52), Marsilius, following Aristotle's general notion, preferred a "pluralitas et distinccio parcium civitatis" (*DP*, 1.4.5 [Scholz, p. 19]), these parts being, of course, under the strict and exclusive control of the human legislator.

35. Richard Scholz, *Unbekannte kirchenpolitische Streitschriften aus der Zeit Ludwigs des Bayern (1327–1354)*, 2 vols. (Rome, 1911–14), 1:255. An analysis containing

because it represents the final and not the active cause of the city, and because Aristotle insisted upon a distinction of offices.[36] They say, he continued, that the priesthood belongs not to judges and soldiers, but to contemplatives who have renounced political action.[37] But the author was not content with this view. After demonstrating the necessity of unity in the Christian state, he declared that its primary ruler must be the pope, as is proved by three arguments. The second of these, the argument from the dignity of offices, is based on Aristotle's six parts of the state. The author claims that priests, as former judges, retain or surpass the dignity of judges. Aristotle had made it clear that elderly judges are to dwindle into priests. To this author they rather rise into the priesthood, when they are most fit for the speculative life, as Peter of Auvergne had suggested. When the hierarchy of the church is grafted onto this ascending scale of dignities, the greatest of priests becomes the greatest of judges.[38]

Scholz has shown that Alvarus Pelagius was sufficiently impressed by this inversion of the political order of Aristotle (and, by extension, of Marsilius) to use it in *De planctu ecclesiae*, 1.40.[39] The argument of Alvarus, which often follows the anonymous treatise word for word, makes additions and subtractions but has the same burden and uses the argument based on the dignity of the priesthood, to reach the same equation between priests and judges.[40]

In these examples one part of Aristotle's description of the offices of the state, that is, the serial identity of judges and priests, was taken by clerical supporters to endow the latter with the dignity of the former, perhaps a feeble compliment for the clergy. This description could serve the clergy in other ways. We should not forget what was said about priests as magistrates in 4.15, for though this may seem perfectly to suit the purposes of Marsilius and those of his mind, Moerbeke's translation of the central phrase can be interpreted in two quite different ways.

---

parts of the treatise, from Cod. Paris 4046, is given here on pp. 250–56. The complete text is given from the same manuscript in Jean Leclerq, "Textes contemporains de Dante sur les sujets qu'il a traités," *Studi medievali*, 3d ser., no. 6, fasc. 2 (1965): 507–17.

36. *Politics*, 4.15.1299a.

37. Scholz, *Streitschriften*, p. 252.

38. Leclerq, "Textes," pp. 513–14.

39. Scholz, *Streitschriften*, 1:255, gives 1330–32 as the date of the first version of this treatise.

40. "Summum sacerdotium summo iudici et econverso" (cited from the unpaginated Ulm edition of 1474). The text is clearly based on the one summarized above at note 38.

About ten years later, Alvarus returned to this theme in his *Speculum regum*. He listed the six necessary parts of the city, as they appear in *Politics*, 7.8.1328b, with the order of judges and priests reversed. (Here he had the modest goal of inculcating respect for the church and did not make high claims for the papacy.) See Miguel Pinto de Meneses, ed., *Frei Alvaro Pais, Bispo de Silves, Espelho dos Reis*, 2 vols. (Lisbon, 1955), 1:34, and Marino Damiata, *Alvaro Pelagio: Teocratico Scontento*, Studi Francescani 81, 3–4 (Florence, 1984), p. 573.

Walter Burley was one who took Aristotle's separation of priests from the political magistracies to imply superiority rather than subordination. We do not see this in his exposition of 4.15 itself. There, his comments are neutral: he simply says that the clergy represents an authority different from that of the public magistrates.[41] His defense of the spiritual power comes rather in his comments on 6.8.1322b, where Aristotle apparently considered priests to be some sort of public officers. But the defense does not seem to be provoked by this text, or by the statement that the managers of public sacrifices "are in some states called archon, in others king, and in others prytaneis."[42] He simply chose to insert at this point what Daly calls "one of his rare *notanda.*"[43]

While this expansiveness is unusual, the argument is not. It is an example of the metaphysic described in Grabmann's article. To take it somewhat out of Burley's order: the unity which Aristotle considers necessary to the city requires order, which in turn demands subordination. So far Marsilius would not disagree. But Burley, like the author of the *De potestate ecclesiae,* took the matter to a different conclusion. For Burley it was clear that divine things are superior to all others, so that the religious power dominates the others in some way, apparently leaving the immediate direction of inferior things to the temporal power.[44]

What is striking here is not the metaphysic, but the way he introduces it. He denies the superiority of temporal authority to spiritual authority, because Aristotle said that these two powers do not belong to the same class.[45] This may be a reference to the division of offices in 6.8.1322b, as though Aristotle's demarcation between religious and other offices were taken by Burley to be stronger than was intended. But it may hark back to 4.15.1299a, to the comment that the priestly authority is unlike political authority. In any case he was clearly thinking of a distinction between types of offices, which is found in the *Politics.* Where Aristotle makes an incidental observation that priests are something other than (perhaps less

41. His *Politics* commentary, written in the 1340s, is cited from Cambridge MS Gonville and Caius 490 (fols. 11a–74va), with this comment on fol. 36vb.

42. *Politics,* 6.8.1322b; Barker, p. 277.

43. Lowrie J. Daly, "The Conclusions of Walter Burley's Commentary on the *Politics,* Books V and VI," *Manuscripta* 13 (1969): 149.

44. "Philosophus vult civitatem habere unam unitatem conexionis sed habere unitas non potest esse nisi principatus in ea sunt ordinati sed non est ordo in eis nisi unus sit sub alio. . . . principatus politici inmediate applicat se ad ista inferiora ordinanda sed principatus divinus inmediate convertit se ad divina non ordinans ea sed rogans Deum quatenus omnia dirigat et conservet in bono statu" (fol. 51va).

For a summary, see Daly as cited above. See also F. E. Cranz, "Aristotelianism in Medieval Political Theory: A Study of the Reception of the Politics" (Ph.D. diss., Harvard University, 1938), p. 203, and Conor Martin, "Some Medieval Commentaries on Aristotle's *Politics,*" *History* 36 (1951): 40.

45. "Et notandum est quod principatus politicus non est super principatum divinum quia dicit quod hoc genus principatum divinorum est aliud genus a genere principatuum politicorum" (fol. 51va).

[153]

than) magistrates, Burley assumes that any distinction of offices must in principle involve a subordination based on final causes, not independence alone for the priesthood, but superiority.

Here he differs from Marsilius: in fact, his premises are so foreign to those of Marsilius, and so likely to be rejected out of hand by Marsilius, that they do not seem to represent a reaction or response to the *Defensor pacis*.

It was also possible to meet Marsilius on his own ground, by interpreting these texts from the *Politics* somewhat more literally than did these clericalist writers. That is, one could try to see the whole state in Aristotelian terms, to discover what is necessary for political life in general and what is required by each part in particular. This meant that the writer must look for principles in the texts rather than inflate what was incidental, that is, the identity of judges and priests, or import metaphysical notions such as unity and the final cause. His solution would thus be plausible, coherent, and in the spirit of Aristotle, more so than the *Defensor pacis* itself.

Separation of priests from political magistrates could be construed to give the clergy a foundation more secure than a pedestal and more practical than moral supremacy, that is, a foundation of independence. We have seen a sign of this in Albertus's commentary: priests, who are concerned with sacred things, are not subject to the political order.[46] That is to say, he took Moerbeke's *praeter* to mean "beyond" rather than "other than" or "apart from." But this is as far as he went. If he thought that this interpretation had a bearing upon the church, he did not explain what it might be.

In Nicole Oresme's French version of the *Politics*, however, this text forms part of a coherent defense of the rights of the clergy. Although he was off the mark in translating the passage, Oresme could explicate it in good company. He chose the reading of "an expositor," undoubtedly Albertus, his most favored predecessor, who had said that "Aristotle means that priests are not subject to political, that is, temporal, authority."[47] Oresme did not mention the Marsilian version of this passage, although

46. Albertus, *Opera omnia*, 8:405b.
47. This glossed translation, dating from about 1371–74, has been edited from Avranches MS 223 by Albert Douglas Menut, *Maistre Nicole Oresme: Le Livre de politiques d'Aristote*, Transactions of the American Philosophical Society, n.s., 60, 6 (Philadelphia, 1970). See also Susan M. Babbitt, *Oresme's Livre de Politiques and the France of Charles V*, Transactions of the American Philosophical Society, n.s., 75, 1 (Philadelphia, 1985).
Oresme's translation of this text reads in part: "Et ce princey est a mettre autre que ne sunt princeys politiques, et est aucune chose hors telz princeys" (*Livre de politiques*, 4.21 [fols. 156d–57a, p. 196a: column letters have been added to page numbers to allow easier reference]). His comment follows on fol. 157a, p. 196a.

he knew the *Defensor pacis,* cited it in the *Livre de politiques,* and was considered sympathetic to this work (so much so that he was among those accused of translating it into French).[48] He may not have thought of this version when he wrote his gloss, or he may simply have preferred the version of Albertus, which is more consistent with his own notion of an independent clergy.

This notion is worth attention, because Oresme made a more extensive application of the *Politics* to questions of spiritual and temporal power than any previous commentator. With one exception, he used every one of the texts mentioned here as the basis for remarks about the Christian clergy.[49] He acknowledged that Aristotle did not pay particular attention to the priesthood and noted, as none of the other commentators had, that in one enumeration of the parts of the city he had omitted it altogether.[50] Nevertheless, Oresme took it upon himself to show the necessity of the sacerdotal element in the state and to defend his application of the *Politics* to the "ecclesiastical polity."[51]

It should be noted that when he used this expression he referred to the clergy rather than to the mass of believers (although in one gloss he did say that all those who were, are, or shall be members of the "catholic communion" might be considered as a city).[52] By equating church and clergy he secured two advantages. First, his notion of the church suited a clerical association whose wealth, power, and jurisdiction were like those of a state. Second, he avoided some of the trouble arising from Marsilius's identification of the church with the multitude within the political unit,

48. For mention of the *DP* in the *Livre de politiques,* see 3.14 (fol. 96c, p. 137a; fol. 97a, p. 137b). For mention of "la plus vaillant partie" or similar phrases, see 3.23 (fol. 117d, p. 157a), 4.12 (fol. 141d, p. 181a), and 5.24 (fol. 200a, p. 241a). As Gewirth says (*Defender,* 1:184), such usage is "an almost certain sign of Marsilian influence." For mention of the "legislateur humaine," see 7.21 (fol. 269c, p. 311b; fol. 270c, p. 312a).

On the investigation of the French translation of the *DP,* see Menut's edition, pp. 5a–11a, which includes a reference to the record of the inquest to be found in Heinrich Denifle and Emile Chatelain, *Chartularium universitatis parisiensis,* 4 vols. (Paris, 1891–99), 3 (1894): 223–27. See also the source of this account, Charles du Plessis d'Argentré, *Collectio iudiciorum de novis erroribus,* 3 vols. (Paris, 1724–36), 1:397–400.

49. The one exception is Aristotle's division of the directors of the state into priests and magistrates (*Politics,* 7.12.1331b; *Livre de politiques,* 7.25 [fol. 276b, p. 318b]). As noted above, the writers mentioned in this essay seem to have done nothing with this passage.

50. *Livre de politiques,* 7.25 (fol. 277a, p. 319b); 4.5 (fol. 133d, p. 172b), the latter from *Politics,* 4.4.1291a. Oresme has a sensible explanation for this omission: priests do not rule; therefore, they do not vary constitutions.

51. *Livre de politiques,* 7.16 (fols. 260b–63a, pp. 302a–4b), from *Politics,* 7.8.1328b; 3.3 (fol. 79a, p. 120a); 3.24 (fols. 123d–24a, p. 160b); 5.25 (fol. 201c–d, p. 243a) and 7.25 (fol. 277a–c, pp. 319b–20a), with reference to this discussion in the "Table des Notables," fol. 321c, p. 366a. There are over a score of references to the "policie ecclesiastique" by this or another designation.

52. *Livre de politiques,* 3.3 (fol. 78d, p. 120a).

which put the clergy into a peculiar limbo, deprived of both the prerogatives of their office and the right to full citizenship within the state.
Oresme could afford to be less equivocal because he made a consistent
assumption that "the law of Jesus Christ is not discordant with [good
government]."[53] Moreover, he could at the same time maintain the independence of the church within the city or monarchy and discuss the
internal problems of an ecclesiastical organization without reference to
secular government.

This brings us back to the question of priests as magistrates. The position of Oresme is not without unease, for while he wished to give priests
their due as public officers,[54] he could not entirely accept the argument
from nomenclature used by the author of the *De potestate ecclesiae* and
by Alvarus Pelagius. If priests are called princes and kings, and if they are
associated with judges, what can one make of this? Oresme was inclined
to treat it as a metaphor, which proves nothing and does not alter the
distinction between offices in the state but does suggest the dignity of the
sacerdotal office.[55] Certainly he did not want to blur the distinction
between the parts of the state, to cause one part to assimilate another.

He would admit a certain transference of honor from judges to priests.
How improper it would be, he said in one of the glosses criticizing voluntary poverty, if those who had been brave knights and worthy counselors
were to end their days as mendicants! But here judges are judges and
priests, priests.[56] What is important is the common membership of these
officers in the better, propertied class rather than a quality transmitted

53. Ibid., 2.6 (fol. 40c, p. 83b). For other glosses in which Aristotelian notions of good
government are applied to church organization as such, see 3.24 (fols. 122c–25a, pp.
159b–61b); 4.10 (fols. 138d–39b, p. 178a–b); 4.16 (fols. 149d–50c, p. 189a–b); 4.22 (fol.
160c, p. 200a); 5.4 (fol. 170d, p. 210a); 5.5 (fol. 171b–c, p. 210b—two glosses are involved
here); 5.14 (fol. 184c–d, p. 225a–b); 5.14 (fol. 185d, p. 226b); 6.2 (fol. 217c, p. 258a); 6.12
(fol. 232a–b, p. 274b); 7.10 (fol. 247b, p. 289b), and 7.19 (fol. 267a, p. 308b).

54. For example, the priesthood is described as the "office sacerdotal" and "dignité
sacerdotal" in 7.19 (fol. 265c, p. 307a), and see also, in the same gloss, fol. 266c, p. 308a.
It is described as an "honneur publique" in 7.36 (fol. 290d, p. 335b).

55. There are incidental references to princes of the church in 3.24 (fol. 122d, p. 159b);
4.10 (fol. 139b, p. 178b); 4.22 (fol. 160c, p. 200a), and 6.12 (fol. 232a, 274b). There are
discussions of clergymen as princes in 4.21 (fol. 157a, p. 196a); 6.13 (fol. 232d, p. 275b);
7.19 (fol. 265a, p. 306b), and 7.21 (fol. 269d, p. 311b).

In 7.21 (fol. 269d, p. 311b), Oresme denied, while making arguments against his own
position, that this usage is made except "par methaphore et par similitude pour l'excellence de ceste dignité." When taking up his own arguments he did not actually say that
this usage transformed priests into princes or vice versa, but he made the claim, at once
slippery and reasonable, that priests could hardly be compared to kings if they lacked
jurisdiction over their own personnel and possessions (fols. 270d–71a, p. 312b).

56. *Politiques*, 7.19 (fol. 267a, p. 308b). He did not accept an identity between the two
groups, for as he noted, not all priests need have been soldiers and judges, and not all
soldiers and judges should become priests, although "le procés d'aucuns tres bons est
tel" (fols. 266d–67a, p. 308b).

from one to another.[57] One of the arguments presented against the commutative jurisdiction of the clergy is that Aristotle established judges as well as priests in his ideal city. In his response to this argument Oresme did not claim that priests are judges, only that the cognizance of judges is not all encompassing, so that the church retains control over the persons and property that allow it to fulfill its function.[58] Such a jurisdiction would be anathema to Marsilius, but Oresme was not preoccupied with the unity of authority within a state. This allowed him to designate a limited competence as proper to the clergy without compromising the public good or the prerogatives of other officials.

The right to jurisdiction, as we have noted, is closely associated with the right to property. Oresme was able to use Aristotle to show that clerical property should suffice to maintain a modest existence and should be freely held.[59] His reasoning was simple. Priests are citizens and as such should have property at their disposal. Furthermore, they are by Aristotle's account old men deserving rest.[60] How can they have rest, or the liberty that has been granted to the priesthood in all states of good repute, if their persons and goods are under the jurisdiction of others?[61] (A corollary of this rule, which Oresme was only too happy to derive, was that mendicants are no part of the city.)[62]

57. Oresme accepted Aristotle's restrictions on admission to the priesthood: see *Politiques*, 7.19 (fols. 264d–65c, pp. 306b–7a), where the gloss says that priests should be honorable "en generation, en corps, en meurs et en estat" because they are called princes and kings (fol. 265a, p. 306b).

58. *Politiques*, 7.21 (fols. 270c–71d, pp. 312b–13b). See also 6.13 (fol. 232d, p. 275b), where the same conclusion arises from Aristotle's remark that religious officials are sometimes called kings (*Politics*, 6.8.1322b).

59. From the "Tables des Notables," fol. 317c, p. 362b.

60. *Politiques*, 7.19 (fol. 265c–d, p. 307a); 7.21 (fol. 270d, p. 312b).

61. Ibid., fol. 270d, p. 312b. Oresme described the support of the priesthood in well-reputed states in 7.19 (fol. 266a–c, pp. 307b–8a).

62. Ibid., 5.31 (fol. 209d, p. 251a). Aristotle said (*Politics*, 5.11.1315a) that the city is made up of the poor and the rich. But by the poor, said Oresme, he means laborers and craftsmen, not mendicants, who are no part of the city. Like John of Jandun (see note 23 above) he distinguished priests from contemplatives, with whom they share some functions, and placed the latter outside the city (*Politiques*, 7.7 [fol. 243b–c, p. 285b] and 7.16 [fol. 260c, p. 302b, and fol. 262c, p. 304a]).

In questions written on the *Politics* during the fifteenth century, John Versor argued on Aristotelian grounds for the necessity and civil function of the clergy, while judging (sincere) mendicants to be somewhat outside the city, and (false) mendicancy to be more harmful to the city than moderate clerical possessions. See Martin Grabmann, "Die mittelalterlichen Kommentare zur Politik des Aristoteles," *Sitzungsberichte der Bayerischen Akademie der Wissenschaften zu München: Philosophisch-historische Abteilung 2*, 10 (1941): 65–75. See also Charles H. Lohr, "Medieval Latin Aristotle Commentaries. Authors: Johannes de Kanthi-Myngodus," *Traditio* 27 (1971): 290–99. I have used the 1497 Cologne printing, where the discussion of priests in the city (from book 7) appears on fols. 104rb–6va. On fol. 105vb he says: "Et non dubito quod mendicitas plus noceat quam moderate divitie."

Susan M. Babbitt

Oresme's defense of clerical property was supported on several occasions by the example of the kings of the Heroic Age (*Politics*, 3.14.1285b), who were lords "of all and any property and possessions not belonging to priests."[63] The ancient kings' lack of jurisdiction over clerical goods sorted very well with Oresme's notion of priesthood not subject to secular control; in fact he referred to the kings "of the good old days" just after giving his interpretation of *praeter politicos principatus ponendum*.[64] As far as I can tell, no writer before him had used the text in this way, or indeed in any way, except as a subject of literal exposition. This is just as well, for the text had been incorrectly translated and bears a meaning opposite to the one that was so convenient for Oresme. Aristotle had actually said that these monarchs had charge of the sacrifices (not the possessions) that were not reserved for priests, so that the independence of the religious officials was compromised rather than secured.[65] The distortion is more important as evidence of the fragility of the transmission of ancient texts than as part of the problem of priests in the city, however, because it involves only one text (and one writer) among those consulted here.

No one would claim that Oresme's glosses have the force of the *Defensor pacis*. In the long view they may be insignificant, but they show that it was possible to form an Aristotelian theory of the church that was more coherent than that of Marsilius and more consistent with the principles of the *Politics* than that of the "Aristotelian, rather than Christian."[66] Actu-

63. *Politiques*, 3.20 (fol. 107c–d, p. 148a).
64. Ibid., 4.21 (fol. 157a, p. 196a). They are also mentioned in 6.13 (fol. 232d, p. 275b) and 7.21 (fol. 271a, p. 312b), in both of these latter cases in close proximity to the notion of priests as princes or kings.
65. Moerbeke had said that these kings "erant praesulatus secundum bellum et substantiarum, quaecunque non sacerdotales" (Susemihl, p. 217, lines 8–9), thus translating (as I imagine) *ousia* rather than *thysia*. Albertus Magnus and Peter of Auvergne had no choice but to follow him (Peter: Spiazzi, p. 171, no. 483; Albertus: *Opera omnia* 8:289i). Walter Burley, like Peter, speaks of *possessiones* (Cambridge MS Gonville and Caius 490, fol. 23vb).
The situation is further complicated by Aristotle's summary of the varieties of kingship, in which he said that the king of the Heroic Age was "head of religious observances" (*Politics*, 3.14.1285b; Barker, p. 139). Moerbeke properly rendered this as "eorum quae ad deos dominus" (Susemihl, p. 218, line 9). Albertus, (*Opera omnia*, 8:290l) and Peter (Spiazzi, p. 171, no. 485) did not try to explain this contradiction, although Peter said that these kings were not lords "in omnibus" (as Oresme said that judges lacked all-encompassing jurisdiction) and that their lordship in religious matters concerned things "sicut electionis sacerdotis, punitionis et talium, sed non possessionum." In Walter Burley's listing of the types of kingship he spoke, like Moerbeke, of "substantiarum quaecunque non sacerdotales" (fol. 26va). In his gloss on the summary Oresme was careful, while allowing that these kings may have chosen priests "et . . . teles choses," to deny them control over the possessions of priests (*Politiques*, 3.21 [fol. 108a–b, p. 148a–b]), so that his solution was like that of Peter.
66. This was judgment of Albertus Pighius, in *Hierarchia ecclesiastica*, 5.1, ed. J. T. Rocaberti, *Bibliotheca maxima pontificia*, 21 vols. (Rome, 1697–99), 2:122a.

ally Marsilius, whatever his feelings may have been, was anxious to justify himself as a Christian as well as an Aristotelian. Indeed his priesthood, which stands anomalous and incompetent in the city of the world, is more like that of the early church than that of pagan Greece. It is the views of Aristotle that suffer the most distortion in this notion of the church.

Oresme, on the other hand, kept Aristotle in the foreground, so that he could judge by a single standard and could set apart (not deny) the spiritual functions of the clergy. He did not disregard the New Testament; rather, he wrote as a Christian who accepted the church as an institution in which spiritual ends could be served through political wisdom. What is repugnant in political life is not to be commended in the church.[67] Oresme's priests are political animals. As citizens, they have property; as public officers they have a right to the leisure and independence that allow them to perform their duties. Oresme could allow them an independent jurisdiction because he, like Aristotle and unlike Marsilius, took a moderate view of the need for unity and sovereignty. He was not convinced that public power must be concentrated at a single point, so he did not regard clerical jurisdiction as an irregularity to be explained away as a coincidence of names.

It was possible to give priests a secure and honorable place within the state described in the *Politics*, neither exalting them by blurring the distinctions between one set of officials and another nor humbling them by compounding the (incompatible) disadvantages of their classical and Christian estates. A grasp of principle, not wishful thinking alone, could sustain the illusion that the Philosopher walked along the *via media*.

67. See note 53 above. These opinions are expressed in *Politiques*, 2.6 (fol. 40c, p. 83a–b). See also 7.19 (fol. 266c, p. 308a), for a rejection of mendicancy as unsuited to a good state.

# [9]

## Epistemology and Omnipotence: Ockham in Fourteenth-Century Philosophical Perspective

### REGA WOOD

Someone who calls Ockham a philosophical skeptic usually means he denied that our knowledge of the external world is based on certain apprehensions. To discuss this claim requires an understanding of Ockham's doctrine of intuitive cognition. According to Ockham, knowledge of our internal states and the external world is acquired by an intuitive grasp of the facts of existence and presence. Modern interpreters of the doctrine of intuitive cognition, like interpreters of Ockham's ecclesiology, are divided between those who consider Ockham a radical innovator and those who point to the traditional elements in his thought.

In declining to deal with the philosophical elements of Ockham's thought, Brian Tierney points out correctly that there is no correspondence between philosophical nominalism and Ockham's theory of the church. But as Tierney had earlier indicated, there is no need to postulate schizophrenia in order to explain his works. One intellectual trait found in both his political and his philosophical works is Ockham's determination to deal first with hard cases. As Tierney showed, Ockham's ecclesiology was animated throughout "by a conviction that virtually the whole body of Christians might apostatize from the truths of Scripture."[1]

A substantial portion of this essay appears in *From Ockham to Wyclif*, ed. Anne Hudson and Michael Wilks, Studies in Church History, Subsidia 5 (Oxford, 1987), pp. 51–61; it is used here by permission of the Ecclesiastical History Society.

1. Brian Tierney, *Origins of Papal Infallibility, 1150–1350* (Leiden, 1972), pp. 207–8. In 1986 Tierney allowed that a study of Ockham's philosophy might be helpful to a student of his political theory. But he concluded that the unusual tenets of Ockham's philosophy were never reflected in the unusual tenets of his political theory. "Natural Law and Canon Law in Ockham's *Dialogus*," in *Aspects of Late Medieval Government and Society: Essays Presented to J. R. Lander* (Toronto, 1986), p. 5.

Without wishing to embrace the view that hard cases make bad philosophy, I should like to point to a similar fundamental principle in Ockham's philosophy and theology: God is limited only by the principle of contradiction.[2] This principle led Ockham always to consider first not what God does and has ordained, but rather what he could do, considering only what we know about his power. The phrase with which Ockham refers to this distinction, *de potentia Dei absoluta,* signifies God's power, the power to do anything not implying a contradiction. Ockham considers it important to determine what is possible absolutely speaking because there are many things God could do and does not wish (*vellet*) to do.[3] That the phrase "*de potentia Dei absoluta*" and the phrase "logically possible" are equivalent in this context can be seen by enumerating some of the things which are possible and impossible for God. *De potentia Dei absoluta* God could cause an effect without its cause or an accident without its subject, but he could not cause contradictories to be true simultaneously or wish something impossible.

Regarding the doctrine of intuitive cognition, a less general corollary is relevant, the theological principle: Whatever God *can* accomplish through second causes, he *can* accomplish immediately and independent of second causes. Interestingly, this principle can be considered a conservative element in Ockham's thought, since it was affirmed in the Paris condemnations of 1277. But it was in Ockham's hands a powerful and radical tool and an important motive for his critique of Scotus's vastly influential doctrine of intuitive cognition. It led Ockham to emphasize intuitive cognition of nonexistence.

I have not tried to decide the extent to which Ockham was a radical innovator in philosophy, but I do attempt to shed light on Ockham's doctrine of intuitive cognition by examining its history. I discuss first the writings of John Duns Scotus, whose doctrine of intuitive cognition Ockham held must be modified in accordance with the principle of omnipotence. Then I consider the views of those like Ockham who studied and criticized Scotus while adopting large parts of his doctrine. The views of those who studied and criticized Ockham are treated next. Finally, I suggest some parallels between Ockham's philosophical views and his political theory.

2. The fundamental importance of this principle is widely recognized. See, for example, Paul Vignaux, *Nominalism au XIVe siècle* (Paris, 1948), p. 22; Heiko Oberman, *Archbishop Thomas Bradwardine* (Utrecht, 1958), p. 39; Juergen Miethke, *Ockham's Weg zur Sozialphilosophie* (Berlin, 1969), pp. 137–56. John Boler, however, calls it disparagingly "Ockham's favorite if unfortunate device for displaying necessary connection" (with some justification, since he focuses on Ockham's philosophical views). See "Intuitive and Abstractive Cognition," in *Cambridge History of Later Medieval Philosophy* (Cambridge, 1981), p. 469.

3. *Quodlibet VI,* q. 1, ed. Joseph Wey, Opera Theologica 9 (St. Bonaventure, N.Y., 1980), pp. 585–86.

Rega Wood

## John Duns Scotus

For Scotus human certitude regarding the existence of objects is based on intuitive cognition. In virtue of intuitive cognition, we affirm or deny contingent propositions, we become aware of our mental acts, and the blessed apprehend of God's being.[4]

Scotus distinguishes intuitive cognition from abstract cognition. In abstract cognition, the object is apprehended in a way that implies nothing regarding the existence or presence of the object; in intuitive cognition, the object is apprehended as something existent and present. The efficient cause (*ratio formalis motiva*) of intuitive cognition is the thing apprehended in its proper existence. In abstract cognition, the efficient cause is a species similar to the thing or "something in which the thing has intelligible existence" (*esse cognoscibile*). From Scotus's distinction between the causes of abstract and intuitive cognition, there follows a further distinction between the relations necessarily established between the observer and the thing observed. When a person apprehends something intuitively, a real relation is necessarily established between the observer and the thing he observes. In abstract cognition there need be no real relation, since the object apprehended need not exist.[5]

## Peter Aureol

On the subject of intuitive cognition, perhaps Scotus's most influential critic was Peter Aureol, a Franciscan who lectured at Bologna and, after having gained the favorable notice of Pope John XXII, at Paris, Aureol argued that the distinction between abstract and intuitive cognition must be reformulated. Scotus was wrong to say that intuitive cognition could arise only in the presence of its object, while abstract cognition could arise whether its object existed or not. Instead abstract and intuitive cognition were distinguished by the way their objects were presented. The objects of abstract cognition appeared in a quasi-imaginary mode (*quasi modo imaginario et absente*); intuitive cognition was direct rather than discursive,

4. Scotus, *Opus Oxon*, IV, d. 45, q. 2, n. 12; q. 3, n. 17; d. 49, q. 8, n. 5, ed. Luke Wadding, *Opera omnia*, vol. 10 (Lyons, 1639), pp. 182, 207, 498; *Quodlibet VI*, a. 1, nn. 20–21, ed. Felix Alluntis (Madrid, 1968), pp. 214–15.

5. *Quodlibet VI*, a. 1, nn. 18–19; *Quodlibet XIII*, a. 2, nn. 27–42 (ed. Alluntis, n. 212, pp. 455–62); *Opus Oxon*, IV, d. 49, q. 12, n. 6 (ed. Wadding, 10:574). For a further account of Scotus's views see Sebastian Day, *Intuitive Cognition* (St. Bonaventure, N.Y., 1947); Camile Bérubé, *La connaissance de l'individuel* (Paris, 1964), pp. 176–224; Ludger Honnefelder, *Ens inquantum ens, Beitraege zur Geschichte der Philosophie des Mittelalters*, n.s. 16 (1979): 218–53; Boler, "Intuitive and Abstractive Cognition," pp. 460–78.

and it conveyed the impression that its objects existed and were actually present.[6]

Aureol argued against Scotus's version of the distinction between abstract and intuitive cognition in two ways: on *a priori* grounds and on *experiential* grounds. Aureol's *a priori* argument is based on the principle that God can cause or preserve directly anything which is ordinarily caused by or based on secondary causes or on the more general principle that God can do anything that does not impy a contradiction. To preserve intuitive cognition independent of the object known does not imply a contradiction, since the object known and our knowing it are independent of one another. Therefore God could preserve our intuitive cognition of an object without the object's continued presence or, more precisely, in the absence of its presentiality.

Aureol formulated the theological principle regarding secondary causes as follows: God can suspend the efficient causality of any created thing while maintaining its effects. Our knowledge of an object is effectively caused by that object. Therefore in the absence of that object, God could preserve that knowledge. Aureol's *experiential* argument consists of a series of examples of naturally occurring sensory illusions. In all these cases, the object of sight or intuitive cognition does not exist. Since what is the case is possible, Aureol argues that intuitive cognition of objects does not require the existence and presence of its objects. This reasoning looked to Aureol's contemporaries like a powerful argument against natural certainty, or confidence in our perceptions of presence and existence. But it is a curious fact that Aureol himself did not recognize this implication. He held that intuitive cognition would not lead the intellect to err.[7]

Another aspect of Aureol's theory of intuitive cognition which seemed to some of his contemporaries to threaten certainty was his theory of *esse apparens* or *esse visum*. According to Aureol, when a thing is apprehended, the act of apprehension posits or produces that thing in *esse apparenti* within the intellect. In other words, when apprehended the thing achieves another mode of being; it achieves (*capit*) apparent or intentional being. To the objection that on this view the thing itself is not apprehended, Aureol replies that what is apprehended is indeed the thing itself, "having *esse apparens*."[8] *Esse apparens* is not a real separate entity

6. Aureol, *Scriptum*, I, prol., q. 2, a. 2, nn. 102–111, ed. Eligius Buytaert (St. Bonaventure, N.Y., 1952), pp. 203–6.

7. Aureol, *Scriptum*, I, prol., q. 2, a. 2, nn. 93–95; a. 4, n. 120 (ed. Buytaert, 1:200–2, 209); Aureol's experiential argument and the reaction against it are described in Rega Wood, "Adam Wodeham on Sensory Illusions," *Traditio* 38 (1982): 213–34.

8. Petrus Aureolus, *Scriptum*, I, d. 3, c. 3, a. 1; a. 3 (ed. Buytaert, pp. 696–701, 712–15); I *Sent.*, d. 9, p. 1, a. 1; d. 27, p. 2, a. 2; II *Sent.*, d. 3, q. 2, a. 4 (Rome, 1596, 1:323a, 626a; 3:70a). The relevant passages are cited in the excellent article by A. F. Prezioso, "La teoria dell'essere apparente nella gnoseologia di Pietro Aureolo," *Studi Francescani* 46 (1950): 15–43.

distinct from the object apprehended and the apprehending intellect, but an entity which exists only as a mental object. As an *esse obiectivum* it has only an incomplete or diminished existence and does not interfere with our apprehension of the object.

Evidently Aureol did not intend to treat *esse apparens* as something distinct from extramental things (as more recent philosophers have treated sense data as distinct from the material things which cause them). Instead, the *esse apparens* of a thing was for Aureol the thing itself as it appears to a mind.[9] Perhaps this is why Aureol believed that no skeptical consequences follow from his view.

## Godfrey of Fontaines

As Peter Aureol recognized, there was a way to defend the principle that there is no vision in the absence of the visible object without abandoning the principle that whatever God could do by means of particular agents, he could accomplish without them—namely, by maintaining another theory of vision. This is precisely what the secular master Godfrey of Fontaines did, claiming that vision was not only an absolute entity, but also a relational one. That is, the vision of an object for Godfrey is the visual faculty as it is informed by the thing seen. On this theory, the thing seen is not only the cause of vision, but also its object. God could supply the place of the thing seen as a cause of vision by making a given object (the sun, for instance) appear to the visual sense. Thus there could be an act of vision whose object is the sun but whose cause is God alone and not the sun. But without the sun as an object, we cannot see the sun, since God could not supply the place of the sun as object.

Godfrey is familiar with and rejects the view that vision and its object are related as light and a luminous body are related. He claims that though God could not produce vision without its object, he could produce lighted air without the luminous object. For apart from being an effect of a luminous body, lighted air has no necessary relation to the luminous body. Vision, on the other hand, not only is caused by its object but bears a necessary relation thereto. Godfrey prefers to liken vision to science. The thing known may exist without science, but not science without the thing known.

In Godfrey's formulation, the principle that God can supply the causality of any secondary cause is preserved. But since it involves a contradiction to cause vision in the absence of its object, God cannot cause vision in the absence of its object.[10]

9. But see Wood, "Adam Wodeham," p. 217 n. 19.
10. *Quodlibet XII*, q. 1, ed. Jean Hoffmans, *Les philosophes Belges*, vol. 5 (Louvain,

## Hervaeus Natalis

Hervaeus Natalis, or Harvey Nedellec, was a Dominican and a master of theology at Paris in 1307.[11] Later as General of the Order he successfully championed Thomas's canonization. As a Thomist, he resisted Scotus's concept of intuitive cognition, adopting it relatively late in his scholastic career. In *Quodlibet 2*, q. 5, an attack on Scotus's view on the abstract apprehension of the divinity, he describes Scotus's two forms of cognition, intuitive and abstract, but prefers himself to use terms such as *cognitio quidditativa* for abstract cognition. *Cognitio non praesupponente alia*, *cognitio naturalis*, and *cognitio terminata ad entitatem rei ut est in se* are used in preference to *cognitio intuitiva*. As late as *Quodlibet 3* Hervaeus says that some call *"cognitio rei prima . . . in suo esse reali"* intuitive cognition while abstaining from using that terminology himself.[12]

Hervaeus was a contemporary of Peter Aureol. He was attacked by Aureol for the views he stated in *Quodlibet 2*, q. 5. Hervaeus in turn attacked Aureol's view that intuitive cognition does not presuppose the existence of its object in *Quodlibet 4*, q. 11.[13] But despite this fact, in the fourth *Quodlibet* Hervaeus changed his views on cognition of nonexistent beings to accommodate Aureol's argument. In *Quodlibet 2*, q. 5, Hervaeus claimed it was absurd to hold that God could cause intuitive cognition in the absence of its object (*sine praesentia obiecti exsistentis*), but later in *Quodlibet 4*, he allowed cognition in the absence of its object in all but one case.

In *Quodlibet 4* Hervaeus defined intuitive cognition as a term meaning either cognition presupposing no other cognition, cognition terminating at a thing as existing, or certain cognition. Taken as cognition which does not presuppose another cognition, or as cognition which is certain, intuitive cognition does not require the presence of the object known. Such a requirement would have to be in virtue of the motion caused by the object or in virtue of the object as the terminus of cognition. But Hervaeus argues

---

1932), pp. 78–82.

11. See Bernardus Guidonis as quoted in J. Quetif and J. Echard, *Scriptores ordinis praedicatorum*, vol. 1, 2 (Paris, 1719–23; reprint New York, 1959), p. 533.

12. *Quodlibet II*, q. 5; *Quodlibet III*, q. 12 (Venice, 1513), fols. 41va, 42rb–va, 84vb).

13. Hervaeus's *Quodlibet IV*, q. 11, is a reply to the *Reportatio* preserved in Borgh. 123, not to the *Scriptum* of 1316. Hervaeus's *Quodlibet IV*, q. 11, quotes briefer versions of Aureol's arguments than found in the *Scriptum*, and it includes two arguments not found in the *Scriptum*—an argument *de rebus remotis* and an argument that things which appear curved or prominent at a distance may in fact be flat or straight. Aureol, *Scriptum*, prol., q. 2, a. 2, nn. 93–95 (ed. Buytaert, 1:200–2); Hervaeus, *Quodlibet IV*, q. 11, (ed. Venice, 1503), fol. 100rb, misnumbered 107rb; Philotheus Boehner, "*Notitia Intuitiva* of Non Existents According to Peter Aureoli," *Franciscan Studies* 8 (1948): 412–13.

contrary to Godfrey that no such object need be present as an object of cognition, on the ground that a nonexistent thing can be the terminus of an intuitive cognition. This could happen either naturally, as when species produced in previous acts of cognition persist after their objects have ceased to exist, or supernaturally, as when God causes men to see nonexistent objects.

Even when intuitive cognition is understood as cognition terminating at an object as it actually exists, Hervaeus allows for the possibility that the object need not be present. False cognition does not require the existence of its object; only true cognition requires this. Thus the only form of intuitive cognition which requires that its object be as it appears is true intuitive cognition of the object as it now is.[14]

## William of Ockham

Like Aureol in his a priori argument and like Hervaeus, William of Ockham argued against Scotus that an object need not be present in order to be apprehended, since God could preserve intuitive cognition in the absence of an object.

As often happens when he is discussing Scotus's views, Ockham borrows the form of his argument from Scotus. In this case he argues that the object of intuitive cognition must be either the final, formal, material, or efficient cause of intuitive cognition. For various reasons, he eliminates the object as final, formal, and material cause. But if the object is the efficient cause of intuitive cognition, then God can supply the cause. God can cause directly by himself whatever can be accomplished by means of efficient causes.[15]

Like most of his contemporaries, Ockham formulated a new definition of intuitive cognition. Intuitive cognition of a present and existing object is that cognition in virtue of which we know that the object exists. In the case of a nonexistent object, intuitive cognition leads to the judgment that its object does not exist. Thus Ockham holds with Aureol that, in itself and necessarily, intuitive cognition pertains no more to existent than to nonexistent objects.[16] But Ockham objects strenuously to Aureol's theory of intuitive cognition because he agrees with Scotus that there is no case of a nonexistent object's leading to a judgment of presence or existence.

Ockham rejects both Aureol's experimental argument against Scotus and the theory of *esse apparens*. Ockham argues that if *esse apparens* is

14. *Quodlibet II*, q. 5; q. 8; q. 11 (ed. Venice, 1503, fols. 41va–vb, 78rb–79rb, 110rb–111ra).
15. Guillelmus de Ockham, *Scriptum in I Sent.*, prol., q. 1, ed. Gedeon Gál and Stephen Brown, *Opera theologica (OTh)*, vol. 1 (St. Bonaventure, N.Y., 1967), p. 35.
16. Ockham, *Scriptum*, I, prol., q. 1 (*OTh*, I, 31, 70–71).

understood as an objective being—that is, a being which exists only as a mental object—then either the senses never apprehend a true quality of object or in every case two objects are apprehended—namely, the real quality and something which has only objective being. Further, the senses must have real sensible beings as their objects. Aureol's *esse apparens* does not fit this description, since it is an unreal entity, an *ens rationis*, and hence cannot be apprehended by the senses.

Ockham concedes that *intellectio* is *apparitio* and that the thought or *intellectio* of an object is a similitude. But he denies that the object so perceived attains *esse apparens*. Caesar may have his picture painted, and then he may be present to someone viewing the picture as an object is present to the intellect. But Caesar gains no being by being painted. Besides, Ockham claims, we no more make an object present to ourselves by thinking of it than we make Caesar present to us by viewing his picture.[17]

For Ockham, "false cognition" is a contradiction in terms. That is, it involves a contradiction to say that someone knows a nonexistent object exists. Judgments of such contingent facts as "you are sitting" or "I live and understand," based on intuitive cognition are both true and evident. And since evident cognition of the proposition "a thing is present" means that the thing is present, evident knowledge of this proposition in the absence of the thing would mean that the thing was both present and not present, a contradiction. In the case of existent objects, such judgments are caused by the object and our cognition of it; intuitive cognition without its object causes judgment of nonexistence.[18]

But though for Ockham intuitive cognition never leads to error, even when a nonexistent object is apprehended, this does not exclude even naturally induced cases of false belief. Ockham's explains the delusions adduced by Aureol as instances of false judgment based on apprehensions which cause error. Thus the straight stick which appears broken in water elicits apprehensions equivalent to those elicited by a broken stick in the air, and when elicited by a broken stick those same apprehensions cause correct judgment. Indeed, the apprehension of such things as a straight stick in water elicits false beliefs in their natural operation, although

17. *Scriptum*, I, d. 27, ed. Girard Etzkorn and Frank Kelley, *Opera theologica*, vol. 4 (St. Bonaventure, N.Y., 1979), pp. 238–58.

18. At the end of his quodlibetal treatment of this subject, Ockham adds an incomplete and puzzling reply to Chatton which seems somewhat to resemble Mirecourt's later treatment of the subject. Ockham holds that it is a fallacy to claim that God could cause evident cognition of an object's presence by himself without the object. But instead of pointing to the meaning of evident knowledge, he says that it is similar to the fallacious argument: Since God can cause a meritorious act by means of the will of a creature, he could do so on his own. The fallacy arises because of the different connotations of the terms in the antecedent and the conclusion. *Summa logicae* (*OTh*, 1:506); *Scriptum*, prol., q. 1 (*OTh*, 1:71); *Quodlibet V*, q. 5 (*OTh*, 9:496, 498–500).

some observers may avoid the error through other knowledge and judgment.[19]

Ockham is not committed to the view that God cannot deceive us. Certainly God could cause false creditive acts according to Ockham; God could cause the belief that something existed in its absence.[20] It seems likely, however, that Ockham would have argued that since to deceive connotes injustice or wickedness, it could not be predicated of God, although apart from this connotation, every absolute act involved in deception could be performed by God.[21]

## John Reading

John Reading is the probable author of the *Quodlibetal* or disputed questions preserved in the Florentine manuscript of his *Sentence Commentary*.[22] A Franciscan and a Scotist, Reading responded to the problem of intuitive cognition of nonexistents as posed by Aureol by redefining intuitive cognition. He agrees with Ockham that although cognition is normally caused by its object, this causal relation cannot be the specific difference between intuitive and abstract cognition. For God can supply the causality of the object in producing vision or intuitive cognition. And without God's cooperation even the presence of the object, at the proper distance, in absence of an obstacle, with eyes open in a lighted room would not cause vision or intuition.

For Reading, the difference between intuitive and abstract cognition lies in the proper form of each. Intuitive cognition is clear, and abstract cognition is obscure in some sense. More precisely, Reading defined intuitive cognition proper in terms of species. Intuitive cognition is evident, clear, and not obscure cognition of an object *unrepresented* by any species except the idea of itself; it is cognition which cannot be caused by a species in the absence of the object.

Intuitive cognition properly understood is divided into four modes or

19. *Scriptum*, I, d. 27 (*OTh*, 4: 243–50).

20. Boler criticizes Ockham for not telling "us how to distinguish cognitions from deceptive creditive acts." But if we could make such a distinction, then how could we be deceived, except by ourselves? Potentially infallible cognition for people would be a much greater limitation on God's power than any of the participants in this discussion even discussed. "Intuitive cognition," p. 471; Ockham, *Quodlibet V*, q. 5 (*OTh*, 9:498).

21. See the similar case of commanding evil, *Quaestiones in II Sententiarum*, q. 19, ed. Gedeon Gál and Rega Wood, *Opera theologica*, 5:352–54.

22. Reading lectured on the *Sentences* before Ockham, but then revised his *Sentence* commentary to include a critique of Ockham. In the *Commentary* as we now have it, there are references to the *Quodlibet* according to Longpré. Thus the *Quodlibet* belongs like Ockham's lectures to the period before the final revision to the *Sentence Commentary* and should probably be dated about 1321 when Reading was regent master at Oxford. Ephraim Longpré, "Jean de Reading et le B. Jean Duns Scot," *France Franciscaine* 7 (1924): 109; Stephen Brown, "Sources for Ockham's Prologue to the Sentences," *Franciscan Studies* 26 (1966): 36–51.

grades. The first and paradigmatic mode is a clear cognition of an object, present in itself, as one angel sees another and as we see colors which are directly in front of us. Here the thing is not represented except by or in itself. In the second and third mode the object seen or intuited is reflected in some manner, not seen directly. Finally, the influence of Aureol led Reading to define a fourth mode of cognition. This is to cover the case in which God immediately causes in the intellect a clear vision of a nonexistent rose, by informing the intellect with the quality of vision.[23]

Thus, though intuitive cognition of nonexistents is possible, it must be clear. But whether this clear intuition could cause error cannot be ascertained in this *Quodlibet*. For Reading, the problem of certainty was not directly relevant to the discussion of intuitive cognition. In his *Sentence Commentary* he argued that the certitude of our knowledge that objects exist could not be used as an argument for intuitive cognition as Ockham defined it. Certitude and knowledge that an object exists, as opposed to knowledge of the terms, pertain to abstract cognition.[24]

Reading did not criticize Ockham's confidence in the possibility of certain cognition of contingents; he simply argued that Ockham had misused it in the argument. This probably also indicates that Reading saw no skeptical consequences in Aureol's reformulation of the theory of intuitive cognition.

## Walter Chatton

Walter Chatton's *Reportatio* of 1322–23 is a sustained polemic against Ockham. But like Ockham, he criticized Aureol's *esse apparens* as inter-

23. *Quodlibet*, q. 3, cod. Florence, BN, Conv. soppr., D. 4.95, fols. 285r–86v: Deus solus possit esse causa visionis rei re non [con]causante. Sed distinctio simpliciter necessario istius cognitionis est per formas proprias quae sunt alterius rationis, et per hoc quod visio est necessario cognitio clara. Cognitio abstracta est cognitio obscura. . . . Sexto modo accipitur intuitiva cognitio proprie pro cognitione evidenti et clara non obscura rei incomplexo non repraesentante per speciem nisi per ipsam intentionem. Nec ista cognitio potest causari per speciem rei in absentia rei. . . . de cognitione intuitiva proprie dicta notandum quod ipsa habet quattuor gradus. . . . Nam aliqua est cognitio intuitiva quae est clara cognitio rei in se praesente secundum existentiam sicut angelus unus videt alium sibi praesentem, et visus videt colorem praesentem, et hoc in directo aspectu praesentem, et illa res in nullo est repraesentata nisi in se tantum. Alia est . . . clara, non tamen ita clara ut prima, . . . sicut visus videt rem in speculo. . . . Tertio modo est . . . sicut Deus clare videt in essentia sua animam Antichristi. . . . Quartus modus est quod intellectus creatus . . . videat clare rosam non existentem. . . . Et quod hoc possit esse probo: si omnis intellectio sit qualitas a quocumque causetur, potest Deus supplere causalitatem illius et solus causare eam in intellectu. Sed intellectum informari visione rosae est eum videre rosam. . . . Unde sciendum ad hoc quod aliquis videat rem non est imaginandum quod hoc sit quia res est ibi praesens et oculus apertus et nullum obstaculum medium et medium illuminatum. Quia istis omnibus habitis non sequitur quod sit visio, etiam oculos bene disposito . . . , quia Deus non cooperante sicut potest libere non cooperari, et tunc non erit visio.

24. Ioannes de Reading, *Super Sententias*, I, d. 3, q. 3, ed. Gedeon Gál, "Ioannis de Reading de necessitate specierum intelligibilium," *Franciscan Studies* 29 (1969): 134–39.

fering with true vision or cognition. If, for example, the *esse visum* of whiteness were seen, this would interfere with sight of the whiteness itself, since *esse apparens*, or in this case *esse visum*, as described by Aureol., is neither the act of seeing nor the whiteness but some third entity distinct from both. But in fact whiteness is seen, so it is false to suppose that we see some object distinct from whiteness when we see something white.[25]

Like his contemporaries, Chatton reformulated the definitions of intuitive and abstract cognition. Intuitive cognition is proper only to incomplex objects and prior to any mental manipulations of such cognitions; abstract cognition is not proper to any single object, and it is frequently discursive. Intuitive cognition is likened to the operation of the senses and abstract cognition to the imagination.[26]

Most important, intuitive cognition always leads to the judgment that its object exists, whether or not it exists in fact. Abstract cognition leads neither to a judgment of existence nor to a judgment of nonexistence. According to Chatton, intuitive cognition of a nonexistent results in the false judgment that its object exists.[27] Thus if God caused a nonexistent object to appear, as he *could*, then the result would be false cognition. As Chatton recognized, this represents a threat to certainty. And it is perhaps Chatton's greatest contribution to the discussion of intuitive cognition that he focused it on the issue of certainty.

Against Aureol, Chatton claimed that if vision could be caused in the absence of an object, then the certitude of all our naturally acquired knowledge about the sensible world would perish. Further, he argued that vision depends as much on the presence of the object seen as light depends on the existence of a luminous body. Just as light could not be naturally produced in the absence of a luminous body, vision could not naturally be produced in the absence of its object.

Having raised the issue of certainty in this form, Chatton's response was equivocal. For in his view the phenomenon of afterimages showed that light could remain in the absence of luminous body. No more difficulties are involved in maintaining that vision remains in the absence of the object seen than in maintaining that light remains in the absence of a luminous body. Therefore, there can be no objection to maintaining that vision can persist for a short time in the absence of the object seen.[28]

## Adam Wodeham

Like Chatton, Wodeham was a Franciscan. He was present at Chatton's lectures, and in his later writings he frequently defended Ockham against

25. Gualterus Chatton, *Lecturae in I Sent.*, prol., q. 2, ed. Jeremiah O'Callaghan, "The Second Question of the Prologue to Walter Chatton's Commentary on the Sentences," in *Nine Mediaeval Thinkers*, ed. J. R. O'Donnell (Toronto, 1955), pp. 241–42.
26. Chatton, *Lecturae in I Sent.*, prol., q. 2 (ed. O'Callaghan, pp. 248–49).
27. Chatton, *Lecturae in I Sent.*, prol., q. 2 (ed. O'Callaghan, pp. 242–43, 248–49).
28. Chatton, *Lecturae in I Sent.*, prol., q. 2 (ed. O'Callaghan, pp. 244–45).

Chatton. But he followed Chatton in believing that intuitive cognition of nonexistents would lead to the mistaken judgment that the object exists. If God caused intuitive cognition of whiteness to persist in the absence of whiteness, we would judge mistakenly that whiteness existed. The same act without any change in its nature could not at one time cause assent to the proposition that the object of intuitive cognition exists and at another time cause dissent.

Here Wodeham is ignoring Ockham's statement that the judgment of existence is caused by the cognition together with the object, while the judgment of nonexistence is caused by the cognition in the absence of its object. But he correctly points out that Ockham's view is the inevitable result of holding that intuitive cognition leads to evident knowledge of existence or nonexistence.[29]

In Wodeham's redefinition of intuitive cognition, the possibility that God could deceive the observer is conceded, which is unusual in the context of this debate.[30] Thus intuitive cognition for Wodeham is that cognition on which an evident judgment can be based, provided that God is not deceiving the observer.[31]

Like Chatton, Wodeham was preoccupied with the issue of certainty. Against Chatton, he argued that it could not be conceded that intuitive cognition could naturally be *preserved* for a *short time* in the absence of its object. According to Wodeham, neither the principle that vision must be caused by a visible object nor the certainty of human knowledge could be defended on these grounds.

Whenever an object is seen, on Chatton's view it might have ceased to exist a short time previously. Therefore the sight of a thing is no guarantee of its existence. Even at the first instant a thing is seen, there is no certainty of its existence. For an act of judgment presupposes the formation of a proposition and does not occur instanteously. Hence all judgments of existence may refer to a thing that has gone out of existence.

Nor is Chatton's theory consistent. For Chatton holds that vision can be preserved, but not caused, in the absence of its object. But acts such as vision are always in the process of being created and never cease to be dependent on the object causing them. Hence, as Scotus argued, creation and conservation do not differ in such cases except in that one connotes prior existence and the other prior nonexistence. Thus if Chatton allows

29. Wodeham, *Lectura secunda*, prol., q. 6, quoted in Wood, "Adam Wodeham," p. 220n.

30. Though John Rodyngton, a Franciscan who incepted at about 1330, says that many concede that God can deceive, of the authors studied here only Wodeham does so. Rodyngton, for example, admits the possibility that God can cause error while denying that God deceives on the grounds that deception implies bad will. Ioannes de Rodyngton, *Sent.* I, d. 2, q. 3 (cod. Vat. lat. 5306, fol. 70vb); quoted in Prezioso, "Teoria," p. 40 nn. 1–3.

31. Wodeham, *Lectura secunda*, prol., q. 6, nn. 77–78 (cod. Cambridge, Gonville-Caius 281/674), fol. 127ra.

that vision can be preserved in the absence of its object, he should also concede that it can be caused in the absence of its object.[32]

Wodeham argued that the species Chatton postulated no more need coincide with the presence of the object seen than Aureol's *esse apparens*. Neither theory is consistent with the view that the object is the immediate cause, or even a partial immediate cause, of vision. For an effect will cease in the absence of an immediate cause on which it necessarily depends, not persist for a short time.

Wodeham distinguishes what is "seen" in the case of delusions such as those caused by afterimages from the judgment based thereon. Only false judgment, arising from a strong imagination, could cause an observer to believe that what he sees in an afterimage is the same as what he sees when the principal object is present.[33]

Like Ockham, Wodeham conceded that there were a number of cases in which apprehensions led naturally to false judgments under normal conditions of perception. To deal with this situation and to meet Chatton's challenge to preserve certainty, Wodeham defined three grades of evidence. A first and least degree of evidence pertains to an apprehension or proposition formed by the intellect which cannot fail to appear to signify correctly and will incline the intellect to assent even when it does not signify correctly. The second degree pertains to evident propositions which once posited not only cannot fail to appear to signify correctly, but cannot signify incorrectly. The third degree of evidence excludes all doubt and deception and even the possibility of dissent, since *"stante generali Dei influentia"* it necessitates the intellect.

The first degree of evidence covers the case of propositions whose formation is caused by illusions; the second, true categoric propositions concerning contingent facts; and the third, self-evident propositions and logical rules and the conclusions of perfect syllogisms. Contingent propositions cannot be certain in the third degree, since God can deceive us, and knowing this the intellect can withhold its assent.[34]

## John of Mirecourt

Mirecourt was a Cistercian at Paris, writing about ten years after Wodeham. Although Mirecourt was familiar with most of the views I have been discussing, the temporal gap makes it impossible to determine exactly how his views fit into the discussion.[35] Like Chatton and Wodeham,

32. Wodeham, *Lectura secunda*, prol., q. 3, nn. 32–34 (ed. Wood, pp. 241–42).

33. Wodeham, *Lectura secunda*, prol., q. 3, nn. 34–35, 43, 49–59 (ed. Wood, pp. 242–47).

34. Wodeham, *Lectura secunda*, prol., q. 6, quoted in Wood, "Adam Wodeham," p. 232n.

35. For example, Mirecourt quotes and replies to Aureol in the fourth question of the prologue to his *Sentence* commentary; he mentions and conditionally approves Ock-

Mirecourt was concerned to preserve the certainty of knowledge. Mirecourt is of special interest to us here because his attempt to make the theory of intuitive cognition consistent with divine omnipotence may involve a revision in the principle that God can produce the effect of a second cause without the cause.

Mirecourt follows Wodeham in defining grades of certainty. Like Wodeham, Mirecourt limits the highest grade of certainty ("special certainty," which compels assent and allows of no reasonable doubt) only to necessary truths.[36] Contingent propositions for Mirecourt are only "naturally certain." Natural certainty allows for reasonable doubt, because the certainty is conditional—*stante Dei generali influentia et non facto aliquo miraculo.* Mirecourt does not define a least degree of certainty, but like Wodeham he admits that there are objects which naturally cause error unless they are rectified.[37] The qualified certainty of contingent propositions does not mean for Mirecourt that we should doubt them any more than we doubt necessary truths.

Like Godfrey, Mirecourt holds that it is impossible that a thing should be seen or intuited unless the thing itself at least partially causes or conserves the sight or intuition. But he denies that this can be the basis of certainty. Thus when we know something apart from ourselves, we cannot be certain that something apart from ourselves exists, even though from "I know that something is" it does follow that "something is." Presumably Mirecourt's point here is that even when I know something apart from me, I may not be certain that I know this; I may not be able to distinguish this case from one where God, either by himself or through secondary causes, brings it about that I judge falsely that I know.[38]

It has been suggested that Mirecourt limits the possibility of God's interfering in the natural order by holding that although God can cause

---

ham's theory of intuitive cognition of nonexistents; he explains some of the illusions discussed by Aureol using the concept of the strong imagination postulated by Chatton and Wodeham. Ioannes de Mirecourt, *Sent.*, prol., q. 3, 4, ed. Anna Franzinelli, "Questioni inedite di Giovanni di Mirecourt sulla conoscenza," *Rivista critica di storia della filosofia* 13 (1958): 323, 328, 415–28.

36. The truths specified by Mirecourt here are the principle of contradiction and truths known by a priori demonstration, such as the evidence of God, inferred from the existence of a dependent being, the soul. But note that Mirecourt does not allow the existence of God to be demonstrable except in the narrowest sense, namely, that an independent being exists. *Sent.*, prol. q. 4, q. 6 (ed. Franzinelli, pp. 424, 437–49); *Apologia prima*, ed. Friedrich Stegmueller, "Die zwei Apologien des Jean de Mirecourt," *Recherches de théologie ancienne et médiévale* 5 (1933): 66–67.

37. *Nisi aliunde rectificare.* Unlike Wodeham, however, Mirecourt does not specify *per rationem vel experientiam aliunde.* Roy J. Van Neste, "A Reappraisal of the Supposed Skepticism of John of Mirecourt," *Recherches de théologie ancienne et médiévale* 44 (1977): 107.

38. *Apologia prima* (ed. Stegmueller, p. 67); *Sent.*, prol., q. 1, 6 (ed. Franzinelli, pp. 323–28, 445–46).

error, he cannot deceive.[39] Mirecourt's point, however, is that "deception" connotes evildoing or doing other than one ought, which cannot be predicated of God. Yet although God cannot do evil in the sense of willing evilly, he can and does will evil. Our sin is evidence that he wills evil efficaciously and with *velle beneplaciti*, even though he reprobates sin. Hence Mirecourt's denial that God can deceive is intended not to guarantee the certainty of our knowledge but only to prevent us from imputing an evil will to God.[40]

Mirecourt distinguishes intuitive cognition from abstract cognition by saying that intuitive cognition is that in virtue of which we can judge what is here and now. *Formaliter* and *causaliter* the two cognitions are distinguished in terms of their causes. Naturally (that is, excluding miracles) the thing known is the partial effective immediate cause of intuitive cognition. The cause of abstract cognition, on the other hand, is intuitive cognition or a *habitus* inclining us toward abstract cognition.

To this fairly standard distinction, Mirecourt adds two rather novel twists. First, God cannot by himself cause the intuitive cognition of an object but must act through the object as a secondary cause *per se vel per accidens*. By adding the qualification *per accidens*, Mirecourt is admitting that the thing seen may not exist. Hence, although the sight of Peter is evidence that he exists, the sight of something we think is Peter is not evidence of his existence, because in the latter case the thing we see is caused by Peter only *per accidens*.[41]

Second, Mirecourt defines intuitive cognition as a quality and an action of the soul, which must connote a relation to the soul. Thus God can cause any action of the soul by himself, but an act caused solely by God would not be an act of the soul, since to be an act of the soul requires that the soul itself should act. Mirecourt therefore holds that although it is true that God could supply the action of any second cause, it is false to say that God could thereby cause the action of an agent other than himself. God could cause Socrates' cognition to be in Plato's intellect, but this no more causes *Plato* to know than if God had caused Socrates' cognition to occur in a stone.[42] Hence for Mirecourt it will turn out to be a contradiction in terms for God to cause the intuitive cognition of a nonexistent object.

This is an interesting argument, but it seems inadequate because it turns on the causality of the knowing agent rather than on that of the object known. Perhaps, however, we can construct the right sort of argument using a simile employed by Mirecourt. Mirecourt says that God can preserve the light of a luminous body in the absence of the body, for

39. Van Neste, "Supposed Skepticism," pp. 107–8, 125.
40. *Apologia prima* (ed. Stegmueller, pp. 51–56).
41. *Sent.*, prol., q. 1, 2, and 6 (ed. Franzinelli, pp. 323–30, 445–46); *Apologia prima* (ed. Stegmueller, pp. 66–68).
42. *Sent.*, prol., q. 2 (ed. Franzinelli, pp. 329–30); *Apologia prima* (ed. Stegmueller, p. 68).

example, the light given by the sun without the sun. In this case, however, although the light might be in all other respects the same, it could not be sunlight. The parallel argument about intuitive cognition might be that although God could preserve in me that state of my soul by which I have intuitive cognition of an object in the absence of the object, this would not be a case of his preserving intuitive cognition of that object, because the state of my soul would lack the relation to the secondary cause in virtue of which it can be called that object's action on me, and hence my intuition of that object.[43]

Mirecourt does not conceive of himself as denying the theological principle that God can supply the causality of any created agent, since he proposes a new definition of cognition rather than a retraction of the theological principle.[44] But in effect Mirecourt does set limits on what God can accomplish by replacing the causality of a second cause with his own immediate causality. Whereas most earlier authors had agreed that in this way God could bring about intuitive cognition of nonexistents in the human intellect, Mirecourt regards such cognition as involving a contradiction and hence beyond the scope even of divine omnipotence.

## Conclusion

Scotus's theory of intuitive cognition provided an attractive account of evident knowledge of contingent facts. But its combination with the view that cognition was an absolute entity which could exist independently and the theological principle that God could supply the effective causality of any secondary cause created a difficult problem. Godfrey and Mirecourt denied that cognition was an absolute entity and argued that it connoted or created a relation to the thing known.

But failing that solution, all those who discussed the problem allow for the cognition of nonexistents. Once intuitive cognition of nonexistents is postulated, the result of that cognition will be either judgment of existence or nonexistence. Ockham chose the second alternative, because he did not want to sacrifice the theory that intuitive cognition could provide the basis for evident knowledge.

Those who chose to hold that God could cause intuitive cognition of nonexistent objects, and that such cognition would cause us to judge that the object existed, had to qualify the view that intuitive cognition led to evident knowledge. Hence we find such expressions as Hervaeus's *cognitio falsa*. Similarly, Wodeham allows even in the normal course of events a least degree of certainty compatible with error. Absolutely speaking, for Wodeham there could be no certainty concerning contingent facts, because God could cause erroneous cognitions. On this issue, Mirecourt

43. *Sent.*, prol., q. 2 (ed. Franzinelli, pp. 322–30).
44. *Sent.*, prol., q. 2 (ed. Franzinelli, p. 329).

[175]

agreed with Wodeham, though he denied that there could be cognition of nonexistents.

It was Walter Chatton who first suggested that intuitive cognition of nonexistents imperiled the certainty of our knowledge of contingent facts. The issue of the certitude, as opposed to the evidence of our knowledge, was not an important topic in the discussion of intuitive cognition among the philosophers of Ockham's period. It is true that it was the scholars who were his first critics who raised the issue, but they were responding not to Ockham but to Aureol.

Seen in this context, Ockham's theory of the intuitive cognition of nonexistents has as few untoward consequences as could be expected. Indeed he had little alternative, given that he was unwilling to abandon either the certainty of intuitive cognition or the view that cognition was an absolute entity or the principle of divine omnipotence. This was perhaps an inappropriate area in which to emphasize that God could cause directly whatever could be caused mediately by secondary causes. But it should be clear that Ockham's originality did not consist in applying the theological principle of omnipotence in a manner dangerous to the certainty of human knowledge. Every author we know of reflected on this principle in the context of his discussion of intuitive cognition. Rather, what is unusual about his treatment of the subject was that he failed to draw the conclusion that intuitive cognition was fallible. Ockham was confident that we have evident knowledge about the world of contingent facts, and his views on intuitive cognition of nonexistents are a direct consequence of his unwillingness to call that evident knowledge into question.

Ockham's unusual views on intuitive cognition are not the result of skeptical tendencies but result from his adherence both to the principle of divine omnipotence and to the view that experiential knowledge could be certain. Once we see Ockham in this typically Franciscan context, his philosophical views may shed some light on his political views. Ockham's view that virtually the whole church might apostatize can be seen as yet another case where he argues that extreme causes must be taken seriously, for any possibility may be actualized by an omnipotent God. Ockham's views on knowledge based on intellectual intuition parallel his view that Catholic dogma may be based on postapostolic revelation. Just as Ockham claimed that experiential perceptions of the external world and our own internal states could form the basis for certain knowledge, he held that postapostolic revelation might establish Christian doctrine, provided the inspired teaching reached the universal church undoubted.[45] Thus Ockham's philosophical commitments, like his understanding of canon law, help us to understand him as a political thinker.

45. Ockham, *Dialogus*, part 1, lib. 2, c. 5, *Opera plurima*, vol. 1 (Lyons, 1495; reprint London, 1962), fol. 8va.

# PART III

# [10]

## Clericis Laicos and the Canonists

### THOMAS M. IZBICKI

In 1296 Pope Boniface VIII attempted to deprive England and France of the sinews of war by issuing the bull *Clericis laicos*. The Gregorian Decretals contained texts permitting the clergy to make voluntary contributions to princes but requiring papal consent for any taxation of the clergy. Boniface attempted to extend this requirement of papal consent to include voluntary contributions. Laymen who imposed taxes on the clergy without permission and clergy who paid them, even under the guise of gifts, incurred automatic excommunication. These censures were absolvable only by the pope except *in mortis articulo*.[1] Boniface's policy had some effect in England, where Archbishop Winchelsey led the campaign to regularize clerical consent to royal taxation.[2] On the Continent many princes were willing to acquiesce, but not Philip IV of France, who made a two-pronged response. The export of specie from France was forbidden at a time when the pope was at war with the Colonna. At the same time a propaganda campaign was begun, which denounced the clergy for accepting the laity's protection without being willing to help defray the costs of that protection. Nor was the French clergy eager to support the pope

I gave a luncheon paper on this topic at University of California, Berkeley in 1974. Invaluable information used in its revision was supplied by Professor Stephan Kuttner, Professor Bernard Schimmelpfennig, Professor Constantin Fasolt, and Doctor Jacqueline Brown.

1. Friedberg, *CIC*, 2:1662–63: Sext. 3.23.3. The relevant texts are c. *Non minus* (X 3.49.4: ed. cit., 2:654–55) and c. *Adversus* (X 3.49.7: ed. cit., 2:656).

2. E. J. Smyth, "*Clericis Laicos* and the Lower Clergy in England," in *Studies in Medievalia and Americana: Essays in Honor of William Davis, S. J.*, ed. G. G. Steckler et al. (Spokane, Wash., 1973), pp. 77–87; J. H. Denton, *Robert Winchelsey and the Crown, 1294–1313* (Cambridge, 1980), pp. 80–135.

against the king.[3] At last Boniface found it necessary to make peace with France. In 1297 he issued a series of bulls, among them *Etsi de statu*, which granted to the French king the right to tax the clergy for the defense of the realm without papal consent.[4]

*Clericis laicos*, however, did not suddenly go out of circulation. A year later (3 March 1298) the same document appeared in a new official collection of canon law, the *Liber sextus*, as chapter 3 of the title *De immunitate ecclesiarum, coemeteriorum et aliorum locorum religiosorum* (Sext. 3.23.3). We should not dismiss this republication, as Boase did, with the remark that *Clericis laicos* "has in its law book setting a less aggressive sound than when the legates proclaimed it in France."[5] Such an offhand dismissal ignores the realities of an age in which canon law was supposed to affect, at least indirectly, the lives of all Christians. The canonists, moreover, were among the most sophisticated medieval political theorists; and the popes never were reluctant to influence their teachings by circulating their political decretals in official collections transmitted to the schools.[6] Thus the universal diffusion of *Clericis laicos* as part of the canon law was no mere gesture of defiance by a defeated pope. Boniface VIII was not a tactful man, but he must have been aware that he was risking a new rupture of relations with France during a time of truce.[7]

This point is underlined by the nature of the *Liber sextus*, which was intended to revise and codify the canon law. The curialists charged with the work of compilation sifted a half-century's production of papal letters and of conciliar canons. Thus no canon appeared in the *Sextus* by mere accident.[8] Boniface, moreover, gave the collection a personal imprint,

3. G. Digard, *Philippe le Bel et le Saint-Siège de 1285 à 1304*, vol. 1 (Paris, 1936), pp. 246–97; J. Rivière, *Le problème de l'église et de l'état au temps du Philippe le Bel* (Louvain, 1926), pp. 63–70; J. A. McNamara, "Simon de Beaulieu and *Clericis Laicos*," *Traditio* 25 (1969): 155–70; J. Marrone and C. Zuckermann, "Cardinal Simon of Beaulieu and Relations between Philip the Fair and Boniface VIII," *Traditio* 31 (1975): 195–222; R. Scholz, *Die Publizistik zur Zeit Philipps des Schönen und Bonifaz VIII* (Stuttgart, 1903; reprint 1969), pp. 166–72; J. O'Callaghan, "The Ecclesiastical Estate in the Cortes of Leon-Castille, 1252–1350," *Catholic Historical Review* 67 (1981): 183–313 at p. 212.

4. *Les registres de Boniface VIII*, ed. G. Digard et al., vol. 1, 2354 (Paris, 1884), pp. 941–43. For a rare appearance of *Etsi de statu* in a collection of *extravagantes*, see Vat. lat. 12571, fols. 504v–5v with its executory letter at fol. 506r. The gloss at the bottom of fol. 504v describes it, in its own terms, as a declaration of *Clericis laicos*. The same point, coupled with a contention that *Etsi* was revoked by Clement V, is made by Aegidius Bellamera, *Commentaria in extravagantes*, Vat. Ross. 817, fols. 63vb–64ra.

5. T. S. R. Boase, *Boniface VIII* (London, 1933), pp. 92–93.

6. W. Ullmann, *Medieval Papalism* (London, 1955); J. A. Watt, *The Theory of the Papal Monarchy in the Thirteenth Century* (New York, 1965).

7. In this period King Philip circulated the provision of the *Liber sextus* requiring royal officials to cooperate with inquisitors; see Boase, *Boniface VIII*, p. 119.

8. A. Stickler, *Historia iuris canonici*, vol. 1 (Turin, 1950), pp. 257–64; S. Kuttner, "The Code of Canon Law in Historical Perspective," *Jurist* 28 (1968): 129–48 at p. 144; G. LeBras, "Boniface VIII, symphoniste et modérateur," in *Mélanges d'histoire du Moyen Age dédiés à la mémoire de Louis Halphen* (Paris, 1951), pp. 383–94.

incorporating into it texts aimed at his enemies. Thus *Clericis laicos* appears, but *Etsi de statu* does not. The Colonna and their friends among the Spiritual Franciscans argued that the abdication of the preceding pope, Celestine V, had been illegal, having been obtained by foul means. The pope replied by including in the *Sextus* the chapter *Quoniam aliqui*, which emphasized the validity of his predecessor's renunciation of the Roman see. Another chapter, *Ad succidendos*, charged the Colonna cardinals with the crime of schism and expelled them from the Sacred College. In such company *Clericis laicos* has the aggressive sound of an assertion of papal supremacy, of a vindication of the reigning pope, Boniface VIII.[9]

A more concrete political motive for this inclusion can be discerned in the possibility that the pope might once more try to cut off the revenues of princes. This threat could affect the papacy's Angevin allies, locked in the long struggle over Sicily, as well as England or France.[10]

We are concerned here, however, with the papacy's attempt to influence learned opinion on the question of lay taxation of the clergy. When copies of the *Liber sextus* were sent to the universities, *Clericis laicos* became a subject of classroom lecture and of written commentary. The most obvious parallel here is that of Innocent III's decretal *Per venerabilem*. This refusal to legitimate a nobleman's bastards became a vehicle for ideas about papal temporal power. The canonists were compelled to expound the meaning of this text in their lectures, presenting papalist ideas to their students.[11] Boniface, who was interested in the education of the clergy, may have hoped to raise up a generation of clerics less amenable to the will of princes than were the French bishops and priests of his own day.[12]

An examination of commentaries on the *Liber sextus* shows Boniface successfully influencing learned opinion in his own time but failing after his death. This eventual failure reflected the realities of church and state relations in the later Middle Ages, including the French ascendancy over the papacy during its years at Avignon.[13] During the remaining years of Boniface's reign, the canonists accepted *Clericis laicos* without demurrer. This is evident in the case of the first commentary on the *Liber sextus*, that of Iohannes Monachus. Although Monachus was a protégé of Celestine V, no friend of Boniface himself and an advocate of an increased role for the Sacred College in the affairs of the church, there is no sign of

---

9. Sext. 1.7.1: ed. cit., 2.971, and Sext. 5.3.un.: ed. cit., 2.1078–80.

10. Boase, *Boniface VIII*, pp. 151–56.

11. B. Tierney, "*Tria Quippe Distinguit Iudicia*. . . : A Note on Innocent III's Decretal *Per Venerabilem*," *Speculum* 37 (1962): 48–59; K. Pennington, "Pope Innocent III's Views on Church and State: A Gloss to *Per Venerabilem*," in *Law, Church and Society: Essays in Honor of Stephan Kuttner*, ed. K. Pennington and R. Somerville (Philadelphia, 1977), pp. 49–67.

12. L. Boyle, "The Constitution *Cum ex Eo* of Boniface VIII: Education of Parochial Clergy," *Medieval Studies* 24 (1962): 263–302.

13. Rivière, *Problème*, pp. 98–121; G. Mollatt, *The Popes at Avignon*, trans. J. Love (New York, 1965), pp. 229–49.

Thomas M. Izbicki

disagreement with papal policy in his commentary on *Clericis laicos*.[14] Monachus described this text as a valid addition to the canon law and, using words drawn from Lucan, as a valuable one: " 'We strive that it should always be prohibited, and we desire the denial,' that is as to the power [of unlicensed taxation]."[15] Monachus also considered the possibility that a prince might try to collect a tax from the lay dependents of the clergy rather than from the clergy themselves, a maneuvre he denounced as fraudulent.[16]

   The ordinary gloss on the *Sextus* was composed by the great Bolognese canonist Iohannes Andreae. Completed in Boniface's lifetime, this work includes an extensive discussion of *Clericis laicos*. A version of the ordinary gloss is found in most copies of the *Sextus*, but the later printings must be used with care. The manuscripts and incunabula give the original set of *casus* for each chapter; but the more commonly available sixteenth-century printings, including the *editio Romana*, replace these with the *casus* of Elias Regnier.[17] In his gloss on *Clericis laicos*, Iohannes, having passed beyond his own brief *casus* to the letter of the text, echoed Monachus's defense of papal policy on lay taxation of the clergy. Discussing the pope's words about prelates who fear princes more than they do God, Iohannes commended to the reader's attention the more courageous examples of Naboth and of St. Ambrose.[18] Iohannes Andreae also argued that *Clericis laicos* merely put more teeth into existing regulations: "This therefore does not correct [canon law], but it adds a penalty."[19] The ordinary gloss on *Clericis laicos* concludes with the argument that Boni-

   14. Iohannes Monachus, *Glossa aurea super sexto decretalium libro*, ed. Philippus Probus (Paris, 1513; reprint 1968), fol. 334va–b. J. F. von Schulte, *Die Geschichte der Quellen und Litteratur des canonischen Rechts*, vol. 2 (Stuttgart, 1877; reprint 1956), pp. 191–93; R. Steckling, "Jean Lemoine as Canonist and Political Thinker" (Ph.D. diss., University of Wisconsin, 1964), pp. 99–102; B. Tierney, *Foundations of the Conciliar Theory* (Cambridge, 1955), pp. 178–98.
   15. Monachus, *Glossa aurea*, fol. 334va, "Hec decretalis adiicit ac c. proximorum et ad c. Non minus et c. adversus . . . [in vetitum] iuxta illud lucani. Nitimur in vetitum semper. cupimusque negata. [quam]: idest. quantum potestas. extra de constitutionibus ecclesia et c. que in ecclesiarum xcvi. dist. bene quidem circa finem."
   16. Monachus, *Glossa aurea*, fol. 334va, "Quid si hec impositio non fiat ecclesiasticis personis sed hominibus earundem dic in hoc fieri fraudem legi."
   17. Iohannes' *casus* on *Clericis laicos* appears in the Basel 1477 printing of the *Sextus* at fol. 115vb as well as in the manuscripts I examined, e.g., Vat. lat. 1393, fol. 227vb. Regnier's *casus* appears in the Venice 1525 printing at fol. 182rb–va and in his unpaginated *Casus longi sexti et clementinarum* (Strasbourg, 1488) at Sext. 3.23.3. Schulte, *Geschichte*, 2:205–29, 374; S. Kuttner, "Johannes Andreae and His *Novella* on the Decretals of Gregory IX," *Jurist* 24 (1964): 393–408. On a related problem, see idem, "Notes on the *Glossa Ordinaria* of Bernard of Parma," *Bulletin of Medieval Canon Law* 11 (1981): 86–93. Iohannes' *casus* on *Clericis laicos* can also be found in collections of *casus in sextum*; e.g., Yale Law School MS JC 69, no. 1, at fol. 99r; Vat. Chigi lat. E.IV.80 at fol. 71rb. For another *casus* on the same text, see Wurzburg Mp theol. fac. 122, fols. 32ra–45rb at 41rb.
   18. Sext. 3.23.3: ed. cit., 2.1063, "Plus timentes maiestatem temporalem offendere quam aeternam" *Glo. ord. in Sextum* at 3.23.3 s.v. "Eternam."
   19. Ibid., s.v. "Sedis eiusdem," "Non ergo corrigit ista: sed penam adiicit."

face VIII was able to cancel or modify any previous papal concession concerning lay taxation of the clergy.[20]

At about the same time that Iohannes Andreae was composing the ordinary gloss on the *Sextus*, Boniface's fortunes first waxed and then waned. Buoyed by Philip IV's military failure in Flanders and by the Jubilee Year (1300), the pope issued the constitution *Unam sanctam*, which declared subjection to Rome to be necessary for salvation. In 1301, however, King Philip felt able to flout canon law by arresting the bishop of Pamiers, Bernard Saisset. This act brought the pope and the king into mortal conflict. Boniface called the French bishops to Rome for consultations and canceled all concessions made to the French crown. Philip responded with a new propaganda campaign and by renewing old ties with the Colonna. In 1303 Boniface was captured at Anagni by forces led by Sciarra Colonna and Guillaume de Nogaret. Shortly after being released from this brief captivity, the pope died a broken man.[21]

Boniface's successor, Benedict XI, sought peace with France, but not at any price. He threatened to excommunicate Nogaret; but he also made concessions, restricting the penalties imposed by *Clericis laicos* to attempts at unlicensed taxation of the clergy. This left the way open once more for payment of voluntary subsidies by the clergy to the crown. This bull of concession, *Quod olim* (1304), did not appease the French king; nor was the pope happy. When he died suddenly in 1304, Benedict was preparing to excommunicate Nogaret.[22] *Quod olim* remained in circulation, and it eventually found a place, with an apparatus by Iohannes Monachus, in the *Extravagantes communes*.[23]

Only one commentary on the *Sextus* reflects that moment when *Clericis laicos* had been restricted but not revoked. This work was composed by Iohannes Andreae's teacher, Guido de Baysio, archdeacon of Bologna.[24] Like the commentaries of Iohannes Monachus and of Iohannes Andreae, that by the Archdeacon speaks harshly of lay interference with ecclesiastical immunities and urges prelates to defend those immunities.[25] Guido

20. Ibid., s.v. "Non obstantibus."

21. Boase, *Boniface VIII*, pp. 297–301; T. F. Ruiz, "Reaction to Anagni," *Catholic Historical Review* 65 (1979): 385–401.

22. P. Funke, *Papst Benedikt XI* (Münster, 1891), pp. 72–74; *Les registres de Benoit XI*, ed. C. Grandjean, vol. 3 (Paris, 1885), pp. 792–93, no. 1269. For a contemporary reference to *Quod olim*, see Vat. lat. 2498, fol. 75rb *mg.*

23. For example, it is found among the *extravagantes* in Ambrosiana I 83 sup. at fols. 75vb–76ra. (*Clericis laicos* itself appears in the same collection at fol. 131ra–b.) *Extrav. commun.* 3.5.un.: Friedberg, *CIC*, 2:1287–88. Monachus's gloss, with an addition by Petrus Bertrandi, appears in the Venice 1525 printing of the collection at fols. 45vb–46rb. An anonymous *casus* on *Quod olim* appears in Vat. lat. 4990 at fol. 22v.

24. Schulte, *Geschichte*, 2:188–90; F. Liotta, "Appunti per una biografia del canonista Guido da Baisio arcidiacono di Bologna," *Studi Senesi*, ser. 3, 13 (1964): 7–52 at pp. 25–26.

25. T. M. Izbicki, "Guido de Baysio's Unedited Gloss on *Clericis Laicos*," *Bulletin of Medieval Canon Law* 13 (1983): 62–67 at 65.

Thomas M. Izbicki

made specific reference to *Quod olim* as the current interpretation of *Clericis laicos* by the papacy, forbidding unauthorized exactions but permitting voluntary contributions. (An addition to one copy of this text argues that *Quod olim* does nothing more than Boniface had done in *Etsi de statu*.[26] The Archdeacon, like Iohannes Monachus, denounced as fraudulent the collection of unauthorized taxes from the lay dependents of the clergy.[27] At a later date, when Clement V had revoked *Clericis laicos,* the Archdeacon canceled his gloss on the text. We cannot be sure whether he did this because the decretal had been deprived of legal force or because he did not wish to discuss the revocation, regarding it as an insult to the memory of his deceased benefactor, Boniface VIII.[28]

Clement suffers in the eyes of later generations because he was subservient to Philip of France, especially in the affair of the Templars. Perhaps the pope really feared the intermittent French campaign for the posthumous condemnation of Boniface VIII. The king's pose in these proceedings was that of a zealously orthodox grandson of St. Louis.[29] In this spirit of politic piety, Philip the Fair set about having Clement undo any of Boniface VIII's bulls which were offensive to the French Crown. Thus the pope issued the constitution *Meruit,* which declared France to be no more subject to the Crown because of *Unam sanctam* than it had been before the issuing of that bull.[30] The Capetians were permitted once more to have their corpses divided for burial at several sites, a practice forbidden in *Detestandae feritatis.*[31] In practical terms the most important of Clement's concessions was contained in the constitution *Pastoralis* (1306), which repealed *Clericis laicos,* along with its declarations *Etsi de statu* and *Quod olim.* This was a matter of positive law, one pope undoing the acts of his predecessor. The canons *Non minus* and *Adversus* once more were the key texts concerning lay taxation of the clergy. Voluntary contributions were legal, and the pope could authorize the levying of taxes by the king at the beginning of his reign and in the presence of Philip IV. Clement felt the need to justify his action, citing as its just cause the scandals caused by *Clericis laicos.*[32]

26. Ibid., p. 66.
27. Ibid., p. 66.
28. Ibid., p. 64.
29. Mollatt, *Avignon,* pp. 229–49; F. J. Pegues, *The Lawyers of the Last Capetians* (Princeton, 1962), pp. 47–60; Strayer, *Medieval Statecraft,* pp. 300–14; G. Lizerand, *Clement V et Philippe le Bel* (Paris, 1910), pp. 56–57.
30. *Meruit* appears among the *extravagantes* in Ambrosiana I 83 sup. at fol. 76ra and in *Extrav. commun.* 5.7.1: ed. cit., 2.1300. *Unam sanctam* appears in ibid. 1.8.1: ed. cit., 2.1245–46. J. Muldoon, "The Avignon Papacy and the Frontiers of Christendom: The Evidence of Vatican Register 62," *Archivum historiae pontificiae* 17 (1979): 125–95 at p. 142.
31. *Detestandae* appears in *Extrav. commun.* 3.6.1: ed. cit., 2.1272–73. E. A. R. Brown, "Death and the Human Body in the Later Middle Ages: The Legislation of Boniface VIII on the Division of the Human Corpse," *Viator* 12 (1981): 221–70.
32. *Registrum Clementis papae* V, ed. monachi O.S.B., vol. 1 (Rome, 1885), pp. 166–67, no. 906.

Even if Philip's intention in pressing for revocation of *Clericis laicos* had nothing to do with its possible impact of future generations of canonists, the effect of the pope's decision to revoke it was soon felt in legal circles. *Pastoralis* was circulated in its original form, finding its way into at least two collections of *extravagantes*.[33] It reached a wider audience as the chapter *Quoniam* in the last official canonistic collection of the Middle Ages, the *Constitutiones Clementinae*. This was the only chapter under the title *De immunitate ecclesiarum*, the title under which *Clericis laicos* had appeared in the *Sextus*.[34] This text soon became a locus classicus for the discussion of one pope's power to revoke the decisions of another, particularly to avoid scandal.[35] Because of the pope's sovereign power in matters of positive law, no one argued that the revocation of *Clericis laicos* was invalid. Iohannes Andreae, echoed by Baldus de Ubaldis, did complain of the influence of the French king on Clement's decision.[36]

The effects of *Pastoralis* and of *Quoniam*, the version in the Clementines, soon became apparent in commentaries on the *Sextus*. Although neither the text of *Clericis laicos* nor its ordinary gloss was ever deleted from a manuscript of that collection, numerous notes were made in the margins of manuscript copies recording the revocation. Most of them cite the relevant chapter of the *Clementinae*.[37] The revocation was also recorded in the *casus* literature on both the *Sextus* and the *Clementinae*.[38] The same fact was even noted in the margin of a copy of Raymond of Peñafort's *Summa de poenitentia*.[39] A loud dissent on the revocation of *Clericis laicos*, based on the wisdom rather than the validity of the decision, can be found in a Vatican manuscript of the *Liber sextus*, whose

33. *Pastoralis* appears in Ambrosiana I 83 sup. at fol. 88rb–va and in Vat. lat. 3984 at fol. 124va. It also appears in *Extrav. commun.* 3.13.1: ed. cit., 2.1288.

34. Clem. 3.17.un.: Friedberg, *CIC*, 2:1178. S. Kuttner, "The Date of the Constitution *Saepe*, the Vatican Manuscripts and the Roman Edition of the Clementines," in *Mélanges Eugene Tisserant*, vol. 4 (Vatican City, 1964), pp. 427–52.

35. *Glo. ord. in Clementinas* at 3.17.un. s.v. "Pro infectis"; Ps. Bonifacius de Vitalinis (Bonifacius Ammanati), *Commentaria in Clementinis constitutionibus* (Venice, 1521), fols. 177vb–78rb; Franciscus de Zabarella, *Super Clementinis*, Vat. lat. 2529 fols. 251vb–52vb; Petrus de Ancharano, *Super Clementinis facundissima commentaria* (Bologna, 1580), p. 229A; Nicolaus de Tudeschis (Panormitanus), *Super Clementinis*, Vat. Palat. lat. 666, fol. 147rb; Iohannes de Imola, *Commentaria in libros Clementinarum* (Lyons, 1555), fols. 124va–25ra. D. Maffei, "Profilo di Bonifacio Ammanati giurista e cardinale," in *Genèse et débuts du Grand Schisme d'Occident* (Paris, 1980), pp. 239–51.

36. *Glo. ord. in Clementinas*, s.v. "Quoniam"; Baldus de Ubaldis, *Summula super Clementinis*, Vat. lat. 5925, fols. 42ra–49vb at 48rb–va. T. M. Izbicki, "Notes on Late Medieval Jurists," *Bulletin of Medieval Canon Law* 4 (1974): 49–54 at p. 54.

37. Vat. lat. 1392, fol. 63r *mg.*; Vat. lat. 2497, fol. 81ra *mg.*; Vat. lat. 2502, fol. 73vb *mg.*; Vat. lat. 2503, fol. 83rb *mg.*; Vat. lat. 1395, fol. 86ra *mg.*; Vat. lat. 1396, fol. 70rb *mg.*; Vat. lat. 13265, fol. 76rb *mg.*

38. *Casus Sexti et Clementinarum*, Harvard Law School MS 74, fol. 263v, ad *Clericis laicos*, fol. 264r, ad *Quoniam*.

39. Yale University Marston MS 127, fol. 98v *mg.*

owner made this note next to the text of the canceled decretal: "This is revoked today, that is in the Clementines, and badly for the Church of God. May God be merciful to the revoker."[40]

The revocation of *Clericis laicos* occurred early in the long career of Iohannes Andreae. Late in life (ca. 1340), when he composed his *Novella in sextum*, Iohannes recited the history of the restriction and revocation of this chapter. He concluded that one need not dwell on it and, perhaps from a lapse of memory, that the Archdeacon, Guido de Baysio, had not glossed it.[41] Several owners of manuscript copies of the *Sextus* copied this passage from Iohannes' *Novella* in the margin next to the text of *Clericis laicos* or made it the basis of their own annotations on that chapter.[42] The same passage from the *Novella* appears in all sixteenth-century printings of the ordinary gloss on the *Sextus*, placed between Regnier's *casus* and Iohannes' gloss on the letter of the text.[43] At least one commentator on the *Sextus* incorporated this passage from the *Novella* into his own work without mention of its author's name.[44]

The Italian canonists of the fourteenth century who commented the *Sextus* or the *Constitutiones Clementinae* labored in the shadow of Iohannes Andreae. Some simply composed additions to his ordinary glosses on those collections. One of the most conscientious of these annotators was Lapus Tactus, abbot of San Miniato. In his additions to the ordinary gloss on the *Sextus*, when discussing *Clericis laicos*, Lapus referred back to Iohannes Monachus's denial that princes could exact unauthorized taxes from the lay dependents of the clergy. Repeating the opinion of the Picard cardinal, Lapus branded this a fraudulent device.[45] Later generations of Italian canonists, almost to the man, adopted Lapus's restatement of Monachus's opinion. This gave *Clericis laicos* a half-life in legal literature as the place at which this discussion of fraudulent tactics

---

40. Vat. lat. 2504, fol. 98vb *mg.*, "Hoc revocatum est hodie, i.e. quo in clem. et male pro ecclesia Dei. Parcat Deus anime revocantis."

41. Iohannes Andreae, *In sextum decretalium librum novella commentaria* (Venice, 1581; reprint 1966), fol. 130va, "*Clericis. [laicos]*. Benedictus in sua extrava. quae incipit, quod olim, restrinxit hanc decre. ad exigentes tantum. Sed Clemens revocavit hanc decre. cum suis declarationibus, ita quod voluit haberi pro non facta per suam extrava. quae incipit, pastoralis, quae est inter cle. eo. tit. et incipit, quoniam. et vide ibi dixi i. glo. circa istam igitur instandum non est et Arc. etiam (*leg.* eam) non glossavit."

42. Vat. lat. 2498, fol. 74va *mg.*; Vat. lat. 5929, fol. 69rb *mg.*; Vat. Arch. S. Pietro A.38, fols. 94va *mg.*–95ra *mg.* Notes based on Iohannes' text appear in Vat. lat. 1393, fol. 277vb *mg.*; Vat. lat. 1396, fol. 70rb *mg.*; Vat. lat. 2500, fol. 108rb *mg.*; Vat. Urb. lat. 160, fol. 89vb *mg.*

43. E.g., Venice, 1525, fol. 187va. The distinction between *novella* and *additio* made in the printings does not appear in the manuscripts.

44. *Commentaria in Sextum*, Vat. Palat. lat. 651, fol. 274r–v.

45. Lapus Tactus, *Super libro sexto decretalium* (Rome, 1589), fol. 149ra–b. T. M. Izbicki, "New Notes on Late Medieval Jurists," *Bulletin of Medieval Canon Law* 10 (1980): 62–65 at p. 63.

was reproduced.[46] It was possible, however, for Petrus de Ancharano to ignore Lapus's contribution and simply repeat the well-known history of the restriction and revocation of *Clericis laicos.*[47]

To this point we have discussed only canonists resident in Italy. Nor is there much to be said of the Parisian school, because the available materials are sparse. The one substantial commentary on the *Sextus* from that milieu readily available is that of Iohannes de Borbonio, canon of Rheims, who made extensive use of the works of Iohannes Monachus, Iohannes Andreae, and Guido de Baysio.[48] This canonist summarized the acts of Benedict XI and of Clement V, saying that the older regulations remained in force. A nationalistic note can be heard in this author's description of *Clericis laicos* as "vain, harsh and dangerous."[49]

The canonists of the Midi were less inclined to nationalism, and they felt less overawed by Monachus, the ordinary gloss, and the Archdeacon. The earliest of these writers was Bernardus Raimundi; both versions of his commentary on the *Sextus* were composed after the revocation of *Clericis laicos.*[50] Raimundi's interpretation of the text is irenic, arguing that even Boniface had permitted the clergy to make free gifts to kings. (This may be a tacit reference to *Etsi de statu.*)[51]

Guilelmus de Monte Lauduno, who was often employed by the Avignon popes, gave a historical summary of the fortunes of *Clericis laicos*, including an eyewitness account of its revocation by Clement V on the insis-

46. *Commentaria in Sextum*, Vat. lat. 11501, at fol. 149v; Petrus Maurocenus, *Commentaria super Sexto*, Vat. lat. 2274, at fol. 416ra–b; Dominicus de S. Geminiano, *In sextum librum decretalium volumen commentaria* (Venice, 1578), fol. 26orb; Philippus Franchus, *In sextum decretalium librum commentarii* (Basel, 1581), p. 756; Benedictus de Benedictis (Capra), *Commentaria in Sextum*, Ambrosiana E 40, inf. fol. 143vb.

47. Petrus de Ancharano, *Super sexto decretalium acutissima commentaria* (Bologna, 1583), p. 372.

48. Iohannes de Borbonio, *Commentaria in Sextum*, Rheims Bibl. Mun. MS 736, at fol. 97ra. P. Fournier, "Jean de Bourbon, canoniste," *Histoire littéraire de la France* 36:591–95; Schulte, *Geschichte*, 2:241.

49. Iohannes de Borbonio, *Commentaria*, fol. 50ra, "Clericis. Hec decretalis fuit a principio vana, dura et periculosa, et ideo per Benedictum XI moderationem accepit postea in quadam decretale que incipit Quod olim, ut videlicet in solventibus aut recipientibus a sponte dantibus vendicet sibi locum quoad penam sive penas hic insertas. Postea per Clementem quintum fuit quo ad suas penas totaliter revocata et annullata, et ideo argumentum eius exponi non est ulterius laborandum extra, et solum servanda sunt iura extra eodem Non minus et c. Adversus."

50. Bernardus Raimundi, *Suplectiones in Sextum*, Paris BN lat. 4088, fols. 11a–61vb at 48vb–49ra (recension1); Bologna Collegio di Spagna MS 217, fols. 69vb–118rb at 108vb–9ra (recension 2), which adds a reference to the lay dependents of the church. F. Cantelar Rodriguez, "El apparatus de Bernardo Raimundo al Libro Sexto de Bonifacio VIII," in *Proceedings of the Fifth International Congress of Medieval Canon Law*, ed. S. Kuttner and K. Pennington (Vatican City, 1980), pp. 213–58; idem, "Bernardo Raimundo y Gencelino de Cassanis," *ZRG*, Kan. Abt., 67 (1981): 248–63.

51. Bernardus Raimundi, *Suplectiones* (recension 2) at fol. 108vb, "Doni. Nisi esset omnino liberale, et nisi pro libertatibus ecclesie acquirendis. Sic fuit interpretato conditor decretalis eiusdem, et accipe eo ipso etc. quod est infra."

tence of the king of France. Montlauzun justified his glossing the text at
length, despite the revocation, by contending that it was of "good memory" and because it had not perished entirely.[52] Montlauzun's contemporary, Iesselinus de Cassanis, argued that Boniface VIII and Benedict XI
both had permitted free gifts by the clergy to princes. His mention of the
revocation of *Clericis laicos* was more impersonal.[53] Iesselinus also composed a *casus* on *Clericis laicos* which repeated its provisions, including a
reminder that the censures it imposed could be absolved only by the pope
except *in mortis articulo*.[54]

Aegidius Bellamera, although accustomed to using Iesselinus's works
in the composition of his own, ignored that canonist's discussion of
*Clericis laicos*. Bellamera recited the familiar history of restriction and
revocation before wrongly noting that the ordinary gloss, the Archdeacon's apparatus, and that by Iohannes de Borbonio did not discuss that
chapter. Bellamera also repeated Iohannes Monachus's discussion of attempts to tax the lay dependents of the clergy.[55] A more influential
opinion on this topic was expressed by the last of our Occitanian canonists, Elias Regnier. As has been noted above, his *casus* on *Clericis laicos*
appears in sixteenth-century printings of the *Sextus* with ordinary gloss.
In Regnier's works we encounter once more the sort of French nationalism displayed by Iohannes de Borbonio. His *casus* on *Clericis laicos*, like
that on *Quoniam*, which is printed with the *Constitutiones Clementinae*,

52. Guilelmus de Monte Lauduno, *In sextum decretalium interpretatio* (Toulouse,
1524), fol. 111vb, "Hec sumpta est ex hiis que not. extra eodem Non minus. et fuit facta
hec constitutio ante confectionem sexti libri. cito post creationem Bonifacii: sed post-
modum superius a statim post coronationem Clementis pape V per eum Lugduni: ad
instantiam domini regis Francie ibidem presentis me ibi presente et audiente ut quid
ergo membranas occupat xix di. Si Romanorum. sed que eius memoria bona et quia
perimi non in totum suspensaret idcirco aliqua exponamus." Schulte, *Geschichte*,
2:197–99; P. Fournier, *Histoire littéraire de la France*, 35:467–503. Montlauzun also
mentioned King Philip's presence in Lyons in *Commentaria in Clementinas*, Vat. lat.
2583, fols. 1ra–82vb at 66vb.
53. Iesselinus de Cassanis, *Super Sexto*, Paris BN lat. 4087, fols. 1ra–94ra at 76ra,
"Bonifacius VIII istam decretalem et sic interpretatus ad instanciam regis Francie. Idem
fecit Benedictus XI per suam constitutionem que incipit Cum (!) olim eodem titulo.
Clemens autem V hanc constitutionem et omnes declarationes super ipsam factas et
omnino ex eis revocavit sed decretales extra eodem Non minus, Adversus servari
precipit." Schulte, *Geschichte*, 2:199–200; P. Fournier, "Jesselin de Cassagnes, canoniste," *Histoire littéraire de la France*, 35:348–61; J. Tarrant, "The Life and Works of
Jesselin de Cassagnes," *Bulletin of Medieval Canon Law* 9 (1979): 37–64. See also
Iesselinus de Cassanis, *Commentaria in Clementinas*, Vat. lat. 2583, fols. 101ra–211vb
at 188ra.
54. Iesselinus, *Super Sexto* at fol. 76rb. A version without that reminder appears in
Vat. lat. 13265 at fol. 76rb *mg*.
55. Aegidius Bellamera, *Commentaria in Sextum*, Vat. Barb. lat. 1475 at fol. 212ra–b.
Schulte, *Geschichte*, 2:274–75; H. Gilles, *Gilles Bellemàre, canoniste* (Paris, 1967);
Tarrant, "Jesselin de Cassagnes," pp. 48–49.

stresses Boniface's hatred of Philip IV and the scandals this hatred caused among the faithful.[56]

The last word on *Clericis laicos,* however, does not belong to Elias Regnier. In the sixteenth century Bartolomé de Las Casas invoked the authority of that chapter, as if it were valid still, when denouncing royal officials who had violated clerical immunities.[57] The commentary of Iohannes Monachus, moreover, was brought back into circulation in printed form. In 1535 the Parisian jurist Philippus Probus reissued the Picard cardinal's apparatus with his own additions.[58] After reciting Monachus's opinion that churches find wealthy subjects useful, Probus added that the same was true of princes.[59] But he argued, using the authority of Baldus de Ubaldis, that it was improper for princes to downgrade their subjects, since "the honor of the king is increased by the dignity of his subjects, and the status of the king is more powerful and more honorable and more to be feared."[60]

It is fitting to conclude our study of *Clericis laicos* and the canonists with this advice to kings. When Philip IV brought down Boniface VIII, the papacy seemed to possess a very real temporal power. In Probus's day the papacy was at a disadvantage in dealing with princes, who were much more able to obtain subsidies from the clergy of their own realms. The question of the limits of royal power was becoming more important than that of the relationship of church and state. This triumph of the princes is mirrored by the fortunes of *Clericis laicos.* In its author's lifetime, even after his first unsuccessful contest with the French king, the canonists regarded this chapter of the *Sextus* as a valid restriction on lay taxation of the clergy. This restriction, however, was only a matter of positive law. Thus the canonists accepted *Quod olim, Pastoralis,* and *Quoniam,* the version of *Pastoralis* in the *Constitutiones Clementinae,* with little complaint. The old papal means of influencing learned opinion on political issues by inserting a new text into the canon law failed, but it did not fail because of the canonists. The legislator, the pope himself, yielded to the

56. For Regnier's *casus* on *Clericis laicos,* see note 17 above. For Elias Regnier *casus* on *Quoniam,* see *Casus longi* ad Clem. 3.17.un. For an example of this same *casus* on *Quoniam* printed as part of the ordinary gloss on the *Clementinae,* see the Venice 1525 printing at fol. 8orb. There are no *casus* in the ordinary gloss to the *Clementinae;* cf. Vat. lat. 1397.

57. H. R. Parish and H. Weidmann, *Las Casas en Mexico* (forthcoming).

58. See Appendix on Philippus Probus.

59. Iohannes Monachus, *Glossa aurea,* fol. 324vb, referring to another *additio* at fol. 327vb.

60. Iohannes Monachus, *Glossa aurea,* fol. 324vb, "Adde dictum Baldi in c. Intellecto sub numero 5 extra de iure iurando quod 'honor regis augetur per dignitatem subditorum et fit status regis magis potens et magis honorabilis et magis timendus.'" Cf. Baldus de Ubaldis, *In decretalium volumen commentaria* (Venice, 1595; reprint 1971), fol. 261va.

Thomas M. Izbicki

pressures of practical politics. Capitulation by the legislator entailed capitulation by the commentators.⁶¹ The vestigial survival of *Clericis laicos* does not upset these conclusions. That chapter continued to evoke comment on fraud, most of it copied from Iohannes Monachus by way of Lapus Tactus, just as *Quoniam* continued to evoke discussions of scandal; but the papacy ceased presenting any real obstacle to lay taxation of the clergy.

## Appendix
## Philippus Probus

Philippus Probus of Bourges was active in Parisian legal circles until his death about 1551. He served as avocat of the Parlement of Paris and then as official of Amiens. Probus already was an avocat in 1535 when he published Iohannes Monachus's commentary on the *Sextus* with his own additions. In 1542 he did a supplement to Arnulphus Ruzaeus, *Tractatus iuris regaliae* (Paris, 1551).⁶² Three years later Probus, inspired by Paul III's second convocation of the Council of Trent, edited Guilelmus Durantis the younger, *De modo celebrandi conciliorum* (Paris, 1545).⁶³ He also published an edition of the *Pragmatica sanctio* (Paris, 1546) and one of Iohannes Staphilaeus, *Tractatus de litteris gratiae* (Paris, 1547). (A second printing of Probus's edition of the *Pragmatica sanctio* [Paris, 1555] refers to him as a papal chaplain.) Probus is reported to have done additions to Guilelmus de Monteserrato, *De reservationibus per papam ex rationabili causa factis* (Paris, 1666).

Notices on Probus are many but not very useful. Among them are Schulte, *Geschichte*, 2:196 n. 4, 3/1 (Stuttgart, 1875; reprint 1956), p. 533; R. Naz, "Jean le Moine," *Dictionnaire de Droit Canonique* 4:112–13; H. Hurter, *Nomenclator literarius theologiae catholicae . . .* , 2d ed. (Innsbruck, 1906; reprint 1963), p. 861, no. 426; O. Martin, *L'Assemblée de Vincennes* (Paris, 1909), p. 57. More useful are C. Fasolt, "A New View of William Durant the Younger's *Tractatus de modo generalis concilii celebrandi*," *Traditio* 37 (1981): 291–324 at 295 n. 15; idem, "The Manuscripts and Editions of William Durant the Younger's *Tractatus de modo generalis concilii celebrandi*," *Annuarium historiae conciliorum* 10 (1978): 290–309 at 307.

61. J. Muldoon, "Boniface VIII's Forty Years of Experience in the Law," *The Jurist* 11 (1971): 449–77; Scholz, *Publizistik*, pp. 131, 333–52.
62. The work also was published in Petrus Rebuffus, *Praxis beneficiorum* (Paris, 1644) and as *Tractatus de iure regalia* in *Tractatus Universi Iuris* XII (Venice, 1584), fols. 389ra–408va.
63. This is the less accurate of the two editions published in this period according to Fasolt, "A New View of William Durant the Younger's *Tractatus*," pp. 313–15 (cited below).

# [II]

# Papal Reserved Powers and the Limitations on Legatine Authority

## ROBERT C. FIGUEIRA

The medieval church—understood as the collectivity of individual believers—had available to it only a primitive communications apparatus
and thus was too intractable for any one man to supervise effectively and
rule personally. Its government and administration were managed not
only through the papacy but also through smaller units: the diocese with
its bishop, the parish with its priest, and the monastery with its abbot.
Much of what we would today call "ecclesiastical government" occurred
on these local levels. This chapter focuses on an institution or administrative device that medieval popes used to share governmental tasks exercised under their traditional or newly claimed authority—papal legation. Like all agents of government, legates provided a means by which
information and resources were transmitted to the center of power, decisions were executed, commissioned jurisdiction was applied, and physical
resources were transferred outward from that center.

Such activities depended in part on authorization and supervision. How
could the pope communicate to his legate and also to the church at large
which papal powers this agent was empowered to exercise? At the same
time, how could the pope satisfy himself that his unique jurisdiction was
not diminished by employing a legate? The answer to both of these questions, when viewed from the theoretical standpoint of canon law, lies in a
consideration of papal mandates and of powers normally reserved to the
pope alone.

We must first consider a legate's powers and authorization. Medieval

I wish to acknowledge the insightful advice of Professor Robert L. Benson (University of
California, Los Angeles) regarding an earlier draft of this essay.

Abbreviations used in this chapter are listed in appendix I.

popes and canonists alike agreed that legates could perform certain tasks purely as a function of their office, "by right of legation" (*iure legationis*). The minimal prerogatives of this office were considered fixed and were comprehended within the generic terms "general legation" (*generalis legatio*) and its authorization, the "general mandate" (*generale mandatum*). In addition, the pope could authorize a legate (or anyone else, for that matter) to accomplish any task whose performance normally pertained to or was reserved for the pope's jurisdiction alone. These powers could be transferred through "special concession" or "special mandate" (*speciale mandatum*). This system of classification usually occurred in decretist glosses in a variety of formulations. The best method for analyzing the specific powers encompassed by these terms would be both to investigate some of the actual decretals from the *Liber extra* wherein mention of these powers is made and to compile from decretalist glosses a detailed list of the specific powers both reserved to the pope and normally prohibited to legates. Up until now a systematic treatment of canonistic texts in this regard has not been attempted.

## Legatine Mandates in the *Liber Extra*

While on legation in Sicily during 1199–1200, Cardinal Cinthius of St. Laurence in Lucina attempted to transfer or translate the bishop of Troia to the vacant metropolitan see of Palermo.[1] For this act Pope Innocent III roundly denounced Cinthius in a series of decretals (X 1.30.3, 4). Nonetheless, faced with the fait accompli of the translation and aware of the personal importance of the bishop under consideration (he was the chancellor of the kingdom of Sicily), Innocent eventually acquiesced in the translation. Yet he considered it to have been an altogether abnormal act by his legate.[2] Innocent's complaints offered a concise statement of many of the factors relevant to legatine powers.

> by the lesson of punishment you ought to recognize how much you overstep. . . . you, who to the scorn of both canonical sanctions and general custom have presumed by your own will . . . to transfer de facto . . . the bishop of Troia . . . from the church of Troia to that of Palermo without our special mandate.[3]
> Although a general legation was committed to you within the kingdom of Sicily, without special mandate you nevertheless ought not to have stretched forth your hand to those things reserved to the Supreme Pontiff

1. See Zimmermann, p. 29, and Maleczek, pp. 105–6, for details regarding this legation.
2. See X 1.8.3.
3. X 1.30.3.

as a sign of singular privilege. And . . . if some of these matters already seemed permitted to legates by the office of legation itself, matters which often had been granted to legates by special concession (such as the absolution of those persons who incur the canon of a promulgated sentence on account of raising sacrilegious hands against clerics), did you reckon that you could subject the church of Palermo to the church of Messina, and, by conceding the privilege of primacy to the latter, set it over the former, just because we committed to you as legate the fulfillment of our representation? Or do you think that by virtue of the same reason you are permitted to unite two bishoprics or divide a single one without a special license?[4]

For Innocent III a grant of general legation alone clearly did not permit the legate to transfer bishops, to divide or unite bishoprics, or strictly speaking even to absolve persons excommunicated automatically for presuming violence against clerics. A special papal mandate or license could, however, authorize these very actions. As regards the absolution of violent excommunicates, Innocent did not cite an earlier decretal of Clement III (X 5.39.20) whose substance was reaffirmed in a later decretal of Gregory IX (X 1.30.9). These two decretals showed that grants of special papal license in this matter to cardinal-legates or legates *de latere* had been so common and routine during the late twelfth century and early thirteenth that this prerogative of absolution had become standard for this most exalted type of legate in all situations and eventually was accepted even without special mandate.[5] Other types of legates were more limited in their ability to absolve such men, but even they may have transcended such restrictions when empowered "by special grace" of the Apostolic see.

A special papal mandate not only empowered a legate (or anyone else) to perform something beyond his own inherent powers or beyond a general commission, but simultaneously defined a discrete and more specific type of activity as well. In other words, any special mandate derogated, superseded, or cancelled in some specific matter anyone's general commission. A decretal of Celestine III (X 1.30.2) exemplified this phenomenon when it

---

4. X 1.30.4.

5. Although Clement himself did not expressly say that legates *a latere* may normally absolve in such cases *without* a special mandate, this was precisely the inference drawn by the rubricator ("Legati de latere absolvere possunt excommunicatos pro iniectione manuum in clericos") and by subsequent decretalists—Abbas antiquus, *Lectura aurea . . . super quinque libris Decretalium* (Strasbourg, 1510), at X 5.39.20: "Casus"; *Glossa ordinaria ad X,* 5.39.20: "CASUS. . . . Nota quod legati qui mittuntur a latere domini papae, licet non habeant mandatum speciale, absolvere tamen possunt excommunicatos. Bernardus." Both Bernard of Parma and Hostiensis maintained that this prerogative derived from customary usage: *Glossa ordinaria ad X,* 1.17.17: "*non obstante*"; Hostiensis, *Summa,* p. 319: "*Quid pertinet.*"

distinguished between the jurisdictions of legates and of papal judges-delegate.

> You have taken pains to inquire from us, whether a general legate in a province, a person other than him to whom we delegated a case, can himself take cognizance of a case either before or after [the delegate's own] cognizance, or can in such a way impede the progress of our commission transmitted to a delegate judge. . . . we respond that a legate . . . cannot impede a commission made specially to another . . . , because a special mandate derogates a general one; whence, if a sentence has already been promulgated according to the form of our mandate, the same judge cannot disturb it in any way whatsoever, unless he should receive a special mandate concerning this matter.

Indeed, the primacy of a special over a general mandate was raised in an objection against a legate in a similar case reported in the *Liber extra* (X 5.1.22). At the request of Walter, abbot of Corbie, three clerics were delegated by Innocent III to conduct a visitation of that monastery. After their arrival at Corbie a cardinal-legate (Guala Bicchieri) appeared and conducted the visitation himself.[6] Thereupon the legate summoned Walter (who seemed to have been compromised somewhat by the legate's findings) to Paris to state any objections to the visitation the abbot might have. Innocent reported that in Paris the abbot objected, among other things, "that he [the legate] could not proceed as regards the correction of the monastery which had been committed beforehand by our [the pope's] authority to the aforesaid judges [the three visitors]." At this point the abbot appealed to the pope. Nonetheless he was subsequently deposed by the legate, and the monks elected a successor.[7] As it happened, the pope eventually decided the case against Walter for reasons which did not address the validity of the abbot's assertion that the visitor's special mandate had precluded legatine action.

## Papal Reserved Powers

That legates required special authorization to perform certain activities within the purview of papal power necessitated a special category of

6. Guala was at that time (1208–9) cardinal-deacon of St. Mary in Portico; for details on his legation see Zimmermann, p. 41; Maleczek, p. 142. The decretal explains *in parte decisa* that the visitors' task had been contumaciously impeded by certain unnamed monks, and that in their frustration they intended to invoke the secular arm to coerce obedience. This controversy probably impelled the legate to act.

7. The details of oral argument before the pope are reported *in parte decisa* of the decretal. Walther repeated there his major objection, that because the masters had begun and then deferred their visitation the legate could not proceed in the meantime.

"reserved powers," that is, powers normally reserved to papal judgment alone and not transferable by any grant of general legation.[8] We have already seen how in X 1.30.4 Innocent III characterized the activities requiring a special mandate as "reserved to the Supreme Pontiff as a sign of his singular privilege."[9] Nearly all the important decretalists of the thirteenth century provided lists of papal reserved powers and prohibitions of the performance of certain actions by legates. Sometimes they reiterated the individual items of these lists when glossing specific texts. Although they clearly built on the decretists' rather advanced discussion of this same subject, unlike previous canonists the decretalists firmly joined their discussion onto the context of legatine jurisdiction, either within a section entitled "on legates" or in some gloss commenting on a decretal featuring papal legation.[10] The decretalists and decretists were heirs to an ecclesiological tradition when they listed papal reserved powers. The most striking early manifestations of this tradition dated from the Investiture Struggle and its aftermath, in such texts as the *Dictatus papae* (found in Gregory VII's register) and the *Proprie auctoritates apostolice sedis.*[11] Finally, in the steady growth of decretalist lists of papal

---

The abbot believed himself justified "because a general mandate does not derogate a special mandate." The new abbot, who was also present before the pope, advanced counterobjections: Walter's initial acceptance of the legate's visitation, and the necessity for legatine action "by virtue of the office of legation committed to him" in a perilous situation incurred by the visitors' encounter with resistance.

8. Gregory the Great already spoke of such a category (although he did not use this specific term) when he entrusted his authority (*vices*) in Sicily to Bishop Maximus, whom later canonists considered a legate. Maximus was empowered to deal with minor matters (*minimae causae*), whereas more difficult and major cases (*difficilia, maiorae causae*) demanded the direct attention of the pope himself. Gregory's remarks appeared in the *Liber extra* as X 2.23.6; the relevant portions were, however, *in parte decisa* of the decretal.

9. *In parte decisa* of X 1.6.30 Innocent III recounted the actions of his legate, John of St. Paul, during a disputed election to the metropolitan see of Toulouse. John refused to accede to one group's request (postulation) to transfer their candidate, the bishop of Comminges, to the archiepiscopal see. The legate realized that such power of transfer was normally reserved for the pope, and that he had no special authorization. The legate's only course of action was to appeal for Innocent's decision in the matter. John was cardinal-priest of St. Prisca; for this legation see Zimmermann, pp. 30–31, and Maleczek, p. 116.

10. I plan to discuss the decretist analysis of papal reserved powers in a forthcoming study.

11. The only explicit reference to legates in either of these works is in the *Dictatus papae*, number 4: "Quod legatus eius omnibus episcopis presit in concilio etiam inferioris gradus et adversus eos sententiam depositionis possit dare" (*Das Register Gregors VII*, 2d ed., ed. Erich Caspar [Berlin, 1955], *MGH Epp*, 2:203). See Hubert Mordek, "Proprie auctoritates apostolice sedis: Ein zweiter Dictatus papae Gregors VII?" *DA* 28 (1972): 105–32, for the best edition of this work and for some hypotheses concerning its author and date of composition. Friedrich Kempf, "Ein zweiter Dictatus papae? Ein Beitrag zum Depositionsanspruch Gregors VII.," *Archivum historiae pontificiae* 13 (1975): 119–39, subjects Mordek's hypotheses to careful scrutiny. He notes

reserved powers during the thirteenth century one can view a process of accretion contemporaneous with the expansion of papal monarchy and the greater frequency of papal legatine missions.

We may start with Johannes Teutonicus's gloss to the *Compilatio tertia*, which listed sixteen reserved powers: questions of faith; "major matters" (*maiora negotia*); depositions, restitutions, and transfers of bishops; transfers of confirmed bishops-elect; the acceptance of episcopal resignations; the exemption of bishops from metropolitan control; dispensations in cases of major crimes; adjustment of onerous local customs; commutation of vows; the convocation of universal councils; absolution of persons excommunicated by himself or by his judges-delegate; the granting of a benefice or prebend that is not yet vacant (i.e., the grant of an expectancy); and the capability to adjudicate an original complaint or even an appeal to the neglect of all other judicial instances.[12] Johannes's insistence that this final prerogative pertained solely to the pope and not also to his legates resulted partly from an idiosyncratic interpretation of a decretal of Alexander III (X 1.30.1) which occurred in this same canonist's gloss on the *Decretum*.[13] Johannes likewise ran into problems in attempting to reconcile the reservation of certain powers as beyond a legate's capabilities with the

that the *Proprie auctoritates*, unlike the *Dictatus papae*, made no mention of a papal prerogative to depose emperors. Thus Kempf concludes that the *Proprie auctoritates* postdated Gregory's death and was written sometime before 1123/24 by a moderate adherent to the Reform party. A pre-Gratian canonistic work—the *Collectio canonum* of Cardinal Deusdedit (compiled 1083–87) grouped various *canones* under legal maxims that were essentially statements of papal reserved powers; see *Die Kanonessammlung des Kardinals Deusdedit*, ed. Wolf von Glanvell (Paderborn, 1905), pp. 6–12.

12. *Glossa ad Comp. III*, 1.19.2 (= X 1.30.4), pp. 129–30: "*pontifici reservata. . . .*" Pennington counts seventeen reserved powers in Johannes' gloss; in my opinion two separate phrases in the gloss represent only one power, namely, the statements that "likewise only to him [the pope] alone can one appeal despite all other intervening jurisdictions," and "a legate cannot be approached by simple complaint," that is, be a court of first instance. See Kenneth Pennington, "A Study of Johannes Teutonicus' Theories of Church Government and of the Relationship between Church and State, with an Edition of His Apparatus to Compilatio Tertia" (Ph.D. diss., Cornell University, 1972), 1:160–61. Regarding Johannes' thought about legates in general see Kenneth Pennington, "Johannes Teutonicus and Papal Legates," *Archivum historiae pontificiae* 21 (1983): 183–94.

13. *Glossa ordinaria on the Decretum*, Johannes Teutonicus's and Bartholomeus Brixiensis's gloss as found in the Turin 1670 and Lyons 1671 editions of the *Corpus iuris canonici*, at C. 25 q. 2 c. 3: "*Praetermitti.*" Here Johannes insisted that an archbishop of Canterbury's metropolitan power, not his legatine power, allowed intervention in matters regarding a suffragan's clerics. This interpretation reversed the intent of the decretal text (X 1.30.1) itself and was refuted by Johannes' reviser Bartholomeus Brixiensis. For a detailed discussion of this matter see Robert C. Figueira, "The Canon Law of Medieval Papal Legation" (Ph.D. diss., Cornell University, 1980), pp. 77–79. To place Johannes' opinion within the context of his thought regarding legates see Pennington, "Johannes Teutonicus," pp. 185, 187–88, 194. Pennington agrees that Johannes' "interpretation of *Cum non ignoretis* [= X 1.30.1] twisted Alexander's clear intention" and argues that this was deliberate, for the canonist's interpretation dovetailed with his distrust of "any attempt to give legates power which could undermine the jurisdictional rights of the diocesan bishop."

content of a particular *Decretum* text (C. 16 q. 1 c. 52). There Gregory the Great permitted his *responsales* in Constantinople (= apocrisiars whom decretists considered to be legates) to judge "concerning cases of crime or faith . . . , if the matter is minor." Instead of using Gregory's own implied system of reserved powers to obviate this seeming contradiction, Johannes opted for a legally unsatisfactory alternative, asserting lamely that legates could do these things but ought to refrain.

Goffredus de Trano's list was even smaller—he repeated only three of Johannes' items, while adding three more of his own:[14] dispensations in cases concerning benefices with cure of souls; dispensations for priests holding churches in which their own fathers had been the previous incumbents; the position of the pope as ultimate court of appeal. This last item was akin, but not identical, to Johannes' claim that only the pope might be appealed to *omissis mediis*. Goffredus also alluded to the existence of a larger list of reserved powers preserved in the form of a poem, whose incipit he cited: "*restituit papa.*" As one may subsequently see, both Hostiensis and Bernard of Parma gave renderings of this same poem. Innocent IV merely repeated three of the categories of reserved powers already listed by Goffredus.[15] In view of the exponential growth of lists (to be illustrated shortly) for papal reserved powers found in contemporary and later canonistic literature, one can assume that neither Goffredus nor Innocent IV wished to provide exhaustive lists in this context. Instead they presented exemplary material to illustrate the concept of reserved powers itself.

The most prolific list compilers among thirteenth-century decretalists were all active during or after Innocent IV's pontificate: Hostiensis, Bernard of Parma, and Durantis. The last two greatly depended on the first, who in his *Summa* amassed examples of sixty-three papal reserved powers, for which see appendix 2 below. Some of his statements deserve special scrutiny here. Hostiensis disputed Johannes Teutonicus's assumption that appeals could not be made to a legate in neglect of all other inferior ecclesiastical tribunals.[16] Although previous decretalists had claimed that only the pope could grant a benefice not yet vacant, Hostiensis maintained that a legate *de latere* might nonetheless ex officio reserve to his own nomination the first benefice in an area to become vacant, even if this benefice should possess an ecclesiastical patron.[17]

In addition, Hostiensis attacked Huguccio's belief (which Laurentius Hispanus and Johannes Teutonicus also supported) that a legate needed a special mandate to convoke all types of councils. To be sure, the convoca-

14. Goffredus, fol. 52r–v: "*Ingressus* autem provinciam. . . . *Item* dispensare"; fol. 16r: "*Pertinet*. . . ."
15. Innocent IV at X 1.30.4: "*privilegii*. . . ."
16. Hostiensis, *Summa*, p. 324: "*Quid pertinet*. . . . Quid si una pars appellat ad legatum."
17. Ibid., p. 325: "*Viventisque locum concedit*. . . ."

tion of a general council was reserved to the pope. Nonetheless, since primates, metropolitans, and even ordinary bishops convoked provincial and diocesan councils, the legate (who was in no way their inferior) might do likewise ex officio in the province assigned him.[18]

Hostiensis applied the doctrine of legatine absolution of persons excommunicated for violence against clerics to a discussion of the absolution accorded to all persons excommunicated for "light" offenses. In his opinion, the popes reserved for themselves only the absolution of persons excommunicated for "grave and enormous" crimes, such as those who burned churches or counterfeited papal seals or letters.[19] Another example of such a "grave" case would be the absolution of a cleric either excommunicated for performing his ministry after having been deposed or suspended, or deposed for performing it after having been excommunicated. To such persons the pope can grant absolution without distinction, yet his legate is prohibited from granting the same without a special papal mandate.[20]

For a "light" injury, however, either the pope or his legate "by office of legation" could absolve, the latter according to the regulations listed in X 1.30.9 for absolution of excommunicates for violence against clerics: legates *de latere* could do this everywhere, legates "who do not emanate *de latere*" could do so only within their own provinces for persons who either lived there or had committed their offenses there, and legates "by reason of their dignity" could not at all absolve persons excommunicated for "light" offenses. Furthermore, the pope could at any time change these regulations through the grant of special privilege. Yet Hostiensis never adequately listed what could be considered "light" offenses. Finally, there existed for this canonist a class of even more trivial cases of excommunication which might be absolved by a bishop alone.[21]

In addition, Hostiensis also provided a fairly long rendering of the poem mentioned briefly by Goffredus. In thirty-two verses he compactly listed approximately sixty examples of activities, privileges, and prerogatives reserved solely for the pope himself. Indeed, these examples are often stated so tersely in the poem that the actual nature of the reservation is

18. Ibid., p. 324: "Concilium generale facit . . ."; p. 327: "Sed nunquid legatus potest facere concilium?"

19. This list can be found in the *Summa* (Lyons, 1537) at X 5.39 *de sententia excommunicationis*, fol. 294r: "*Quis possit ab hac sententia absolvere.*" Curiously enough, here Hostiensis even listed as a reserved papal power the absolution of persons excommunicated for violence against clerics, but without mention of X 1.30.9, which allowed certain types of legates this same right ex officio in certain circumstances. See the text cited in note 21 for his application of X 1.30.9 for persons excommunicated on account of "light" offenses.

20. Hostiensis, *Summa*, at X 5.27 *de clerico excommunicato deposito vel interdicto ministrante*, p. 1675: "*An cum eis dispensari* possit. . . ."

21. Ibid., at X 5.39 *de sententia excommunicationis*, pp. 1911–12: "*Quis possit ab hac sententia absolvere.* . . ."

unclear. Furthermore, Hostiensis prefaced the entire list with the admonition that no one should interfere in any of these cases without a special mandate,[22] and he subsequently filled several pages in the printed edition of the *Summa* with a full-blown expansion of the nuances of these reservations and copious examples from both Roman and canon law showing their operation. This dispels a considerable part of the confusion engendered by the poem itself. Let the poem and the material found in appendix 2 suffice to elucidate these examples of papal reserved rights.

> The pope restores, he alone deposes, and he himself
> Divides and joins, exempts and approves.
> He loosens restrictions, makes a general synod,
> Transfers, alters; no one may appeal from him. . . .
> If the pope is catholic, no one may judge him.

22. Ibid., pp. 319–20: "*Quid pertinet* . . . utrum tamen his quae sedis Apostolica sibi specialiter reservavit, propria temeritate se intromittere non debet sine speciali mandato. que autem sint illa, consueverunt his versibus comprehensi:

> Restituit Papa, solus deponit, et ipse
> Dividit ac unit, eximit, atque probat.
> Articulos solvit synodum facit generalem,
> Transfert, et mutat, appellat nullus ab ipso. . . .
> Si sit catholicus Papa, non iudicat ullus.
> Erigit, et subiicit cathedras, dividit, unit.
> Mutat vota, crucis, restaurat, et eximit ad se.
> Maiores causae referuntur, legitimatque.
> Promovet, appellare vetat, prohibet profiteri,
> Deponit, transfert, suppletque, renunciat illi.
> Praesul et exemptus, simon iurans anathema
> Vel proprium vel legati, vel lex utriusque.
> Nequaquam participans, et si quem sponte salutat.
> Quem canon damnat: sibi soli quando reservat.
> Solvitur a Papa, necnon quem regula damnat:
> Addas suspensum casum cum fertur ad ipsum.
> Rescriptum fidei, dubium quod confert bona plura
> Irritat infectum, legem condit generalem.
> Approbat imperium, firmat, deponit et ungit
> Concilium generale facit, sanctit quoque sanctos.
> Ens non esse facit, non ens fore pallia semper
> Portat, concedit, legi nec subditus ulli.
> Appellatur ad hunc medio sine, iudiciumque
> Est pro lege suum, monachum revocat renuentem.
> Maius adulterio solvit, generaliter arctat,
> Et laxat, quicquid sponsis nocet, ordinat extra
> Tempora dando sacrum, promotum promovet idem.
> Ordinat, atque die qua consecratur, et ipse.
> Viventisque locum concedit, iureque privat.
> Insignit laico, sacra donat chrisma ministro.
> Summa sede sedet, plenusque vicarius extat.
> Si sit catholicus Papa, non iudicat ullus."

Hostiensis announced at the end of his explication of texts supporting the poem (p. 326): "Si bene computaveris, in supradictis versibus 61 casus specificatos et explicitos, exceptis inclusis et implicitis, poteris reperire." I have verified the same total.

He erects, subjects, divides, unites bishoprics.
Commutes vows, even of the Cross; renews them, and takes them for
    himself.
Major cases are referred to him; he legitimates,
Promotes, forbids appeal, prohibits professions [of vows to enter
    religion].
He deposes, transfers, makes [defects] good; to him
The prelate and exempt cleric proffer resignation; the simoniac and
    oath-swearer [alike are absolved by him]; anathema,
Whether it had been inflicted by himself, by his legate, or by their own
    statute [is absolved by him].
In no wise is he who participates [with excommunicates in divine office
    absolved other than by the pope], and if he [the pope] should greet
    such a person [he is automatically absolved].[23]
When the pope reserves for himself alone [the case of one] whom a
    canonical precept
Or rule condemns, he is absolved by the pope.
Add the case of suspension when it is brought to him.
Doubts concerning his own rescript, or the Faith [are solved by him]; he
    confers a plurality of benefices [to a single person].
He provokes the undone to be done, and makes general law.
He approves emperors, confirms, deposes, and anoints [the emperor-
    elect].
He makes a general council, also canonizes saints.
He makes what exists, not exist; what is not, to exist; he always
Bears the pallium, and concedes [its use by others]; he is not subject to
    any law.
Appeals are made to him without intermediate instance, and his
    sentence
Is law; he may summon an unwilling monk [out of cloister].
He absolves in the grave case of adultery, and generally makes penalties
Or relaxes them in matters harming spouses; in giving Holy Orders
He ordains outside [customary] times; he promotes those
    [originally] promoted [by himself].
And he ordains [clerics] even on the day of his own consecration.
He concedes a benefice belonging to a living incumbent; he justly
    deprives [someone of his benefice].
He confers insignia; gives sacred [rights] to laymen, chrism [even] to
    priests.
He sits on the highest seat, and is the complete vicar.
If the pope is catholic, no one may judge him.

The origin of this poem certainly did not lie with Hostiensis. Goffredus
had already noted its incipit in his own *Summa* some years previously,

23. In his subsequent remarks Hostiensis clarified that this was what he meant in
these abbreviated verses—see *Summa*, p. 322, "Nequaquam participans scilicet excommunicato a papa ex certa scientia in divinis officiis."

[200]

and Hostiensis himself noted after the first four verses (and first eleven examples) that Raymond of Peñafort had expounded twenty-four reserved cases in his *Summa iuris* (1219–20).[24] Raymond likewise quoted the first four verses of the poem and actually mentioned more than three dozen papal reserved rights.[25] In the absence of other evidence one can hypothesize that perhaps Hostiensis added on verses five through thirty-two to introduce his subsequent discussion of more than sixty reserved cases. Be that as it may, Hostiensis closed his analysis of papal reserved cases by reminding his reader that "a legate ought not usurp the aforesaid rights, unless he wishes to be confounded . . . and unless he should possess a special privilege concerning these rights, you may know him to usurp one of them."[26] Implicit in this remark is the concept that legates could perform any of these reserved activities if properly authorized by the pope.

It is important to note the poem's character as a mnemonic device to aid canonists in recalling a series of dissociated (yet mutually suggestive) prerogatives that composed a single jurisprudential whole—papal reserved powers. Thus it is not surprising that the accretion of reserved powers from Goffredus's analysis to Hostiensis's stands in direct relation to the increase of verses in the poem.

Bernard of Parma listed nineteen papal reserved rights in his *Glossa ordinaria*, of which the great majority had already appeared in Hostiensis's *Summa*. In several cases, however, he provided exceptions to these direct prohibitions of legatine activity. The reservation of deposition did not extend to priests, as they could be deposed by a legate acting in conjunction with several bishops. Furthermore, certain types of legates could judge cases involving exempt prelates in certain circumstances.[27]

---

24. Ibid., p. 319: "Ex quibus 11 casus possunt elici. Raymundus vero in summa de casibus 24 notat: tu dic quod 60 sunt, et plures, quos his versibus comprehendes."

25. San Raimundo de Penyafort, *Summa iuris* (Barcelona, 1945), pp. 48–49. The discrepancy between Hostiensis's report of twenty-four items and Raymond's actual list of reserved powers can perhaps be attributed to scribal error. For Bernard of Parma's citation of the poem's first verse see the *Glossa ordinaria ad X*, 1.30.4: "*reservata.*" A gloss on Comp. II attributed by John Watt to Tancred (at 5.13.4 = X 5.31.8) likewise made reference to the poem's first four verses (and eleven reserved powers) in what might be their earliest chronological appearance; see the reference to London BM MS Roy. 11. C. VII, fol. 109v, in "The Use of the Term 'Plenitudo Potestatis' by Hostiensis," in *Proceedings of the Second International Congress of Medieval Canon Law* (Vatican City, 1965), p. 165 n. 19.

26. Hostiensis, *Summa*, same rubric, p. 326: "Legatus igitur praedicta usurpare non debet, nisi velit confundi . . . et ipsum hoc usurpare intelligas, nisi super his privilegium habeat speciale, argumen. infra de privilegiis porro. et c. sane" (X 5.33.7, 9).

27. *Glossa ordinaria ad X*, 1.30.1: "*legationis tamen obtentu*. . . . Sed presbyterum posset deponere adiunctis sibi aliis episcopis. xv quaestio vii foelix et c. si autem" (C. 15 q. 7 cc. 4, 5). Bernard first posited two preconditions for legatine judgment of *exempti*— their own willingness to be judged, and the nature of the exemption; at X 1.30.1: "*universas*. . . . Dicas quod isti legati per suam legationem non possunt punire exemptos, vel audire causas quae movuntur contra eos, nisi velint respondere sub eis, et hoc de his quae in eorum privilegiis continentur. et tota sua potestas consideranda est ex forma privilegii. Alii vero legati cardinales vel alii qui mittuntur de latere domini papae,

Robert C. Figueira

Moreover, Goffredus's reservation for the pope alone of the dispensation of a priest's son was granted by Bernard also to legates *de latere*.[28] Other cases represented new types of reservations heretofore unmentioned: the removal of bishops from the administration of their sees[29] and the granting of indulgences in matrimonial matters.[30] Bernard even maintained that any concession of benefices and prebends in prejudice of lay rights of patronage required the "special grace" of the pope. In this he expanded an earlier statement of Johannes Teutonicus.[31] Also implicit in Bernard's gloss was the reminder that those legitimate activities not reserved by the pope for his own exclusive use should be considered free for the use of his legates, most notably those of the *de latere* class.[32] Unlike Hostiensis, however, Bernard did not especially stress the possibility that even papal reserved rights might be exercised by legates possessing special mandates.

---

habent maiorem iurisdictionem tam contra exemptos quam contra omnes alios, salvis his tantum quae sedi Apostolicae specialiter reservantur." Note that the different capabilities of different types of legates were left very vague. While glossing another decretal Bernard dropped all consideration of the exempt's wishes and restricted judgment of their cases purely to legates *de latere*; in this matter he disagreed with Johannes Teutonicus. At X 1.30.4: "*reservata.* . . . Sed nunquid legatus talis missus a latere papae potest iudicare de exemptiis qui substunt tantum domino papae? Argu. quod non xvii dist huic [D. 17 c. 3]. Argum. quod potest xvi quaestio i frater noster [C. 16 q. 1 c. 52]. Joannes dicit quod non potest, et melius facit si abstineat. argumentum inducit ff de officio proconsulis nec quicquam [Dig. 1.16.9]. Et credo quod potest cognoscere de causis quae contra ipsos moventur, non obstantibus privilegiis suis: quia per privilegia illa eximuntur solum a iurisdictione episcoporum in quorum territorio commorantur: sed a iurisdictione ipsius papae vel legatorum non eximuntur."

28. Ibid., at X 1.17.17: "*Non obstante.* . . ."

29. In X 3.4.11 Cardinal-priest Benedict of St. Susannah, while on legation to the Latin empire of Constantinople, was empowered to remove certain delinquent Greek bishops from the administration of spiritualities in their sees. *Glossa ordinaria ad X*, 3.4.11: "*Removeat.* Ex isto mandato speciali si sunt episcopi, alias non posset legatus ex generali mandato. supra de officio legati quod translationem" [X 1.30.4]. For details regarding this legation see Zimmermann, p. 37; Maleczek, pp. 135–36.

30. In X 4.14.3 Celestine III mentioned the general dispensation granted by a legate (Nicholas Breakspear, cardinal-bishop of Albano) in Norway which allowed the contracting of marriage within the heretofore prohibited sixth degree of consanguinity. Bernard remarked, at X 4.14.3: "*indulgentiam.* quae de auctoritate speciali domini papae facta fuit, alias non tenuisset quia solus papa in tali facto dispensat. infra eodem quia circa [X 4.24.6] et supra de translatione capitulo ultimo" [X 1.7.4]. For Nicholas's legation see Wolfgang Seegrün, *Das Papsttum und Skandinavien bis zur Vollendung der nordischen Kirchenorganisation (1164)* (Neumünster, 1967), pp. 146–72. Nicholas became Pope Hadrian IV shortly after his return to the curia.

31. In X 1.30.6 Innocent III maintained that a legate could confer a vacant benefice even when it pertained to the presentation of another cleric. Johannes Teutonicus mentioned (as also will Bernard) the Roman law maxim that "only the prince can deprive someone of his right," and concluded that the legate can confer a benefice under such conditions only on the basis of some "personal grace"; *Glossa ad Comp. III*, 1.19.4 (= X 1.30.6), p. 131: "*in concessione.* . . ." For Bernard's assertion regarding the relative immunity of lay rights of patronage see *Glossa ordinaria ad X*, 1.30.6: "*in concessione.* . . ."

32. *Glossa ordinaria ad X*, 1.30.5: "*transtulerat.* . . ."; at X 1.30.9: "*commissam.* . . ."

Papal Reserved Powers and Legatine Authority

Hostiensis did not repeat in the *Commentaria* his vast list of reserved powers from the *Summa*. For the most part he reiterated the few examples already found in the *Glossa ordinaria*, while adding seven new cases and referring readers to the relevant section of the *Summa*.[33] He noted that special papal mandates were required for the conferral of control over a monastery to any clergyman not of that monastery, for a "perpetual donation" of church property,[34] for degrading bishops,[35] and for depriving rebellious clerics of their benefices.[36] Hostiensis never elaborated on what he meant by "perpetual donation"; perhaps he was speaking of an unconditional alienation. Regarding degradations the canonist further noted that a legate who was not a bishop must in addition have the cooperation of other bishops to actually degrade a bishop after he had pronounced sentence. In addition, Hostiensis maintained that only the pope could commission someone to preach a crusade or to release a crusader from his vow, and that only he could dispense in minor crimes or absolve a person excommunicated by a bishop.[37] These last two reserved powers ran in direct contradiction to other statements in Hostiensis's *Summa*, such as were discussed above. There he maintained that certain legates could absolve ex officio persons excommunicated for "light" injuries, and that even bishops could provide absolution for more trivial cases of excommunication. In addition, the decretals cited by Hostiensis in the *Commentaria* for his later statements did not directly support him. X 2.1.4 asserted that bishops could dispense in minor crimes, and X 1.31.11

33. Hostiensis, *Commentaria ad X*, 1.30.4: "*reservata*."
34. In X 2.30.9 Honorius III wrote concerning the collation by his legate in Constantinople (John, cardinal-priest of St. Prassede) of control over monasteries as regards both their spiritualities and their temporalities. See Hostiensis, *Commentaria ad X*, 2.30.9: "*contulit. . . .*" For John's legation see Zimmermann, p. 74; Maleczek, pp. 158–59.
35. In X 3.4.11 the legate (Benedict of St. Susannah; see note 29 above) was not commanded by the pope to degrade bishops. Hostiensis nonetheless inferred that this legate did have the requisite special powers to do so. Note especially the bantering tone of his analysis. *Commentaria ad X*, 3.4.11: "*Degradationis sententiam*. Innuit, quod iste Cardinalis haberet potestatem degradandi, quod intelligas de speciali concessione. Sed nunquid erat congruum, quod presbyter episcopos degradaret? Amice non audemus ponere eos in coelum, nam et talibus plerunque concedit Papa episcopalia, ut XCV distin. pervenit [D. 95 c.1]. Vel dic, quod non est incongruum, quod possit pronunciare degradationem, sed incongruum esset, quod degradare posset, ergo sententiam proferre, ut hic dicit, et per episcopos legationis suae ipsum factum exequi non inhibetur, sicut notatur de electo confirmato, supra de electione nosti" (X 1.6.9).
36. In X 3.8.5 Innocent III commanded his legate (Peter of Capua, cardinal-deacon of St. Mary in Via Lata) to compel clerics disobedient to their archbishops to resign illegally acquired benefices and privileges; if they were contumacious the legate was to deprive them of these acquisitions. Hostiensis referred to the legate in question as a "delegate"; *Commentaria ad X*, 3.8.5: "*Et substrationem. . . .*" For Peter's legation see Zimmermann, pp. 23–24; Maleczek, p. 120. It is noteworthy that Peter was not to disturb clergy already holding benefices "vel . . . speciali mandato apostolicae sedis vel auctoritate Lateranensis concilii ab Eboracensi capitulo."
37. Hostiensis, *Commentaria ad X*, 1.30.4: "*reservata. . . .*"

[203]

Robert C. Figueira

merely maintained that persons excommunicated by a papal *delegate* could normally receive absolution only from the pope. These contradictions cannot be resolved on the basis of Hostiensis's statements, in either the *Summa* or the *Commentaria*. But neither do they appear in any subsequent canonistic work.

Durantis's list of reserved powers was larger than all other decretalists' lists, and it mentioned in addition thirty-one cases not already specified. In two of these cases Durantis added specific prohibitions of legatine activity: legates needed a special mandate to alienate any thing (*rem*) pertaining to the Apostolic see, and cardinal-legates required special papal permission to exercise cognizance during an imperial vacancy over cases involving laymen subject to the empire.[38] All in all Durantis listed eighty-nine papal reserved powers (see appendix 2). That he was writing the *Speculum iuris* in the years following his own participation at the Second Council of Lyons (1274) provided a curious twist to his discussion of reserved rights. At this council the Byzantine emperor Michael VIII Palaeologus and the Greek church formally submitted to papal primacy. Hence Durantis treated the rank and stature of the two patriarchs of Constantinople and Alexandria with a modicum of respect. They possessed the only two of five historic patriarchal sees without a Latin incumbent, and their broad powers within their own churches had to be recognized. Thus the Speculator asserted that these patriarchs also possessed by right some of the prerogatives normally reserved for the pope (Durantis named four examples) and were thus, in a certain sense, "superior" to a papal legate.[39]

## Conclusion

When viewed by the aforementioned canonists, papal legation represented an important tool for the medieval pope, since it provided him with

38. Durantis, fols. 46b, 53a: "*Quae sint ei interdicta, et soli sedi Apostolicae reservata.*"

39. Ibid., fol. 52b, rubric as above: "*Quod autem dixi, legatum posse quicquid patriarcha potest, fallit in quibusdam casibus. Nam ille conferret pallia, et facit ante se crucem ferri . . . legatus non. Item patriarcha Constantinopolitanus deponit episcopos suos, et etiam Alexandrinus: quod legatus facere non potest. . . . Item ad illos duos potest omissis mediis appellari . . . quod in legato non obtinet, secundum quosdam. . . . Item licet alii prelati baculo pastorali utantur, non tamen Papa, vel eius legatus: tum propter historiam, tum propter mysticam rationem ut extra de sacra unctione c. unico §fi.*" (X 1.15.1). For more information concerning the absence of the crosier in papal usage since the eleventh century see Patrick Morrisroe, "Crosier," in *The Catholic Encyclopedia* (New York, 1908), 4:515, and the following decretalists: *Glossa ad Comp. III*, 1.11.1 (= X 1.15.1), p. 102: "*ystoriam*"; Innocent IV at X 1.15.1: "*per historiam*"; *Glossa ordinaria ad X*, 1.15.1: "*pastorali . . . propter historiam . . . mysticam rationem*"; Hostiensis, *Commentaria ad X*, 1.15.1: "*Tum propter historiam. . . . Misticam rationem.*" In Durantis's day the patriarchate of Constantinople had an absentee titular Latin claimant.

a flexible means of making his increasingly inimitable jurisdiction opera-
tive at the local level throughout Latin Christendom. This exercise of
power by agents in localities was truly exceptional for monarchical government in the mid-thirteenth century. Only the contemporary kings of
England and Sicily possessed similarly effective deputies, but within narrower geographic confines and among smaller populations than the Western church under papal supervision.

A legate literally embodied the pope's own person. He was his alter ego,
and in many cases even wore the papal purple while on legation.[40] The
results of this research provide some substance to these commonplaces,
for within the concept of representation is the tacit recognition that the
thing or person represented is not fully present in actuality or potency.
Hence the discussion of representation—whether it be formal, descriptive, symbolic, or substantive—must always confront the question of
limitation. By distinguishing between general and special authorization,
and by delineating a category of powers normally reserved for papal exercise alone, medieval popes successfully combined two divergent tendencies inherent in their use of legates: (1) the desire to maximize the
effectiveness of such subordinates when the latter were confronted with
myriad possible legal and administrative situations; and (2) the necessity
of retaining strict control over the authorization of these subordinates'
actions in extraordinary situations. By use of special mandates the pope
could tailor his legate's powers to the complexity of the matter at hand or
to possible unforeseen complications. By having categorized certain powers as normally reserved only to his own exercise, the medieval pope
ensured that the gulf between papal and legatine jurisdiction remained by
definition unbridgeable. Much as Francis Bacon would write many centuries later when describing the subordination of royal judges to the king,
medieval papal legates "must be lions, but yet lions under the throne; they
must shew their stoutness in elevating and bearing up the throne."[41]

40. The theoretical categorization of representation appears in Hanna Fenichel Pit-
kin's seminal work, *The Concept of Representation* (Berkeley and Los Angeles, 1967).
For a discussion of physical and legal identification between the pope and his legate see
Figueira, "Canon Law," pp. 332–48, 380–89, and "*Legatus Apostolicae Sedis:* The
Pope's *Alter Ego* according to Thirteenth-Century Canon Law," *Studi medievali* 27
(1986): 527–74.
41. Francis Bacon, *Letters and Life*, ed. J. Spedding (London, 1862–74), 6:201, speech
to Justice Hutton.

## Appendix 1
## Abbreviations Used in This Chapter

Durantis = Gulielmus Durandus, *Speculum iuris* (Venice, 1585), the section
 *de legato, pars prima*, vol. 1, chap. 2.
*Glossa ad Comp. III* = *Johannis Teutonici Apparatus glossarum in Compila-
 tionem tertiam*, ed. Kenneth Pennington, *Mon. iur. can.*, ser. A, vol. 3, tom.
 I (Vatican City, 1981).

# Robert C. Figueira

*Glossa ordinaria ad X* = Bernard of Parma's ordinary gloss to the *Liber extra* as found in the Turin 1670 and Lyons 1671 editions of the *Corpus iuris canonici*.

Goffredus = Goffredus Tranensis, *Summa super titulis decretalium* (Lyons, 1519; reprint Aalen, 1968).

Hostiensis, *Commentaria ad X* = Hostiensis, *In libros decretalium commentaria* (Venice, 1581; reprint Turin, 1965).

Hostiensis, *Summa* = Hostiensis, *Summa aurea* (Venice, 1579; reprint Turin, 1963), the section *de legato* (unless otherwise noted).

Innocent IV = Innocentius IV, *Apparatus super V libris decretalium* (Lyons, 1535).

Maleczek = Werner Maleczek, *Papst und Kardinalskolleg von 1194 bis 1216* (Vienna, 1984).

Zimmermann = Heinrich Zimmermann, *Die päpstlichen Legation in der ersten Hälfte des 13. Jahrhunderts (Vom Regierungsantritt Innocenz III bis zum Tode Gregors IX 1198–1241)* (Paderborn, 1913).

Quotations from the *Liber extra* are from the edition by Emil Friedberg, *CIC*, vol. 2, exclusive of the *partes decisae*.

## Appendix 2

Table of Papal Reserved Powers: The Decretalists

| | Power | JT | G | I | GO | HS | HC | D |
|---|---|---|---|---|---|---|---|---|
| 1) | cannot be judged | | | | | x | | x[1] |
| 2) | is *legibus solutus* | | | | | x | | x |
| 3) | can do whatever he wishes so long as it is not against the faith | | | | | x | | x[2] |
| 4) | can make something out of nothing | | | | | x | x[3] | x |
| 5) | can make good a defect through use of *plenitudo potestatis* | | | | | x | | x |
| 6) | can forbid future actions (elections or provisions) | | | | | x | | x |
| 7) | can deprive, transfer, or confer rights (*iura*) | | | | | x | | x |
| 8) | cannot be appealed from | | | | | x | | x |
| 9) | can be appealed to *omissis mediis* | x[3] | | | x | x[4] | x | |
| 10) | can forbid appeals | | | | | x | | |
| 11) | can always and everywhere wear the pallium | | | | | x | | x |
| 12) | can decide *maiora negotia et causae maiores* | x | | | x | x | | x |
| 13) | can decide questions of faith | x | | | x | x | x | x[5] |
| 14) | can approve theological writings and written memoranda of others | | | | | | | x |
| 15) | can commit a spiritual cause to a layman | | | | | | | x |
| 16) | can commit a case *appellatione remota* | | | | x | x | | x |

# Papal Reserved Powers and Legatine Authority

| | Power | JT | G | I | GO | HS | HC | D |
|---|---|---|---|---|---|---|---|---|
| 17) | can reserve cases sent to him | | x | | | | | x |
| 18) | can ordain outside four fixed times of year | | | | x[6] | x | x[7] | x |
| 19) | can ordain on the day of his consecration | | | | | x | | x |
| 20) | can canonize saints | | | | | x | | x |
| 21) | can judge concerning contentious papal rescripts, confirmations, or extravagant decretals | | | | | x | | x[8] |
| 22) | can legitimate sons | | | | | x | x[9] | x |
| 23) | allows to regain office those who had resigned a prelacy (pontifical office) in order to enter a religious order | | | | | | | x |
| 24) | can, on the same day, promote one person to two holy orders | | | | | | | x |
| 25) | allows Christians to transport arms to Saracens (for example, to redeem captives) | | | | | | | x |
| 26) | makes confirmations which are irrevocable by others | | | | | | | x |
| 27) | can judge concerning bishops | | | | | x | | x[10] |
| 28) | can depose bishops | x | | | x | x | x | x[11] |
| 29) | can degrade bishops | | | | | | x[12] | |
| 30) | can receive renunciation of a bishop | x | | | x | x | | x[3] |
| 31) | can restore bishops | x | | | | | x | |
| 32) | can transfer a bishop | x | x | | x | x | x | x |
| 33) | can postulate a bishop to a metropolitan see | | | | | | | x |
| 34) | can remove bishops from the administration of their sees | | | | x | | | |
| 35) | can exempt bishops from metropolitan control | x | | | x | x | x | x |
| 36) | can transfer a confirmed *electus* | x | | | | | | |
| 37) | can transfer an *exemptus* | | | | | x[12] | | x[24] |
| 38) | can receive the resignations of exempt abbots or priors | | | | | | | x |
| 39) | can depose simoniacs | | | | | x | | x |
| 40) | can restore degraded clerics | | | | | x | | x[13] |
| 41) | can withdraw an unwilling monk from cloister | | | | | x | | x |
| 42) | can unmake a monk | | | | | x | | |
| 43) | can prohibit professions of religion | | | | | x | | x[14] |
| 44) | can convoke a universal or general council | x[3] | | | x | x | x | x |
| 45) | can "go against a council" (i.e., conciliar statutes derive validity from the pope) | | | | | x | | x |
| 46) | can grant indulgences in matrimonial matters | | | | x | | | |
| 47) | can extend or restrict canonical impediments to marriage | | | | | x | | x |
| 48) | can make general laws | | | | | x | | x |
| 49) | can relax a papal or legatine statute | | | | | x | | |

| | Power | JT | G | I | GO | HS | HC | D |
|---|---|---|---|---|---|---|---|---|
| 50) | can change onerous customs | x | | | | | | |
| 51) | can approve an otherwise inexcusable custom | | | | | x | | x |
| 52) | can promote in orders persons suffering defects (minors, illegitimates, bigamists) | | | | | x | | x |
| 53) | can promote a cleric ordained by a pope | | | | | $x^{12}$ | | x |
| 54) | can promote to higher orders persons not already in lower orders | | | | | x | | |
| 55) | can permit a prelate to have a cross borne before him | | | | | x | | x |
| 56) | can allow priests to confirm in the bishop's absence | | | | | x | | x |
| 57) | can allow clergy to pay taxes to lay authorities | | | | | x | | |
| 58) | concedes to deacons and clerics permission to wear certain garments (episcopal sandals, vestments of the Roman city clergy) | | | | | | | x |
| 59) | concedes episcopal insignia (miter, ring, staff, sandals) to others | | | | | x | | x |
| 60) | grants the pallium | | | | | x | | |
| 61) | grants "sacred things" (sacra) to laymen (e.g., the right of election granted to a lay person) | | | | | x | | x |
| 62) | grants permission to preach a crusade | | | | | | x | |
| 63) | can depose an emperor | | | | | x | | x |
| 64) | can have cognizance over cases involving laymen subject to the empire during a vacancy in the imperial throne | | | | | | | $x^{24}$ |
| 65) | can confirm or reject an imperial election | | | | | x | | x |
| 66) | can define questions concerning royal unction | | | | | | | x |
| 67) | can supply for the lack of royal authority during a vacancy | | | | | | | x |
| 68) | can erect a cathedral church | | | | | x | | x |
| 69) | can divide a cathedral church | | | | | x | x | x |
| 70) | can subject one cathedral church to another | | | | | x | | x |
| 71) | can transfer a see from one place to another | | | | | | | x |
| 72) | can concede a prebend in prejudice of lay patronage rights | | | | x | | | |
| 73) | can grant an expectancy | $x^3$ | x | $x^3$ | $x^3$ | $x^{15}$ | x | x |
| 74) | can make two prebends from one | | | | | $x^3$ | | |
| 75) | can confer a monastery to other clerics | | | | | | $x^{12}$ | |
| 76) | can deprive rebels of benefices | | | | | | $x^{12}$ | |
| 77) | can make a perpetual donation of church property | | | | | | x | |

| | Power | JT | G | I | GO | HS | HC | D |
|---|---|---|---|---|---|---|---|---|
| 78) | can alienate a matter (*rem*) pertaining to the Apostolic see | | | | | | | x[12] |
| 79) | can exempt someone from payment of tithe | | | | | x | | x |
| 80) | can dispense persons from paying tithe | | | | | | | x |
| 81) | can dispense for major crimes | x | | | x | | | |
| 82) | can dispense for minor crimes | | | | | | x | |
| 83) | can dispense for major adulteries | | | | | x | | x |
| 84) | can dispense in grave cases of affinity and consanguinity | | | | | | x | x[3] |
| 85) | can dispense so that regular clergy studying law or medicine may be promoted | | | | | | | x |
| 86) | can dispense in cases of suspension caused by celebration of divine office with an excommunicate | | | | | | | x |
| 87) | can dispense in cases where benefices having care of souls are concerned | | x | | | x[16] | | x[17] |
| 88) | can dispense sons holding churches where their fathers had been the previous incumbents | | x | | x[23] | | x[3] | x |
| 89) | can dispense in cases of irregularity | | | | | x | | x |
| 90) | can dispense an ordained apostate | | | | | | | x |
| 91) | can dispense an unordained person who had performed a ministry, in order that he may ascend to higher orders | | | | | | | x |
| 92) | can dispense in cases where a novice or religious of another profession is to become an abbot | | | | | | | x |
| 93) | can dispense so that monks, laymen, or persons in minor orders may become bishops | | | | | | | x |
| 94) | can dispense excommunicates or persons under suspension who nonetheless received benefices | | | | | | | x[18] |
| 95) | can dispense from canonically fixed penances for enormous crimes | | | | | | | x[18] |
| 96) | can dispense excommunicates who have knowingly received orders | | | | | | | x |
| 97) | can dispense a person ordained by a schismatic | | | | | | | x[19] |
| 98) | can dispense from a crusading vow | | | | | | | x |
| 99) | can dispense from vows of continence | | | | | | | x |
| 100) | can commute vows | | x | | | | | |
| 101) | can arrange the redemption of a crusading vow | | | | | | x | x |
| 102) | can alter a crusading vow | | | | | x | | x |
| 103) | can nullify oaths | | | | x | x | | x[20] |
| 104) | can absolve killers of clerics | | | | | | | x |
| 105) | can absolve a cleric who knowingly participated in the divine office with an excommunicate | | | | | | | x |

| Power | JT | G | I | GO | HS | HC | D |
|---|---|---|---|---|---|---|---|
| 106) can absolve incendiaries | | | | | | | x |
| 107) can absolve an excommunicate merely by being in communion with him | | | | | | | x |
| 108) can absolve persons excommunicated by judges-delegate | x[3] | x | x | x | x | x | x[21] |
| 109) can absolve a person excommunicated by a pope | x | | x | x | x | x[22] | x |
| 110) can absolve persons condemned for ministering sacraments to heretics | | | | | x | | x |
| 111) can absolve persons condemned for irregularity | | | | | x | | |
| 112) can absolve a person excommunicated ipso facto by a law | | | | | x | | |

*Key:*
JT      *Glossa ad Comp. III* 1.19.2 (= X 1.30.4): *"pontificis reservata,"* pp. 129–30.
G       Goffredus, fol. 52r–v: *"Ingressus . . . Item."*
I       Innocent IV at X 1.30.4: *"reservata"*; at X 1.17.17: *"non obstante."*
GO      *Glossa ordinaria ad X* 1.30.4: *"reservata"*; 1.17.17: *"non obstante."*
HS      Hostiensis, *Summa,* pp. 319–26: *"Quid pertinet."*
HC      Hostiensis, *Commentaria ad X* 1.17.17: *"Non obstante"*; 1.30.4; 1.36.11: *"Casibus"*; 2.30.9: *"Contulit"*; 3.4.11: *"Degradationis sententiam"*; 3.8.5: *"Et substrationem"*; 3.38.28: *"Primo vacare contingeret."*
D       Durantis, fols. 45a–53a: *"Quae sint ei interdicta, et soli sedi apostolicae reservata."*

*Notes:*
    1. Except in case of heresy.
    2. That is, what he wills is law, or his judgment is law, if that is his intention.
    3. That is, a legate cannot do this.
    4. A legate can do this.
    5. He reminds the reader that C. 16 q. 1 c. 52 allows legates and bishops (so he claims) to have cognizance concerning minor matters of faith; this chapter actually accords this right to a *responsalis.*
    6. That is, subdeacons on Sundays.
    7. That is, subdeacons outside four fixed times a year.
    8. Just concerning contentious papal rescripts.
    9. That is, he dispenses illegitimate sons.
    10. But a legate can judge a criminal case concerning a bishop only with special permission.
    11. The pope alone may also depose a bishop who deserts his see, while a legate *de latere* may do this specially; furthermore, the patriarchs of Constantinople and Alexandria can also depose their own bishops.
    12. That is, a legate may do this with a special mandate.
    13. But restorations or dispensations according to common law can be done by a bishop.
    14. Professions by eighteen-year-old island inhabitants.
    15. But a legate can reserve the first church to become vacant, even if it has an ecclesiastical patron.
    16. Can confer multiple benefices with cure of souls.
    17. Can dispense from holding multiple benefices with cure of souls.

18. Some authorities claim this.

19. But some authorities claim that even a bishop may do this.

20. That is, he can decide whether an oath is licit and to be obeyed, and he can also dispense from an oath when a threat to salvation is present; a bishop or legate *de latere* can dispense from observance of extorted oaths, but this is best left to the pope; a bishop can dispense *ex causa* from licit oaths.

21. That is, a legate cannot revoke, relax, or impede the sentence of a judge-delegate.

22. And also a person excommunicated by a bishop.

23. A legate *de latere* can also do this.

24. A legate *de latere* can do this with a special mandate.

# [12]

# Preventing Crime in the High Middle Ages: The Medieval Lawyers' Search for Deterrence

## RICHARD M. FRAHER

Originality was not the virtue which made the *Speculum iudiciale* the most widely read textbook on legal procedure in the Middle Ages and the Renaissance. William Durantis, the Speculator, not only assembled the learning of his predecessors in the field of procedure, he devoured the *Ordo iudiciarius* and the *Libelli* of Tancred and Roffredus Beneventanus, reproducing them "down to the last comma."[1] For this reason alone, it is striking to read the sentences with which Durantis introduced book 3, the section on criminal procedure in which the great proceduralist suggested that this area of the law reflected a recent development:

> Above, in the proceding section, we have explained at length how one proceeds in civil cases. But because criminal judgments occur frequently, and because it is in the public interest that malefactions not remain unpunished . . . [a list of legal citations] . . . according to this "you shall not suffer evildoers to live" [Ex. 22:18], therefore we have foreseen that it might be useful to dispute a few things regarding the new teaching [*nova doctrina*] of this matter.[2]

The great German legal historians of the previous century and their twentieth-century disciples such as Dahm, Kantorowicz, and Walter Ull-

1. The literature on William Durantis is summarized briefly in J. A. Clarence-Smith, *Medieval Law Teachers and Writers, Civilian and Canonist* (Ottawa, 1975), par. 77. See Friedrich von Savigny, *Geschichte des römisches Rechts im Mittlelalter* (reprint Graz, 1961), 5:539; Robert Naz, *Dictionnaire du droit canonique* (Paris, 1935–65), 5:1014; and Johan Friedrich von Schulte, *Die Geschichte der Quellen und Literatur des canonischen Rechts* (reprint Graz, 1956), 2:144–56.
2. Guilelmus Durantis, *Speculum iudiciale* (Lugduni, 1521), book 3, fol. 2.

mann had no trouble defining the nature of this "new doctrine."[3] Professor Ullmann, the last of the exponents of the traditional *Geistesgeschichte* to write on this subject, portrayed the rebirth of Roman law and the rediscovery of Aristotle as the agents of a thoroughgoing rationalization of law and legal procedures and of the birth of public institutions which prefigured the modern state.[4] According to this view, the "new states" found in the Roman law a relatively sophisticated model for the creation of public institutions aimed at the suppression of crime. The two most significant changes in the criminal law were the adoption of inquisitorial procedure, which has usually been seen as a response to heresy, and the "resurrection" of a purportedly rational Roman system of proofs. Therefore 1215 was cast as a critical year, primarily because Innocent III and the Fourth Lateran Council forbade clerics to participate in ordeals, and secondarily because the council sanctioned the regular use of inquisitorial procedure.

This cheerful portrayal of a ruling elite prodding the law toward rationality has not escaped criticism in recent years. Works by John Baldwin, Rebecca Colman, and Paul Hyams have challenged the notion that a rational legal order, imposed from on high, displaced an irrational criminal law.[5] As Hyams put it: "In the early middle ages legal change seldom emerged directly from positive public decisions motivated by a driving desire for a higher rationality. Perhaps it never does."[6]

In the High Middle Ages, without doubt the public authorities did consciously strive after a higher rationality, but John Langbein has recently pointed out that rationalizing efforts aimed at consistency did not necessarily produce an efficient or effective criminal procedure. Langbein claims that the Romano-canonical jurists adopted a criminal process con-

---

3. H. Kantorowicz, *Albertus Gandinus und das Strafrecht der Scholastik*, 2 vols. (Berlin, 1907–26); W. Engelmann, *Irrtum und Schuld nach der italienischen Lehre und Praxis des Mittelalters* (1922); G. Dahm, *Das Strafrecht Italiens im ausgehenden Mittelalter* (1931); idem, *Untersuchungen zur Verfassungs- und Strafrechtsgeschichte der italienischen Stadt im Mittelalter* (Hamburg, 1941).

4. W. Ullmann, *Law and Politics in the Middle Ages: Introduction to the Sources of Medieval Political Ideas* (Ithaca, 1975). Ullmann's earlier works on criminal law include "Reflections on Medieval Torture," *Juridical Review* 56 (1944): 123–37; *The Medieval Idea of Law as Represented by Lucas de Penna: A Study in Fourteenth-Century Legal Scholarship* (London, 1946), chap. 7, "The Idea of Crime"; "Medieval Principles of Evidence," *Law Quarterly Review* 62 (1946): 77–87; "Some Medieval Principles of Criminal Procedure," *Juridical Review* 59 (1947): 1–28; and "The Defence of the Accused in the Medieval Inquisition," *Irish Ecclesiastical Record* 73 (1950): 481–89.

5. J. Baldwin, "The Intellectual Preparation for the Canon of 1215 against Ordeals," *Speculum* 36 (1961): 613–36; Rebecca Colman, "Reason and Unreason in Early Medieval Law," *Journal of Interdisciplinary History* 4 (1974): 571–91; P. Hyams, "Trial by Ordeal: The Key to Proof in the Early Common Law," in *On the Laws and Customs of England: Essays in Honor of Samuel E. Thorne*, ed. M. S. Arnold, T. A. Green, S. A. Scully, and S. D. White (Chapel Hill, N.C., 1981), pp. 90–126.

6. Hyams, "Trial by Ordeal," p. 125.

Richard M. Fraher

taining an impossibly stringent law of proof, which in turn left the new criminal procedure hopelessly incapable of resolving difficult criminal cases, where suspicion was strong but direct proof was lacking.[7] The widespread use of torture was, according to Langbein, the logical, albeit inhumane, result of a formally consistent but totally impractical law of proof. I believe that both the traditional picture of the birth of the "new" Romano-canonical criminal law and the recent criticisms of that picture have failed to convey an accurate explanation for the appearance of the inquisitorial process and the emergence of an incipient criminal jurisprudence in thirteenth-century Europe. I think that we have all been misled by Durantis's allegation that he was dealing with a *nova doctrina* in 1270 or so, and we have therefore concentrated too exclusively upon the thirteenth century and too narrowly on the single issue of heresy and the Inquisition. In addition, our long romance with the purported rationalism of the new law has led us to overemphasize the law of proof without examining the other social and legal developments that created the need to change the law governing evidence and proofs in criminal cases.

This article suggests that when we look for the causes of the new developments the focus should be changed from the question of proof to the problem of social control through deterrence, and from a period just beginning in 1200, when legislators and jurists began to rationalize wholesale changes in the criminal law, to a longer time frame, beginning in the later eleventh century, when the Gregorian reformers, as a part of their program to establish a distinct clerical elite directed from Rome, committed the hierarchy to detecting, punishing, and eradicating clerical misbehavior, especially simony and concubinage.

I venture the suggestion that the commitment to criminal deterrence was a new development originating in the Gregorian reform movement because the fathers of the Latin church had decidedly rejected the preoccupation of fifth-century Roman law with maintaining social control through harsh penal sanctions. Although Ambrose, Augustine, Jerome, and Gregory the Great filled their letters and sermons with the vocabulary of the Roman law, so that sin, *peccatum*, became synonymous with *crimen*, *delictum*, and *maleficium*, the Latin fathers employed these terms without accepting the conceptual framework from which the vocabulary was drawn.[8] If the voice of Christian experience in the age of martyrs did not sufficiently discredit the brutal Roman approach to crimi-

7. John Langbein, *Torture and the Law of Proof: Europe and England in the Ancien Régime* (Chicago, 1977), pp. 3–8.

8. *Crimen*, *delictum*, and *maleficium* had already been blurred together by the postclassical Roman law, before the Christian emperors borrowed *peccatum* as the generic term for all manner of wrongdoing. See Adolf Berger, *Encyclopedic Dictionary of Roman Law* (Philadelphia, 1953), s.v. "crimen." For the generic use of the term *peccata*, see Dig., 47.10.18: "Peccata enim nocentium nota esse et oportere et expedire." The Vulgate does not reflect any clear distinction between *delictum* and *peccatum*, which appear to be more frequently and more flexibly employed than *crimen* and

[214]

nal law, the authority of Scripture, cautioning the Christian not to accuse his brother, certainly suggested toleration.⁹ It was not that any sin would fail to meet its just desert, but that Augustine and Gregory were not confident of society's ability to enforce the divine law in this world and therefore felt safer in leaving vengeance to God and restricting the aims of the church in *this* world to corrective, medicinal ends through penance.¹⁰ Augustine's letters to Faustus and to Count Boniface point out the one major exception to this approach. Heretics, the bane of Augustine's episcopal career, constituted a threat to the sacred mission of the church in this world, and as such they merited special efforts toward detection and eradication.¹¹ Otherwise, though the state in its role as protector and divinely sanctioned hangman might pursue malefactors, the church would follow the example of Christ's toleration of Judas. Hence the principle that "ecclesia de occultis non iudicat."¹²

In the era following the Germanic invasions criminal procedures were far from conforming to the patristic ideal. Accusatory procedures culminating in purgatory oaths or in ordeals made more sense in early medieval communities than did the witness proofs prescribed by surviving epitomes of Roman law and by the Fathers.¹³ So thoroughly did vulgar procedures displace the formal processes prescribed by the Fathers that by the eleventh century even the Gregorian reformers, self-proclaimed restorers of the virtues of a pristine Christianity, seized upon procedures by ordeal when they began their campaign to purify the church by stamping out simony and clerical concubinage.¹⁴ What was new in the criminal

---

*maleficium.* Medieval commentary began with Titus 1:7: "Oportet enim episcopum sine crimine esse." Jerome and Augustine both argued that *crimen* in this case meant sin, and medieval glosses made this reading standard: "Crimen est querela, idest peccatum accusatione et dampnatione dignum." See Gratian's *Decretum*, Dist. 25 dictum post c. 3 and the gloss s.v. "Nomine autem."

9. Peter Brown, *The Cult of the Saints: Its Rise and Function in Latin Christianity* (Chicago, 1981), p. 102, portrays the martyrs as protectors of persons rightly or wrongly accused of crimes. Brown cites the *Miracula Sancti Stephani*, 2.5.851, and in a more general note concerning "the known horrors of late Roman judicial practice" he refers to Prudentius, *Peristephanon*, 2.313–488, and Symmachus, *Relatio*, 21. For scriptural injunctions, see Rom. 14:10 and 2 Thess. 3:15.

10. The most influential of Augustine's and Gregory's writings on ecclesiastical toleration of wrongdoing are collected in Gratian's *Decretum*, C. 23 q. 4. The argument against penal sanctions and in favor of penitential reconciliation is summarized in Gratian's dictum at C. 23 q. 4 post c. 15.

11. Among Augustine's works, see *Contra Faustum*, Epistola 200, in the Maurist edition, and *Retractationes*, 2.79.

12. Stephen Kuttner, "Ecclesia de occultis non iudicat: Problemata ex doctrina poenali decretistarum et decretalistarum a Gratiano usque ad Gregorium pp. IX," in *Actus Congressus Internationalis* (Rome, 1936), 3:225–46.

13. Colman, "Reason and Unreason," pp. 571–73, used comparative and anthropological legal studies to suggest this point.

14. Colin Morris, "*Iudicium Dei:* The Social and Political Significance of the Ordeal in the Eleventh Century," *Studies in Church History* 12 (1975): 97.

Richard M. Fraher

enforcement of the Gregorian reformers was not the procedure, but the
commitment to enforcement through vigorous efforts to detect occult
crimes and to prevent further deviant behavior, all of this necessary because Augustine's transcendant church, his "City of God," which might
be threatened by heresy or schism but not by occult sin, was abandoned
for the Gregorian reformers' conception of a visible elite community of
clerics, a community which, like a human body, was injured by the
wounds inflicted upon it.[15] Simony, in particular, subverted the ecclesiastical hierarchy of grace, and therefore simony was classified as a
heresy, the sort of crime which had always merited efforts aimed at
detecting deviancy and preventing its spread. Clerical concubinage, a
source of grave public scandal, was perceived in only slightly less horrific
terms. Accordingly, as soon as the reformers gained control of the papacy
with the elevation of Leo IX in 1049, they launched a campaign to stamp
out simony and clerical cohabitation. Adam of Bremen tells us that at the
Council of Mainz in 1049, Sibico, bishop of Speyer, was forced to clear
himself of a charge of adultery by performing a sacrificial oath.[16]

Vulgar procedures remained perfectly useful, so long as a pope was forc-
ing reluctant bishops to toe the line. But the reformers in the hierarchy
quickly discovered to their dismay that they had sprung upon themselves
two problems whose solutions tended in opposite directions. The first difficulty was that the very canons, which the papal partly cited as the basis
for their reforming efforts, contained the doctrines of the Latin fathers,
who had cared so little for penal institutions and processes and so had
saddled their successors with a doctrine of "due process" compounded by
a very difficult requirement for proof in criminal cases: testimony from
two eyewitnesses, or confession.[17] In case after case, knowledgeable clerical malefactors insisted upon their right to be tried according to the
canonical process, with a right of appeal which strung out some cases over
twenty years, and with a standard of proof which lent a considerable
advantage to the defendant.[18]

This difficulty became compounded by a second inconvenience when
the papal reformers discovered that the hierarchy was not the only group
zealous to prosecute wayward clerics. During the 1060s a wide-eyed re-

15. See Gerd Tellenbach, *Church, State, and Christian Society,* trans. R. F. Bennett
(reprint New York, 1970), chap. 5, esp. pp. 131–32.
16. Adam of Bremen, *Gesta Hammaburgensis Ecclesie Pontificium,* ed. B. Schmeid-
ler, *MGH, SS* (Hannover and Leipzig, 1917), pp. 172–73.
17. See H. Jaeger, "La preuve judiciaire d'après la tradition rabbinique et patristique,"
*La preuve: Recueils de la Société Jean Bodin* 16 (1964): 415–594 at p. 450. The most
influential single text was Cod. Theod., 9.40.1 interp., transmitted through the Lex
Romana visigothorum, 9.30.1, to the Capitula Angilramni, Burchard's *Decretum* (16.6),
Ivo's *Decretum* (2.83) and *Tripartita* (1.62), Anselm of Lucca (3.79 and 3.89.26), and
Gratian's *Decretum,* C. 2. q. 1 c. 2.
18. *Summa causae inter regem et Thomam,* in *Materials for the History of Arch-
bishop Thomas Becket,* ed. J. C. Robertson (London, 1879), 4:202.

form-minded faction of Florentine citizenry, inspired by some Vallam-
brosan monks, assailed their bishop, Peter Mezzabarba, with a charge of
simony.[19] One of the tub-thumping Vallambrosans, a fellow called Peter
and subsequently known as Igneus, "proved" the accusation against Peter
Mezzabarba by walking unscathed through a roaring blaze. This case by
itself did not convince the reforming party at Rome to abandon ordeals,
but a repetition of the same pattern at Milan in 1103 and the proliferation
of incidents in which urban mobs were stirred into action against the local
clergy during the twelfth century convinced clerical leaders that the prelates had to limit opportunities for lay enthusiasts to turn the reformers'
war against clerical crime into an attack upon the elite position of the
clergy as a whole.[20]

This dilemma was the stuff from which Gratian created his *Decretum*,
or *Concordance of Discordant Canons*, about 1140. Gratian's work reflects the fact that the reformers' priorities still dominated the thinking of
the canon lawyers, for the problem of simony received pride of place in
Causa 1.[21] That the Gregorian initiative against simony had led more or
less directly to practical problems concerning criminal procedure is suggested by the fact that Gratian moved directly from his simony case to a
thorough consideration of "due process" and sufficiency of proof according to the canons. Causa 2 is a case of a cleric despoiled of his office
without proper canonical trial and without sufficient proof of his crime by
eyewitness testimony.[22] The real world of the reformers and their prob-

19. Morris, "*Iudicium Dei*," pp. 105–6, recounting this episode from Andreas, *Vita
Gualberti, MGH, SS*, 30.2 (1934): 1086.
20. Morris, "*Iudicium Dei*," p. 109, details the trial by fire at Milan in 1103. Further
instances of reform agitation leading to violent anticlericalism include Tanchelm's
preaching at Utrecht, 1112–14; Henry of Le Mans's turbulent career; and the activities
of Peter of Bruys between 1112 and 1131. The appearance of heretics only compounded
the problem faced by a hierarchy committed to high standards of clerical discipline and
equally committed to defending the elite status of all clerics against attack by unauthorized meddlers. On the heresiarchs, see W. Wakefield and A. Evans, *Heresies of the
High Middle Ages* (New York, 1969), pp. 95–126.
21. The case of the simoniacal bishop, which Gratian placed first among the *causae*
in the *Decretum*, genuinely vexed the ecclesiastical reformers. *Quaestio sexta*, for
example, carried on a long-standing discussion concerning the validity of orders conferred by simoniacal prelates, and *quaestio septima* raised the ticklish matter of
whether a confessed simoniac could be restored to his episcopal office. *Causa prima* was
the longest case in the *Decretum*, and it continued to occupy a disproportionate amount
of space in the decretists' *summae*. See Friedberg, *CIC*, 1:356–438; and the lengthy
discussions of *causa prima* in the *Summa Parisiensis*, ed. T. McLaughlin (Toronto,
1952); *Summa Magistri Rolandi*, ed. F. Thaner (Innsbruck, 1874); Stephan of Tournai,
*Summa decreti*, ed. J. F. von Schulte (Giessen, 1891); and Rufinus, *Summa decretorum*,
ed. H. Singer (Paderborn, 1902).
22. Gratian suggests the connection between the two *causae* in his dictum post C. 1
q. 7 c. 27: "His breuiter premissis ad ea ueniamus, que ecclesia seueritate disciplinae
parata est ulcisci, ostendentes quibus accusantibus uel testificantibus quilibet sint
conuincendi.... Et ut facilius pateat quod dicturi sumus, exemplum ponatur sub

Richard M. Fraher

lems is peering out at us from Gratian's dialectical exercise, and Gratian's
solutions to these procedural problems suggest that in the middle of the
twelfth century the canonists were, at least for the moment, as concerned
with protecting what we would call the procedural rights of clerical defendants as they were with the detection and punishment of clerical deviancy. Gratian systematically elaborated on the "due process" requirements which the Fathers had contrived to protect sacramental ministers
from the suspicions of their flocks, and Gratian extended this protection
to mean that any cleric, no matter how notoriously concubinous, was
innocent until proved guilty.[23]

At the same moment as Gratian was composing his carefully crafted
opus, another zealous reforming pope, Innocent II, was presiding over the
Second Lateran Council, which torpedoed Gratian's ideas about "due
process" for suspect priests. The council forbade the laity to attend masses
celebrated by concubinous clerics without stipulating any procedural pre-
requisites to such a boycott.[24] Innocent II thought it more important to
maintain pressure on wayward priests than to maintain a strict standard
of "due process," and in general after 1050 papal and conciliar legislation
tended to emphasize detection and prevention as opposed to tolerance of
occult and unproved offenses. Canonists therefore had to create categories
of exceptions to their principle that "ecclesia de occultis non iudicat."[25]
Homicide and simony, although characteristically committed in secret
rather than in public, struck most twelfth-century decretists as crimes
sufficiently enormous to merit special efforts aimed at prosecution and
punishment. By 1200, heresy and usury would join the ranks of crimes
which demanded particular attention.[26] By the middle of the thirteenth
century, Hostiensis enumerated ten *crimina maiora* that merited prosecution on account of their enormity.[27]

oculis, in quo auctoritates hinc inde controuersantes distinguantur, et quid sanctorum
patrum sentiat auctoritas liquido intimetur."

23. C. 15 q. 8 c. 5: "Non statim qui accusatur reus est, sed qui conuincitur crimi-
nosus." See my essay "Ut Nullus Describatur Reus Prius Quam Convincatur: Presumption of Innocence in Medieval Canon Law?" in *Proceedings of the Sixth International
Congress of Medieval Canon Law: Monumenta Iuris Canonici*, ser. C, subsidia, vol. 7
(Vatican City, 1985).

24. Concilium Lateranense II, c. 7: "Ad haec predecessorum nostrorum Gregorii VII,
Urbani, et Paschalis Romanorum pontificium vestigiis inhaerentes, praecipimus ut
nullus missas eorum audiat, quos uxores vel concubinas habere cognovit." *Conciliorum
oecumenicorum decreta*, ed. J. Alberigo et al. (Bologna, 1973), p. 198.

25. Kuttner, "Ecclesia de occultis non iudicat," see note 12 supra.

26. For conciliar concern with heresy and usury before 1200, see Concilium Lateranense II, c. 13 and Concilium Lateranense III, c. 27. Simony, clerical concubinage,
heresy, and usury became the major stimuli in the development of the canon law on
crime. Devices invented to cope with any one of these crimes were quickly adapted to
other high-priority concerns. Modern scholarship attributes too exclusive a role to the
war on heresy.

27. Hostiensis, *Summa aurea* (Venice, 1605), Rubr. De penitentiis et remissionibus,
col. 1758. He included heresy, sins against nature, homicide, treason, sacrilege, incest,
conspiracy, adultery, giving false testimony, simony, and usury.

With the age of the lawyer-popes, beginning with Alexander III in 1159, early ham-fisted attempts at enforcement of the prohibitions on simony and concubinage began to give way to carefully considered attempts to resolve particular practical problems through the application of consistent, rational principles. It was Alexander III who articulated the distinction, based upon Abelard's intentionist theories, that offenses against the church in this world were the object of the *forum externum*, which punished transgressors in the here and now.[28] Every crime therefore was defined by the canonists as a public crime, an offense against the Christian community.[29]

By 1200, the canon lawyers settled upon two central principles as a simple theoretical basis for the criminal law that was growing out of the reformers' agenda. Paradoxically, while both ideas were borrowed from the *Corpus iuris civilis*, both marked departures from earlier medieval ideas about law. The first, which I have treated in another essay, was the notion that punishing crime is a matter of public interest.[30] By the end of the twelfth century, with the spirit of reform triumphant at Rome, the hierarchy had long since abandoned the policy that earthly misdeeds should be tolerated in this life and left to divine judgment. In the middle of the thirteenth century even the conservative Innocent IV, who preferred the traditional view that concealing one's brother's occult wrongs was meritorious and therefore taught that witnesses ought not to be forced to testify in criminal cases, recognized an exception in cases where the deviant behavior posed a societal danger. Innocent found *periculum*, and taught that it justified prosecutorial intervention through *inquisitio*, in cases of heresy, because an undetected heretic could infect others, and in cases of simony, homicide, and misappropriation of ecclesiastical property.[31] The maxim "public interest demands that crimes not go unpun-

28. For Abelard's distinction between divine and human judgment, see Kuttner, "Ecclesia de occultis non iudicat," p. 244. On Alexander III, see W. Ullmann, *The Growth of Papal Government in the Middle Ages*, 2d ed. (London, 1964), p. 379 n. 2. More generally, see P. Anciaux, *Le théologie du sacrement de penitence au xiie siècle* (Louvain, 1949), and D. Luscombe, *The School of Peter Abelard* (Cambridge, 1970), esp. pp. 218–23.

29. This became a notorious point of contrast between canon law and Roman law. See, for example, Innocent IV, *In quinque libros decretalium commentaria* (Venice, 1610), fol. 602, at X 5.22.2, s.v. "preteribat": "Secundum canones autem fere omne crimen esse publicum puto." Roman law recognized as *crimina* only those deeds which could be prosecuted by any citizen in the public *iudicia* established by statute.

30. R. M. Fraher, "The Theoretical Justification for the New Criminal Law of the High Middle Ages: 'Rei Publicae Interest, Ne Crimina Remaneant Impunita,'" *Illinois Law Review*, 1984, p. 577.

31. Innocent IV, *In quinque libros decretalium commentaria*, at X 2.21.1: "Ubi autem celare veritatem non est peccatum, ut quando agitur criminaliter . . . vel alio modo ad penam tantum, non dicimus [testes] cogendos, quia celare veritatem non est peccatum sed meritorium, scilicet celare crimen fratris, arg. 2 q. 1. Si peccaverit, . . . nisi esset crimen de quo esset periculum quod esset occultum, sicut heresis, delapidatio. Nam in his dicimus testes cogendos etiam si sit occultum, quia nequeunt sine periculo dissimulari." At X 5.1.24, commenting on Innocent III's assertion that *inquisitio* was to

ished" crystallized the new approach to active prosecution wherever deviant behavior posed a threat to social order. Although the phraseology came from ancient Roman law, the canonists employed the argument from public interest to reach radically new conclusions, including the rule that every crime is a public offense.

Deterrence, the second "new" idea, was also based on the vocabulary of the ancient Roman jurists. One might tend to think of deterrence as a quintessentially modern notion of social engineering, but the idea appeared in the *Corpus iuris civilis*, and the medieval canonists made energetic use of it. So far as one can tell, it was Innocent III who steered the decretalists toward adopting a deterrence theory, when he wrote that failure to punish malefactors creates "an audacity of impunity, through which those who were bad become worse."[32] The decretalists' glosses to this passage point out its grounding in Roman law. From the Code came an imperial prohibition on the early release of prisoners who had been sentenced to hard labor, with a word of explanation that it is against public interest to grant remission of punishments, "lest people be encouraged to dare to commit crimes."[33] From the Digest came three citations pointing out the social value of inflicting punishment. A snippet from Gaius asserted simply that there is a *magna ratio* that penalties should be paid for crimes, but the passage did not explain what this "powerful argument" might be.[34] Two further texts, however, drawn from Tryphonius and Callistratus, suggest that Gaius's *magna ratio* was deterrence. Tryphonius posed a question arising from the case of an individual convicted of a capital crime. If a creditor came forward and demanded payment of the condemned man's debt before the state confiscated all of his goods, should the money go to the creditor or to the fisc? Tryphonius concluded that the state should confiscate the money, in order to teach the sharpest possible lesson. "A person who has done wrong ought to suffer indigence publicly, so that by his example to others he serves to

---

be used where toleration of wrongdoing would pose a danger, Innocent IV glossed the word *periculo:* "Aliorum, puta si dicatur hereticus, cum periculum sit ne alios inficiat, vel quia periculum est quod aliquis non occidat alium vel occidatur, et sic est multa exempla invenire. Et potest dici quod ubi timetur periculum, etiam sine multa infamia proceditur." Innocent IV also argued that the enormity of certain crimes justified the coercion of witnesses; at X 2.21.9 he wrote: "In maioribus criminibus dicunt cogendos testes, ut heresi, simonia, homicidio . . . propter enormitatem criminis."

32. X 5.39.35: "Et per impunitatis audaciam fiant qui nequam fuerant nequiores."

33. Cod. 9.47.14. "Cum non remittere poenam facile publicae intersit, ne ad maleficia quisquam prosiliat."

34. Dig. 46.1.70.5. "Nam poenas ob maleficia solvi magna ratio suadet." Perhaps no explanation was needed, given the Digest's introductory note on the "priestly" function of jurists: "Iustitiam namque colimus et boni et aequi notitiam profitemur . . . bonos non solum metu poenarum, uerum etiam praemiorum quoque exhortatione efficere cupientes." A carrot and stick approach to social control was implied throughout imperial law.

deter wrongdoing."[35] Callistratus, writing more generally about the functions of punishment, observed that many authorities had found it advisable for two reasons to hang notorious bandits in the neighborhood they had haunted. Graphically visible punishment of the brigands supposedly gave solace to relatives of the bandits' victims. But pride of place was given to the argument that the sight of criminals hanging from a gibbet would deter others from committing the same crimes.[36] Both Tryphonius and Callistratus used forms of the verb *deterreo*, and the context leaves no doubt as to their meaning: punishing a criminal creates an incentive to obey the rules not only for one convict, but for others who might be tempted to go astray.

Similar ideas had circulated during the earlier Middle Ages, for example, in St. Ambrose's dictum that making reconciliation too easy for malefactors created an incentive to delinquency.[37] But not until the Scholastic jurists fashioned a rationale for the ecclesiastical reformers' "war on crime" did deterrence emerge as a fundamental touchstone of European criminal law. It is almost needless to say that public officials charged with maintaining clerical discipline or social order tended to favor arguments that made detection, prosecution, and punishment easier and more efficient and justified their innovations as a means to deterrence, while it is perhaps surprising to discover that the jurists, both civilian and canonist, tended to give nearly equal emphasis to considerations of fairness, consistency, and "due process." But one cannot push this distinction too far, for despite the caricatures of the hysterical heretic-hunting inquisitor and the bloodthirsty *podestà*, public officials were clearly aware of the legal rules governing criminal process, while even the most humane of the jurists insisted that crime must be punished even if one had to compromise the fairness of the process.[38]

---

35. Dig. 16.3.31. "Nam male meritus publice, ad exemplum aliis ad deterrenda maleficia sit, etiam egestate laborare debet."

36. Dig. 48.19.28.15. "Famosos latrones in his locis, ubi grassati sunt, furca figendos compluribus placuit, ut et conspectu deterreantur alii ab isdem facinoribus et solatio sit cognatis et adfinibus interemptorum eodem loco poena reddita, in quo latrones homicidia fecissent."

37. Quoted in Gratian's *Decretum*, Q. 23 q. 4 c. 33. "Facilitas enim veniae incentivum tribuit delinquendi."

38. Attitudes toward criminal behavior seem to have been correlated with many different variables. Sarah Blanshei has suggested that popular, as opposed to aristocratic, governments strove harder to suppress crime in medieval Italy, and that the integration of trained jurists within the ruling circles of Bolognese society was an important factor in the development of a more severe, impersonal criminal law in that commune. See her "Criminal Law and Politics in Medieval Bologna," *Criminal Justice History: An International Review* 2 (1981): 1–30; "Crime and Law Enforcement in Medieval Bologna," *Journal of Social History* 16 (1982): 121–38; and "Criminal Justice in Medieval Perugia and Bologna," *Law and History Review* 1 (1983): 251–75. The assimilation of trained canon lawyers within the power structure of the Latin church helps to explain the rapid pace of change in the canon law from about 1140 to about 1378.

Richard M. Fraher

As I have suggested, Innocent III's pontificate remains a significant turning point in the history of medieval criminal law, for this pontiff not only crystallized in concise phrases the principles which would govern subsequent juristic discussion, but also fashioned a criminal procedure which met the conflicting needs of the hierarchy. In 1203, William of Ste. Mere Eglise, bishop of London, wrote to Innocent to enquire about proper criminal procedures against incorrigible clerics. Innocent responded, in the decretal *Ut fame*, with three rationales for using coercion against criminals. First, it was the function of prelates to correct the excesses of their subjects. Second, public interest demanded the punishment of crimes. And third, perhaps explaining the nature of public interest, Innocent argued that failure to punish made bad people worse.[39] These ideas, which Durantis borrowed in the preface to book 3 of his *Speculum iudiciale*, reappeared in the works of virtually every subsequent canonist, civilian, or proceduralist writer, including Hostiensis, Innocent IV, Albertus Gandinus, Bartolus of Saxoferrato, and Franciscus Zabarella.[40]

Hostiensis's *Lectura* on *Ut fame* stressed the connection between public utility and deterrence. Glossing Innocent's use of the term "public utility," Hostiensis wrote, "Here you have a notable passage, which we often use, saying that it is a matter of public interest or utility that crimes not go unpunished.... A *magna ratio* argues that penalties should be paid ... lest someone be inclined to dare to commit crimes." Commenting on Innocent's argument that failure to punish created "an audacity of impunity," Hostiensis commented that "being too easy with forgiveness creates an incentive for the delinquent ... and the infliction of punishment cultivates terror and restrains others from sinning."[41] To jurists of the High and later Middle Ages, the refrain "ne crimina remaneant impunita," and the belief that prompt, savage retribution would deter potential criminals, justified such innovations as the replacement of accusatory by inquisitorial procedures, the virtually automatic use of torture as an investigative and perhaps punitive tool in criminal cases, the employment of lesser standards of proof when witnesses were lacking, and the creation of summary procedures to deal with "enormous" crimes.[42]

---

39. *Liber extra*, 5.39.35, in med.: "et publicae utilitatis intersit, ne crimina remaneant impunita."

40. Durantis, *Speculum iudiciale*; Hostiensis, *In quinque libros decretalium commentaria* (Venice, 1581), at X 5.39.35, s.v. "et publice"; Innocent IV, *Commentaria*, at X 3.2.8, s.v. "notorium"; Albertus Gandinus, *Tractatus de maleficiis*, rubr. "Quid sit accusatio," c. 4; Franciscus de Zabarellis, *Lectura super i–v Libris decretalium* (Venice, 1502), at X 3.2.7, no. 13; Bartolus de Saxoferrato, *In XII. libros codicis commentaria, una cum additionibus Alexandri de Imola* (Lugduni, 1505), at Cod. 2.4.18.

41. Hostiensis, *Lectura in quinque libros Gregorii Noni decretalium libros* (Paris, 1512), at 5.39.35. "Nam facilitas venie incentivum tribuit delinquenti ... et pene inflictio terrorem incutit et retrahit alios a peccatis."

42. For the first point, see Zabarella, *Lectura*, at X 5.1.24, s.v. "Hunc Tamen," no. 10, quoting Dynus to the effect that "inquisitio est remedium ordinarium" and Cynus

[222]

Despite Innocent III's characteristic fondness for a bon mot, and despite the huge success of this particular decretal, it is important to remember that the pope was at least as concerned with the practical problems raised by continuing efforts to maintain clerical discipline as he was with general principles. In 1200 the church remained vulnerable to public scandal arising from accusations against bishops and priests. Gratian's attempts to resolve this problem had, if anything, rendered the situation more difficult, for the *Decretum*, as we have seen, had established an almost impossible standard of proof within a context of strict due-process requirements, all of which served as a barrier to malicious accusations but also interdicted successful prosecution of genuinely criminal clergymen. Innocent moved to resolve both difficulties. In 1206, in a letter to the bishop of Vercelli, Innocent acknowledged that bishops were frequently subjected to malice and snares, which had caused the fathers of the church to make it difficult to accuse prelates.[43] But as Innocent pointed out, clerics ought not to sin insolently, and so he ordered the bishop of Vercelli to proceed against wayward clerics via *inquisitio* rather than permitting individuals to proceed against prelates *per accusationem*. In 1215, the Fourth Lateran Council made this decree, *Qualiter et quando*, the law of the universal church. Later, in a world in which *inquisitio* had become ubiquitous, jurists looked back to the promulgation of *Qualiter et quando* as the moment when the pope and council "invented" a new *remedium ordinarium* in the ecclesiastical courts, introduced in the public interest, in order to punish crimes where the accusatorial process had failed to do so.[44] By the end of the Middle Ages, the ideology of deterrence was extended to explain the origins and functions of *inquisitio*. Bonifacius de Vitalinis and Angelus Aretinus believed that the inquisitorial process prevented crimes by punishing criminals.[45] The fourteenth- and fifteenth-

---

arguing the contrary "quia processus inquisitorius est adinventus ut crimina non remaneant impunita." Angelus Aretinus, *Tractatus de maleficiis* (Venice, 1578), rubr. "Hec est quedam inquisitio," no. 29: "Accusatio de quolibet crimine est permissa, ergo et inquisitio, que succedit loco eius. . . . Et sic ad eundem effectum, ne crimina remaneant impunita." On torture, see Gandinus, *Tractatus de maleficiis*, rubr. "De questionibus et tormentis," passim. On lesser standards of proof, the most influential text was Thomas de Piperata, *Tractatus de fama*, printed in Zilettus, *Tractatus universi iuris* (Venice, 1584), 11.1.8. On summary procedures, the literature on heresy and on the criminal ban of the Italian city-states contains numerous examples.

43. X 5.1.17: "Et quia non possunt omnibus conplacere, cum ex officio teneantur non solum arguere sed etiam increpare, quin etiam interdum suspendere, nonnunquam vero ligare, frequenter odium multorum incurrent et insidias patiuntur. Et ideo sancti patres provide statuerunt, ut accusatio prelatorum non facile admittatur, ne concussis columnis corruat edificium."

44. *Glossa ordinaria*, at X 5.1.24, s.v. ad inquirendum: "Sed melius est quod inquirat, quia periculosum est accusare, quia de facili nullus accusaret." Cynus concluded (note 41 above) that *inquisitio* had been invented as an extraordinary measure to enhance the efficiency of the criminal process.

45. Bonifacius de Vitalinis, *Tractatus de maleficiis*, rubr. "De inquisitione et earum formis": "Vel inquisitio est iudicis officium ad inveniendum malorum delicta et pena

century jurists did not realize that Innocent III had in fact accomplished two purposes when he adopted the inquisitorial process. *Inquisitio* permitted the hierarchy to continue its war on clerical deviancy without fostering "malicious" attacks upon the clergy.

Innocent enjoyed less immediate success in fashioning a decisive resolution to the seemingly intractable problem of the law of proof, especially in cases of sexual misdemeanors, which were the bête noire of the reforming party within the hierarchy. So strong was the aversion toward clerical concubinage, and so difficult was it to prove sexual transgressions by eyewitness testimony, that in trying to create effective deterrence, reforming popes consistently overstepped the bounds of due process as defined by the canon law. During the 1180s Pope Lucius III in the decretal *Vestra* commended the "holy zeal" of laypersons who boycotted masses celebrated by notoriously concubinous priests, "so that license to sin may be denied to others."[46] The *glossa ordinaria* to the *Decretales* commented that Lucius's decree was a canon "famous [or infamous] both for its intrinsic content and for its extrinsic material, that is, *notorium.*"[47] The glossators also noted that this decretal was "very difficult and perilous," because Lucius's decree was simply unworkable, both from the point of view of criminal procedure and from the perspective of ecclesiastical politics. Innocent III, very early in his pontificate, tried to close the gaping loopholes created by his zealous predecessor. According to Innocent's decretal *Tua nos*, if parishioners alleged that a priest was "notoriously" living in sin, the clergyman could not be punished or subjected to any shortcuts in the formal procedure unless an ecclesiastical judge decided that his malefaction were so obvious, on the basis of widely known evidence, that his guilt "could not be hidden by any tergiversation."[48] Hence, Innocent recognized that genuine notoriety (*notorium*) obviated the stringencies of the law of proof, but the pope declared that an ecclesiastical court, rather than the laity, constituted the arbiter of what could be considered a *crimen notorium*. Moreover, Innocent armed the judge in such cases with weapons for use against the recalcitrant defendant, for if scandal had arisen, the prelate hearing of the rumors could force the

---

debita punienda, favore rei publice introductum. . . . Nam rei publice interest, ne committantur maleficia." Angelus Aretinus de Gambilionibus, *Tractatus de maleficiis* (Venice, 1578) rubr. "Hec est quedam inquisitio": [Discussing whether a private accuser should be able to prosecute a criminal case to the exclusion of a public *inquisitio*] . . . "Item quia in iudice est maior ratio, quia prosequitur vindictam publicam et offensi; et cum ex suo officio incumbat inspicere, ne maleficia committantur, fortius ut commissa puniantur."

46. X 3.2.7.

47. *Glossa ordinaria*, at X 3.2.7, s.v. "Vestra": "Famosum est tum propter materiam intrinsecam ipsius, tum propter materiam extrinsecam, scil. notorii, et utraque est multum difficilis et periculosa."

48. X 3.2.8.

suspect to undergo a purgative oath. *Purgatio* served at least two functions, for a successful purgation publicly and officially put an end to any existent scandal, while an unsuccessful purgation allowed the judge to pronounce a punitive sentence, even in the absence of other proof of guilt.[49] An entire subcategory of jurisprudence concerning *notorium, manifestum, fama,* and *evidentia* grew up in the course of the thirteenth century. Modern scholarship has made much of the Roman legal principles that in criminal cases proof had to be "clearer than the light at midday" and that the judge was bound to adjudicate according to the law and not according to his conscience.[50] What has escaped attention is that Innocent III promoted the policy of deterrence through efficient prosecution when he created an important new genre of proofs by recognizing notoriety as a sufficient, if merely presumptive, proof based upon external evidence, and by leaving it to judicial discretion to decide whether an individual case was notorious. The medieval jurists recognized the seminal influence of the decretals of Lucius III and Innocent III, for the entire juristic discussion of the subject of fashioning proof from circumstantial evidence was ultimately based on two canons under the unlikely rubric "on the cohabitation of clerics and women." Every jurist from Durantis to Bartolus gives evidence in his citations that the law of evidence had its origins in the hierarchy's war upon clerical concubinage.[51]

49. Innocent's decretal established a hierarchy of procedural devices. *Notorium facti,* that is, notoriety based upon undeniable public evidence, relieved the presiding judge of responsibility for establishing any further proof, for securing a formal accusation against the accused, or for conducting a formal joinder of issues. Mere *fama,* in contrast, did not obviate the need for the judge to follow the full, formal *ordo iudiciarius,* including citation of the accused, establishment of full proof, and examination of the suspect's defense. Subsequent legislation in Innocent's pontificate did, however, make *fama* sufficient grounds for conducting an inquisition. Finally, if *fama* gave rise to scandal, the judge had the discretionary power to require the suspect to undergo a purgatory oath, even in the absence of proof.

50. Langbein, *Torture and the Law of Proof,* p. 6: "The system of statutory proofs insists upon objective criteria of proof. The judge who administers it is an automaton. He condemns a criminal upon the evidence of two eyewitnesses, evidence which is in the famous phrase 'as clear as the light of day.'" See Knut W. Nörr, *Zur Stellung des Richters im gelehrten Prozess der Frühzeit* (Munich, 1967), for a learned discussion of the implications of the principle that "iudex secundum leges, non secundum conscientiam suam iudicare debet." This literature distorts criminal procedure to the extent that the authors have ignored the wide scope of judicial discretion in every step of the Roman-canon law's procedures short of pronouncing a definitive sentence. Another commonplace among the medieval jurists held that "arbitrium dat potestatibus largas habenas." I plan to conduct further research on the subject of judicial discretion.

51. See, for example, Gandinus, *Tractatus de maleficiis,* rubr. "Quomodo de maleficio cognoscitur quando crimen est notorium," c. 4; Durantis, *Speculum iudiciale,* pt. 3, rubr. "De notoriis criminibus," no. 4. Although civilians such as Thomas de Piperata and Jacobus de Bellovisu made exclusive use of Roman law citations in discussing this subject, Bartolus was more honest about the actual source of ideas about *notorium:* "Quero que dicantur crimina notoria? Tractatum de notoriis criminibus non habemus in iure nostro, set canonistae habent tractatum longum," Bartolus, *In ius universe civile*

Richard M. Fraher

Innocent III and his successors made extensive use of presumptive proofs and summary procedures in their efforts to eradicate those crimes which most distressed the hierarchy during the thirteenth and fourteenth centuries: heresy and usury. Although heresy was not the sole stimulus which underlay the development of the new criminal law, the clerical campaign to extirpate heresy does follow a pattern which is very instructive about medieval efforts to control crime.[52] The problem of heresy had emerged as an urgent priority for the entire Roman church by the second half of the twelfth century, and the Third Lateran Council responded with the traditional excommunications, anathemas, and confiscations.[53] Merely reiterating traditional sanctions did not prevent heretics from proselytizing, and the formalities of the criminal procedure, especially the difficulty of proof and the right of appeal, were perceived to be a hindrance to successful prosecution, so in 1184 at the Council of Verona, Lucius III turned his "holy zeal" against heretics, as he had done against adulterous clerics. At the discretion of the ecclesiastical judge, defendants suspected of heresy might be forced to prove their innocence by purgation, and a suspect who had once abjured and was subsequently apprehended for heresy faced automatic relegation to a secular court for punishment "without any further hearing."[54] Innocent III and the Fourth Lateran Council added that the ecclesiastical judge could pronounce an interim sentence of excommunication against a suspected heretic who answered a summons but failed to cooperate in the investigation.[55] Later developments included a ban on the right to counsel; recognition of the validity of testimony against suspected heretics, even if the source were an "infamous" person, such as another heretic or a convicted perjurer; prosecutions against deceased suspects; and Alexander IV's ruling that a party suspected of heresy who failed to answer a summons could be held as convicted and liable to the death penalty after a year.[56] Hostiensis explained the rationale for such zealous prosecution of heretics in terms

---

commentaria (Basel, 1562), at Dig. 48.16.6.3 at no. 3. The tractatus longus de notorio among the canonists customarily appeared in the decretalists' discussion of X 3.2.7.

52. Modern historical scholarship overemphasizes the causal ties between heresy and the invention of inquisitorial procedures. W. Ullmann, in his introduction to H. C. Lea, The Inquisition of the Middle Ages: Its Organization and Operation (New York, 1969), p. 44, suggested that the difficulty of proving heresy gave rise to the use of fama and indicia as circumstantial evidence. In fact, clerical cohabitation and the difficulty of proving sexual misconduct led to the development of new evidentiary principles in the course of the twelfth-century implementation of the Gregorian reform program. During the thirteenth century, heretical inquisitors and communal magistrates alike exploited the new evidentiary principles.

53. Concilium Lateranense III, c. 27.

54. X 5.7.9.

55. Concilium Lateranense IV, c. 3.

56. Sext. 5.2.4 and 5.2.8.3; Sext. 5.2.8.7; Sext. 5.2.7.

of the injury done to everyone when anyone deviated from the faith.[57] Bonifacius de Vitalinis was closer to the spirit of the age when he wrote that imposing public penance and making a confessed heretic wear a cross on his clothes would deter others.[58]

The jurists, as a group, probably came near to the medieval popes in terms of orthodoxy in the faith, but the lawyers were evidently more sympathetic to the plight of suspected heretics, who were being stripped of all procedural protections. The canonists by and large rationalized away their hesitations, but some lawyers sought to resist the excesses of the Inquisition by claiming that defendants handed over to the secular authorities for execution had a right to a new hearing on the substance of the charges before the secular judge could pronounce sentence.[59] As early as the 1260s, Pope Urban IV responded to such legal obstructionism by pronouncing invalid any statute which impeded or retarded the work of the inquisitors and threatening local officials with ecclesiastical censure.[60] Even if the jurists did not share in the hierarchy's enthusiasm for hounding heretics, expediency dictated that one should not quibble over the niceties of "due process" in the face of the clerical imperative to extirpate heresy.

While the jurists did not distinguish themselves in defense of suspected heretics, the matter of usury provoked a different response. Usury never became quite so compelling a priority on the hierarchy's "hit list" of heinous crimes as simony, clercial concubinage, and heresy.[61] Usurers, moreover, almost by definition enjoyed social and economic advantages that accused heretics typically would have lacked. The ranks of accused usurers included prosperous bankers who could afford to pay the costs of appealing to reverse a conviction on technical grounds. Meanwhile, mer-

57. Hostiensis, *Summa Aurea*, rubr. "De hereticis," col. 1528: "Qua pena feriatur? Et certe magna et non solum una, sed multa et diversis. Et hoc ideo, quia hereticus omnes offendit. Quod enim in religionem divinam committitur in omnium fertur iniuriam."

58. Bonifatius de Vitalinis, *Tractatus de maleficiis*, rubr. "De crimine heresis": "Item quia eis inducitur publica penitentia per crucis impositionem, ut ex hoc alii terreantur."

59. See, for example, Johannes Teutonicus's gloss to IV Lat. c. 3, s.v. "ex tunc uelut heretici condempnentur": "Vehemens presumptio non statim condempnat aliquem de heresi, set facit hoc quod est procedendum contra eum quasi contra suspectum. Et licet presumptio de qua hic agitur primo fuerit probabilis, tamen propter cursum temporis et quia noluerunt se expurgare et quia per annum steterunt in excommunicatione, et pro conuictis habentur, ut xi. q. iii. *Rursus et Quicumque* [c. 36–37]. *Secus tamen est in aliis criminibus.*" A. Garcia y Garcia, ed., *Constitutiones Concilii quarti Latearnensis, una cum commentariis glossatorum* (Vatican City, 1981), p. 189. For the jurists' speculations concerning new trials before secular magistrates, see Martinus de Fano, *Tractatus de brachio seu auxilio implorando per iudicem ecclesiasticum a iudice seculari vel e contra*, ed. Zilettus, *Tractatus universi iuris*, 11.2.408.

60. Sext. 5.2.9.

61. Part of the canonists' fascination with usury lay in the very difficulty of proof. Zabarella called it "causa arduissima usurarii." *Lectura*, at X 5.1.22 at no. 11.

Richard M. Fraher

chants, bankers, and scholars could and did make an argument concerning usury that one could not make concerning heresy, that is, that the substantive law defining the offense was wrongheaded and needed to be changed. The canon lawyers gradually enunciated a system of exceptions to the blanket prohibition on usury, while popes and councils continued to hammer at the need for enforcement. The ecclesiastical legislation aimed at eradicating usury follows the now-familiar pattern of procedural shortcuts and impatience with obstructionism, culminating in 1311, when the Council of Vienne reiterated the traditional prohibition against usury along with the traditional sanctions, concluding with a threat to proceed with heresy charges against anyone who argued that usury was not mortally sinful.[62]

Assaulting the traditional teaching on the wrongfulness of usury was a course too perilous to recommend itself to the medieval jurists. Instead, they successfully argued in the classroom that the traditional definition of the offense was overinclusive, while in the courtroom they equally successfully demanded the acquittal of accused usurers on procedural grounds. The *consilia* of the fourteenth- and fifteenth-century jurists, canonist and civilian alike, bulge with cases of defendants condemned as "manifest" usurers in ecclesiastical courts of first instance only to be exonerated by appellate jurisdictions on the basis of a jurist's advice that the conviction rested upon insufficient evidence.[63] In this matter, the jurists' commitment to the legal principles of "due process" and sufficiency of proof, heftily fortified by the economic and social standing of the defendants, withstood the hierarchy's assault on such procedural niceties as stood in the path of effective prosecution.

The evidence I have presented points toward the conclusion that the motivation behind the development of the new criminal procedures which Durantis called a *nova doctrina* was the perceived need for efficient enforcement of the canon law, for the purpose of deterring deviant behavior. I believe that the substance of the Roman-canon law concerning crime reflects as much the influence of the reforming popes as that of

62. See J. T. Noonan, *The Scholastic Analysis of Usury* (Cambridge, Mass., 1957); J. T. Gilchrist, *The Church and Economic Activity in the Middle Ages* (New York, 1969); the conciliar legislation that moved toward summary procedures for convicting "notorious" usurers appears in II Lyons, c. 26; Vienne, c. 29.

63. For example, Baldus de Ubaldis, *Consiliorum sive responsorum volumina v* (Venice, 1580) vol. 3, cons. 277; vol. 4, cons. 459; and vol. 4, cons. 465, which includes a long discussion on the nature of *crimen manifestum* and the traditional law of proof in criminal cases. An interesting opinion contrary to Baldus's appears in Nicolas de Tudeschis, *Consilia, Tractatus, Questiones, et Practica* (Venice, 1571) at cons. 181, in which Panormitanus argued that a certain Ser Stephanus might not be denied Christian burial as a manifest usurer on the basis of the evidence brought against him, but that "saltem quoad poenas speciales" Ser Stephanus could be condemned, despite an admitted prejudice to his rights, because "expedit animabus ipsorum usurariorum et aliorum, ut facilius arceantur."

Justinian's lawyers. The juristic literature of the High Middle Ages suggests that the ecclesiastical authorities and the canon lawyers built upon the slender foundations of the Roman criminal law an elaborate new structure, and that the Italian city-states which employed the Roman-canon *ius commune* relied heavily upon the decretalists for the structure of their criminal law.[64] But the communal governments, not nearly as politically secure as the papacy of the High Middle Ages, and not nearly as constrained by a class of jurists who perceived themselves as the guardians of authoritative tradition, moved much further than did the ecclesiastical government in subverting the position of defendants in the interest of detection and deterrence. The communes had their own priorities in the development of substantive criminal law, including the repression of crimes of violence, sedition, insurrection, crimes against morality, and—surprisingly—gambling. The city-states also employed much greater flexibility than did the church in the area of penal law. It was common wisdom in the thirteenth century that a rise in criminal activity should be met by the imposition of harsher penal sanctions to deter any further increase.[65] Albertus Gandinus thought that the communal judges should, as a matter of course, increase or decrease penalties in relation to the incidence of crime, "so that sentencing is an example when many people are breaking the laws, so that the punishment of one might be the fear of many."[66] By the end of the fourteenth century, Bonifacius de Vitalinis listed a truly remarkable array of offenses that resulted in the death penalty, which Bonifacius justified because "delinquents should be punished with their deserved penalty, so that others will not dare to be delinquent."[67] In penal law, the argument for deterrence justified the brutality of a cruel age.

What William Durantis called a *nova doctrina*, then, was a criminal procedure based on a relatively recent consensus that public interest demanded the detection and punishment of deviant behavior, which in

64. Lucas de Penna, *Lectura super tribus libris codicis* (Lugduni, 1538), is a good example. Although this was a civilian work, Lucas's discussion of inquisitio at Cod. 10.10.5, s.v. "Si vacantia," allows that inquisition was not the standard criminal procedure in Roman law, but "materia autem inquisitionis per doctores iuris canonici diffuse tractatur. Item nota prout dicit Innocentius, extra. de elect. Bonae memoriae Magunt. Et sic servat totus mundus."

65. Hostiensis, *Summa Aurea*, col. 1587, Rubr. "De penis raptorum corporum" (Venice, 1605): "Sed crimine crescente debet maiorem [penam] imponere ad terrorem."

66. Gandinus, *Tractatus de maleficiis*, rubr. "Utrum poena possit augeri": "Ut quando multis grassantibus et delinquentibus opus est exemplo, ut pena unius sit metus multorum."

67. Bonifacius de Vitalinis, *Tractatus de maleficiis* (Lugduni, 1555), rubr. "Quibus ex causis quis possit ad mortem vel in membro condemnari": "Quia expedit ne maleficia remaneant impunita, . . . et ut delinquentes debita pena puniantur, ad hoc ut alii temere ad delinquendum non prosiliant, videmus in quibus casibus possit quis condemnari ad mortem."

turn would serve as a deterrent to further criminal activity. The result was that public authorities experimented with a host of new legal devices, all aimed at increasing the efficiency of the criminal process. Many jurists, following the lead of Albertus Gandinus, espoused an almost bloodthirsty enthusiasm about the *nova doctrina* which led the scholastic lawyers to blur the lines between investigative and penal procedures. It is clear, for example, that Gandinus believed that the threat of judicial torture served precisely the same function as the Roman jurist Callistratus had associated with public hangings. Gandinus posed the question, which he claimed was one that arose frequently in fact, whether a judge could torture a detainee of ill fame and low condition if there was no evidence against the suspect at all, except for a public outcry, originating after the detainee had been arrested, that he was guilty of some earlier, unsolved crime. Gandinus thought that such a suspect ought to be tortured, even though it was against the law, and even though it was unclear who might have committed the crime in question. After a bow to the ubiquitous argument from public interest, Gandinus made an argument that the use of torture was useful as social theater. The judge should make himself appear terrifying to a person of ill repute and should torture this kind of defendant *maxime*, so that the unfortunate detainee could serve as an example to others in order to deter the commission of crimes.[68] So concerned had Gandinus become about controlling crime by making examples of socially marginal defendants that the jurist employed an investigative device, which everyone knew to be a *res fragilis* that produced fear and false confessions, in place of the penal sanctions that could not legally be used in the absence of positive proof that the defendant was guilty. Gandinus was aware of the traditional "due process" guarantees, and he cannot have been unmindful of a thirteenth-century Florentine statute barring torture in the absence of "violent presumptions" against the defendant,[69] but he sidestepped any assertion that the law prohibited torture in the hypothetical case by invoking a principle of estoppel: a person of ill repute who lives outside the law does injury to the state in which he lives and cannot be heard to invoke the protection of the laws of that state.[70] In

68. Albertus Gandinus, *Tractatus de maleficiis*, rubr. "A quo vel a quibus possit fama incipere et ex quo tempore," c. 5: "Et propterea adversus eum tamquam famosum et denotatum iudex cause criminis debet se terribilem prebere. . . . Et ideo videtur, quod iudex, animadvertendo in eundem ut iniuriosum et male meritum, possit, ut terribilem se ostendens, de dicto crimine inquirere per tormenta et maxime, ut publice aliis ad terrenda maleficia sit exemplum. . . . Sed licet incertum sit, quis illud maleficium commiserit, tamen, cum de ipso detento et captum malum exemplum habeatur, dum se sua sponte constituit et se fecit hominem male fame, videtur, quod iudex ex officio suo et de bono regimine possit de crimine occulto ad questiones procedere contra illum."

69. See, for example, *Statuti Bolognesi*, book 4, rubr. 17, "De tondolo et tormento": "Ordinamus quod nullus possit . . . tormentari . . . nisi in casibus infrascriptis. . . . Et in quolibet predictorum casuum cum violente presumptiones invente fuerint."

70. Gandinus, *Tractatus de maleficiis*, rubr. "A quo vel a quibus possit fama incipere et ex quo tempore," c. 5: "Ergo ut denotatus et male meritus hic, de quo queritur, non

the absence of a theory of inviolable individual rights, and in an age when public authorities perceived themselves as being seriously threatened by criminal behavior, it was difficult for even the most scrupulous jurist to make a convincing argument that the policies favoring procedural fairness should outweigh the policies that favored zealous prosecution in pursuit of deterrence. Moreover, it seems not to have dawned upon Gandinus or his contemporaries that cultivating fear of the law might undercut, rather than reinforce, the legitimacy of social norms. Even Bartolus of Saxoferrato, who would have classified Gandinus as one of those "stupid judges who force a defendant to confess [by torture] as soon as they have bits of evidence against him," nevertheless found himself constrained by the requirements of judicial office to put suspects to the question before exonerating them, "so that at syndication it might not be said, 'You should have tortured him.'"[71] Durandus of St. Pourçain spoke for the majority of the populace when he wrote: "It is possible that for some time men will do good only under terror of punishment. . . . Some are not born to obey reverently, but out of terror, not to shun evil out of shame, but on account of penalties. . . . Now it is expedient for the state that bad men should live in want, so that through the example of their penalties others may be restrained from evil. . . . It is natural that the delinquent should be punished, and this conclusion rests upon a natural principle. Or one might say that the *ius gentium* says this is good, the *ius civile* says it is expedient."[72]

The expediency of criminal deterrence was the unifying idea the jurists used to explain the development of the Roman-canon criminal law during the High Middle Ages. The reformed papacy's campaign against simony and clerical concubinage, and later against heresy and usury, lies at the heart of the development, and the search for deterrence in these areas explains in large part the emergence of inquisitorial procedures and the new law of proof in the twelfth and thirteenth centuries. The adoption of *inquisitio* in place of *accusatio*, the emergence of police functions, the development of a theory of circumstantial evidence, and the widespread use of torture all followed from the conviction that crime *had* to be deterred by public authority, and that the only effective deterrent was efficient prosecution and punishment. The decretalists and civilians all shared the conviction that public interest demanded that criminals be punished, but the more thoughtful lawyers, especially the best of the jurists, such as Bartolus, felt that ecclesiastical and secular authorities, in their pursuit of the expedient, deterrence, exceeded the bounds of reason and of the law.

---

poterit ipsius civitatis . . . contra cuius mores commisit, pro se aliquod auxilium invocare, quia frustra iuris civitatis implorat auxilium, qui contra illud commisit."
71. Bartolus, *Commentaria*, at Dig. 48.18.20, s.v. "Qui sine."
72. Durandus de St. Pourçain, *Tractatus de legibus* (Paris, 1506), fol. 15–15v.

Richard M. Fraher

Conclusion

The history of the Roman-canon law of crime reflects two interrelated processes unfolding from about 1050 to 1350. The decisive first step was the commitment of public authorities to the detection and prevention of crime. During the eleventh century the Gregorian reformers resolved to eradicate certain forms of deviant behavior. From the eleventh century through the fourteenth there was a continuous elaboration of new substantive law accompanied by experiments with new institutions and procedures whose purpose was to catch and punish malefactors.

The second process, intimately intertwined with the first after 1200, was the articulation of a nascent criminal jurisprudence. First the scholastic jurists, particularly the canonists, ransacked the *Corpus iuris civilis* and the canonical sources for a legal vocabulary that lent legitimacy and theoretical consistency to the new policy aimed at eradicating crime. The Roman law terms that assumed a new lease on life were public interest and deterrence. Neither of these ideas occupied a conscious part of the ecclesiastical reformers' intellectual universe in 1050. But after Innocent III's pontificate, popes, decretalists, civilian jurists, and communal legislators alike justified innovations in criminal law and procedure by pointing to the public interest in punishing and hence deterring crime.

The law schools did more than present the champions of the new criminal law with a concisely articulated ideology. Most eminent scholastic jurists routinely held official functions in the administration of justice. Gandinus and Bartolus were communal judges. After serving as a papal *auditor generalis*, William Durandus as bishop of Mende held ordinary jurisdiction in his own diocese. Henricus de Segusia was archdeacon of Paris, bishop of Sisteron, and archbishop of Embrun before becoming cardinal-bishop of Ostia, whence he acquired the name Hostiensis. Sinibaldus Fieschi learned Roman law from Accursius and canon law from Johannes Teutonicus before assuming the papal tiara as Innocent IV in 1243. Public policy largely dictated the pattern of substantive and procedural development, even as expounded in the scholarly literature of the schools. The jurists, with an eye to the "war on crime" being waged outside the lecture halls, pursued prosecutorial efficiency even at the expense of legal definitions and distinctions that once had been regarded as fundamental. As we have seen, the criminal process itself, rather than the penal sanctions that followed conviction, came to be cast in the role of a deterrent. Once the jurists decided to attribute to the investigatory stage of the *inquisitio* the deterrent functions traditionally reserved to penal law, the carefully crafted "due process" doctrines of the patristic age no longer protected a defendant's life or limbs. Traditional notions of fairness were sacrificed so that inquisitorial courts could more efficiently produce examples of the lesson that crime would be repaid with asperity.

[232]

The medieval lawyers' search for deterrence suggests at least one general lesson for contemporary scholarship in legal history. Given the dialectical mind-set of the medieval law school curriculum, it is clear that the scholastic lawyers did in fact pursue a higher rationality in legal development, in contrast to what Paul Hyams has found for the early Middle Ages. But unblemished consistency and logical symmetry were not the jurists' sole, or even their primary, concern. Even the most scrupulous, theoretically conservative of the thirteenth-century decretalists, Innocent IV, displayed a pragmatic concern with manipulating legal doctrines and institutions to produce an efficient, effective criminal process. The lesson for legal historians seems to be that even in an age when lawyers are consciously committed to principled arguments and formal consistency as the tools of legal development, the real motor of legal change lies not in logic, but in experience, in the social vision and practical aspirations of the people who have power to change the law.

# [13]

## "More Easily and More Securely": Legal Procedure and Due Process at the Council of Constance

### Thomas E. Morrissey

In the decree *Haec sancta* (6 April 1415) the Council of Constance defined itself, asserted its authority, and grounded the legitimacy of its actions in the ends toward which it strove—namely, union and reform. In stating these goals, the council said that it would attain them, *"facilius, securius, liberius et uberius"* ("more easily, more securely, more freely and more fruitfully").[1] As I have shown elsewhere, Cardinal Zabarella, a very careful lawyer, had a hand in framing this decree,[2] and there were other good lawyers at Constance, such as Peter Ancharano and Cardinal Fillastre. It is unlikely, therefore, that these words were added without serious consideration and purpose. The intent of this chapter is to show the importance of this phrase and explain its meaning, by looking at the way the council resolved the crucial question of how to deal with the three papal claimants and secure the election of a new pope.

We can understand the import of the words by referring to contempo-

Part of this paper was presented at the Conference on Conciliarism and Conciliarity in the Late Middle Ages: Perspectives East and West, sponsored by the Center for Medieval Studies at Fordham University, Bronx, New York, in March 1983.

1. *Acta* of the Council of Constance are for the most part to be found in three standard sources: Heinrich Finke et al., *Acta concilii Constanciensis*, 4 vols. (Münster, 1896–1928); Hermann von der Hardt, ed., *Magnum oecumenicum Constantiense concilium*, 6 vols. (Frankfurt and Leipzig, 1696–1700), and vol. 7, *Index* (1742); Mansi, vols. 26, 27, 28. These works will henceforth be cited as: Finke, *Acta Constanciensis*; von der Hardt; Mansi. In this instance the text is found in Mansi, 27:585–86.

2. On Zabarella's relation to this decree see my "The Decree 'Haec Sancta' and Cardinal Zabarella: His Role in Its Formulation and Interpretation," *Annuarium historiae conciliorum* 10 (1978): 145–76; Brian Tierney, *Foundations of the Conciliar Theory* (Cambridge, 1955), c. iv: "Franciscus Zabarella," pp. 220–37. On the decree see also: A. J. Black, "Council and Pope: The Modern Relevance of Conciliarism," *New Blackfriars* 56 (1975): 82–88.

rary events in England, Germany, France, and Italy, of which the council fathers were well aware. In England, as Peter McNiven has shown, there was at that time a crisis of authority caused by the deposition of Richard II in 1399.[3] Henry IV's right to the throne was questioned on numerous occasions, and he faced many rebellions.[4] McNiven showed that increasingly Henry's claims to legitimacy came to depend on parliamentary consent but that these claims were not yet fully accepted when Henry V succeeded to the throne.[5]

In Germany, one year after Richard was deposed, some of the prince-electors became exasperated with Emperor Wenceslaus and declared him deposed. In his place they elected Ruprecht of the Rhine Palatinate, one of their own members.[6] These actions led to a period of political uncertainty because Wenceslaus did not accept the action, and when Ruprecht died in 1410, he renewed his claims to the imperial throne. There followed a brief period during which there were three imperial claimants, until Sigismund of Hungary reached an agreement with Wenceslaus, and in the meantime the third claimant, their cousin Jobst of Moravia, died.[7]

In France, events took a more violent turn. In 1408, the dispute between the Orleanists and Burgundians for the control of the incapacitated king led to the assassination of Louis, duke of Orléans. When Jean Petit wrote a tract justifying the deed as tyrannicide, he caused a great argument over the legitimacy of power that rested on such acts.[8] Ultimately this quarrel came before the Council of Constance.

Finally, the Venetians' conquest of Padua in 1404–5, and their execution of many members of the Carrara clan, the leading Paduan family,[9]

3. Peter McNiven, "Legitimacy and Consent: Henry IV and the Lancastrian Title, 1399–1406," *Mediaeval Studies* 44 (1982): 470–88.

4. Ibid., p. 482.

5. Ibid., pp. 487–88. Christopher Brooke, *The Structure of Medieval Society* (New York, 1971), p. 67, phrased well the mishmash of justifications that were used: "When Henry usurped the throne in 1399, it was given out that Richard had voluntarily resigned the throne and designated Henry as his successor, that he had proved unsatisfactory as king and had to be removed, that Henry had been elected by the magnates of the realm, and that he was in any case king by hereditary right."

6. Louis Salembier, *The Great Schism of the West*, trans. M. D. (London, 1907), p. 179.

7. Ibid., pp. 269–70.

8. Among the many writings on this topic one should consult: Leon Mirot, "L'assassinat de Louis duc d'Orléans et la théorie du tyrannicide au xve siècle," *Revue des études historiques* 100 (1933): 139–50; Bernhard Bess, *Frankreichs Kirchenpolitik und der Prozess des Jean Petit über die Lehre von Tyrannenmord bis zur Reise Sigismunds* (Marburg, 1891); and Alfred Coville, *La question du tyrannicide au commencement du xve siècle* (Paris, 1932); Amnon Lindner, "The Knowledge of John of Salisbury in the Later Middle Ages," *Studi medievali* (Centro Italiano di Studi sull'Alto Medioevo), 3d ser. 18 (1977): 315–66, esp. pp. 349–52, for the course of events in the Petit case, and Howard Kaminsky, *Simon de Cramaud and the Great Schism* (New Brunswick, N.J., 1983), for the political context, esp. pp. 288–90.

9. Ernst Bernheim, "Ein Episode aus der venezianischen Geschichte (Der Sturz des Hauses Carrara)," *Zeitschrift für allgemeine Geschichte: Kultur- Literatur- und Kunstgeschichte* 4 (1887): 103–23, at pp. 120, 122.

raised questions about the legitimacy of Venetian rule. Could legitimate authority rest upon conquest and violence?

The council fathers at Constance had these secular events and issues in mind, but they also could reflect on recent ecclesiastical history. In 1409 the colleges of cardinals of the two obediences had given up their respective papal claimants to join in the Council of Pisa, which they hoped would elect a new, universally recognized pope and reform the church.[10] At Pisa the cardinals declared both the Roman line's Gregory XII and his Avignon rival, Benedict XIII, deposed and proceeded to elect Alexander V.[11] This did not end the schism, however, and so another general council was called at Constance to achieve union and reform.

An examination of the work of the Council of Constance shows that participants were conversant with the issues raised by contemporary events and were aware of the consequences should they fail to take careful, precise steps to attain their goals. It is in this awareness that the meaning of the words of *Haec sancta* is to be found. Cardinal Zabarella was one of the principal vehicles through which these events affected the council fathers.[12] He had been asked to give a verdict on the legitimacy of the imperial deposition in 1400.[13] As a citizen of Padua—where he taught

10. The events leading up to this and the Council of Pisa are briefly described by Salembier, *Great Schism*, pp. 224–64. On Pisa see also Johannes Vincke, *Schriftstücke zum Pisaner Konzil: Ein Kampf um die öffentliche Meinung* (Bonn, 1942); R. N. Swanson, *Universities, Academics and the Great Schism*, Cambridge Studies in Medieval Life and Thought, 3d ser., 12, (Cambridge, 1979).

11. The Council of Pisa declared that Gregory XII and Benedict XIII were "notorious schismatics, . . . notorious heretics" (*notorios schismaticos . . . notorios haereticos*) and had "deviated from the faith" (*a fide devios*), and so neither was pope any longer. The condemnation at Pisa is found in von der Hardt, 2:136–39, and in Mansi, 26:1226ff. Thus Pisa took a conservative view and used the most restrictive grounds for action against a pope, that is, heresy, see Walter Ullmann, *The Origins of the Great Schism* (London, 1948), p. 189. Constance removed John XXIII on the charges of notorious crime, that is, heresy in the widest sense. At Pisa they were aware that they were choosing this narrower interpretation; Otto Gunther, "Zur Vorgeschichte des Konzils von Pisa (Unbekannte Schriftstücke aus einer Danziger Handschrift)," *Neues Archiv* 41 (1917–19): 633–76, at p. 663. Cardinal Bertrand, a defender of papal rights, said bluntly: "Against a bad pope, not a heretic, the remedy is that the faithful pray for him, and that the cardinals convoke a general council if the pope refuses to do this" (in Joseph Lecler, "Les théories democratiques au Moyen Age," *Etudes* 225 [1935]: 2–25, 168–89, at p. 172). For earlier responses on papal immunity, see Brian Tierney, "Pope and Council: Some New Decretist Texts," *Mediaeval Studies* 19 (1957): 197–218.

12. Zabarella died in part from his labors in the dispute over the method to be used in the election of the new pope, a dispute which went on through most of 1417. His declining health is documented by many references to his absence from sessions at the council because of illness; see Finke, *Acta Constantiensis*, 2:3–21, 45–72, 95. For Zabarella's involvement in the disputes, see my "Emperor-Elect Sigismund, Cardinal Zabarella and the Council of Constance," *Catholic Historical Review* 79 (1983): 353–70.

13. Heinrich Finke drew attention to this legal brief of Zabarella, "Ein Gutachten Zabarellas über die Absetzung des römischen Königs Wenzel," *Mitteilungen des Instituts für österreichischen Geschichtsforschung* 11 (1890): 631–33; the text of Zabarella's opinion is included in his *Concilia* (Milan, 1515), fol. 76v.

law—he experienced the events of 1404–5. The Venetians specifically asked him to participate in the formal surrender of the city.[14] Meanwhile, he had gone to Paris in search of support for Padua, and there he became familiar with the problems and debates in France. He gave two addresses on the issues during this mission to the royal court.[15] Finally, Zabarella's tract *De scismate* finished in the crucial year of 1408, provided the legal justification for the summoning of the Council of Pisa,[16] and he was then the chief negotiator with King Sigismund for the convocation of the Council of Constance.[17] It is no surprise that he was a major spokesman at the council in its early months[18] and remained prominent in the council affairs.[19]

14. Zabarella's formal speech of surrender of the city in which he was acting on behalf of the university exists in a number of manuscripts. The text is unusual for him in that it exists in both an Italian and a Latin version. It is the only work of Zabarella that I have seen in Italian, and it is unclear whether the original was in Italian and he later provided a Latin version or vice versa. The text can be found in Milan, Biblioteca Ambrosiana, Lat. cod. D 462 inf., fols. 202r–8v (Latin); Padua, Biblioteca Universitaria, cod. 2231, fols. 77–83 (Italian); Padua, Museo Civico Biblioteca, BP 1013:xix (Italian); BP 133:xvi (= MS 117) (Latin); BP 5 (= 1418), fols. 1–20 (Latin); BP 802:xvii, fols. 199–222 (Italian). The decision on who was to partake in the ceremony and who was to form the embassy that would represent the city on that day was made at a meeting on 31 December 1405. All classes and groups were to be included among the sixteen delegates. Zabarella's friend and humanist Ognibene della Scola was chosen to represent the civil jurists, and one of the official witnesses was the Greek scholar Emmanuel Chrysoloras, who would work with Zabarella for the Council of Constance; see Andrea Gloria, ed., *Monumenti della Universita di Padova (1318–1405)*, 2 vols. (Padua, 1888), 1:57–58; *I libri commemoriali*, pp. 312–13, documents 13–14.

15. The two addresses Zabarella gave at this time have been edited by Gaspare Zonta, *Francesco Zabarella (1360–1417)* (Padua, 1915), App., pp. 144–49.

16. Vincke, *Schriftstücke zum Pisaner Konzil*, p. 136, where the council explicitly cited Zabarella's tract in its own defense, "Idem tenet Franciscus de Zabarellis in suo consilio seu tractatu de modo uniendi ecclesiam." Zabarella had written the *De scismate* originally as *Consilia* in three parts between 1403 and 1408 and had finally issued it as a complete work in that same year.

17. In November 1413 Zabarella acted as a delegate for Sigismund to receive the oath of obedience from Filippo Maria Visconti of Milan; see Peter Partner, *The Papal State under Martin V* (London, 1958), p. 27; also Finke, *Acta Constantiensis*, 1:246. Zabarella left the papal curia in October 1413 to meet with Sigismund to settle the time and place for the new council. In November they met at Lodi and decided on Constance; von der Hardt, 1, 9:540, "Nam fuit inprimis auctor huius loci statuendi." In the early spring of 1414 Zabarella was once again sent by John XXIII to negotiate with Sigismund for an alliance against Ladislaus of Naples, who was causing trouble and anxiety by his military advance into central Italy; see Finke, *Acta Constanciensis*, 1:251–55.

18. On numerous occasions Zabarella was the official spokesman for the council in the reception and integration of members of the Avignonese obedience into the council; see my "The Call for Unity at the Council of Constance: Sermons and Addresses of Cardinal Zabarella (1415–1417)," *Church History* 53 (1984): 307–18.

19. Both Pier Paolo Vergerio and Poggio Bracciolini claimed that Zabarella was the chief influence in making John XXIII stand by his commitment to hold the council at Constance and to appear there in person; see Carlo A. Combi and Luciano Tomaso, eds., *Epistole di Pietro Paolo Vergerio Seniore*, Monumenta storici pubblicati dalla R. Deputazione Veneta di storia Patria, ser. 4, Miscellanea 5 (Venice, 1887), letter 122, p. 186; von der Hardt, 1, 9:540.

Thomas E. Morrissey

The council wrote *Haec sancta* under the influence of Zabarella, and in those words of the decree, it was stating that it would proceed according to strict legal requirements, so that no one could attack the legitimacy of its actions. Only if it achieved this end would the council resolve the schism and bring about reform easily, securely, freely, and fruitfully.

In spite of disputes and the attempts of some to lead the council fathers to precipitous or high-handed actions, the council did follow a moderate, careful path. Having stated that it would act legitimately, it consistently observed legal procedure and due process. At the beginning, the council fathers rejected a maneuver by John XXIII's faction to declare Constance a continuation of Pisa, so that the condemnations of Popes Gregory and Benedict would merely be confirmed there.[20] The council fathers realized that such action would have closed off hope of any cooperation from the Roman or Avignon obediences. Therefore they adopted a more moderate yet firm position which rejected the Roman and Avignon papal claims but left the door open to accommodation and compromise.

Repeatedly they put pressure on John XXIII to resign, countering his subterfuges with a consistent stance. When he broke faith with them and fled the city on 20–21 March 1415, they were compelled to act in defense of the integrity of the council. Yet even here in the decree *Haec sancta*, the wiser and calmer voices among the council members warned their brethren to avoid precipitous action which could be misconstrued and might become the basis for a challenge to their decree. Only two days after John's escape, Zabarella warned that this pope had not definitively broken his commitment to resign or to work for reform. No one, he said, should assume this until it was proved.[21] The council kept up negotiations with John until he finally did resign, accepting the council's decree of deposi-

20. Albert Lenne, "Der erste literarische Kampf auf dem Konzil im November und Dezember 1414," *Römische Quartalschrift* 28 (1914): 3–40, 61–86, at pp. 19ff.; Julius Hollerbach, "Die gregorianische Partei, Sigismund und das Konstanzer Konzil," *Römische Quartalschrift* 23 (1909): 127–65, 24 (1910): 3–39, 121–40, esp. vol. 24 (1910): 8. See also Heinrich Finke, *Forschungen und Quellen zur Geschichte des Konstanzer Konzils* (Paderborn, 1889), p. 250, and idem, *Acta Constantiensis*, 2:197. One of the points was that the Council of Pisa had not been closed but only suspended by Alexander V in 1409; see von der Hardt, 4:23–24, Mansi, 27:581. Zabarella had proposed that the council consider the matter of Gregory's and Benedict's claims as closed so as not to leave any illusions with them or their supporters that their position had not been irreversibly changed (Finke, *Acta Constanciensis*, 2:197, and Lenne, "Erste literarische Kampf," p. 29), but he also hoped to obtain cooperation from them in the form of cession (Zonta, *Francesco Zabarella*, pp. 80–81). Thus the council acted very prudently; while maintaining a firm stance on the legal status of Gregory, it was most amenable in what it would do in the way of accommodation on the de facto level, for example, its reception and honors accorded his envoys, and so the council obtained in the end its desired goal, the removal of Gregory. Not all at the council had been willing to be so flexible.

21. Von der Hardt, 4, 3:101, "Et usque huc ipsis non fuit visum juxta ejus scripta et dicta, quod declinaret in contrariam (malam) viam."

tion.[22] He was ultimately released from captivity and allowed to spend his last years in a position of honor.

With Gregory XII the council followed a similar policy. In the opinion of the council fathers he had already been condemned and deposed at Pisa,[23] but if it was expedient and useful to treat him as if he were pope in order to obtain his cooperation, the majority of them were prepared to do so.[24] They received his delegate, Giovanni Dominici, whom they treated with all the honor due a cardinal.[25] They allowed Dominici to act as though Gregory were the legitimate pope and his meager following represented the whole church. Soon a second representative of Gregory arrived, Charles of Malatesta, who was allowed to make a solemn entrance into the city. After some negotiations, Malatesta and Dominici were permitted to go through the motions of a formal convocation of the council in Gregory's name which led to the integration of Gregory's obedience into the council. Finally, Malatesta proclaimed Gregory's resignation, and the

22. Zabarella with Cardinal Fillastre spent late April of 1415 on an embassy to John XXIII after he had fled from Constance; Finke, *Acta Constanciensis*, 2:29–33. Only when he had been taken prisoner did the reality of his situation begin to intrude on John's consciousness, but even then he attempted to avoid the inevitable disposition of his case. He tried to appoint Fillastre, Zabarella, and d'Ailly as his proctors without consulting them, but not surprisingly they refused this task (von der Hardt, 4, 3:282). Fillastre expressed their attitude well: "It is difficult to take up a defense against the whole world" (von der Hardt, 4:167). Before acting against John the council sent a commission that included Zabarella to get John's acceptance of the verdict of the council which was pronounced on 29 May 1415 (von der Hardt, 4:28–29, Finke, *Acta Constanciensis*, 2:39–40). The cardinals got John to acquiesce (ibid., 2:247–48), but also the articles of condemnation were toned down so as not to weaken the papal office in the decree against the person of John (ibid., 2:245–46). In the judicial process Zabarella on several occasions acted to give full benefit of the law to John and to protect him against mere accusation and unfounded report. Not all the statements were to be taken as evidence; some were mere hearsay (ibid., 3:20, 158, 167–68, 171, 183, 191, 193). John may have been guilty of simony before he was pope, but there was not convincing evidence that he had employed simony to obtain the papacy (ibid., 4:817–20). John was not to be charged with the crime of heresy, since he was not deviant in faith in the strict sense (Konradin Zähringer, *Das Kardinalkollegium auf dem Konstanzer Konzil bis zur Absetzung Papst Johanns XXIII.* [Münster, 1935], p. 133). On 31 May 1415 John accepted the decision of the council, and so this precluded any later claims that it was a forced abdication (von der Hardt, 4:291).

23. Many in the Italian nation at the start of the council had thought this way and saw the decisions as merely aimed at the other claimants, Gregory and Benedict (Salembier, *Great Schism*, p. 286).

24. There were protests when Giovanni Dominici posted on the doors of the Augustinian house where he resided the coat of arms of Gregory XII, whom he was representing as envoy (see Mansi, 27:540). Karl A. Fink has shown the care with which the official documents referred to the various claimants in his "Sic in sua obedientia Nuncupatus," *Quellen und Forschungen aus italienischen Archiven und Bibliotheken* 60 (1980): 189–199.

25. There was controversy on the reception accorded Giovanni Dominici; see Lenne, "Erste literarische Kampf," p. 20. Zabarella and d'Ailly agreed that Pisa was merely a step on the road to union and reform and was not to be seen as a stopping point or allowed to become a stumbling block (Zähringer, *Kardinalkollegium*, p. 62).

council accepted it immediately. Gregory too was accorded a position of honor for the rest of his days.[26] Thus two-thirds of their initial task—the elimination of schism—had been achieved, mostly by peaceful means.[27]

With the third papal claimant, Benedict XIII, the council showed equal forbearance. A mission headed by King Sigismund went to negotiate with him and his followers.[28] Since he proved totally recalcitrant, one by one most of his supporters were persuaded to abandon his cause. Over a period of months they or their delegates came to Constance, where they were ceremoniously received and integrated into the council.[29] At the same time, the legal process of judgment was pursued until 26 July 1417, when the council condemned Benedict for heresy and schism and, since he refused to resign, deposed him.[30] Once again the council had taken all reasonable precautions in this affair. Defectors from Benedict's obedience, such as the Count of Foix, were treated with respect similar to that shown to those of Gregory XII's obedience.[31] Whereas in 1409 the Council of Pisa

26. The council acceded to Gregory's condition that Sigismund preside at the council, since Gregory had refused to acknowledge any council at which John XXIII presided. John's absence removed this obstacle, and so the abdication through Gregory's proxies took place on 4 July 1415 (von der Hardt, 4, 3:177–78, 192–93); see also Jacques Lenfant, *Histoire du concile de Pise*, 2 vols. (Amsterdam, 1724), 1, 3:381, and Finke, *Acta Constanciensis*, 2:45–47.

27. There had been fighting between the forces of King Sigismund and those of Frederick of Austria, who functioned briefly as John's protector, but Louis of Bavaria succeeded in winning Frederick over to submission to Sigismund (Finke, *Acta Constanciensis*, 2:34).

28. The timing and the political context of this mission were very complex, as has been shown by Bernhard Bess, "Die Verhandlung zu Perpignan und die Schlacht bei Agincourt (1415)," *Historisches Jahrbuch* 22 (1901): 688–709; Heinrich Finke, "Zur spanischen Kirchengeschichte der Jahren 1414–1415," *Römische Quartalschrift* 7 (1893): 165–79; W. Prinzhorn, "Die Verhandlungen Sigismunds mit Benedickt XIII. und seiner Obödienz in Perpignan. Aug.–Dez. 1415." (diss., Freiburg, 1925 [Maschinenschrift]); Herbert Immenkötter, "Ein avignonesischer Bericht zur Unionspolitik Benedikt XIII.," *Annuarium historiae conciliorum* 8 (1976): 200–49.

29. The agreement to abandon Benedict had been reached at Narbonne on 13 December 1415 (Finke, *Acta Constanciensis*, 2:55–56, 3:480–81). Aragon was delayed because of the transition after the death of its king and the accession of its new king who, however, continued the policies of his father; see von der Hardt, 2, 18:540. On 15 June 1416 the delegation from Portugal came to Constance (Finke, *Acta Constantiensis*, 2:301–3). On 10 September 1416 the ambassador of the king of Aragon was accredited at the council (von der Hardt, 4, 9:856–59). On 15 October 1416 these two groups came together to form the Spanish nation at the council; see Bernhard Fromme, *Die spanische Nation und das Konstanzer Konzil* (Münster, 1896), pp. 46ff. In December 1416 the count of Foix was accepted (von der Hardt, 4, 9:1012).

30. On 28 November 1416 Zabarella presented a summary of the commission's report on Benedict (Finke, *Acta Constantiensis*, 2:80). Benedict was formally presented with the legal citation at Peniscola on 21 January 1417 (ibid., 3:400) and was finally removed as "a supporter of the schism . . . notorious and suspected of heresy" (von der Hardt, 4, 9:981). Benedict was condemned on 26 July 1417 as incorrigible, a notorious heretic and a schismatic (ibid., pp. 1128, 1314); see also Margaret Harvey, "Papal Witchcraft: The Charges against Benedict XIII," *Studies in Church History* 10 (1973): 109–16.

31. Von der Hardt, 4:997.

had merely declared Gregory and Benedict deposed, in accord with one school of canonistic thought as schismatics and fomenters of schism who were automatically self-deposed,[32] the fathers at Constance went further. They made clear the link between schism and heresy. Benedict was formally judged and condemned for heresy on the evidence of his actions in continuing the schism.[33] In this act of condemnation and deposition, the council fathers at Constance showed that they agreed with the views of the other major school of canonistic thought, of which Zabarella was a leader.[34] In either case, Benedict could be deposed because according to both theories he had lost his office and his right to it.[35] The council could then move on to the election of a new pope acceptable to all.

This next step was not readily achieved, for legal problems arose again, threatening apparently irreconcilable conflicts. Controversy flared up in the early summer of 1415 in the form of anger and resentment against John XXIII's flight. Some council fathers, since they could do little directly to John XXIII, turned their anger against those associated with him, especially the cardinals who had made up his curia. Some spoke against the right of these cardinals to take part in the activities of the council along with the other members.[36] The most extreme voices even said that the pope should not be allowed to have any voice in the activities of the council, but fortunately John Maurotius, the Latin patriarch of Antioch and no friend of John, effectively countered such arguments by his statement that the pope could not legally be excluded from conciliar affairs.[37]

Twice that summer the council issued declarations on the election of a new pope, in which there are some intriguing textual differences. On 29 May 1415, at the Twelfth General Session, the council decreed that "they [the cardinals] should not proceed [in the election] without the deliberation and consent of this holy general council."[38] In the foreword to this declaration the decree *Haec sancta* was quoted, including in particular the desire to attain unity and reform "more easily, more swiftly,

---

32. The views of this school which stressed papal immunity are presented in studies such as A. M. Königer, "Prima sedes a nemine iudicatur," in *Festgabe A. Ehrhard. Beitraege zur Geschichte des christlichen Altertums und der byzantinischen Literatur* (Bonn and Leipzig, 1922), pp. 273–300; James L. Moynihan, *Papal Immunity and Liability in the Writings of the Medieval Canonists*, Analecta Gregoriana 120 (Rome, 1961), pp. 46ff; Brian Tierney, "Pope and Council," 197–218.

33. The distinction between the actions of the two councils has been pointed out by Arnulf Vagedes, *Das Konzil über dem Papst? Die Stellungnahme des Nikolaus von Kues und des Panormitanus zum Streit zwischen dem Konzil von Basel und Eugen IV.*, 2 vols. (Paderborn, 1981), 1:246–47 and n. 88, 2:280.

34. Vagedes, 2:280 n. 88 refers to Zabarella, Cesarini, Tudeschis, and other adherents of this theory.

35. Von der Hardt, 4:1128.

36. Von der Hardt, 2, 13:285–88.

37. Von der Hardt, 2, 13:295–98 291–92 (*sic*; mistaken pagination).

38. Von der Hardt, 4:28, "Nullo modo procedatur sine deliberatione et consensu huius sacri generalis concilii."

more freely, and more usefully."[39] Then on 4 July 1415 at the Fourteenth General Session the council issued several decrees asserting more strongly its claim to control a papal election. Nothing was to be done without its deliberation and consent (a repetition of the 29 May text); any action to the contrary was null and void (*irritum et inane*); all positive laws, decrees of councils, customs, orders, privileges, and so forth, in this matter were to be suspended; and the method, form, and place of the election were to be chosen by the council. An additional provision specified that in the election of the new pope, none of the three claimants was to be reelected.[40] The language found in the body of these two decrees clearly echoes the text of *Haec sancta*. The first decree speaks of attaining union "more easily, more freely, and more usefully" (*facilius, liberius et utilius*), while the second refers to doing this "better, more sincerely, and more securely" (*melius, sincerius et securius*). Thus the two decrees of 4 July 1415 split "more easily" (*facilius*) and "more securely" (*securius*). Although the earlier decree from 29 May had added the phrase "more quickly" (*celerius*),[41] in reality these decrees would have the effect of delaying the papal election for almost two and a half years, creating a situation in which the election of a new pope could not be achieved more easily, more securely, or more quickly. They implied that only the council's voice would be decisive in the election. One faction at the council justified the exclusion of the cardinals with the claim that there were no valid cardinals then in existence.[42] These decrees were an extreme assertion of conciliar authority in a form which ignored all other rights and traditions. Fortunately for the church and for the Council of Constance, the cardinals responded not just adversarially but rather with an approach to the problem which manifested restraint, moderation, and concern for due process that ultimately led to a resolution of the conflict.

The council had staked its claim to share in the election of a new pope. Did this mean that the legitimate rights of the cardinals in a papal election were to be ignored or violated?[43] What response could the cardinals make? What claims to legitimate right could they invoke? They did not let the initial assertion of the council go unchallenged but rather initiated numerous arguments, charges, and rebuttals,[44] and they rejected the attempt to exclude them from taking part in the business of the council.[45] Cardi-

---

39. Von der Hardt, 4:282–85, "Facilius, celerius, liberius et utilius."
40. Von der Hardt, 4:375.
41. Von der Hardt, 4:282–85, 375.
42. Finke, *Acta Constanciensis*, 4:78–80.
43. Pope Nicholas II in 1059 had issued the decree which first specified the rights of the cardinals in papal elections, and this decree was taken over into canon law (Friedberg, *CIC*, 1:77–79, D. XXIII, c. 1) and so was well known by all; see on the decree Brian Tierney, *The Crisis of Church and State, 1050–1300* (Englewood Cliffs, N.J., 1964), pp. 33ff.
44. Von der Hardt, 2, 20:584ff.
45. Von der Hardt, 2, 13:287–96.

nal d'Ailly, in a tract on the method and form for the election of the new pope, put the cardinals' case succinctly: "To them [the cardinals] the right of electing [the pope] belongs by legal right" (*ad quos de iure pertinet ius eligendi*).[46] Thus d'Ailly, who was himself not a canonist but a philosopher-theologian, defended the cardinals' prerogative not as a matter of mere historical accident but as one of legal rectitude and so reinforced and repeated the position of canonists such as Zabarella.[47]

In this fashion the two positions had taken shape, and the question of how they were to be reconciled simmered for months. This problem was complicated by the further issue of whether the election of the pope should take priority over reform in the church or whether a new pontiff, if and when he was ever elected, should be presented with a series of reforms already in place as a fait accompli. This dispute was linked in addition with the ambivalent feelings of some council fathers, especially some among the cardinals, toward Emperor-Elect Sigismund's motives and the role he proposed to take in the council. Was it merely coincidental that in those critical days of early July 1415, when the council was advancing its claims to decide the papal election process, Sigismund sat in the center of the council fathers and presided over them?[48] Was it surprising then that the council appealed to him,[49] or that one of the cardinals protested all these developments?[50] The council had turned to Sigismund to obtain his aid as defender and protector of the church.[51] This was precisely the same basis on which Zabarella had earlier sought the emperor's cooperation in having the council assemble, because in his capacity as protector and defender of the church an emperor had an obligation and a right to act in an emergency.[52] As time passed, with no progress toward a settlement of the issue of a papal election, there was enormous pressure on the cardinals to accept the decrees of the council concerning the election of the pope or else face the possible loss of their status.[53] But the cardinals held firm

46. Von der Hardt, 2, 20:586–87.

47. Long before he was ever named a cardinal, as a canonist Zabarella had written in his commentaries: "Papam enim eligunt cardinales" *Comm. ad X*, 1.6. "Rubrica," fol. 112rb (Venice, 1502); in his *De scismate*, fol. 118vb (in the Venice 1502 edition included as an appendix to his commentary on 1.6.6) Zabarella had further specified: "Ubi considerandum quod in hiis que concernunt electionem pape collegium cardinalium representat universalem ecclesiam et eius vice fungitur."

48. Odilo Engels, "Der Reichsgedanke auf dem Konstanzer Konzil," *Historisches Jahrbuch* 86 (1966): 90.

49. Finke, *Acta Constanciensis*, 2:45–47.

50. Ibid., 3:266ff.

51. Mansi, 27:739.

52. See his *Comm. ad X*, 1.6.34, fol. 167ra (Venice, 1502), and his *De scismate* (an appendix to his commentary on 1.6.6), fols. 117ra–20vb in that same edition, as well as his *In Clem.*, 2.9.9, fol. 84ra (Venice, 1602). For a discussion of the difference between Zabarella's view on Sigismund's role as a facilitator and protector versus the emperor functioning as head or leader of the council, see my "Emperor-Elect Sigismund," pp. 357, 361–62, 369.

53. Finke, *Acta Constanciensis*, 2:98.

## Thomas E. Morrissey

against what they viewed as the undue influence of Sigismund and his desire to control the election.[54] In the end the policy of patience, Sigismund's long absence from the council, and political events outside of the council shifted the balance in the cardinals' favor.[55]

By the spring of 1417 the cardinals had acquired a new ally and had a new angle from which their assertion of the rights of the college of cardinals could be focused and exploited. In early April 1417 the delegates of the kingdom of Castile raised the question whether freedom existed at the Council in Constance. The cardinals objected that because the council reserved the right to establish the form, matter, place, and time of the election they were not free.[56] This posed a serious problem, for if the cardinals could claim that they acted in fear, especially fear caused by undue pressure and threats, this could reduce whatever election might be held to the same status as the election of 1378, which had started the schism. The danger existed that just as it had not been possible to resolve the question of the validity of the 1378 election, a similar morass would ensue following any election held in similar circumstances in 1417.[57]

However this question might be answered, the cardinals decided to press their case aggressively in May 1417, by objecting once again to the decrees the council had issued on the papal election. They argued that they were not seeking merely to defend their own right or to protect their own interests (*non pro defensione sui iuris, vel pro suo interesse*), but by a

54. In the midst of these quarrels Cardinal Fillastre spoke in his diary of Sigismund's desire to push the electoral form toward achieving his own will, "modos faciendi papam ad voluntatem regis" (Finke, *Acta Constanciensis*, 2:118). In June 1417 when Sigismund had returned to Constance after a long absence, he was seen as demanding a virtual power over the choice of the new pope (ibid., 2:123–26).

55. Sigismund was absent from Constance from 18 July 1415 until 27 January 1417. When he returned at that time after the successful completion of the negotiations with the members of the Avignon obedience and various diplomatic dealings, for example, a treaty with England, it first appeared that he was at the height of his power and influence. He made a festal entrance into the council and was greeted in the name of the council by his chief supporter in the English nation, Robert Hallam, bishop of Salisbury. He even took his place in the seat formerly occupied by the pope (Finke, *Acta Constanciensis*, 3:387). But the alliance with England had alienated the French, the Italians were suspicious, and the Spanish nation as it took form was hesitant about the influences that were dominant in the council and seemed to limit freedom (see the note below). Two events mark the turn of the tide away from Sigismund; six months after his return, when Benedict XIII was formally declared deposed from office, the council by this time had reverted back to the customary procedure of having the session presided over by a cardinal rather than by Sigismund (ibid., 2:111), and in September 1417, only shortly before the death of Cardinal Zabarella, the bishop of Salisbury passed away (ibid., 2:144), and thus Sigismund's ability to control the English nation weakened.

56. Finke, *Acta Constanciensis*, 2:105.

57. The rumor had spread at one point that Sigismund had planned to seize some of the cardinals (or all of the cardinals, according to one rumor) and some other prelates (Finke, *Acta Constanciensis*, 2:144). The delegates from Castile in part prepared to leave Constance, and some had started to leave, but the cardinals intervened to prevent a further outbreak of schism (ibid., 2:140).

brilliant stroke they asserted that the mode of papal election that they were defending, if implemented, would achieve a perfect and undisputed union (*ad perfectam et indubitatam unionem consequendam*). Invoking the words of *Haec sancta*, they explained that this mode of papal election could achieve such a union because it was "juster, easier and more secure" (*iustior, facilior et securior*).[58] Their plan, as one of their defenders at that time pointed out, deserved these attributes because it was a legal right of the cardinals to elect the pope.[59]

Various members of the council intervened in opposition to this view. An anonymous attack by a member of the German nation was among the first.[60] One group objected that the proposal of the cardinals was contrary to the claim of the council to superiority—that is, that it was contrary to *Haec sancta*.[61] But other voices, such as that of the influential member of the French nation Simon de Cramaud, supported the cardinals' position.[62] The controversy dragged on through the summer of 1417. Two sermons, one by Poggio and the other anonymous, delivered as eulogies on the death of Cardinal Zabarella (26 September 1417), stressed the role this careful lawyer and leading canonist had played in these most turbulent days of the council. Poggio noted that in his last intervention at the council, just a few days before his death, Zabarella, then very ill, had expressed his willingness to make a strong defense of the inclusion of the cardinals in the electoral process as his last testament spoken for the sake of the unity of the church.[63] The other sermon reiterated this theme, saying that Zabarella had died in the struggle for the conservation and rebuilding of the church.[64]

It is fascinating that the proposal of the cardinals which caused such controversy was basically a very reasonable one, a compromise in the true sense of the word, which balanced the traditional rights of the cardinals and the claims of the council for a decisive voice in the election of the new pope. Their proposal ultimately derived from the tract of Cardinal d'Ailly, who had first proposed a way out of the dilemma.[65] D'Ailly had suggested, even while defending the de jure right of the cardinals to elect the new pope, delegates from each nation, in a number not to exceed the number of cardinals, should participate in the election. In this scheme, the successful candidate would need a two-thirds vote of both electoral bodies. This

58. Ibid., 2:105.
59. Ibid., 3:621, "Cardinales ad quod pertinet ius eligendi Romanum et summum pontificem," *Cedula ad Laudem* (29 May 1417), again an invocation not only of mere positive law but of basic right founded in tradition and practice accepted for centuries.
60. Ibid., 3:624ff. (29 May 1417).
61. Ibid., 3:645, between 29 May and 18 June 1417.
62. Ibid., 3:653.
63. Von der Hardt, 1, 9:544.
64. Von der Hardt, 1, 9:551.
65. D'Ailly's *De modo vel forma eligendi novum pontificem* (von der Hardt, 2, 20:586–87.

was the plan the cardinals put forward in the summer of 1417, and it was the one that Zabarella had defended.[66]

The solution was breathtaking in its simplicity and in its comprehension, for the extraordinary electoral process by which Cardinal Odo de Colonna became Martin V on 11 November 1417 satisfied all questions. The Council of Constance had claimed special rights of consultation, involvement, and control over this election which were realized through the creation of a body of electors chosen by the nations at the council. These electors were to choose a new pope by a two-thirds vote. It should be noted that a successful candidate needed a two-thirds vote from each nation.[67] But the traditional rights of the cardinals and the full letter of the law were also respected. Cardinal Colonna had to obtain a two-thirds vote from his confreres as well. The solution finally adopted which ended the schism thus embodied both the claims of *Haec sancta* on behalf of the council for the highest authority and the traditional forms favored by the cardinals. Both sides could be satisfied and agree that this method of election by a bicameral electoral college would achieve final unity more easily and more securely (*facilius et securius*). No one had grounds later to question Martin V's accession, because all such protests had been obviated by careful legal groundwork. Due process had been consistently and strictly observed throughout the whole series of events.

This observance of strictly legal procedure was followed to a greater or lesser degree in many other disputes and issues that came before the council. Although in some instances it appears that due process failed, this failure should not be seen as the result of a desire of the participants to ignore due process or to neglect or trample upon just rights. Even when in some cases extreme views prevailed, the voices of moderation, of technically correct procedure and respect for legal rights, were heard in opposition. Cases such as those of John Hus and Jerome of Prague, the dispute over Jean Petit's defense of tyrannicide and the bitter quarrel between the Teutonic Knights and the kingdom of Poland provide further opportunity to explore this theme. Extended analysis, similar to that pursued here on the question of the papal election, is needed for these cases, but a preliminary examination strongly suggests that the spirit of legal restraint and respect for law colored these proceedings as well. The discussion and debate on the method and form of the papal election at Constance has shown how necessary it is to read the proceedings and reports from Constance carefully, and it allows us to draw some conclusions about the pervasive spirit of scrupulous respect for legal procedure. The able lawyers

66. Finke, *Acta Constanciensis*, 3:621. For a discussion of Zabarella's disagreements with Sigismund during that summer of 1417, see my "Emperor-Elect Sigismund," pp. 366–70.
67. Bernhard Fromme, "Die Wahl Martins V," *Römische Quartalschrift* 10 (1896): 140.

present in Constance whose voices were heard prevented greater problems from developing precisely because they, as jurists, recognized the legal implications of the council's work, the importance of the careful observance of legal procedure, and the need for all the council's actions be grounded in a solid legal foundation. Nevertheless, law and the legal process could not be divorced from the political arena. The failure of legal process at Constance when it occurred was a human failure, an aberration which does not negate the constructive spirit of the council as a whole. What is remarkable about the Council of Constance is the extent to which the expressed desire for the observance of legal forms was realized through due process, demonstrating that the goals of the conciliarists could thereby be achieved more easily and more securely.

# PART IV

# [14]

# Recent Historiography on the Medieval
# Church and the Decline of European Jewry

## Jeremy Cohen

The Catholic church in western Europe first took official note of the Jewish community in its midst at one of its earliest episcopal synods, the Council of Elvira held at the beginning of the fourth century. Even before the Roman Empire had chosen to tolerate Christianity, Spanish prelates must have viewed the Jews as a sufficiently significant element in society to warrant legislating against excessive social intercourse with them.[1] Throughout the Middle Ages, the Jews constituted the only nonbelieving group consistently allowed to live in Latin Christendom on any regular and prosperous basis. Nevertheless, by the middle of the sixteenth century few Jews remained in western Europe. Expelled from England in 1290, France in 1394, Spain and Sicily in 1492, Portugal in 1497, and the Kingdom of Naples in 1541, European Jews could then live only in portions of Germany and Italy. Most of those who remained found themselves subject to increasingly harsh and humiliating forms of discrimination, ranging from ghettoization and exclusion from respectable occupations to excessive taxation and the public degradation of their religion.

How ought one to account for the dramatic downfall of European Jewry—a community which had once stood at the forefront of Jewish economic and cultural productivity—during the closing centuries of the medieval period? Historians have grappled incessantly with this question

The text of this chapter was first delivered at a joint meeting of the American Historical Association and the American Catholic Historical Association in December 1983 in San Francisco, California; it was submitted for publication in the spring of 1984.

1. Mansi, 2:8 (16), 14 (49–50), 18 (78). See also my "Roman Imperial Policy toward the Jews from Constantine until the End of the Palestinian Patriarchate (ca. 429)," *Byzantine Studies* 3 (1976): 3ff.

Jeremy Cohen

since the rise of critical Judaic scholarship in nineteenth-century Germany, and the subject has still not been exhausted. Virtually every authority on the period has had something new to add to the discussion, so that the pertinent historiography now abounds and itself demands recognition as a primary source for more recent intellectual history.

This chapter neither reviews the history of medieval Jewry nor accounts for the development of Jewish historical study over the past 150 years. But in tribute to the scholarly opus of Brian Tierney, which has illuminated the diverse influences of medieval Christian civilization on its European heirs, it focuses on a narrower subject: the role of the medieval church in fashioning an early modern Europe that was nearly *Judenrein*. Clarifying this more limited issue, surveying the relevant scholarly literature, and analyzing several particularly provocative interpretations, this chapter assesses the accomplishments of recent research and identifies avenues along which fruitful inquiry might now proceed.

The church's role in the decline of medieval European Jewry constitutes a complex question, whose difficulty is underscored by the decisiveness with which some historians have discounted it. The church did not contribute to the downfall of the medieval Jewish community, Gavin Langmuir and Kenneth Stow have argued, because medieval popes themselves never abandoned the patristic doctrine, first formulated as an institutional policy by Pope Gregory the Great, that the Jews had a rightful place in Christian society. *Sicut Iudeis*, the title of the papal edict of protection for the Jews issued repeatedly during the High Middle Ages, faithfully captured the spirit of ecclesiastical Jewish policy: "Just as license ought not to be granted the Jews to presume to do . . . more than the law permits them, just so ought they not to suffer curtailment in those [privileges] which have been conceded them."[2] Christian theology, to be sure, generated often virulent anti-Judaism in medieval society; but, in Kenneth Stow's words, "as the formal executive and legislative—and theological—center of the Church, it was the papacy which established what, for want of a better word, may be called the official policy toward the Jews. And it was to the papacy that Jews, from all the countries of Latin Europe, turned in time of crisis and tried to secure guarantees against attacks."[3]

2. Kenneth R. Stow, *Catholic Thought and Papal Jewry Policy, 1555–1593*, Moreshet: Studies in Jewish History, Literature and Thought 5 (New York, 1977), pp. xi–xxviii; Gavin I. Langmuir, "The Jews and the Archives of Angevin England: Reflections on Medieval Anti-Semitism," *Traditio* 19 (1963): 183–244. The text and a translation of *Sicut Iudeis* appear in Solomon Grayzel, *The Church and the Jews in the XIIIth Century* (1933; reprint New York, 1966), pp. 92–95. See also Solomon Katz, "Pope Gregory the Great and the Jews," *Jewish Quarterly Review*, n.s. 24 (1933–34): 113–36; and Grayzel, "The Papal Bull *Sicut Judaeis*," in *Studies and Essays in Honor of Abraham A. Neuman*, ed. Meir Ben-Horin et al. (Leiden, 1962), pp.243–80.
3. Stow, *Catholic Thought*, p. xix. Stow has since developed, refined, and strengthened his thesis in "Hatred of the Jews, or Love of the Church: Papal Policy toward the

[252]

The Medieval Church and the Decline of European Jewry

Ought our discussion to end here? Should we reformulate our concern as the *religious component* in (rather than the ecclesiastical causes of) late medieval anti-Judaism, or may we recall that the medieval church viewed itself as embodying not only the papacy but all of Christian society? Semantic considerations aside, distinctions between the upper echelons of the ecclesiastical hierarchy, particular clerics or clerical factions, and the masses of the European laity acting on religious impulse deserve mention in any treatment of the church and the Jews.[4] And just as expressions of popular Christian piety often failed to comport with "official" church policy, so too did that policy at times develop for reasons having little to do with theology and doctrine; the anti-Jewish legislation of late medieval popes, for example, was seldom enforced thoroughly in the Papal States.[5] Moreover, since most would agree that medieval Jewry declined for a variety of interrelated reasons, how ought one to isolate and calculate the responsibility of the church? If anti-Jewish teachings permeated Christian theology when the Jews prospered as well as when they suffered, can one fairly deem them the cause of Jewish misfortune? Lacking extensive physical control over the life of the late medieval layman, does the church deserve blame for his actions undertaken in the name of its God? These and other questions have moved scholars to differentiate between "origins" and "causes" in evaluating the responsibility of the church for medieval anti-Judaism,[6] or to advance equivocal summary judgments, like that of James Parkes: "The Church saw to it that the Jew should not climb back to equality; the medieval popes found that they could not protect from violence those whom they proclaimed the fitting objects of oppression and contempt. In this sense the Church was directly responsible for the decline in the status of the Jew . . . but the new position which he came to assume . . . had its origin more in Germanic than in ecclesiastical concepts." Moving on to the question of Jewish usury, for

---

Jews [in Hebrew]," in *Antisemitism through the Ages*, ed. S. Almog (Jerusalem, 1980), pp. 91–111; and in *The "1007 Anonymous" and Papal Sovereignty: Jewish Perceptions of the Papacy and Papal Policy in the High Middle Ages*, Hebrew Union College Annual Supplements 4 (Cincinnati, 1984).
  4. Among many others, see in this regard Peter Browe, "Die Judenbekämpfung im Mittelalter," *Zeitschrift für katholische Theologie* 62 (1938): 197–231, 349–84, "Die religiöse Duldung der Juden im Mittelalter," *Archiv für katholisches Kirchenrecht* 118 (1938): 3–76, and *Die Judenmission im Mittelalter und die Päpste*, Miscellanea historiae pontificiae 6 (Rome, 1942); and Joshua Trachtenberg, *The Devil and the Jews: The Medieval Conception of the Jew in Its Relation to Modern Antisemitism* (New Haven, 1943), esp. chaps. 11ff.
  5. Moritz Güdemann, *Geschichte des Erziehungswesens und der Cultur des abendländischen Juden während des Mittelalters und der neueren Zeit*, 3 vols. (1880–88; reprint Amsterdam, 1966), 2:74ff.; Solomon Grayzel, "The Avignon Popes and the Jews," *Historia Judaica* 2 (1940): 1–12; and Salo Wittmayer Baron, *A Social and Religious History of the Jews*, 2d ed., 17 vols. (New York, 1952–80), 9:44–50—among others.
  6. Langmuir, "Jews," p. 230.

Parkes a key factor in popular anti-Judaism, he adds: "If the main responsibility for usury as a whole lies with the Church . . . the special responsibility for the usury of the Jews lies with the medieval princes."[7]

Finally, our subject is complicated still further by its interrelationship with other matters of scholarly dispute—notably, the alien legal status of medieval Jewry. All would concur that European Jews eventually lost the privileges of Roman citizenship which they had come to enjoy during the late imperial period, largely as a result of the Catholicization of Europe. Generally, as long as the Germanic tribes who invaded the Roman Empire in the West espoused their Arian form of Christianity, they continued to treat the Jews as Roman citizens, preserving their rights and privileges under imperial legislation. But as Goths, Franks, Lombards, and Burgundians converted to Catholicism, the legal distinction between Germanic tribesman and Roman citizen faded; Roman law itself no longer ensured the toleration or status of the Jews.[8] Disagreement remains, however, over *when* the Jews actually forfeited their civil rights and *how* this development contributed to the decline of the medieval Jewish community; and permutations of different answers to each of these questions abound. Johannes Scherer and Salo Baron, for example, maintain that the Jews' alien status dates from the dawn of the Middle Ages. Scherer attributes the worsening plight of the Jews to the integration of ecclesiastical legislation into systems of secular law, a process which began in the twelfth and thirteenth centuries with the emergence of Jewish serfdom, while Baron argues that both canon law and the status of "serfdom" served to safeguard, rather than undermine, the security of medieval Jewry.[9] Others, including Heinrich Graetz, Bernhard Blumenkranz, and Guido Kisch, who postpone the onset of the Jews' loss of civil rights at least until after the Carolingian era and link it with a marked deterioration of their condition in Christendom, often fail to demonstrate convincingly the alleged connection between religious animus and legal station.[10] Kisch, for instance,

7. James Parkes, *The Jew in the Medieval Community: A Study of His Political and Economic Situation* (1938; reprint New York, 1976), pp. 383–86.

8. See Parkes, *The Conflict of the Church and the Synagogue: A Study in the Origins of Antisemitism* (London, 1934), pp. 206–23, 307–70; Solomon Katz, *The Jews in the Visigothic and Frankish Kingdoms of Spain and Gaul* (Cambridge, Mass., 1937); Solomon Grayzel, "Jews and Roman Law," *Jewish Quarterly Review*, n.s. 59 (1968): 93–117; and Bernard S. Bachrach, *Early Medieval Jewish Policy in Western Europe* (Minneapolis, 1977).

9. Johannes E. Scherer, *Die Rechtsverhältnisse der Juden in den deutschen-österreichischen Landern*, Beiträge zur Geschichte des Judenrechtes im Mittelalter 1 (Leipzig, 1901), pp. 1–105; Baron, *History*, 4:48–50, 9:3–11, 135–47; idem, "Medieval Nationalism and Jewish Serfdom," in *Studies and Essays in Honor of Abraham A. Neuman*, ed. Meir Ben-Horin et al. (Leiden, 1962), pp. 17–48; and idem, " 'Plenitude of Apostolic Power' and Medieval 'Jewish Serfdom,' " in his *Ancient and Medieval Jewish History: Essays*, ed. Leon A. Feldman (New Brunswick, N.J., 1972), pp. 284–307, 525–33.

10. Heinrich Graetz, *Geschichte der Juden*, vol. 5, 2d ed. (Leipzig, 1871), pp. 219ff., and vol. 6, 3d ed. (Leipzig, 1894), pp. 93, 226–28; Bernhard Blumenkranz, *Juifs et*

considers Emperor Frederick II's formal initiation of chamber serfdom (*Kammerknechtschaft*) in 1236 the major turning point in the status of medieval Jews; Frederick allegedly based his edict on a decretal of Innocent III emphasizing Jewish servitude and issued in 1205, but supposedly not available to the emperor until its inclusion in Gregory IX's *Liber extra* of 1234. Frederick, however, had previously referred to Sicilian Jews as *servi nostre camere*, and the inclusion of Innocent's decretal *Etsi Iudeos* in the *Compilatio tertia* (5.3.un.) resulted in its publication long before 1234. In view of these facts, as well as the fierce ongoing struggle between Frederick and the papacy, Kisch's explanation for the onset of chamber serfdom appears questionable.[11] Yet it demonstrates the entanglement of our concern with the issue of the Jews' status in secular law, although the connection between them need not have been direct.

Against this background, we may proceed to classify the noteworthy scholarly literature, characterized by two opposing schools of thought. On the one hand stand those interpretations which ascribe a major role in the decline and virtual disappearance of medieval Jewry to theological factors—reflected in official church policy or popular piety and belief, expressed in a substantive shift in Christian ideology, or manifested simply in the diligent application of hitherto unenforced doctrinal principles. The most popular tendency among such opinions, first evidenced clearly over a century ago by Otto Stobbe, views 1096 and the anti-Jewish violence which accompanied the Crusades as a decisive turning point, after which the status of the Jew declined steadily. The massacres of Franco-German Jewish communities in the name of Catholic piety revealed the inadequacy of existing legal safeguards for the person and property of the Jews. Their need for greater protection enhanced their dependence on, and weakness before, Christian princes, without whose goodwill the Jews remained at the mercy of an increasingly hostile European society. The physical persecution of the Jews, although technically illegal, simultaneously awakened Latin Christendom to their anomalous situation. Why were the enemies of Christ permitted to remain and to thrive within the borders of Christian Europe, which was expending its resourcs in holy wars against the infidels abroad? Haim Hillel Ben-Sasson has thus concluded: "The Jews now realized that charters alone could not provide absolute security against mob fury. Christian religious fervour had kindled a fire in the tents of Jacob and had led to slaughter in his habitations. The blood of the Jews had, as it were, been made free for the Christian masses. In respect to legal formulations, security and possibilities of live-

---

*Chrétiens dans le monde occidentale, 430–1096* (Paris, 1960), pp. 352, 386ff.; Guido Kisch, *The Jews in Medieval Germany: A Study of Their Legal and Social Status* (1949; reprint New York, 1970), pt. 2.

11. Frederick's Sicilian legislation is cited in Baron, *History*, 9:143, 311; and see Aemilius Friedberg, ed., *Quinque compilationes antiquae* (1882; reprint Graz, 1956), p. 130.

Jeremy Cohen

lihood, the First Crusade inaugurated a new and harsh epoch for Jews in Christian lands."[12] This outlook is reflected in the periodization which underlies major works of recent Judaic scholarship, despite a disinclination to view the crusading period as a "watershed" in general or Christian historiography.[13] Insightful variations on this theme include the argument of Hans Liebeschütz, that the ideas of Cluniac and Gregorian reform turned Christendom against the Jews even before the Council of Clermont in 1095. Amos Funkenstein has noted a new conception of medieval Jews as irrational and even heretical in the polemical writings of twelfth-century theologians. Lester Little, moreover, has argued that in the wake of the Crusades, European society first projected onto the Jews, who had played a dominant role in early medieval trade and commerce, the guilt derived from its own emergent "profit" economy. Christendom subsequently dispensed with the Jews altogether once new types of spirituality had mollified such pangs of conscience, and the presence of the Jews with their investment capital was no longer essential.[14] Nevertheless, the continuing prosperity of the western European Jewish community during the 150 years after 1096 has led other writers to discern religious causes for its decline only after the early Crusades. Heinrich Graetz, Moritz Güdemann, George Caro, and above all Solomon Grayzel have located such developments in the anti-Jewish legislation of Innocent III and his papal successors, who, according to Grayzel, sought to translate into law the full weight of patristic *Adversus Judaeos* doctrine. "The exclusion of the Jews," Grayzel writes, "which characterized Christian society of the west

12. Otto Stobbe, *Die Juden in Deutschland während des Mittelalters in politischer, socialer und rechtlicher Beziehung* (1866; reprint Amsterdam, 1966), pp. 15, 103ff., 163–93; Haim Hillel Ben-Sasson et al., *A History of the Jewish People,* trans. George Weidenfeld (Cambridge, Mass., 1976), p. 414. Cf. also Simon Dubnow, *Weltgeschichte des jüdischen Volkes,* 10 vols. (Berlin, 1925–30), 4:269ff.; Browe, "Judenbekämpfung im Mittelalter," pp. 198, 211–23; Parkes, *Jew,* pp. 81ff.; George LaPiana, "The Church and the Jews," *Historia Judaica* 11 (1949): 117–44; Trachtenberg, *Devil,* p. 167; and Leon Poliakov, *The History of Anti-Semitism,* vol. 1, trans. Richard Howard and Natalie Gerardi (New York, 1965), pt. 2.

13. For examples of the tendency in Jewish historiography, see Benzion Dinur, *Israel in the Diaspora, II: From the Persecutions of 1096 until the Black Death* (in Hebrew), 2d ed., vol. 1 (Tel Aviv, 1965), esp. pp. 1–6; Blumenkranz, *Juifs et Chrétiens;* Cecil Roth, ed., *The Dark Ages: Jews in Christian Europe, 711–1096,* World History of the Jewish People 11 (New Brunswick, N.J., 1966); and the original Hebrew of Ben-Sasson, *History of the Jewish People,* vol. 2, *The Middle Ages* (in Hebrew) (Tel Aviv, 1969), pp. 21, 83. Robert Chazan's *European Jewry and the First Crusade* (Berkeley, 1986) did not appear in time for consideration in this essay.

14. Hans Liebeschütz, "The Crusading Movement in Its Bearing on the Christian Attitude towards Jewry," *Journal of Jewish Studies* 10 (1959): 97–111; Amos Funkenstein, "Changes in the Patterns of Christian Anti-Jewish Polemic in the Twelfth Century" (in Hebrew), *Zion,* n.s. 33 (1968): 125–44, and idem, "Basic Types of Christian Anti-Jewish Polemics in the Later Middle Ages," *Viator* 2 (1971): 373–82; Lester K. Little, *Religious Poverty and the Profit Economy in Medieval Europe* (Ithaca, N.Y., 1978), pp. 42–57, 216.

at the end of the Middle Ages was the result of a process which had been going on for more than a thousand years. It began with the triumph of Christianity in the Roman Empire and terminated in the total expulsion from the westernmost countries of Europe."[15] Kisch, as noted above, located the point of transition in the proclamation of chamber serfdom by Frederick II and the Jews' ensuing loss of the right to bear arms (*Waffenrecht*). And I have stressed the ideas and activities of the new mendicant friars, who called for the exclusion of the Jews from Europe on theological grounds, just as the thirteenth-century *Ecclesia* was attempting to regiment all of Western society into a perfectly integrated Christian commonwealth, often conceived organically as the mystical body of Christ. Scrutinzing the Talmud and other works of postbiblical Judaism, Dominican and Franciscan friars claimed that medieval Jews had forsaken their Old Testament heritage for a heretical, rabbinic perversion thereof and had thereby forfeited their privilege of inclusion in a properly ordered Christendom. Instead of the blind witnesses to the Christological truth of biblical prophecy whom church fathers like Augustine had perceived in the Jews, the friars now depicted them as deliberate unbelievers, ones who had killed the divine messiah intentionally and whose books and traditions could serve the church no constructive purpose.[16]

On the other hand, various scholars minimize the significance of religious factors in explaining the changing plight of medieval European Jewry. "Expansion and contraction of West-European Jewry," Salo Baron asserts categorically, "coincided with the great rise and decline in the temporal power of the Roman Church. . . . As a matter of principle, the Church continued its traditional policy of extending to Jews sufferance with severe qualifications. The innovations of the later Middle Ages consisted [merely] in more detailed exposition and clarification of these relationships."[17] Only as the power and political influence of the papacy waned did the rulers of Europe expel their Jews. To explain this, Wilhelm

15. Graetz, *Geschichte*, 6:226f., and ibid., vol. 7, 3d ed. (Leipzig, 1894), pp. 3–18; Güdemann, *Geschichte*, 2:84ff.; Georg Caro, *Sozial- und Wirtschaftsgeschichte der Juden im Mittelalter und der Neuzeit* (1908–18; reprint Hildesheim, 1964), 1:228–453; and of the many works of Solomon Grayzel, see, above all, *Church and the Jews*, esp. pp. 1–82; "The Beginning of Exclusion," *Jewish Quarterly Review*, n.s. 61 (1970): 15–26 (quotation on p. 15), and "Popes, Jews, and the Inquisition from 'Sicut' to 'Turbato,' " in *Essays on the Occasion of the Seventieth Anniversary of Dropsie University*, ed. Abraham I. Katsch and Leon Nemoy (Philadelphia, 1979), pp. 151–88. Cf. also Louis I. Rabinowitz, *The Social Life of the Jews of Northern France in the XII–XIV Centuries as Reflected in the Rabbinical Literature of the Period* (1938; reprint New York, 1972), p. 18.

16. See my *The Friars and the Jews: The Evolution of Medieval Anti-Judaism* (Ithaca, N.Y., 1982), "The Jews as the Killers of Christ in the Latin Tradition, from Augustine to the Friars," *Traditio* 39 (1983): 1–27, and "Scholarship and Intolerance in the Medieval Academy: The Study and Valuation of Judaism in European Christendom," *American Historical Review* 91 (1986): 592–613.

17. Baron, *History*, 9:3, 5.

Jeremy Cohen

Roscher contended in 1875 that the commercial jealousies of a nascent Christian bourgeoisie turned late medieval rulers against the Jewish community, which had virtually monopolized European commerce before the Crusades but by the thirteenth and fourteenth centuries could no longer be deemed indispensable:

> For a number of centuries the Jews remained the commercial guardians of the young nations, to the advantage of the latter and not without open recognition of this advantage. But every tutelage becomes burdensome when it continues longer than the dependency of the ward. Entire nations emancipate themselves from the tutelage of other nations, even as individuals used to, only by means of struggle. The Jewish persecutions of the later Middle Ages are in large measure a product of trade jealousies. These persecutions are intimately related to the first flowering of a national merchants' caste.

Despite the probable affinity between Roscher's views and German anti-Semitism of the late nineteenth century which Toni Oelsner has identified and vehemently condemned, many scholars, Jewish as well as Christian, have accepted this idea at face value and assumed it to be valid.[18] Others have suggested that the socioeconomic impact of Jewish moneylending, or perhaps even the emptiness of royal treasuries, caused the downfall of Jewish communities and the confiscation of their assets.[19] True to his theory that the Jews throughout history have fared worst in Gentile states of single nationalities, Baron himself explains that incipient medieval nationalism underlay the expulsions from England, France,

18. Wilhelm Roscher, "Die Stellung der Juden im Mittelalter, betrachtet vom Standpunkte der allgemeinen Handelspolitik," *Zeitschrift für die gesamte Staatswissenschaft* 31 (1875): 503–26, the relevant portion of which has been translated by Solomon Grayzel as "The Status of the Jews in the Middle Ages Considered from the Standpoint of Commercial Policy," *Historia Judaica* 6 (1944): 13–26 (quotation on p. 20). The nature and influence of Roscher's views have been discussed by Guido Kisch, "The Jews' Function in the Medieval Evolution of Economic Life," *Historia Judaica* 6 (1944): 1–12; and Toni Oelsner, "Wilhelm Roscher's Theory and the Economic and Social Position of the Jews in the Middle Ages: A Critical Examination," *Yivo Annual of Jewish Social Science* 12 (1958–59): 176–95, and idem "The Place of the Jews in Economic History as Viewed by German Scholars," *Yearbook of the Leo Baeck Institute* 7 (1962): 188–91. Subsequent advocates of Roscher's approach to our question have included Karl Gottfried Hugelmann, "Studien zum Recht der Nationalitäten im deutschen Mittelalter," *Historisches Jahrbuch* 48 (1928): 578–81; Raphael Straus, "The Jews in the Economic Evolution of Central Europe," *Jewish Social Studies* 3 (1941): 15–40; Karl W. Deutsch, "Anti-Semitic Ideas in the Middle Ages," *Journal of the History of Ideas* 6 (1945): 248, 250; and Abraham Leon, *The Jewish Question: A Marxist Interpretation* (New York, 1970).

19. P. Elman, "The Economic Causes of the Expulsion of the Jews in 1290," *Economic History Review*, 1st ser. 7 (1936–37): 145–54; Parkes, *Jew*, chap. 10; Trachtenberg, *Devil*, chap. 13; Simon Schwarzfuchs, "The Expulsion of the Jews from France (1306)," in *Seventy-fifth Anniversary Volume of the Jewish Quarterly Review*, ed. Abraham A. Neuman and Solomon Zeitlin (Philadelphia, 1967), pp. 482–89.

Spain, and Portugal. "Religion and economics played prominent roles in Jewish history . . . but they were not the sole nor even the chief causes for the changes which occurred from time to time in attitudes of monarchs and states toward the Jews. They were merely the contributing, or sometimes the immediate, the efficient causes." As medieval kingdoms grew into nation-states during the fourteenth and fifteenth centuries, their rulers and populations could not tolerate the presence of a distinct, alien population whose religious and ethnic distinctiveness subverted the basis for national unification. Baron thus accounts for the survival of Jews in portions of early modern Italy and Germany, which failed to coalesce into national polities before the nineteenth century.[20] Yet another school of thought has stressed the changing configurations of political alliances involving king, aristocracy, and bourgeoisie, in which the Jews were not directly involved but from whose volatility they often had most to lose.[21]

From this spectrum of interpretations, three stand out as especially helpful in illuminating and clarifying the complexities of our subject. In a lengthy article titled "The Jews and the Archives of Angevin England: Reflections on Medieval Anti-Semitism," Gavin Langmuir grapples with the question through his analysis of H. G. Richardson's *English Jewry under the Angevin Kings* and exemplifies the tendency to disregard almost completely the role of the church in the decline of medieval Jewry. Criticizing "an archival perspective in medieval studies . . . whose horizon is limited by a concern to establish as much detailed information on a given topic as the state of the archives will permit . . . but the level of [whose] insight into the implication of the facts so discovered tends to be low,"[22] Langmuir demonstrates the extensive ramifications of medieval anti-Judaism as a historical and historiographical problem. Popular prejudices both medieval and modern join with the complex legal, socioeconomic, and theological status of the Jews so as to require of the historian an imaginative and discerning disposition as well as a scientific one. As for the church's contribution to the persecution and eventual expulsion of English Jews in the thirteenth century, assumed by Richardson to be significant, Langmuir proceeds to the opposite extreme. Not only must one distinguish between ecclesiastical policies properly implemented by clerical authorities and unlicensed actions of individual churchmen, but one must also look beyond the reason why the Jews in particular suffered

20. Salo Wittmayer Baron, "Nationalism and Intolerance," *Menorah Journal* 16 (1929): 503–15 (quotation on p. 504), 17 (1929): 148–58; idem, *History* 10:116–17, 11:188–283, 12:3–4.

21. Benzion Netanyahu, *Don Isaac Abravanel, Statesman and Philosopher*, 3d ed. (Philadelphia, 1972), chaps. 1–2, passim; Barnett D. Ovrut, "Edward I and the Expulsion of the Jews," *Jewish Quarterly Review*, n.s. 67 (1977): 224–35.

22. Langmuir, "Jews," p. 185; H. G. Richardson, *English Jewry under the Angevin Kings* (London, 1960).

during the Middle Ages and consider European society's need for a scape-
goat in the first place. Although the church had always condemned Judaism, it consistently called for toleration; and "what is remarkable in the
Middle Ages is not that the doctrine on the Jews was emphasized, but that
it underwent so little change."[23] Such constancy in Christian doctrine
was hardly duplicated in the actual treatment of the Jews—hence "the
existence of the doctrine is a very insufficient explanation" for their
downfall, especially in view of the simultaneously waning influence of
the church over European kings. Instead, Langmuir calls for further research into the effects "of a new social, political, and economic order" on
late medieval Jewry, and into the changing nature of irrational popular
attitudes toward the Jews between 1096 and 1400.[24]

Writing only two years after Langmuir, Lea Dasberg presents a sound
case that religious ideas did contribute heavily to the anti-Jewish persecutions of the High and late Middle Ages, beginning with the massacres
accompanying the Crusades.[25] Dasberg argues effectively against attribut-
ing these hostilities to commercial rivalries, still a popular scholarly
tendency. The Jews did not dominate European commerce to the extent
that many have assumed, nor was it the Christian merchant who typically
turned against them.[26] Although sympathetic with Kisch's view of 1236
as the commencement of Jewish serfdom in Germanic law, Dasberg's
argument demonstrates the gap so characteristic of the relationship between imperial policy and lawbook. In this case, "Jewry law" lagged far
behind important changes in "Jewish policy," which in turn emerged
from a new religious orientation two centuries in its development. For the
changing conceptions of the Jews evident in the massacres of 1096 derived
from the spirit of Cluniac reform in the tenth century, a new idealism
vis-à-vis worldly issues which within several generations had influenced
the policies of the papacy. While the church endeavored to raise the

23. Langmuir, "Jews," p. 235. On attitudes to Jewish history in modern historiography, see also idem, "Majority History and Post-Biblical Jews," *Journal of the History of
Ideas* 27 (1966): 343–64.
24. Langmuir, "Jews," pp. 235–44. In "L'absence d'accusation de meurtre rituel à
l'ouest du Rhône," in *Juifs et judaisme de Languedoc: XIIIe siècle–début XIVe siècle,*
ed. Marie-Humbert Vicaire and Bernhard Blumenkranz, Collection Franco-Judaica
6/Cahiers de Fanjeaux 12 (Toulouse, 1977), pp. 235–49, Langmuir subsequently applied
his perspective to the popularity of the ritual murder accusation in northern Europe of
the later Middle Ages and its virtual absence in southern Europe. Socioeconomic and
psychological factors, not the doctrine of the church, underlay the realia of anti-Jewish
persecutions. In the south, Langmuir explains (pp. 245–46), "l'hostilité populaire exis-
tait, bien sûr, mais elle fut bien moindre qu'en Europe du Nord, peut-être parce que, en
Europe du Sud, le développement précoce du commerce et du crédit chrétien avait rendu
les Juifs moins distincts; y contribuaient également le pluralisme culturel, l'instruction
générale, et la complexité de l'organisation sociale. De plus, il semble que les croyances
religieuses aient joué un rôle plus circonscrit dans cette vieille société bien romanisée."
25. Lea Dasberg, *Untersuchungen über die Entwertung des Judenstatus im 11. Jahrhundert* (Paris, 1965).
26. See also Oelsner, "Roscher's Theory."

esteem of the simple man and transformed basically economic issues into religious-ethical ones, it also began to pose itself against the established political-economic power held responsible for such social injustice—the secular princes and, by extension, the Jews under their protection. Dasberg treats the Investiture Controversy and the anti-Jewish violence of the Crusades as two stages of the same conflict, that of reformers versus the simoniacal establishment, and even classifies the respective reactions of burghers, princes, and bishops to the violence according to their stance in the papal-imperial conflict. Coupled with a surge of apocalyptic fervor calling for the conversion of the infidel, the piety which sustained the Crusade understandably precipitated the persecution of the Jews.

In a brief but penetrating essay published at the end of the previous decade, Israeli historian Maurice Kriegel proposes a qualitatively new "organic" model to account for the expulsion of Jews from England, France, and Spain (and even from portions of Germany)—a theory which in many ways balances the opposing viewpoints of Langmuir and Dasberg.[27] This interpretation properly considers each of the traditional explanations—theological, socioeconomic, or political—unsatisfactory on its own, either because it fails to account for the complexity of the process which culminated in the expulsions or because the events of the specific expulsions simply fail to substantiate it. Instead, Kriegel argues, decrees of banishment in fact derived from royal attempts to integrate and mobilize previously fragmented societies, through the consolidation of territorial domains, the strengthening of urban power centers, the institution of a governmental bureaucracy—in a word, through the construction of a state. Realization of these goals depended in large measure on the successful manipulation of public opinion to engender a unity of spirit among diverse elements of the population. Here Kriegel's thesis departs from the nationalistic interpretation of Salo Baron. For the goal of unity induced Edward I of England, Philip IV of France, and Ferdinand and Isabella of Spain to exploit the traditional religious sentiments of their subjects, seeking to characterize their monarchies as sacred, heavenly kingdoms. Appeal to popular religious belief and custom allowed these monarchs to rally their constituencies around policies which often lacked theological derivation, without impinging upon their ability to generate and pursue such policies autocratically. Not by accident did Philip IV clothe his struggle with the Templars, or Ferdinand and Isabella theirs against Granada, in soteriological garb. In the case of France, Kriegel observes, "On a pu qualifier Phillipe le Bel de roi 'constitutionnel.'" While the epithet is

27. Maurice Kriegel, "Mobilisation politique et modernisation organique: Les expulsions de Juifs au bas Moyen Age," *Archives de sciences sociales des religions* 46 (1978): 5–20. Kriegel has developed his interpretation of the expulsion from Spain more extensively in "La prise d'une décision: L'expulsion des Juifs d'Espagne en 1492," *Revue historique* 260 (1978): 49–90. Cf. also his *Les Juifs à la fin du Moyen Age dans l'Europe méditerranéenne* (Paris, 1979), esp. chap. 6.

hardly accurate from a strictly juridical point of view, it has validity "si l'on veut dire par là qu'il ne bouscula pas les lois et la coutume, qu'il gouverna par le truchement de mécanismes éprouvés, qu'il ne chambarda pas les équilibres donnés: ce roi qui prend Saint Louis pour modèle, l'imite aussi en se montrant respectueux des droits traditionels et des normes coutumières." Desire for political and economic gain did not preclude the sincerity of their piety; such was "le paradoxe de la double présence de la religiosité et de la convoitise."[28] Sociopolitical mobilization and modernization built upon age-old Christian beliefs and institutions, and the need for valuable unanimity in religious ideology outweighed any benefits which accrued from the Jewish presence. Curiously, concludes Kriegel, the emergence of the modern state united with traditional religious fervor to induce the expulsion of the Jews, *ad maiorem Dei gloriam.*

Each of the three scholars mentioned here signals progress achieved in recent historiography as well as directions in which research into this question must still advance. The problematic relationship between popular piety and official ecclesiastical doctrine notwithstanding, the teachings and policies of the medieval church clearly played a part in the downfall of the European Jewish community together with numerous other factors. These require careful identification and definition, while their interaction with Christian theology and popular prejudice demands analysis. We need to know precisely how religious ideas were brought to bear upon political policy and socioeconomic reality. The arguments of Langmuir, Dasberg, and Kriegel have shown that the answer is far from simple. Any convincing interpretation of the demise of medieval Jewry must consider factors which ultimately had little to do with the Jews and Judaism—Cluniac or Gregorian reform, the development of popular superstition and prejudice, and the drive toward sociopolitical integration on a national scale. In much the same way as John Boswell has shown how the general penchant for order and uniformity in twelfth-century Christendom triggered the persecution of homosexuals, who previously had enjoyed toleration, historians of the Jews must integrate their particular concerns with the larger tendencies and processes of medieval European history in general.[29] Moving in this direction, Langmuir, Dasberg, and Kriegel succeed in discrediting traditional and simplistic interpretations of earlier historians, but the full value of their respective theories has not yet been appreciated. Their speculative suggestions have yet to be tested thoroughly, and the applicability of their explanatory models must be shown to transcend medieval political boundaries, in order to do justice to our historical puzzle.

28. Kriegel, "Mobilisation," p. 17.

29. John Boswell, *Christianity, Social Tolerance, and Homosexuality: Gay People in Europe from the Beginning of the Christian Era to the Fourteenth Century* (Chicago, 1980), pt. 4. See also my *Friars,* esp. chap. 10, which seeks to establish a similar basis for the anti-Judaism of thirteenth- and fourteenth-century Dominicans and Franciscans.

# [15]

# Fraternal and Lay Images of
# St. Francis in the Thirteenth Century

## WILLIAM R. COOK

In the study of almost any aspect of late medieval history, the friars, especially the Franciscans, play a critical role. In areas ranging from the history of science to missionary activity in China, the friars are central. And the story of the development of the Franciscans is especially stormy and dynamic whether it is told in the pages of the most learned tomes or in *The Name of the Rose.* Two useful symbols of how the order changed in the thirteenth century may be helpful. Francis had urged his friars always to remain lesser brothers and not to accept positions of authority; he also urged the ecclesiastical hierarchy not to call friars to prelacies. By the end of the thirteenth century, however, there had been not only many Franciscan bishops but also a Franciscan pope. Francis loved poor and humble churches and had special love for the tiny church below the city of Assisi called the Porziuncola. By the end of the century, the center of the order was the splendid Gothic church and convent in Assisi. That church in 1300 already contained works of Cimabue and several Roman masters as well as the magnificent frescoes of the life of the saint which are still the most striking works in the basilica.[1] And during the next three decades,

Several years ago, when applying for a grant to study the paintings of the life and miracles of Francis, I asked Brian Tierney for a letter of recommendation. He wrote back saying that he had once begun a study of these works and had traveled in Italy for that purpose. He never completed this work, however. Thus, although I did not pursue research in the areas of canon law or constitutional history, I am happy to be able to offer this work to Brian Tierney, knowing that it is a study he began many years ago.

1. There is passionate disagreement among scholars concerning the dating of the cycle of the life of Francis in the Upper Church. The most recent attempt to date the frescoes argues for a date as late as the 1340s for their completion. See James Stubblebine, *Assisi and the Rise of Vernacular Art* (New York, 1985). I do not find Stubblebine convincing. The more-or-less standard dating for the frescoes is that they were

William R. Cook

Giotto, Simone Martini, Pietro Lorenzetti, and many other artists of note would bring their genius to its walls.

One approach to studying the development of the order is to examine the ways the Franciscans told the story of their founder's life. Within the order itself, the life of Francis was preserved and developed in the commissioned lives of the saint; the earliest of these was the *Vita prima* of Friar Thomas of Celano, written in connection with the saint's canonization in 1228. Almost twenty years later, Celano wrote a second life, primarily consisting of stories not known to him at the time he wrote the *Vita prima*. A few years later he appended to this a treatise containing a large number of mostly posthumous miracles. In 1260 Bonaventure, the minister general, was commissioned to write a new life of Francis, known as the *Legenda maior*. This was presented to the general chapter in 1263, and three years later all other versions of the saint's life including Celano's were ordered destroyed.[2]

Although these lives all contain valuable information about the life of Francis, none is a biography in the modern sense. It is clear that the authors were not so much interested in exactly what happened and in what sequence as they were concerned to proclaim the holiness of the man and to provide an inspiration and a model for the friars who were reading or listening to the life. Scholars have often recognized that these lives tell us as much about the authors' conceptions of the order and the issues current at the time of writing as they do about the historical Francis, in much the same way that the gospels inform us as much about the intellectual history of the early church as they do about the thoughts and words of the historical Jesus.[3]

These early lives of the saint were written in Latin, primarily for the

complete or almost complete by 1307. For that argument, see John White, "The Date of 'The Legend of St. Francis' at Assisi," *Burlington Magazine* 98 (1956): 344–51. I am convinced that the frescoes were executed about the year 1292. The representation of the porch of the Lateran basilica, completed in 1291, presents a terminus post quem. A chalice in Assisi, commissioned by Pope Nicholas IV (d. 1292), contains an enamel of the stigmatization closely related to the fresco in the Upper Church and in all probability modeled on it. See Dieter Blume, *Wandmalerei als Ordenspropanda: Bildprogramme in Chorbereich franziskanischer Konvente Italiens bis zur Mitte des 14. Jahrhunderts* (Worms, 1983), p. 168. For a discussion of the chalice, a work of the Sienese Guccio di Mannaia, see Dora Liscia Bemporad, "Oreficerie e avori," in *Il tesoro della basilica di San Francesco ad Assisi* (Assisi, 1980), pp. 123–25.

2. All three lives plus selections from Celano's treatise containing posthumous miracles are translated in *St. Francis of Assisi: Omnibus of Sources*, ed. Marion Habig (Chicago, 1973). In the text as well as the notes, I will use the standard citations: I Celano for the *Vita prima*, II Celano for his *Vita secunda*, and *Legenda maior*.

3. For two rather different treatments of the early lives, see Rosalind Brooke, "The Lives of St. Francis," in *Latin Biography*, ed. T. A. Dorey (New York, 1967), pp. 177–98, and John Fleming, *An Introduction to the Franciscan Literature of the Middle Ages* (Chicago, 1977), pp. 32–72.

friars themselves, although copies circulated outside the order.[4] To a great extent, then, these were internal texts. In them, the authors paid a great deal of attention to issues that the friars themselves were concerned with—the role of learning in the order, the precise meaning and implications of poverty, and so forth.

The friars went to great length to present their founder to the laity. They wanted to establish his cult and make Assisi a pilgrimage center, but also to explain who they were and what their role was in the life of the church and, for that matter, in the entire history of salvation. One way this occurred was through their preaching; several thirteenth-century Latin sermons about Francis survive and probably served as models for countless vernacular sermons throughout Europe.[5] The other primary means by which the friars presented Francis to the laity was commissioning works of art. In Italy alone, mostly in Tuscany and Umbria, about one hundred paintings survive from the thirteenth century which contain representations of Francis,[6] the vast majority coming from Franciscan houses. Many of these paintings are "portraits" of the saint either alone or with other saints. About twenty show Francis at the foot of the cross in a crucifixion scene. There are also fourteen works consisting of at least two stories from the life and miracles of Francis. It is this last group that I wish to examine in some detail.[7] To see which stories were selected and how they were

4. The general chapter ordered the two lives by Celano destroyed in 1266; surviving manuscripts are from non-Franciscan institutions, since the general chapter had authority only over the friars minor.

5. Five sermons by Bonaventure and another by Odo of Châteauroux have been translated and analyzed in *The Disciple and the Master: St. Bonaventure's Sermons on St. Francis of Assisi*, trans. and ed. Eric Doyle (Chicago, 1983). For a discussion of Franciscan sermons, see D. L. d'Avray, *The Preaching of the Friars: Sermons Diffused from Paris before 1300* (Oxford, 1985).

6. There is no complete catalog of these works. The single most comprehensive catalog of thirteenth-century paintings is Edward Garrison, *Italian Romanesque Panel Paintings: An Illustrated Index* (Florence, 1949). As the title suggests, this book does not deal with frescoes or stained glass, and several more works have been discovered and published since 1949. I have recently completed a study of the surviving works with a catalog appended.

7. These fourteen, in approximate order of execution, are: dossal with six stories of the life and miracles of Francis by Bonaventura Berlinghieri, dated 1235, San Francesco, Pescia (province of Pistoia); dossal with six miracles, Pisan school, about 1250, Pinacoteca, Pisa; dossal with twenty stories of the life and miracles, Bardi St. Francis Master, about 1250, Santa Croce, Florence; dossal with four miracles, about 1255, Giunta Pisano or follower, Il Tesoro, San Francesco, Assisi; dossal with four miracles, about 1260, follower of Giunta Pisano, Vatican Museum, Rome; dossal with eight stories of the life and miracles, 1250s, Florentine, Museo Civico, Pistoia; dossal with four stories of the life and miracles, about 1260, Sienese, Museo Diocesano, Orte (province of Viterbo); fresco cycle with two stories of the life, about 1260, North Italian, San Fermo Maggiore, Verona; fresco cycle with five stories of the life, about 1265, St. Francis Master, Lower Church, San Francesco, Assisi; stained-glass window with six stories of the life, about 1265, cartoons perhaps by the St. Francis Master, Upper Church, San Francesco, Assisi; fresco cycle with two stories of the life, about 1280, Umbrian school,

depicted, and what changes occurred during the course of the thirteenth century, will provide some new insights into how the Franciscans interpreted the material contained in the lives of the saint and what the friars wanted the laity to believe about Francis and the order he founded.

I propose that, despite their different audiences, there is a parallel development between the written and painted accounts of the life of Francis. We have the two earlier lives of Francis superseded by the *Legenda maior* of Bonaventure, which eliminated or reinterpreted many of the stories found in I and II Celano and became the standard, official life of the saint. In like manner, we have several early panel paintings consisting of scenes from the life and miracles of Francis based on I and II Celano; by the mid-1260s there is a shift in what is represented, although the new emphases in the representation of the life of Francis became "codified" in an authoritative form only with the painting of twenty-eight scenes from his life and miracles, all taken directly from the *Legenda maior*, in the Upper Church of San Francesco in Assisi about 1292.

In examining the early written lives and noting changes in developments in the way the life of Francis was interpreted, I am focusing on issues that were vitally important to the friars in defining their own vocation and spirituality; to a great extent, these issues were not of great concern for the laity, and one also suspects that the friars did not want to parade their internal struggles before that audience. In the examination of the development of the visual representations of the saint's life, I am concentrating on the way the art is meant to present an image of the saint himself and increasingly of his order as a way of explaining to the laity what the friars were about and what their role was in the church.

One issue that can be examined in I and II Celano and the *Legenda maior* is Francis and the brothers' asceticism. I Celano reports that the brothers used a variety of penitential devices, including "instruments of iron around their bodies . . . and . . . wooden girdles of penance."[8] According to I Celano, the Franciscan order was founded as a brotherhood to preach penance, and Innocent III expressly commissioned Francis and the friars to do so.[9] II Celano presents the pope's commission to the friars as preaching generally, however, with no specific reference to penance.[10] Furthermore, Celano modified his earlier words about penitential devices. He reported that the friars used such devices but described Francis as a moderating influence: "They would very often have succumbed had they

---

San Francesco, Gubbio; wing of a triptych with two stories of the life, about 1290, Christ Church Master (Sienese), Fogg Museum, Cambridge, Massachusetts; dossal with eight stories of the life, about 1290, follower of Guido da Siena, Pinacoteca, Siena; fresco cycle with twenty-eight stories of the life and miracles, about 1292, several artists (traditionally Giotto), Upper Church, San Francesco, Assisi.

8. I Celano, 40.
9. I Celano, 33.
10. II Celano, 17.

not relaxed the rigor of such abstinence at the earnest advice of their kind shepherd [Francis]."[11] And the story which follows this passage is about discretion and moderation with respect to food. But, II Celano does describe Francis subjecting "his own innocent body to scourgings and want, multiplying its wounds without cause."[12] II Celano also speaks approvingly of a friar who wore an iron corset next to his skin.[13] Thus, on this issue there is a certain ambiguity, caused by Celano's desire to see the friars imitate Francis combined with his awareness of the need for certain modifications of the founders' rigid ascetic practices.

Although 90 percent of the material in Bonaventure's *Legenda maior* comes directly from I and II Celano, he left out all the material on penitential rigors described above. He did use a story about discretion found in II Celano 21, however, immediately following the description of penitential devices. In fact, Bonaventure retold that story with the following introduction: "Francis did his utmost to encourage the friars to lead austere lives, but he had no time for exaggerated self-denial which excluded tender compassion or was not tempered with discretion."[14] Bonaventure made it clear that Francis practiced asceticism, but by choosing stories in which Francis used more traditional ascetic practices such as fasting, dressing poorly, and fighting off evil desires. As an example of the last, Bonaventure told how Francis threw himself into the snow when faced with the temptation of lust. His source is II Celano, but he reshaped the story, bringing it into close parallel with the familiar story of Benedict's throwing himself into a thornbush.[15] Bonaventure did recount the story of Francis's having himself treated like a criminal in the town square of Assisi after eating some meat. But while I Celano, Bonaventure's source, treated this as an edifying account which brought an immediate response from the audience to confess their sins, Bonaventure warned that "his action certainly seemed to have been intended rather as an omen reminiscent of the prophet [Isaiah] than as an example" and noted that the friars observing this event realized that "his humility was rather to be admired than imitated."[16] In the *Legenda maior* this event has become a unique and prophetic one rather than serving as a model for literal imitation.

What we discover in the *Legenda maior* is a recasting of early Franciscan material so that it addressed the changing realities of the order. By Bonaventure's time, the friars did not perceive the order primarily as a penitential brotherhood, nor was its primary activity the preaching of

11. II Celano, 21.
12. II Celano, 129.
13. II Celano, 208.
14. *Legenda maior*, V, 7.
15. The source is II Celano, 116–17. See my "Tradition and Perfection: Monastic Typology in St. Bonaventure's *Life of St. Francis.*" *American Benedictine Review* 33 (1982): 6–7.
16. *Legenda maior*, VI, 2. Cf. Isa. 20:23.

penance.[17] The order under Bonaventure was led by one of the century's most brilliant and subtle theologians, and his conception of it was much more complex than Francis's had been. Bonaventure himself had little patience with the eccentric ascetics of the order, for they were doing little to rebuild the church, Francis's and the friars' great mission.[18] In practice, the order was becoming more like the established cloistered orders; thus, the *Legenda maior* emphasized traditional monastic forms and examples of penance.

Another interesting issue we can trace through I and II Celano and the *Legenda maior* is the question of the friars' doing manual labor. In both lives by Celano, it is clear that all the friars who were able should labor "with their hands."[19] In II Celano Francis stated: "I want all my brothers to work and to be employed, and those who do not know how should learn some crafts."[20] Immediately following this passage is a lament that many friars were working too little and talking too much. Bonaventure ignored most of this material about manual labor. The *Legenda maior* does warn against idleness[21] and points out that Francis curbed his lower nature by self-discipline and useful work. There is no call for the friars to work with their hands, however, and II Celano recognized that even by the 1240s the friars no longer widely practiced manual labor.[22] The most obvious reason for this deemphasis on manual labor is that the order had changed from a group of simple lay penitents into one of primarily well-educated, clerical members who, along with the papacy, had broadened the role of the order in the church far beyond what its original members had envisioned or intended.[23] And the very number of friars would require modification of the rules about manual labor, for where would all of them find work if they sought it?[24]

17. John Moorman, *A History of the Franciscan Order from Its Origins to the Year 1517* (Oxford, 1968), p. 141. Moorman points out that for Bonaventure, the friars' task was "to make good the defects of the clergy."

18. *Legenda maior*, II, 1. After Bonaventure described how the cross at San Damiano spoke to Francis and told him to rebuild the church, he commented that "[Francis] was quite willing to devote himself entirely to repairing the ruined church of San Damiano, although the message really referred to the universal Church which Christ won for himself at the price of his own blood."

19. I Celano, 39.

20. II Celano, 161.

21. *Legenda maior*, V, 6.

22. II Celano, 162. Here the author laments that there were friars who were "working more with their jaws than with their hands."

23. The best account of the years between the death of Francis and the generalate of Bonaventure, which began in 1257, is Moorman, pp. 84–139. The friars had become much more involved in administering the sacrament of penance, active in the universities, and highly clericalized.

24. Many years ago, Brian Tierney made this commonsense, but often unarticulated, point in a lecture he delivered to my students and colleagues at the State University of New York at Geneseo. It is one thing for a handful of friars to seek work or to beg, but a large number of friars in a small community made working and begging untenable as the sole sources of survival.

The question of the relationship of books and learning to the Franciscan vocation is a complex one. Celano's *Vita prima* contains no discussion of the issue, but several passages in II Celano address it. Thomas of Celano must have wrestled with this issue a great deal; for although he tended to be conservative and to argue for a simple lay order, he was also well educated and a writer of books.[25] In II Celano Francis is presented as a person without much formal education but also as a devoted reader of Scripture, though not of modern biblical commentaries,[26] and he made no use of philosophical distinctions or rhetorical techniques.[27] Celano also presented Francis as saying that he envisioned a time when books" would be an occasion of ruin" for the order.[28]

None of these statements about learning was incorporated into the *Legenda maior*. Bonaventure instead thoroughly rewrote a passage from II Celano that reported Francis's answer to the question whether learned friars should continue to study Scripture: "I do not mind, provided that they do not neglect prayer after the example of Christ of whom we are told that he prayed more than he studied. They should not study merely in order to have something to say; they should study so as to practice what they have learned and then encourage others to do likewise."[29] In other words, Francis permitted the friars to study in order to improve their lives so that they could preach by example and by word, just as Francis himself had done without book learning. Bonaventure realized that what Francis had grasped intuitively from Scripture, others lacking his spiritual gifts could obtain only by study. Ultimately, Francis's kind of knowledge is superior, as illustrated by a story Bonaventure summarized from II Celano in which a learned Dominican asked Francis to interpret a particularly thorny passage from Ezekiel. After Francis explicated the text, the theologian could only exclaim: "His theology soars aloft on the wings of purity and contemplation, like an eagle in full flight, while our learning crawls along the ground."[30] Bonaventure's positive interpretation of Francis's attitude toward study not only provided a justification for much of the order's work—including Bonaventure's own contributions—but also tried to deal realistically with how friars without Francis's spiritual intuition and gift for contemplation could do the work of Francis—rebuilding the church.

25. For the life and thought of Thomas of Celano, see Silvana Spirito, *Il frances-canismo di Fra Tommaso da Celano* (Assisi, 1963).

26. II Celano, 102.

27. II Celano, 107, 164.

28. II Celano, 195.

29. *Legenda maior*, XI, 1. This passage is Bonaventure's thorough rewriting of II Celano, 195, cited above. In this chapter, Celano quoted Francis as saying, "For tribulation will come . . . such that books, useful for nothing, will be thrown out of windows and into cubbyholes." Celano continued by telling the story of a friar who asked Francis for permission to have a psalter; Francis instead offered him ashes.

30. *Legenda maior*, XI, 2, based on II Celano, 103.

William R. Cook

I have chosen asceticism, manual labor, and intellectual activity as
examples of concerns of Thomas of Celano and Bonaventure that would
have been of little direct interest to the laity. The friars had no need to
involve the laity with these essentially internal matters. In the beginning,
however, it was vital for the friars to present Francis to the laity as a holy
man and his shrine in Assisi as a pilgrimage center, for proof of his sanctity
was an important way to propagate the order, since the older orders like the
Benedictines and Camaldolese were founded by saints who had worked
many miracles. As the order grew and its expanding role in the church was
challenged about midcentury, it became necessary for the order to assure
the laity that the friars were living in accord with the ideals of their saintly
founder. Furthermore, the friars needed to proclaim the order's establishment by the pope, its orthodoxy, and its proper relation to the secular
clergy as well as defining its roles of preaching and administering the
sacraments. The development of the images of Francis for the laity can be
traced by a careful examination of the surviving thirteenth-century works
of art in Italy depicting Francis, especially the fourteen early works that
illustrate events in his life and his miracles. With rare exceptions, the
sources for these works are the two lives by Thomas of Celano and the
*Legenda maior*.[31] The artists did not merely illustrate the texts, however;
they interpreted them. This often involved adapting the traditional iconography of Christ or an established saint and events from his or her life as
well as stories from the life of Christ. Obviously, the choices an art-
ist/patron made were important for establishing the context in which
Francis was understood.[32] For example, the fresco in the Upper Church in
Assisi that depicts Francis's body being taken to San Damiano makes use
of the iconography of Christ's triumphal entry into Jerusalem. Furthermore, there were hundreds of stories about Francis to choose from; yet
only a few were represented with any frequency in the visual arts. Several
stories which appeared frequently in the earliest works of Franciscan art
drop out of the later cycles, and other stories enter the visual accounts.
With these concerns in mind, we can turn to this largely ignored body of

31. Of the 105 painted episodes in these fourteen cycles, perhaps as few as four have
no direct source in the writings of Thomas of Celano or Bonaventure. One is a scene in
the Pistoia dossal where Francis is preaching penance, but it does not appear to be the
representation of a particular event described in I or II Celano. Two are posthumous
miracles in the Bardi dossal, which some scholars have erroneously identified with
stories in Celano's treatise on miracles. The fourth is a posthumous miracle in the Orte
dossal.
32. Lack of evidence makes it impossible to know about the relationship between
patrons and artists at this time, although it is generally believed that artists were rather
carefully guided by the ecclesiastics for whose churches they were painting. A contract
between the bishop of Arezzo and Pietro Lorenzetti survives from the year 1320; it
suggests that the selection of even the minor figures in the altarpiece for Santa Maria
della Pieve was left to the bishop; see S. Borghesi and L. Bianchi, *Nuovi documenti per la
storia dell'arte senese* (Soest; reprint 1970), p. 10.

source material for the development of Franciscan thought and propaganda.

One obvious observation about the cycles painted in the first thirty years or so after Francis's death is that they primarily contained posthumous miracles. I Celano recounts several of these, but they account only for twenty-four of the 150 chapters. Celano's second life contains almost no posthumous miracles, but he later wrote a separate work on miracles after being criticized for failing to include them. Bonaventure also described posthumous miracles, but they make up less than 25 percent of the *Legenda maior*. In the seven earliest panel paintings, however, slightly more than half of the scenes are posthumous miracles. If one excludes the somewhat unusual dossal in the Bardi Chapel of Santa Croce in Florence, 72 percent of the scenes in these early panels are of posthumous miracles.[33] Three of these panels—those in Pisa, Assisi, and the Vatican—contain posthumous miracles exclusively. This representation of Francis as thaumaturgist was an important means of demonstrating the sanctity of one recently canonized. By contrast, of all the cycles that can be dated between 1265 and 1290, there is not a single posthumous miracle, or at least not more than one in a total of twenty-three scenes.[34] Of the twenty-eight frescoes in the cycle of the Upper Church of San Francesco in Assisi, only four represent posthumous miracles.

The miracles which appear frequently in the early panels include cures of cripples and lepers and also exorcisms; these are typical miracles associated with many of the popular saints of Europe as well as with Christ himself, and they had established visual iconographies. Artists could also adapt stories with established iconographies to Francis's posthumous miracles. For example, an eleventh-century or early twelfth-century fresco in the crypt of San Clemente in Rome shows a miracle at the tomb of St. Clement. In the story, a mother comes into the chapel containing St. Clement's tomb, which is underwater except on his feast day, to look for her son, who accidentally had been left there the year before and was

33. Four of six in the Pescia dossal, six of six in the Pisa dossal, four of twenty in the Bardi dossal (the scene of the death of Francis also shows the cure of cripples), four of four in the Assisi and Vatican dossals, four of eight in the Pistoia dossal, one of four in the Orte dossal.

34. A scene in the window of the Upper Church in Assisi between that of the cross speaking to Francis at San Damiano and that of Innocent III's dream of the Lateran is usually identified as Francis's posthumous cure of Bartholomew of Narni because of its iconographic similarity to the way that story is represented in several of the early dossals, for example, in Pescia. There are some good reasons for rejecting this identification, however. First, it would be completely out of sequence temporally. Second, that story is not in the *Legenda maior*, the written source for this window. Third, the cure takes place at a bath, but in the window there is no water. I suspect that the artist has borrowed and adapted the iconography of the cure of Bartholomew of Narni but has reworked it slightly to represent Francis curing lepers, a story which fits chronologically between the vision at San Damiano and the dream of Innocent III.

presumed drowned. She leaned over the body of the child at the saint's tomb and discovered miraculously he was still alive. She then held the child up to proclaim the miracle.[35] This iconography is adapted, probably indirectly, by Bonaventura Berlinghieri in his 1235 dossal in San Francesco, Pescia, the earliest dated painting of Francis and probably the earliest to contain scenes from the saint's life.[36] In Francis's first posthumous miracle, a mother brings her deformed daughter to Francis's tomb on the day of his burial. At the tomb, the girl is cured, but in fear she runs off crying.[37] In Berlinghieri's painting, however, the mother lifts the girl on her shoulders to proclaim this great miracle that Francis had performed (see fig. 1). And as in the fresco in San Clemente, the canopied altar/tomb is on the right and a crowd of witnesses on the left.

This and other "typical" miracles that are found in the earliest paintings contrast with the much more unusual miracles of Francis illustrated in the cycle of the Upper Church in Assisi. By the time this cycle was executed about 1292, it was the unique role of Francis and his order in the history of salvation that the friars wanted to publicize. After all, the sanctity of Francis was not in doubt, and he was well known throughout Christendom. There was no need to "prove" that he was a saint by showing that he did what saints do. None of the miracles illustrated in the early panels is found in the Upper Church.[38] Instead, those selected from the *Legenda maior* document Francis's unique likeness to Christ and the special role of his order. The first illustrates a story about the reality of the often-disputed side wound of Francis, revealed to Pope Gregory IX in a dream.[39] The second is concerned with the healing power of the stigmata,

35. For a discussion and photograph of this painting, see Otto Demus, *Byzantine Art and the West* (New York, 1970), pp. 107–8. See also Enzo Carli, Cesare Gnudi, and Roberto Salvini, *Pittura italiana: Medioevo, romanico e gotico* (Milan, 1959), p. 16. The story is retold in the thirteenth century by Jacobus de Voragine, *The Golden Legend*, trans. Granger Ryan and Helmut Ripperger (New York, 1941), p. 706.

36. Miklòs Boskovits has argued for the precedence of the Pisa dossal; see his "Giunta Pisano: Una svolta nella pittura italiana del duecento," *Arte illustrata* 6 (1973): 345–46. I agree with Enzo Carli, who argues that the Pisa dossal was painted shortly after 1250, since two of its scenes are based on stories in Celano's treatise on miracles. See his *Pittura medievale pisana*, vol. 1 (Milan, 1958), p. 39. A seventeenth-century drawing of a lost dossal from San Miniato al Tedesco contains the date 1228. There are good reasons for distrusting this date, however; see Benvenuto Bughetti, "Vita e miracoli di San Francesco nelle tavole istoriate dei secoli XIII e XIV," *Archivum franciscanum historicum* 19 (1926): 715–16.

37. I Celano, 127.

38. Although the particular miracles so popular in the early dossals are not included in the *Legenda maior* and thus could hardly have been represented in Assisi, there were similar stories of miraculous cures in the last portion of Bonaventure's text.

39. There was significant controversy over the reality of the stigmata in the thirteenth century. Gregory IX, Alexander IV, Nicholas III, and Nicholas IV all issued bulls affirming their reality. And there was even greater controversy specifically about the side wound. See André Vauchez, "Les stigmates de Saint François et leurs détracteurs dans les derniers siècles du Moyen Age," *Mélanges d'histoire et d'archéologie* 80 (1968): 595–625. The story of the vision of Gregory IX is in the *Legenda maior*, part 2, I, 2.

*Figure 1.* San Francesco, Pescia. Detail of a dossal by Bonaventura Ber-linghieri, 1235. Francis's first posthumous miracle, the cure of a crippled girl at the saint's tomb. All photographs by the author.

emphasizing again the side wound, since Francis heals a man with an injury in his side by placing his hand in that wound. The third involves Francis's raising from the dead a woman who had failed to confess a mortal sin so that she could confess to a friar minor. This clearly suggests that the order was not only to call people to repentance but also to mediate God's grace through sacramental confession.[40] The fourth story, Francis interceding for the release in Rome of a reformed heretic named Peter, testifies to his concern for orthodoxy at a time when some friars were under suspicion of heresy.[41] Furthermore, in the story a bishop comes to understand and appreciate the work of Francis; by this time, attacks had

40. This reinforces a story from Francis's life that dealt with the same issue and was also painted in the Upper Church—the death of the knight of Celano.

41. These three stories are found in the *Legenda maior*, part 2, I, 5; II, 1; and V, 4.

[273]

been made on behalf of the secular clergy against the whole concept of mendicancy, and there was great tension and debate between the two groups about spiritual territoriality.[42] This last story also puts Francis in a position analogous to that of the angel in the familiar story where St. Peter is freed from his chains.

There is another element to the choice of posthumous miracles in the thirteenth century. In the early works, most miracles were associated with Francis's tomb in Assisi, thus promoting and celebrating pilgrimage to the new basilica. In fact, the early dossal from Assisi shows in one scene a gate into the city of Assisi and in two others the Lower Church's altar, which was dedicated in 1253.[43] By the end of the century, however, Assisi was a well-established pilgrimage center, and there was no need to emphasize miracles that took place there. Rather, the miracles in the fresco cycle of the Upper Church dealt with controversial issues of the day such as the reality of the fifth wound of Francis, thus totally identifying him with Christ Crucified, the role of the order in administering the sacrament of penance, and the friars' orthodoxy and relationship with the secular clergy.

The event in Francis's life depicted most often throughout the thirteenth century was the stigmatization.[44] The earliest surviving painting of this event is in Bonaventura Berlinghieri's Pescia dossal of 1235 (see fig. 2).[45] It shows a seraph with a human face, hands, and feet appearing to Francis. The seraph has no nimbus and looks toward the viewer rather than toward Francis. Berlinghieri tried to render faithfully Celano's description of "a man . . . like a seraph,"[46] although the painter ignored Celano's statement that the man/seraph was fastened to a cross. It is difficult to find a reason for the lack of a cross in the earliest representation of the stigmatization, but perhaps the artist simply did not dare to present something as unusual and startling as a crucified angel.[47] According to I Celano, the marks did not appear on Francis's body until after the

42. See Moorman, pp. 127–31, for a discussion of the attacks on mendicancy by William of St. Amour and how the mendicants responded to them. One of the clearest and most succinct discussions of some of the issues in the mendicant/secular controversy is in Brian Tierney, *The Origins of Papal Infallibility, 1150–1350* (Leiden, 1972), esp. pp. 72–82.

43. P. Scarpellini, "Assisi e i suoi monumenti nella pittura dei secoli XIII–XIV," in *Assisi al tempo di San Francesco: Atti del V convegno internazionale, Assisi, 13–16 ottobre 1977* (Assisi, 1978), pp. 81–88.

44. The stigmatization is part of ten of the fourteen cycles being discussed here; of the other four, three have only posthumous miracles and the fourth (Gubbio) is probably incomplete. At least twelve other representations of the stigmatization survive from the thirteenth century and the very beginning of the fourteenth.

45. The most detailed analysis of Berlinghieri's rendering of the stigmatization is William Miller, "The Franciscan Legend in Italian Painting in the Thirteenth Century" (Ph.D. diss., Columbia University, 1961), pp. 17–28.

46. I Celano, 94.

47. See H. Matrod, "Le stimmate di S. Francesco nella representazione più antica che si conosca," *Miscellanea francescana* 10 (1906): 9–12, 17.

*Figure 2.* San Francesco, Pescia. Detail of a dossal by Bonaventura Berlinghieri, 1235. The stigmatization.

vision had ended. The painter saw the need to include both the vision and
its results, however, and thus had to telescope two separate parts of the
narrative into one scene. We must realize how difficult it was to translate
this story into a visual medium, for as Brother Elias wrote in 1226, the
stigmatization was a new and unique miracle. The vision was not of a
seraph, for which there was an established iconography, but rather of a
man like a seraph. The artist had to adapt traditional seraph iconography
to this unique vision.[48] What Berlinghieri gives us is neither entirely
human nor angelic. It is important to note that there is no explicit indication in the Berlinghieri paintings or in I Celano, his source, that what

48. Miller, pp. 17–28. An excellent example of seraph iconography is found in a
mosaic in the apse of the Sicilian cathedral of Cefalù.

Francis saw was the crucified Christ. In the depiction of Francis himself in the Berlingheri stigmatization, the hand and foot wounds are clearly visible; but there is no indication of the side wound, whether by a tear in the habit or by a reddened portion of it. The artist tried to show the connection between the two fingers by placing a wide gold band, interrupting the geography, between Francis and the man/seraph.

Two paintings now in Florence and dating from about the middle of the thirteenth century[49] show the man/seraph with a nimbus, suggesting an emphasis on the angelic nature of Francis's vision at LaVerna. One of these, the Uffizi stigmatization, has the further innovation of attaching the man/seraph to a cross. This change brings the depiction of the stigmatization close to Celano's description. This work also presents a more intimate relationship between Francis and the seraph because the angel's head is turned toward the saint. Both of these paintings also have three thick gold lines that connect the man/seraph with the gold nimbus of the saint instead of Berlinghieri's gold band.

An Assisi fresco of about 1265 shows the man/seraph with a human face and with the head inclined toward Francis, again suggesting an intimate relationship with the saint; unfortunately, the figure of Francis had been destroyed, so that it cannot be determined if there is anything new in the way the saint is represented.[50] In two panels from the late thirteenth century from Siena, one ascribed to Guido da Siena and the other to a follower of his,[51] we find the nimbus, the cross, and the inclined head of the seraph. And in the autograph work of Guido, there are also three thin lines from the mouth of the seraph to the head of Francis. In a Sienese panel now in the Fogg Museum in Cambridge, Massachusetts, dated about 1290,[52] we see for the first time all five wounds of Francis in a stigmatiza-

49. One is part of a diptych (the other half being lost) now in the Uffizi. See Luisa Marcucci, *I dipinti toscani del secolo XIII* (Rome, 1958), pp. 30–32. The other is a scene in the dossal in the Bardi Chapel of Santa Croce. Two important recent studies of this much-written-about work are Judith Stein, "Dating the Bardi St. Francis Master Dossal: Text and Image," *Franciscan Studies* 36 (1976): 271–95, who dates the work to after 1254 because of what I believe is the incorrect assumption that the eighteenth and nineteenth stories are based on Celano's treatise on miracles. See also Blume, *Wandmalerei als Ordenspropaganda*, pp. 14–17.

50. The expression on the face of the man/seraph is somehow gentler and more compassionate than that of the figure in the Uffizi stigmatization. These frescoes have been much written about, and their dating is the subject of much controversy. For a good analysis but a late date, see Jürgen Schultze, "Zur Kunst des 'Franziskusmeisters,'" *Wallraf-Richarts-Jahrbuch* 25 (1963), esp. pp. 123–34. For another interpretation and an earlier date see Serena Romano, "Le storie parallele di Assisi: Il Maestro di San Francesco," *Storia dell'arte* 44 (1982): 63–81. See also Blume, pp. 29–32. The best theological analysis of the frescoes is Gerhard Ruf, *Das Grab des hl. Franziskus: Die Fresken der Unterkirche von Assisi* (Freiburg, 1981).

51. James Stubblebine, *Guido da Siena* (Princeton, 1964), pp. 20–22, 69–71.

52. James Stubblebine, *Duccio di Buoninsegna and His School* (Princeton, N.J., 1979), 1:121–22.

tion scene, the side wound being shown through a tear in the habit, a device used in other contexts beginning about 1255.[53]

In the fresco of the stigmatization in the cycle of the Upper Church in Assisi, we see for the first time a cruciform nimbus and five wounds on the seraph (see fig. 3). Furthermore, its facial characteristics are those of contemporary paintings of Christ at his crucifixion. There are also lines from each of the seraph's five wounds to the marks in Francis's body, and both of their side wounds bleed. A 1307 painting by Giuliano da Rimini in the Isabella Stewart Gardner Museum in Boston, generally acknowledged to be inspired by the Assisi fresco,[54] makes the identification of the seraph with Christ complete by adding the cross, inexplicably missing in the Upper Church fresco. From the first decade of the fourteenth century on, depictions of the stigmatization clearly show Christ Crucified appearing to Francis at LaVerna. Giotto's version in Santa Croce, Florence, over the entrance to the Bardi Chapel, suggests the mystical nature of Francis's encounter with Christ by showing that Christ revealed himself completely to Francis, whereas part of Christ is shielded from the viewer's sight by one pair of wings.

To understand fully the changes of the representation of the stigmatization, we need to examine the text of the *Legenda maior*. It describes the vision as consisting of the image of a man crucified in the midst of the six wings of a seraph. Later, Bonaventure informed his readers that this was a

53. It is possible that the depiction of the side wound through a tear in Francis's habit originated with enamel painters in Limoges shortly after Francis's death. M. M. Gauthier dates two reliquaries showing Francis with the side wound, now in the Louvre, to shortly after 1228. See her *Emaux du Moyen Age occidental*, 2d ed. (Paris, 1973), p. 184. A stained-glass window in the Franciscan church in Erfurt, Germany, also shows the side wound and is usually dated about 1230. See Erhard Drachenburg et al., *Die Mittelalterliche Glasmalerei in den Ordenskirchen und im Angermuseum zu Erfurt* (Berlin, 1976), pp. 72–78. Artists from Thuringia worked on the Upper Church in Assisi and may have introduced the image of Francis with the side wound into Italy. For the German presence in Assisi, see Giuseppe Marchini, "Le vetrate della Basilica di San Francesco," in *Giotto e i giotteschi in Assisi*, ed. Giuseppe Palumbo (Assisi, 1979), p. 273. Richard Offner believes that a panel in the Louvre storage room showing Francis with the side wound is from southern Italy and can be dated about 1230, but I am not at all convinced it is that early. If Offner's date is correct, this is an isolated iconographic development. See Offner's "Note on an Unknown St. Francis in the Louvre," *Gazette des beaux-arts* 39 (1952): 129–33. The representation of Francis with the side wound was probably made popular by the St. Francis Master, who painted a famous "portrait" of the saint, now in the Museum of the Porziuncola in Assisi, with a prominent side wound. He also is responsible for the frescoes in the Lower Church, one of which shows the side wound being examined through a tear in the habit at the saint's death. It is possible that the fresco in that cycle of the stigmatization also showed Francis with the side wound, but the figure of the saint was destroyed in the fourteenth century. For the works of the St. Francis Master, see Schultze and Romano.

54. See White, "Legend of St. Francis," p. 347. Stubblebine, *Assisi and the Rise of Vernacular Art*, pp. 70–74, challenges the authenticity of the painting's inscription but still believes that the stigmatization in Giuliano's painting is derived from the Assisi fresco.

*Figure 3.* Upper Church, Basilica of San Francesco, Assisi. Detail of a fresco of the stigmatization from a cycle of the saint's life by unknown artists (traditionally attributed to Giotto), about 1292. Christ Crucified in the wings of a seraph.

vision of Christ, "sub specie Seraph."[55] He did not mention a side wound as part of the vision, however, although he reported Francis's side wound.

55. *Legenda maior*, XIII, 3.

Clearly, Bonaventure wanted his readers to understand this vision as a unique experience of Christ which brought the final transformation of Francis into a perfect image of Christ Crucified. In addition, Bonaventure understood the stigmata as the seal of authenticity on the life of St. Francis and thus also on the life of those who faithfully imitated him: "And you bear . . . the seal of the supreme High Priest Christ, so that your words and example must be regarded by everyone as genuine and sound beyond all cavil."[56]

Obviously, the artists who painted the stigmatization from the *Legenda maior* account had a difficult task to create a work of art that would make clear Bonaventure's interpretation of the event. They tried to communicate intimacy between Christ and Francis. And gradually they added the bloody side wound to Francis,[57] gave the seraph the traditional attributes of Christ, and linked the wounds of Christ to Francis by connecting lines. Thus, there is a rather clear line of development of the iconography of the stigmatization from a heavenly vision into Francis's unique experience of and transformation into Christ Crucified.

Apparently by the end of the thirteenth century it had become obligatory to include in any cycle a scene that explicated Francis's and the friars' relationship with the papacy. This had not always been the case. The 1235 Berlinghieri panel in Pescia contains no such scene. Neither does the dossal in Orte, which I suspect dates from the 1250s or early 1260s.[58] But two dossals probably dating between 1250 and 1260—those in the Bardi Chapel of Santa Croce in Florence and the Museo Civico in Pistoia—show Innocent III granting Francis and his followers approval of their rule.[59] In this decade the friars' way of life was seriously challenged, and some friars, including John of Parma, minister general of the order, fell under suspi-

56. *Legenda maior*, XIII, 9.

57. The importance of the side wound as part of the iconography of the stigmatization is especially important in the Upper Church fresco cycle, for three subsequent scenes in the cycle focus on it. There is the authentication of the stigmata, in which the knight Jerome, like doubting Thomas, thrusts his fingers into the wound (*Legenda maior*, XV, 4). In the scene where Francis's body is taken to San Damiano before burial, Clare thrusts her hand into the side wound, a detail not found in Bonaventure's account (cf. *Legenda maior*, XV, 5). Finally, there is the vision of Gregory IX, discussed above (*Legenda maior*, part II, I, 2).

58. There is a traditional date of 1282 for this painting that several scholars have accepted. See, for example, Luisa Mortari, *Museo diocesano di Orte* (Viterbo, n.d.), pp. 14–15. Miller, pp. 100–2, prefers a date in the third quarter of the thirteenth century. Since one of the scenes in the panel is a story from II Celano, which was ordered destroyed in 1266, I doubt that the painting can be later than this. It is generally accepted now that the painting is Sienese, and it is sometimes attributed to the same artist who did the famous John the Baptist altar now in the Pinacoteca of Siena. See Cesare Brandi, "Il meastro del paliotto di S. Giovanni Battista a Siena," in *Scritti di storia dell'arte in onore di Mario Salmi*, vol. 1 (Rome, 1961), pp. 351–61. There are two essays of varying quality about this panel in *San Francesco e storie della vita nella tavola del Museo Diocesano di Orte* (Orte, 1985).

59. See above, note 7.

cion of heresy. It was a good idea to assure the public that the friars' way of life was papally sanctioned and that Francis's obedience to the pope was beyond challenge. When Bonaventure composed the *Legenda maior,* he too wanted to emphasize the order's papal approbation, for he incorporated *all* the stories from I and II Celano concerning Francis's meeting with Innocent III, including three distinct visions.[60]

The fresco cycle in the Lower Church in Assisi, probably executed shortly after the publication of the *Legenda maior,* contains Innocent III's dream in which he saw the Lateran basilica being held up by a man who, he later realized, was Francis. Innocent interpreted this vision, according to Bonaventure, to mean that "by [Francis's] work and teaching, he will uphold Christ's church."[61] Furthermore, as a result of this vision, Innocent agreed to Francis's request to approve his way of life and "promised to give the friars greater powers in the future."[62] And the dream of the Lateran further suggests that in the reform and rebuilding of the church, even the pope relied on Francis and his brotherhood. The friars clearly wanted to convey these messages to the laity, for the dream of the Lateran appears in all but one of the later thirteenth-century cycles. In the fresco cycle in the Upper Church in Assisi, the confirmation of the rule by Innocent III immediately follows the dream of the Lateran. In this cycle, no fewer than five of the twenty-eight scenes show the three important popes in the life of Francis and in the establishment of the order—Innocent III, who originally sanctioned the rule; Honorius III, who promulgated the *Regula bullata* in 1223; and Gregory IX, protector of the order as a cardinal and later the pope who canonized Francis in 1228.[63]

Of the seven cycles that show Francis with Innocent III, five also present the story of Bishop Guido's covering Francis's nakedness as he renounces his earthly father and goods (see fig. 4).[64] This story not only strengthens in a general sense the friars' legitimacy, but also suggests that the episcopacy should protect and nurture the order and its way of life. This is a potent message in the second half of the thirteenth century, during which time there were numerous clashes between the secular clergy and the mendicants, the former resenting the friars' assuming functions traditionally performed by diocesan clergy as well as their independence of the episcopacy. In the fresco cycle in the Upper Church, there also appears the story of Bishop Guido's vision of Francis's death. The last scene in the cycle illustrates a bishop giving thanks for Francis's intecession on behalf

60. *Legenda maior,* III, 8–10.
61. *Legenda maior,* III, 10.
62. Ibid.
63. Innocent III is shown in his dream of the Lateran and in the approval of the rule. Honorius III listens to a sermon that Francis preached. Gregory IX appears at Francis's canonization and in his vision of Francis that confirmed the reality of the side wound.
64. The Bardi and Siena dossals and the Lower Church, Upper Church, and Gubbio frescoes.

*Figure 4.* Pinacoteca, Siena. Detail of a dossal by a follower of Guido da Siena, about 1290 (from San Francesco, Colle Valdesa). Francis renounces his worldly goods and is clothed by the bishop.

[281]

# William R. Cook

of an imprisoned but reformed heretic. These stories also are meant to convey the proper relationship between the friars and the bishops. Francis respectfully "informs" his bishop, through a vision, of his death and entry into the kingdom of heaven; the bishop in the last scene is rightly grateful to Francis. All together, eight of the twenty-eight scenes in the Upper Church contain popes or bishops (29 percent), compared with a total of five in fifty-two scenes in the seven earliest panels (9 percent).[65]

One major iconographic development in the visual representation of the life of St. Francis occurs in the way his death was treated. The story appears in five of the fourteen cycles being studied here;[66] it was especially important in the Upper Church in Assisi, for three of the twenty-eight scenes are stories about the saint's death. The earliest representations, based on I Celano, are in the Bardi and Pistoia dossals. In the latter we see friars and clerics gathered around the bier of Francis. The most significant detail is Francis's soul being taken to heaven; in I Celano, an unnamed friar had a vision of the ascension of Francis's soul,[67] but none of the friars in the painting is looking toward it. Thus, it is the viewer who sees the vision, which reassures him or her that Francis is indeed a saint and that the anniversary of his death is the celebration of his birthday in heaven. The Santa Croce panel similarly shows people gathered around the body as the soul is taken to heaven. Kneeling below are four suppliants, crippled and diseased, calling on *Saint* Francis to intercede for them. This reminds the viewer that although Francis is not physically present to preach and teach, he is present in heaven, where he can aid those in need who call upon him and make pilgrimages to his tomb.

The fresco of Francis's death in the Lower Church in Assisi follows the tradition of showing his soul ascending to heaven (see fig. 5). There are two innovations, however. First, there are friars adoring or kissing the wounds in Francis's hands; damage to the fresco prevents us from knowing if there are also friars at Francis's feet, but it seems likely.[68] There is also a friar pointing to the side wound, visible through a tear in Francis's habit; a second friar stares at it while a third contemplates it. The purpose of this representation is not merely to show that Francis is a saint; primarily it draws attention to the stigmata and in particular to the side wound, thus identifying Francis completely with Christ Crucified and in a general sense presenting Bonaventure's theology of Francis.

The late thirteenth-century dossal from Colle Valdelsa, now in the

65. Of the five, four are in the Bardi dossal; the other is the approval of the rule in the Pistoia dossal.
66. The Bardi, Pistoia, and Siena dossals and the Lower Church and Upper Church frescoes.
67. I Celano, 110.
68. Although I Celano, 113, reports the kissing of the hands and feet, Bonaventure emphasizes the friars' joy and amazement (*Legenda maior*, XV, 3), which I believe is reflected in this fresco.

*Figure 5.* Lower Church, Basilica of San Francesco, Assisi. Detail of a fresco cycle of the life of St. Francis by the St. Francis Master, about 1265. The death of Francis.

Pinacoteca of Siena, repeats the friars around the bier. A friar kisses the foot wounds. But a bishop is also standing behind the bier. Nowhere in any of the written accounts is a bishop present at Francis's death or funeral, but the *Legenda maior* tells that Bishop Guido of Assisi had a vision of Francis's death while on a pilgrimage.[69] I believe that the Siena panel shows us Bishop Guido mystically present at Francis's death through his

69. *Legenda maior*, XIV, 6.

vision. This argument is strengthened by the fact that opposite this scene is one showing Bishop Guido, depicted in an identical fashion to the bishop in the death scene, wrapping his cloak around the naked Francis when he renounces his earthly goods. Showing Bishop Guido in the first and last scenes of this panel again suggests Francis's legitimacy, and thus that of his order, and the proper relationship between the friars and the episcopacy. The bishop protected Francis at his renunciation; Francis dutifully and courteously informed Guido of his death and sanctity even though the bishop was away from Assisi. There is no soul ascending to heaven in the death scene of the Siena dossal; all attention is focused on Francis and Bishop Guido and by extension on the relationship of the friars to the secular clergy and to the church in general.[70]

In the Upper Church in Assisi, there are three stories concerning Francis's death. The first shows the dead Francis, friars kissing the hand and foot wounds; above, his soul is taken to heaven by angels. In the second, we see two visions of Francis's death—that of Bishop Guido and another of a friar named Augustine.[71] The third shows the incredulous knight Jerome putting his fingers in Francis's side wound through a tear in his habit. Thus, in this fresco cycle, there are many themes present in the depictions of Francis's death. First, Francis is a saint, as evidenced by his soul's being taken to heaven. Second is the reality of the stigmata, especially the side wound that fully identifies him with Christ Crucified. Finally, the two visions of Francis's death are given to a mendicant and a secular; this suggests Francis's concern for his brothers, but also for the church as a whole. These visions represented together even suggest the ideal of a positive relationship between the friars and the secular clergy. The scene following these shows Francis's body taken to San Damiano before its burial in Assisi. The themes of the death scenes are reinforced by the iconography, which is an adaptation of Christ's entry into Jerusalem, thus identifying Francis with Christ and also reminding the viewer of *Saint* Francis's entry into the heavenly Jerusalem. And Clare inserting her hand into Francis's side wound confirms Jerome's authentication of the stigmata.

One story that is found in I Celano, the *Legenda maior*, and nine of the fourteen thirteenth-century cycles is Francis's sermon to the birds.[72] In the final analysis this story is not central to the meaning of Francis in

70. This artist was particularly concerned with the friars' relationship to the secular clergy and to the church in general; for in addition to the two scenes described here, this dossal contains the cross speaking to Francis at San Damiano and Innocent III's dream of the Lateran.

71. *Legenda maior*, XIV, 6. Presumably because of Brother Augustine's privileged vision, Dante placed this rather obscure friar with the doctors of the church in *Paradiso* XII.

72. The Pescia, Bardi, Orte, and Siena dossals; the Fogg triptych; the Verona, Lower Church, and Upper Church frescoes; and the Upper Church window.

salvation history and does not define the nature of the friars minor,[73] but both written and visual sources suggest that it struck a responsive chord in thirteenth-century audiences. It is a good story to illustrate the dynamic relationship between text and painting.

In Celano's *Vita prima*, the sermon to the birds is a miracle.[74] Bonaventura Berlinghieri presented it that way in his 1235 dossal in Pescia. In Celano's account, Francis left his companions to preach to the birds; but in the Pescia dossal two friars are beside Francis, and one spreads his hands in a traditional gesture of wonder.[75] Once again, the artist made use of traditional iconography, in this case to convey the miraculous nature of the event. Essentially, the iconography does not change much in the thirteenth century, although we find a greater variety of birds in the later depictions and there is less emphasis on the miraculous. The meaning of the story does change significantly in the *Legenda maior*, however. For Bonaventure, the sermon to the birds is primarily a lesson from nature about how people should respond to Francis and by extension to the friars who are his brothers and imitators: "A person would certainly have to be really perverse and obstinate to refuse to listen to Saint Francis' preaching,"[76] since creatures not endowed with reason did so. Thus, although the story is not central to an understanding of Francis or his order, I believe it retained its popularity in art at least in part because its meaning was changing so that it addressed contemporary concerns of the friars and their relationship with the laity.

Another story to be considered in text and painting is that of Francis rescuing a lamb he saw among goats. According to I Celano, the only written source, Francis was reminded by what he saw of Christ among the chief priests and pharisees; thus, Francis had a strong desire to rescue the lamb.[77] There is one painting of this story; it is one of the twenty stories in the Bardi dossal (see fig. 6). The artist has gone beyond the text in such a way as to fundamentally alter the story's message. He has turned it into an allegory of the Last Judgment through his positioning of the figures—Francis with the sheep moving to the right toward a lush mountain with four flowing rivers, the shepherd and his goats moving left toward a barren hill. The artist even added a pig, an unclean animal, to the goats to reinforce this interpretation of the story. In this judgment allegory, Francis is analogous to an angel with the soul of one of the saved. I am

73. It is important to remember that there is a long tradition of holy men exercising control over wild creatures; thus, the representation of this event is a traditional way of proclaiming Francis's sanctity. For a study of this tradition, see Edward Armstrong, *Saint Francis: Nature Mystic* (Berkeley, 1973), pp. 42–100.

74. I Celano, 58–59.

75. Evelyn Sandberg-Vavalà, *La croce dipinta italiana* (Verona, 1929), p. 720.

76. The story is told in *Legenda maior*, XII, 3; the conclusion, referring to this and other stories, is in XII, 6.

77. I Celano, 77.

*Figure 6.* Bardi Chapel, Santa Croce, Florence. Detail of a dossal by the Bardi St. Francis Master, about 1250. Francis rescues a sheep from among goats.

reasonably certain that the artist would have been guided by a friar, and I suggest that this story may well have acquired its eschatological significance in sermons and that the friars at Santa Croce wished this story to be represented with the meaning they rather than Celano attached to it.

Finally, I turn briefly to one nonnarrative form of representing Francis in thirteenth-century Italian painting. There survive more than twenty representations of St. Francis at the foot of the cross. Eleven of these are large crucifixes that hung above altars or were attached to altar screens, such as are depicted in two of the frescoes of the life of Francis in the Upper Church in Assisi.[78] There are also four processional crosses with Francis and eight panel paintings and frescoes of the crucifixion with him, the most famous of which is Cimabue's fresco in the Upper Church in

78. The twelfth fresco of the cycle, depicting the story of the Christmas crib at Greccio, shows the back of an altar screen with a large wooden cross mounted on it. The twenty-first scene shows the knight Jerome authenticating the stigmata; behind is the front of an altar screen with a large cross and two other paintings attached to the top of it.

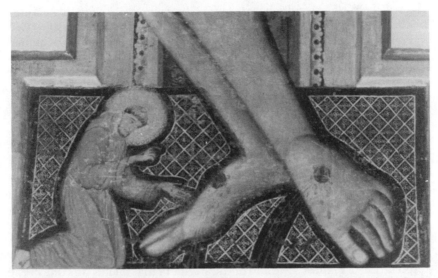

*Figure* 7. Galleria Nazionale dell'Umbria, Perugia. Detail of a crucifix by the St. Francis Master, 1272 (from San Francesco al Prato, Perugia). Francis kneeling before the feet of Christ.

Assisi.[79] This image was first created by Giunta Pisano in 1236, when Brother Elias, then minister general, commissioned a cross for the basilica in Assisi. Unfortunately this work was destroyed in the seventeenth century, but we know about it from written descriptions and works derived from it.[80] In all probability, a rather tiny Francis knelt to the viewer's left of Christ's feet, his hands in a gesture of prayer and his head bowed; two crosses probably painted in the 1250s and derived from Giunta in museums in Faenza and Bologna illustrate this pose.[81] A 1272 cross in Perugia attributed to the St. Francis Master is a development of this type of representation (see fig. 7). In it Francis gestures toward the nail in Christ's foot, however; furthermore, in the outlining of the figures, Francis and Christ's feet are united and set off from the patterned background. There are four other large crosses from the last two decades of the century that are closely related iconographically to this cross.[82]

A second version of Francis at the crucifixion exists in three surviving

79. This fresco is in the left transept of the Upper Church. A similar one in the right transept is usually ascribed to followers of Cimabue. See Enio Sindona, *L'opera completa di Cimabue ed il momento figurative pregiottesco* (Milan, 1975), pp. 101, 108–9.

80. For details including the inscription on the cross, see Oswald Sirén, *Toskanische Maler im XIII. Jahrhundert* (Berlin, 1922), pp. 150–51.

81. For a discussion of these crosses, see Victor Lazarev, "Un crocefisso firmato di Ugolino di Tedice," *Paragone* 67 (1955): 9.

82. These are in the local museums in Gualdo Tadino, Nocera Umbra, and Montefalco and in the church of Sant'Andrea in Spello. All these towns are within a few miles of Assisi.

crosses, the earliest of which is in Santa Chiara in Assisi. Probably painted in the 1260s,[83] it presents Francis kneeling on a rock, representing Calvary. Francis cradles the foot of Christ and holds his face next to the nail piercing that foot. Christ's blood drips onto Francis. Perhaps the most interesting variation on this theme is the cross in San Francesco, Arezzo.[84] We see in a crucifixion scene for the first time all five wounds in Francis' body (see fig. 8). Francis's hand and foot wounds are miniature versions of the nails in Christ's body, and his side wound bleeds exactly like Christ's, which is directly above it. Even the left-leaning of Francis's body parallels Christ's body hanging asymmetrically on the cross. This is perhaps the most dramatic representation of Francis transformed into Christ Crucified. Although we know that the image of Francis at the foot of Christ's cross was invented in 1236, there are only two surviving crucifixions with Francis dating from before the 1260s, while there are about nineteen that date from the last forty years of the century. This is remarkably different from the survival of the early cycles, about half of which date from about 1260 or before. I think it is reasonable to suggest that it is Bonaventure's interpretation of Francis's life and of the stigmata that makes this one of the most popular images of Francis of Assisi in the latter part of the *duoento*.

That the life of St. Francis was uniquely popular in the thirteenth century is clear from the enormous body of literature and art which has survived into the twentieth century. During the first seventy-five years after Francis' death, however, the accounts and interpretations of Francis's life and teachings changed in response to developments within the Franciscan order as well as evolving relationships between the mendicants and secular clergy. Furthermore, different versions of the life of Francis had different audiences—the Latin texts primarily for the friars and the paintings largely for the laity. Thus, the artists and the friars who commissioned and guided them had to translate for a different audience and into a different medium the essence of Francis and the order he founded. How that was done and what some of the specific elements of translation entailed have constituted much of the substance of this chapter—research possible only because of the extraordinary quantity and quality of evidence left by a large number of mostly anonymous Italian painters. Looking at the means that the friars used to have their founder continue to address current issues within and beyond the order broadens our understanding of how the friars perceived themselves and how they wished the faithful to perceive them.

83. Several scholars date this cross in the 1270s or 1280s, but I accept the argument that it was executed shortly after the patron, Abbess Benedicta, died in 1260 and probably in time for the consecration of the church in 1265. See Garrison, *Italian Romanesque Panel Paintings*, no. 542. For the argument for a later date, see Sandberg-Vavalà, pp. 841–44.

84. For this cross, see Sandberg-Vavalà, p. 873. The other cross with this basic iconography is a much-cut-down work in the collection of Harold Acton in Florence. See Sandberg-Vavalà, pp. 834–35.

*Figure 8.* San Francesco, Arezzo. Detail of a crucifix by an Umbrian or Tuscan artist, about 1290. Francis embracing the feet of Christ.

# [16]

## An English Conciliarist?
## Thomas Netter of Walden

### KIRK STEVAN SMITH

"It has long been incumbent upon Englishmen, especially upon us clergy, to restore and unify the seamless garment of Christ. . . . yet we are said to have done little or nothing, and the result is to diminish the conspicuous good name of England."[1] So wrote the Canterbury cleric Henry Ware in the midst of the crisis affecting the church at the beginning of the fifteenth century, the period known to church historians as the Conciliar Epoch.

Scholars have long shared Ware's conclusion that English thinkers contributed little to the rich ferment of ecclesiological debate leading up to the councils of Pisa and Constance.[2] This lack of concern, it is argued, may have been due to pressure from King Henry V, who viewed the councils not as a means for effecting reform, but simply as an arena for furthering his own foreign policy against France.[3] Then too, there was the English chagrin over their image as "the nursemaid of heresy," a country which had produced John Wyclif and the Lollards and their continental offspring, the Hussites.[4] It was perhaps this overwhelming preoccupation

1. Quoted in E. F. Jacob, "English Documents of the Conciliar Movement," *Bulletin of the John Rylands Library* 15 (1931): 3.

2. "The Council of Constance did not hold a very large place in the interests of contemporary Englishmen as a whole, whether they were clerks or laymen." C. M. D. Crowder, "Correspondence between England and the Council of Constance," *Studies in Church History* 1 (1964): 185.

3. Ibid. Cf. E. F. Jacob, "Reflections upon the Study of the General Councils in the Fifteenth Century," *Studies in Church History* 1 (1964): 80–98.

4. That England suffered under this image can be seen clearly from contemporary accounts. The Richtental Chronicle mentions "Oxenford, where flourished John Wyclif the heretic" (quoted by R. N. Quirk, "Bishop Robert Hallum and the Council of Constance," *Friends of Salisbury Cathedral Annual Report*, May 1952, p. 4). When Pope

with heresy that caused English churchmen to neglect more important and subtle issues of ecclesiastical reform.[5]

Yet this general lack of interest in conciliar issues does not mean that England was totally lacking in reform-minded clerics. Even before delegates had left for Pisa, a plan for reform had been suggested by Richard Ullerston in his *Petitiones pro ecclesias militantis reformatione*,[6] a work commissioned by the bishop of Salisbury, Robert Hallum. Hallum, who was the leader of the delegation to Pisa, and who later participated at Constance, seems to have collected around him a large group of reformers, most of whom were connected with Oxford University.[7]

Among these young university scholars was Thomas Netter of Walden (1372–1430), a figure destined to become, in the words of Dom David Knowles, "perhaps the most distinguished friar of any order between the Age of Ockham and the Dissolution."[8] His career, which saw him as confessor to two kings, prior provincial to his fellow English Carmelites, and leading intellectual opponent of the Lollards, has only recently begun to receive the attention it deserves.[9] His works had a considerable impact far beyond the time they were written and are now viewed as containing much which is noteworthy and unique to late medieval ecclesiology.[10] Of special importance to us here is a section of his massive anti-Wycliffite

---

John XXIII called the council into session he asked the delegates to "consider the errors which for some time past have been springing up in certain regions; those especially that originated with a certain John called Wyclif." Cf. Louise Loomis, *The Council of Constance* (New York, 1961), p. 205.

5. "The English to their discredit had produced the arch-heretic; it was now their duty to use all their influence against heresy." E. F. Jacob, *Archbishop Henry Chichele* (London, 1967), p. 35.

6. H. van der Hardt, *Magnum oecumenicum concilium Constantiense* (Frankfurt, 1697), 1:1126–70. Cf. Margaret Harvey, "English Views on the Reforms to Be Undertaken in the General Councils: 1400–1418" (diss., Oxford University, 1963).

7. On Robert Hallum, a sadly neglected figure of the English conciliar epoch, see Quirk, "Bishop Robert Hallum." Cf. J. M. Wilkinson, "The Register of Robert Hallum, Bishop of Salisbury" (B. litt. thesis, Oxford University, 1962). The universities, including Oxford, played a major role in the formation of conciliar thought; see Guy Fitch Lytle, "Universities as Religious Authorities in the Later Middle Ages and Reformation," in *Reform and Authority in the Medieval and Reformation Church*, ed. Guy Fitch Lytle, (Washington, D.C., 1981), pp. 69–98. Cf. R. N. Swanson, *Universities, Academics, and the Great Schism* (Cambridge, 1979).

8. David Knowles, *The Religious Orders in England* (Cambridge, 1955), 2:146.

9. A complete biography of Netter may be found in my dissertation, "The Ecclesiology of Controversy: Scripture, Tradition, and Church in the Theology of Thomas Netter of Walden" (Ph.D. diss., Cornell University, 1983), chap. 1. Cf. D. J. DuBois, "Thomas Netter of Walden, OC. (B. litt. thesis, Oxford University, 1978). A brief notice may be found in the *Dictionary of National Biography*, 14:232. Netter's extant letters and other information about him are collected in Benedict Zimmerman, *Monumenta historica Carmelitarum* (Lerins, 1907), pp. 442–84.

10. In addition to Smith, "Ecclesiology," see also F. X. Siebel, "Die Kirche als Lehrautorität nach dem 'Doctrinale antiquitatum fidei catholicae ecclesiae' des Thomas Waldensis (1372–1431)," *Carmelus* 60 (1969): 3–70, and Michael Hurley, "Thomas Netter, a Pre-Tridentine Theology of Tradition," *Heythrop Journal* 4 (1963): 348–99.

compendium the *Doctrinale antiquitatum fidei catholicae ecclesiae*,[11] which sets forth clearly his view of general councils in the governance of the church.

Netter's interest in councils was more than just academic. In 1408, perhaps because of his growing reputation as a preacher, he was selected to attend the Council of Pisa.[12] There he quickly established himself as an advocate of the *via concilii*, the view which purposed ending the schism by deposing the two rival popes and electing a third. Such was the tone of a *consultatio theologorum* attended by Netter in the spring of 1409.[13] Its members decided that both Benedict XIII and Gregory XII "were, according to divine law, found to be pertinacious schismatics and fomenters of the ancient schism and also heretics, in the strict sense of the word. And, as such pertinacious schismatics and heretics, ought to be declared by the sacred general council to be de jure ejected from office."[14]

These conclusions Netter brought home to the council in a series of sermons preached before the emperor and the assembled delegates, sermons later collected and published by his friend and fellow Oxford delegate John Luk.[15]

The period between councils saw Netter engaged in the trials of many of the early Lollards, including the most famous proceeding of his time, the case of Sir John Oldcastle.[16] His reputation as an inquisitor and apologist may have helped him secure election as prior provincial of his order in 1414.[17]

Given Netter's considerable status, it comes as no surprise that he was among those asked to attend a new council to be held at Constance "pro

11. Several editions. By far the most complete is the one used here, edited by Bonaventura Blanciotti (Venice, 1757); reprint Gregg Press, 1967).

12. The contents of the royal summons (in Thomas Rymer, *Foedera* [London, 1816], 1:146) give no names, specifying only that the two archbishops are to attend with four doctors, and five bishops with five doctors each.

13. Mansi, 27:399–412.

14. Mansi, 27:400, "In jure divino fundatos fore pertinaces schismaticos et antiquite schismatis nutritores, et haereticos, haeresis termino stricte sumpto. Et per consequens per sacrum generale concilium et tales pertinaces schismatici antiquo schismate et haeretici sunt declarandi de jure ejecti."

15. Johannes Pit, *Relationium historicarum de rebus Anglicis liber* (Paris, 1619), p. 619. Pit provides the most complete list of titles attributed to Netter, among them three sermons: *Responsa in Concilio Pisano, Ad Clerum in eodem Concilio*, and *Coram Sigismundo Caesare Oratio*. John Luk (d. 1435) was senior proctor of the university while Netter was there. It was probably Netter's friendship with Luk which brought him into contact with Bishop Hallum and the reformers connected with him. Cf. Smith, "Ecclesiology," p. 24.

16. An interesting account of Netter's activity at this trial is preserved by John Bale, "A brefe Chronycle concernynge the Examination and Death of the Blessed Martyr of Chryst syr Johan Oldescastell, the Lorde Cobham, first collected by John Bale" (London, 1544), reprinted in *Harleian Miscellany* (London, 1808), 2:249–81.

17. BL Harleian MS 3838, fol. 35.

pace et exaltatione ecclesiae ac tranquillitate Christianorum,"[18] to try once again to resolve the schism left unsolved by the Council at Pisa. Accounts of Netter's presence at Constance are vague and in some cases contradictory. Some scholars have doubted that Netter attended at all.[19] It may well be that he traveled there not as an official delegate, but simply as an observer.[20]

Whatever Netter's official role at Constance, he most certainly would have been deeply interested in the process which led up to the council's condemnation of John Wyclif in April of 1415.[21] It may have been that Netter's personal reaction to events there came in the form of his encyclopedic anti-Wycliffite work the *Doctrinale*, published in three volumes over the years 1421–28.[22]

The purpose of this work was to provide a thoroughgoing defense of the church against the attacks of John Wyclif and his followers. Appealing to Scripture and the church fathers, Wyclif had claimed that the church of his day had departed from the pristine faith of the ancient church and had fallen into corruption and decay. In response, Netter used the same scriptural and patristic witnesses to demonstrate the essential continuity between the church of his time and the apostolic faith.[23] By so doing, he showed clearly how a historic exemplar could be used not as an instrument of radical dissent, but as a buttress to orthodoxy. The goal of the *Doctrinale* was thus to provide precise historical evidence supporting the

18. The papal summons is printed in E. F. Jacob, ed., *The Register of Henry Chichele, Archbishop of Canterbury* (Oxford, 1943), 1:17–20.

19. It should be noted that E. F. Jacob, by far the greatest scholar of this period, doubts that Netter was at Constance (quoted in J. Crompton, "Fasciculus Zizaniorum," *Journal of Ecclesiastical History* 12 [1961]: 165 n. 5). Such an opinion is easy to understand, for there is no record of his name on the official envoy list. There is also evidence that he was in England for a Carmelite synod early in 1416 (*Dictionary of National Biography*, 14:272). There also exists a letter, unfortunately undated, from Netter to Prior General John Grosse, asking to be excused from attending. Cf. Zimmerman, *Monumenta*, p. 477. This evidence is called into question, however, by another letter in the same collection from Henry V to the council commending Netter to them: ibid., p. 447, "Exhibitorem praesentium fratrem Thomam Walden . . . in regno nostro Angliae priorem provincialem hujus nostrae voluntatis et virtutum suarum intuitu vestris habendis favoribus in Domino specialiter commendatum."

20. John Bale, Netter's earliest and most important biographer, is insistent that Netter attended the council. Bodleian, Bodl. MS 73, fol. 81, "Missus est unus ad consilium generalium constancie." Bodleian, Bodl. MS Selden Supra 41, fol. 177, "Hunc rex habuit ambassiatorem, ano. do. 1415 ad consilium generale Constancie per republicam Anglicanam missus est." Cf. Crowder, "Correspondence," p. 186 n. 4.

21. The condemned statements are in Mansi, 28:57–156.

22. A manuscript copy of the *Doctrinale* (Bodleian Madl. Col. 153, fol. 8) contains an illuminated miniature of a Carmelite friar presenting the work to the pope.

23. Smith, "Ecclesiology," chap. 4. My view is in contrast to those who hold that use of Scripture and the Fathers is the distinguishing mark of a "pre-Reformation thinker." Cf. Gordon Leff, "The Apostolic Ideal in Later Medieval Ecclesiology," *Journal of Theological Studies* 18 (1967): 71ff., and "The Making of a Myth of a True Church in the Later Middle Ages," *Journal of Medieval and Renaissance Studies* 1 (1971): 1–15.

doctrines and practices attacked by the English Lollards and Bohemian Hussites—the doctrine of the Eucharist, the prerogatives of the papacy, the legality of the mendicant orders.

Fundamental to Netter's ecclesiology was his conception of "primitive church" as the norm for Christian belief. It is faith in this "creedal" or "universal" church which Christians profess when they acknowledge "one Holy Catholic and Apostolic Church."[24] The faith of this primitive church comes to us through many channels, most importantly through Holy Scripture and the teaching tradition of the church, tradition meaning for Netter above all the writings of the church fathers.[25] For Netter, all organs of authority within the church must be defined in relation to this apostolic deposit. Bishops, popes, councils, all were important instruments for preserving and transmitting this deposit, but none of them had any power whatever to add to it or change it.[26] The original and pure faith had been determined once and for all in the time of the apostles. It was henceforth fixed, static, and immutable.[27]

> Now that we may return to a definition of the catholic church, you see that multiple grades of authority are followed in it: All catholic doctors, especially those holy bishops who presided over the original apostolic churches, above all the Roman bishop. Even greater authority than these is possessed by a general council. But the pronouncements of none of these ought to be obeyed, I think, as if they were the faith itself, that is to say, the primitive faith of Scripture and the creedal church of Christ, but rather simply as institutions of elders and admonitions of fathers. They ought to be obeyed, nonetheless, without question, unless a higher authority proscribes them.[28]

It is with this understanding that Netter turns to an examination of the powers of a general council.

It is clear from the outset that Netter's defense of conciliar power is not a systematic treatment of the subject; rather, it is a direct response to the charges Wyclif made against the authority of such councils. Wyclif had

24. *Doctrinale*, 1:326.
25. *Doctrinale*, 1:357, "Et qui de primitivis fidei cognoverunt, patres fidei appellantur."
26. *Doctrinale*, 1:341.
27. *Doctrinale*, 1:346, 353.
28. *Doctrinale*, 1:384, "Jam ut ad definitionem Ecclesiae Catholicae redeamus, videtis sequendam esse in Ecclesia Catholica gradatim authoritatem multiplicem: Doctorum scilicet Catholicorum omnium, Antistitum Sanctorum magis, Ecclesiarum Apostolicarum potius, et ex eis amplius Romanae Ecclesiae: et abundatius his omnibus Authoritatem Concilii Generalis. Nec tamen alicui jam dictae ita obediendum censeo, et tam prono fide, sicut primae fidei Scripturae, vel Ecclesiae Christi Symbolicae; sed sicut institutionibus Seniorum, et monitioni Paternae. Obediatur, dico, sine scrupulis questionum nisi quatenus id quis doceat quod jam juste proscripsit superioris auctoritas."

made the statement (it is one of those rare instances where Netter does not provide us with a cross-reference) that modern councils were in no way equal to their ancient counterparts, the great ecumenical gatherings of the early church.[29] For Wyclif, it was not even necessary to consult such modern councils, since the Word of God as contained in Scripture was quite enough for the governance of the church.[30]

Netter, naturally, was of a different mind. Fundamental for him was the notion that although a council was not in itself equal to the universal church, it was nearer (propinquior) to it than any institution of the visible church.[31] In this assertion, Netter shows his true conciliarist colors, namely, his appeal to the congregatio fidelium as represented in a general council as the ultimate source of authority in the church. There can be no doubt that Netter deserves the label "conciliarist."[32]

Netter is quick, however, to qualify his exaltation of the power of councils with his all-important notion of the primitive church. As close as a council might be to the ideal of the creedal or universal church "as is possible in this life, in this time and place," its decrees could never possess the same weight as the teachings of the Scriptures and the church fathers.[33] A general council, therefore, could never be considered the final arbiter of truth in the church. That place was reserved for Netter's apostolic church and its teachings alone.

But if Netter is not in precise alignment with those who feel that a general council is always the legitimate expression of the will of the church universal, he does agree with them that the church ought to be governed in common.[34] This principle helps to define even the position of a pope, for, as Netter flatly states, "It is widely said that a pope is preeminent in a council. However, he is not preeminent over a council, for the church must be governed in common."[35]

29. As a continual minority voice in the church, Wyclif had some harsh things to say about the principle of "majority rule" in church councils. "Ideo blasphema est regula; quod si major pars talium sententiae cuicunque consenserit, tunc est vera, laudabilis, et tenenda; atque eo magis omni catholico reverenda." Quoted in Doctrinale, 1:371.

30. Again quoting Wyclif, ibid., "Non quaeramus, ergo superflue concilium qualiter facere debeamus, cum verbum Dei, quod est Scriptura sacra, et impulsus Spiritus in recte viventibus satis doceat."

31. Doctrinale, 1:376, "Ipsa convocatio Synodi est tam conformis Ecclesiae universali; non tamen est universalis Ecclesia, nec ejus decretum, ut sit fides Symbolica; sed Ecclesiae Catholicae imago propinquior, et de omnibus Ecclesiis catholicis ex sacris Antistitibus, quantum in hac vita uno tempore et uno loco convenire possunt, simillima genitura; et ideo est universali Ecclesiae in authoritate multum consimilis, quamvis secundum rei veritatem disparis ponderis."

32. "The appeal to the underlying authority of the church, understood as the congregatio fidelium, was the very essence of the conciliar position." Brian Tierney, Foundations of the Conciliar Theory (Cambridge, 1955), p. 4.

33. Doctrinale, 1:376.

34. Doctrinale, 1:382.

35. Doctrinale, 1:384, "Et sic communiter dicitur, Papam in Consilio praeesse, non autem praeesse Consilio, quia in communi debet Ecclesia regi."

When it comes to getting beyond these general principles, however, Netter becomes rather vague. On one hand, he often lashes out against the pope. The council should be able to expel him for any reason.[36] At one point, this notion is even couched in language echoing that of the "charter of independence" of the Council of Constance, the decree *Haec sancta:* A general council ought to have power to reform all orders of the church "no matter how great," and that it must be obeyed, "sub poena contumaciae."[37] Such extreme limits on papal power might seem openly contradictory of what Netter says elsewhere in his work about papal sovereignty.[38] This contradiction is best understood by keeping in mind the underlying purpose of the *Doctrinale*. The intricacies of papal-conciliar relations were not of prime interest to the Oxford inquisitor. What was of interest was the council's utility, its effectiveness in combating heresy. It might help to remember that the Council of Constance was for Netter the orthodox council par excellence. It had gone on record with a public condemnation of Wyclif's doctrines and had culminated its antiheretical activities with the famous trials of John Hus and Jerome of Prague. It is no wonder that Netter was concerned with vindicating such conciliar activities, not only against the vicissitudes of changing papal politics, but also against the more serious charge that such modern councils were in some way inferior to their great counterparts of the past. If such modern councils were not legitimate, then neither were their anti-Wycliffite activities legitimate.

For this reason, Netter steers his discussion of general councils away from theoretical questions of their nature and authority and spends most of his time establishing their role as teaching organs of the church. It was for this reason that they were called into existence in the first place, for correction of believers led astray; led astray to such an extent that a greater weight of authority was needed to bring them back to correct belief than could be provided by a pope alone.[39]

A council possesses this greater weight of authority for two reasons, according to Netter. The first is theological. Christians believe that the

36. *Doctrinale,* 1:403.

37. *Doctrinale,* 1:385, "Ubi ex omnibus liquet authoritas Generalis Concilii; quia illi cedunt cuncta scripta Pontificum et Doctorum, et reformatari per ipsum debent Concilia minora regnorum, immo et priora, quamvis plenaria. Tanti ergo valet authoritas Ecclesiae jam praesentis, ut singulis in ea ordinate jubentibus obediri debent a subjectis plus vel minus secundum superius et inferius, sub poena contumaciae." To this statement Netter's editor, Blanciotti, adds in the margin, "Hoc declaravit magna Synodus Constantiensis, cui Waldensis interesse meruit. Nam sessione 4. definivit, Concilium Generale habere a Christo immediatam authoritatem, cui omnis obedire tenetur, etiamsi Papalis Dignitatis existat."

38. Mostly found in the *Doctrinale,* 1:399–525. Cf. Smith, "Ecclesiology," pp. 232–44.

39. *Doctrinale,* 1:380, "Secundo, quia ad corrigendum populum, plurimum valet auctoritas et consensus multorum in una sententia, et nedum populum, sed clerum errantem vel dubium."

Holy Spirit will be among them "wherever two or three are gathered together." How much more, asks Netter, may we expect that Spirit to be present when the leaders of the entire church are assembled together?[40] Of course, as we have seen before, there are limits to this conciliar authority. A council must remain true to the apostolic model. But "provided that it remains uncorrupted, it possesses the rightful spirit for defining the faith."[41] Hence councils in no way detract from the ultimate authority of Scripture but serve, along with the Fathers, as organs for defining and transmitting the universal faith; for telling us "quid Scriptura docet."[42]

The theological legitimacy of general councils is also buttressed by their historical legitimacy. They are not recent inventions of the church, but have their origins in that period of history when the church felt itself threatened by the inroads of the great heretics, the Donatists, the Arians, the Manicheans. This was the period of the first great councils, Chalcedon, Nicea, Constantinople. Previous to such councils the fathers of the church were not able to combat the heretics adequately. By banding together, they discovered, they could be much more effective. Ever since those days councils have been considered the highest court of appeal in doctrinal matters, and it is precisely for this reason that Wyclif feared them so much.[43]

Incidentally, the form of the past councils remains for Netter the model modern ones should follow. For example, he is violently against the idea that councils ought to include members of the laity. The reason? No laypeople are mentioned as having taken part in the earliest "protocouncils" mentioned in the Book of Acts. If one is to proceed in this matter "according to apostolic form, we read that they did not call laity to their councils."[44] Perhaps some might have been present "silenter," yet the prominent laymen we find mentioned elsewhere in the Gospel accounts are conspicuous by their absence. Likewise, St. Paul's accounts of the gatherings in which he was involved mention only apostles and priests (sic).[45] A general council was for Netter an episcopal institution above all.[46]

40. *Doctrinale*, 1:376.

41. *Doctrinale*, 1:382, "Ita ergo plenariis Conciliis Ecclesiae, si tamen maneant incorrupta, Spiritus Sanctus adest, et definit de fide. . . . Ecce quod multorum Sanctorum concursus in Conciliis praestat plenitudinem authoritatis."

42. *Doctrinale*, 1:378.

43. *Doctrinale*, 1:381, "Post tempora namque Apostolorum, fide jam nunciata per orbem, coepit Christianorum persecutio ingrassari, unde non poterant Ecclesiae Patres uno consensu suo haereses, quae tunc licenter intrabant, extinguere, usque ad tempora Constantini. Tunc ergo coactis Conciliis tot suffocabant communi authoritate Ecclesiae immanes haereses, quot Concilia celebrabant."

44. *Doctrinale*, 1:383, "Sed si sequendam putemus in hac re formam Apostolicam, ipsos non legimus ad Concilia sua laicos convocasse."

45. Ibid., "Solos Apostolos et Presbyteros legimus esse collectos."

46. Ibid., "Nec movere quemquam debet, quod talem concordem professionem Patrum praeposui decreto generalis Concilii, etiamsi de toto orbe convenirent Episcopi."

Where did this leave the laity, the major part of the church? Were they to have no role at all? Laity certainly were included in the Councils of Pisa and Constance, yet Netter defines their role in strictly utilitarian terms. Their presence was not necessary, but it was useful in that it helped to expedite the business of the council.[47] In addition, and here Netter begins to backpedal a bit, they also helped to add weight to the pronouncements of the council, since "greater numbers carry with them a greater truth."[48] This notion finds justification in the Bible, for in Acts we notice that even the apostles were anxious to have their statements endorsed by the faithful and so often presented them before a large crowd. Take, for example, Acts 15, where in choosing Paul and Barnabas for a mission to the Gentiles "it seemed good" to the other apostles "to act with the whole church."[49] For Netter this was scriptural proof of the principle that "the opinion of the multitude is of no small import."[50]

What may one conclude? First, that Netter's conciliar thought is highly erratic, at times even contradictory. A council is to be the representative body of the whole church, but its membership includes only priests and bishops. The presence of the laity serves only a utilitarian purpose, yet it also increases the authority of the council. A council has authority over a pope, yet a pope meeting with a council has even more authority. A council is the supreme dogmatic organ of the church, but it must remain faithful to the apostolic teaching, and so on. It is no wonder that even the best theologians of subsequent generations were confused about Netter's exact stand on certain issues. Yet behind this welter of seeming contradictions there is visible the concern which led Netter to make them in the first place. That concern was his overwhelming desire to uphold *all* institutions in the church that he felt could combat heresy. This power Netter vested primarily in the throne of St. Peter, yet he knew that in the aftermath of the abuses of papal power, abuses that had led to councils like Pisa and Constance, simple appeals to papal arbitration were no longer enough. The legitimacy of those two recent councils which had taken bold anti-Wycliffite action must be upheld against heretical "biblical-historical" attack. Both pope and council had to be vindicated as correct (and that meant for Netter, apostolic) means for dealing with the menace of Lollardy and Hussitism. His goal remained, therefore, not a well-structured description of the interrelation of the two ecclesiastical organs, the obsession of most conciliar thinkers of his day, but only a polemical defense of the right of both institutions to serve as channels for the true faith.

Cf. *Doctrinale*, 1:342. For Netter a frequent synonym for "concilium generalis" is "Synodus Antistitum generalis." Ibid.
47. *Doctrinale*, 1:383, "Non ergo tamen posse vocari Laicos potentes vel simplices, si sic expedire negocio videntur Ecclesiae."
48. Ibid., "Semper major numerus authoritatem accumulat veritatis."
49. *Doctrinale*, 1:384.
50. Ibid., "Ergo opinio multitudinis non erit parvi momenti."

Thus it would be wrong finally to claim that Netter's use of conciliar ideas in his inquisitorial arsenal somehow invalidates those ideas or makes Netter less of a conciliarist than his reform-minded contemporaries. True, he was not preoccupied with the same questions of church polity as were his Continental peers. Their enemies were tyrannical pontiffs, his heretical Hussites. Still, their overarching concern was the same as his: the protection of orthodoxy and the preservation of the "one, Holy, Catholic, and Apostolic Church."

# [17]

## An Episcopal Election in
## Quattrocento Florence

### David S. Peterson

In early August 1445 Florence's archbishop, Bartolomeo Zabarella, died while making a trip to Rome. Immediately, and to some observers with unseemly haste, the Florentines directed their attention to finding a successor.[1] Zabarella had not yet been buried when, on 8 August, the city's chancellor, Carlo Marsuppini, wrote separate letters to Pope Eugenius IV on behalf of five Florentine candidates: Donato de' Medici, bishop of Pistoia; Benozzo Federighi, bishop of Fiesole; Roberto Cavalcanti, bishop

I am grateful to Professor Tierney for helping me prepare this essay, though he did not know it would be this chapter.

In citations, the following abbreviations will be used: *ASI, Archivio storico italiano; AFP, Archivum Fratrum Praedicatorum.* The *Pergamene* are in Florence's Archivio del Capitolo, cited by the catalog numbers of Ignazio Paur (1843) and Luigi Strozzi (1681) and the date. For series in Florence's Archivio di Stato (ASF), note: *CP, Consulte e pratiche; DO, Deliberazioni dei signori e collegi, ordinaria autorità; LC, Signori, carteggi, missive, legazioni e commissarie; MAP, Mediceo avanti il principato; Missive, Signori, carteggi, missive, I cancelleria; NA, Notarile antecosimiano; PR, Provvisioni registri.* Documents cited from the Vatican Archives (ASV) include: *RL, Registra Lateranensia;* and *RV, Registra Vaticana.*

1. The exact dates and locations of Zabarella's death and burial remain obscure. At a meeting of the cathedral canons held on 14 August, Tommaso della Bordella announced that Zabarella had died and been buried on 12 August, but the notary present, Ser Jacopo di Ser Antonio di Jacopo di Piero da Romena, added the words "seu alio verior." ASF, NA, I 9 (1443–45), fol. 401r (14 August 1445). On 10 August the priors approved the deputation of two *mazzerii* to guard the archiepiscopal palace on behalf of its patrons, and custodians during vacancies, the Visdomini and Tosinghi. ASF, DO, 62, fols. 35v–36r (10 August 1445). For contemporary comments on the Florentines' haste, see *Leonardo Dati . . . epistolae XXXIII,* ed. Laurentius Mehus (Florence, 1743), 30:53–55, to Cardinal Lodovico Scarampi (1445); and *Hieronymi Aliotti Arretii . . . epistolae et opuscula,* ed. Gabriele Maria Scarmalli, vol. 1 (Arezzo, 1769), 2, 25:120, to Jacopo Lavagnolo (1445). See also note 47 below.

of Volterra; and Giovanni di Nerone di Nigi Dietisalvi and Andrea di Domenico d'Andrea Fiochi, both cathedral canons. In the next few months Marsuppini would dispatch a total of thirty-one letters to the pope, various cardinals, and other Roman officials. The Medici, too, would demonstrate their interest in the choice of a new archbishop, as would the cathedral chapter, the custodians of the see, the candidates themselves, various Tuscan clerics, and several officials in Rome. In filling the vacancy, Eugenius necessarily signaled not only his own intentions for the archdiocese but his estimation of the competing claims of the interested parties, including those of clergy and laity who had not found spokesmen. Such a flurry of activity was unusual but not unprecedented in quattrocento Florence,[2] pointing beyond the continuing importance of the archbishopric in Florentine and papal affairs to the matrix of ecclesiastical and civic, pious and political interests that converged upon it, within which the successful candidate would in turn exercise his authority.

The first letter recorded in the city's registers is the one Marsuppini wrote to Eugenius on behalf of Donato de' Medici. After a flourish of lamentations over the death of Archbishop Zabarella, balanced by an appeal for equanimity, he urged finding a replacement "from among our citizens, pleasing to the city and devoted to the present regime [status]."[3] Marsuppini pointed out that Florence had hosted a succession of foreigners as archbishops, and its citizens now wished to have one of their own head the church. Donato fit the twin requirements of local birth and piety. He was, moreover, "descended from the celebrated family of the

2. In 1423 the commune sponsored six Florentine candidates for the cardinalate, offering Martin V, however, one simple list. ASF, *Missive,* 31, fol. 12r (21 November 1422). I discuss the role of the archbishop in Florentine politics more fully in "Archbishop Antoninus: Florence and the Church in the Earlier Fifteenth Century" (Ph.D. diss., Cornell University, 1985), particularly pp. 29–41. Roberto Bizzocchi has examined the Florentine aristocracy's influence on the local church in "Chiesa e aristocrazia nella Firenze del Quattrocento," *ASI* 142 (1984): 191–282, and he surveys fifteenth-century episcopal elections in *Chiesa e potere nella Toscana del Quattrocento,* Annali dell'Istituto Storico Italo-germanico, Monografia 6 (Bologna, 1987), pp. 195–217. Useful surveys of electoral politics and local ecclesiastical institutions in Italy around this period are Mauro Ronzani's "Vescovi, capitoli e strategie famigliari nell'Italia comunale," and Giorgio Chittolini's "Stati regionali e istituzioni ecclesiastiche nell'Italia centrosettentrionale del Quattrocento," both in *La Chiesa e il potere politico dal Medioevo all'età contemporanea,* Storia d'Italia, Annali 9, ed. Giorgio Chittolini and Giovanni Miccoli (Turin, 1986), pp. 101–46, 149–93. Denys Hay furnishes an ample bibliography in *The Church in Italy in the Fifteenth Century* (Cambridge, 1977).

3. "[A]liquem e nostris civibus . . . civitati gratus et presentis status studiosus." *Missive,* 36, fol. 123v (8 August 1445), pub. in Raoul Morçay, *Saint Antonin archevêque de Florence (1389–1459)* (Paris, 1914), pp. 432–33. The word *status* carried a variety of significations in Florentine discourse, often meaning the regime, the government, or an existing state of affairs but rarely anything as abstract as the modern term "state." See Nicolai Rubinstein, "Notes on the Word *Stato* in Florence before Machiavelli," in *Florilegium Historiale: Essays Presented to Wallace K. Fergusson,* ed. J. G. Rowe and W. H. Stockdale (Toronto, 1971).

Medici, . . . and by virtue of his parentage most pleasing and loyal to this regime."[4] Marsuppini closed with a summation of Donato's virtues, emphasizing his faith, learning, and popularity, and sent a copy of this letter, "eiusdem tenoris et effectus, mutatis mutandis," to the College of Cardinals and to Lodovico Scarampi, formerly Florence's archbishop, now cardinal of Aquilia.[5]

The proposal to make Donato archbishop rested on three criteria: his piety, his Florentine citizenship, and his membership in the ruling elite of Florence's citizens. On the first point there are no positive grounds for skepticism. Donato had been serving as bishop of Pistoia since 1436, having previously been a parish priest (plebanus) of Santa Maria a Dicomano and metropolitan provost in Florence.[6] He appears to have been much less active in ecclesiastical power broking than either his kinsman Cosimo or Cosimo's son Giovanni, to whom he in fact refused several favors.[7] Nor were Marsuppini and the priors he spoke for necessarily cynical in claiming piety to be a factor in their considerations. To be sure, they often sought to advance the commune's interests by lobbying for the appointment of favorites to ecclesiastical office, particularly to monasteries, parishes, and bishoprics in the outlying regions of the territory, where communal control was tenuous.[8] Yet communal correspondence often reveals, alongside the desire to manipulate churchmen and benefices, a belief that public stability, and that of any reggimento, was better served by conscientious, even inspiring clergy than by those who might be

4. "[E]x clarissima medicorum familia ortus est . . . et familie genere gratiosissimus ac fidissimus huic statui sit." Missive, 36, fol. 123v. Certainly the Medici regime was not the first to set a premium on family ties to the ruling elite. Under the Albizzi, in 1431, the city recommended Antonio Peruzzi to the pope for an unspecified high honor, noting that his family was "ex intimo regiminis nostri." Missive, 34, fol. 33r–v (24 November 1431). See also Missive, 32, fol. 124r–v (12 September 1429).

5. Scarampi had held the archbishopric of Florence in 1438–39. C. Eubel, Hierarchia Catholica Medii Aevi, vol. 2 (Munich, 1898), p. 7.

6. Salvino Salvini, Catologo cronologico de' canonici della chiesa metropolitana fiorentina (Florence, 1782), p. 39.

7. Donato di Nicola di Messer Vieri de' Medici was from the line of Lippo de' Medici, Cosimo was from that of Averardo. ASF, MAP, filza 9, contains a number of letters from Donato to Giovanni. See MAP, 9, 93 (25 September 1454) and 9, 354 (11 February 1459), among numerous refusals of assistance for Giovanni's clients. Many were, to be sure, embarrassingly poor candidates. A variety of petitions to Giovanni are in filze 6, 7, and 8. MAP, 6, 301 (29 November 1457), for example, contains an appeal for a chaplaincy from the sacristan Antonio di Bartolomeo, who promised: "Io mi v'obligho essere schiavo e servidore sempre mai."

8. At least a third of the Missive touch on clerical affairs, of which appointments were a prime concern. The dioceses of Arezzo, Cortona, and Volterra were of exceptional interest to the commune. Regarding the bishopric of Arezzo, the priors wrote Francesco Condulmer that "est necessarium ut persona sit fidelis et de qua merito confidere valeamus, considerata auctoritate maxima quam episcopus habet in illa urbe." Missive, 34, fol. 74r–v (2 November 1433). In 1447 the commune urged the pope either to send more friars to a monastery in Livorno or to allow it to use the income of the house to supply a garrison there. ASF, LC, 12, fol. 20v (10 July 1447).

a source of *scandalo*.[9] Marsuppini's presumption that piety and state service complemented each other was likely no more willfully hypocritical than the identification members of any *reggimento* made between their partisan interests and Florence's *ben comune*.[10]

The second and third points of Marsuppini's recommendation, however, which emphasized Donato's Florentine citizenship and his family's membership in the city's ruling elite, while apparently compatible and even complementary, had in the course of Florentine history stood in conflict with each other. Although the commune opposed allowing foreigners to hold benefices in Florence,[11] it had traditionally taken the reverse position respecting the archbishopric. Realizing that its desirability might stir contention among the city's greater families, and thus civic strife, the commune had passed a law as far back as the thirteenth century prohibiting Florentines from accepting election or appointment to the bishoprics of Florence or Fiesole.[12] This had formed part of the antimagnate legislation of the time, but a similar measure had been passed in 1375 and reissued in 1415.[13] When in 1427 the commune yielded to Martin V in striking some of its old antiecclesiastical legislation, it had specifically retained the law limiting access to the archbishopric.[14]

Nevertheless the law had been only selectively enforced, having become an instrument by which those of any *reggimento* might prevent suspect families from reinserting themselves into civic life through ecclesiastical channels. Since the War of the Eight Saints five members of the Florentine patriciate had occupied the see.[15] Amerigo Corsini (1411–35), however,

9. See *Missive*, 32, fol. 1r–v (29 October 1428), chastising the Aretine bishop both for absenteeism and for despoiling the diocese. The city regularly invited outstanding preachers to the city, particularly to deliver the Lenten sermons at Santa Croce, the leading Franciscan house in Florence. For example, *Missive*, 34, fol. 39v (30 January 1432), to Paolo d'Assisi.

10. Dale Kent, *The Rise of the Medici: Faction in Florence 1426–1434* (Oxford, 1978), p. 204.

11. ASF, *PR*, 83, fols. 212v–14r (10 December 1394); *PR*, 93, fols. 71v–72v (18 July 1404), *PR*, 95, fol. 63r (15 June 1406); *PR*, 105, fols. 232v 33v (10 December 1415); all touching foreigners, absenteeism, and the sequestration of income from vacant benefices.

12. Romolo Caggese, ed., *Statuti della repubblica fiorentia*, vol. 1, *Statuto del Capitano del Popolo degli anni 1322–1325* (Florence, 1910), 5, 78:273–74.

13. The law of 1375 is *PR*, 63, fol. 70v (7 July 1375), printed in part in Antonio Panella, "La guerra degli Otto Santi e le vicende della legge contro i vescovi," *ASI* 99 (1941): 45–47. It was reissued in the compilation of 1415, pub. in *Statuta populi et communis Florentiae . . . anno salutis MCCCCXV*, vol. 1 (Freiburg, 1778), 3, 46: 262.

14. *PR*, 117, fols. 35r–36r (17 May 1427).

15. Angelo Ricasoli (1370–83), Angelo Acciaiuoli (1383–85), Onofrio (Onorio) Visdomini (1390–1401), Alamanno Adimari (1401), and Amerigo Corsini (1411–35). Luca Giuseppe Cerrachini, drawing on the work of Ughelli, Migliore, and Borghini, dates Corsini's archiepiscopate 1411–30. *Chronologia sacra de' vescovi e arcivescovi di Firenze* (Florence, 1716), p. 134. Notarial documents support the contention of the

was the only one to have done so since the turn of the century, and granted that he officiated for over twenty years, his archiepiscopate was bounded by those of Jacopo Palladini (1401–10) from the Abruzzo and Francesco Zabarella (1410–11) from Padua, by Giovanni Vitelleschi (1435–37) from Corneto, and by Lodovico Scarampi (1438–39) and Bartolomeo Zabarella (1440–45), both again from Padua.[16] For most of these foreigners the office had represented a mere *passaggio* in their careers.[17] Bartolomeo Zabarella was the only one of them actually to stay in office until his death, though in the event he was off to Rome to receive the cardinalate for legations that he had carried out in Germany, France, and Spain.[18]

The Florentines might reasonably have desired an archbishop who both knew the city and might be willing to stay there awhile. Already, in 1435, the city's councils had suspended the law prohibiting Florentines from becoming archbishop to enable Vitelleschi, from Corneto in the Florentine territory, to accept the office, and in 1439, although Eugenius had set Zabarella in the see, the councils had suspended the law for five years "desiring that the cathedrals of Florence and Fiesole may be provided with those from the city and territory of Florence."[19] Donato's candidacy, however, raised the specter of political intrigue surrounding the office in a particularly acute way, for not only was he Florentine, he was a Medici, and his nomination was firm evidence of his family's hand in Florentine politics.

Eugenius was being asked to provide an episcopal candidate who was "fidissimus huic statui." The Medici had spent the past ten years seeking to consolidate their hold on the Florentine government and by 1445 appeared to have gotten control of its electoral and legislative apparatus. In October 1443 they had succeeded in extending by three years the period during which electoral officials, the *accoppiatori*, could fill the election

chronicler Paolo di Pietrobuoni that he died in March 1435. *Priorista*, Florence, Biblioteca Nazionale, *Conv. Sopp.*, C.4.895, fol. 135r.

16. Cerrachini, passim.

17. Palladini moved to the bishopric of Spoleto and served as nuncio to Ladislaus of Poland in 1417. Zabarella's subsequent career as a cardinal is well known. Vitelleschi came to Florence after having served already as an apostolic protonuncio, legate to the Marches, bishop of Corneto (Tarquinia), bishop of Recanati, and patriarch of Alexandria. He left in 1437 to assume his cardinalate and leadership of the papal armies. Scarampi came to Florence from the bishopric of Trogir (Traù) and moved on to be patriarch of Aquilia, cardinal of San Lorenzo in Damaso, papal vice-chamberlain, and superintendent of the papal troops in Rome. On Vitelleschi, see Ludwig von Pastor, *History of the Popes*, trans. F. I. Antrobius, vol. 1 (London, 1923), pp. 296–302. On Scarampi, see Pio Paschini, *Lodovico Cardinal Camerlengo*, Lateranum, n.s. 1 (Rome, 1939).

18. Cerrachini, pp. 150–51.

19. "[C]upientes quod ecclesie cathedrali florentine et fesulane etiam de civibus comitatinis et districtualibus provideri possit." *PR*, 130, fol. 271r–v (18 December 1439, printed in Panella, p. 49). The law of 1435 is *PR*, 126, fol. 163r–v (18 August 1435). See *Missive*, 35, fols. 55v and 56r (4 July 1436), letters to Eugenius and Scarampi (bishop of Trogir) complaining that the Vallumbrosans were being mismanaged by outsiders.

bags with the names of candidates by hand (*a mano*), a technique that increased and extended Medici control over nominations to political office in Florence. In May the following year they had gone further, extending by ten years the sentences of citizens banished in 1434 and establishing an extraordinary commission, or *balìa*, of five years' duration with further powers over electoral scrutinies and financial legislation.[20] One of its first measures was to repeal for good the law prohibiting Florentines from holding the archbishopric,[21] and in the period of the episcopal vacancy the Medici-dominated councils would in fact initiate a review of all Florentine legislation to bring it into conformity with their own designs.[22]

Complementing such tactics, the Medici had asserted their leadership in the broader spheres of Florentine social, cultural, and inevitably, religious life. They had cultivated a network of connections among churchmen, sponsoring the transfer of the Observant Dominicans from Fiesole to the monastery of San Marco, just up the street from their palace, while across the way they had supported the growth of the collegiate church of San Lorenzo to such an extent that it rivaled the cathedral chapter.[23] Although they had enjoyed good relations with Vitelleschi and Scarampi, Zabarella had been less accommodating.[24] The election of one of their own to the archbishopric would open direct avenues to patronage and

20. Nicolai Rubinstein, *The Government of Florence under the Medici (1434–94)* (Oxford, 1966), pp. 17–19, 74–77.

21. ASF, *Balìe*, 26, fol. 62r (21 August 1444).

22. *PR*, 136, fols. 186v–87v (11 October 1445). This was done, as Giovanni Cambi put it, "per poter achonciare lo stato a suo modo." Giovanni Cambi, *Istorie fiorentine*, in *Delizie degli eruditi Toscani*, ed. P. Ildefonso di San Luigi, vol. 20 (Florence, 1785), p. 250.

23. Anthony Molho, "Cosimo de' Medici: *Pater Patriae* or *Padrino?*" *Stanford Italian Review* 1 (1979): 5–33; E. H. Gombrich, "The Medici as Patrons of Art," in *Italian Renaissance Studies*, ed. E. F. Jacob (London, 1960), pp. 279–311; Isabelle Hyman, *Fifteenth Century Florentine Studies: The Palazzo Medici and a Ledger for the Church of San Lorenzo* (New York, 1977); Kent, pp. 69–71. Myriad examples of Medici involvement in ecclesiastical patronage can be drawn from the *MAP* collection. Apart from the examples cited below, touching Florence and Rome, it is noteworthy that they were active also in the countryside, as evidenced by the gratitude of the prior of the Camaldoli hermits, and as early as 1435 could support candidates to southern bishoprics such as Tropea. *MAP*, 8, 372 (19 November 1453), and *MAP*, 4, 322 (24 July 1435). Civic patronage could be exchanged for ecclesiastical, as when Bishop Leonardo Salutati of Fiesole asked Piero di Cosimo that his nephew, Tedice di Giovanni di Simone Altoviti, be made a prior of Florence. *MAP*, 17, 319 (8 February 1453).

24. On Scarampi, *MAP*, 12, 197 (6 July 1440). On Vitelleschi, *MAP*, 11, 197 (18 December 1438); *MAP*, 11, 205 (2 January 1436); and *MAP*, 11, 292 (4 July 1439). While in Florence, Vitelleschi stayed with the Medici. *Pergamene*, 1002/814 (26 April 1438). See, however, the desperate appeal of his nephew, Bartolomeo, to Cosimo and Lorenzo, on the eve of Giovanni's capture and murder in Castel Sant'Angelo. *MAP*, 13, 110 (26 March 1440). Zabarella was willing to overrule Medici designs by appointing his chamberlain to a benefice, telling Cosimo: "Ve raccomando la confermatione del [l']autorità mia e la ragione del camerlingo mio." *MAP*, 12, 215 (9 July 1444). But a letter to Piero indicates that his own motives were not disinterested. *MAP*, 17, 37 (19 July 1444).

David S. Peterson

would confirm their status as the leading family of a new Florentine *reggimento*. Vespasiano da Bisticci relates that Cosimo himself wrote to Eugenius urging that he choose a candidate appropriate to Florence, though he was not so crude as to mention Donato specifically.[25]

Arguably he did not have to. The close ties that existed between Eugenius and the Florentines in the 1430s need no great elaboration. At a moment of acute weakness, which saw the papal state under attack by Francesco Sforza and Eugenius's legitimacy being contested at Basel, the pope had found a refuge in Florence.[26] He arrived in June 1434, having been chased out of Rome by angry mobs, and remained almost continuously until 1443. The commune not only defrayed the expense of his stay in the Dominican monastery of Santa Maria Novella but helped underwrite the expense of the council of Florence,[27] a boost to papal prestige at a time when the council of Basel was working, as it seemed to Eugenius, to undermine it. Eugenius himself had been given very preferential terms for his investments in the Monte, Florence's public debt, against which the Medici advanced him additional sums of money.[28]

Whether as a foil to their support for Donato or to hedge their bets, the Signoria on 8 August also sent a recommendation to the pope on behalf of Giovanni di Nerone di Nigi Dietisalvi. A canon of the Florentine cathedral, trained in law at the *studio fiorentino*, Giovanni was the provost of the Fiesolan diocese and had been an apostolic judge delegate in Tuscany. He was also the brother of Dietisalvi di Nerone di Nigi Dietisalvi, one of Cosimo's most devoted partisans.[29] Marsuppini's letter is similar to the one he had written for Donato; indeed, he employed many of the same stock forms of praise. Again the pope was reminded of the Florentines'

25. Vespasiano da Bistici, *Le vite,* ed. Aulo Greco, vol. 1 (Florence, 1970), p. 225.

26. Filippo Rinuccini, *Ricordi storici . . . dal 1282 al 1460,* ed. G. Aiazzi (Florence, 1840), p. 64. Cambi asserts that the commune even paid the expenses of the trip. Cambi, p. 191. Negotiations had in fact been initiated as early as December 1433 by the Albizzi regime. *LC,* 9, fols. 88v–91r (13 December 1433).

27. Touching the council, the priors sought first to defray the city's expenses with a levy on the clergy and, failing that, set a limit of 1,700 florins per month, still a substantial sum. See the city's instructions to Lorenzo di Giovanni de' Medici, Florence's ambassador to Eugenius in Ferrara in 1438, printed in Angelo Fabroni, *Magni Cosmi Medicei vita,* vol. 2 (Pisa, 1789), 64:135–37. See also Peter Partner, "Florence and the Papacy in the Earlier Fifteenth Century," in *Florentine Studies: Politics and Society in Renaissance Florence,* ed. Nicolai Rubinstein (London, 1968), p. 397. *PR,* 129, fols. 232r–33r (24 December 1438) called on the Monte officials to set aside 4,000 florins for the pope's visit.

28. Julius Kirshner, "Papa Eugenio IV e il Monte Comune: Documenti su investimento e speculazione nel debito pubblico di Firenze," *ASI,* 126 (1969): 339–83. In 1438 the Medici lent Eugenius 10,000 florins directly. ASV, *RV,* 366, fol. 286r (17 April 1438). The commune also worked out special deals for Vitelleschi and Scarampi. *Balìe,* 25, fols. 129r–30r (31 December 1434); *PR,* 125, fols. 211r–12r (5 February 1435); *PR,* 131, fols. 267v–69r (29 November 1440).

29. Nerone di Nigi Dietisalvi served as Florence's ambassador in negotiations between Eugenius and Sforza. *LC,* 11, fols. 25v–27r (13–14 October 1444). Pietrobuoni lists him as one of the eight citizens charged in October 1445 to review the city's laws. *Priorista,* fol. 147v. On the Medici and Dietisalvi families, see Kent, pp. 131–32. On

great desire for a citizen archbishop: "This whole people yearns in every way that this dignity be committed not to a foreigner, but to some citizen of their own."[30] Like Donato, Giovanni was "fidissimus huic statui." Copies went out not just to the pope but to the College of Cardinals, to Cardinal Jean le Jeun of Contay, and to Cardinal Scarampi. There is a note in the *Missive* that letters were also written on behalf of the bishops of Fiesole and Volterra, and the Florentine canon Andrea Fiochi, who was also a papal secretary, "mutatis tamen mutandis, ut supra." All were recommended also to the College of Cardinals. Cavalcanti and Fiochi were recommended to Cardinal Scarampi, Federighi to Cardinal Jean le Jeun.[31]

Thus in one day the Signoria sent out sixteen letters on behalf of five Florentine candidates. But of these five candidates, the registers of *Missive* reflect only the commune's subsequent support of Giovanni. If this indicates an early suggestion of disfavor on Eugenius's part it must have come swiftly, for Florence's next letter in favor of Giovanni went out only eight days after the first. There were no further letters for any of the other candidates. Vespasiano's account of Eugenius's reply to Cosimo's letter supporting the Florentine candidates does reflect, if not *freddezza*, at least a willingness to be as coy about his intentions as Cosimo had been: "The pope replied that they should have no doubt that he would elect them such a pastor as would please them."[32]

Whatever favors the Medici had done Eugenius, the pope may well have felt that he had repaid them. When he came to Florence in 1434 the Medici were in exile and the Albizzi were in power. Contemporaries clearly believed that he had been instrumental in the Medici restoration. The chronicler Giovanni Cavalcanti relates that at a critical moment in October, when the struggle between the Albizzi and Medici factions had come down to street fighting, it was Eugenius who persuaded Rinaldo degli Albizzi to lay down arms,[33] and according to Giovanni Cambi, Cosimo

---

Giovanni, see Salvini, p. 41. For Giovanni as an apostolic judge delegate, *NA*, I 9 (1443–45), fol. 466r (8 December 1444).

30. "[U]niversus hic populus omni studio exoptet hanc dignitatem non alicui alieni-gene sed alicui suo civi esse demandandam." *Missive*, 36, fols. 123v–24r (8 August 1445), pub. in Morçay, pp. 433–34.

31. That Marsuppini did not bother transcribing letters for these candidates may suggest the desultory manner in which they were proposed. Federighi and Cavalcanti were both from leading Florentine families, not as *intimo* with the Medici as Donato, but since they were prelates in Tuscany it would have been slighting not to have mentioned their names along with his. Cavalcanti had also served as *procurator* for the cathedral canons, and the Federighi were important ecclesiastical patrons. *Pergamene*, 984/412 (1434); *LC*, 12, fol. 38r–v (18 August 1447). Proposing Andrea to Eugenius was likely also a courtesy. He had been at the cathedral since 1427 and was an intimate of the pope. Salvini, p. 36.

32. "Il papa rispose che non dubitassino punto, che elegerebe loro tale pastore che sarebono contenti." Vespasiano, p. 226.

33. Giovanni Cavalcanti, *Istorie fiorentine*, ed. Filippo Polidori, 2 vols. (Florence, 1838–39), 1:581–610. Cavalcanti's bias was clearly against the Medici, and his estima-

and followers shortly afterward "went to visit the bishop of Recanati [Giovanni Vitelleschi], and then His Holiness the Pope, to thank him for the aid they had received from His Holiness in returning to the patria."[34] Within a year Eugenius named Vitelleschi, who had engineered the meeting between Rinaldo and himself, to the see of Florence.[35] In 1436 he elevated Donato to the bishopric of Pistoia, replacing the deceased Ubertino degli Albizzi, in a gesture that could not have been without significance to contemporaries.[36] Three years later he elevated Scarampi to the cardinalate at Cosimo's request. Meanwhile the Medici enjoyed the profits which accrued to them as the pope's preferred bankers.[37] Were this not going far enough, Eugenius had given the commune permission in 1444 to levy a 60,000 florin impost on the Florentine clergy.[38]

By 1445 Eugenius may have felt not only that he had discharged his obligations toward Florence and the Medici, but that he had been abused by them. In 1441 tensions in the diplomatic alliance between Florence, Venice, and the papacy had come into the open.[39] Both Florentine and Venetian armies were eating into the papal state, and in that year in the Peace of Cavriana the Florentines, by secret agreement, reconciled themselves with Sforza at the expense of the church.[40] With the collapse of

---

tion of Eugenius was not much higher: "Molte cose disse Eugenio al cavaliere, per le quali messer Rinaldo il ringraziò, non s'avvedendo che le infinite lagrime del Papa con quelle del coccodrillo uscivano d'un medesimo fonte." Ibid., 1:586.

34. "Senandarono a visitare el Veschovo di Richanati, e dipoi la Santità del Papa per ringraziarela del benefitio ricievuto di tornare alla patria per mezzo di Sua Santità." Cambi, p. 197. Pietrobuoni's comment is balder but does not contradict the other two chroniclers. Priorista, fol. 133r. The most extreme judgment of these events comes from Neri Capponi, who ascribed to Eugenius the desire to take over the city himself, presumably using the Medici as his tools: "Il Papa aveva l'animo a volere il dominio della città, perché gliene fu data intenzione." Quoted in Gino Capponi, Storia della repubblica di Firenze, vol. 2 (Florence, 1876), p. 224.

35. Eugenius had previously sent Vitelleschi to straighten out some clerical problems in the Florentine diocese, and Cavalcanti relates that during his sojourn Vitelleschi became well acquainted with Florentine politics: "Molte amicizie impetrò coi nostri cittadini: ed ancora che, nel tempo che avemmo la guerra duchesca di Romagna, a Roma non si trovò nessun cherico più amico del nostro comune, che questo messer Giovanni." Cavalcanti, 1:581. Congratulating him on receiving the archbishopric, the priors expressed their wish that "promotionem istam vostram non solum ad animarum curam, verum etiam ad molta nostre rei publice negotia fructus uberrimos esse nobis populoque nostro allaturam." Missive, 35, fol. 117r-v (14 August 1436).

36. Eubel, p. 246. The commune expressed its appreciation in Missive, 35, fol. 54r (30 June 1436).

37. Eugenius made their papal agent his depositary general. Raymond de Roover, The Rise and Decline of the Medici Bank: 1397–1494 (Cambridge, Mass., 1963), pp. 198–202, 216.

38. RV, 367, fols. 164v, 164v–65r (28 January 1444), letters to the priors of Florence and to Archbishop Zabarella. Notably, legislation in Florence was handled by the new balìa of 1444. Balìe, 26, fol. 62r-v (22 August 1444).

39. Partner, pp. 396–400.

40. According to Cavalcanti: "Questa cotale dimostrazione indusse il Papa a tanto irato sdegno, che cercò piuttosto iniqua vendetta che giusta lamentanza." Cavalcanti, 2:167.

Angevin aspirations in 1442, Eugenius acquired Visconti support against Sforza and excommunicated him. The next year he made a very tense departure from Florence and relieved Roberto Morelli, head of the Medici bank's "Rome branch," of his position as papal depositary general.[41]

In these same years the commune was tightening its grip on the Tuscan religious establishment. In February 1444 it passed a law curtailing the rights of the officeholding class to meet in groups of *laudantes*,[42] and in August it legislated that no foreigner could accept a benefice in Florence without first being approved by the priors.[43] A commission of five citizens continued to survey the transfers of property from laymen to ecclesiastics and other tax-exempt groups,[44] and in 1445 the tax Eugenius had just conceded to Florence broke down in mutual recriminations. Eugenius refused to allow it to go forward until the city paid overdue interest on his Monte shares, while the city claimed that it could not do so until it had received the revenues due from the clerical levy.[45]

It is thus not surprising that Donato and three of the other Florentine candidates soon dropped from consideration for the archbishopric. But the commune found new grounds to pursue the candidacy of Giovanni di Nerone di Nigi Dietisalvi. On 16 August Marsuppini again wrote to Eugenius, the College of Cardinals, Cardinal Jean le Jeun, Cardinal Giovanni Tagliacozzo, and Cardinal Pietro Bembo announcing that Giovanni was now the choice of the cathedral canons and that "since the chapter of cathedral canons has elected him with full consensus, on that account it does not seem out of place to write again to Your Beatitude."[46] He cataloged Giovanni's fine points and appealed on behalf of the citizens of Florence, his well-wishers, "as well as the canons who choose him," that he be awarded the position.

Giovanni in fact had won a bare majority of his fellows' votes. Tommaso della Bordella, acting on the authority of the absent provost, Giovanni Spinelli, had convened the canons earlier on 16 August, four days after Zabarella's presumed burial, and in a first round of secret balloting Giovanni had been chosen by thirteen out of the twenty-two canons assembled.[47] His nearest rival was Francesco Legnamino of Padua, an apos-

41. De Roover, p. 198.
42. *PR*, 134, fols. 208v–9r (18 February 1444).
43. *Balìe*, 26, fols. 61v–62r (21 August 1444).
44. *PR*, 132, fols. 328r–30r (16 January 1442).
45. *LC*, 11, fols. 39v–40v (9 January 1445), and fols. 63r–64r (17 June 1445).
46. "Cum collegium canonicorum cathedralis ecclesie summo consensu eum elegerint, non alienum nobis visum est pro eo iterum ad vestram beatitudinem scribere." *Missive*, 36, fol. 126r (16 August 1445), pub. in Morçay, pp. 434–35.
47. Tommaso di Petruccio di Zetto della Bordella had been a cathedral canon since 1428 and had served as vicar general for archbishops from Corsini onward. He first convened twenty of the canons on 14 August to announce Zabarella's death and burial two days earlier (see note 1) and to call a vote for two days hence. *NA*, I 9 (1443–45), fol. 401r–v (14 August 1445). The canon Antonio degli Agli had to be summoned from Impruneta. Ibid., fols. 401v–2v. The meeting of 16 August was held in the cathedral

David S. Peterson

tolic treasurer who had recently been in Tuscany overseeing clerical levies, who attracted seven votes, four from canons with close ties to papal administration like Andrea Fiochi.[48] Niccolò Banducci cast a courteous vote for Bishop Benozzo Federighi, Giovanni's titular superior in Fiesole, and Giovanni himself modestly supported the elderly canon Michaele Capponi. Announcing the numerical results to the assembled canons, Bordella praised Giovanni's training in law, honest customs, and legitimate birth, and inquired publicly whether the canons were content with the electoral result. He then swiftly declared Giovanni to have won the consensus of the "maiorem et saniorem partem" of the canons, and thus archbishop elect, "per formam consilii generalis," and in the Holy Spirit.[49]

The commune's support of a canonically elected candidate raised a delicate point in the electoral process. The Florentine cathedral chapter had not enjoyed much influence on episcopal appointments since the early fourteenth century.[50] In advancing Giovanni's candidacy, some of

sacristy. Having assured their privacy by threatening excommunication of interlopers, the canons set up a scrutiny committee of Bordella, Jacopo di Giovanni Ugolini, and Gimignano di Ser Niccolò di Messer Tedaldo Giudice Inghirami ("da Prato"). These retired to "unum angulum" of the sacristy, where each canon individually conferred his vote, "secretum et sigillatum." Ibid., fol. 403r (16 August 1445). But the notary, Ser Jacopo di Antonio di Jacopo di Piero da Romena, recorded them. Bordella cast the first vote for Giovanni, followed by Gimignano, then Filippo di Paolo di Piero degli Albizzi, Mico di Piero d'Agnolo Capponi, Bernardo d'Agnolo di Luigi degli Spini, Manente di Gherardo di Lorenzo Buondelmonti, Antonio di Tommaso di Jacopo Pecori, Antonio di Simone di Nofri de' Antella, Antonio di Bellincione di Bernardo degli Agli, Antonio di Ser Matteo di Domenico Picchini, Masetto di Luca di Maso degli Albizzi, Zaccheria di Giovanni d'altro Giovanni Strozzi, and Salvino di Berto di Miliano Salvini. Ibid., fols. 403v–6r.

48. *RV,* 376, fols. 194v–95r (29 September 1444). Francesco was also the *plebanus* of San Donato di Calenzano in the Florentine diocese. *NA,* I 9 (1443–45), fol. 403v. His supporters were Jacopo di Giovanni Ugolini (an apostolic abbreviator), Andrea di Domenico d'Andrea Fiochi (a papal secretary), Coluccio d'Arrigo di Messer Coluccio Salutati, Ugolino di Filippo di Niccolò Giugni (an apostolic protonotary), Niccolò di Dino Corbizzi, Antonio di Giovanni d'Andrea Giachini (an apostolic collector), and Catalano Bartoli. Ibid., fols. 403v–6r, 407v.

49. Only Niccolò di Giovanni di Banduccio Banducci appears to have formally changed his vote, from Federighi to Giovanni. Ibid., fols. 406v, 407v.

50. The canons' deliberation as to how to hold the scrutiny for Giovanni's election may have been more than pro forma. Ibid., fol. 403r–v. John XXII's appointment of Francesco di Silvestro da Cingoli in 1321 over the capital's candidates, Guglielmo de' Frescobaldi and Federico di Bartolo de' Bardi, had signaled the definitive loss of this prerogative by the canons. Elena Rotelli, "I vescovi nella società fiorentina del trecento," in *Eretici e ribelli del xiii e xiv secolo,* ed. Domenico Maselli (Pistoia, 1974), p. 209. This did not prevent Antoninus from reciting the technicalities of capitular elections in his *Summa theologica,* 4 vols. (Verona, 1740; reprint Gratz, 1959), 3, 19, 2:cols. 1048–56. He nevertheless acknowledged the pope's *plenitudo potestatis* respecting all inferior prelates in Ibid., 3, 22, 3, 5:cols. 1191–93. For the canon law on episcopal elections, see Robert Benson, *The Bishop Elect* (Princeton, 1968); Jean Gaudemet, *Les élections dans l'église latine des origines au XVIe siècle* (Paris, 1979); Geoffrey Barraclough, *Papal Provisions: Aspects of Church History Constitutional, Legal and Administrative in the Later Middle Ages* (Oxford, 1955); and of course, Brian Tierney,

the canons may have hoped to exploit Eugenius's difficulties with the council of Basel to revive their former electoral prerogative. But more likely their motives lay in recent politics in Florence and within the Florentine church. For decades the cathedral canons had been the objects of jealousy and resentment among other elements of the clergy, who felt that they did not carry their fair share of the clergy's fiscal burdens. In the 1430s Eugenius himself had investigated and tried to straighten out their finances.[51] They were increasingly overshadowed by the growing canonry of San Lorenzo but had resented also the efforts of the commune to counter such evidence of Medici patronage by inflating their own numbers.[52] They were likewise tied up in a struggle with the Dominican friars of Santa Maria Novella for precedence in the procession of Corpus Domini.[53] By the early 1440s, however, several of the canons were from families allied to the Medici, most notably Antonio di Tommaso di Jacopo Pecori, and Giovanni himself.[54] The commune's support of a Medici partisan, nominated by a faction of the cathedral canons, presented Eu-

---

*Foundations of the Conciliar Theory: The Contribution of the Medieval Canonists from Gratian to the Great Schism* (Cambridge, 1955), pp. 127–32.

51. When, for example, the clergy drew up a constitution of their own shortly after 1415 (discussed below), they allotted only one of eleven proctorships to the cathedral chapter. *Constitutiones sinodales cleri florentini*, Florence, Biblioteca Nazionale, Cl. 32, cod. 31, pub. in Richard C. Trexler, *Synodal Law in Florence and Fiesole, 1306–1518*, Studi e testi 268 (Vatican City, 1971), 1:249. On Eugenius's efforts to order capitular finances, *Pergamene*, 977/1078 (1431), and also *Pergamene*, 406 (1433) and 984/412 (1434), in which the canons made Roberto Cavalcanti their procurator to resist the apostolic commissioner in Tuscany.

52. The Medici had been patronizing San Lorenzo since 1419, but in 1428 they substantially increased their endowments to provide for two more canons. Gombrich, p. 282; *MAP*, 155, fols. 11r–13r (documents from 28 November 1428 to 27 January 1430). The cathedral canons, already resentful of the prerogatives that the Lana guild (woolen cloth manufacturers) had acquired in their affairs to help complete the building of the new cathedral, resented further the commune's efforts to counter the Medici by inflating their numbers. On the canons and the Lana guild, see Margaret Haines, *The "Sacrestia delle Messe" of the Florentine Cathedral* (Florence, 1983), pp. 34–42. The law expanding their numbers is *PR*, 117, fols. 119r–20r (26 June 1427). The canons' appeal to Martin V is in *Pergamene* 954/1086 (1427), discussed in *Missive*, 31, fol. 34r–v (17 June 1427). Despite assurances from Martin V and Eugenius IV that older canons would not have to share their incomes with newcomers, they continued discontented. *Pergamene*, 990/1077 (1435). So did the commune, which protested to Eugenius the continuing diminution of the cathedral's honor. *Missive*, 34, fols. 56v–57v, 58r (13 and 15 October 1432).

53. P. Vincenzio Fineschi, *Della festa e della processione del Corpus Domini in Firenze* (Florence, 1768), pp. 21–37.

54. I have compared the lists of canons in Salvini, pp. 38–43, with the list of apparent Medici friends and partisans in Kent, pp. 352–54. It may be a further indication of growing Medici influence on the cathedral chapter that Roberto Cavalcanti had been admitted in 1429, Donato de' Medici in 1432, and Giovanni Vitelleschi's nephew Bartolomeo in 1434. In the 1430s two canons were brought in from San Lorenzo, Giovanni di Tommaso di Marco Spinelli and Antonio di Bellincione di Bernardo degli Agli.

genius with a double challenge: a reassertion of Medici interests garbed in the prerogatives of the local church and, conversely, the canons' effort to assert their largely bygone electoral rights, and their standing in the local church, by allying themselves to the Medici.

Three days later Marsuppini wrote again to Eugenius for Giovanni, this time because several of the canons were heading to Rome to lobby for him in person.[55] A change in the officers of the Signoria offered yet another occasion to write, this time to the College of Cardinals, on 3 September, because "many things urge us to do so."[56] Marsuppini reduced the grounds for Giovanni's candidacy in serial fashion to three. Priority went to his honest life. Second, his family was "fidissima huic statui." Finally, Giovanni had been elected with the "full consensus of the canons."[57] Clearly some sort of party had formed in Florence behind the candidacy of Giovanni, manifest in the effective collaboration between communal officials, the Medici, and a part of the capitolo.

Copies of these letters went out to another group of cardinals: Guillaume d'Estouteville, Prospero Colonna, and Alfonso Borgia. In all, Eugenius had received seven letters in favor of Florence's candidates, the College of Cardinals eight, Scarampi and Jean le Jeun five apiece, and five other cardinals had been approached in the process. The Florentines aimed to generate support for Giovanni in the college, perhaps even to create pressures there that Eugenius would find difficult to resist. Scarampi in particular exercised considerable influence on affairs touching the local church.[58] On 19 August and 3 September Marsuppini wrote to another Roman power broker, Francesco of Padua himself, perhaps seeking his neutrality but formally soliciting his support.[59] Explaining that he had informed the pope that the commune now stood behind Giovanni, "especially because the cathedral canons have chosen him in full consensus," Marsuppini urged Francesco to intervene with Eugenius, for "we know how much favor and authority you wield with the pope."[60]

55. Missive, 36, fol. 128r (19 August 1445), pub. in Morçay, p. 435. Giovanni Spinelli convened the chapter, which chose Manente Buondelmonte and Antonio degli Agli to lobby for Giovanni before Eugenius. Notably, none of the canons who had voted against Giovanni attended the meeting. NA, I 9 (1443–45), fol. 410r–v (19 August 1445).

56. "Plura et enim ad id faciendum nos hortantur." Missive, 36, fol. 128v (3 September 1445), pub. in Morçay, p. 436.

57. "Primum honestas morum viteque probitas, tum etiam eruditio non mediocris. Secundum quod his parentibus ea que familia ortus est, que et fidissima huic statui et universo huic populo gratiosa existit. Deinde quod summo consensu a canonicorum ecclesie cathredalis [sic] collegio in locum demortui archiepiscopi fuit optatus." Ibid.

58. This is evident in Leonardo Dati's appeals to Cardinal Scarampi for a benefice on the occasion of Zabarella's death. Dati . . . Epistolae, 30:53–55, (1445), et passim.

59. Missive, 36, fols. 127v–28r (19 August 1445), and fol. 130r (3 September 1445), pub. in Morçay, pp. 435–36.

60. "[P]resertim cum iam eum summo consensu canonici cathedralis ecclesie delegerint," and further: "[S]ciamusque quantum apud sanctissimum patrem et gratia et auctoritate valeatis." Missive, 36, fols. 127v–28r.

Giovanni himself confided in Francesco, sending the treasurer a letter that reveals both the complexities of the election and the mixture of patrician ambition and political apprehension that this bestirred in him. Giovanni confessed embarrassment, not simply because of the precipitousness with which the canons had rushed to nominate him, but because it was common opinion in Florence that Francesco too had been eyeing the see "toto desiderio." Giovanni humbly, even servilely offered to stay off the treasurer's ground "inasmuch as you are my most special lord."[61] The patrician canon was quite willing to stand aside for one of Eugenius's favorites, provided he was an outsider. What he found appalling was the prospect of losing in competition to another Florentine. "That which I implore of you above all else," he continued, "is that it not be allowed to come to pass that another of our people be preferred to myself, for clearly an injury will be done me if, having not been elected, another should be preferred in my place."[62] Despite these misgivings, Giovanni was prepared to fight for the post, even in the face of many citizens who, he acknowledged, had "stiffened their necks" against the repeal of the law barring Florentines from holding the archbishopric.[63] Marsuppini's insistence that Giovanni, and the other candidates the priors had proposed, enjoyed the support of Florence's whole populace clearly belied the intensity of family and political rivalries that lay behind the pursuit of the archbishopric.

By early September, Eugenius's silence must have convinced many Florentines that Giovanni's candidacy had failed and that Francesco's Roman connections would procure him the Florentine see. A humbler order of aspiring clients now scrambled to congratulate the presumed archbishop. Girolamo Aliotti, a Benedictine monk from Arezzo, who had been the sometime secretary of Archbishop Zabarella and had composed Giovanni's letter to Francesco for him, must have been typical of a flock of lower-level ecclesiastical humanists who carried before them the example of Ambrogio Traversari's career. In a volume of his letters filled with appeals for preferment and deprecating the provincialism of his circumstances is one he wrote to Francesco, felicitating him on his appointment and, in flagrant contradiction of what appears to have been common knowledge, urging him to abandon the contemplative life in order to take

---

61. "Ego, quantum ex me est, paratus sum ceptis vestris reverenter cedere, tanquam Domini mei singularissimi." *Aliotti . . . Epistolae,* 2, 26:121. The letter is dated only 1445, but it fits logically into the period between 21 August 1445, when Florence repealed its law against allowing citizens to hold the archbishopric, and early September, when Aliotti rushed to congratulate Francesco on having been nominated, as he presumed. See below.

62. "Id tamen a vobis multis precibus contendo, ne patiamini, quemquam ex nostris conterraneis mihi praeferri; iniuria enim mihi facta videretur, si non electus electo mihi praeferatur." Ibid.

63. "Nostrorum civium cervices obduruisse in hac re videntur." Ibid.

David S. Peterson

up the active life of an archbishop, to be "like another Aaron beside the Apostle."[64] On this note he requested the abbacy of San Savino, observing that "it is rich, but that wealth does not deter me."[65] A month later members of the Visdomini family, jealous of their prerogatives as custodians of the archbishopric during vacancies and sensitive to the criticism they had received for refurbishing the archiepiscopal palace, urged Francesco to accept the post "more for our sake, and that of our church, than for yours."[66]

Nothing more touching the archbishopric emerged until 10 January 1446, when Eugenius issued a bull to Antonino Pierozzi, an Observant Dominican who had just stepped down after six years as prior of San Marco, designating him to succeed Zabarella.[67] The document provides few clues to why Eugenius waited five months to name a successor or why he chose Antoninus in particular. Arguably he may have been waiting on military developments in the Romagna, or the return of Scarampi from Bologna,[68] although in these months Florentine-papal relations only continued to deteriorate, both on the diplomatic front and with respect to the stalled levy on the clergy.

Touching the circumstances of the election, Eugenius asserted that at Zabarella's death he had specially reserved provision of the archbishopric to himself, hoping thereby to spare the Florentine church an inconvenient vacancy. In fact, Eugenius had been willing in the past to allow the see to stand vacant for up to a year, redirecting episcopal income into other channels,[69] and even on this occasion a five-month delay was scarcely *celer*. But he argued further that it would be "irritum et inane" if it should be filled in any other way. Eugenius was not about to concede any prerogatives to the cathedral canons, nor would he allow anyone else "of whatever authority, knowingly or unknowingly" to interfere with his choice.[70]

---

64. "[T]anquam Aaron, iuxta Apostolum." Ibid., 2, 30:126 (7 September, 1445).
65. "Peto transferri ad monasterium Sancti Savini . . . quoniam, ut dicitur, est opulentum; sed ea opulentia non me deterret." Ibid.
66. "[M]agis nostra nostreque ecclesie quam vestra de causa." Ibid., 2, 36:135–36 (23 November 1445). On disputes touching the Visdomini, see ibid., 2, 25:120 (1445), and 2, 55: 158–59 (28 January 1446). Cf. *DO*, 62, fols. 35v–36r (10 August 1445), and footnote 1.
67. ASV, *RL*, 421, fols. 162v–63r (10 January 1446), pub. in Morçay, pp. 437–38.
68. This is the suggestion of Morçay, p. 112.
69. *RV*, 373, fols. 161r–62r (19 March 1435) to the bishop of Trogir, Tommaso Tommasini, acting as "administratorem . . . ecclesie florentine." *RV*, 367, fol. 111v (17 march 1438), to Giovanni Spinelli, and *Pergamene*, 1003/833 (1439). Antoninus expressed disapproval of this policy in his *Chronica*, ed. Giles and Jacob Huegetan, 3 vols. in 1 (Lyons, 1543), 3, 22, 10, 6:140, excerpts pub. in Raoul Morçay, *Chroniques de Saint Antonin: Fragments originaux du titre xxii (1378–1459)* (Paris, 1913), pp. 56–57.
70. "[N]os cupientes eidem ecclesie . . . ydoneam preesse personam provisionem ipsius ecclesie ordinationi et dispositioni nostre duximus ea vice specialiter reservandam, decernentes ex tunc irritum et inane, si secus super hiis per quoscumque, quavis auctoritate, scienter vel ignoranter, contingeret attemptari." He added: "[D]e qua nullus

To underscore the point, he issued a second bull the same day to all of his "beloved sons and vassals of the Florentine church," ordering them to acknowledge and obey the new archbishop or face apostolic penalties for "rebelles."[71] Clearly, Eugenius's concern to defend his papal authority was a factor in his rejection of the Florentine candidates brought before him by the commune and the *capitolo*. Why he nevertheless appointed another Florentine, Antoninus, rather than a papal insider like Francesco of Padua is a more complex issue.

Indirect contemporary evidence suggests that Antoninus's fellow Dominican Fra Angelico may have proposed his name to Eugenius while he was working in Rome.[72] Angelico's fame as a painter, and Antoninus's subsequent canonization in 1523, have reinforced the appeal of the story, but even if it is true, Eugenius's choice would have been shaped by considerations beyond his respect for the painter, or even for Antoninus's holy reputation. Antoninus's biographer, Raoul Morçay, was shrewd to note that in selecting Antoninus, the son of a Florentine notary, Eugenius was able to satisfy the Florentines' avowed desire for a native archbishop while at the same time skirting communal politics by reaching below the level of the city's patriciate to choose a candidate from neutral social territory, thus signaling his own independence without directly rebuffing the commune, the Medici, or their opponents.[73] It is likely also, as Morçay believed, that beyond this Eugenius weighed both Antoninus's character and Florence's politics with an eye to church reform. But Morçay's tendency to delineate reform in terms of disciplining clerical morals, or of recovering the church's "anciennes libertés" from a usurping commune, is too simple. Quattrocento debate on reform encompassed complex political and administrative issues. Eugenius's character was multifaceted, as was the structure of the Florentine church and its relationship to the Floren-

---

preter nos ea vice se intromittere potuerat sive potest, reservatione et decreto obsistentibus supradictis, ne ecclesia ipsa longe vacationis exponeretur incommodis." *RL*, 421, fol. 162v.

71. "Dilectis filiis universis vasallis ecclesie florentine salutem." A copy of the bull, dated 10 January 1446, is transcribed in *NA*, I 10 (1445–47), fol. 525r (13 March 1446).

72. The case has been advanced most recently by Creighton Gilbert, based on the assertion of Antoninus's companion, Francesco da Castiglione, that Eugenius got Antoninus's name from some "viris religionis," and the testimony of six (out of 283) witnesses at the process for Antoninus's canonization, held in 1518. Creighton Gilbert, "Fra Angelico's Fresco Cycles in Rome: Their Number and Dates," *Zeitschrift für Kunstgeschichte* 38 (1975): 248–49. Francesco da Castiglione, "Vita Beati Antonii de Florentia," in *Acta Sanctorum*, ed. Daniel Papebroch, vol. 14 (2 May) (Paris, 1866), p. 319. The testimony of witnesses is preserved in Florence, Biblioteca Laurenziana, San Marco, 882, 883, 884. Notably, however, neither of Antoninus's other contemporaries, Vespasiano da Bisticci and Baldovino Baldovini, mentions such a rich anecdote. Baldovini's life of Antoninus is in Florence, Biblioteca Riccardiana, MS 1333, fols. 52v–84v, excerpts pub. in Morçay, *Saint Antonin*, pp. 427–31.

73. Morçay, *Saint Antonin*, pp. 101–23.

David S. Peterson

tine community. Similarly, Morçay's assertion that Antoninus's key cre-
dential as an episcopal candidate and reformer was his autonomy regarding Florentine politics obscures the delicacy of his, and the Observant
Dominicans', relations with the city and its leaders, particularly the Medici.

In his bull of nomination Eugenius certainly acknowledged Antoninus's religious zeal, scholarship, honest customs, and various other merits. But the characteristic to which he recurred most often was his skill in
handling temporal and administrative affairs. His expression of hope that
the Florentine church might prosper under good government was formu-
laic and generic, but it is a point to which Eugenius returned throughout
his bull.[74] With the demise of Basel and his return to Rome, Eugenius
aimed to revamp diocesan administration and to restore the independence
of regional churches in Italy from the peninsula's growing temporal powers. There is evidence that he had these objects before him in appointing to
other dioceses.[75] Having lived in Florence himself for nearly ten years, he
would have had to agree with Marsuppini that the church had suffered
from ineffective leadership, although beyond this their aims diverged.

Since the schism, competing communal and Roman claims to control
of the Florentine church, particularly its financial resources, had inflamed
clerical fractiousness and spawned a debate over the locus of authority
within the diocese itself. In 1419 Florence's clergy had appealed to Pope
Martin V for relief from both Florentine and papal taxes, while at the same
time they had drafted their own *constitutiones sinodales cleri florentini*,
drawing on conciliar principles and the model of Florence's guild-based
priorate to form a corporation encompassing eleven constituencies, by
which they aimed to govern themselves independently of episcopal supervision.[76] By the late twenties Martin was able to curb the Florentines'
fiscal exactions on the church and even to force them to repeal several

74. "[Q]uod . . . per tue circumspectionis industriam et studium fructuosum, re-
getur utiliter et prospere dirigetur." *RL*, 421, fol. 162v. Several times he referred to
Antoninus's "temporalium circumspectione."
75. Study of the Genoese diocese at this time shows that Eugenius there likewise
asserted his right of nomination over local claims and, when his appointee proved too
conservative and tolerant of local patrician influence on the church, sent his own agent
to pressure the bishop and eventually to reform local houses himself. Valeria Polonio,
"Crisi e riforma nella chiesa genovese ai tempi dell'Arcivescovo Giacomo Imperiale
(1439–1452)," in *Miscellanea di studi storici*, ed. Geo Pistarino, Collona storica di fonte
e studi (Genoa, 1969), pp. 265–363.
76. ASV, *Registra supplicationum*, 120, fols. 68v–69r (14 January 1419). The constitutions are cited above, note 51. Professor Tierney called my attention to the likely
interaction of conciliar and "civic humanist" ideas and raised the point in *Religion,
Law, and the Growth of Constitutional Thought, 1150–1650* (Cambridge, 1982), p. 87. I
will discuss these constitutions more fully in "Florence's *Universitas Cleri* in the Early
Fifteenth Century," *Renaissance Studies* 2 (1988), and "Conciliarism, Republicanism,
and Corporatism: The 1415–20 Constitution of the Florentine Clergy," forthcoming in
*Renaissance Quarterly*.

antiecclesiastical statutes passed in the fourteenth century.[77] But he was in turn so rigorous in pursuing clerical revenue that the Florentines themselves urged him to relent.[78] Just as Archbishop Corsini had seemed to be successfully exploiting clerical factions to assert his own authority, Martin had sent Vitelleschi as his commissioner to investigate Corsini and the clergy's finances. When Vitelleschi in turn became embroiled in local clerical politics, Martin chose to remove him and to buttress Corsini's hierarchical authority over the clergy with an apostolic commission.[79]

But Corsini was at best a compromised clerical leader, and in any case Eugenius failed, on his death, to promote strong successors to the archbishopric. Rather, in the absence of Archbishops Vitelleschi and Scarampi, residing in Florence himself, he sought to reorganize the affairs of the diocese through his own commissioners, defending the clergy from usurious loans and the city's court of *mercanzia*, investigating the cathedral's finances, and sending his agents into Tuscany to reform the monasteries and to survey the clergy's wealth, privileges, and immunities.[80] Nevertheless, he was so beholden to Florentine hospitality that he was forced to sanction levies conducted without his prior consent,[81] while the breakdown of the levy he conceded in 1444 indicates how little progress his commissioners had made. The issue of the clergy's Monte interest emerged only after Eugenius's program to review clerical exemptions, and to carry out an inventory of clerical wealth similar to Florence's Catasto, had become stalled.[82]

Having left Florence, and having witnessed the failure of his own efforts at reform by means of visiting commissioners, Eugenius would have been well disposed to support an episcopal candidate sufficiently familiar with the local church to carry forward the reordering of its administration. But

77. A proposed levy of 100,000 florins is discussed in a letter to Florence's Roman ambassadors in 1426. *Missive*, 31, fol. 31r–v (27 July 1426). Martin's refusal is printed in Cesare Baronio, Augostin Theiner, and Odorico Rinaldi, *Annales Ecclesiastici*, vol. 28 (Paris, 1875), p. 74. Rinaldi's date of 1429 can be corrected to 1426–27. In 1427 the Florentines instead levied a tax of 25,000 florins on the clergy. *PR*, 117, fols. 308r–9r (18 August 1427). The repeal of antiecclesiastical laws is ibid., fols. 35r–36v (17 May 1427).

78. *Missive*, 31, fols. 4v–5r (13 July 1422).

79. The notarial registers of Ser Francesco di Ser Francesco di Giannino da Castelfranco, Valdarno, are filled with documents touching these events. See particularly ASF, *NA*, F 507 (1427–30), fols. 112r–17v (14 April 1429) and my article on "Florence's *Universitas Cleri.*"

80. On usurious loans, *NA*, M 344 (1397–1432), fols. 255r–57v (25 August 1431). On the *mercanzia*, *RV*, 374, fols. 10v–12r (4 December 1435). Antoninus discusses Eugenius's reform of the monasteries in the *Chronica*, 3, 22, 10, 5:140 (Morçay, *Chroniques*, pp. 51–54). Eugenius's instructions to his commissioners are in *RV*, 373, fol. 54r–v (21 September 1434), and fols. 161r–62r (19 March 1435), and a very instructive letter to Archbishop Vitelleschi is in *RV*, 374, fol. 95r–v (17 December 1435).

81. This was done in 1431 and 1438. *Missive*, 33, fol. 51v (22 September 1431). ASV, *Armadio* 39, 7a, fols. 184v–85r (10 August 1438).

82. *RV*, 367, fol. 169r (9 November 1444).

David S. Peterson

he needed one also who was independent enough to contest an aggressive, administratively sophisticated communal government. No one in Florence was without political interests, but Antoninus's Florentine origins ensured his familiarity with the local church, while his membership in the Observant Dominican community had afforded him a view of the church beyond, if not entirely above, the city's querulous religious establishment.

Born to a prosperous Florentine notary in 1389, Antoninus had been among Giovanni Dominici's first followers, helping him found a new Observant Dominican house in San Domenico di Fiesole, of which he became prior in 1418. He rose rapidly in the new order, becoming vicar of the Tuscan province in 1424 and later traveling to Naples and then to Rome, where he became prior of Santa Maria sopra Minerva in 1430 and an auditor general of the Rota.[83] By 1435 he had returned to Florence, serving by 1437 as vicar general of the Observants in Tuscany.[84] In 1438 he assumed the priorate of San Marco, the convent to which the Fiesolan Observants had moved in 1435–36.

This move, however, points directly to the Observants', and Antoninus's, ties to the Medici. As archbishop, Antoninus on various occasions stood up to the Medici and the commune in defense both of ecclesiastical prerogatives and of the city's political traditions. In 1456 he sent a stinging missive to Giovanni di Cosimo, who had sought a pardon for one of his clients, declaring: "In judicial affairs, no exception is made of persons. You (and your friends) are all great and powerful citizens, and the church takes the place of an orphan [pupillo], small and weak. But 'it is small, the better for you to listen,' says God. . . . Therefore I intend to take care of this matter properly, and not in a hurry."[85] In his Summa theologica he

83. Antoninus's early years are narrated by Morçay, Saint Antonin, pp. 3–97. Additional details have been added by Stefano Orlandi, S. Antonino: Studi bibliografici, 2 vols. (Florence, 1959, 1960), 1:1–40; and Dom Carlo C. Calzolai, Frate Antonino Pierozzi dei Dominicani Arcivescovo di Firenze (Rome, 1960), pp. 17–98. On the early history of San Domenico di Fiesole, see Orlandi, 2:3–180.

84. Orlandi suggests he may have returned to Tuscany as vicar general in 1432. Orlandi, 2:78. The chronicles of San Domenico and San Marco both assert that he held the office in 1435. San Domenico di Fiesole, Convento di San Domenico, Cronica quadripartita, fol. 3r. Florence, Biblioteca Laurenziana, San Marco, cod. 370, Annalia Conventus Sancti Marci, fol. 4r, pub. in Raoul Morçay, "La cronaca del convento fiorentino di San Marco," ASI 71, 1 (1913): 7. Both were composed in the early sixteenth century and rely on an earlier work by Fr. Giuliano Lapaccini, who joined the community of Fiesole before 1436. Cronica quadripartita, fols. 1r, 36r. Annalia, fol. 146r. Florentine notarial documents refer to Antoninus as vicar general in 1435. Orlandi, 2:137. But Raymond Creytens argues that the office was suppressed by the master general of the order until 1437. "Les actes capitulaires de la congrégation Dominicaine de Lombardie (1482–1531)," AFP 31 (1961): 227–28.

85. "In iudiciis personarum acceptio non est habenda. Tutti siete potenti cittadini e grandi, e la chiesa tiene e[l] luogo del pupillo, picolo e debole. 'Et parvum, ut magnum audietis,' dicie idio. . . . Maturamente adunqua intendo di governare questa causa, e non in fretta." MAP, 6, 208 (8 December 1456).

spoke harshly of the Florentine practice of exiling political opposition, and he criticized the political innovations of his own day, while in 1458 he publicly defied Luca Pitti and other Medici supporters when they attempted to impose new voting procedures in the city's councils.[86] At the same time, even as archbishop, Antoninus knew when to compromise. In his *Chronica*, written at the end of his life, he commended Cosimo for his generosity, offered a very sympathetic account of his return to Florence in 1434, not obscuring Eugenius's role, and in fact praised Cosimo for not having been vindictive toward his enemies.[87]

Whether it was Antoninus's independence or his ability to accommodate Florentine realities that was apparent to Eugenius in 1445 is more difficult to determine than his biographers, emphasizing the continuity of his character, have allowed. From the outset Dominici's Observant followers had been skillful at attracting support and benefactions from leading ecclesiastics and Florentines.[88] By the time Cosimo persuaded Eugenius to fulfill the Observants' long-standing aim of moving to San Marco, they were already shareholders in the Monte and settling property disputes in the communal courts.[89] The necessary ousting of the Silvestrians from San Marco was undertaken against the advice of Eugenius's reform commission and over the protests of Florence's government.[90] Fra

86. *Summa*, 3, 3, 4:cols. 189–93. On 26 July 1458, he issued a public protest against a proposal for open balloting in the city councils. Baldovino Baldovini, fols. 62r–64v, pub. in Morçay, *Saint Antonin*, pp. 429–30. See Rubinstein, chap. 5, on the consolidation of the *reggimento* in 1458.

87. "Nec visus est vindictam expetere de adversariis suis, nisi iustitia exigente." *Chronica*, 3, 22, 10, 3:139 (Morçay, *Chroniques*, p. 48). Cosimo returned to the city "cum ingenti gaudio populi, ingressi civitatem, pontificem visitavit." Ibid., p. 47. In these same sections, however, Antoninus also reflects full awareness of how Cosimo was already manipulating the system of drawing officers for the city: "Et qui fuerant in priori mutatione relegationis Cosme admoniti, id est ab officiis remoti, in secunda postea, revocato eo, fuerunt exaltati, ad officia omnia admissi cum amicis suis." Ibid.

88. Bishop Jacopo Altoviti of Fiesole was their first benefactor, but his grant of land to the Observants was accompanied by a privilege from Pope Gregory XII, procured by Rinaldo di Maso degli Albizzi, representing the commune. *Cronica quadripartita*, fols. 1r, 4r. ASF, *Diplomatico*, San Domenico di Fiesole, 14 June 1408. When the Observants failed to meet the terms of his grant, Altoviti tried to transfer it to the Dominican friars at Santa Maria Novella, but he was overruled when Master General Leonardo Dati intervened with Martin V. *Cronica quadripartita*, fol. 2r–v; Orlandi, 2:93–104. See ibid., pp. 104–54, passim, for a selection of early benefactions.

89. The credits were held for them by Palla Strozzi. *Diplomatico*, San Domenico di Fiesole, 28 January 1430; and Orlandi, 2:119–22. On courts, see *Diplomatico*, San Domenico di Fiesole, 6 March 1431.

90. The Fiesolan Observants had been eyeing the convent since 1419. Morçay, *Saint Antonin*, p. 61. An appeal to Martin V had failed, perhaps because in 1417 the commune had taken the convent under its protection, requiring that it display the "arma et signa populi et comunis florentium et partis guelforum, et non alterius." *PR*, 107, fols. 52v–53r (26 April 1417), cited in Richard C. Trexler, "Ritual Behavior in Renaissance Florence: The Setting," *Medievalia et humanistica*, n.s. 4 (1973): 142 n. 17. An inquest initiated by Eugenius's commissioners in 1435 found the Sylvestrians performing their proper duties, and the populace well content with them. Nevertheless, Eugenius went

David S. Peterson

Cipriano da Raggiolo, not Antoninus, was prior of San Domenico at the time of the move, but chroniclers of both convents insisted that as vicar general Antoninus had been instrumental.[91] Two years later he became joint prior of the convents as the Medici were beginning a munificent building program which included Michelozzo's library, a new chapel, and an altarpiece consecrated by Eugenius and emblazoned with the Medici *scudo.*

Antoninus's biographers have insisted that he was indifferent to the blandishments of Cosimo and faithful to the Observant ideal of poverty.[92] While Cosimo came regularly to his cell at San Marco to pray, legend has it, Antoninus clandestinely organized the Buonuomini di San Martino to aid his political victims among the *poveri vergognosi.*[93] But the food distributed by the *buonuomini* was scarcely translatable into political power, the artisans who for the most part received it cannot be identified as members of Florence's political class, and the confraternity's leading benefactor was Cosimo himself.[94] Antoninus should rather be credited with steering Cosimo's munificence, and his social attentions, beyond the institutional church into the expanding realm of ecclesiastically sponsored charity. As an administrator his application of the rule of poverty

ahead and ordered the transfer. Antoin Brémond, ed. *Bullarium ordinis Fratrum Praedicatorum,* vol. 3 (Rome, 1731), p. 57 (21 January 1436). According to the chronicle of San Marco, this was done "procurantibus civibus et praecipue magnificis Cosma et Laurentio gemanis, . . . (sine quibus facta minus fuisset permutatio de ecclesia in ecclesiam)." Morçay, "Cronaca," p. 8. Similarly, *Cronica quadripartita,* fol. 3r, pub. in Orlandi, 2:111. One detects a note of resentment in the halls of the communal government, for having committed sixty florins to the support of the Silvestrians in 1435 (*PR,* 126, fol. 282r–v, [22 October 1435]), it sent an indignant letter to Eugenius after the transfer had taken place, complaining of the Observants' arrogance and cupidity: "Satis erat pepulisse Silvestrinos de conventu suo antiquo et consueto. Nunc vero ultra queritur, scilicet spoliare eos bonis. In qua quidem re videmus convictam esse superbiam cum avaritia." *Missive,* 35, fol. 61r–v (17 July 1436).

91. *Cronica quadripartita,* fol. 3r; Morçay, "Cronaca," p. 7. In his own account, Antoninus insisted that Eugenius transferred the Silvestrians "cum fama eorum obscura esset et ingrata populo dicte ecclesie." *Chronica,* 3, 22, 10, 5:140 (Morçay, *Chroniques,* p. 53).

92. Vespasiano (p. 229) set the tone when he asserted that: "Autorità di persona apresso di lui non valeva."

93. Morçay, *Saint Antonin,* pp. 85–89, following Giuseppe Richa, *Notizie istoriche delle chiese fiorentine,* vol. 1 (Florence, 1757), pp. 207–17; and Luigi Passerini, *Storia degli stabilimenti di beneficenza della città di Firenze* (Florence, 1850), pp. 501–16.

94. Richard C. Trexler, "Charity and the Defense of Urban Elites to the Italian Communes," in *The Rich, the Well Born, and the Powerful,* ed. Frederick Jaher (Urbana, Ill., 1973), pp. 87–99, 105–9. Amleto Spicciani, "The 'Poveri Vergognosi' in Fifteenth-Century Florence: The First Thirty Years' Activity of the Buonuomini di S. Martino," in *Aspects of Poverty in Early Modern Europe,* ed. Thomas Riis (Florence, 1981). Trexler questioned Antoninus's role as founder of the confraternity (p. 88), and Spicciani concedes that positive evidence is lacking (p. 162 n. 10). His presence as a benefactor on the first page of the confraternity's register of *entrate* seems strong circumstantial evidence confirming subsequent assertions that he was. Florence, Biblioteca Nazionale, *Fondo Tondi* 18, *filza* 2, fol. 1r.

was as pragmatic as it was scrupulous.[95] Again he was a key figure, but not the prior, when in 1445 San Domenico and San Marco separated in a rupture provoked by the difficulties of administering the two houses jointly, and particularly by disputes touching the allotment of benefactions.[96] As archbishop he continued to support San Marco, and the chronicle of San Marco credits him with helping Cosimo procure Pope Calixtus III's official relaxation of the rule in 1455.[97]

Arguably an altarpiece was little to yield for a library, and not all compromises produce clients. The prestige Cosimo derived from patronizing San Marco may have meant as much to him as his benefactions meant to Antoninus. Though he was scarcely leading Florence's *résistance* to the Medici, neither was Antoninus a Medici creation. Five years before the Medici returned to Florence, the commune had acknowledged his popularity by urging the master general of the Dominicans to transfer him back to Fiesole from Naples.[98] His travels, and the circulation of his early *Confessionale* and *consilia*, made him well known outside the city.[99] His reputation as a moderate on the property issue got him invited to Bologna in 1441 to settle a dispute between the city and the Observants there,[100] and at the time of his nomination he had left Florence to return to Naples.[101]

The shrewd Eugenius would have admired Antoninus's adroit handling of the Medici and Florence's politics. His rise in the sometimes controversial order of Observant Dominicans pointed both to his reforming zeal and to his administrative abilities, while he had evidenced also an element of

95. This is neatly telescoped in *Diplomatico*, San Domenico di Fiesole, 22 August 1441. Forced either to sell within a year property bequeathed to them (income from which sales would support building projects at San Domenico and San Marco) or to turn the bequest over to the hospital of Santa Maria Nuova, Antoninus repeatedly convened his brothers ("iterum . . . et iterum et denovo") and reminded them ("monuit") "qualiter . . . in eorum constitutionibus inter alia continetur quod non debent tenere bona propria sed stare in paupertate, et quod etiam nisi vendabantur dicta bona infra certum tempus, devolvantur."

96. Both chronicles insist that this was done by Antoninus as vicar general, on account of the "inconvenientia" occasioned by a dual priorate which produced "plures murmurationes inter fratres." Morçay, "Cronaca," p. 18. Similarly the *Cronica quadripartita*, fol. 3v, which notes the existence of two dissenters. Shortly thereafter, the monks of San Domenico referred to the split in instituting new procurators, "iustis causis motus." *Diplomatico*, San Domenico di Fiesole, 25 January 1445 (1446).

97. See the *Ricordanze* of San Marco. Florence, Biblioteca Laurenziana, *San Marco*, 502, fol. 32r. On his intervention with Calixtus, Morçay, "Cronaca," p. 28. The bull itself only mentions Cosimo. Brémond, p. 340.

98. *Missive*, 32, fols. 74v–75r (11 May 1429).

99. He completed the *Confessionale* by the time of his second trip to Naples. Morçay, *Saint Antonin*, pp. 404–7. See also Raymond Creytens, "Les cas de conscience soumis à Saint Antonin de Florence par Dominique de Catalogne, O.P.," *AFP* 28 (1958): 149–218, and "Les 'consilia' de Antonin de Florence, O.P.," *AFP* 37 (1967): 263–343.

100. Raymond Creytens, "Saint Antonin de Florence, syndic et procureur général de Saint-Dominique de Bologne (1441)," *AFP* 26 (1956): 320–31.

101. Morçay, *Saint Antonin*, p. 97.

David S. Peterson

personal appeal in the city and, if not political cunning, astuteness. Eugenius would have known Antoninus both at the Rota and in Florence and had already deployed him to reform some of the monasteries in the region[102] and to help collect a papal tithe.[103] Antoninus's enthusiasm for the Observant cause had, in his early years, led him to resist authorities further up the church hierarchy[104] but had brought him also to decidedly warm papalist sentiments touching church councils that would have convinced Eugenius of the compatibility of their views on both the goals and the means of church reform.[105] Nor could the Medici, or the commune, complain of his appointment.

But Antoninus did.[106] Fully two months passed before he submitted to a modest consecration ceremony on 13 March 1446.[107] In the interim he showed more than the requisite reluctance, indeed rather considerable peevishness, in accepting the post. This may have been reassuring to Florentines who looked forward to tidy relations with an old friar newly named archbishop, but it was a source of annoyance as well. On 29 January Marsuppini wrote to Eugenius that "no one your holiness might have raised to that office could be more acceptable and pleasing," but he went on to suggest that Eugenius resort to apostolic penalties should Antoninus prove recalcitrant.[108]

102. *RV*, 367, fol. 154r (14 June 1444).
103. This is the suggestion of Morçay, *Saint Antonin*, p. 116, following a comment of Aliotti's to the bishop of Arezzo: "Ego interim sollicitabo rem cleri nostri apud fratrem Antonium." *Aliotti . . . Epistolae*, 2, 38:138 (13 December 1445).
104. In 1409 he fled with Dominici and the other Fiesolan Observants to Foligno, then Cortona, rather than follow Florence and Master General Thomas of Fermo in recognizing the election of Alexander V at Pisa. Orlandi, 2:13–18. *Cronica quadripartita*, fol. 2r–v. This occasioned the quarrel with Bishop Altoviti (note 88, above). Antoninus's emergence as vicar of a Tuscan congregation in 1437 was also part of the Observants' struggle for independence of the master general of the order. Creytens, "Actes capitulaires," p. 227.
105. Antoninus denied the legitimacy of Pisa and Basel for having been convoked without papal authority. *Summa*, 3, 23, 2, 1. In his *Chronica* (3, 22, 5, 2; Morçay, *Chroniques*, p. 15) he specifically distinguished Constance from Pisa as having been convened by popes as well as cardinals. Notably, Gregory XII had made Dominici a cardinal in 1408. *Cronica quadripartita*, fol. 2v. Antoninus denounced Basel as a "synagoga satane auctoritate." *Chronica*, 3:22, 10, 4 (Morçay, *Chroniques*, p. 49). The Silvestrians took their case against the Observants to Basel in 1437. Antoninus's friend Giovanni Turrecremata acted as procurator for the Observants. Morçay, "Cronaca," p. 11. Ulrich Horst correctly notes that the issue of declaring articles of faith led Antoninus to waffle on the respective authority of popes and councils, but he goes a bit far in suggesting that at Vatican I "Beide Parteien konten sich zu Recht auf die ihnen passenden Elemente beziehen." "Papst, Bishöfe und Konzil nach Antonin von Florenz," *Recherches de théologie ancienne et médiévale* 32 (1965): 116. Though he stopped short of carrying the Petrine doctrine into an argument for papal inerrancy (*Summa*, 3, 22, 3, 1:col. 1187), he followed an Ockhamist line of reasoning to assert that neither were councils repositories of the church's inerrancy (*Summa*, 3, 23, 2, 6:col. 1270).
106. Vespasiano, p. 226. The story became a staple of Antoninus's hagiographers.
107. This is narrated in lavish detail by Morçay, *Saint Antonin*, pp. 122–25.
108. "Ei officio nemo a vestra sanctitate prefici potuit, qui cunctis nostris civibus esset aut acceptior aut gratior." *Missive*, 36, fol. 156v (29 January 1446), pub. in Morçay,

In congratulating Antoninus Marsuppini urged him to accept the post, deploying his best Ciceronian rhetoric to weave together civic and religious ideals of the *vita activa* and Christian *renovatio* in an appeal that fused piety and patriotism. Contrasting the active and contemplative lives, he insisted that "though a tranquil life and great leisure may appeal to you, it is better to consider that we are not born for ourselves alone, but rather that we may serve the *patria*, our neighbors, our friends, and, indeed, the whole human race."[109] Though the ancient fathers commended the merits of the hermits, the priesthood had been established for leading others to the faith. Marsuppini could name innumerable men in the episcopate who had earned not only fame and honor among men, which were always "fluxa et fragilis," but also divine honors. Lest the Florentines, he concluded, "raised to such hope and expectation, suffer frustration, you ought rather to comply with the urging of the *patria*, the order of the pope, and the calling of God."[110]

Domenico Capranica also intervened on Eugenius's behalf,[111] and Antoninus was persuaded to reverse his course from Naples back to Florence. While Aliotti and Dati rushed to congratulate him,[112] Antoninus continued his soul-searching, disparaging himself in sermons of the time.[113] But if his biographer Castiglione is correct he also called together leading figures from the city and the Florentine church for counsel,[114] and these meetings, if a further demonstration of humility, also provided an opportunity to begin consolidating his position. By mid-February he had begun appointing his officers,[115] and at his consecration in March he cast aside all hesitation, swearing an oath of his own devising that amounted to a militant pledge of loyalty to the Roman see.[116]

---

*Saint Antonin*, pp. 440–41. Castiglione (p. 320) asserts that Cosimo also sent a letter of support.

109. "Si vita quieta et magis otiosa vos delectaret, illud profecto est cogitandum, non nobis solis esse natos, sed patrie, sed propinquis, sed amicis, sed denique ut pro viribus, humano generi universo usui adque adiumento simus." *Missive*, 36, fol. 152v (24 January 1446), pub. in Morçay, *Saint Antonin*, pp. 439–40.

110. "Ne universum hunc populum, tanta spe et expectatione erectum, frustratum esse patiamini, immo potius poscenti patrie, iubenti Pontifici, vocanti deo obtemperetis." Ibid., fol. 153r.

111. Castiglione, p. 320.

112. *Aliotti . . . epistolae*, 2, 54:156–57 (26 January 1446); *Dati . . . epistolae*, 32:56–58 (28 March 1446).

113. See the extracts from his *Sermo in coena Domini*, Florence, Biblioteca Riccardiana, MS 308, fol. 149r (2 March 1446), pub. in Orlandi, 1:43.

114. Castiglione, p. 320.

115. *NA*, T 96 (16 February 1446), in which he named Martino de' Bianchi to be his vicar general.

116. This is contained in a collection of documents pertaining to Antoninus's consecration, *NA*, I 10 (1445–47), fols. 521v–22r (13 March 1446), pub. in Orlandi, 1:182–83. Antoninus also had Eugenius's two bulls of 10 January reread to the assembled clergy. He swore in his "custodes et vassalles," members of the Ughi family, on 19 March. *NA*, F 507 (1400–1445), fols. 192r–93v (19 March 1446).

Antoninus went into action immediately. He quickly rebuffed a suave effort by the canons to procure the *pallium* for the "metropolitan church" by deputing their syndics as archiepiscopal procurators instead.[117] In April he convened his first synod, proclaiming that in the future archiepiscopal synods would be held annually.[118] In August he began visiting the diocese,[119] but he rushed back to the city to brandish an excommunication at the commune's leaders when, in their ongoing struggle with Eugenius over taxes and Monte interest, they took Francesco of Padua hostage.[120] He made his authority felt by clergy and laity alike. In 1447 the commune yielded to him and repealed its law touching foreigners and Florentine benefices,[121] and in 1452 at his insistence it struck its legislation on confraternities, as well as a recent initiative to tax the clergy.[122] Meanwhile he extended his visitations into suffragan dioceses, toured the Vallumbrosan houses and other monasteries, and settled disputes from as far away as Pisa.[123]

In appointing Antoninus, Eugenius had sidestepped the Medici and had resumed Martin V's policy of buttressing episcopal authority in Florence. From the outset Antoninus functioned as an apostolic commissioner.[124] But it was owing less to the formal instruments of episcopal power than to his ability to exploit the web of competing interests surrounding his office, set in relief by the process of his election, that Antoninus was able to make his influence felt. In the course of his thirteen-year archiepisco-

117. The syndics were to seek the pallium on behalf of the "metropolitana ecclesia florentina" and to acknowledge the "plenitudo pontificalis ufficii." *NA*, I 10 (1445–47), fols. 525v–27r (14 March 1446). Antoninus redeputed them on 23 March, with directions to submit themselves to the "summo pontifici." Ibid., fol. 528r–v (23 March 1446).

118. *Pergamene* 1012/1084 (1446), a copy of Eugenius's bull nominating Antoninus, contains the addendum: "Presentatus clero sinodaliter congregato in cathedrali ecclesia florentina, die xxii mensis Aprilis, 1446." His statute is published in Trexler, *Synodal Law*, p. 279.

119. Pub. in Orlandi, 1:130–78.

120. Antoninus's role in this incident is described only by Castiglione (p. 320), but his account of events is corroborated by *Missive*, 36, fol. 186r–v (10 July 1446), and fols. 187r–88r (11 July 1446).

121. ASF, *CP*, 52, fol. 19v (14 July 1447).

122. The repeal of legislation on confraternities is in *PR*, 143, fols. 32v–33v (3 April 1452). In 1451 the commune imposed a tax on transfers of property to ecclesiastics and other tax-exempt groups. *PR*, 142, fols. 216r–17v (9 September 1451). Antoninus's protest, and the commune's amendment of this law, are in *DO*, 74, fol. 23v (5 April 1452). For further details, see my dissertation, pp. 296–332.

123. On his visitations of the diocese of Pistoia, see his letters to Donato of 4 March and 7 October 1451. Pistoia, *Archivio Vescovile*, pub. in Morçay, *Saint Antonin*, pp. 464–65; also *NA*, B 1322 (1435–48), fol. 36r (14–22 October 1447). On settling disputes in Pisa, see *Missive*, 40, fol. 58v (16 July 1454). On visiting the Vallumbrosan houses, see Orlandi, 1:188–91. In 1452 Antoninus presided over a meeting of their chapter general. *NA*, M 342 (1439–82), fols. 3r–4r (4 February 1452).

124. He is always designated thus in the notarial registers of Ser Baldovino Baldovini, *NA*, B 382, 384, 386, and of Ser Filippo di Bernardo Mazzei, *NA*, M 342, 343, 344.

pate he balanced the concerns of the papacy, commune, patriciate, clergy, and populace in such a manner as to put himself at their center in affairs touching the Florentine church. While shielding it from impinging pressures, he advanced his reforming objectives and expanded archiepiscopal authority in the diocese, indeed throughout Tuscany.[125] One thing he could not do, however, was choose his successor. Donato de' Medici finished his career in Pistoia, but in 1462, three years after Antoninus's death, Florence's archbishopric at last came into the hands of Giovanni di Nerone di Nigi Dietisalvi.[126]

125. I will discuss these points more fully in a book I am preparing on the Florentine church in the early quattrocento.
126. Eubel, pp. 216, 154. Orlando Bonarli held the see in the intervening three years.

# Bibliography of the Works of Brian Tierney, 1951–87

## Del Sweeney

### 1951

"A Conciliar Theory of the Thirteenth Century." *Catholic Historical Review* 36:415–40.

Review
Charles Edward Smith, *Innocent III: Church Defender. Catholic Historical Review* 37:300–301.

### 1953

"The Canonists and the Mediaeval State." *Review of Politics* 15:378–88.

Review
David C. Douglas and George Greenaway, eds., *English Historical Documents*, vol. 2, *1042–1189. Catholic Historical Review* 39:332–34.

### 1954

"Ockham, the Conciliar Theory, and the Canonists." *Journal of the History of Ideas* 15:40–70.*
"Some Recent Works on the Political Theories of the Medieval Canonists." *Traditio* 10:594–625.*

Review
Andrew Browning, ed., *English Historical Documents*, vol. 8, *1660–1714. Catholic Historical Review* 40:329–30.

*Reprinted in the Variorum Reprint edition.
*Note:* Book reviews of less than one page have not been included.

## 1955

*Foundations of the Conciliar Theory: The Contribution of the Medieval Canonists from Gratian to the Great Schism.* Cambridge: Cambridge University Press. xi, 280 pp. (Reprinted 1968.)

"Grosseteste and the Theory of Papal Sovereignty." *Journal of Ecclesiastical History* 6:1–17.*

## 1957

"Pope and Council: Some New Decretist Texts." *Mediaeval Studies* 19:197–218.*

Review

Alan Gewirth, trans., *Marsilius of Padua: The Defender of the Peace,* vol. 2, *The Defensor Pacis. Catholic Historical Review* 43:186–87.

## 1958

Review

Hubert Jedin, *A History of the Council of Trent. Catholic Historical Review* 44:179–81.

## 1959

*Medieval Poor Law: A Sketch of Canonical Theory and Its Application in England.* Berkeley and Los Angeles: University of California Press. xi, 169 pp.

"The Decretists and the 'Deserving Poor.'" *Comparative Studies in Society and History* 1:360–73.*

"Two Anglo-Norman Summae." *Traditio* 15:483–91.

## 1960

Reviews

Ludwig Buisson, *Potestas und Caritas. American Historical Review* 65:584–85.

John W. Baldwin, *The Medieval Theories of the Just Price. Journal of Economic History* 20:320–22.

Rosalind B. Brooke, *Early Franciscan Government. Speculum* 35:432–34.

## 1961

Review

S. and S. Stelling-Michaud, *Les juristes suisses à Bologne. Renaissance News* 14:99–100.

## 1962

"'Tria quippe distinguit iudicia . . .': A Note on Innocent III's Decretal *Per Venerabilem." Speculum* 37:48–59.

Reviews

Joseph Balon, *Lex Iurisdictio. American Historical Review* 67:382–83.

J. A. Watt, J. B. Morrall, and F. X. Martin, eds., *Medieval Studies Presented to Aubrey Gwynn, S.J. Catholic Historical Review* 48:220–22.

## 1963

"Bracton on Government." *Speculum* 38:295–317.

"Innocent as Judge." In *Innocent III: Vicar of Christ or Lord of the World?* ed. James M. Powell, pp. 59–66. New York: D. C. Heath. (Slightly revised version of "'Tria quippe distinguit iudicia . . .': A Note on Innocent III's Decretal *Per Venerabilem,"* 1962.)

"*Natura id est Deus:* A Case of Juristic Pantheism?" *Journal of the History of Ideas* 24:307–22.*

"'The Prince Is Not Bound by the Laws': Accursius and the Origins of the Modern State." *Comparative Studies in Society and History* 5:378–400.* (Reprinted in *Atti del Convegno internazionale di studi accursiani, Bologna, 21–26 ottobre 1963,* 3:1245–74. Milan, 1968.)

Review

David Knowles, *The Evolution of Medieval Thought. Catholic Historical Review* 49:428–29.

## 1964

*The Crisis of Church and State, 1050–1300.* With selected documents. Englewood Cliffs, N.J.: Prentice-Hall. xi, 211 pp.

Reviews

M. J. Wilks, *The Problem of Sovereignty in the Later Middle Ages. Catholic Historical Review* 50:248–50.

Franklin J. Pegues, *The Lawyers of the Last Capetians. Manuscripta* 8:55–57.

## 1965

"Collegiality in the Middle Ages." *Concilium* 7:5–14.

"The Continuity of Papal Political Theory in the Thirteenth Century: Some Methodological Considerations." *Medieval Studies* 27:227–45.*

Reviews

Giles Constable, *Monastic Tithes from Their Origins to the Twelfth Century. Speculum* 40:716–18.

Bibliography of the Works of Brian Tierney, 1951–87

Gaines Post, *Studies in Medieval Legal Thought*. *Harvard Law Review* 78:1502–6.

## 1966

"Die konziliare Theorie am Hofe Kaiser Friedrichs II." In *Stupor Mundi, zur Geschichte Friedrichs II. von Hohenstaufen*, ed. Gunther Wolf, pp. 455–58. Darmstadt: Wissenschaftliche Buchgesellschaft.

"Medieval Canon Law and Western Constitutionalism." *Catholic Historical Review* 52:1–17. (Reprinted in *Creation: The Impact of an Idea*, ed. Daniel O'Connor and Francis Oakley, pp. 225–38. New York: Scribner, 1969.)

## 1967

(Ed. with Donald Kagan and L. Pearce Williams) *Great Issues in Western Civilization*. Vol. 1, *From Periclean Athens through Louis XIV*, xii, 716; vol. 2, *From the Scientific Revolution through the Cold War*, xii, 735. New York: Random House.

"'Sola Scriptura' and the Canonists." *Collectanea Stephan Kuttner*. 1. *Studia Gratiana* 11:347–66. (Reprinted Bonn, 1967.)

"Boniface VIII, Pope," "Capitulations," "Conciliarism (History of)," "Constance, Council of," "Marsilius of Padua," "Praemunire, Statute of," and "Provisors, Statute of." *New Catholic Encyclopedia* 2:671–73, 3:90, 4:109–11, 218–23, 9:297–98, 11:660, 924–25.

Reviews

Thomas N. Bisson, *Assemblies and Representation in Languedoc in the Thirteenth Century*. *Catholic Historical Review* 52:575–76.

John A. Watt, *The Theory of Papal Monarchy in the Thirteenth Century*. *American Historical Review* 72:1371–72.

## 1968

"The Roots of Western Constitutionalism in the Christian Tradition: The Significance of the Council of Constance." In *We the People of God: A Study of Constitutional Government for the Church*, ed. James Coriden, pp. 113–28. Huntington, Ind.: Our Sunday Visitor Press.

## 1969

"Hermeneutics and History: The Problem of *Haec Sancta*." In *Essays in Medieval History Presented to Bertie Wilkinson*, ed. T. A. Sandquist and M. R. Powicke, pp. 354–70.* Toronto: University of Toronto Press.*

"Limits to Obedience in the Thirteenth Century: The Case of Robert Grosseteste." In *Contraception: Authority and Dissent*, ed. Charles E. Curran, pp. 76–100. New York: Herder and Herder. (Based on "Grosseteste and the Theory of Papal Sovereignty," 1955.)

Del Sweeney

## 1970

(With Sidney Painter) *Western Europe in the Middle Ages, 300–1475.* New York: Knopf. xi, 522, xvii pp. (Revision of Sidney Painter, *A History of the Middle Ages, 284–1500,* 1953.)

*The Middle Ages.* vol. 1, *Sources of Medieval History,* ix, 344 pp; vol. 2, *Readings in Medieval History,* ix, 346 pp. New York: Knopf.

"Innocent as Highest Judge." In *Church and State in the Middle Ages,* ed. Bennett D. Hill, pp. 156–64. New York: Wiley.

Reviews

Antonio Marongiu, *Medieval Parliaments. Catholic Historical Review* 56:725–26.

Francis Oakley, *Council over Pope? Toward a Provisional Ecclesiology. Jurist* 30:398–99.

## 1971

*Ockham, the Conciliar Theory, and the Canonists.* With an introduction by Heiko A. Oberman. Facet Books, Historical Series 19. Philadelphia: Fortress Press. xxi. 42 pp. (Reprint of article of same title, 1954.)

"Origins of Papal Infallibility." *Journal of Ecumenical Studies* 8:841–64.

Reviews

Marjorie Reeves, *The Influence of Prophecy in the Later Middle Ages. American Historical Review* 76:140–41.

Walter Brandmüller, *Das Konzil von Pavia-Siena, 1423–1424,* vol. 1, *Darstellung. Catholic Historical Review* 57:500–501.

A. J. Black, *Monarchy and Community: Political Ideas in the Later Conciliar Controversy, 1430–1450. Journal of Ecclesiastical History* 22:263–65.

## 1972

*Origins of Papal Infallibility, 1150–1350: A Study on the Concepts of Infallibility, Sovereignty and Tradition in the Middle Ages.* Studies in the History of Christian Thought 6, ed. Heiko A. Oberman. Leiden: E. J. Brill. x, 298 pp.

(Ed. with Donald Kagan and L. Pearce Williams) *Great Issues in Western Civilization.* 2d ed. 2 vols. New York: Random House.

"From Thomas of York to William of Ockham: The Franciscans and the Papal *sollicitudo omnium ecclesiarum,* 1250–1350." *Communione interecclesiale, collegialità, primato, ecumenismo* 2:607–58.

Review

Giuseppe Alberigo, *Cardinalato e collegialità. Speculum* 47:99–100.

## 1973

*The Middle Ages.* Vol. 1. *Sources of Medieval History.* 2d ed. New York: Knopf. xiv, 356 pp.

"Ursprünge der päpstlichen Unfehlbarkeit," trans. A. Berz. In *Fehlbar? Eine Bilanz,* ed. Hans Küng, pp. 121–45. Zurich: Benziger. (German translation of "Origins of Papal Infallibility," 1971.)

Reviews

Stanley Chodorow, *Christian Political Theory and Church Politics in the Mid-Twelfth Century. Journal of Ecclesiastical History* 23:410–11.

Colin Morris, *The Discovery of the Individual, 1050–1200. Journal of Ecclesiastical History* 23:295–96.

Joseph R. Strayer and Donald E. Queller, eds., *Post Scripta (Festschrift Gaines Post). American Historical Review* 78:413–15.

## 1974

*The Middle Ages.* Vol. 2. *Readings in Medieval History.* 2d ed. New York: Knopf. xi, 363 pp.

(With Sidney Painter) *Western Europe in the Middle Ages, 300–1475.* 2d ed. New York: Knopf. xiii, 562, xvii pp.

"On the History of Papal Infallibility: A Discussion with Remegius Bäumer." *Theologische Revue* 70:185–94.

"Infallibility in Morals: A Response [to G. J. Hughes]." *Theological Studies* 35:507–17.

## 1975

" 'Divided Sovereignty' at Constance: A Problem of Medieval and Early Modern Political Theory." *Annuarium historiae conciliorum* 7:238–56.*

"Infallibility and the Medieval Canonists: A Discussion with Alfons Stickler." *Catholic Historical Review* 61:265–73. (Translated into Italian as "L'infallibilità e i canonisti medievali." *Rivista di storia della chiesa in Italia* 29:221–30.)

"Modèles historiques de la papauté." *Concilium* 108:65–74.

Review

Arthur Stephen McGrade, *The Political Thought of William of Ockham. Medium aevum* 44:329–31.

## 1976

(Ed. with Donald Kagan and L. Pearce Williams) *Great Issues in Western Civilization,* 3d ed. Vol. 1, *From Periclean Athens through Louis XIV,*

Del Sweeney

576 pp.; vol. 2, *From the Scientific Revolution through the Cold War,* 576 pp. New York: Random House.

"Hostiensis and Collegiality." *Proceedings of the Fourth International Congress of Medieval Canon Law* (Toronto, 21–25 August 1972), ed. Stephan Kuttner, pp. 401–9. Monumenta Iuris Canonici, ser. C, vol. 5. Vatican City: Bibliotheca Apostolica Vaticana.

"Ockham, die konziliare Theorie und die Kanonisten." In *Die Entwicklung des Konziliarismus: Werden und Nachwirden der konziliaren Idee,* ed. Remigius Bäumer, pp. 113–15. Darmstadt: Wissenschaftliche Buchgesellschaft. (Extracts, in German translation, from "Ockham, the Conciliar Theory, and the Canonists," 1954.)

"A Scriptural Text in the Decretales and in St. Thomas: Canonistic Exegesis of Luke 22–32." *Mélanges G. Fransen. 2. Studia Gratiana* 20:363–77.*

### 1977

"Ockham's Ambiguous Infallibility." *Journal of Ecumenical Studies* 14:102–5.

" 'Only the Truth Has Authority': The Problem of 'Reception' in the Decretists and in Johannes de Turrecremata." In *Law, Church and Society: Essays in Honor of Stephan Kuttner,* ed. Kenneth Pennington and Robert Somerville, pp. 69–96. Philadelphia: University of Pennsylvania Press.

Review

John T. Gilchrist, ed., *Diuersorum patrum sententie siue Collectio in LXXIV titulos digesta. Catholic Historical Review* 63:110–11.

### 1978

(With Sidney Painter) *Western Europe in the Middle Ages, 300–1475.* 3d ed. New York: Knopf. xv, 587, xvii pp.

*The Middle Ages.* Vol. 1. *Sources of Medieval History.* 3d ed. New York: Knopf. xiv, 378 pp.

Review

Robert E. Rodes, Jr., *Ecclesiastical Administration in Medieval England. Catholic Historical Review* 64:258–59.

### 1979

*Church Law and Constitutional Thought in the Middle Ages.* Collected Studies Series 90. London: Variorum Reprints. 340 pp.

"Aristotle, Aquinas, and the Ideal Constitution." *PMR* (Proceedings of the Mid-Atlantic States Conference on Patristic, Mediaeval, and Renaissance Studies) 4:1–11.

Review
August Bernhard Hasler, *Pius IX (1846–1878), päpstliche Unfehlbarkeit und I. Vatikanisches Konzil. Journal of Ecclesiastical History* 30:396–97.


## 1980

(Ed. with Peter Linehan) *Authority and Power: Studies on Medieval Law and Government Presented to Walter Ullmann on His Seventieth Birthday.* Cambridge: Cambridge University Press. x, 274 pp.
"Public Expediency and Natural Law: A Fourteenth-Century Discussion on the Origins of Government and Property." In ibid., pp. 167–82.
"A Letter to the Editor." *Catholic Historical Review* 66:700–701.


Review
Clarence Gallagher, *Canon Law and the Christian Community: The Role of Law in the Church According to the Summa Aurea of Cardinal Hostiensis. Catholic Historical Review* 66:654–55.


## 1981

"Papal Infallibility: A Response to Dr. D'Avray." *Catholic Historical Review* 67:275–77.
(With Larry D. Benson and Laurence K. Shook) "Harry Caplan." *Speculum* 61:693–94.


## 1982

*The Middle Ages.* Vol. 1, *Sources of Medieval History,* 4th ed., xv, 375 pp.; vol. 2, *Readings in Medieval History,* 3d ed., xi, 343 pp. New York: Knopf.
*Religion, Law and the Growth of Constitutional Thought, 1150–1650.* Wiles Lectures, 1979, given at the Queen's University of Belfast. Cambridge: Cambridge University Press. xi, 114 pp. Japanese translation: *Rikken shiso shigen to Tankai.* Tokyo, 1988.
"Sovereignty and Infallibility: A Response to James Heft." *Journal of Ecumenical Studies* 19:787–93.


## 1983

(With Sidney Painter) *Western Europe in the Middle Ages, 300–1475.* 4th ed. New York: Knopf. xiv, 633, xx pp.
"L'idée de répresentation dans les conciles d'occident au Moyen Age." *Concilium* 187:24–30.
"Tuck on Rights: Some Medieval Problems." *History of Political Thought* 4:429–41.

Del Sweeney

## 1984

(With Joan Scott) *Western Societies: A Documentary History*. New York: Knopf. Vol. 1, xx, 525 pp.; vol. 2, xxiii, 599 pp.

## 1985

"John Peter Olivi and Papal Inerrancy: On a Recent Interpretation of Olivi's Ecclesiology." *Theological Studies* 46:315–28.

Review
Harold J. Berman, *Law and Revolution. Catholic Historical Review* 71:431–32.

## 1986

"Natural Law and Canon Law in Ockham's Dialogus." In *Aspects of Late Medieval Government and Society: Essays Presented to J. R. Lander*, ed. J. G. Rowe, pp. 3–24. Toronto: University of Toronto Press.

## 1987

"Hierarchy, Consent, and the 'Western Tradition.'" *Political Theory* 15:646–52.

"Religion and Rights: A Medieval Perspective." *Journal of Law and Religion* 5:163–75.

"Ockham's Infallibility and Ryan's Infallibility." *Franciscan Studies* (in press).

"Canon Law and Church Institutions in the Late Middle Ages." Proceedings of the Seventh International Congress of Medieval Canon Law (in press).

"Villey, Ockham and the Origin of Natural Rights." In *The Weightier Matters of the Law: Essays on Law and Religion*, ed. Frank C. Alexander and J. Witte (in press).

"Concilarism, Corporatism, and Individualism: The Doctrine of Subjective Rights in Gerson." *Christianesimo nella Storia* (in press).

Review
Eric Methen, *Das Basler Konzil als Forschungsproblem der europäischen Geschichte. Zeitschrift der Savigny-Stiftung für Rechtsgeschichte* (Kan. Abt.) 104:384–86.

Ulrich Horst, *Zwischen Konziliarismus und Reformation. Journal of Ecclesiastical History* 38:297.

# Index

Persons are indexed according to Christian name, rather than surname.

# Index

Honorius III, pope, 36–37n., 40, 42, 44, 45, 47, 59, 280
Hormisdas, pope, 99
Hostiensis, canonist, 66–67, 193n., 197–201, 202, 203–4, 218, 222, 226–27, 232
Hugh, archbishop of Lyons, 8
Hugolino, cardinal bishop of Ostia (Pope Gregory IX), 39
Huguccio, canonist, 197
Humbert of Silva-Candida, 7n.
Hungary, 26–52

Imre, king of Hungary, 45
Innocent II, pope, 132, 218
Innocent III, pope, 26–52, 66, 181, 192–95, 202n., 203n., 213, 219n., 220, 222–24, 226, 255, 256, 271n., 279, 280, 284n.
Innocent IV, pope, 66, 197, 219, 232
Innocent VIII, pope, 72
inquisitio, 219–20, 223–24, 227
Inter caetera, letter of Pope Alexander VI, 71
Investiture controversy, 3–25
Iohannes. See Johannes
Isabella, queen of Castile, 261
Ivo of Chartres, 8, 14

Jacobus, archbishop of Capua, 53, 57–59
Jacopo Altoviti, bishop of Fiesole, 319n., 322n.
Jacopo di Antonio di Jacopo di Piero da Romena, notary, canon of Florence, 310n.
Jacopo di Giovanni Ugolini, 310n.
Jacopo Palladini, archbishop of Florence, 304
James of Viterbo, 151n.
Jean Chappuis, canonist, 70
Jean de Voivre, prior of Clairvaux, 103
Jean le Jeun of Contay, cardinal, 307, 309, 312
Jean Petit, 235, 246
Jerome, St., 104
Jerome of Prague, 246, 296
Jesselinus de Cassanis, canonist, 188
Jews: decline of European, 251–62; and Crusades, 255–56, 261; in England, 259, 261; in France, 261–62; Frederick II and, 255, 257; legal status, 254–55
Joannes. See Johannes
Jobst of Moravia, 235
Johannes Andreae, canonist, 182–83, 185–87

Johannes de Borbonio, canon of Reims, canonist, 187–88
Johannes Monachus, canonist, 64–65, 70, 181, 183–84, 186–87, 189
Johannes Staphilaeus, 190
Johannes Teutonicus, canonist, 196–97, 202, 227n.
John VIII, pope, 94, 98
John XXII, pope, 70, 74–88, 162
John XXIII, antipope, 236n., 237n., 238–39, 240n., 241
John, archbishop of Esztergom, 33, 42
John Duns Scotus, 161–63, 165
John Grosse, prior general of the Carmelites, 293n.
John Hus, 246, 296
John Luk, 292
John Maurotius, patriarch of Antioch, 241
John of Belna, 77–78n.
John of Jandun, 150n.
John of Limoges, abbot of Zirc (Cistercian), 31
John of Mirecourt, 172–75
John of Parma, minister general of the Franciscans, 279
John of Salisbury, 148
John of St. Paul, cardinal priest of St. Prisca, 195n.
John of Winterthur, 77n.
John Oldcastle, 292
John Reading, 168–69
John Rodyngton, 171n.
John Wyclif, 290, 293–95
Juan de Solórzano y Pereira, 62–63, 69, 71–73
Judge delegates in Hungary, 26–52
Julius II, pope, 72

Ladislaus of Naples, 237n.
Ladislaus of Poland, 304n.
Lapus Tactus, abbot of San Miniato, canonist, 186–87, 190
László IV, king of Hungary, 35
Laurentius Hispanus, canonist, 197
Lay investiture, 3–25
Legates, papal, 191–211
Leo IX, pope, 216
Leo Brancaleone, cardinal of Santa Croce in Gerusalemme, papal legate in Hungary and Bulgaria, 44–45
Leonardo Dati, master general of the Observant Dominicans, 312n., 319n., 323
Lewis of Bavaria, emperor, 88, 240n.
Liber Augustalis. See Constitutions of Melfi

[339]

# Index

# Index

Peter of Narni, archbishop of Spalato (Split), 26
Peter Olivi, 75, 78–88
Peter Pierleoni (antipope Anaclet II), 3n.
Petrus Bertrandus, canonist, 64, 65–66, 67, 70
Petrus de Ancharano, canonist, 187, 234
Petrus de Vinea, 53, 58n.
Philip, bishop of Bayeux, 102, 107–9
Philip the Fair, king of France, 64, 69, 148, 179, 180n., 183, 184, 261
Philippus Probus, canonist, 189–90
Pierleoni, 3, 4n., 23n.
Pier Paolo Vergerio, 237n.
Pierre d'Ailly, 239n., 243, 245
Pierre de la Palu, 80–85
Pietro Bembo, cardinal, 309
Pietro da Moglio, 111
Pietro Lorenzetti, 264, 270n.
Pliny the Younger, 104, 107
Poggio Bracciolini, 237n., 245
Pomponius Mela, 107
Poverty, Franciscan, 74–88
Praeceptae Pithagorae, 104
pravilegium (Paschal II's grant of investiture to Henry V), 5
Primitive church, 295
Proof, standards of, 212–15, 224–26
Prospero Colonna, cardinal, 312
Proverbia Philosophorum, 104
Pseudo-Isidore, 95–101
Pseudo-Plautus, Querolus, 104

Qualiter et quando, decree of the Fourth Lateran Council, 223
Querolus, Pseudo-Plautus, 104
Quintilian, 123, 131, 137, 139
Quod olim, letter of Pope Benedict XI, 183–84, 189
Quoniam, part of Pastoralis, letter of Pope Clement V, 185, 188–90
Quoniam aliqui, letter of Pope Boniface VIII, 181

Radbert of Corbie, 97–98, 100
Rainerius, archbishop of Spalato (Split), 27–28
Raymond of Peñafort, canonist, 185, 201
Reform, church, 115, 135–38
regalia, 4–10, 14, 23
Regnum and sacerdotium, 67
Reinhard, bishop of Halberstadt, 15, 16n., 20
Renaissance, Carolingian, 93–95
Rhetoric, 122–27, 131, 134–37, 139–40, 142–44
Richard II, king of England, 235

Richard de Pan, canon of Aire, archdeacon of St.-Omer, 95n.
Richard Ullerston, 291
Rinaldo degli Albizzi, 307, 319n.
Robert, count of Flanders, 19
Robert Hallam, bishop of Salisbury, 244n., 291–92
Robert of Lille, master, royal chancellor, provost of Székesfehérvár, bishop of Veszprém, 33–34, 42
Robert Winchelsey, archbishop of Canterbury, 179
Roberto Cavalcanti, bishop of Volterra, 300–301, 307, 311nn.
Roberto Morelli, 309
Roffredus Beneventanus, canonist, 212
Rule of St. Francis, 79
Rupert of Deutz, 129, 131
Ruprecht of the Rhine Palatinate, Holy Roman Emperor, 235
Ruthard, archbishop of Mainz, 11–13, 16n., 20

Sacerdotium, 67
St. Abraham, monastic house (Hungary), 33
St. Egidius (Benedictine), Somogy, disputed abbatial election, 35, 36–37
St. Mary in Sala, church, 33
Salvino di Berto di Miliano Salvini, canon of Florence, 310n.
Santa Maria in Turri, 3–4, 22. See also Agreement of Sutri
Sciarra Colonna, 183
Seneca, 104
Sententiae Philosophorum, 104
Sibico, bishop of Speyer, 216
Sicut Iudeis, letter of Pope Alexander III, 252
Sidonius, 104–5
Sigebert of Gembloux, 10n., 18n.
Sigismund, emperor, 235, 237, 240, 243–44
Simon de Cramaud, 245
Simone Martini, 264
Sinibaldus Fieschi. See Innocent IV, pope
Somnium viridarii (Songe du Vergier), 149n.
Spiritual Franciscans, 74–88
spiritualia, 8–9, 18
Stephen, king of Hungary, 39
Stephen of Fossanova, cardinal priest of the Basilica of the Twelve Apostles, papal chamberlain, 43
stigmata. See Francis, St.
Suger, abbot of St. Denis, 16n., 17

[341]

# Index

Sutri. *See* Agreement of Sutri
Swords: theory of the two, 64–66, 70–71
Symmachus, pope, 96, 98; fifth synod of, 98n.
Synod, Benevento (1108), 23
Synod, Lent (1110), 15
Synod, Lent (1112), 5, 24

Tanchelm, heretic, 217n.
Tancred, canonist, 201n., 212
Taxation of clergy, 179–90, 306n., 316–17
Templars, 261
*temporalia*, 18
Teutonic Knights, 69
Theodoric, king of the Ostrogoths, Ennodius's panegyric, 91
Theodulf of Orléans, 94
Thomas, provost of Veszprém, 33
Thomas, archdeacon of Spalato (Split), 34
Thomas Aquinas, St., 77n., 147
Thomas Netter of Walden, 290–99
Thomas of Celano, Franciscan, 264, 265n., 266–71, 274–76, 279n., 280, 282, 284–86
Thomas of Fermo, master general of the Observant Dominicans, 322n.
Thomas of York, 75n.
Tommaso della Bordella, canon of Florence, 309–10
Tryphonius, 220–21
*Tua nos*, letter of Pope Innocent III, 224
Tyrannicide, 235, 246

Ubertino degli Albizzi, bishop of Pistoia, 308
*Unam sanctam*, letter of Pope Boniface VIII, 63–73, 183
Urban II, pope, 23n.

Urban IV, pope, 227
Urias (Oros), abbot of Pannonhalma (Benedictine), 31, 33–34, 40–41, 44–45, 48
Usury, 227–28, 253–54
*Ut fame*, letter of Pope Innocent III, 222
Uto, bishop of Hildesheim, 16n., 20

Vespasiano da Bisticci, 306–7
*Vestra*, letter of Pope Lucius III, 224
Vincent of Beauvais, 106
Visconti, 309
*vita activa*, 133
*vita apostolica*, 117–18, 131–33
*vita contemplativa*, 133
Vital du Four, cardinal, 76–77

Walcher, deposed bishop of Cambrai, 20–21
Walter, abbot of Corbie, 194, 195n.
Walter, archbishop of Ravenna, 132
Walter Burley, 153–54
Walter Chatton, 167n., 169–72
Welf V, duke of Bavaria, 16, 21
Wenceslaus, emperor, 235
Wido, bishop of Chur, 13
William. *See also* Guilelmus
William de Nogaret. *See* Guillaume de Nogaret
William Durand. *See* Guilelmus Durand
William of Laudin, 80n.
William of Moerbeke, 145–48, 152, 154
William of Ockham, 160–61, 166–68, 171
William of St. Amour, 274n.
William of Ste. Mere Eglise, bishop of London, 222
Wiprecht, count of Groitsch, 16

Zaccheria di Giovanni d'altro Giovanni Strozzi, canon of Florence, 310n.

[342]

Library of Congress Cataloging-in-Publication Data

Popes, teachers, and canon law in the Middle Ages.

   Bibliography: p.
   Includes index.
   1. Church history—Middle Ages, 600–1500. 2. Canon law—History.
3. Tierney, Brian. I. Sweeney, James Ross. II. Chodorow, Stanley.
BR253.P6   1989     270     88-47930
ISBN 0-8014-2264-7 (alk. paper)